Computer Concepts

FIFTH EDITION – ILLUSTRATED

INTRODUCTORY ENHANCED

Computer Concepts
FIFTH EDITION – ILLUSTRATED

INTRODUCTORY ENHANCED

June Jamrich Parsons / Dan Oja

THOMSON
COURSE TECHNOLOGY

Australia • Canada • Mexico • Singapore • Spain • United Kingdom • United States

Computer Concepts, Fifth Edition—Illustrated Introductory, Enhanced
is published by Course Technology.

Adapting Author:
Rachel Biheller Bunin

Developmental Editor:
Pamela Conrad

Executive Editor:
Nicole Jones Pinard

Senior Product Managers:
Christina Kling Garrett,
Amanda Young Shelton

Production Editor:
Jennifer Goguen

Associate Product Manager:
Emilie Perreault

Editorial Assistant:
Shana Rosenthal

Marketing Manager:
Joy Stark

Interior Designer:
Betsy Young

Photo and Video Researcher:
Christina Micek

Composition:
GEX Publishing Services

Media Developers:
Donna Mulder, Fatima Lockhart,
Keefe Crowley, Tensi Parsons

Photographers:
Greg Manis, Joe Bush, David S. Bunin

Illustrator:
Eric Murphy

CD Development:
MediaTechnics Corporation

Student Edition ISBN 0-619-27355-0
Instructor Edition ISBN: 1-4188-4276-1

Author Acknowledgements

Thanks to Dan Oja and June Parsons for entrusting me and the Illustrated team to adapt their best-selling New Perspectives Concepts book into the Illustrated format. My most heartfelt appreciation and admiration go to Pamela Conrad, the Developmental Editor, who has worked with me on this project through all five editions. Pam is a master of the trade, contributes insight and vision to the content, has a great sense of humor, and keeps the project on schedule and all together with its many parts. Thank you, Pam, for being a true friend and terrific colleague. Special thanks to Nicole Pinard, for having the vision five editions ago to let us create the first Concepts Illustrated book and for keeping me and Pam together as a team for all the editions and enhanced editions. This enhanced edition gives us a chance to address some of the more exciting and interesting topics in technology today. My gratitude to Christina Kling Garrett who contributed extraordinary leadership as the Project Manager and kept us going through the project. Thanks to Summer Hughes and Jennifer Goguen, our terrific Production Editors. Many thanks to our reviewers for their comments and insights - Anthony Barbis, University of Missouri; Raphael De Arazoza, Miami-Dade College; Hazel Kates, Miami-Dade College; Theresa Savarse, San Diego City College; and John Walsh, Gibbs College. On behalf of the entire Illustrated team, we hope you find this book a valuable resource for your students.

- Rachel Biheller Bunin, Adapting Author

We offer heartfelt thanks to all of the members of the Illustrated team for contributing their vision, talent, and skills to make this book a reality. Special thanks to Rachel Biheller Bunin for her fast and efficient work as the adapting author; Pamela Conrad for her insights as the developmental editor; Jennifer Goguen for her solid work as the production editor; and Christina Kling Garrett for tracking all the bits and pieces of this project. Whether you are a student or instructor, we thank you for using our book and hope that you find it to be a valuable guide to computers and software.

- June Parsons, Dan Oja, and MediaTechnics for the New Perspectives Series

Contents

◉ = CD   ✦ = Info Web   ∿ = Lab   📺 = TechTV

UNIT C   Computer Software   71

UNIT D   Digital Electronics and File Management   105

📺 UNIT H   Digital Media   245

Preface

Welcome to *Computer Concepts, Fifth Edition—Illustrated Introductory, Enhanced*. This Enhanced Edition contains the same page-for-page content as the Fifth Edition, but includes two bonus units at the end:

- **Trends in Technology unit:** Provides students with 8 lessons of new material covering the most recent developments in computer technology. The unit also includes a new Tech Talk, a Computers in Context, and a new Issue. All new end-of-unit exercises add to your course, while the organization of the unit makes it easy to incorporate into an already existing curriculum.

- **Bonus Issues and Up-to-Dates unit:** Includes 8 additional Issues, a bonus Computers in Context, and 9 Up-to-Date exercises that provide additional options for reinforcement and correspond in topic area to each of Units A-H. The exercises challenge students to expand their knowledge, and can be assigned at the end of each unit or at the end of the course.

About the Illustrated Approach

What makes the information in this book so easy to access? It's quite simple. As shown in this sample lesson, each concept is presented on two facing pages, with the main points discussed on the left page and large, dramatic illustrations presented on the right. Students can learn all they need to know about a particular topic without having to turn the page! This unique design makes information extremely accessible and easy to absorb, and makes a great reference for after the course is over. The modular structure of the book also allows for great flexibility; you can cover the units in any order you choose, and you can skip lessons if you like.

Icons in the margins indicate that a technology element is featured for that lesson

A single concept is presented in a two-page "information display" to help students absorb information quickly and easily

Easy-to-follow introductions to every lesson focus on a single concept to help students get the information quickly

Details provide additional key information on the main concept

---

UNIT B

Comparing storage media and devices

When trying to determine the best storage media for a job, it is useful to apply four criteria: versatility, durability, speed, and capacity. Versatility is the ability of a device and its media to work in more than one way. After storing data using this storage technology, can that data be changed? Durability determines the ability of the device or media to last. How long will it work? How long will the data be accessible? Speed is the time it takes to retrieve or access the data, a factor that is very important in determining how efficiently you work. Finally, capacity is the amount of data each technology can store.

DETAILS

- Versatility. Some storage devices can access data from only one type of medium. More versatile devices can access data from several different media. A floppy disk drive, for example, can access only floppy disks, but a DVD drive can access data DVDs, DVD movies, audio CDs, data CDs, and CD-Rs.

- Durability. Most storage technologies are susceptible to damage from mishandling or other environmental factors, such as heat and moisture. Some technologies are less susceptible than others. Optical and solid state technologies tend to be less susceptible than magnetic technologies to damage that could cause data loss.

- Speed. Not surprisingly, fast storage devices are preferred over slower ones. **Access time** is the average time it takes a computer to locate data on the storage medium and read it. Access time for a personal computer storage device, such as a disk drive, is measured in **milliseconds** (thousandths of a second). Lower numbers indicate faster access times. For example, a drive with a 6 ms access time is faster than a drive with an access time of 11 ms. Random-access devices have the fastest access times.

    Random access (also called "direct access") is the ability of a device to "jump" directly to the requested data. Floppy disk, hard disk, solid state, CD, and DVD drives are random-access devices. A tape drive, on the other hand, must use slower **sequential access**, which reads through the data from the beginning of the tape. The advantage of random access becomes clear when you consider how much faster and easier it is to locate a song on a CD (random access) than on a cassette tape (sequential access).

    Data transfer rate is the amount of data that a storage device can move from the storage medium to the computer per second. Higher numbers indicate faster transfer rates. For example, a CD-ROM drive with a 600 KBps (kilobytes per second) data transfer rate is faster than one with a 300 KBps transfer rate.

- Capacity. **Storage capacity** is the maximum amount of data that can be stored on a storage medium, measured in kilobytes (KB), megabytes (MB), gigabytes (GB), or terabytes (TB). The amount of data that a disk stores—its capacity—depends on its density. **Disk density** refers to the closeness of the data on the disk surface. The higher the disk density, the more data it can store. Higher capacity is almost always preferred. Table B-1 compares the capacity of various storage devices and media.

FYI

Storage media is divided into tracks and then into sectors to create electronic "addressable bins" in which to store data.

Adding storage devices to a computer

Computer users frequently want to upgrade their hard drives to gain capacity or to add CD or DVD drives to make their systems more versatile. The system unit case for a desktop computer contains several storage device "parking spaces" called drive bays. See Figure B-6. If you have an empty bay that is the right type and size, you can add a storage device. Bays come in two widths—5 ¼" and 3½". CD and DVD drives require 5¼" bays; a floppy disk drive fits in a 3½" bay. Some drive bays provide access from the outside of the system unit, a necessity for a storage device with removable media, such as floppy disks, CDs, tapes, and DVDs. Internal drive bays are located inside the system unit and are designed for hard disk drives, which don't use removable storage media.

40 COMPUTER CONCEPTS

News to Use boxes relate the lesson material to real-world situations to provide students with additional practical information

Tables provide quick
reference information

TABLE B-1: Capacities of storage media

DEVICE	CAPACITY	COMMENTS
Floppy disk	1.44 MB	Low capacity means that the disk can hold small files but not large files; not suitable for graphics-intensive files
SuperDisk	120 MB or 240 MB	SuperDisks are manufactured by Imation; Zip disks are manufactured by Iomega; each holds much more than a floppy; each requires its own proprietary drive; a full system backup requires multiple disks
Zip disk	100 MB, 250 MB, and 750 MB	
Fixed hard disk	80 GB (average)	High storage capacity, fast and convenient, economical storage-cost/megabyte, is susceptible to damage or theft of your computer
External hard drive	80 GB	Fast, but transfer rate depends on computer system; drive can be removed and locked in a secure location
Removable hard disk	2.2 GB (average)	Fast, limited capacity, but disks can be removed and locked in a secure location
CD	700 MB	Limited capacity, can't be reused, long shelf life
CD-RW	700 MB	Limited capacity, reusable
Writable DVD	4.7 GB	Good capacity, standards still in development
Tape	30 GB (average)	Good capacity, reasonable media cost, convenient—you can let backups run overnight, but slow—it can take 15-20 minutes to back up 1 GB of data

FIGURE B-6: Drive bays

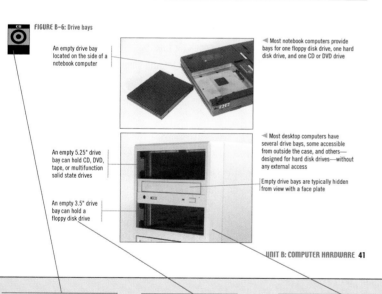

An empty drive bay located on the side of a notebook computer

Most notebook computers provide bays for one floppy disk drive, one hard disk drive, and one CD or DVD drive

An empty 5.25" drive bay can hold CD, DVD, tape, or multifunction solid state drives

An empty 3.5" drive bay can hold a floppy disk drive

Most desktop computers have several drive bays, some accessible from outside the case, and others—designed for hard disk drives—without any external access

Empty drive bays are typically hidden from view with a face plate

UNIT B: COMPUTER HARDWARE 41

Icons to the left of the figure captions direct students to the CD for a Video or ScreenTour, bringing the book to life

The callouts point out key elements on each illustration

Large photos and screenshots illustrate the lesson concepts

Unit Features
Each unit contains the following features, providing a flexible teaching and learning package.

- **InfoWebs** The computer industry changes rapidly. Students can get up-to-date information by exploring the concept on the InfoWebLinks Web site, when indicated by an InfoWeb icon.

- **TechTV clips** TechTV clips help students stay on top of emerging technologies and challenges students to further investigate topics related to the units.

- **Tech Talk** Each unit ends with a Tech Talk lesson. These lessons go into greater depth on a technical topic related to the unit. Instructors have the option of assigning this lesson or skipping it, depending on the expertise of the students and the course goals.

- **Computers in Context** Each unit includes a **new** Computers in Context two-page spread, which highlights how computers and computer technologies are used in various disciplines, such as medicine, law enforcement, and sports.

- **Issue** Each unit contains an interesting Issue article, followed by two types of questions to encourage students to form and express their own opinions. Interactive Questions can be collected electronically, and Expand the Ideas are open-ended, essay questions.

- **Key Terms** Students can use this handy list to review bold terms that represent key concepts from the unit. Definitions are provided in the glossary.

- **Unit Review** After completing the Unit Review, students will have synthesized the unit content in their own words.

- **Fill in the Best Answer** Students can complete this in the book or on the Interactive CD and get immediate feedback on how well they have learned the unit content.

- **Independent Challenges** These exercises enable students to explore and develop critical thinking skills Challenges with E-Quest icon point student to the Web to complete the exercise.

- **Lab Assignments** Assignments let student work further with the interactive labes features on the CD.

- **Visual Workshop** Based on a screenshot or illustration, Visual Workshops encourage independent thinking to explore a concept further.

Instructor Resources

The Instructor Resources CD is Course Technology's way of putting the resources and information needed to teach and learn effectively into your hands. With an integrated array of teaching and learning tools that offer you and your students a broad range of technology-based instructional options, we believe this CD represents the highest quality and most cutting edge resources available to instructors today. Many of these resources are available at **www.course.com**.

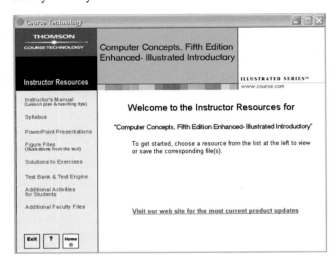

- Solutions to Exercises—Solutions to Exercises contain files from the End-of-Unit material and Extra Independent Challenges.

- **Test Bank & Test Engine**—ExamView is a powerful testing software package that allows you to create and administer printed, computer (LAN-based), and Internet exams. ExamView includes hundreds of questions that correspond to the topics covered in this text, enabling students to generate detailed study guides that include page references for further review. The computer-based and Internet testing components allow students to take exams at their computers, and also saves you time by grading each exam automatically.

- Instructor's Manual—Available as an electronic file, the Instructor's Manual is quality-assurance tested and includes a lecture note for every lesson, Teaching Tips, Quick Quizzes and Classroom Activities.

- Syllabus—Prepare and customize your course easily using this sample outline.

- **PowerPoint Presentations**—Each unit has a corresponding PowerPoint presentation that you can use in lecture, distribute to your students, or customize to suit your course.

- Figure Files—Includes every image from the book which you can use to create transparencies or a PowerPoint presentation.

- Additional Activities for Students—Materials provided here are Extra Independent Challenge exercises, a first-time buyer's guide, a guide to the Interactive CD and our Classic Labs.

- Additional Faculty Files—In this section, you will find a WebTrack Guide on using your WebTrack account, and other helpful documents.

Bring computer concepts to life with Student Edition Labs, the highly-interactive, multimedia-enriched labs. This free, web-based software features up-to-the-minute content, eye-popping graphics, and rich animation to help your students master computer concepts on a variety of topics. Students learn through the proven teaching method of dynamic observation, step-by-step practice, and challenging review questions.

You can add the power of assessment and detailed reporting to your Student Edition Lab assignments with SAM Computer Concepts. SAM Computer Concepts helps you energize your training assignments by allowing students to learn and quiz on hundreds of essential computer skills in an active, hands-on environment.

Online Offerings We offer a full range of content for use with MyCourse 2.0, BlackBoard and WebCT to simplify the use of Computer Concepts in distance education settings, or to supplement your traditional class. Visit **www.course.com** for more information.

About the Technology

These indicators in the book tell you when to use the Interactive CD and InfoWebLinks Web site.

CD Videos and ScreenTours

Videos and ScreenTours enhance learning and retention of key concepts. A CD icon next to a figure or text indicates you can view an interactive concept on the CD.

InfoWebs

InfoWebs connect you to Web links, film, video, TV, print, and electronic resources, keeping the book and URL's up-to-date. An InfoWeb icon indicates you can link to further information on the topic by accessing the InfoWeb site, using your browser and an Internet connection.

Interactive Exercises

A CD icon next to an exercise indicates that you can also complete this activity on the Interactive CD. Interactive exercises include the Issues, Fill in the Best Answers, Practice Tests, and Labs.

New Perspectives Labs

Concepts come to life with the New Perspectives Labs—highly interactive tutorials that combine illustrations, animations, digital images, and simulations. Labs guide you step-by-step through a topic, and present you with QuickCheck questions to test your comprehension. You can track your QuickCheck results using a Tracking Disk. (See the Before You Begin section for more information.) Lab assignments are included at the end of each relevant unit. A Lab icon on the left page of a lesson indicates a Lab is featured for the lesson concept. The following Labs are available with the Interactive CD.

Unit A
Making a Dial-Up Connection
Browsing and Searching
Using E-Mail

Unit B
Working with Binary Numbers
Operating a Personal Computer

Unit C
Using the Windows Interface
Installing and Uninstalling Software

Unit D
Benchmarking
Working with Windows Explorer

Unit E
Tracking Packets
Securing Your Connection

Unit F
Backing Up Your Computer

Unit G
Working with Cookies

Unit H
Working with Bitmap Graphics
Video Editing

Computer Concepts, Fifth Edition Illustrated Web Site

Our integrated **Web site** provides a wealth of online resources including pre-assessment tools, interactive games, InfoWeb links, TechTV clips, additional projects, study tips, and Student Edition Labs to reinforce the concepts presented in this edition. To take advantage of this exclusive password protected site, visit **www.course.com/illustrated/concepts5** using the pincode included in the back of your book.

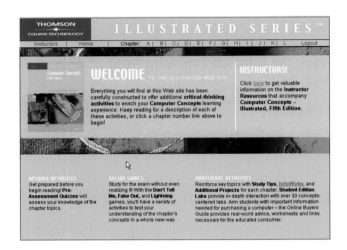

STUDENT EDITION LABS

You can master hundreds of computer concepts, including input and output devices, file management and desktop applications, computer privacy, virus protection, and much more using the **Student Edition Labs**. The interactive Student Edition Labs help you learn through dynamic observation, step-by-step practice, and challenging review questions. Student Edition Lab Assignments challenge you to apply the skills learned in the labs to realistic case problems.

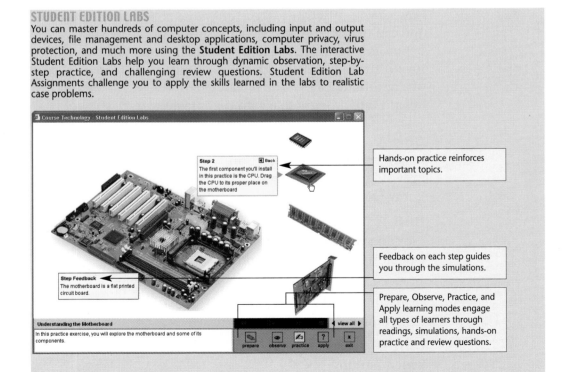

Hands-on practice reinforces important topics.

Feedback on each step guides you through the simulations.

Prepare, Observe, Practice, and Apply learning modes engage all types of learners through readings, simulations, hands-on practice and review questions.

TechTV Video Clips Library

Ever wondered what it is like to program your own video game? What are the social implications of a digital system that tracks patrons at a neighborhood bar? Stay on top of emerging technologies and technology-related issues with our library of TechTV video clips. Go to the Student Online Companion at **www.course.com/illustrated/concepts5** to link to each clip.

Unit A: Computer and Internet Basics
Getting Started

Unit B: Computer Hardware
The Army's Virtual World

Unit C: Computer Software
Making FlowCharts Using Office XP
Download of the Day: Synergy
Confessions of a Software Pirate

Unit D: Digital Electronics and File Management
PC Pioneer Trail

Unit E: Networks and the Internet
Free Wi-Fi Blankets San Francisco

Unit F: Data Security
Sasser Worm
Controversial Digital Bouncers Track Bar Patrons

Unit G: The Web and E-Commerce
Find the Best Deals Online

Unit H: Digital Media
Online Music Stores and Services
P2P's Cloudy Future

Unit Trends: Computer I/O components
High-Tech Helmets
Download of the Day: Synergy

Unit Trends: Storage
Online Storage

Unit Trends: Networking and wireless connectivity
Get News, Weather, Reports and More Delivered to your Desktop

Unit Trends: Security and privacy
MS Windows Security Hole

Unit Trends: The Internet and e-Mail
GMail Database Privacy

Unit Trends: Software
Software Vending Machines

Unit Trends: Leisure technology
Design Your Own Video Game

Unit Trends: End of Unit Independent Challenge 5
PC Pioneer Trail

Bonus: Up-To-Date: E-Voting: questions and concerns
E-Voting Controversy

Before You Begin

It's a snap to start the Interactive CD and use it on your computer. The answers to the FAQs (frequently asked questions) in this section will help you begin.

Will the Interactive CD work on my computer? The Interactive CD works on most computers that run Windows. Just follow the steps below to start the CD. If you have trouble, check with your instructor or technical support person. The link on the Main Menu screen will provide you with Frequently Asked Questions as well as contact information for technical support. This information is available at **www.mediatechnics.net/np5cd/support.htm**.

How do I start the CD? Follow these simple steps to get started:

1. Make sure your computer is turned on.
2. Press the button on your computer's CD-ROM drive to open the drawer-like "tray."
3. Place the Interactive CD into the tray with the label facing up.
4. Press the button on the CD-ROM drive to close the tray.
5. Wait about 15 seconds. During this time, the light on your CD-ROM drive should flicker. Soon you should see a screen that displays the Computer Concepts menu. The first time you use the Interactive CD, your computer will check for several necessary Windows components. Any missing components will be automatically installed. When this process is complete, you might be prompted to reboot your computer, and then you can continue to use any of the options on the Computer Concepts menu.
6. *Manual Start*: Complete these steps only if the menu did not appear after completing Step 5:
   a. Use the mouse to position the arrow-shaped pointer on Start, then click the left button on your mouse.
   b. When the Start menu appears, click Run.
   c. Type d:\start.exe, then click the OK button. If your CD-ROM drive is not "d" you should substitute the letter of your drive, for example, q:\start.exe.

How do I use the Interactive CD? A menu bar provides the options you'll need to navigate through the CD. See Figure 1. To read the text at the bottom of a page, drag the scroll box, or click the scroll bar at the side of the screen.

What if I don't see any Annotation or Syllabus buttons? These buttons only appear if your instructor has provided a link to the syllabus, or a note for a page, and you are using a Tracking Disk. When you send Tracking Disk data to your instructor, the Syllabus and Annotation links are downloaded to your Tracking Disk. If you do not see any Annotation or Syllabus links, first use your Tracking Disk to send any results to your instructor. If you still do not see any Annotation or Syllabus links, check with your instructor.

FIGURE 1: CD navigation from Unit A home page

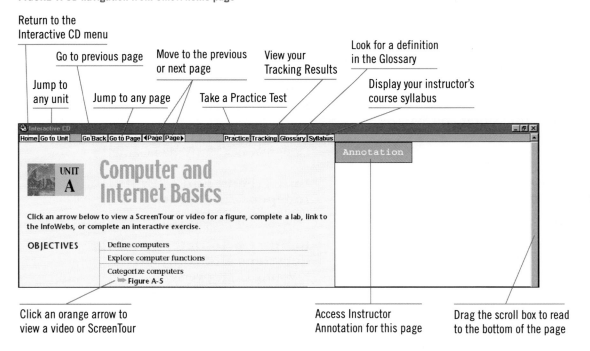

Return to the Interactive CD menu

Go to previous page

Move to the previous or next page

View your Tracking Results

Look for a definition in the Glossary

Jump to any unit

Jump to any page

Take a Practice Test

Display your instructor's course syllabus

Click an orange arrow to view a video or ScreenTour

Access Instructor Annotation for this page

Drag the scroll box to read to the bottom of the page

How do I view videos and ScreenTours? Each unit has a home page (See Figure 1), which lists the objectives for the unit and provides links to all the CD and Web elements for that unit. To view a video or ScreenTour, simply click the arrow next to that figure.

How do I access the InfoWebs? You can link directly to the Illustrated Computer Concepts Fifth Edition InfoWeb home page from the CD menu, or click the link from the unit home page on the Interactive CD. Or, type **www.course.com/illustrated/concepts5** in the Address bar of your browser.

The InfoWebs work only if you have a browser and an Internet connection. When you link to the InfoWebs from the CD menu or the unit home page, the Interactive CD will automatically start your Web browser software. When you complete your exploration of the InfoWebs, you can return to the CD by closing your browser.

How do I access the Interactive Exercises? The interactive exercises include a variety of activities you can use to review the unit material. You can link directly to the exercise on the CD you want to complete from the unit home page, or navigate through all the interactive exercises by clicking the Page navigation buttons on the menu bar. Additionally, you can take a Practice Test by clicking the Practice link on the menu bar.

How do I access the Labs? You can link to a Lab in two ways. You can link to the Lab from the unit home page in the Objectives list. Or, you also can link to the lab from the Lab Assignments in the Interactive Exercises list.

How do I complete the Interactive Exercises and Labs with a Tracking Disk? To complete an activity, simply follow the instructions for these activities to enter your answers. When you complete the Interactive Questions for the Issue, you'll see a message that asks you if you want to save your answers. If you click the OK button, you will be prompted to insert your Tracking Disk, then your score will be saved on it.

When you complete a Lab, the Fill in the Best Answer activity, or a Practice Test, your responses are automatically checked and you are provided with a score. Then, you'll see a message that asks you if you want to save your score. If you click the OK button, you will be prompted to insert your Tracking Disk, then your score will be saved on it. For Practice Tests, you will also receive a study guide to help you find the answers to questions that you answered incorrectly. You can print the study guide by following the instructions on the screen.

The first time you save a score, you must follow the directions on the screen to create a Tracking Disk. To do so, click the Create button and insert a blank, formatted floppy disk. You can also select a location, which could be a folder on drive C: or an alternative storage device, such as a USB flash drive. You only need to create a Tracking Disk one time. Once you create the Tracking Disk, just insert it into the floppy disk drive or your computer when you start the Interactive CD, or when prompted to do so.

You can view or print a summary report of all your scores by clicking the Tracking button on the menu bar. Your Issue responses are not listed here, but are submitted with your Tracking Data. If your instructor wants you to submit your Tracking Data to track your progress, simply click the "Send your Student Tracking Data to your Instructor" link on the CD menu.

Can I make the type appear larger on my screen? If the type in the Interactive CD appears small, your monitor is probably set at a high resolution. The type will appear larger if you reduce the resolution by using the Start menu to select Settings and open the Control Panel. Double-click the Display icon, then select the Settings tab. Move the Screen Area slider to 800 × 600. This setting is optional. You can view the Interactive CD at most standard resolutions.

How do I end a session? You must leave the Interactive CD in the CD-ROM drive while you use it. Before you remove it, exit the program by clicking the Exit button from the CD menu.

What if I have additional questions about how to use the Interactive CD or Web site? For answers to technical questions, click the Technical Support link on the Interactive CD menu. Additional technical information is provided in the Readme.doc file on your Interactive CD.

SYSTEM REQUIREMENTS

- A computer running Windows 98, ME, 2000, or XP is recommended. (This product can be used on older Windows 95 and Windows NT 4.x systems, but they might require updates for Microsoft Internet Explorer and Windows Media Player. The Interactive CD will not run on Windows 3.x)
- Microsoft Internet Explorer 4 (or higher)
- High-color or True Color graphics with a resolution of at least 800 × 600 or 1024 × 768 resolution recommended
- A floppy disk drive, or other writable storage database, configured as drive A: is recommended, but the software can be configured to store Tracking Data on the C: drive or other drives, such as USB flash drives.
- A properly configured CD-ROM drive
- A properly configured sound card and speakers
- A Pentium processor, preferably 400 MHz or faster
- Required RAM depends on the operating system and other loaded programs, but should typically have a minimum of 256 MB
- Computer lab users must have Write rights to the Windows Registry and to the Windows Temporary folder (typically c:\windows\temp). If using a custom Tracking Data location such as a USB flash drive, users must also have write rights to C:\.

CREDITS

Credits

UNIT A

Computer and Internet Basics

OBJECTIVES

Unit A provides an overview of computer and Internet technologies. The unit begins by defining the basic characteristics of a computer system and then provides a quick overview of data, information, and files. You will be introduced to application software, operating systems, and platform compatibility. You will get a basic overview of the Internet, the Web, and e-mail. The Tech Talk discusses the boot process, the sequence of events that happens when you turn on your computer. You will also have an opportunity to look at computers in the context of sports and the Issue looks at the effects of ever-present computing.

Defining computers

Whether you realize it or not, you already know a lot about computers. You've picked up information from commercials and magazine articles, from books and movies, from conversations and correspondence, and perhaps even from using your own computer and trying to figure it out. This lesson provides an overview designed to help you start organizing what you know about computers, provide you with a basic understanding of how computers work, and get you up to speed with basic computer vocabulary.

DETAILS

- The word "computer" has been part of the English language since 1646, but if you look in a dictionary printed before 1940, you might be surprised to find "computer" defined as a person who performs calculations! Prior to 1940, machines that were designed to perform calculations were referred to as calculators and tabulators, not computers. The modern definition and use of the term "computer" emerged in the 1940s, when the first electronic computing devices were developed.

- Most people can formulate a mental picture of a computer, but computers do so many things and come in such a variety of shapes and sizes that it might seem difficult to distill their common characteristics into an all-purpose definition. At its core, a **computer** is a device that accepts input, processes data, stores data, and produces output, all according to a series of stored instructions.

- A **computer system** includes hardware, peripheral devices, and software. Figure A-1 shows two examples of a basic computer system. **Hardware** includes the electronic and mechanical devices that process data. The term "hardware" refers to the computer as well as components called peripheral devices. **Peripheral devices** expand the computer's input, output, and storage capabilities.

- An **input device**, such as a keyboard or mouse, gathers input and transforms it into a series of electronic signals for the computer. An **output device**, such as a monitor or printer, displays, prints, or transmits the results of processing from the computer memory.

- A computer requires instructions called **software**, which is a **computer program** that tells the computer how to perform particular tasks.

- A **computer network** consists of two or more computers and other devices that are connected for the purpose of sharing data and programs. A **LAN (local area network)** is simply a computer network that is located within a limited geographical area, such as a school computer lab or a small business.

FYI

The term "personal computer" is sometimes abbreviated as "PC." However, "PC" is usually used for a specific type of personal computer that runs Windows software.

Exploring computer functions

To really understand computers, you need to understand the functions they perform. Figure A-2 illustrates the basic computer functions—accept input, process data, store data, and produce output—and shows the components that work together to accomplish each function.

DETAILS

- Accept input. A computer accepts input. Computer **input** is whatever is put into a computer system. Input can be supplied by a person, by the environment, or by another computer. Examples of the kinds of input that a computer can accept include the words and symbols in a document, numbers for a calculation, pictures, temperatures from a thermostat, music or voice audio signals from a microphone, and instructions from a computer program.

- Process data. A computer processes data. In the context of computing, **data** refers to the symbols that represent facts, objects, and ideas. Computers manipulate data in many ways, and we call this manipulation **processing**. Some of the ways that a computer can process data include performing calculations, sorting lists of words or numbers, modifying documents and pictures, and drawing graphs. The instructions that tell a computer how to carry out the processing tasks are referred to as a computer program, or simply a "program." These programs are the software. In a computer, most processing takes place in a **processor** (also known as a microprocessor) called the **central processing unit (CPU)**, which is sometimes described as the "brain" of the computer.

- Store data. A computer stores data so that it will be available for processing. Most computers have more than one location for storing data, depending on how the data is being used. **Memory** is an area of a computer that temporarily holds data waiting to be processed, stored, or output. **Storage** is the area of a computer that holds data on a permanent basis when it is not immediately needed for processing. For example, while you are working on it, a document is in memory; it is not in storage until you save it. After you save the document, it is still in memory until you close the document, exit the program, or turn off the computer. Documents in memory are lost when you turn off the power. Stored documents are not lost when the power is turned off.

- Produce output. **Output** consists of the processing results produced by a computer. Some examples of computer output include reports, documents, music, graphs, and pictures. An output device displays, prints, or transmits the results of processing. Figure A-2 helps you visualize the input, processing, storage, and output activities of a computer.

FIGURE A-2: Basic computer functions

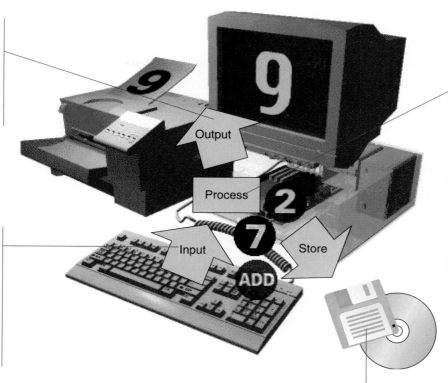

A computer produces output. You use an output device, such as a printer or display screen, to see the results of processing, that is, the computer output

A computer processes data. The CPU retrieves the numbers and the instruction, and then processes the numbers by performing addition; the result, 9, is temporarily held in memory; from memory, the result can be output, usually to a monitor, printer, or storage medium

A computer accepts input. You use an input device, such as a keyboard, to input numbers, such as 2 and 7, along with the instruction ADD; the instruction and the numbers are temporarily held in memory

Output

Process

Input

Store

ADD

A computer stores data. You can permanently store data on disks and CDs

Understanding the importance of stored programs

Early computers were really no more than calculating devices designed to carry out a specific mathematical task. To use one of these devices for another task, it was necessary to rewire or reset its circuits—a task best left to an engineer. In a modern computer, the idea of a **stored program** means that instructions for a computing task can be loaded into a computer's memory. These instructions can easily be replaced by different instructions when it is time for the computer to perform a different task. The stored program concept allows you to use your computer for one task, such as word processing, and then easily switch to a different type of computing task, such as editing a photo or sending an e-mail message. It is the single most important characteristic that distinguishes a computer from other simpler and less versatile devices.

Categorizing computers

Computers are versatile machines, but some types of computers are better suited to certain tasks than others. Computers are categorized according to criteria such as usage, cost, size, and capability to help consumers associate computers with appropriate tasks. To reflect today's computer technology, the following categories are appropriate: personal computers, handheld computers, workstations, videogame consoles, mainframes, supercomputers, and servers.

DETAILS

- A **personal computer**, also called a **microcomputer**, is designed to meet the computing needs of an individual. It typically provides access to a wide variety of computing applications, such as word processing, photo editing, e-mail, and Internet access. Personal computers include **desktop computers**, as illustrated in Figure A-3, and **notebook computers** (sometimes called "laptop computers"), as illustrated in Figure A-4. A desktop has separate components, while laptops have a keyboard, monitor, and system in one compact unit. Laptops can be more expensive than comparable desktops.

- A **handheld computer**, such as a Palm, an iPAQ, or a PocketPC, features a small keyboard or touch-sensitive screen and is designed to fit into a pocket, run on batteries, and be used while you are holding it. See Figure A-5. A **PDA (Personal Digital Assistant)** is typically used as an electronic appointment book, address book, calculator, and notepad. Inexpensive add-ons make it possible to send and receive e-mail, use maps and global positioning to get directions, maintain an expense account, and make voice calls using cellular service. With its slow processing speed and small screen, a handheld computer is not powerful enough to handle many of the tasks that can be accomplished using desktop or notebook personal computers.

- A **tablet computer** is a portable computing device featuring a touch-sensitive screen that can be used as a writing or drawing pad. A "pure" tablet configuration, like the one in Figure A-6, lacks a keyboard (although one can be attached) and resembles a high-tech clipboard. A "convertible" tablet computer is constructed like a notebook computer, but the screen folds face up over the keyboard to provide a horizontal writing surface.

- Computers that are advertised as **workstations** are usually powerful desktop computers designed for specialized tasks such as design tasks. A workstation can tackle tasks that require a lot of processing speed, such as medical imaging and computer-aided design. Some workstations contain more than one processor, and most have circuitry specially designed for creating and displaying three-dimensional and animated graphics.

"Workstation" can also mean an ordinary personal computer that is connected to a local area network.

- A **videogame console** (see Figure A-7), such as the Nintendo® GameCube™, the Sony PlayStation®, or the Microsoft XBox®, is a computer. In the past, a videogame console was not considered a computer because of its history as a dedicated game device that connects to a TV set and provides only a pair of joysticks for input. Today's videogame consoles, however, contain processors that are equivalent to any found in a fast personal computer, and they are equipped to produce graphics that rival those on sophisticated workstations. Add-ons make it possible to use a videogame console to watch DVD movies, send and receive e-mail, and participate in online activities, such as multiplayer games.

- A **mainframe computer** is a large and expensive computer capable of simultaneously processing data for hundreds or thousands of users. Mainframes are generally used by businesses, universities, or governments to provide centralized storage, processing, and management of large amounts of data where reliability, data security, and centralized control are necessary. Its main processing circuitry is housed in a closet-sized cabinet. See Figure A-8.

- A computer is a **supercomputer** if, at the time of construction, it is one of the fastest computers in the world. Because of their speed and complexity, supercomputers can tackle tasks that would not be practical for other computers. Typical uses for supercomputers include breaking codes and modeling worldwide weather systems. A supercomputer CPU is constructed from thousands of processors.

- In the computer industry, the term "server" has several meanings. It can refer to computer hardware, to a specific type of software, or to a combination of hardware and software. In any case, the purpose of a **server** is to "serve" the computers on a network (such as the Internet or a LAN) by supplying them with data. Just about any personal computer, workstation, mainframe, or supercomputer can be configured to perform the work of a server.

FIGURE A-3: A desktop personal computer

▲ A desktop computer fits on a desk and runs on power from an electrical wall outlet; the main unit can be housed in either a vertical case (like the one shown) or a horizontal case

FIGURE A-4: A notebook personal computer

▲ A notebook computer is small and lightweight, giving it the advantage of portability; it can run on power supplied by an electrical outlet, or it can run on battery power

FIGURE A-5: A handheld computer

▲ Many handheld computers feature a small keyboard, while others accept handwriting input

FIGURE A-6: A tablet computer

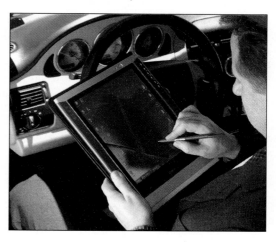

▲ A tablet computer is similiar in size to a notebook computer, but features a touch-sensitive screen that can be used for input instead of a keyboard

FIGURE A-7: A videogame console

▲ A videogame console includes circuitry similiar to a personal computer's, but its input and output devices are optimized for gaming

FIGURE A-8: A mainframe computer

▲ This IBM S/390 zSeries 900 mainframe computer weighs about 1,400 lbs and is about 6.5 feet tall

Examining personal computer systems

The term "computer system" usually refers to a computer and all of the input, output, and storage devices that are connected to it. Despite cosmetic differences among personal computers, see Figure A-9, a personal computer system usually includes standard equipment or devices. Devices may vary in color, size, and design for different personal computers. Figure A-10 illustrates a typical desktop personal computer system. Refer to Figure A-10 as you read through the list of devices below.

DETAILS

- **System unit**. The system unit is the case that holds the power supply, storage devices, and the circuit boards, including the main circuit board (also called the "motherboard"), which contains the processor. The system unit for most notebook computers also holds a built-in keyboard and speakers.

- **Display device**. Most desktop computers use a separate **monitor** as a display (output) device, whereas notebook computers use a flat panel display screen that is attached to the system unit.

- **Keyboard**. Most computers are equipped with a keyboard as the primary input device.

- **Mouse**. A mouse is a common input device designed to manipulate on-screen graphical objects and controls.

- **Storage devices**. Computers have many types of storage devices that are used to store data when the power is turned off. For example: A **floppy disk drive** is a storage device that reads data from and writes data to floppy disks. A **hard disk drive** can store billions of characters of data. It is usually mounted inside the computer's system unit. A small external light indicates when the drive is in use. A **CD-ROM drive** is a storage device that uses laser technology to read data that is permanently stored on data or audio CDs. A **DVD drive** can read data from data CDs, audio CDs, data DVDs, or DVD movie discs. CD-ROM and DVD drives typically cannot be used to write data onto discs. "ROM" stands for "read-only memory" and means that the drive can read data from discs, but cannot be used to store new data on them. Many computers, especially desktop models, include a **CD-writer** or **DVD-writer** that can be used to create and copy CDs and DVDs. There are a wide variety of CD-writers and DVD-writers including CD-R, CD-RW, DVD-R, and DVD+RW.

- **Speakers** and **sound card**. Desktop computers have a rudimentary built-in speaker that's mostly limited to playing beeps. A small circuit board, called a sound card, is required for high-quality music, narration, and sound effects. A desktop computer's sound card sends signals to external speakers. A notebook's sound card sends signals to speakers that are built into the notebook system unit. The sound card is an input and an output device, while speakers are output devices.

- **Modem**. Many personal computer systems include a built-in modem that can be used to establish an Internet connection using a standard telephone line. A modem is both an input and an output device.

- **Printer**. A computer printer is an output device that produces computer-generated text or graphical images on paper.

What's a peripheral device?

The word "peripheral" dates back to the days of mainframes when the CPU was housed in a giant box, and all input, output, and storage devices were housed separately. Today, the term "peripheral device" designates equipment that might be added to a computer system to enhance its functionality. A printer is a popular peripheral device, as is a digital camera, zip drive, scanner, joystick, or graphics tablet. Though a hard disk drive seems to be an integral part of a computer—after all, it's built right into the system unit—by the strictest technical definition, a hard disk drive is classified as a peripheral device. The same goes for other storage devices and the keyboard, monitor, sound card, speakers, and modem.

FIGURE A-9: Typical personal computer systems

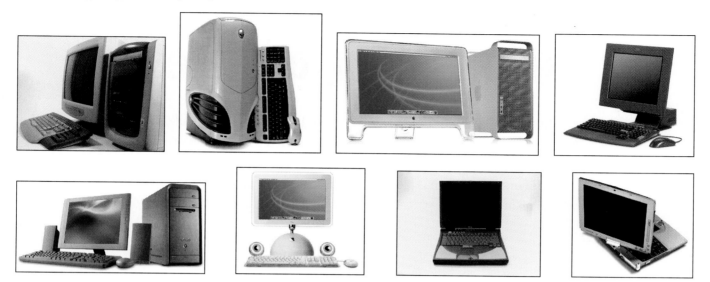

FIGURE A-10: Components of a typical computer system

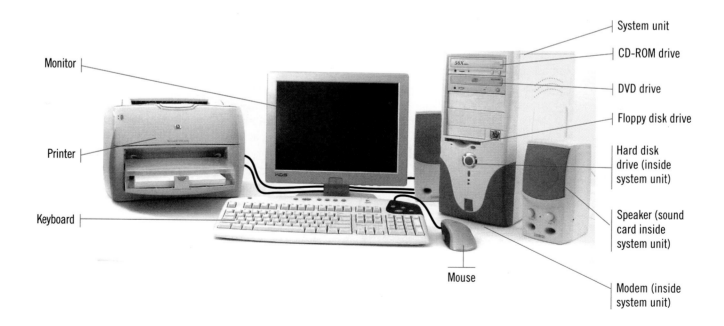

Exploring data, information, and files

In everyday conversation, people use the terms "data" and "information" interchangeably. Nevertheless, some computer professionals make a distinction between the two terms. They define **data** as the symbols that represent people, events, things, and ideas. Data becomes **information** when it is presented in a format that people can understand and use. As a rule of thumb, remember that data is used by computers; information is used by people. See Figure A-11.

DETAILS

- Have you ever gotten a computer file you couldn't read? It could be because the data has not been converted to information. Computers process and store data using the binary number system and several other codes designed expressly for electronic data. The **binary number system** has only two digits: 0 and 1. The binary number system can represent number data using only 0s and 1s.

- Computers use these codes to store data in a digital format as a series of 1s and 0s. Each 0 or 1 is a **bit**, and 8 bits are called a **byte**. The bits and bytes that are processed and stored by a computer are data. The output results of processing data—the words, numbers, sounds, and graphics—are information.

- A computer stores data in files. A **computer file**, usually referred to simply as a **file**, is a named collection of data that exists on a storage medium, such as a hard disk, a floppy disk, or a CD. Although all files contain data, some files are classified as "data files," whereas other files are classified as "executable files."

- A **data file** contains data. For example, it might contain the text for a document, the numbers for a calculation, the specifications for a graph, the frames of a video, or the notes of a musical passage.

- An **executable file** contains the programs or gives the instructions that tell a computer how to perform a specific task. For example, the word processing program that tells your computer how to display and print text is stored as an executable file.

You can think of data files as passive because the data does not instruct the computer to do anything. Executable files, on the other hand, are active because the instructions stored in the file cause the computer to carry out some action.

- Every file has a name, the **filename**, which often provides a clue to its contents. A file also has a **filename extension** usually referred to simply as an "extension" that further describes a file's contents. For example, in Pbrush.exe, "Pbrush" is the filename and "exe" is the extension. As you can see, the filename is separated from the extension by a period called a "dot." To tell someone the name of this file, you would say, "P brush dot e-x-e."

Executable files typically have .exe extensions. Data files have a variety of extensions, such as .jpg, .bmp or .tif for a graphic, .mid for synthesized music, .wav for recorded music, or .htm for a Web page. Each software program assigns a specific filename extension to the data files it creates. As a user, you do not decide the extension; rather, it is automatically included when files are created and saved, for example .xls for files created with Excel or .doc for files created with Word. Depending on your computer settings, you may or may not see the filename extension assigned to a file. Figure A-12 shows a list of files, including the filename extensions.

FIGURE A-11: The difference between data and information

The computer reads the data in the file and produces the output image as information that the viewer can understand

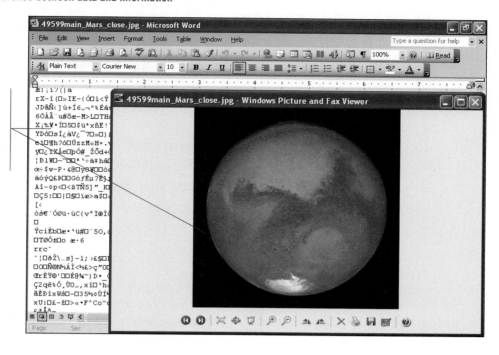

FIGURE A-12: Filenames and filename extensions

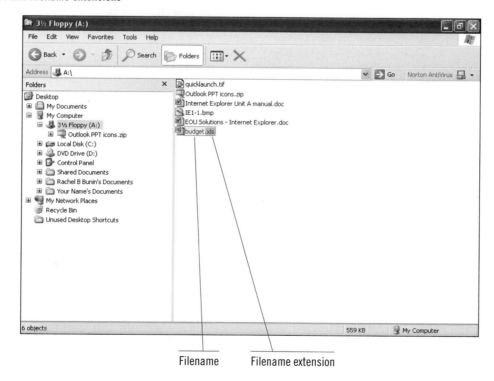

Filename   Filename extension

Introducing application and system software

A computer's application software and operating system make a computer run. As a computer user, you are probably most familiar with application software. In fact, you probably use many different types of application software that are installed on your computer. As a computer user, your computing experience is driven by the operating system. There is usually only one operating system on your computer; the operating system is not another type of application software. You can run many applications at one time, but only one operating system at one time.

Info Web
APPLE COMPUTERS

DETAILS

- **Application software** is a set of computer programs that helps a person carry out a task. Word processing software, for example, helps people create, edit, and print documents. Personal finance software helps people keep track of their money and investments. Video editing software helps people create and edit home movies and even some professional, commercially-released films.

- An operating system is essentially the master controller for all of the activities that take place within a computer. An **operating system** is classified as **system software**, not application software, because its primary purpose is to help the computer system monitor itself in order to function efficiently. Unlike application software, an operating system does not directly help people perform application-specific tasks, such as word processing. Most of the time people interact with the operating system without realizing it. However, people do interact with the operating system for certain operational and storage tasks, such as starting programs and locating data files.

- Popular personal computer operating systems include Microsoft Windows and Mac OS. Microsoft Windows Mobile and Palm OS control most handheld computers. Linux and UNIX are popular operating systems for servers. Microsoft Windows (usually referred to simply as "Windows") is probably the most widely used operating system for personal computers. As shown in Figure A-13, the Windows operating system displays menus and simulated on-screen controls designed to be manipulated by a mouse.

- Windows software is not the same as the Windows operating system. The term "Windows software" refers to any application software that is designed to run on computers that use Microsoft Windows as their operating system. For example, a program called Microsoft Word for Windows is a word processing program; it is an application program that is referred to as "Windows software."

- An operating system affects compatibility. Computers that operate in essentially the same way are said to be "compatible." Two of the most important factors that influence compatibility and define a computer's platform are the processor and the operating system. A **platform** consists of the underlying hardware and software of the computer system. Today, two of the most popular personal computer platforms are PCs and Macs.

  PCs are based on the design for one of the first personal computer "superstars"—the IBM PC. A huge selection of personal computer brands and models based on the original PC design and manufactured by companies such as IBM, Hewlett-Packard, Toshiba, Dell, and Gateway are on the shelves today. The Windows operating system was designed specifically for these personal computers. Because of this, the PC platform is sometimes called the "Windows platform." Most of the examples in this book pertain to PCs because they are so popular.

  Macs are based on a proprietary design for a personal computer called the Macintosh, manufactured almost exclusively by Apple Computer, Inc. The stylish iMac is one of Apple's most popular computers, and like other computers in the Mac platform, it uses Mac OS as its operating system. See Figure A-14.

- The PC and Mac platforms are not compatible because their processors and operating systems differ. Consequently, application software designed for Macs does not typically work with PCs. When shopping for new software, it is important to read the package to make sure that it is designed to work with your computer platform.

  Different versions of some operating systems have been created to operate with more than one processor. For example, one version of the Linux operating system exists for the PC platform and another version exists for the Mac platform.

FIGURE A-13: The Windows interface

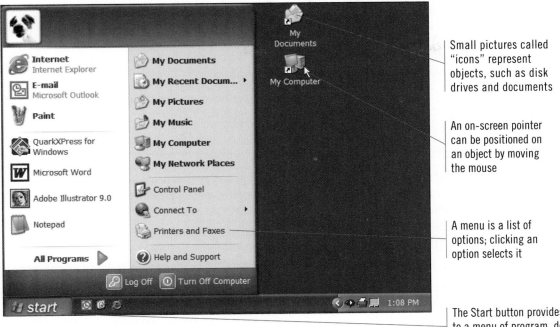

Small pictures called "icons" represent objects, such as disk drives and documents

An on-screen pointer can be positioned on an object by moving the mouse

A menu is a list of options; clicking an option selects it

The Start button provides access to a menu of program, document, and customization options

▲ The Windows operating system displays on-screen icons, menus, buttons, and other graphical controls designed to be manipulated by a mouse

FIGURE A-14: The Mac OS

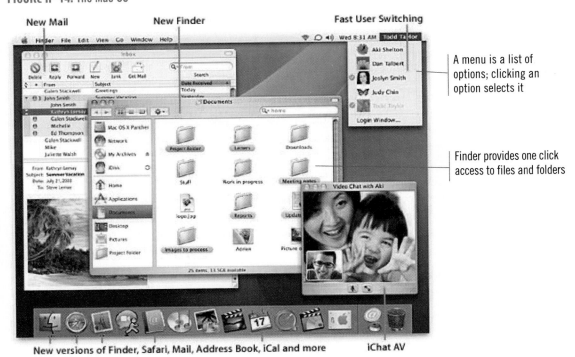

A menu is a list of options; clicking an option selects it

Finder provides one click access to files and folders

New Mail

New Finder

Fast User Switching

New versions of Finder, Safari, Mail, Address Book, iCal and more

iChat AV

▲ The Mac OS displays on-screen icons, menus, buttons, and other grapical controls designed to be manipulated by a mouse

Defining Internet basics

Sometimes referred to as "cyberspace," the **Internet** is a collection of local, regional, national, and international computer networks that are linked together to exchange data and distribute processing tasks. If you're looking for information, if you want to communicate with someone, or if you want to buy something, the Internet offers abundant resources.

DETAILS

- The **Internet backbone** defines the main routes of the Internet. See Figure A-15. Analogous to interstate highways, the Internet backbone is constructed and maintained by major telecommunications companies. These telecommunications links can move huge amounts of data at incredible speeds.

- In addition to the backbone, the Internet encompasses an intricate collection of regional and local communications links. These links can include local telephone systems, cable television lines, cellular telephone systems, and personal satellite dishes that transport data to and from millions of computers and other electronic devices.

- Communication among all of the different devices on the Internet is made possible by **TCP/IP (Transmission Control Protocol/Internet Protocol)**, which is a standard set of rules for electronically addressing and transmitting data.

- Most of the information that is accessible on the Internet is stored on servers. These servers use special **server software** to locate and distribute data requested by Internet users.

- Every device that's connected to the Internet is assigned a unique number, called an **IP address** that pinpoints its location in cyberspace. To prepare data for transport, a computer divides the data into small chunks called **packets**. Each packet is labeled with the IP address of its destination and then transmitted. When a packet reaches an intersection in the Internet's communications links, a device called a **router** examines the packet's address. The router checks the address in a routing table and then sends the packet along the appropriate link towards its destination. As packets arrive at their destinations, they are reassembled into a replica of the original file.

- A **Web site** can provide information, collect information through forms, or provide access to other resources, such as search engines and e-mail.

- The Internet revolutionized business by directly linking consumers with retailers, manufacturers, and distributors through electronic commerce, or **e-commerce**.

- Electronic mail, known as **e-mail**, allows one person to send an electronic message to another person or to a group of people. A variation of e-mail called a **mailing list server**, or "listserv," maintains a public list of people who are interested in a particular topic. Messages sent to the list server are automatically distributed to everyone on the mailing list.

- **Usenet** is a worldwide bulletin board system that contains thousands of discussion forums on every imaginable topic called **newsgroups**. Newsgroup members post messages based on their interests to the bulletin board; these messages can be read and responded to by other group members.

- The Internet allows real-time communication. For example, a **chat group** consists of several people who connect to the Internet and communicate in real time by typing comments to each other. A private version of a chat room, called **instant messaging**, allows people to send typed messages back and forth. **Internet telephony** allows telephone-style conversations to travel over the Internet. Internet telephony requires special software at both ends of the conversation and, instead of a telephone, it uses a microphone connected to a computer.

- The Internet carries radio shows and teleconferences that can be broadcast worldwide. Internet radio is popular because broadcasts aren't limited to a small local region.

- Internet servers store a variety of files including documents, music, software, videos, animations, and photos. The process of transferring one of these files from a remote computer, such as a server, to a local computer, such as your personal computer, is called **downloading**. Sending a file from a local computer to a remote computer is called **uploading**. See Figure A-16.

- P2P file sharing. A technology known as **peer-to-peer (P2P)** file sharing makes it possible to access files stored on another Internet user's hard disk—with permission, of course. This technology is the basis for popular music and file exchange Web sites, such as Morpheus, WinMX, and Kazaa.

FIGURE A-15: The Internet backbone

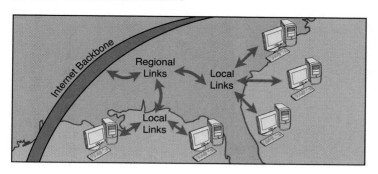

◄ Personal computers are connected to regional and local communications links, which in turn connect to the Internet backbone; data transport works seemlessly between any two platforms—between PCs and Macs, and even between personal computers and mainframes

FIGURE A-16: Web sites provide files

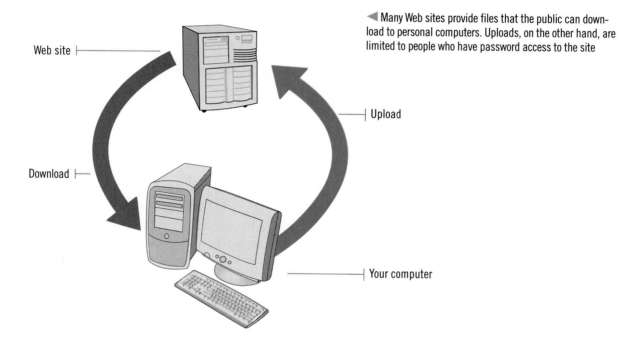

◄ Many Web sites provide files that the public can download to personal computers. Uploads, on the other hand, are limited to people who have password access to the site

Web site

Upload

Download

Your computer

What is a blog?

The term **blog**, derived from the phrase "WeB LOG," refers to a personal journal posted on the Web for access by the general public. Blogs can focus on a single topic or cover a variety of issues. A typical blog includes commentary by the author as well as links to additional information. Blogs have become a popular way of disseminating information over the Internet. Blog directories, such as the one shown in Figure A-17, provide links to blogs on all sorts of topics.

FIGURE A-17: Blogs

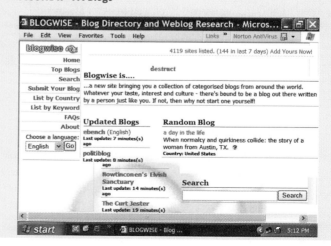

Connecting to the Internet

To take advantage of the Internet, you'll have to establish a communications link between your computer and the Internet. Possibilities include using your existing telephone line, a cable television line, a personal satellite link, wireless or cell phone service, or special high-speed telephone services. Being on the Internet is often referred to as being **online**.

LAB

MAKING A DIAL UP CONNECTION

DETAILS

- A **dial-up connection** requires a device called a **voice band modem**, or "modem," which converts your computer's digital signals into a type of signal that can travel over telephone lines. Figure A-18 shows various types of computer modems.

    To establish a dial-up connection, your computer's modem dials a special access number, which is answered by an Internet modem. Once the connection is established, your computer is "on the Internet." When you complete an Internet session, you must "hang up" your modem. You can choose to disconnect automatically or manually; either way the connection is discontinued until the next time you dial in.

    Theoretically, the top speed of a dial-up connection is 56 K, meaning that 56,000 bits of data are transmitted per second. Actual speed is usually reduced by distance, interference, and other technical problems, however, so the speed of most 56 K dial-up connections is more like 45 K. This speed is useable for e-mail, e-commerce, and chat. It is not, however, really optimal for applications that require large amounts of data to be transferred quickly over the Internet.

- **Cable modem service** is offered to a cable company's customers for an additional monthly charge and usually requires two pieces of equipment: a network card and a cable modem. A **network card** is a device that's designed to connect a personal computer to a local area network. A **cable modem** (see Figure A-19) is a device that changes a computer's signals into a form that can travel over cable TV links.

    Cable modem access is referred to as an **always-on connection**, because your computer is, in effect, always connected to the Internet, unlike a dial-up connection that is established only when the dialing sequence is completed. A cable modem receives data at about 1.5 million bits per second (1.5 Mbps) more than 25 times faster than a dial-up connection. This speed is suitable for most Internet activities, including real-time video and teleconferencing.

- Many telephone and independent telecommunications companies offer high-speed, always-on connections. **ISDN (Integrated Services Digital Network)** provides data transfer speeds of either 64 K (bits per second, or bps) or 128 K (bps). Given data

transfer speeds that are only marginally better than a 56 K dial-up connection and substantial monthly fees, ISDN ranks low on the list of high-speed Internet options for most consumers. **DSL (Digital Subscriber Line)** is a generic name for a family of high-speed Internet links, including ADSL, SDSL, and DSL lite. Each type of DSL provides different maximum speeds from twice as fast to approximately 125 times faster than a 56 K dial-up connection. Both ISDN and DSL connections require proximity to a telephone switching station, which can be a problem for speed-hungry consumers who don't live near one.

- Another Internet connection option is **DSS (Digital Satellite Service)**, which today offers two-way Internet access at an average speed of about 500 K. Consumers are required to rent or purchase a satellite dish and pay for its installation.

- An **ISP (Internet Service Provider)** is a company that maintains Internet computers and telecommunications equipment in order to provide Internet access to businesses, organizations, and individuals. Some parts of the Internet (such as military computers) are off limits to the general public. Other parts of the Internet limit access to paid members.

- User IDs and passwords are designed to provide access to authorized users and to prevent unauthorized access. A **user ID** is a series of characters, letters, and possibly numbers that becomes a person's unique identifier, similar to a social security number. A **password** is a different series of characters that verifies the user ID, sort of like a PIN (personal identification number) verifies your identity at an ATM machine.

- Typically, your ISP provides you with a user ID and password that you use to connect to the Internet. You will accumulate additional user IDs and passwords from other sources for specific Internet activities, such as reading New York Times articles or participating in an online auction. The process of entering a user ID and password is usually referred to as "logging in" or "logging on." See Figure A-20. The rules for creating a user ID are not consistent throughout the Internet, so it is important to read all of the instructions carefully before finalizing your ID.

FIGURE A-18: Computer modems

▲ To determine whether a computer has a modem, look for a place to plug in a standard phone cable

▲ A modem card slides into a notebook computer's PC card slot

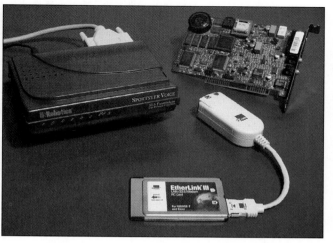

▲ An external modem (top left) connects to the computer with a cable; an internal modem (top right) is installed inside the computer's system unit; a PC card modem (bottom center) is typically used in a notebook computer

FIGURE A-20: Entering a password

▲ Typically, when you log in and enter your password, a series of asterisks appears on the screen to prevent someone looking over your shoulder from discovering your password; don't share your password with anyone, or write it down where it could be found; your password should be a sequence of characters and numbers that is easy for you to remember, but would be difficult for someone else to guess

FIGURE A-19: Cable modem

▲ A cable modem can be a standalone device set up close to a computer, or it can be integrated with other electronic components in a "set-top box" on top of a television

What services does an Internet Service Provider provide?

To access the Internet, you do not typically connect your computer directly to the backbone. Instead, you connect it to an ISP that in turn connects to the backbone. An ISP is a point of access to the Internet. An ISP typically provides a connection to the Internet and an e-mail account. Some ISPs offer proprietary services that are available only to subscribers. These services might include content channels with articles on health, hobbies, investing, and sports; activities specially designed for kids and teens; anti-spam and security software; a variety of voice and text messaging services; and free (and virus-free) software. ISP customers arrange for service, in this case for Internet access, for which they pay a monthly fee. In addition to a monthly fee, an ISP might also charge an installation fee. The ISP that you select should provide service in the places that you typically use your computer. If your work takes you on the road a lot, you'll want to consider a national ISP that provides local access numbers in the cities that you visit.

Understanding World Wide Web basics

In the 1960s, long before personal computers or the Internet existed, a Harvard student named Ted Nelson wrote a term paper in which he described a set of documents, called **hypertext**, that would be stored on a computer. He envisioned that while reading a document in hypertext, a person could use a set of "links" to view related documents. A revolutionary idea for its time, today hypertext is the foundation for a part of the Internet that's often called "the Web" by the millions of people who use it every day.

DETAILS

● One of the Internet's most captivating attractions, the **Web** (short for "World Wide Web") is a collection of files that are interconnected through the use of hypertext. Many of these files produce documents called **Web pages**. Other files contain photos, videos, animations, and sounds that can be incorporated into specific Web pages. Most Web pages contain **links** (sometimes called "hyperlinks") to related documents and media files. See Figure A-21.

● A series of Web pages can be grouped into a **Web site**—a sort of virtual "place" in cyberspace. Every day, thousands of people shop at online department stores featuring clothing, shoes, and jewelry; visit research Web sites to look up information; and go to news Web sites, not only to read about the latest news, sports, and weather, but also to discuss current issues with other readers. The Web encompasses these and many other types of sites.

● Web sites are hosted by corporations, government agencies, colleges, and private organizations all over the world. The computers and software that store and distribute Web pages are called **Web servers**.

● Every Web page has a unique address called a **URL (uniform resource locator)**. For example, the URL for the Cable News Network Web site is http://www.cnn.com. Most URLs begin with http://. **HTTP (Hypertext Transfer Protocol)** is the communications standard that's instrumental in transporting Web documents over the Internet. When typing a URL, the http:// can usually be omitted, so www.cnn.com works just as well as http://www.cnn.com.

● Most Web sites have a main page that acts as a doorway to the rest of the pages at the site. This main page is sometimes referred to as a **home page**. The URL for a Web site's main page is typically short and to the point, like www.cnn.com.

● The site might then be divided into topic areas that are reflected in the URL. For example, the CNN site might include a weather center www.cnn.com/weather/ and an entertainment desk www.cnn.com/showbiz/. A series of Web pages will then be grouped under the appropriate topic. For example, you might find a page about hurricanes at the URL www.cnn.com/weather/hurricanes.html or a page about El Niño at www.cnn.com/weather/elnino.htm. The filename of a specific Web page always appears last in the URL—hurricanes.html and elnino.htm are the names of two Web pages. Web page filenames usually have an .htm or .html extension, indicating that the page was created with **HTML** (Hyptertext Markup Language), a standard format for Web documents. Figure A-22 identifies the parts of a URL.

● A URL never contains a space, even after a punctuation mark. An underline character is sometimes used to give the appearance of a space between words, as in the URL www.detroit.com/restaurants/best_restaurants.html. Be sure to use the correct type of slash—always a forward slash (/)—and duplicate the URL's capitalization exactly. The servers that run some Web sites are case sensitive, which means that an uppercase letter is not the same as a lowercase letter. On these servers, typing www.cmu.edu/Overview.html (with an uppercase "O") will not locate the page that's stored as www.cmu.edu/overview.html (with a lowercase "o").

FIGURE A-21: A Web page

URL

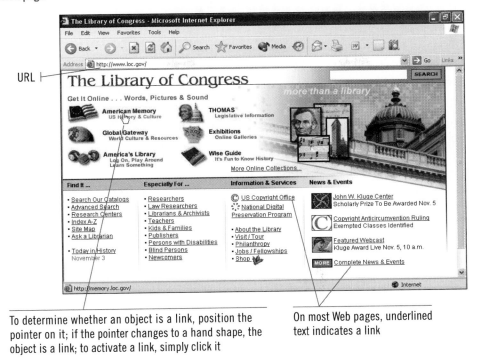

To determine whether an object is a link, position the pointer on it; if the pointer changes to a hand shape, the object is a link; to activate a link, simply click it

On most Web pages, underlined text indicates a link

FIGURE A-22: A URL

http://www.cnn.com/showbiz/movies.htm

Web protocol standard

Web server name

Folder name

Document name and filename extension

◀ The URL for a Web page indicates the computer on which it is stored, its location on the Web server, a folder name, its filename, and its filename extension

Using search engines

The term "search engine" popularly refers to a Web site that provides a variety of tools to help you find information on the Web. A keyword is any word or phrase that you type to describe the information that you're trying to find. Based on your input, the search engine provides a list of pages. Depending on the search engine that you use, you may be able to find information by entering a description, filling out a form, or clicking a series of links to review a list of topics and subtopics (Topic Directory). To use a topic directory, simply click a general topic. When a list of subtopics appears, click the one that's most relevant to the information you are trying to locate. If your selection results in another list of subtopics, continue to select the most relevant one until the search engine presents a list of Web pages. You can then link to these pages just as though you had used a keyword query. See Figure A-23. Without search engines, using the Internet would be like trying to find a book in the Library of Congress by wandering around the stacks. To discover exactly how to use a particular search engine effectively, refer to its Help pages.

FIGURE A-23: Search engines

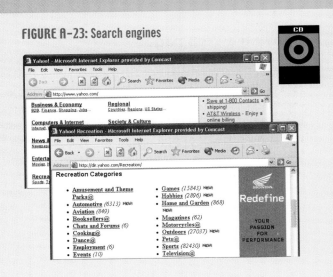

Using browsers

A Web browser, usually referred to simply as a **browser**, is a software program that runs on your computer and helps you view and navigate Web pages. See Figure A-25. A browser provides a window in which it displays a Web page. The borders of the window contain a set of menus and controls to help you navigate from one Web page to another. Today's most popular browsers are Microsoft Internet Explorer® (IE) and Netscape Navigator® (Navigator).

INFO WEB — BROWSER   LAB — BROWSING AND SEARCHING

DETAILS

- Whether it's called a "URL box," an "Address box," or a "Location box," most browsers provide a space for entering URLs.

- If you want to view the Web page www.dogs.com/boxer.html, you enter the URL into the Address box provided by your browser. When you press [Enter] on the keyboard, the browser contacts the Web server at www.dogs.com and requests the boxer.html page. The server sends your computer the data stored in boxer.html. This data includes two things: the information that you want to view and embedded codes, called **HTML tags**, that tell your browser how to display the information. The tags specify details such as the color of the background, the text color and size, and the placement of graphics. Figure A-26 shows that a browser assembles a document on your computer screen according to the specifications contained in the HTML tags.

- Web browsers offer a remarkably similar set of features and capabilities. HTML tags make it possible for Web pages to appear similar from one browser to the next.

- The browser's Back button lets you retrace your steps to view pages that you've seen previously. Most browsers also have a Forward button, which shows you the page that you were viewing before you clicked the Back button.

- Your browser lets you select a **home page**, which is the Web page that appears every time you start your browser. Whenever you click the Home button, your browser displays your home page. This home page is different than the home page of a Web site.

- Typically, a browser provides access to a print option from a button or a menu, allowing you to print the contents of a Web page. You should always preview before printing because a Web page on the screen may print out as several printed pages.

- To help you revisit sites from previous sessions, your browser provides a **History list**. You can display this list by clicking a button or menu option provided by your browser. To revisit any site in the History list, click its URL. Many browsers allow you to specify how long a URL will remain in the History list.

- If you find a great Web site and you want to revisit it sometime in the future, you can add the URL to a list, typically called **Favorites** or **Bookmarks** so you can simply click its URL to display it.

- Sometimes a Web page takes a very long time to appear on your screen. If you don't want to wait for a page, click the Stop button.

- If you're looking for information on a Web page, use the Find option on your browser's Edit menu to locate a word or phrase.

Copying a Web page

Most browsers let you save a copy of a Web page and place it at the storage location of your choice. Most allow you to save a copy of a graphic or sound that you find on a Web page. Most browsers also provide a Copy command that allows you to copy a section of text from a Web page, which you can then paste into one of your own documents. To copy a passage of text from a Web page, highlight the text (see Figure A-24), click the Edit menu, then select Copy. Next, switch to your own document and use the Paste option. To keep track of the source for each insertion, you can also use the Copy command to copy the Web page's URL from the Address box, and then paste the URL into your document.

FIGURE A-24: Selecting text on a Web page

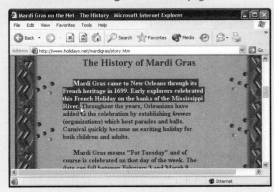

FIGURE A-25: Internet Explorer browser

Navigation buttons   Stop   Home   Search button   Favorites   History list   Print

Title bar

Menu bar

Toolbar

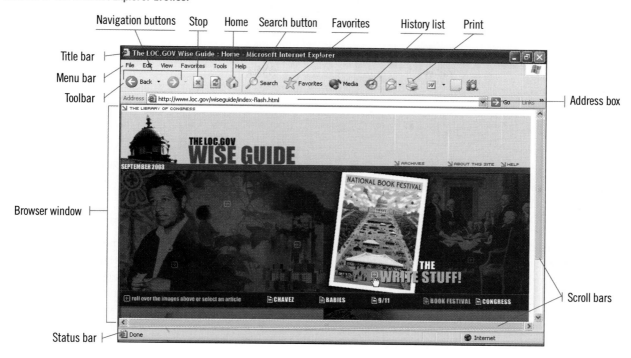

Address box

Browser window

Scroll bars

Status bar

FIGURE A-26: A Web page in Internet Explorer and the HTML code used to display it

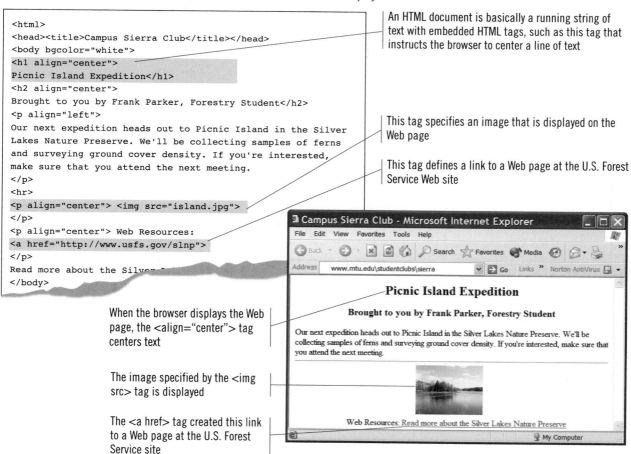

```
<html>
<head><title>Campus Sierra Club</title></head>
<body bgcolor="white">
<h1 align="center">
Picnic Island Expedition</h1>
<h2 align="center">
Brought to you by Frank Parker, Forestry Student</h2>
<p align="left">
Our next expedition heads out to Picnic Island in the Silver
Lakes Nature Preserve. We'll be collecting samples of ferns
and surveying ground cover density. If you're interested,
make sure that you attend the next meeting.
</p>
<hr>
<p align="center"> <img src="island.jpg">
</p>
<p align="center"> Web Resources:
<a href="http://www.usfs.gov/slnp">
</p>
Read more about the Silver
</body>
```

An HTML document is basically a running string of text with embedded HTML tags, such as this tag that instructs the browser to center a line of text

This tag specifies an image that is displayed on the Web page

This tag defines a link to a Web page at the U.S. Forest Service Web site

When the browser displays the Web page, the <align="center"> tag centers text

The image specified by the <img src> tag is displayed

The <a href> tag created this link to a Web page at the U.S. Forest Service site

UNIT A

Understanding e-mail basics

The Internet really took off when people discovered electronic mail. Billions of e-mail messages speed over the Internet each year. E-mail can refer to a single electronic message or to the entire system of computers and software that transmits, receives, and stores e-mail messages. Any person with an e-mail account can send and receive e-mail. Basic e-mail activities are discussed in Table A-1.

DETAILS

- An **e-mail account** provides the rights to a storage area, or mailbox, supplied by an e-mail provider, such as an ISP. Each mailbox has a unique address that typically consists of a user ID, an @ symbol, and the name of the computer that maintains the mailbox. For example, suppose that a university student named Dee Greene has an electronic mailbox on a computer called rutgers.edu. If her user ID is "dee_greene," her **e-mail address** would be dee_greene@rutgers.edu.

- An **e-mail message** is a document that is composed on a computer and transmitted in digital or "electronic" form to another computer. Every message includes a message header and the body of the message, usually displayed in a form, as shown in Figure A-27. Basic e-mail activities include writing, reading, replying to, and forwarding messages. Messages can be printed, kept for later reference, or deleted.

- Any file that travels with an e-mail message is called an **e-mail attachment**. A conversion process called **MIME (Multi-Purpose Internet Mail Extensions)** provides a way of transporting digital photos, sounds, and other media as plain ASCII text that can travel over the Internet as e-mail attachments. An electronic message incorporated in the e-mail header provides your e-mail software with the information that allows it to reconstruct the attachment into its original form.

- After you receive an e-mail message, you can use the Forward feature to pass it on to other people. When you initiate the forward process, the original e-mail message is copied into a new message window, complete with the address of the original sender. You can then enter the address of the person to whom you are forwarding the message. You can also add a note about why you are passing the message along.

- Today, most e-mail software allows you to create e-mail messages in HTML format. Why use HTML format for your e-mail? HTML messages can contain fancy formatting. The only limitation is that your e-mail recipients must have HTML-compliant e-mail software; otherwise, your message will be delivered as ASCII text.

- Although e-mail is delivered quickly, it is important to use proper netiquette when composing a message. **Netiquette (Internet etiquette)** is a series of customs or guidelines for maintaining civilized and effective communications in online discussions and e-mail exchanges. For example, typing in all caps, such as "WHAT DID YOU DO?" is considered shouting and rude.

- An **e-mail system** is the equipment and software that carries and manipulates e-mail messages. It includes computers and software called **e-mail servers** that sort, store, and route mail.

- E-mail is based on **store-and-forward technology**, a communications method in which data that cannot be sent directly to its destination will be temporarily stored until transmission is possible. This technology allows e-mail messages to be routed to a server and held until they are forwarded to the next server or to a personal mailbox.

- Three types of e-mail systems are widely used today: POP, IMAP, and Web-based mail. **POP (Post Office Protocol)** temporarily stores new messages in your mailbox on an e-mail server. See Figure A-28. Most people who use POP have obtained an e-mail account from an ISP. Such an account provides a mailbox on the ISP's **POP server**, which is a computer that stores your incoming messages until they can be transferred to your hard disk. Using POP requires e-mail client software. This software, which is installed on your computer, provides an Inbox and an Outbox. When you ask the e-mail server to deliver your mail, all of the messages stored in your mailbox on the POP server are transferred to your computer, stored on your computer's disk drive, and listed as new mail in your Inbox. You can then disconnect from the Internet, if you like, and read the new mail at your leisure.

    IMAP (Internet Messaging Access Protocol) is similar to POP, except that you have the option of downloading your mail or leaving it on the server. **Web-based e-mail**, the most commonly used, keeps your mail at a Web site rather than transferring it to your computer. Examples of Web-based e-mail are Yahoo mail and Hotmail. Before you can use Web-based e-mail, you'll need an e-mail account with a Web-based e-mail provider.

FIGURE A-27: Composing a message

When you compose an e-mail message, you'll begin by entering the address of one or more recipients and the subject of the message

You can also specify one or more files to attach to the message

The body of the e-mail message contains the message itself

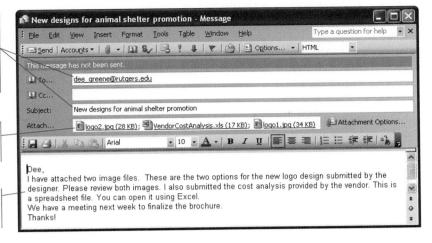

When the message is sent, your e-mail software adds the date and your e-mail address to identify you as the sender

FIGURE A-28: Incoming and outgoing mail

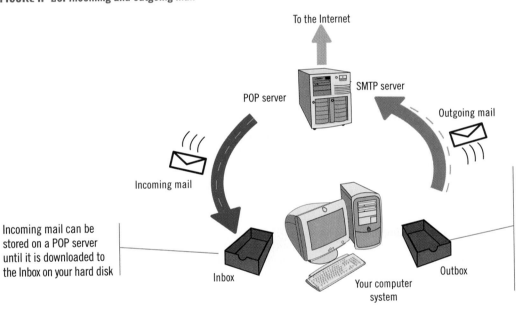

Incoming mail can be stored on a POP server until it is downloaded to the Inbox on your hard disk

An Outbox temporarily holds messages that you composed and completed, but that haven't been transmitted over the Internet; when you go online, you can send all the mail that's being held in your Outbox; outgoing mail is routed by an SMTP (Simple Mail Transfer Protocol) server, instead of by the POP server

Table A-1: Basic e-mail activities consist of writing, reading, replying to and forwarding messages

FEATURE/ ACTIVITY	USE TO	FEATURE/ ACTIVITY	USE TO
Reply	Send a reply to recipients of an e-mail; includes the original message	Group	Create an e-mail "group" that consists of several e-mail addresses
Forward	Pass an e-mail on to other people	Priority	Assign a priority level to your e-mail messages
Cc:	Send a "carbon copy" of a message to one or more recipients	Sort	Sort e-mail messages by date received, sender name, subject, or priority
Bcc:	Send a "blind carbon copy" of a message to one or more recipients	Automate	Automate replies to messages when you will not be responding for a few days
Address book	Maintain contact information	Block	Refuse messages that arrive from a particular e-mail address

The sequence of events that occurs between the time that you turn on a computer and the time that it becomes ready to accept commands is referred to as the **boot process** or "booting" your computer. Your computer boots up by first loading a small program, called a "bootstrap" program, into memory, then it uses that small program to load a large operating system. Your computer's small bootstrap program is built into special ROM (read-only memory) circuitry housed in the computer's system unit. When you turn on a computer, the ROM circuitry receives power and it begins the boot process.

What is the purpose of the boot process? The boot process involves a lot of flashing lights, whirring noises, and beeping as your computer performs a set of diagnostic tests called the **power-on self-test (POST)**. The good news is that these tests can warn you if certain crucial components of your computer system are out of whack. The bad news is that these tests cannot warn you of impending failures. Also, problems identified during the boot process usually must be fixed before you can start a computing session.

The boot process serves an additional purpose—loading the operating system from the hard disk into memory so that it can help the computer carry out basic operations. Without the operating system, a computer's CPU is basically unable to communicate with any input, output, or storage devices. It can't display information, accept commands, store data, or run any application software. Therefore, loading the operating system is a crucial step in the boot process.

Most of a computer's memory is "volatile" random access memory (RAM), which cannot hold any data when the power is off. Although a copy of the operating system is housed in RAM while the computer is in operation, this copy is erased as soon as the power is turned off. Given the volatility of RAM, computer designers decided to store the operating system on a computer's hard disk. During the boot process, a copy of the operating system is copied into RAM, where it can be accessed quickly whenever the computer needs to carry out an input, processing, output, or storage operation. The operating system remains in RAM until the computer is turned off.

Six major events happen during the boot process:

1. Power up. When you turn on the power switch, the power light is illuminated, and power is distributed to the computer circuitry.

2. Start boot program. The processor begins to execute the bootstrap program that is stored in ROM.

3. Power-on self-test. The computer performs diagnostic tests of several crucial system components.

4. Identify peripheral devices. The operating system identifies the peripheral devices that are connected to the computer and checks their settings.

5. Load operating system. The operating system is copied from the hard disk to RAM.

6. Check configuration and customization. The processor reads configuration data and executes any customized startup routines specified by the user.

What if I turn on a computer and nothing happens? The first step in the boot process is the power-up stage. Power from a wall outlet or battery activates a small power light. If the power light does not come on when you flip the "on" switch, you should check all the power connections and be sure everything is plugged in properly.

What kinds of problems are likely to show up during the power-on self-test? The POST checks your computer's main circuitry, screen display, memory, and keyboard. It can identify when one of these devices has failed, but it cannot identify intermittent problems or impending failures. The POST notifies you of a hardware problem by displaying an error message on the screen or by emitting a series of beeps. A **beep code** provides your computer with a way to signal a problem, even if the screen is not functioning. You can check the documentation or Web site for your computer to find the specific meaning of numeric error codes. The printed or online reference manual for a computer usually explains the meaning of each beep code.

Should I try to fix these problems myself? If a computer displays error messages, emits beep codes, or seems to freeze up during the boot process, you can take some simple steps that might fix it. First, turn the computer off, check all the cables, wait five seconds, then try to start the computer again. Refer to Figure A-29 for a power-up checklist. If you still encounter a boot error after trying to restart the computer several times, contact a technical support person.

What's the long list of stuff that appears on my screen during the boot process? After the POST, the bootstrap program tries to identify all of the devices that are connected to the computer. The settings for each device appear on the screen, creating a list of rather esoteric information.

On occasion, a device gets skipped or misidentified during the boot process. An error message is not produced, but the device doesn't seem to work properly. To resolve this problem, shut down the computer and reboot it. If a device is causing persistent problems, you may need to check the manufacturer's Web site to see if a new software patch will improve its operation.

Do computers have trouble loading the operating system or applying customization settings? Problems during the last stages of the boot process are rare, except when a disk has been inadvertently left in the floppy disk drive. Before computers were equipped with hard disk drives, floppy disks were used to store the operating system and application software. As a legacy from these early machines, today's computers first check the floppy disk drive for a disk containing the operating system. If it doesn't find a disk in the drive, it proceeds to look for the operating system on the hard disk. However, if a floppy disk happens to be left in drive A, the computer will assume that you want to boot from it and will look for the operating system on that disk. The error message "Non-system disk or disk error" is the clue to this problem. Remove the floppy disk and press any key to resume the boot process.

FIGURE A-29: Power-up checklist

How do I know when the boot process is finished? The boot process is complete when the computer is ready to accept your commands. Usually, the computer displays an operating system prompt or main screen. The Windows operating system, for example, displays the Windows desktop when the boot process is complete.

If Windows cannot complete the boot process, you are likely to see a menu that contains an option for Safe Mode. **Safe Mode** is a limited version of Windows that allows you to use your mouse, monitor, and keyboard, but not other peripheral devices. This mode is designed for troubleshooting, not for real computing tasks. If your computer enters Safe Mode at the end of the boot process, you should use the Shut Down command on the Start menu to shut down and turn off your computer properly. You can then turn on your computer again. It should complete the boot process in regular Windows mode. If your computer enters Safe Mode again, consult a technician.

- ☑ Make sure that the power cable is plugged into the wall and into the back of the computer.
- ☑ Check batteries if you're using a notebook computer.
- ☑ Try to plug your notebook into a wall outlet.
- ☑ Make sure that the wall outlet is supplying power (plug a lamp into it and make sure that you can turn it on).
- ☑ If the computer is plugged into a surge strip, extension cord, or uninterruptible power supply, make sure that it is turned on and functioning correctly.
- ☑ Can you hear the fan in your desktop computer? If not, the computer's power supply mechanism might have failed.

Computers are helping athletes optimize their perform-ance. In the mid-1960s researchers first used mainframe computers to perform complex computations for biome-chanics, the study of the motion of living things. Biomechanics can be applied to many sport-related activities, such as determining the optimal take-off position for an ice skater's triple jump or discovering the best wrist action for a basketball free-throw. Figure A-30 shows how a computer helps with a golf swing.

On a very simple level, biomechanics views the human body's bones and joints as a series of interconnected lines, called vectors. Your arm, for example, is composed of two vectors connected at the elbow. When you bend your arm, the angle formed by the two vec-tors decreases. The size of the vectors and the angles they form can be expressed and manipulated mathematically, allowing biome-chanics researchers to model the entire human body as a series of vectors. Because the human body doesn't operate in a vacuum, bio-mechanical analyses must take into account physical factors, such as gravity, mass, speed, and the fluid dynamics of air or water in which the athlete performs. Calculations for all the factors in bio-mechanical analyses involve many data points and complex equations—definitely a job for computers.

Today, researchers can use powerful processors, wireless electro-magnetic sensors, digital video cameras, and sophisticated model-ing software to study an athlete's movement. Small sensors are attached to key joints of the athlete's body. At rates up to 120 times per second, each sensor sends its location as X, Y, and Z coordi-nates to a computer. A computer then uses the sensor data to con-struct a 3-D animation of the athlete's movements. The data can be superimposed on an animated skeletal model so that athletes and coaches can look for fundamental athletic performance problems. A series of performances can be compared on a split screen display or with strobe-like multiple shots.

Another way to enhance athletic performance is with computer-controlled simulators. Similar to a flight simulator, a sports simulator creates a computer-generated environment that the athlete can manipulate. Simple and inexpensive software-based simulators for sports such as golf, sailing, and BMX racing run on standard per-sonal computers. Most software-based sports simulators are essentially games. Simulators that depict settings based on real locations, however, help athletes familiarize themselves with a course or track before competing on it. More sophisticated sports simulators include hardware components that simulate the total sports experience. For example, a bobsled simulator developed at The University of California includes a computer-controlled capsule equipped with a screen display, realistic steering controls, an audio system that generates the sound of a sled on a track, and a motion control system designed to realistically roll and vibrate the cockpit. Data from competition tracks in Salt Lake City, Lillehammer, Calgary, and Albertville can be fed into the computer. Based on the driver's steering input, the computer generates an image of the track ahead, sends messages to the motion control system, and returns force-feedback to the driver through the steering handles. Bobsled drivers are typically limited to four or five daily practice runs on a real track, but with the bobsled simulator they can take many practice runs, concentrate on difficult sections of the track, practice on different tracks without traveling, and compare their runs to other drivers.

FIGURE A-30

The same technology powers arcade style golf, racecar, and snowboard simulators. Simulation technology is also filtering down to consumer fitness equipment, such as stationary bicycles and treadmills.

In addition to optimizing performance, computers make it possible to design stronger, lighter, and more efficient sports equipment, such as mountain bikes, athletic shoes, and snowboards. Refer to Figure A-31. Advances in the fields of computerized engineering and materials science have revolutionized equipment design and manufacturing. Until a decade ago, equipment designers created simple 2-D models on a computer screen, and then hand-tooled a product mockup. Today, powerful computer workstations and 3-D CAD (computer-aided design) software help designers plot their ideas in three dimensions, and then send the design to a CAM (computer-aided manufacturing) device that carves out a physical model from light-reactive plastic or wax. In the past, exorbitantly expensive CAD software, CAM devices, and high-end computer workstations prevented many companies from using CAD/CAM technology. Today, CAD software is much more affordable and runs on consumer-level personal computers. Most athletic equipment manufacturers can also afford to maintain their own CAM equipment in house.

Computer use in sports is not without controversy. The use of high-tech computer gear has raised dissent among some sports fans, who question whether the focus of sports has shifted from athletes to their equipment. Computers and materials science experts can supply pole-vaulters with springier poles, golfers with long-range balls and clubs, and cyclists with ever-lighter

bikes. In races that may be won by a tenth of a second, equipment rather than human performance can make the difference between first and second place.

Some observers believe that fair competition is possible only if all contestants use the same gear. Is the solution to standardize competition gear? Those opposed to this idea argue that standardized equipment would inhibit innovations that contribute to the evolution of sports. International sports associations tend to agree that within limits, competitors can use the best gear that computers, designers, and engineers can produce. As long as this continues to be the case, expect sports equipment manufacturers to continue exercising their CAD/CAM equipment to produce cutting-edge athletic gear. However, even the best gear can't transform an athlete into a champion, so also expect innovations in the use of technology to analyze athletic performance and increase performance skills.

FIGURE A-31

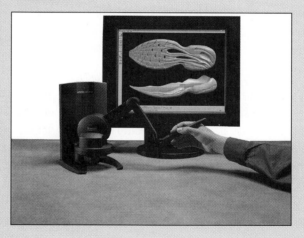

You wake up, put in your contact lenses, and rush over to the computer to check your e-mail. After reading and responding to the messages that came in overnight, you write a few new messages to get the day going, check out world events on several of your favorite news sites, play a quick game of solitaire, and then an hour or two later, remember you haven't yet dressed or had breakfast. Then fast forward to the end of the day...you get home from the job—which may or may not require you to sit at a computer, say a quick hello to your family, and then sit down for a few hours of "leisure" time at the computer.

As computers are becoming more ubiquitous, that is, ever-present in our lives, people are spending more and more time at the keyboard. What are the implications for personal health (physical, emotional, and mental), language usage, and society? How does all this time people are spending at the computer affect society in general? Are we spending too much time online? The Internet is available 24 hours a day, 7 days a week...and as a result people can check their e-mail, stay in touch with work (even when they should be on vacation), research their stocks, and so on any time of the day or night. Is all this time at the computer necessary, or are we computer-addicted?

Computer users who spend excessive amounts of time at the keyboard are prone to a variety of computer-related health issues. Physical health issues include repetitive stress injuries, such as carpal tunnel syndrome. Repetitive stress injuries are caused by repetitive motions, such as using the same arm or wrist motion to enter data, and are not solely computer-related. Other physical health issues include eye strain and fatigue, as well as headaches, which can be the result of sitting for long periods of time looking at a monitor without proper eyewear or at inappropriate distances.

A comprehensive research study on the effects of prolonged daily use of computers, particularly the effects of sitting in front of a monitor, was conducted by researchers at Chiba University in Japan. The study, published in the American Journal of Industrial Medicine (Volume 42, Issue 5, 2002), investigated more than 25,000 workers three times over a 3-year period (1995-1997) using a self-administered questionnaire. The researchers looked at three primary factors: mental, physical, and sleep-related symptoms. Even after adjusting for mitigating factors, they found that there was a significant relationship between the amount of time people sit at a computer and look at a monitor and physical and mental ailments. People working at a computer longer than five hours per day seemed to exhibit the most symptoms. Physical ailments included headache, eyestrain, and joint pain. Mental ailments for people working more than five hours at a computer included increased lethargy, insomnia, anxiety, and fatigue.

The science of ergonomics, which is the study of people and their work environments to improve work conditions and to enhance productivity, has tried to address physical issues related to ubiquitous computing by creating ergonomically-designed workspaces. These workspaces include proper furniture, such as desks that can be adjusted to the needs of the user, special keyboard layouts, and adjustable chairs. Ergonomics also addresses the issue of proper lighting to help reduce eyestrain and headache. The science also provides information on proper posture—a key element in helping to reduce physical injuries.

In addition to physical injuries, healthcare workers are concerned about the emotional and mental issues stemming from excessive computer use. One such problem is that of computer addiction disorder (CAD), sometimes referred to as Internet addiction disorder (IAD). As of this writing, CAD/IAD has not been recognized officially as a psychological or psychiatric diagnosis, but the addiction to computers and computer use is being studied seriously by healthcare professionals.

Apparently, computer usage is affecting not only our physical health but also our language skills. Several major news organizations have reported on the effect of computers in the way students write. Teachers report that essays and school assignments are being submitted with some words written in the language of text messaging (short abbreviations used for communicating over the Internet) rather than full words and correct English. Many teens are incorporating text messaging, which they use when sending instant messages through services such as ICQ and AOL Instant Messaging or when sending text messages on their cell phones, into their school work. For example, "gr8 2 b ur friend cuz u r kewl, c u l8r @ home" may seem like an odd collection of symbols and letters but for a teen it's a simple message: "Great to be your friend because you are cool, see you later at home."

Text messaging is also called Short Message Service. Webopedia defines Short Message Service (SMS) as "the transmission of short text messages to and from a mobile phone, fax machine and/or IP address. Messages must be no longer than 160 alpha-numeric characters and contain no images or graphics." If you only have 160 characters, you tend to get creative, such as using "gr8" for great! Recently, the Oxford University Press added an appendix that includes a glossary of abbreviations used in electronic text messaging to its Concise Oxford Dictionary. These shorthand terms were developed and defined by e-mail users. Some worry that including this glossary of abbreviations in the Concise Oxford Dictionary is a step toward acceptance of these abbreviations as Standard English.

It is a well-known fact that language is always evolving. Each new generation contributes words to its language, words that then become part of the accepted language. However, the Internet generation is pushing the boundaries of written language by suggesting that simply typing "lol" (laughing out loud), "brb" (be right back), and "ttyl" (talk to you later) should be universally accepted as Standard English. Regardless of whether or not these abbreviations are accepted as Standard English, they are clearly impacting language usage by their pervasive intrusion into our written language.

What is the impact on society of ubiquitous computing? Is the computer changing the way we interact with our family and friends? How do you tell your neighbors good news? Bad news? There was a time when you would walk next door or down the block and tell a friend face-to-face about a promotion, a success, or a sad event. With our circles widening in large geographic areas, it's a good thing to be able to stay in touch with people who no longer live down the block. However, are we losing the ability to face people and tell them things personally?

Computer usage will continue to expand. The 24/7 accessibility to computers is changing society—for example, the way businesses do business, the way the economy runs, and the way people work. As it does, we would be wise to consider its impact on our lives.

▼ INTERACTIVE QUESTIONS

○ Yes ○ No ○ Not sure

1. Do you think that computer users who spend more than five hours each day at a keyboard are placing their health at risk?

○ Yes ○ No ○ Not sure

2. Would you be able to understand a simple text message if it arrived on your cell phone or computer?

3. Do you think that the 24/7 availability of computers is having a negative effect on our society?

○ Yes ○ No ○ Not sure

▼ EXPAND THE IDEAS

1. What are the pertinent health issues for computer users who spend more than 5 hours each day at a keyboard? Research two topics on this issue. Write a short paper summarizing two studies or articles.

2. How well do you know the shorthand used in text messaging? Could you understand an Instant message if it came to you? Have you ever used abbreviations (such as b/c for "because" or w/in for "within")? Write a message that is no longer than 160 characters and that uses text messaging. In a group, exchange papers and see if the messages can be interpreted. Discuss the advantages and disadvantages of using these abbreviations.

3. Research the impact of being available 24/7 to marketers and clients. What are the benefits and drawbacks to such extended accessibility? Who is most affected by this accessibility? Comment on how the 24/7 availability of computers affects our society and what we as a society should do about it, if anything.

Issue

End of Unit Exercises

▼ KEY TERMS

Always-on connection
Application software
Beep code
Binary number system
Bit
Blog
Bookmark
Boot process
Browser
Byte
Cable modem
Cable modem service
CD-ROM drive
CD-writer
Central processing unit (CPU)
Chat group
Computer
Computer file
Computer network
Computer program
Computer system
Data
Data file
Desktop computer
Dial-up connection
Display device
Downloading
DSL
DSS
DVD drive
DVD-writer
E-commerce

E-mail
E-mail account
E-mail address
E-mail attachment
E-mail message
E-mail servers
E-mail system
Executable file
Favorites
File
Filename
Filename extension
Floppy disk drive
Handheld computer
Hard disk drive
Hardware
History list
Home page
HTML
HTML tag
HTTP
Hypertext
IMAP
Information
Input
Input device
Instant messaging
Internet
Internet backbone
Internet telephony
IP address
ISDN

ISP
Keyboard
Keyword
LAN (local area network)
Link
Mailing list server
Mainframe computer
Memory
Microcomputer
MIME
Modem
Monitor
Mouse
Netiquette
Network card
Newsgroup
Notebook computer
Online
Operating system
Output
Output device
Packet
Password
PDA
Peer-to-Peer (P2P)
Peripheral device
Personal computer (PC)
Platform
POP
POP server
Power-on self-test (POST)
Printer

Processing
Processor
Router
Safe Mode
Search engine
Server
Server software
Software
Sound card
Speakers
Storage
Storage device
Store-and-forward technology
Stored program
Supercomputer
System software
System unit
Tablet computer
TCP/IP
Uploading
URL
Usenet
User ID
Videogame console
Voice band modem
Web
Web-based e-mail
Web page
Web server
Web site
Workstation

▼ UNIT REVIEW

1. Make sure that you can define each of the key terms in this unit in your own words. Select 10 of the terms with which you are unfamiliar and write a sentence for each of them.

2. Explain the basic functions of a computer: input, processing, storing, and output. Explain why the stored program concept is important to all of this.

3. Identify and describe each of the components of a basic personal computer system.

4. Describe the difference between an operating system and application software.

5. Define computer platform. Then discuss what makes two computer platforms compatible or incompatible.

6. List at least five resources that are provided by the Internet and identify those that are most popular.

7. Make a list of the ways to connect to the Internet presented in this unit and specify characteristics of each.

8. Describe the components of a URL and of an e-mail address.

9. Describe the rules that you should follow when copying text and images from the Internet.

10. Define "browser," then describe how a browser helps you navigate the Web.

▼ FILL IN THE BEST ANSWER

1. The basic functions of a computer are to accept _____, process data, store data, and produce output.

2. A computer processes data in the _____ processing unit.

3. The idea of a(n) _____ program means that instructions for a computing task can be loaded into a computer's memory.

4. The _____ unit is the case that holds the main circuit boards, processor, power supply, and storage devices for a personal computer system.

5. A device that is an integral part of a computer but that can be added to a computer is called a(n) _____ device.

6. Executable files usually have a(n) _____ extension.

7. A(n) _____ system is the software that acts as the master controller for all of the activities that take place within a computer system.

8. The main routes of the Internet are referred to as the Internet _____.

9. Communication between all of the different devices on the Internet is made possible by _____ /IP.

10. Most of the "stuff" that's accessible on the Internet is stored on _____ that are maintained by various businesses and organizations.

11. A dial-up connection requires a device called a(n) _____ band modem.

12. To use a cable Internet connection you need a cable modem and a(n) _____.

13. A cable modem provides an always _____ connection to the Internet.

14. The process of entering a user ID and password is referred to as _____.

15. Every Web page has a unique address called a(n) _____.

16. A browser assembles a Web page on your computer screen according to the specifications contained in the _____ tags.

17. Whenever you start your browser, it displays your _____ page.

18. A(n) _____ fetches and displays Web pages.

19. Store-and-forward technology stores messages on an e-mail _____ until they are forwarded to an individual's computer.

20. For many e-mail systems, a(n) _____ server handles incoming mail, and a(n) _____ server handles outgoing mail.

▼ PRACTICE TESTS

When you use the Interactive CD, you can take Practice Tests that consists of 10 multiple-choice, true/false, and fill-in-the blank questions. The questions are selected at random from a large test bank, so each time you take a test, you'll receive a different set of questions. Your tests are scored immediately, and you can print study guides to determine which questions you answered incorrectly. If you are using a Tracking Disk, insert it in the floppy disk drive to save your test scores.

Exercises

▼ INDEPENDENT CHALLENGE 1

When discussing computers and computer concepts it is important to use proper terminology. Unit A presented you with many computer terms that describe computer equipment. If you would like to explore any of the terms in more detail, there are online dictionaries that can help you expand your understanding of these terms.

1. For this independent challenge, write a one-page paper that describes the computer that you use most frequently.

2. Refer to the Key Terms used in this unit and use terms from this unit to describe your computer components and the functions they perform.

3. In your final draft, underline each Key Term that you used in your paper. Follow your professor's instructions for submitting your paper as an e-mail attachment or as a printed document.

▼ INDEPENDENT CHALLENGE 2

Suppose that producers for a television game show ask you to help them create a set of computer-related questions for the next show. You will compose a set of 10 questions based on the information provided in Unit A. Each question should be in multiple-choice format with four possible answers.

1. Write 10 questions: two very simple questions, five questions of medium difficulty, and three difficult questions. Each question should be on an index card.

2. For each question, indicate the correct answer on the back of each card and the page in this book on which the answer can be found.

3. Gather in small groups and take turns asking each other the questions.

▼ INDEPENDENT CHALLENGE 3

 The Computers in Context section of this unit focused on how computers are applied to sports. For this independent challenge, you will write a two- to five-page paper about how computers and technology have influenced and affected sports and athletics based on information that you gather from the Internet.

1. To begin this Independent Challenge, log on to the Internet and use your favorite search engine to find information on current uses of technology in sports and athletics to get an in-depth look at the topic. Are computers granting an unfair advantage to those who can use them to train and enhance performance? Are computers and technology creating equipment that is so superior that it creates an unfair advantage for those who can afford them?

2. Determine the viewpoint that you will present in your paper about computers in sports. You might, for example, decide to present the viewpoint that it all comes down to the skills of the athlete and computers do not provide any unfair advantage. Whatever viewpoint you decide to present, make sure that you can back it up with facts and references to authoritative articles and Web pages.

3. Place citations to your research (include the author's name, article title, date of publication, and URL) at the end of your paper as endnotes, on each page as footnotes, or along with the appropriate paragraphs using parentheses. Follow your professor's instructions for submitting your paper via e-mail or as a printed document.

▼ INDEPENDENT CHALLENGE 4

 A new ISP is getting ready to open in your area, and the president of the company asks you to design a print ad. Your ad must communicate all pertinent information about the ISP.

1. Before starting on the design, use your favorite search engine to find out more about ISPs in your area. Gather information to use in your ad, such as the type of services offered (dial-up, cable modem, etc.), the speed of service, the geographical coverage, price, and special or proprietary services.

2. Make up a name for your ISP. Design a print ad for the company using a computer or freehand tools. Submit your ad design along with a short written summary that describes how this ad reflects the ISP and the services it offers.

▼ LAB: MAKING A DIAL-UP CONNECTION

1. Start the interactive part of the lab. Insert your Tracking Disk if you want to save your QuickCheck results. Perform each of the lab steps as directed and answer all of the lab QuickCheck questions. When you exit the lab, your answers are automatically graded and your results are displayed.

2. Make a list of at least five ISPs that are available in your area. If possible, include both local and national ISPs in your list.

3. Suppose that you intend to create manually a dial-up connection icon for AT&T WorldNet. What's missing from the following information?

   - AT&T's dial-in telephone number and country

   - AT&T's IP address

   - Your password

4. Provide the following information about the Internet connection that you typically use: Name of ISP, type of Internet connection (dial-up, DSL, cable modem, ISDN, DSS, school network, or business network), connection speed, and monthly fee. (If you don't currently have Internet access, describe the type of connection that you would like to use.)

▼ LAB: BROWSING AND SEARCHING

1. Start the interactive part of the lab. Insert your Tracking Disk if you want to save your QuickCheck results. Perform each of the lab steps as directed and answer all of the lab QuickCheck questions. When you exit the lab, your answers are automatically graded and your results are displayed.

2. Make a note of the brand and location of the computer that you're using to complete these lab assignments.

3. Examine the Favorites or Bookmarks list. How many pages are included in this list? Link to three of the pages, and provide their URLs and a brief description of their contents.

4. Suppose that you want to make your own trail mix, but you need a recipe. In three different search engines, enter the query: "trail mix" AND "recipe". (Refer to the Search Engines InfoWeb for a list of popular search engines.) Describe the similarities and differences in the results lists produced by each of the three search engines.

5. Conduct a second search to find the blue book price for a Taurus. Use the search engine of your choice to determine whether the query: "Blue book price" Taurus -"used car" provides the same results as the query: Blue book price Taurus -"used car".

   Make sure that you enter each query exactly as specified, including the quotation marks and no space after the hyphen. Explain the similarities and differences in the query results.

▼ LAB: USING E-MAIL

1. Start the interactive part of the lab. Insert your Tracking Disk if you want to save your QuickCheck results. Perform each of the lab steps as directed and answer all of the lab QuickCheck questions. When you exit the lab, your answers are automatically graded and your results are displayed.

2. Using the e-mail software of your choice, send an e-mail message to kendra_hill@cciw.com. In the body of your message, ask for a copy of the "Most Influential Person Survey."

3. Wait a few minutes after sending the message to Kendra Hill, then check your mail. You should receive a survey from Kendra Hill. Reply to this message and Cc: your instructor. In your reply, answer each question in the survey, interspersing your answers with the original text. Send the reply, following the procedures required by your e-mail provider.

4. Examine the address book offered by your e-mail software. Describe how much information (name, home address, business address, birth date, telephone number, fax number, etc.) you can enter for each person. In your opinion, would this address book be suitable for a businessperson to use for storing contact information? Why or why not? Send the descriptions and answers to these questions to your instructor in an e-mail.

▼ STUDENT EDITION LABS

Reinforce the concepts you have learned in this unit through the **E-Mail** Student Edition Lab, available online at the Illustrated Computer Concepts Web site.

▼ SAM LABS

If you have a SAM user profile, you have access to additional content, features, and functionality. Log in to your SAM account and go to your assignments page to see what your instructor has assigned for this unit.

▼ VISUAL WORKSHOP

The digital divide is defined as the difference in rates of access to computers and the Internet among different demographic groups. With the explosion of the Internet and the technology that drives the information age, forward-thinking social reformers recognized early on the potential for a divide between the "haves" and the "have nots." See Figure A-32. Not-for-profit organizations, concerned with the impact of the digital divide, designed studies to help them analyze the causes and effects of this phenomenon. These studies have been conducted for the past few decades.

FIGURE A-32

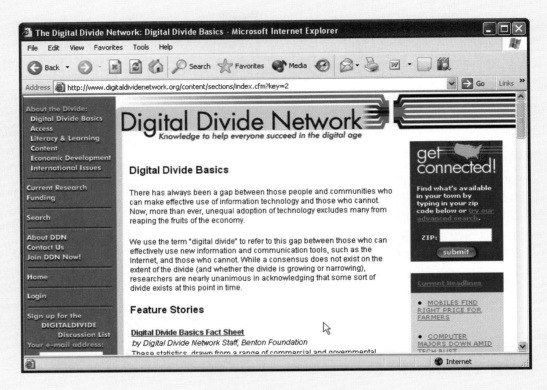

1. Is there a solution to the digital divide? Connect to the Internet and use your favorite search engine to search on the key phrase "digital divide." Find sites that include links to articles and research studies that address the digital divide. Review the findings for two studies or articles. Write a short paper summarizing these studies or articles. In your conclusion, comment on how you feel the digital divide affects our society and what we as a society should do about it, if anything.

2. Could you live without computers? Computers are ubiquitous; beyond the obvious applications, such as using your word processor to write a report, you come in contact with them during the course of your day in simple activities such as shopping in a supermarket or getting cash from your bank's ATM machine. Create a log to track your daily activities that involve computers. Keep the log for one week. At the end of the week, write a summary of any surprises or insights you have as to how computers affect your life.

3. Is there a digital divide in your community? Create a survey that will determine Internet access and computer ownership among people that you know. The survey should consist of 5-10 questions. You want to find out, within a chosen sector, who owns a computer, if they own more than one, what they use the computer(s) for, if they have Internet access, and if they access the Internet from their home or elsewhere. Be sure to survey at least 20 people. The survey should be anonymous but include demographic information. Compile the results of your survey into a chart and write a short summary explaining your findings.

UNIT B Computer Hardware

OBJECTIVES

Introduce storage technology

Compare storage technologies

Compare storage media and devices

Explore floppy disk technology

Explore hard disk technology

Explore CD/DVD technology

Explore solid state storage

Examine input devices

Compare display devices

Compare printers

Understand expansion slots, cards, and ports

Explore peripheral devices

Tech Talk: The Windows Registry

Computers in Context: Military

Issue: Why Recycle Computers?

This unit discusses computer hardware, with several lessons focusing on the various technologies that enable a computer to store and retrieve data and programs. Storage technology defines how computers store data and program files. You will learn the difference between magnetic, solid state, and optical storage. You will learn about input and output devices such as popular printer and display technologies. You will learn about the components of a computer's expansion bus, including various types of expansion slots and cables and how to use the expansion bus to add devices to a computer. You will learn about a variety of peripheral devices including how to install them, and in the Tech Talk, how the Windows Registry tracks installed devices. You will also have an opportunity to look at computers in the context of the military. The Issue discusses computer recycling.

Introducing storage technology

The basic functions of a computer are to accept input, process data, store data, and produce output. When you want to store data permanently, you save the data to a storage device. Computers can be configured with a variety of storage devices, such as a floppy disk drive, Zip drive, hard disk drive, CD drive, or DVD drive. While one storage technology might provide extremely fast access to data, it might also be susceptible to problems that could wipe out all of your data. A different storage technology might be more dependable, but it might also have the disadvantage of providing relatively slow access to data. Understanding the strengths and weaknesses of each storage technology will enable you to use each device appropriately and with maximum effectiveness.

LAB
WORKING WITH BINARY NUMBERS

DETAILS

- The term **storage technology** refers to data storage systems. Each data storage system has two main components: a storage medium and a storage device. A **storage medium** (storage media is the plural) is the disk, tape, memory card, CD, DVD, paper, or other media that holds data. For some examples of storage media, see Figure B-1. A **storage device** is the mechanical apparatus that records and retrieves data from a storage medium. Storage devices include floppy disk drives, Zip drives, hard disk drives, tape drives, CD drives, and DVD drives. For some examples of storage devices, see Figure B-2.

- Data is copied from a storage device into RAM, where it waits to be processed. **RAM** (random access memory) is a temporary holding area for the operating system, the file you are working on (such as a word processing document), and application program instructions. RAM is not permanent storage, in fact RAM is very **volatile**, which means data in RAM can be lost easily. That is why it is important to store data permanently.

- RAM is important to the storage process. You can think of RAM as the connection between your computer's storage devices and its storage media. After data is processed in RAM, it is usually copied to a storage medium for more permanent safekeeping.

- The process of recording or storing data is often referred to as "writing data" or "saving a file" because the storage device writes the data on the storage medium to save it for later use. The process of retrieving data is often referred to as "reading data," "loading data," or "opening a file."

- A computer works with data that has been coded and can be represented by 1s and 0s. When data is stored, these 1s and 0s must be converted into a signal or mark that's fairly permanent but that can be changed when necessary. The data is not literally written as "1" or "0." Instead, the 1s and 0s must be transformed to change the surface of a storage medium. Exactly how this transformation happens depends on the storage technology. For example, floppy disks store data in a different way than CD-ROMs store data.

The science of data representation

Letters, numbers, musical notes, and pictures don't pass from the keyboard through the circuitry of a computer and then jump out onto the screen or printer. So how is it that a computer can work with documents, photos, videos, and sound recordings? The answer to that question is what data representation and digital electronics are all about. Data representation is based on the binary number system, which uses two numbers, 1 and 0, to represent all data. Data representation makes it possible to convert letters, sounds, and images into electrical signals. Digital electronics makes it possible for a computer to manipulate simple "on" and "off" signals, which are represented by the 0s and 1s, to perform complex tasks.

FIGURE B-1: Examples of storage media

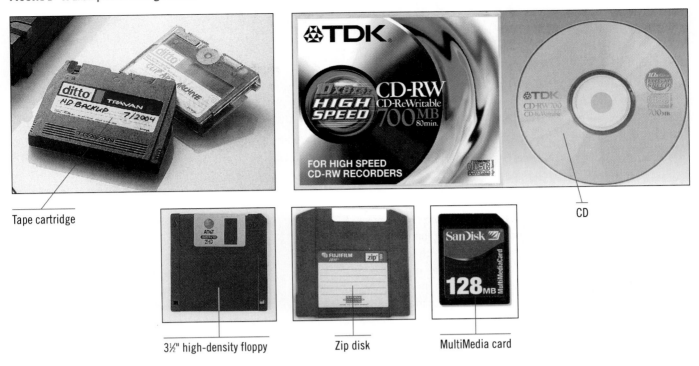

Tape cartridge

CD

3½" high-density floppy

Zip disk

MultiMedia card

FIGURE B-2: Examples of storage devices in a system unit

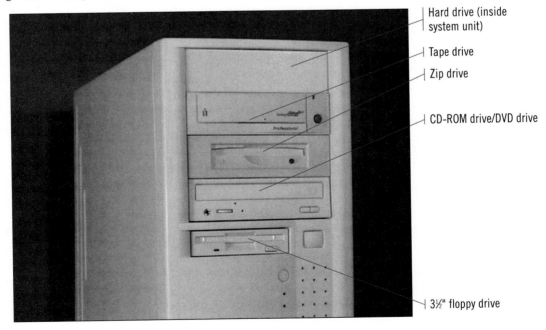

Hard drive (inside system unit)

Tape drive

Zip drive

CD-ROM drive/DVD drive

3½" floppy drive

Comparing storage technologies

Three types of storage technologies are commonly used for personal computers: magnetic, optical, and solid state. Each storage technology has advantages and disadvantages. To compare storage devices, you need to understand how each one works.

DETAILS

● **Magnetic storage**. Hard disk, floppy disk, Zip disk, and tape storage technologies can be classified as magnetic storage, which stores data by magnetizing microscopic particles on the disk or tape surface. The particles retain their magnetic orientation until that orientation is changed, thereby making disks and tape fairly permanent but modifiable storage media. A **read-write head** mechanism in the disk drive reads and writes the magnetized particles that represent data. Figure B-3 shows how a computer stores data on magnetic media.

Before data is stored, the particles on the surface of the disk are scattered in random patterns. The disk drive's read-write head magnetizes the particles and orients them in either a positive or negative direction. These patterns of magnetized particles are interpreted as the 0s and 1s that represent data. Data stored magnetically can be changed or deleted simply by altering the magnetic orientation of the appropriate particles on the disk surface. This feature of magnetic storage provides flexibility for editing data and reusing areas of a storage medium containing data that is no longer needed.

Magnetic media is not very durable. Data stored on magnetic media such as floppy disks can be altered by magnetic fields, dust, mold, smoke particles, heat, and mechanical problems with a storage device. For example, a magnet should never be placed on or near a floppy disk because it will destroy the magnetic particles on the disk. Magnetic media gradually lose their magnetic charge, which results in lost data. Some experts estimate that the reliable life span of data stored on magnetic media is about three years.

● **Optical storage**. CD and DVD storage technologies make use of optical storage, which stores data as microscopic light and dark spots on the disc surface. The dark spots are called **pits**, and it is possible to see the data stored on a CD or DVD storage medium using a high-powered microscope. See Figure B-4. The lighter, non-pitted surface areas of the disc are called **lands**. This type of storage is called optical storage because a low-power laser light is used to read the data stored on an optical disc. When the beam strikes a pit, no light is reflected. When the laser strikes a reflective surface, light bounces back into the read head. The patterns of light and dark between pits and lands are interpreted as the 1s and 0s that represent data. Data recorded on optical media is generally considered to be less susceptible to environmental damage than data recorded on magnetic media. The useful life of a CD-ROM disc is estimated to exceed 200 years.

● **Solid state storage**. A variety of compact storage cards, pens, and sticks can be classified as solid state storage. Solid state media stores data in a non-volatile, erasable, low-power chip. A solid state storage medium stores data in a microscopic grid of cells. See Figure B-5. A card reader transfers data between the card and a computer. Solid state storage provides faster access to data than magnetic or optical storage technology because it includes no moving parts. Solid state storage is very durable—it is virtually impervious to vibration, magnetic fields, or extreme temperature fluctuations. These characteristics make solid state storage a good choice for storing images created by digital cameras and sound files stored on portable listening devices. The capacity of solid state storage does not currently match that of hard disks, CDs, or DVDs. The cost per megabyte of storage is significantly higher than for magnetic or optical storage.

FIGURE B-3: Magnetic storage

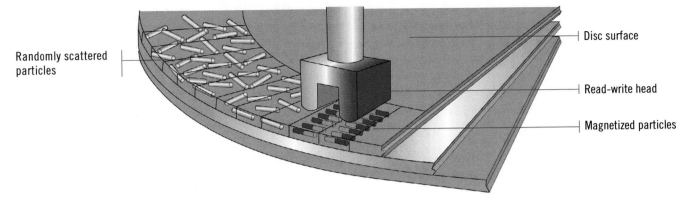

Randomly scattered particles

Disc surface

Read-write head

Magnetized particles

FIGURE B-4: Optical storage

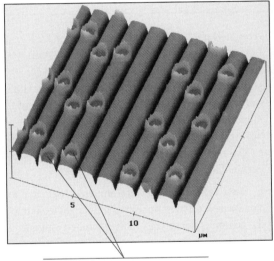

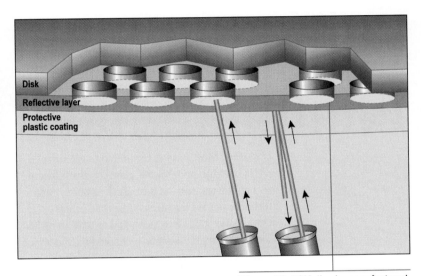

Disk

Reflective layer

Protective plastic coating

The pits on an optical storage disc as seen through an electron microscope; each pit is 1 micron in diameter

When a CD-ROM disc is manufactured, a laser burns pits into a reflective surface; these pits become dark non-reflective areas on the disc

FIGURE B-5: Solid state storage

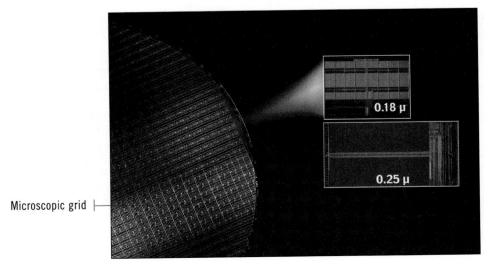

Microscopic grid

0.18 μ

0.25 μ

Comparing storage media and devices

UNIT B

When trying to determine the best storage media for a job, it is useful to apply four criteria: versatility, durability, speed, and capacity. Versatility is the ability of a device and its media to work in more than one way. After storing data using this storage technology, can that data be changed? Durability determines the ability of the device or media to last. How long will it work? How long will the data be accessible? Speed is the time it takes to retrieve or access the data, a factor that is very important in determining how efficiently you work. Finally, capacity is the amount of data each technology can store.

Info Web

STORAGE
FRONTIERS

DETAILS

- Versatility. Some storage devices can access data from only one type of medium. More versatile devices can access data from several different media. A floppy disk drive, for example, can access only floppy disks, but a DVD drive can access data DVDs, DVD movies, audio CDs, data CDs, and CD-Rs.

- Durability. Most storage technologies are susceptible to damage from mishandling or other environmental factors, such as heat and moisture. Some technologies are less susceptible than others. Optical and solid state technologies tend to be less susceptible than magnetic technologies to damage that could cause data loss.

- Speed. Not surprisingly, fast storage devices are preferred over slower ones. **Access time** is the average time it takes a computer to locate data on the storage medium and read it. Access time for a personal computer storage device, such as a disk drive, is measured in **milliseconds** (thousandths of a second). Lower numbers indicate faster access times. For example, a drive with a 6 ms access time is faster than a drive with an access time of 11 ms. Random-access devices have the fastest access times.

   Random access (also called "direct access") is the ability of a device to "jump" directly to the

requested data. Floppy disk, hard disk, solid state, CD, and DVD drives are random-access devices. A tape drive, on the other hand, must use slower **sequential access**, which reads through the data from the beginning of the tape. The advantage of random access becomes clear when you consider how much faster and easier it is to locate a song on a CD (random access) than on a cassette tape (sequential access).

   Data transfer rate is the amount of data that a storage device can move from the storage medium to the computer per second. Higher numbers indicate faster transfer rates. For example, a CD-ROM drive with a 600 KBps (kilobytes per second) data transfer rate is faster than one with a 300 KBps transfer rate.

- Capacity. **Storage capacity** is the maximum amount of data that can be stored on a storage medium, measured in kilobytes (KB), megabytes (MB), gigabytes (GB), or terabytes (TB). The amount of data that a disk stores—its capacity—depends on its density. **Disk density** refers to the closeness of the data on the disk surface. The higher the disk density, the more data it can store. Higher capacity is almost always preferred. Table B-1 compares the capacity of various storage devices and media.

> **FYI**
>
> *Storage media is divided into tracks and then into sectors to create electronic "addressable bins" in which to store data.*

Adding storage devices to a computer

Computer users frequently want to upgrade their hard drives to gain capacity or to add CD or DVD drives to make their systems more versatile. The system unit case for a desktop computer contains several storage device "parking spaces" called **drive bays**. See Figure B-6. If you have an empty bay that is the right type and size, you can add a storage device. Bays come in two widths—5 ¼" and 3½". CD and DVD drives require 5¼" bays; a floppy disk drive fits in a 3½" bay. Some drive bays provide access from the outside of the system unit, a necessity for a storage device with removable media, such as floppy disks, CDs, tapes, and DVDs. Internal drive bays are located inside the system unit and are designed for hard disk drives, which don't use removable storage media.

TABLE B-1: Capacities of storage media

DEVICE	CAPACITY	COMMENTS
Floppy disk	1.44 MB	Low capacity means that the disk can hold small files but not large files; not suitable for graphics-intenstive files
SuperDisk	120 MB or 240 MB	SuperDisks are manufactured by Imation; Zip disks are manufactured by Iomega; each holds much more than a floppy; each requires its own proprietary drive; a full system backup requires multiple disks
Zip disk	100 MB, 250 MB, and 750 MB	
Fixed hard disk	80 GB (average)	High storage capacity, fast and convenient, economical storage-cost/megabyte, is susceptible to damage or theft of your computer
External hard drive	80 GB	Fast, but transfer rate depends on computer system; drive can be removed and locked in a secure location
Removable hard disk	2.2 GB (average)	Fast, limited capacity, but disks can be removed and locked in a secure location
CD	700 MB	Limited capacity, can't be reused, long shelf life
CD-RW	700 MB	Limited capacity, reusable
Writable DVD	4.7 GB	Good capacity, standards still in development
Tape	30 GB (average)	Good capacity, reasonable media cost, convenient—you can let backups run overnight, but slow—it can take 15-20 minutes to back up 1 GB of data

FIGURE B-6: Drive bays

An empty drive bay located on the side of a notebook computer

◄ Most notebook computers provide bays for one floppy disk drive, one hard disk drive, and one CD or DVD drive

An empty 5.25" drive bay can hold CD, DVD, tape, or multifunction solid state drives

An empty 3.5" drive bay can hold a floppy disk drive

◄ Most desktop computers have several drive bays, some accessible from outside the case, and others—designed for hard disk drives—without any external access

Empty drive bays are typically hidden from view with a face plate

Exploring floppy disk technology

A **floppy disk** is a round piece of flexible mylar plastic covered with a thin layer of magnetic oxide and sealed inside a protective casing. If you broke open the disk casing (something you should never do unless you want to ruin the disk), you would see that the mylar disk inside is thin and literally floppy. See Figure B-7. Floppy disks are also referred to as "floppies" or "diskettes." It is not correct to call them "hard disks" even though they seem to have a "hard" or rigid plastic casing.

DETAILS

- Floppy disks provide one type of inexpensive, removable storage for personal computer systems. Floppy disks come in many sizes and capacities. The floppies most commonly used on today's personal computers are 3½" disks with a capacity of 1.44 MB, which means they can store 1,440,000 bytes of data.

- A floppy disk features a **write-protect window**, which is a small square opening that can be covered by a moveable plastic tab on the disk. When you open the window, the disk is "write-protected," which means that a computer cannot write or save data on the disk.

- Two additional storage systems use magnetic technology. **Zip disks**, manufactured by Iomega, are available in 100 MB, 250 MB, and 750 MB versions. **SuperDisks**, manufactured by Imation, have a capacity of 120 MB and 240 MB. Although the increased storage capacity of these types of disks is attractive, they require special disk drives; a standard floppy disk drive will not read them. SuperDisks, however, are backward-compatible with standard floppy disks, which means you can use a SuperDisk drive to read and write to standard floppy disks. Three types of floppy disk drives are shown in Figure B-8.

- The major advantage of floppy disks is their portability. Floppies are still used in many school computer labs so that students can transport their data to different lab machines or to their personal computers.

- A major disadvantage of standard 3½" floppy disks is their relatively low storage capacity. Files that students are creating, such as presentations with graphics and databases, are large. Often, these files will not fit on a 3½" floppy disk, which makes Zip disks, SuperDisks, or CDs that you can read from and write to (called CD-Rs) more attractive.

- Another disadvantage is that a standard 3½" floppy disk drive is not a particularly speedy device. It takes about 0.5 second for the drive to spin the disk up to maximum speed and find a specific sector that contains data. A Zip drive is about 20 times faster, but both are significantly slower than a hard disk drive.

- In the past, floppy disks were extensively used to store data, share files, and distribute software. Today, most software vendors use CDs or DVDs as distribution disks. In addition, local computer networks and the Internet have made it easy to share or distribute files without physically transporting them from one place to another.

What do HD DS and HDD mean?

Today's floppies are "high-density disks" (HD or HDD). When you see "HD DS" on a box of floppy disks it means "high-density double-sided." Although the storage capacity of a standard floppy disk pales beside that of Zip and SuperDisks, there was a time when floppies stored even less. At one time, floppy disks stored data only on one side. Today, however, most store data on both sides. Read-write heads above and below the disk read both sides so that you don't have to turn the disk over.

FIGURE B-7: A 3½" floppy disk

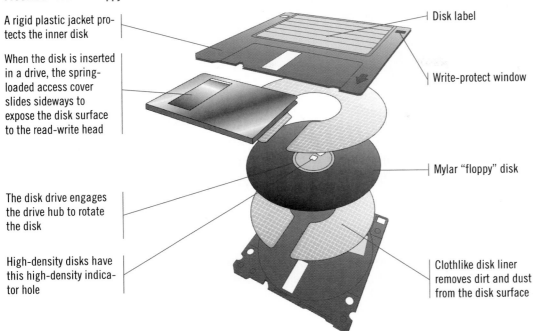

A rigid plastic jacket protects the inner disk

When the disk is inserted in a drive, the spring-loaded access cover slides sideways to expose the disk surface to the read-write head

The disk drive engages the drive hub to rotate the disk

High-density disks have this high-density indicator hole

Disk label

Write-protect window

Mylar "floppy" disk

Clothlike disk liner removes dirt and dust from the disk surface

FIGURE B-8: A floppy disk, a Zip disk, and a SuperDisk

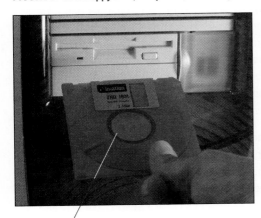

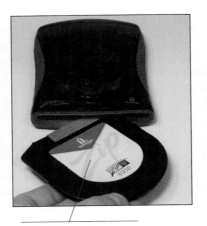

The storage device that records and retrieves data on a floppy disk is a floppy disk drive, shown here with a 3½" floppy disk

A Zip disk requires special disk drives, but is transportable and provides more storage capacity than a floppy disk

A SuperDisk provides an alternative high-capacity, transportable storage option; SuperDisk drives can read standard floppy disks, but a SuperDisk cannot be used in a standard floppy disk drive

Exploring hard disk technology

Hard disk technology is the preferred type of main storage for most computer systems. Hard disks provide more than enough storage capacity for most users and provide faster access to files than floppy disk drives do. In addition, hard disks are more economical than floppy disks. A hard disk typically stores millions of times more data than a floppy disk, but a hard disk drive might cost only three times as much as a floppy disk drive.

DETAILS

- A **hard disk** is one or more platters and their associated read-write heads. A **hard disk platter** is a flat, rigid disk made of aluminum or glass and coated with magnetic iron oxide particles. Personal computer hard disk platters are typically 3½" in diameter. This is the same size as the circular mylar disk in a floppy, but the density of the surface particles on hard disk platters far exceeds that of a floppy disk. The terms "hard disk" and "hard disk drive" are often used interchangeably. The term "fixed disk" is also used to refer to hard disks.

- Hard disk storage capacities of 80 GB and access times of 6 to 11 ms are not uncommon. Computer ads typically specify the capacity and access time of a hard disk drive. So "80 GB 8 ms HD" means a hard disk drive with 80 gigabyte capacity and an access time of 8 milliseconds.

- The access time for a hard disk is significantly faster than that for a floppy disk. Hard disk drive speed is sometimes measured in **revolutions per minute (rpm)**. The faster a drive spins, the more rapidly it can position the read-write head over specific data. For example, a 7,200 rpm drive is able to access data faster than a 5,400 rpm drive.

- Hard disk platters are divided into tracks and sectors into which data is written. You might guess that a hard disk drive would fill one platter before storing data on a second platter. However, it is more efficient to store data at the same track and sector locations on all platters before moving the read-write heads to the next sector. A vertical stack of tracks is called a **cylinder**, which is the basic storage bin for a hard disk drive. Figure B-9 provides more information on how a hard disk drive works.

- A hard drive storage device includes a circuit board, called a **controller**, which positions the disk and read-write heads to locate data. Disk drives are classified according to the type of controller they use. Popular drive controllers include Ultra ATA, EIDE, and SCSI. **Ultra ATA (AT attachment)** and **EIDE (enhanced integrated drive electronics)** use essentially the same drive technology and feature high storage capacity and fast data transfer. Ultra ATA drives, which are commonly found in today's PCs, are twice as fast as their EIDE counterparts. **SCSI (small computer system interface)** drives provide a slight performance advantage over EIDE drives and are typically found in high-performance workstations and servers.

- The storage technology used on many PCs transfers data from a disk, through the controller, to the processor, and finally to RAM before it is actually processed. **DMA (direct memory access)** technology allows a computer to transfer data directly from a drive into RAM, without intervention from the processor. This architecture relieves the processor of data-transfer duties and frees up processing cycles for other tasks. **UDMA (ultra DMA)** is a faster version of DMA technology. DMA and Ultra ATA are companion technologies. A common storage configuration for PCs pairs an Ultra ATA drive with UDMA data transfer.

- Hard disks are not as durable as many other storage technologies. The read-write heads in a hard disk hover a microscopic distance above the disk surface. If a read-write head runs into a dust particle or some other contaminant on the disk, or if the hard disk is jarred while it is in use, it might cause a **head crash**. A head crash damages some of the data on the disk. To help prevent contaminants from contacting the platters and causing head crashes, a hard disk is sealed in its case.

- Removable hard disks or hard disk cartridges can be inserted and removed from the drive much like floppy disks. Removable hard disks increase the storage capacity of your computer system, although the data is available on only one disk at a time. Removable hard disks also provide security for data by allowing you to remove the hard disk cartridge and store it separately from the computer.

The drive spindle supports one or more hard disk platters; both sides of the platter are used for data storage; more platters mean more data storage capacity; hard disk platters rotate as a unit on the spindle to position read-write heads over specific data; the platters spin continuously, making thousands of rotations per minute

▲ Each data storage surface has its own read-write head, which moves in and out from the center of the disk to locate data; the head hovers only a few microinches above the disk surface, so the magnetic field is much more compact than on a floppy disk; as a result, more data is packed into a smaller area on a hard disk platter

Understanding tape storage

Tape is another type of storage technology; it consists of a tape for the storage medium and a tape drive for the storage device. Tape is a sequential, rather than a random-access, storage medium. Data is arranged as a long sequence of bits that begins at one end of the tape and stretches to the other end. As a result, tape access is much slower than hard drive access. In fact, access times for a tape are measured in seconds rather than in milliseconds. A tape may contain hundreds, or in the case of a mainframe, thousands of feet of tape.

The most popular types of tape drives for personal computers use tape cartridges for the storage medium. A **tape cartridge** is a removable magnetic tape module similar to a cassette tape. Figure B-10 shows several different kinds of tape used with personal computer tape drives.

Tape drives are available in either internal or external models. An internal tape drive fits into a standard drive bay. An external model is a standalone device that you can connect to your computer with a cable.

FIGURE B-10: Tape storage options

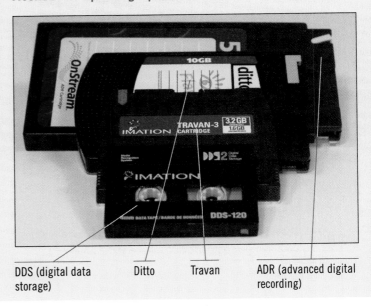

DDS (digital data storage)   Ditto   Travan   ADR (advanced digital recording)

Exploring CD/DUD technology

Optical storage media use one of three technologies: read-only (ROM), recordable, or rewritable. Both **CDs (compact discs)** and **DVDs** ("digital video disc" or "digital versatile disc") use optical storage technologies. The suffix associated with a CD or DVD helps you recognize the type of technology used to create the CD or DVD. The suffixes "ROM," "R," and "RW" denote specific CD and DVD technologies. CD-ROM specifies "read-only" technology, CD-R specifies "CD recordable" technology, and CD-RW specifies "CD rewritable" technology.

Info Web
CD AND DVD

DETAILS

- Optical storage technology provides larger storage capacity than floppy disks, solid state media, Zip disks, or SuperDisks. Standard CD capacity is 700 MB of data. The current capacity of a DVD is about 4.7 GB (4,700 MB).

- **CD drives** and **DVD drives** are storage devices that use laser technology to read data on computer or audio CDs or DVDs respectively. Figure B-11 shows how to place a CD in a CD drive. Figure B-12 illustrates how a CD-ROM drive uses laser technology to read data. CD and DVD drives contain a spindle that rotates the disc over a laser lens. The laser directs a beam of light toward the underside of the disc. Dark "pits" and light "lands" on the disc surface reflect the light differently. As the drive reads the disc, these differences are translated into the 0s and 1s that represent data.

  Most CD drives can read CD-ROM, CD-R, and CD-RW discs. Most DVD drives can read CD and DVD formats. Storing computer data and creating music CDs requires a recordable or rewritable device. As you can see from Table B-2, the most versatile optical storage device is a DVD+R/+RW/CD-RW combo.

- **Read-only (ROM) technology**. A computer CD-ROM or DVD disc contains data that was stamped on the disc surface when it was manufactured, such as commercial software, music, and movies. Examples of CDs and DVDs using read-only optical technology follow:

  CD-DA (compact disc digital audio) is the format for commercial music CDs. Music is typically recorded on audio CDs by the manufacturer.

  DVD-Video (digital versatile disc video) is the format for commercial DVDs that contain feature-length films.

  CD-ROM (compact disc read-only memory) was the original format for storing computer data. Data is stamped on the disc at the time it is manufactured.

  DVD-ROM (digital versatile disc read-only memory) contains data stamped onto the disc surface at the time of manufacture.

For all of these examples, data cannot be added, changed, or deleted from these discs.

- **Recordable technology (R)** uses a laser to change the color in a dye layer sandwiched beneath the clear plastic disc surface. The laser creates dark spots in the dye that are read as pits. The change in the dye is permanent, so data cannot be changed once it has been recorded. Usually, you can record your data in multiple sessions, that is, you add two files to your CD-R disc today and then add more files to thse same disc tomorrow. Examples of CDs and DVDs using recordable optical technology follow:

  CD-R (compact disc recordable) discs store data using recordable technology. The data on a CD-R cannot be erased or modified once you record it. However, most CD-R drives allow you to record your data in multiple sessions.

  DVD+R (digital versatile disc recordable) discs store data using recordable technology similar to a CD-R, but with DVD storage capacity.

- **Rewritable technology (RW)** uses "phase change" technology to alter a crystal structure on the disc surface. Altering the crystal structure creates patterns of light and dark spots similar to the pits and lands on a CD. The crystal structure can be changed from light to dark and back again many times, making it possible to record and modify data much like on a hard disk. Examples of CDs and DVDs using rewritable optical technology follow:

  CD-RW (compact disc rewritable) discs store data using rewritable technology. Stored data can be recorded and erased multiple times, making it a very flexible storage option.

  DVD+RW (digital versatile disc rewritable) discs store data using rewritable technology similar to CD-RW, but with DVD storage capacity.

- A rewritable CD or DVD drive is not a good replacement for a hard disk drive. The process of accessing, saving, and modifying data on a rewritable disc is relatively slow compared to the speed of hard disk access.

FIGURE B-11: Inserting a CD-ROM

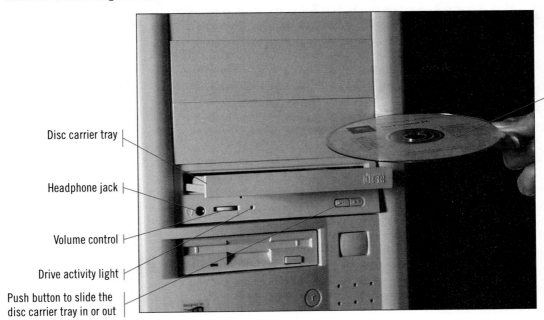

Disc carrier tray

Headphone jack

Volume control

Drive activity light

Push button to slide the disc carrier tray in or out

Data is stored on the bottom of a CD-ROM disc in one continuous track that spirals out from the center of the disc; the track is divided into equal-length sectors; the printed side of the disc does not contain data; it should be face up when you insert the disc because the lasers read the bottom of the disc

FIGURE B-12: How a CD-ROM drive works

Laser lens directs a beam of light to the underside of the CD-ROM disc

Drive spindle spins the disc

Tracking mechanism positions a disc track over the laser lens

Laser pickup assembly senses the reflectivity of pits and lands

TABLE B-2: CD and DVD drive capabilities

	PLAY AUDIO CDS	PLAY DVD MOVIES	READ CD DATA	READ DVD DATA	CREATE MUSIC CDS	STORE DATA ON CDS	STORE DATA ON DVDS
CD-ROM drive	X		X				
CD-R drive	X		X		X	X	
CD-RW drive	X		X		X	X	
DVD/CD-RW drive	X	X	X	X	X	X	
DVD+R/+RW/CD-RW drive	X	X	X	X	X	X	X

Exploring solid state storage

Solid state storage is portable, provides fast access to data, and uses very little power. It is an ideal solution for storing data on mobile devices and transporting data from one device to another. Solid state storage is widely used in consumer devices, such as digital cameras, MP3 music players, notebook computers, PDAs, and cell phones.

DETAILS

● A variety of compact storage cards can be classified as solid state storage, which stores data in a non-volatile, erasable, low-power chip. The chip's circuitry is arranged as a grid, and each cell in the grid contains two transistors that act as gates. When the gates are open, current can flow and the cell has a value that represents a "1" bit. When the gates are closed, the cell has a value that represents a "0" bit. Very little power is required to open or close the gates, which makes solid state storage ideal for battery-operated devices, such as digital cameras. Once the data is stored, it is non-volatile—the chip retains the data without the need for an external power source. Some solid state storage requires a device called a **card reader** to transfer data to or from a computer; others plug directly into a computer's system unit.

● Consumers today can select from a variety of solid state storage media. See Figure B-13.

A **USB flash drive**, such as Sony's MicroVault, is a portable storage device featuring a built-in connector that plugs directly into a computer's USB port. A USB flash drive requires no card reader, making it easily transportable from one computer to another. Nicknamed "pen drives" or "keychain drives," USB flash drives are about the size of a highlighter pen and so durable that you can literally carry them on your key ring. When connected to your computer's USB port, you can open, edit, delete, and run files stored on a USB flash drive just as though those files were stored on your computer's hard disk.

CompactFlash (CF) cards are about the size of a matchbook and provide high storage capacities

and access speeds. CompactFlash cards include a built-in controller that reads and writes data within the solid state grid. The built-in controller removes the need for control electronics on the card reader, so the device that connects to your computer to read the card's data is simply an adapter that collects data from the card and shuttles it to the computer's system unit. With their high storage capacities and access speeds, CompactFlash cards are ideal for use on high-end digital cameras that require megabytes of storage for each photo.

MultiMedia cards (MMC) offer solid state storage in a package about the size of a postage stamp. Initially used in mobile phones and pagers, use of MultiMedia cards has spread to digital cameras and MP3 players. Like CompactFlash cards, MultiMedia cards include a built-in controller, so MMC readers are electronically simple and very inexpensive.

SecureDigital (SD) cards are based on MultiMedia card technology, but feature significantly faster data transfer rates and include cryptographic security protection for copyrighted data and music. SecureDigital cards are popular for MP3 storage.

SmartMedia cards were originally called "solid state floppy disk cards" because they look much like a miniature floppy disk. Unlike other popular solid state storage, SmartMedia cards do not include a built-in controller, which means that the SmartMedia reader manages the read/write process. These cards are the least durable of the solid state storage media and should be handled with care.

FIGURE B-13: Popular solid state storage options

Sony's MicroVault USB
flash drive: 32-512 MB
capacities

CompactFlash card:
8 MB-1 GB capacities

MultiMedia card:
32-256 MB capacities

SecureDigital card:
32 MB-1 GB capacities

SmartMedia card:
32-128 MB capacities

Why use solid state storage?

A solid state memory card in a digital camera can hold data for hundreds of snap-shots. You can remove the card from the camera and insert it into a card reader that's connected to a computer. Once the card is connected to your computer, you can transfer the files to your hard drive so the photos can be edited using the computer's graphics software and transmitted via the computer's Internet connection. Or, moving data the other way, you can download MP3 music files and store them on a solid state memory card. Then you can insert the card into a portable MP3 player so you can hear your favorite tunes while you're on the go. Solid state storage is also ideal for portable computing, that is, transporting data from one computer to another. For example, you can transfer data from your home computer to a solid state storage media and then bring that storage media to a computer in your school lab or your workplace. Whether you are using the solid state memory card with a camera, an MP3 player, or for some other portable computing needs, the data on the memory card can be erased so the card can be reused.

Examining input devices

Most computer systems include a keyboard and pointing device as the primary input devices for basic data input. Although you don't have to be a great typist to use a computer effectively, you should be familiar with the computer keyboard and its special keys. The most popular pointing devices for personal computers include mice, trackballs, pointing sticks, trackpads, and joysticks. Using a pointing device requires some practice in order to become skillful.

LAB

OPERATING A
PERSONAL
COMPUTER

DETAILS

● Most computers are equipped with a keyboard. You can even find keyboards on handheld devices—entering text and numbers is an important part of most computing tasks. A computer keyboard includes the basic **typing keypad** with keys or buttons with letters and numbers as well as several keys with characters and special words to control computer-specific tasks. You use the keys to input commands, respond to prompts, and type the text of documents. Figure B-14 illustrates a variety of keyboards you might encounter on various computing devices. Virtually every computer user interface requires you to use a keyboard.

In addition to the basic typing keypad, desktop and notebook computer keyboards include a **navigation keypad** with keys such as the Home, End, and arrow keys, which you can use to efficiently move the screen-based insertion point or cursor. An **insertion point** (or **cursor**) indicates where the characters you type will appear. The insertion point appears on the screen as a flashing vertical bar. The cursor appears on the screen as a flashing underline. You can change the location of the cursor or insertion point using the arrow keys or the mouse.

Function keys at the top of many keyboards are designed for computer-specific tasks. For example, [F1] often opens a Help window. Most desktop computer keyboards also include a calculator-style **numeric keypad**.

Modifier keys, the [Ctrl], [Alt], and [Shift] keys are located at the periphery of the typing keypad. You can use the [Ctrl], [Alt], and [Shift] keys in conjunction with the other keys on the keyboard to expand the repertoire of available commands. Instead of using the mouse, you might use the [Alt] or [Ctrl] key in combination with letter keys to access menu options. Such combinations are called **keyboard shortcuts**.

● A **pointing device** allows you to manipulate an on-screen pointer and other screen-based graphical controls. A standard desktop computer includes a mouse as its primary pointing device. Many computer owners also add a mouse to their notebook computers. A **mouse** includes one or more buttons that can be "clicked" to input commands. To track its position, a mouse uses one of two technologies: mechanical or optical. See Figure B-15. Most computer owners prefer the performance of an optical mouse because it provides more precise tracking, greater durability, less maintenance, and more flexibility to use the mouse on a wide variety of surfaces without a mouse pad.

● Pointing sticks, trackpads, and trackballs are typically used with notebook computers as an alternative to a mouse. See Figure B-16. A **pointing stick**, or **TrackPoint**, looks like the tip of an eraser embedded in the keyboard of a notebook computer. It is a space-saving device that you can push up, down, or sideways to move the on-screen pointer. A **trackpad** is a touch-sensitive surface on which you can slide your fingers to move the on-screen pointer. A **trackball** looks like a mechanical mouse turned upside down. You use your fingers or palm to roll the ball and move the pointer.

A joystick looks like a small version of a car's stick shift. Moving the stick provides input to on-screen objects, such as a pointer or a character in a computer game. Joysticks, can include several sticks and buttons for arcade-like control when playing computer games.

● Additional input devices, such as scanners, digital cameras, and graphics tablets, are handy for working with graphical input. Microphones and electronic instruments provide input capabilities for sound and music.

FIGURE B-14: Computer keyboards

FIGURE B-15: Mechanical and optical mice

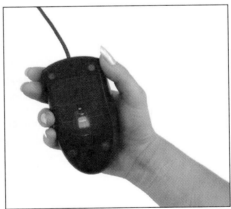

◀ A mechanical mouse (left) reads its position based on the movement of a ball that rolls over a mouse pad placed on a desk; an optical mouse (right) uses an onboard chip to track a light beam as it bounces off a surface, such as a desk, clipboard, or mouse pad

FIGURE B-16: Alternative pointing devices

Pointing stick

Trackpad

Trackball

Joystick

Comparing display devices

A computer display system is the main output device for a computer. Two key components of a computer display system are a graphics card and a display device, such as a monitor or screen. Display devices use one of three technologies: CRT, LCD, and gas plasma. See Figure B-17.

Info Web

DISPLAY DEVICES

DETAILS

- For many years, CRT monitors were the only display devices available for desktop computers. **CRT (cathode ray tube)** technology uses gun-like mechanisms to direct beams of electrons toward the screen and activate individual dots of color that form an image—much like a color TV. CRT monitors offer an inexpensive and dependable computer display.

- Today, an alternative to CRT monitors, are LCD monitors. **LCD (liquid crystal display)** technology produces an image by manipulating light within a layer of liquid crystal cells. LCDs are standard equipment on notebook computers. The advantages of an LCD monitor include display clarity, low radiation emission, portability, and compactness. Standalone LCDs, referred to as "LCD monitors" or "flat panel displays," are available for desktop computers as a replacement for CRT monitors. They are, however, more expensive than CRT monitors.

- A third display device technology is used in gas plasma screens. **Plasma screen technology** creates an on-screen image by illuminating miniature colored fluorescent lights arrayed in a panel-like screen. The name "plasma" comes from the type of gas that fills fluorescent lights and gives them their luminescence. Like LCD screens, plasma screens are compact, lightweight, and more expensive than CRT monitors.

- Image quality is determined by screen size, dot pitch, resolution, and color depth. **Screen size** is the measurement in inches from one corner of the screen diagonally across to the opposite corner. Typical monitor screen sizes range from 13" to 21". On most monitors, the viewable image does not stretch to the edge of the screen. Instead, a black border makes the viewing area smaller than the screen size. Many computer ads include a measurement of the **viewable image size (vis)**. For example, a 15" monitor might have an approximately 13.9" vis.

A monitor's **viewing angle width** indicates how far to the side you can still clearly see the screen image. A wide viewing angle indicates that you can view the screen from various positions

without compromising image quality. CRT and plasma screens offer the widest viewing angles. Graphics artists tend to prefer CRT screens, which display uniform color from any angle.

- **Dot pitch (dp)** is a measure of image clarity. A smaller dot pitch means a crisper image. Technically, dot pitch is the distance in millimeters between like-colored pixels, the small dots of light that form an image. A dot pitch between .26 and .23 is typical for today's monitors.

- The computer's graphics card sends an image to the monitor at a specific **resolution**, defined as the maximum number of horizontal and vertical pixels that are displayed on the screen. Standard resolutions include 800 × 600 and 1024 × 768. Even higher resolutions, such as 1600 × 1200, are possible given enough memory on the graphics card and a monitor capable of displaying that resolution. At higher resolutions, the computer displays a larger work area, such as an entire page of a document, but text and other objects appear smaller. The two screen shots in Figure B-18 help you compare a display at 800 × 600 resolution with a display at 1024 × 768 resolution.

- The number of colors that a monitor and graphics card can display is referred to as **color depth** or "**bit depth.**" Most PCs have the capability to display millions of colors. When you set the resolution at 24-bit color depth (sometimes called "True Color"), your PC can display more than 16 million colors and produce what are considered photographic-quality images. Windows allows you to select resolution and color depth.

- Although you can set the color depth and resolution of your notebook computer display, you might not have as many options as you do with a desktop computer. Typically, the graphics card circuitry is built into the motherboard of a notebook computer, making it difficult to upgrade and gain more video memory for additional resolution and color depth.

FIGURE B-17: Display device technology options

CRT

LCD

Gas Plasma

FIGURE B-18: Comparing screen resolutions

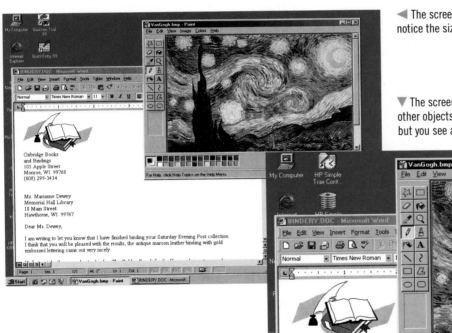

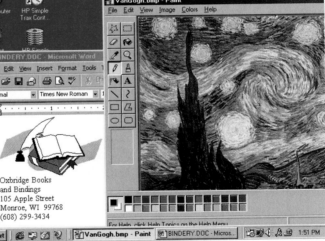

◄ The screen on the left shows 1024 × 768 resolution; notice the size of text and other screen-based objects

▼ The screen below shows 800 × 600 resolution; text and other objects appear larger on the low-resolution screen, but you see a smaller portion of the text and other objects

Graphics cards

A **graphics card** (also called a "graphics board" or a "video card") contains circuitry that generates the signals for displaying an image on the screen. It also contains special video memory, which stores screen images as they are processed before they are displayed. The amount of video memory is the key to how fast a screen updates for fast action games, 3-D modeling, and graphics-intensive desktop publishing. In addition to video memory, most graphics cards contain special graphics accelerator technology to further boost performance. Graphics circuitry can be built into a computer's motherboard or supplied as a small circuit board, like the one in Figure B-19, that plugs into the motherboard.

FIGURE B-19: A PC graphics card

UNIT B

Comparing printers

Printers are one of the most popular output devices available for personal computers. Printers differ in resolution and speed, both of which affect the print quality and price. Today's best-selling printers typically use ink jet or laser technology. Printer technologies for specialized applications include dot matrix, solid ink, thermal transfer, and dye sublimation.

DETAILS

- The quality or sharpness of printed images and text depends on the printer's resolution, the density of the grid of dots that create an image. Printer resolution is measured by the number of dots it can print per linear inch, abbreviated as **dpi**. At normal reading distance, a resolution of about 900 dots per inch appears solid to the human eye, but a close examination of color sections will reveal a dot pattern. Expensive coffee-table books are typically produced on printers with 2,400 dpi or higher.

- Printer speeds are measured either by pages per minute (ppm) or characters per second (cps). Color printouts typically take longer than black-and-white printouts. Pages that contain mostly text tend to print more rapidly than pages that contain graphics. Ten pages per minute is a typical speed for a personal computer printer.

- In addition to printer speed, a printer's **duty cycle** determines how many pages a printer is able to churn out. Printer duty cycle is usually measured in pages per month. For example, a personal laser printer has a duty cycle of about 3,000 pages per month (ppm)—that means roughly 100 pages per day.

- Ink jet printers outsell all of the others because most ink jet printers are small, lightweight, and inexpensive, yet produce very good quality color output. An **ink jet printer** has a nozzle-like print head that sprays ink onto paper to form characters and graphics. You must periodically replace the black ink cartridge and a second cartridge that carries the colored inks. See Figure B-20. Ink jet printers have excellent resolution, which can range from 600 dpi to 2,880 dpi, depending on the model.

- A **laser printer** (see Figure B-21) uses the same technology as a photocopier to produce dots of light on a light-sensitive drum. Personal laser printers produce six to eight ppm (pages per minute) at a resolution of 600 dpi. Professional models pump out 15 to 25 ppm at 1,200 dpi. Laser printers are a popular technology for situations that require high-volume output or good-quality printouts.

- When PCs first began to appear in the late 1970s, dot matrix printers were the technology of choice, and they are still available today. A **dot matrix printer** (see Figure B-22) produces characters and graphics by using a grid of fine wires. A fast dot

matrix device can print at speeds up to 455 cps or about five pages per minute. Unlike laser and ink-jet technologies, a dot matrix printer actually strikes the paper and, therefore, can print multipart carbon forms. Today dot matrix printers are used primarily for "back-office" applications that demand low operating cost and dependability but not high print quality.

- A **solid ink printer** melts sticks of crayon-like ink and then sprays the liquefied ink through the print head's tiny nozzles. The ink solidifies before the paper can absorb it, and a pair of rollers finishes fusing the ink onto the paper. A solid ink printer produces vibrant colors on most types of paper and is used for professional graphics applications.

- A **thermal transfer printer** uses a page-sized ribbon that is coated with cyan, magenta, yellow, and black wax. The print head consists of thousands of tiny heating elements that melt the wax onto specially coated paper or transparency film (the kind used for overhead projectors). This type of printer excels at printing colorful transparencies for presentations, but the fairly expensive per-page costs and the requirement for special paper make this a niche market printer that is used mainly by businesses.

- A **dye sublimation printer** uses technology similar to wax transfer. The difference is that the page-sized ribbon contains dye instead of colored wax. Heating elements in the print head diffuse the dye onto the surface of specially coated paper. Dye sublimation printers produce excellent color quality. The high per page cost, however, makes these printers too pricey for the average consumer.

- A large memory capacity is required to print color images and graphics-intensive documents. For example, a laser printer might have between 2 MB and 32 MB of memory. Some printers accept additional memory, if you find that your printer requires more memory for the types of document you typically print.

- A computer sends data for a printout to the printer along with a set of instructions on how to print that data. **Printer Control Language (PCL)** is the most widely used language for communication between computers and printers, but **PostScript** is an alternative printer language that many publishing professionals prefer.

FIGURE B-20: Ink jet printer

▶ Most ink jet printers use **CMYK color**, which requires only cyan (blue), magenta (pink), yellow, and black inks to create a printout that appears to have thousands of colors

FIGURE B-21: Laser printer

▲ Laser printers are a popular technology when high-volume output or good-quality printouts are required; electrostatically charged ink is applied to the drum, then transferred to paper

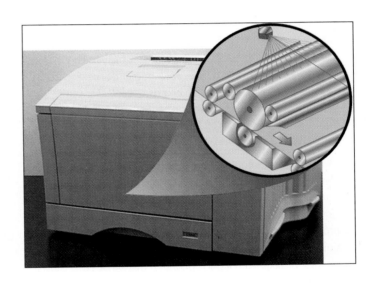

FIGURE B- 22: Dot matrix printer

▲ Dot matrix printers can print text and graphics; some even print in color using a multicolored ribbon; with a resolution of 140 dpi, a dot matrix printer produces low-quality output with clearly discernible dots forming letters and graphics

Print head contains a matrix of thin wires

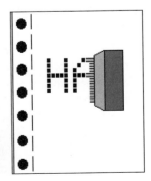

▲ As the print head moves across the paper, the wires strike the ribbon and paper in a pattern prescribed by your PC

Understanding expansion slots, cards, and ports

Within a computer, data travels from one component to another over circuits called a **data bus**. One part of the data bus runs between RAM and the microprocessor; the other part runs between RAM and various storage devices. The segment of the data bus between RAM and peripheral devices is called the **expansion bus**. As data moves along the expansion bus, it may travel through expansion slots, cards, ports, and cables. This lesson takes a closer look at slots, cards, and ports; the next lesson looks at cables.

DETAILS

- An **expansion slot** is a long, narrow socket on the motherboard into which you can plug an expansion card. The motherboard is the main board in the computer that holds the components that control the processing functions. An **expansion card** is a small circuit board that provides a computer the ability to control a storage device, an input device, or an output device. Expansion cards are also called "expansion boards," "controller cards," or "adapters." To insert an expansion card, you slide it into an expansion slot, where it can be secured with a small screw. See Figure B-23.

- Most desktop computers have four to eight expansion slots, but some of the slots usually contain factory installed expansion cards. A graphics card (sometimes called a "video card") provides a path for data traveling to the monitor. A **modem card** provides a way to transmit data over phone lines or cable television lines. A **sound card** carries data out to speakers and headphones, or back from a microphone. A **network card** allows you to connect your computer to a local area network. You might add other expansion cards if you want to connect a scanner or download videos from a camera or VCR.

- A desktop computer may have up to three types of expansion slots. Each expansion card is built for only one type of slot. ISA, PCI, and AGP slots are different lengths so you can easily identify them by opening your computer's system unit and looking at the motherboard. See Figure B-24. **ISA (industry standard architecture)** slots are an old technology, used today only for some modems and other relatively slow devices. **PCI (peripheral component interconnect)** slots offer fast transfer speeds and a 32-bit or 64-bit data bus. This type of slot typically houses a graphics card, sound card, video capture card, modem, or network interface card. **AGP (accelerated graphics port)** slots provide a high-speed data pathway that is primarily used for graphics cards.

- Most notebook computers are equipped with a special type of external slot called a **PCMCIA slot (personal computer memory card international association)**. Typically, a notebook computer has only one of these slots, but the slot can hold more than one PC card (also called "PCMCIA expansion cards" or "Card Bus cards"). PCMCIA slots are classified according to their thickness. Type 1 slots accept only the thinnest PC cards, such as memory expansion cards. Type II slots accept most of the popular PC cards such as those that contain modems, sound cards, and network cards. Type III slots commonly included with today's notebook computers accept the thickest PC cards, which contain devices such as hard disk drives. A Type III slot can also hold two Type 1 cards, two Type II cards, or a Type 1 and a Type II card. Figure B-25 shows a PCMCIA slot and a PC card.

- An **expansion port** is any connector that passes data in and out of a computer or peripheral device. See Figure B-26. Ports are sometimes called "jacks" or "connectors," but the terminology is inconsistent. An expansion port is often housed on an expansion card so that it is accessible through an opening in the back of the computer's system unit. A port might also be built into the system unit case of a desktop or notebook computer. The built-in ports on a computer usually include a mouse port, keyboard port, serial port, and USB port. Ports that have been added with expansion cards usually protrude through rectangular cutouts in the back of the case.

- USB ports are probably the most popular ports for connecting peripheral devices. Most computers feature several USB ports, which provide connectivity for lots of USB devices. On many computer models USB ports are conveniently located on the front of the system unit so that peripherals can be easily connected and disconnected. Many kinds of peripheral devices—including mice, scanners, and joysticks—are available with USB connections. Several types of storage devices, such as USB Flash drives, also use USB connections. Windows automatically recognizes most USB devices, which makes installation simple.

FIGURE B-23: Inserting an expansion card

FIGURE B-24: Types of expansion slots

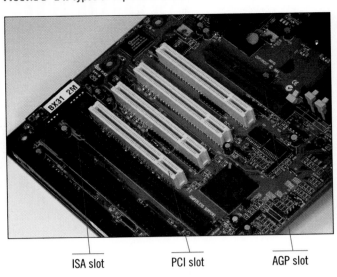

ISA slot   PCI slot   AGP slot

FIGURE B-25: PC card for a notebook computer

PC card

FIGURE B-26: Expansion ports on a typical desktop computer

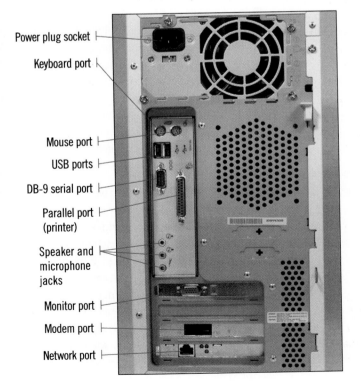

Power plug socket

Keyboard port

Mouse port

USB ports

DB-9 serial port

Parallel port
(printer)

Speaker and
microphone
jacks

Monitor port

Modem port

Network port

Exploring peripheral devices

All computers use peripheral devices to input, output, and store data. **Peripheral devices** are equipment that you connect to the computer to enhance its functionality. They are hardware components that are "outside," or in addition to, the main computer. They are connected to the main computer through the use of expansion slots, cards, ports, and cables.

DETAILS

- Peripheral devices expand and modify your system. Although the keyboard, printer, monitor, disk drives, and mouse can be considered peripheral devices, most people do not consider them to be peripheral devices because they are necessary to perform basic computer functions. Figure B-27 shows examples of several peripheral devices. A **computer projection device** is an output device that produces a large display of the information shown on the computer screen. A **scanner** is an input device that converts a page of text or images just into a digital format. **Multifunction devices** work both as input and output devices to combine the functions of a printer, scanner, copier, fax, and answering machine. A **digital camera** is an input device that records an image in digital format. A **graphics tablet** is an input device that accepts input from a pressure-sensitive stylus and converts strokes into images on the screen. A **Web cam** is an input device used to capture live video and transmit it over the Internet. A trackball and **joystick** are pointing devices that you use as alternative input devices to a mouse. TrackPoints and touchpads are alternative input devices often found on notebook computers.

- In order for a peripheral device to work, a connection must be made between it and the motherboard, often the connection is made using a cable. To install a peripherial device, you must match the peripheral device and a port on the computer. If the right type of port is not available, you might have to add an expansion card. Figure B-28 describes the cable connectors you might need in order to connect a peripheral device to your PC. If a cable is supplied with a peripheral device, you can usually figure out where to plug it in by matching the shape of the cable connector to the port. If you need to purchase a cable, be sure the cable matches the available ports.

- Remember, when you install a peripheral device, you are basically creating a connection for data to flow between the device and the computer. The installation might simply require connecting a cable, or it might require installing an expansion card. If you own a desktop computer, you might have to open the system unit. Before doing so, make sure you unplug the computer and ground yourself—that means that you are releasing static electricity by using a special grounding wristband or by touching both hands to a metal object before opening the system unit.

- Today's PCs include a feature called **Plug and Play** (also known as **PnP**) that automatically takes care of technical details for installing just about every popular peripheral device. Once the peripheral device is connected to the motherboard, PnP should recognize the new device. If not, you'll probably have to install device driver software.

- Each peripheral device requires software called a **device driver** to set up communication between your computer and the device. The directions supplied with your new peripheral device will include instructions on how to install the device driver if it does not happen automatically with PnP. Typically, you'll use the device driver disk or CD once to get everything set up, then you can put the disk away. Be sure to keep the driver disk or CD in a safe place, however, because if you ever need to restore your computer or reinstall the device, you may need to install the driver again. If the peripheral device still doesn't work, check the manufacturer's Web site for a device driver update, or call the manufacturer's technical support department.

FIGURE B-27: Examples of peripheral devices

▲ Scanner

▲ Multifunction device

▲ Computer projection device

▲ Digital camera

▲ Graphics tablet

▲ Web cam

FIGURE B-28: Personal computer cables and connectors

	CONNECTOR	DESCRIPTION	DEVICES
	Serial DB-9	Connects to serial port, which sends data over a single data line one bit at a time at speeds of 56 Kbps	Mouse or modem
	Parallel DB-25M	Connects to parallel port, which sends data simultaneously over 8 data lines at speeds of 12,000 Kbps	Printer, external CD drive, Zip drive, external hard disk drive, or tape backup device
	USB	Connects to universal serial bus (USB), which sends data over a single data line and can support up to 127 devices. USB-1 carries data at speeds up to 12,000 Kbps; USB-2, at 480,000 Kbps	Modem, keyboard, joystick, scanner, mouse, external hard disk drive, MP3 player
	SCSI C-50F	Connects to SCSI port, which sends data simultaneously over 8 or 16 data lines at speeds between 40,000 Kbps and 640,000 Kbps; supports up to 16 devices	Internal or external hard disk drive, scanner, CD drive, tape backup device
	IEEE 1394	Connects to the FireWire port, which sends data at 400,000 Kbps	Video camera, DVD player
	VGA HDB-15	Connects to the video port	Monitor

To many computer owners, the Windows Registry is simply a mysterious "black box" that is mentioned occasionally in articles about computer troubleshooting. It is certainly possible to use a computer without intimate knowledge of the Registry, but it is useful to understand that the Registry is the "glue" that binds together many of the most important components of a PC: the computer hardware, peripheral devices, application software, and system software. See Figure B-29. After reading this Tech Talk section, you should have a basic understanding of the Registry and its role in the operation of a computer system.

Why does a PC need the Registry? You know that you use application software to direct the operations that a computer carries out. For some operations, particularly those that involve hardware, the application software communicates with the operating system. The operating system might communicate with device drivers or, in some cases, it can communicate directly with a peripheral device.

In order to act as an intermediary between software and peripheral devices, your operating system needs information about these components: where they are located, what's been installed, how they are configured, and how you want to use them. A special type of memory called **CMOS memory** holds the most essential data about your computer's processing and storage hardware, but the **Windows Registry** keeps track of your computer's peripheral devices and software so that the operating system can access the information it needs to coordinate the activities of the entire computer system. Some examples of specific data that the Registry tracks include your preferences for desktop colors, icons, pointers, shortcuts, and display resolution; the sounds that are assigned to various system events, such as clicking and shutting down; the capability of your CD-ROM drive for playing audio CDs and autorunning computer CDs; the options that appear on a shortcut menu when you right-click an object; your computer's network card settings and protocols; and the location of the uninstall routines for all installed hardware and software.

FIGURE B-29: Items tracked by the Windows Registry

User preferences for desktop colors, icons, pointers, short-cuts, and display resolution

Sounds that are assigned to various system events, such as clicking and shutting down

The capability of your CD-ROM drive for playing audio CDs and autorunning computer CDs

The options that appear on a shortcut menu when you right-click an object

The computer's network card settings and protocols

The location of the uninstall routines for all installed software.

The contents of the Registry are stored in multiple files in the Windows/System folder of your computer's hard disk and are combined into a single database when Windows starts. Although each version of Windows uses a slightly different storage scheme, the basic organization and function of the Registry is similar in all versions.

Windows stores the entire contents of the Registry in two files: System.dat and User.dat. System.dat includes configuration data for all the hardware and software installed on a computer. User.dat contains user-specific information, sometimes called a "user profile," which includes software settings and desktop settings.

The Registry has a logical structure that appears as a hierarchy of folders, as shown in Figure B-30. There are six main folders in the Registry, and their names begin with HKEY. Each folder contains data that pertains to a particular part of a computer system.

You indirectly change the Registry whenever you install or remove hardware or software. Device drivers and the Windows Plug and Play feature automatically update the Registry with essential information about the hardware's location and configuration. The setup program for your software provides similar update services for newly installed software.

You can also make changes to the Windows Registry by using the dialog boxes for various configuration routines provided by the operating system and application software. For example, if you want to change the desktop colors for your user profile, you can do so by selecting the Settings option from the Start menu, clicking Control Panel, and then selecting the Display option. Any changes that you make to the settings in the Display Properties dialog box (Figure B-31) will be recorded in the Windows Registry.

FIGURE B-30: The Windows Registry is organized as a hierarchy of folders and files

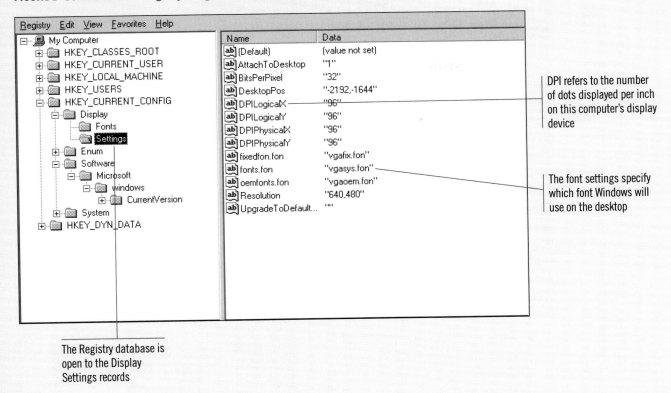

DPI refers to the number of dots displayed per inch on this computer's display device

The font settings specify which font Windows will use on the desktop

The Registry database is open to the Display Settings records

FIGURE B-31: Changes that you make when using the Display Properties dialog box automatically update the corresponding entries in the HKEY_CURRENT_CONFIG folder of the Registry

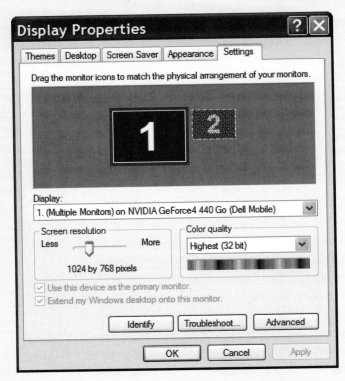

The military, an early pioneer in computer and communication technologies (see Figure B-32), continues to be the driving force behind technologies that have revolutionized everyday life. During World War II, the U.S. military initiated a classified research program, called Project PX, to develop an electronic device to calculate artillery firing tables; each table required weeks of grueling manual calculations. Project PX produced ENIAC (Electrical Numerical Integrator And Calculator), one of the first general-purpose electronic computers. When ENIAC was completed in 1946, the war was over, but ENIAC's versatile architecture could be used for other calculations, such as designing hydrogen bombs, predicting weather, and engineering wind tunnels. ENIAC's technology evolved into the computers used today.

After Project PX, the military continued to support computer research. Like most large corporations, the military used mainframe computers to maintain personnel, inventory, supply, and facilities records and distributed this data to terminals at other locations via rudimentary networks. Because all data communication flowed through the mainframe, a single point of failure for the entire system was a possible risk. A malfunction or an enemy "hit" could disrupt command and control, sending the military into chaos. To eliminate this risk, the armed forces created the Advanced Research Projects Agency (ARPA) to design a distributed communications system that could continue operating without a centralized computer. The result was ARPANET, which paved the way for the data communications system we know today as the Internet.

The U.S. Department of Defense (DoD) currently maintains two data communications networks: SIPRNet, which is a classified (secret-level) network and NIPRNet, which provides unclassified services. The DoD's public Web site, called DefenseLINK, provides official information about defense policies, organizations, budgets, and operations.

Computers and communications technology have also become an integral part of high-tech military operations (see Figure B-33). U.S. Apache helicopters, for example, are equipped with computer-based Target Acquisition Designation Sights, laser range finder/designators, and Pilot Night Vision Sensors. These arcade-style controls are also used by tank drivers in the U.S. Army's 4th Infantry Division. Each vehicle in this "Digitized Division" is equipped with a Force 21 Battle Command Brigade and Below system, which works like a battlefield Internet to transmit data from one vehicle to another using wireless communication regarding the location of friendly and enemy forces.

FIGURE B-32

Much like a video game, the Force 21 touch screen shows friendly troops in blue, and a global positioning satellite (GPS) system updates their positions automatically. Enemy troops spotted by helicopters are shown as red icons. To get information on any friendly or enemy vehicle, a soldier can simply touch one of these blue or red icons. To send text messages—much like cell phone and computer instant messaging—a soldier touches the Message button.

The built-in GPS system provides location and route information, much like sophisticated mapping programs in luxury cars. Force 21 computers are installed in shock-resistant cases and equipped with a cooling system that eliminates the need for a fan, which might pull in dust, dirt, or water. The computers run Sun Microsystem's Solaris operating system because it is less vulnerable to viruses and intrusion attacks than Microsoft Windows. To prevent enemy capture and use, Force 21 computers have a self-destruct mechanism that can be triggered remotely.

In addition to pilots and tank drivers, battlefield soldiers will soon be equipped with "wearable" computer and communications equipment. The $2 billion Land Warrior program will provide high-tech weaponry, such as the Integrated Helmet Assembly Subsystem for soldiers. IHAS is a helmet-mounted device that displays graphical data, digital maps, thermal images, intelligence information, and troop locations. It also includes a weapon-mounted video camera, so that soldiers can view and fire around corners and acquire targets in darkness.

The military has also conducted research in computer simulations that are similar to civilian computer games. "Live" military training is dangerous—weapons are deadly and equipment costs millions of dollars. With computer simulations, however, troops can train in a true-to-life environment without physical harm or equipment damage. Flying an F-16 fighter, for example, costs about $5,000 an hour, but flying an F-16 simulator costs only $500 per hour. The military uses simulators to teach Air Force pilots to fly fighter jets, Navy submarine officers to navigate in harbors, and Marine infantry squads to handle urban combat.

Military trainers agree that widespread use of computer games helps prepare troops to adapt quickly to real situations. A 24-year-old preflight student at Pensacola Naval Air Station modified the Microsoft Flight Simulator game to re-create a T-34C Turbo Mentor plane's controls. After logging 50 hours on the simulator, the student performed so well on a real plane that the Navy used his simulation to train other pilots. Today, a growing cadre of computer and communications specialists is needed to create and maintain increasingly complex military systems.

An army once depended on its infantry, but today's high-tech army depends equally on its database designers, computer programmers, and network specialists. Even previously low-tech military jobs, such as mechanics and dietitians, require some computer expertise. New recruits are finding military computer systems easy to learn, based on their knowledge of civilian technologies, such as the Internet and computer games.

FIGURE B-33

Although most citizens agree that an adequate national defense is necessary, the cost of defense-related equipment, personnel, and research remains controversial. In 1961, President Dwight Eisenhower warned "We must guard against the acquisition of unwarranted influence, whether sought or unsought, by the military-industrial complex." Many socially motivated citizens and pacifists protested diverting tax dollars from social and economic programs to the military-industrial complex that Eisenhower cautioned against. In retrospect, however, military funding contributed to many technologies we depend on today. For example, detractors tried to convince the government that Project PX was doomed to failure, but without ENIAC research, computers might not exist today. Skeptics saw no future for the fruits of ARPANET research, but it led to the Internet, which has changed our lives significantly.

Why Recycle Computers?

Keeping up with technology means replacing your computer every few years, but what should you do with your old, outdated computer? According to the National Safety Council, an estimated 300 million computers will be obsolete by the year 2007. A recycling company called Back Thru the Future Micro Computer, Inc. (BTTF) estimates that 63 million computers will be retired in 2005 alone, compared with 20 million that became obsolete in 1998. BTTF estimates that printer ink cartridges are discarded at the rate of almost eight cartridges every second in the United States alone. A recycling company called GreenDisk estimates that about 1 billion floppy disks, CDs, and DVDs end up in landfills every year.

U.S. landfills already hold more than 2 million tons of computer parts, which contain toxic substances such as lead, phosphorus, and mercury. A computer monitor can contain up to six pounds of lead. An Environmental Protection Agency (EPA) report sums up the situation: "In this world of rapidly changing technology, disposal of computers and other electronic equipment has created a new and growing waste stream." See Figure B-34.

Many computers end up in landfills because their owners were unaware of potential environmental hazards and simply tossed them in the garbage. In addition, PC owners typically are not provided with information concerning the options for disposing of their old machines. Instead of throwing away your old computer, you might be able to sell it; donate it to a local school, church, or community program; have it hauled away by a professional recycling firm; or send it back to the manufacturer.

With the growing popularity of Internet auctions and dedicated computer reclamation sites, you might be able to get some cash for your old computer. At Web sites, such as the Computer Recycle Center (www.recycles.com), you can post an ad for your "old stuff." Off the Web, you can find several businesses, such as Computer Renaissance, that refurbish old computers and sell them in retail stores.

Donating your old computer to a local organization doesn't actually eliminate the disposal problem, but it does delay it. Unfortunately, finding a new home for an old computer is not always easy. Most schools and community organizations have few resources for repairing broken equipment, so if your old computer is not in good working order, it could be more of a burden than a gift. In addition, your computer might be too old to be compatible with the other computers that are used in an organization. It helps if you can donate software along with your old computer. To provide a legal transfer, include the software distribution disks, manuals, and license agreement. And remember, once you donate the software, you cannot legally use it on your new computer unless it is freeware or shareware. If you cannot find an organization to accept your computer donation, look in your local Yellow Pages or on the Internet for an electronics recycling firm that will haul away your computer and recycle any usable materials.

FIGURE B-34

In recent years, about half the states in the U.S. have taken some legislative action to curtail the rampant disposal of obsolete computer equipment. For example, Massachusetts implemented a statewide ban in 2000 on disposing computers in landfills, which helped spur recycling efforts. New Jersey's tough regulations on electronics disposal, which became effective in December 2002, apply to more than 220 pounds or 100 kilograms, which is about eight monitors. Under those regulations, disposal must be at an approved New Jersey facility and disposal records must be kept for three years. Failure to comply can result in a $2,000 fine for each violation. Many lawmakers in the United States, Japan, and the European Union believe that more legislation is necessary but they can't agree on an implementation plan. Basic to the issue is the question of "Who pays?" Should it be the taxpayer, the individual, or the computer manufacturer?

Taxpayers typically pick up the tab for electronic waste disposal through municipal trash pick-up fees or local taxes. For example, the Silicon Valley Toxics Coalition estimates that California taxpayers will spend more than $1 billion to manage electronic waste between 2002 and 2006. But is this approach fair to individual taxpayers who generate very little electronic waste?

To make consumers responsible for the cost of recycling the products they buy, some lawmakers suggest adding a special recycling tax to computers and other electronic devices. A proposal in South Carolina, for example, would impose a $5 fee on the sale of each piece of electronic equipment containing a CRT and require the state treasurer to deposit the fees into a recycling fund for electronic equipment.

Other lawmakers propose to make manufacturers responsible for recycling costs and logistics. Some companies currently participate in voluntary extended producer responsibility programs. Hewlett-Packard, 3M, Nortel, Frigidaire, IBM, Sony, and Xerox, for example, provide recycling options for some products and components. Sony recently implemented a take-back program in Minnesota that allows residents to recycle all Sony products at no cost for the next five years.

IBM recently implemented its PC Recycling Service program, which allows you to ship any make of computer, including system units, monitors, printers, and optional attachments, to a recycling center for a nominal fee. These programs and others are important steps in the effort to keep our planet green.

▼ INTERACTIVE QUESTIONS

○ Yes   ○ No   ○ Not sure
1. Have you ever thrown away an old computer or other electronic device?

○ Yes   ○ No   ○ Not sure
2. Are you aware of any options for recycling electronic equipment in your local area?

3. Would it be fair for consumers to pay a recycling tax on any electronic equipment that they purchase?

○ Yes   ○ No   ○ Not sure

▼ EXPAND THE IDEAS

1. Have you ever thrown away an old computer or other electronic device? If so, how did you dispose of it? Did you donate it, pass it along, or just throw it in the garbage? Write a short essay explaining what your options were at the time, any thoughts about recycling or donating you might have had, and exactly how you got rid of the old computer.

2. Research options for recycling electronic equipment in your local area. Create a chart showing ways to get rid of an old computer, include the positive and negative aspects of each option. Include specific details for recycling or donating the computers, such as names or addresses.

3. Would it be fair for consumers to pay a recycling tax on any electronic equipment that they purchase? Research the current trends. Include any important legislation or pending legislation in your area or around the world that you feel is relevant. Compile your findings in a short report. Include your opinion in the conclusion.

End of Unit Exercises

▼ KEY TERMS

Access time
AGP
Bit depth
Card reader
CD
CD-DA
CD drive
CD-R
CD ROM
CD-ROM disc
CD-RW
CMOS memory
CMYK color
Color depth
CompactFlash (CF) card
Computer projection device
Controller
CRT
Cursor
Cylinder
Data bus
Data transfer rate
Device driver
Digital camera
Disk density
DMA
Dot matrix printer
Dot pitch
Dpi

Drive bay
Duty cycle
DVD
DVD drive
DVD+R
DVD-ROM
DVD+RW
DVD-Video
Dye sublimation printer
EIDE
Expansion bus
Expansion card
Expansion port
Expansion slot
Floppy disk
Function key
Graphics card
Graphics tablet
Hard disk
Hard disk platter
Head crash
Ink jet printer
Insertion point
ISA
Joystick
Keyboard shortcut
Lands
Laser printer
LCD

Magnetic storage
Millisecond
Modem card
Modifier key
Mouse
Multifunction device
MultiMedia card (MMC)
Navigation keypad
Network card
Numeric keypad
Optical storage
PCI
PCMCIA slot
Peripheral device
Pits
Plasma screen technology
Plug and Play (PnP)
Pointing stick
PostScript
Printer control language (PCL)
RAM
Random access
Read-write head
Recordable technology
Resolution
Revolutions per minute (rpm)
Rewritable technology
Scanner
Screen size

SCSI
SecureDigital (SD) card
Sequential access
SmartMedia card
Solid ink printer
Solid state storage
Sound card
Storage capacity
Storage device
Storage medium
Storage technology
SuperDisk
Tape
Tape cartridge
Thermal transfer printer
Touchpad
Trackball
Trackpad
TrackPoint
Typing keypad
UDMA
Ultra ATA
USB flash drive
Viewable image size (vis)
Viewing angle width
Volatile
Web cam
Windows Registry
Write-protect window
Zip disk

▼ UNIT REVIEW

1. Make sure that you can use your own words to define the bold terms that appear throughout the unit.

2. Describe the advantages and disadvantages of magnetic storage, solid state storage, and optical storage.

3. Create a grid with each type of storage device written across the top. Make a list of the corresponding media down the left side of the grid. Working down each column, place an X in cells for any of the media that can be read by the device listed at the top of the column.

4. Summarize important uses for each type of storage technology.

5. Summarize display devices. Be sure to include advantages and disadvantages.

6. Create a table to summarize what you know about the printer technologies that were discussed in this unit.

7. List any peripheral devices that are attached to your computer. Describe what each one does. Be sure to identify each one as input, output, or storage.

8. If possible, open your computer and count the number of expansion slots that are not currently in use and how many are in use.

9. Look at the front of your computer and identify the devices that are in the drive bays.

10. Count the number of cables coming out of the back of your computer. Using Figure B-28 identify each type of cable.

▼ FILL IN THE BEST ANSWER

1. Data on an optical storage medium is stored as _____ and lands.

2. _____ time is the average time that it takes a computer to locate data on a storage medium and read it.

3. A computer can move directly to any file on a(n) _____ access device, but must start at the beginning and read through all of the data on a(n) _____ access device.

4. Higher disk _____ provides increased storage capacity.

5. "HD DS" means _____.

6. EIDE, Ultra ATA, and SCSI refer to the type of _____ used by a hard disk drive.

7. CD-R technology allows you to _____ data on a disk, then change that data.

8. A variety of compact storage cards, pens, and sticks can be classified as _____ storage which store data in a non-volatile, erasable, low-power chip.

9. The _____ bus carries data from RAM to peripheral devices.

10. AGP, PCI, and ISA are types of expansion _____, which are part of a personal computer's motherboard.

11. Many peripheral devices come packaged with device _____ software.

12. A scanner is a type of _____ device.

13. Most people set their monitors to a(n) _____ of 800 × 600 or 1024 × 768.

14. The number of colors that a monitor can display is referred to as bit _____.

15. The advantages of an LCD _____ include display clarity, low radiation emission, and portability.

16. The most popular printers for personal computers are _____, which are inexpensive and produce good-quality color printouts.

17. Today's PCs include a feature called Plug and _____ that automatically takes care of technical details for installing peripheral devices.

18. A _____ key such as the [Ctrl] key is used in conjunction with other keys to expand the abilities of each key.

19. TrackPoints and touchpads are alternative _____ devices often found on notebook computers.

20. A read-write _____ is a mechanism in the disk drive that reads and writes the magnetized particles that represent data.

▼ PRACTICE TESTS

When you use the Interactive CD, you can take Practice Tests that consist of 10 multiple-choice, true/false, and fill-in-the blank questions. The questions are selected at random from a large test bank, so each time you take a test, you'll receive a different set of questions. Your tests are scored immediately, and you can print study guides to determine which questions you answered incorrectly. If you are using a Tracking Disk, insert it in the floppy disk drive to save your test scores.

▼ INDEPENDENT CHALLENGE 1

You know that you're really a tech wizard when you can decipher every term and acronym in a computer ad. But even the most knowledgeable computer gurus sometimes need a dictionary for new terms.

1. For this independent challenge, photocopy a full page from a current computer magazine that contains an ad for a computer system. On the copy of the ad, use a colored pen to circle each descriptive term and acronym.

2. On a separate sheet of paper, or using a word processor, list all of the terms that you circled and write a definition for each term. If you encounter a term that was not defined in the unit, use a computer dictionary or refer to the Webopaedia Web site (www.webopedia.com) to locate the correct definition.

3. Prepare your list to submit to your instructor. Add a summary paragraph indicating why you would or would not purchase the computer in the ad and additional information that you need before making a decision.

▼ INDEPENDENT CHALLENGE 2

Storage technology has a fascinating history. Mankind has evolved many ways to retain and store data. From the ancient days when Egyptians were writing on papyrus to modern day holographic technologies, societies have found ways to retain more and more information in permanent and safe ways.

1. To complete this independent challenge you will research the history of storage technologies and create a timeline that shows the developments. Be sure to include such items as 78-rpm records and 8-track tapes. Your research should yield some interesting technologies and systems.

2. For each technology, list the media, the device used to retrieve the information, two significant facts about the technology, the era in which it was used or popular, and what lead to its demise or obsolescence, or why it is still popular.

3. You can create the timeline using images or just words. This is a creative project. Your best research, artistic, and communication skills come together to create this timeline.

▼ INDEPENDENT CHALLENGE 3

It is important that you are familiar with the type of computer you use daily. You may need to consult your technical resource person to help you complete this independent challenge.

1. Identify the components on your computer. What type of computer are you using? What kind of system unit do you have?

2. What peripheral devices are attached to your computer? List the name, manufacturer, and model number of each device if available.

3. Draw a sketch of your computer. Label each component and identify what it does.

▼ INDEPENDENT CHALLENGE 4

 For this project, use your library and Web resources to research information in order to compare printers.

   1. Use the information in this unit as well as your own resources to create a comparative table of printers.

2. Your column heads might address these questions: What types are available? What technology is used? What is the duty cycle? What is the cost range? What is the average cost per page? Who is the market for this type of printer?

3. Provide a summary statement indicating which printer you would buy and why, based on the information in your table.

▼ INDEPENDENT CHALLENGE 5

 In this unit you learned about peripheral devices. Some of these are standard peripheral devices such as monitors and printers. If your office is tight for space, you might consider purchasing a multifunction device. For this project, use your library and Web resources to research information about multifunction devices.

1. Research and find the types of multifunction devices available. Categorize them by their functions: scanners, fax, phone, copiers, color or black-and-white printing, laser or inkjet. Different manufacturers bundle different capabilities into their devices. The more features a unit has, typically, the more expensive it will be.

2. Research and find the manufacturers and model numbers for three devices you would consider buying. Write a comparison of the features, strengths, and weaknesses of each model.

▼ INDEPENDENT CHALLENGE 6

 The Issue section of this unit focused on the potential for discarded computers and other electronic devices to become a significant environmental problem. For this independent challenge, you will write a short paper about recycling computers based on information that you gather from the Internet.

1. To begin this independent challenge, consult the Internet and use your favorite search engine to search for and find Web pages to get an in-depth overview of the issue.

2. Determine the specific aspect of the issue that you will present in your paper. You might, for example, decide to focus on the toxic materials contained in computers that end up in landfills. Or you might tackle the barriers that discourage the shipment of old computers across national borders. Whatever aspect of the issue you decide to present, make sure that you can back up your discussion with facts and references to authoritative articles and Web pages.

3. You can place citations to these pages (include the author's name, article title, date of publication, and URL) at the end of your paper as endnotes, on each page as footnotes, or along with the appropriate paragraphs using parentheses. Follow your professor's instructions for submitting your paper via e-mail or as a printed document.

▼ LAB: WORKING WITH BINARY NUMBERS

1. Start the interactive part of the lab. Insert your Tracking disk if you want to save your QuickCheck results. Perform each of the lab steps as directed and answer all of the lab QuickCheck questions. When you exit the lab, your answers are automatically graded and your results are displayed.

2. Using paper and pencil, manually convert the following decimal numbers into binary numbers. Your instructor might ask you to show the process that you used for each conversion.

   a. 100   b. 1,000   c. 256   d. 27

   e. 48   f. 112   g. 96   h. 1,024

3. Using paper and pencil, manually convert the following binary numbers into decimal numbers. Your instructor might ask you to show the process that you used for each conversion.

   a. 100   b. 101   c. 1100   d. 10101

   e. 1111   f. 10000   g. 1111000   h. 110110

4. Describe what is wrong with the following sequence:

   10 100 110 1000 1001 1100 1110 10000

5. What is the decimal equivalent of 2^0? 2^1? 2^8?

▼ LAB: OPERATING A PERSONAL COMPUTER

1. Start the interactive part of the lab. Insert your Tracking Disk if you want to save your QuickCheck results. Perform each of the lab steps as directed and answer all of the lab QuickCheck questions. When you exit the lab, your answers are automatically graded and your results are displayed.

2. Make a note of the brand and location of the computer that you're using to complete these lab assignments.

3. Use the Start button to access your computer's Control Panel folder. Describe the status of your computer's power saver settings.

4. Preview the screen savers that are available on the computer that you use most frequently. Select the screen saver that you like the best and describe it in a few sentences.

5. What is the purpose of an Fn key? Does your computer keyboard include an Fn key? Explain why or why not.

6. In your own words, describe what happens when you (a) click the Close button, (b) hold down the Ctrl, Alt, and Del keys, (c) press the reset button, and (d) select the Shut Down option.

▼ STUDENT EDITION LABS

Reinforce the concepts you have learned in this unit through the **Using Input Devices, Peripharal Devices,** and **Maintaining a Hard Drive** Student Edition Labs, available online at the Illustrated Computer Concepts Web site.

▼ SAM LABS

If you have a SAM user profile, you have access to additional content, features, and functionality. Log in to your SAM account and go to your assignments page to see what your instructor has assigned for this unit.

▼ VISUAL WORKSHOP

If you thought a holograph was just the image of Princess Leia saying "Obi-Wan Kenobi, you are my only hope," think again. Holographic storage devices are in development as a means to respond to the growing need for large-volume data storage. Holographic technologies promise data retrieval speeds far exceeding magnetic or optical storage and capacities far beyond anything currently available. Researchers are working to make this technology an affordable reality. Figure B-35 shows a Web page from InPhase Technologies, a company specializing in holographic technologies.

FIGURE B-35

1. Use your favorite search engine to find and read the May 2000 edition of Scientific American (www.sciam.com), which included a feature article about holographic storage. Write a brief summary of the article and, based on what you read, explain the basics of how holographic memory works.

2. Research the current trends in holographic development. Are there any existing applications? How far has the technology come? What companies are working to develop these technologies? How far are we from using holocubes for data storage?

3. Write a scenario that includes the requirements and applications for holographic storage. Under what circumstances do you think such technologies would be useful, and what types of data do you think would best take advantage of this new technology?

UNIT C Computer Software

OBJECTIVES

A computer's versatility is possible because of software—the instructions that tell a computer how to perform a specific type of task. This unit begins with the components of a typical software package and explains how these components work together. Next, you will learn about a computer's most important system software, its operating system. You will get an overview of software applications, including document production, spreadsheets, database, graphics, music, video editing, and games. Finally, the unit wraps up with important practical information on software copyrights and licenses. The Tech Talk reviews how to install and uninstall software. You will also have an opportunity to look at computers in the context of journalism. The Issue discusses software piracy.

Introducing computer software

In common practice, the term "software" is used to describe a commercial product that can be distributed on floppy disks, DVDs, CDs, or made available as a Web download. Computer software determines the tasks that a computer can help you accomplish, such as create documents and presentations, prepare your tax return, or design the floor plan for a new house. You will learn about the components of computer software and how these components work together to help you complete tasks.

DETAILS

- Software is categorized as either application software or system software. **Application software** helps you carry out tasks—such as creating documents, crunching numbers, and editing photographs—using a computer. **System software**—your computer's operating system, device drivers, and utilities—helps your computer carry out its basic operating functions. Figure C-1 shows the types of software that fall into the system software and application software categories.

- **Software** consists of computer programs, support programs, and data files that work together to provide a computer with the instructions and data necessary for carrying out a specific type of task, such as document production or Web browsing.

- Software typically includes files that contain computer programs. A **computer program**, or "program," is a set of self-contained instructions that tells a computer how to solve a problem or carry out a task. A key characteristic of a computer program is that it can be started or "run" by a computer user.

- At least one of the files included in a software package contains an executable program designed to be launched, or started, by users. On PCs, these programs are stored in files that typically have .exe filename extensions and are sometimes referred to as **executable files** or **user-executable files**. When using a Windows PC, you can start an executable file by clicking its icon, selecting it from the Start menu, or entering its name in the Run dialog box.

- Other files supplied with a software package contain programs that are not designed to be run by users. These **support programs** contain instructions for the computer to use with the main user-executable file. A support program can be "called," or activated, by the main program as needed. For example, when you use the spelling checker in a word processing program, the word processing program calls on support programs to run the spelling checker. In the context of Windows software, support programs often have filename extensions such as .dll and .ocx.

- A **data file** contains any data that is necessary for a task, but that is not supplied by the user. For example, word processing software checks spelling by comparing the words in a document with the words in a dictionary file. This dictionary file is a data file that is supplied by the software, not by the user. Data files supplied with a software package have filename extensions such as .txt, .bmp, and .hlp.

- The use of an executable file plus several support programs and data files offers a great deal of flexibility and efficiency for software developers. See Figure C-2. Support programs and data files can usually be modified without changing the main executable file. This modular approach can significantly reduce the time required to create and test the main executable file, which usually contains a long and fairly complex program. The modular approach also allows software developers to reuse their support programs and adapt preprogrammed support programs for use in their software.

- Most software is designed to provide a task-related environment, which includes a screen display, a means of collecting commands and data from the user, the specifications for processing data, and a method for displaying or outputting data. Figure C-3 is a simple computer program that converts a Fahrenheit temperature to Celsius and displays the result.

FIGURE C-1: Software categories

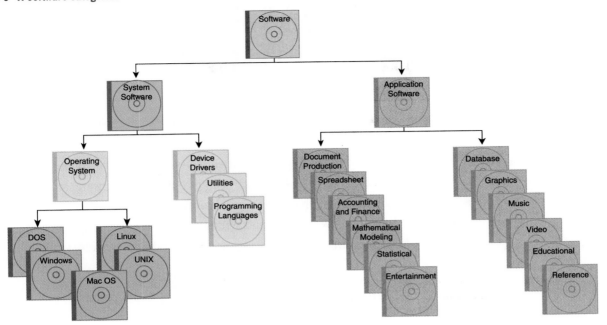

FIGURE C-2: Installed files for a software program

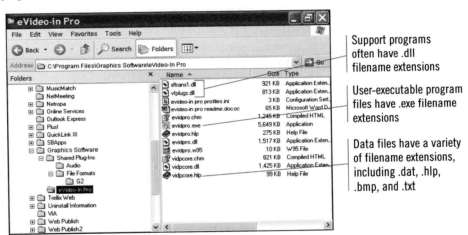

Support programs often have .dll filename extensions

User-executable program files have .exe filename extensions

Data files have a variety of filename extensions, including .dat, .hlp, .bmp, and .txt

FIGURE C-3: A simple computer program

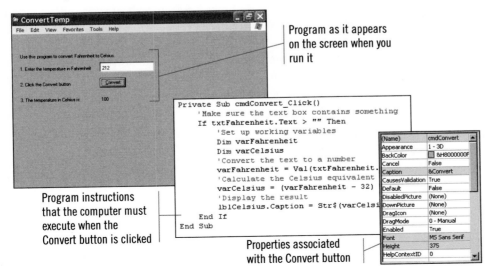

Program as it appears on the screen when you run it

```
Private Sub cmdConvert_Click()
    'Make sure the text box contains something
    If txtFahrenheit.Text > "" Then
        'Set up working variables
        Dim varFahrenheit
        Dim varCelsius
        'Convert the text to a number
        varFahrenheit = Val(txtFahrenheit.
        'Calculate the Celsius equivalent
        varCelsius = (varFahrenheit - 32)
        'Display the result
        lblCelsius.Caption = Str$(varCelsi
    End If
End Sub
```

Program instructions that the computer must execute when the Convert button is clicked

Properties associated with the Convert button

Explaining how computers interpret software

Computer programmers write the instructions for the computer programs and support programs that become the components of a computer software product. The finished software product is then distributed by the programmers themselves, or by software publishers, companies that specialize in packaging, marketing, and selling commercial software. Most businesses, organizations, and individuals purchase commercial software to avoid the time and expense of writing their own. Learning how programmers write the instructions and how a computer's processor translates these instructions will help you understand how software works.

DETAILS

- A **programming** or **computer language** provides the tools that a programmer uses to create software. These languages help the programmer produce a lengthy list of instructions called **source code**. Most programmers today prefer to use **high-level languages**, such as C++, Java, COBOL, and Visual Basic, which have some similarities to human languages and produce programs that are fairly easy to test and modify.

- A computer's processor interprets the programmer's instructions, but the processor can only understand **machine language**—the instruction set that is "hard wired" within the processor's circuits. Instructions written in a high-level language must be translated into machine language before a computer can use them.

- Translating instructions from a high-level language into machine language can be accomplished by two special types of programs: compilers and interpreters. Figure C-4 gives you an idea of what happens to high-level instructions when they are converted into machine language instructions. A simple instruction to add two numbers becomes a long series of 0s and 1s in machine language.

- A **compiler** converts high-level instructions into a compiled program, which is a new file containing machine language instructions. A compiler translates all of the instructions in a program as a single batch, and the resulting machine language instructions, called **object code**, are placed in a new file.

- As an alternative to a compiler, an **interpreter** converts one instruction at a time while the program is running. An interpreter reads the first instruction in a script, converts it into machine language, and then sends it to the processor. The interpreter continues in this way to convert instructions until all instructions are interpreted. See Figure C-5. An interpreted program runs more slowly than a compiled program because the translation process happens while the program is running.

- Figure C-6 illustrates how a video editing program, such as eVideo-In Pro works when installed on a computer that is running Windows. The files included in this software package interact with the hardware when you select commands to edit videos.

FIGURE C-4: Converting a high-level instruction to machine code

High-level Language Instruction	Machine Language Equivalent	Description of Machine Language Instructions
Answer = FirstNumber + SecondNumber	10001000 00011000 010000000	Load FirstNumber into Register 1
	10001000 00010000 00100000	Load SecondNumber into Register 2
	00000000 00011000 00010000	Perform ADD operation
	10100010 00111000	Move the number from the accumulator to the RAM location called Answer

FIGURE C-5: The interpreter converts instructions one instruction at a time

▶ An interpreter converts high-level instructions into machine language instructions while the program is running

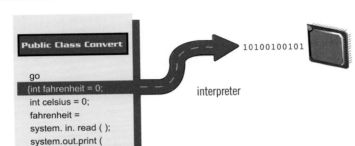

interpreter

◀ An interpreted program runs more slowly than a compiled program because the translation process happens while the program is running

FIGURE C-6: How software works

1. When you start the eVideo-In Pro software, the instructions in the file eVidpro.exe are loaded from disk into RAM and then sent to the processor

2. eVidpro.exe is a compiled program, so its instructions are immediately executed by the processor

3. As processing begins, the eVideo-In Pro window opens and the graphical controls for video editing tasks appear; the program waits for you to select a control by clicking it with the mouse

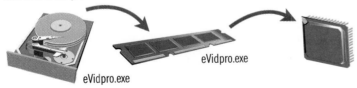

eVidpro.exe

eVidpro.exe

4. Based on your selection, eVidpro.exe follows its instructions and performs the actions you specify; many of the instructions for these actions are included in the main executable file; if not, eVidpro.exe calls a support program, such as Sftrans.dll

5. If you access eVideo-In Pro Help, eVidpro.exe loads the data file eVidpro.hlp

6. eVidpro.exe continues to respond to the controls you select until you click the Close button, which halts execution of the program instructions, closes the program window, and releases the space the program occupied in RAM for use by other programs or data

Sftrans.dll

eVidpro.hlp

Exploring operating systems

The term **operating system (OS)** is defined as system software that acts as the master controller for all of the activities that take place within a computer system. If you understand how an operating system works, you will understand how your computer performs its many functions. For example, when you issue a command using application software, the application software tells the operating system what to do. See Figure C-7. While you interact with application software, your computer's operating system is busy behind the scenes.

DETAILS

- In the context of a computer system, the term **resource** refers to any component that is required to perform work. For example, the processor is a resource. RAM, storage space, and peripherals are also resources. The operating system manages a computer's resources by interacting with application software, device drivers, and hardware.

- Figure C-8 illustrates some common operating system tasks. Your operating system stores and retrieves files from your disks and CDs. It remembers the names and locations of all your files and keeps track of empty spaces where new files can be stored. It communicates with device driver software so that data can travel smoothly between the computer and the peripheral resources. If a peripheral device or driver is not performing correctly, the operating system makes a decision about what to do; usually it displays an on-screen warning about the problem.

- Many activities called "processes" compete for the attention of your computer's processor. To manage all of these competing processes, your computer's operating system helps the processor switch tasks. When you want to run more than one program at a time, the operating system has to allocate specific areas of memory for each program. See Figure C-9.

- While multiple programs are running, the OS must ensure that instructions and data from one area of memory don't "leak" into an area allocated to another program. If an OS fails to protect each program's memory area, data can get corrupted, programs can "crash," and your computer will display error messages.

- Your computer's operating system ensures that input and output proceed in an orderly manner, using queues to collect data and buffers to hold data while the computer is busy with other tasks. By using a keyboard buffer, for example, your computer never misses one of your keystrokes, regardless of how fast you type.

- Many operating systems also influence the "look and feel" of your software by determining the kinds of menus, toolbars, and controls that are displayed on the screen, and how these objects react to your input. Most operating systems today support a **graphical user interface**, which provides a way to point and click a mouse to select menu options and manipulate graphical objects that are displayed on the screen. Graphical user interface is sometimes abbreviated "GUI" and referred to as a "gooey."

- In some computers—typically handhelds and videogame consoles—the entire operating system is small enough to be stored in ROM. For nearly all personal computers, servers, workstations, mainframes, and supercomputers, the operating system program is quite large, so most of it is stored on a hard disk. The operating system's small **bootstrap program** is stored in ROM and supplies the instructions needed to load the operating system's core into memory when the system boots. This core part of the operating system, called the **kernel**, provides the most essential operating system services, such as memory management and file access. The kernel stays in memory all the time your computer is on. Other parts of the operating system, such as customization utilities, are loaded into memory as they are needed. **Utilities** are tools you can use to control and customize your computer equipment and work environment. Table C-1 lists some OS utilities.

- **DOS** stands for Disk Operating System. It was developed by Microsoft, introduced on the original IBM PC in 1982. Although IBM called this operating system PC-DOS, Microsoft marketed it to other companies under the name MS-DOS. Today, users rarely interact with DOS. Operating systems for today's computers are discussed in the next lesson.

FIGURE C-7: How the operating system interacts with application software

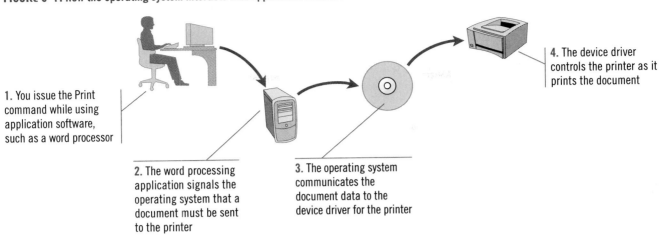

1. You issue the Print command while using application software, such as a word processor

2. The word processing application signals the operating system that a document must be sent to the printer

3. The operating system communicates the document data to the device driver for the printer

4. The device driver controls the printer as it prints the document

FIGURE C-8: Operating system tasks

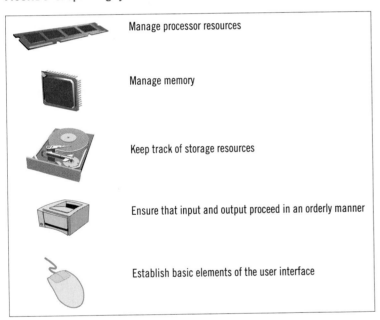

Manage processor resources

Manage memory

Keep track of storage resources

Ensure that input and output proceed in an orderly manner

Establish basic elements of the user interface

FIGURE C-9: The operating system and RAM

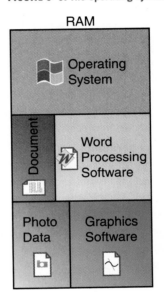

RAM

Operating System

Document

Word Processing Software

Photo Data

Graphics Software

TABLE C-1: Examples of Windows operating system utilities

UTILITY USED TO	WHAT WINDOWS PROVIDES
Launch programs	When you start your computer, Windows displays a "desktop" that contains a collection of graphical objects, such as the Start menu, which you can manipulate to start programs.
Manage files	Windows Explorer allows you to view a list of files, move them to different storage devices, copy them, rename them, and delete them.
Get help	Windows provides a Help system that you can use to find out how various commands work.
Customize the user interface	The Control Panel, accessible from the Start menu, provides utilities that help you customize your screen display and work environment.
Configure equipment	The Windows Control Panel also provides access to utilities that help you set up and configure your computer's hardware and peripheral devices.

UNIT C

Comparing operating systems

The operating system is the master controller of your computer system. It determines how you interact with your computer. This lesson discusses categories of operating systems and compares the main features of popular operating systems.

LAB
USING THE
WINDOWS INTERFACE

DETAILS

● Operating systems are informally categorized using one or more of the following terms:

A **single-user operating system** expects to deal with one set of input devices—those that can be controlled by one user at a time. Operating systems for handheld computers and many personal computers fit into the single-user category.

A **multiuser operating system** is designed to deal with input, output, and processing requests from many users at the same time. One of its most difficult responsibilities is to schedule all of the processing requests that must be performed by a centralized computer, often a mainframe.

A **network operating system**, or **server operating system**, provides communications and routing services that allow computers to share data, programs, and peripheral devices. While a multiuser OS and a network OS may sound the same, a multiuser operating system schedules requests for processing on a centralized computer; a network operating system simply routes data and programs to each user's local computer, where the actual processing takes place.

A **desktop operating system** is one that's designed for either a desktop or notebook personal computer. The computer that you typically use at home, at school, or at work is most likely configured with a desktop operating system. Typically, these operating systems are designed to accommodate a single user, but may also provide networking capability. Some operating system vendors characterize their products as "home" or "professional" versions. The home version typically has fewer network management tools than the professional version.

Today's desktop operating systems invariably provide multitasking services. A **multitasking operating system** provides process and memory management services that allow two or more programs to run simultaneously. Most of today's personal computers use operating systems that offer multitasking services.

● **Microsoft Windows** is installed on over 80% of the world's personal computers. Since its introduction in 1985, Windows has evolved through several versions. Microsoft currently offers several types of operating systems. Home, Professional, and

Workstation editions are designed for personal computers. Server editions are designed for LAN, Internet, and Web servers. Embedded editions are designed for handheld devices, such as PDAs and mobile phones.

● Like Windows, **Mac OS** has been through a number of revisions. Its current version is OS X (version 10).

● Both Mac OS for the Apple Macintosh computer and Windows base their user interfaces on the graphical interface model that was pioneered at Xerox. A quick comparison of Figure C-10 and Figure C-11 shows that both Windows and Mac interfaces use a mouse to point and click various icons and menus. Both interfaces feature rectangular work areas for multitasking services and provide basic networking services. Many of the most prolific software publishers produce one version of their software for Windows and another version for Mac OS.

● The **UNIX** operating system was developed in 1969 at AT&T's Bell Labs. It gained a good reputation for its dependability in multiuser environments. Many versions of it became available for mainframes and microcomputers.

● In 1991, Linus Torvalds developed the **Linux** operating system (see Figure C-12), based on a version of UNIX. Linux is rather unique because it is distributed under the terms of a General Public License (GPL), which allows everyone to make copies for their own use, to give it to others, or to sell it. This licensing policy has encouraged programmers to develop Linux utilities, software, and enhancements. Linux is primarily distributed over the Web.

● **Palm OS** and **Windows Mobil OS** are the two dominant operating systems of handheld computers. PDA and desktop operating systems provide many similar services, but because PDAs tend to be used for less sophisticated tasks, their simpler and smaller operating systems can be stored in ROM. A PDA's operating system is ready almost instantly when the unit is turned on and provides built-in support for touch screens, handwriting input, wireless networking, and cellular communications. **Windows XP Tablet Edition** is the operating system supplied with just about every tablet computer. Its main feature is handwriting recognition, which accepts printed input from the touch-sensitive screen.

FIGURE C-10: Microsoft Windows

Icons represent computer hardware and software

The Start button provides access to a menu of programs, documents, and utilities

◀ The Windows operating system gets its name from the rectangular work areas that appear on the screen-based desktop; each work area can display a different document or program, providing a visual model of the operating system's multitasking capabilities

Two different programs can run in two separate windows

The taskbar indicates which programs are running

FIGURE C-11: Mac OS

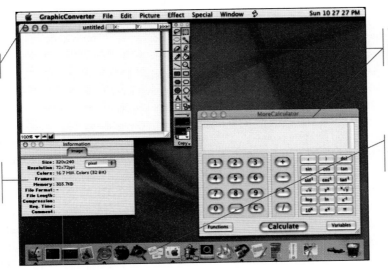

The Apple logo provides access to a menu

Menus and other on-screen objects are manipulated by using a mouse

Two different programs can run in two separate windows

Icons represent computer hardware components and software

FIGURE C-12: Linux

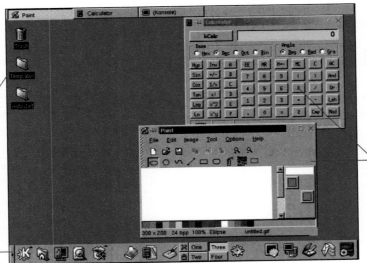

Desktop icons look similar to those on the Windows and Macintosh desktops

A horizontal option bar combines features of the Windows Start menu, Control Panel, and taskbar

◀ Linux users can choose from several graphical interfaces; this is the popular KDE (K Desktop Environment)

Two different programs can run in two separate windows

Defining document production software

Whether you are writing a 10-page paper, writing software documentation, designing a brochure for your new startup company, or laying out the school newspaper, you will probably use some form of **document production software**. This software assists you with composing, editing, designing, printing, and electronically publishing documents.

DETAILS

- Document production software can be classified as one of three types:

  Word processing software is used to produce documents such as reports, letters, and manuscripts. Word processing software gives you the ability to compose a document on the screen before you commit it to paper. Refer to Figure C-13. Microsoft Word is an example of word processing software.

  Desktop publishing software (DTP) takes word processing software one step further by helping you use graphic design techniques to enhance the format and appearance of a document. Although today's word processing software offers many page layout and design features, desktop publishing software provides more sophisticated features to help you produce professional-quality output for publications. QuarkXPress is an example of destktop publishing software.

  Web authoring software helps you design and develop Web pages that you can publish electronically on the Internet. Web authoring software provides easy-to-use tools for composing the text for a Web page, assembling graphical elements, and automatically generating HTML tags. Macromedia Dreamweaver is an example of Web authoring software.

- A description of common features of document production software follows:

  - *Alignment*: determines the position of text as left, right, centered, or fully justified

  - *Autocorrect*: automatically changes a typo, such as "teh" to "the"

  - *Find and replace*: finds all occurrences of a word or phrase and lets you replace it with another word or phrase, such as changing May to August

  - *Formatting options*: allows you to change font, font size, and font style

  - *Line spacing*: determines the space between lines of type, such as single space

  - *Mail merge*: creates personalized letters by automatically combining information in a mailing list with a form letter

  - *Spelling checker/grammar checker*: marks words in a document as misspelled if they do not match words in the spelling dictionary; points out potential grammatical trouble spots, such as run-on sentences

  - *Style*: saved set of formatting options that you apply to text; you can create character, paragraph, table, and list styles

- The **format** for a document refers to how all text, pictures, titles, and page numbers are arranged on the page. The look of your document will depend on formatting factors, such as font style, paragraph style (see Figure C-14), and page layout. You can vary the font style by selecting different fonts, such as Arial and Comic Sans MS, and character formatting attributes, such as bold, italic, underline, superscript, and subscript. You can also select a color and size for a font. The font size for the text in a typical paragraph is set at 8, 10, or 12 pt. Titles can be as large as 72 pt.

- **Page layout** refers to the physical position of each element on a page. A **header** is text that you specify to appear in the top margin of every page automatically. A **footer** is text that you specify to appear in the bottom margin of every page automatically. **Clip art** is a collection of drawings and photos designed to be inserted into documents. A **table** is a grid-like structure that can hold text or pictures. For printed documents, tables are a popular way to provide easy-to-read columns of data and to position graphics. For Web pages, tables provide one of the few ways to position text and pictures precisely.

- Some software allows you to divide each page into several rectangular-shaped **frames** that you can fill with either text or pictures. See Figure C-15. Frames provide you with finer control over the position of elements on a page, such as a figure and a caption on top of it. Since frames are helpful for complex page layout, DTP software is usually frame oriented.

FIGURE C-13: Microsoft Word

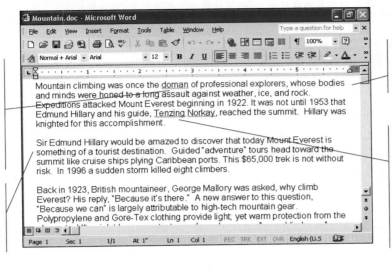

As you type, the spelling checker compares your words with a list of correctly spelled words; words not included in the list are marked with a wavy line as possible misspellings

Even after you type an entire document, adjusting the size of your right, left, top, and bottom margins is simple

Document production software uses word wrap to fit your text automatically within the margins

Proper nouns and scientific, medical, and technical words are likely to be flagged as misspelled even if you spell them correctly because they do not appear in the spelling checker's dictionary

FIGURE C-14: Applying a style

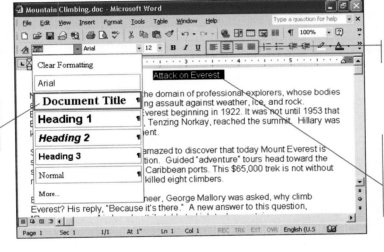

The style called Document Title specifies Times New Roman font, size 18, bold, and centered

Paragraph alignment buttons

Applying the formats assigned to a style simply requires you to highlight the text, then click a style from the list, such as the Document Title style

FIGURE C-15: Using frames

Attack on Everest
by Janell Chalmers

Mountain climbing was once the domain of professional explorers, whose bodies and minds were honed to a long assault against weather, ice, and rock. Expeditions attacked Mount Everest beginning in 1922. It was not until 1953 that Edmund Hillary and his guide, Tenzing Norkay, reached the summit. Hillary was knighted for this accomplishment.

Sir Edmund Hillary would be amazed to discover that today Mount Everest is something of a tourist destination. Guided "adventure" tours head toward the

"Because it's there."
George Mallory

summit like cruise ships plying Caribbean ports. This $65,000 trek is not without risk. In 1996 a sudden storm killed eight climbers.

Back in 1923, British mountaineer, George Mallory was asked, why climb Everest? His reply, "Because it's there." A new answer to this question, "Because we can" may be largely attributable to new high-tech mountain gear. Nylon, polypropylene and Gore-Tex clothing provide light, yet warm protection from the elements. Ultraviolet lenses protect eyes from dangerous "snow-blindness."

One frame holds the centered title and author's byline

A frame can be positioned anywhere on the page, even in the center of two text columns

Wrapping text around a frame adds interest to the layout

Graphical elements such as photos, diagrams, graphs, and pie charts can be incorporated in your documents using frames

Defining spreadsheet software

Spreadsheet software is used for numerical calculations based on simple equations or more complex formulas. Spreadsheets are ideal for projects that require repetitive calculations: budgeting, maintaining a grade book, balancing a checkbook, tracking investments, calculating loan payments, and estimating project costs. Spreadsheet software can turn your data into a variety of colorful graphs and charts.

Info Web

SPREADSHEET
SOFTWARE

DETAILS

- A **spreadsheet** uses rows and columns of numbers to create a model or representation of a real situation. For example, your checkbook register is a type of spreadsheet because it is a numerical representation of the cash flowing in and out of your bank account. **Spreadsheet software** provides tools to create electronic spreadsheets.

- You use spreadsheet software to create an on-screen **worksheet** like the one shown in Figure C-16. A worksheet is based on a grid of columns and rows. Each **cell** in the grid can contain a value, label, or formula and has a unique **cell reference**, or "address," derived from its column and row location. For example, A1 is the cell reference for the upper-left cell in a worksheet because it is in column A and row 1. You can select any cell and make it the active cell by clicking it. Once a cell is active, you can enter data into it. A **value** is a number that you want to use in a calculation. A **label** is any text that is used to describe data.

- The values contained in a cell can be manipulated by formulas that are placed in other cells. A **formula** works behind the scenes to tell the computer how to use the contents of cells in calculations. You can enter a simple formula in a cell to add, subtract, multiply, or divide numbers. Figure C-17 illustrates how a formula might be used in a simple spreadsheet to calculate savings. More complex formulas can be designed to perform just about any calculation you can imagine. You can enter a formula "from scratch" by typing it into a cell, or you can

use a **function**, which is a predefined formula built into the spreadsheet software.

- When you change the contents of any cell in a worksheet, all of the formulas are recalculated. This **automatic recalculation** feature assures you that the results in every cell are accurate with regard to the information currently entered in the worksheet. Your worksheet is also automatically updated to reflect any rows or columns that you add, delete, or copy within the worksheet.

- In order for automatic recalculation to be accurate, you must understand and implement proper cell referencing in your formulas. Unless you specify otherwise, a cell reference is a **relative reference**—a reference that can change if cells are deleted or inserted and the data or a formula moves. See Figure C-18. If you don't want a cell reference to change, you can use an absolute reference. An **absolute reference** never changes when you delete or insert cells or copy or move formulas. Understanding when to use absolute references is one of the key aspects to developing spreadsheet design expertise.

- Most spreadsheet software includes a few templates or wizards for predesigned worksheets, such as invoices, income-expense reports, balance sheets, and loan payment schedules. Additional templates are available on the Web. These templates are typically designed by content professionals and contain all of the necessary labels and formulas. To use a template, you simply plug in the values for your calculation.

FYI

Spreadsheet software is useful for what-if analyses, such as, "Is it better to take out a 30-year mortgage at 5.0% interest or a 15-year mortgage at 4.5% interest?"

QUICK TIP

You can format the labels and values on a worksheet by changing fonts and font size, selecting a font color, and selecting a font style, such as bold.

FIGURE C-16: An on-screen worksheet

Each column is lettered

Cell A1

Each row is numbered

Values in these cells can be used for calculations

Labels, such as Expenses and Profit, identify data

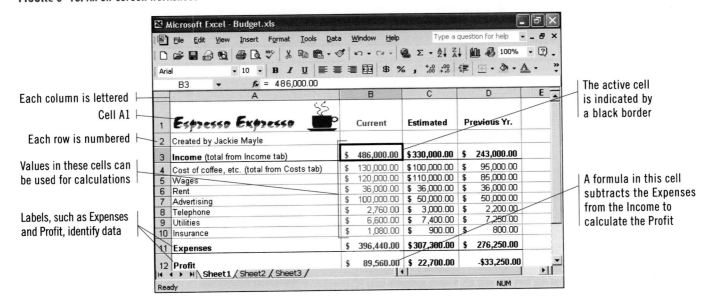

The active cell is indicated by a black border

A formula in this cell subtracts the Expenses from the Income to calculate the Profit

FIGURE C-17: How formulas work

▶ When a cell contains a formula, it displays the result of the formula, rather than the formula itself

The number that appears in cell B6 was calculated by the spreadsheet based on the formula typed in the cell

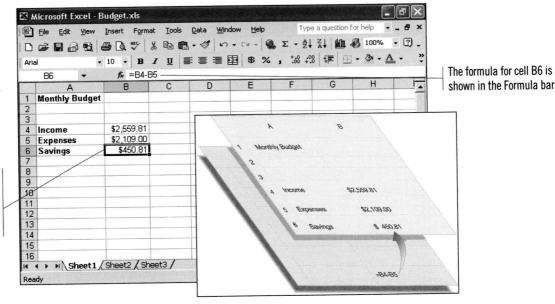

The formula for cell B6 is shown in the Formula bar

FIGURE C-18: Relative vs. absolute references

▶ Relative references within a formula can change when you insert or delete rows and columns or when you copy or move formulas; an absolute reference is "anchored" so that it always refers to a specific cell

Two blank rows

The original formula =B4-B5 uses relative references

When row 3 is deleted, the Income and Expenses values move up one row, which means that these values have new cell references; the formula changes to =B3-B4 to reflect the new cell references

Defining database software

Database software helps you enter, find, organize, update, and report information stored in a database. Databases can be stored on personal computers, LAN servers, Web servers, mainframes, and even handheld computers. This lesson provides an overview of databases and how database software manages the data stored in databases.

DETAILS

- The term **database** has evolved from a specialized technical term into a part of our everyday vocabulary. In the context of modern usage, a database is simply a collection of data that is stored on one or more computers. A database can contain any sort of data, such as a university's student records, a library's card catalog, a store's inventory, an individual's address book, or a utility company's customers.

- Database software stores data as a series of records, which are composed of fields that hold data. A **record** holds data for a single entity—a person, place, thing, or event. A **field** holds one item of data relevant to a record. You can envision a record as a Rolodex or index card and a series of records as a **table** as shown in Figure C-19.

- Database software provides tools to work with more than one collection of records, as long as the records are somehow related to each other. For example, in a jazz music database, one table of database records might contain data about songs with fields such as those shown in Figure C-19. Another table of records might contain biographical data about musicians, including name, birth date, and home town. It might even include a field for the performer's photo. These two sets of records can be related by the name of the performing artist, as shown in Figure C-20.

- Database software provides the tools you need to define fields for a series of records. Figure C-21 shows a simple form you might use to specify the fields for a database. After you've defined fields for a series of records, you can enter the data for each record. Your database software provides a simple-to-use data entry form that allows you to easily fill in the data for each field.

- Instead of typing data into a database, you can also import data from a commercial database, such as a customer mailing list— you can even download databases from the Web, and then import the data into fields you have defined with your database software.

- Many databases contain hundreds or thousands of records. If you want to find a particular record or a group of records, scrolling through every record is much too cumbersome. Instead, you can enter a **query**—a search specification that prompts the computer to look for records in a particular field— and the computer will quickly locate the records. Most database software provides one or more methods for making queries.

- A **query language**, such as **SQL (Structured Query Language)**, provides a set of commands for locating and manipulating data. To locate all performances of Summertime before 1990 from a Jazz Songs database, you might enter a query such as: Select * from JazzSongs where SongTitle = 'Summertime' and Date < '1990'

- Some database software provides **natural language query** capabilities. To make a query, you can simply enter a question, such as: Who performed Summertime before 1990? As an alternative to a query language or a natural language query, the database software might allow you to **query by example (QBE)**, simply by filling out a form with the type of data you want to locate.

- Database software can help you print reports, export data to other programs (such as to a spreadsheet where you can graph the data), convert the data to other formats (such as HTML so that you can post the data on the Web), and transmit data to other computers. Whether you print, import, copy, save, or transmit the data you find in databases, it is your responsibility to use it appropriately. Never introduce inaccurate information into a database. Respect copyrights, giving credit to the person or organization that compiled the data. You should always respect the privacy of the people who are the subject of the data. Unless you have permission to do so, do not divulge names, social security numbers, or other identifying information that might compromise someone's privacy.

FIGURE C-19: Defining a database

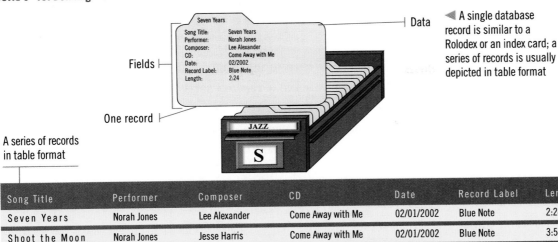

Data

One record

Fields

Seven Years

Song Title:	Seven Years
Performer:	Norah Jones
Composer:	Lee Alexander
CD:	Come Away with Me
Date:	02/2002
Record Label:	Blue Note
Length:	2:24

◄ A single database record is similar to a Rolodex or an index card; a series of records is usually depicted in table format

A series of records in table format

Song Title	Performer	Composer	CD	Date	Record Label	Length
Seven Years	Norah Jones	Lee Alexander	Come Away with Me	02/01/2002	Blue Note	2:24
Shoot the Moon	Norah Jones	Jesse Harris	Come Away with Me	02/01/2002	Blue Note	3:57
Summertime	Sarah Vaughan	George Gershwin	Compact Jazz	06/22/1987	Polygram	4:34

FIGURE C-20: Related records

JAZZ PERFORMERS

Performer	Birth Date	Home Town
Ella Fitzgerald	04/25/1918	Newport News, VA
Norah Jones	03/30/1979	New York, NY
Billie Holiday	04/07/1915	Baltimore, MD

◄ The two sets of records are related by the Performer field; the relationship allows you to select Norah Jones from the Jazz Performers records and jump to any record in the Jazz Songs records that Norah Jones performed

JAZZ SONGS

Song Title	Performer	Composer	CD	Date	Record Label	Length
Seven Years	Norah Jones	Lee Alexander	Come Away with Me	02/01/2002	Blue Note	2:24
Shoot the Moon	Norah Jones	Jesse Harris	Come Away with Me	02/01/2002	Blue Note	3:57
Summertime	Sarah Vaughan	George Gershwin	Compact Jazz	06/22/1987	Polygram	4:34

FIGURE C-21: Specifying fields

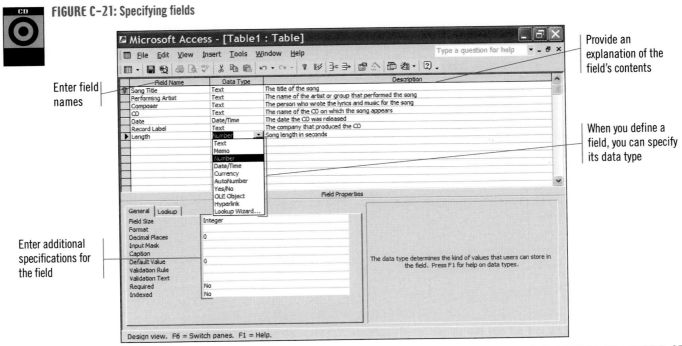

Enter field names

Enter additional specifications for the field

Provide an explanation of the field's contents

When you define a field, you can specify its data type

Defining graphics software

In computer lingo, the term **graphics** refers to any picture, drawing, sketch, photograph, image, or icon that appears on your computer screen. **Graphics software** is designed to help you create, display, modify, manipulate, and print graphics. Many kinds of graphics software exist, and each one typically specializes in a particular type of graphic. If you are really interested in working with graphics, you will undoubtedly end up using more than one graphics software package, such as those described in this lesson.

DETAILS

- **Paint software** (sometimes called "image editing software") provides a set of electronic pens, brushes, and paints for painting images on the screen. Graphic artists, Web page designers, photographers, and illustrators use paint software as their primary computer-based graphics tool.

- **Photo editing software** includes features specially designed to fix poor-quality photos by modifying contrast and brightness, cropping out unwanted objects, and removing "red eye." Photos can also be edited using paint software, but photo editing software typically provides tools and wizards that simplify common photo editing tasks.

- **Drawing software** provides a set of lines, shapes, and colors that can be assembled into diagrams, corporate logos, and schematics. The drawings created with this type of software tend to have a "flat" cartoon-like quality, but they are very easy to modify and look good at just about any size. Figure C-22 provides more information on paint, photo editing, and drawing software.

- **3-D graphics software** provides a set of tools for creating "wireframes" that represent three-dimensional objects. A wireframe acts much like the framework for a pop-up tent. Just as you would construct the framework for the tent, then cover it with a nylon tent cover, 3-D graphics software can cover a wireframe object with surface texture and color to create a graphic of a 3-D object. See Figure C-23.

- **CAD software** (computer-aided design software) is a special type of 3-D graphics software designed for architects and engineers who use computers to create blueprints and product specifications. Scaled-down versions of professional CAD software provide simplified tools for homeowners who want to redesign their kitchens, examine new landscaping options, or experiment with floor plans.

- **Presentation software** provides all of the tools you need for combining text, graphics, graphs, animations, and sound into a series of electronic **slides**. See Figure C-24. You can display the electronic slides on a color monitor for a one-on-one presentation or use a computer projection device for group presentations. You can also output the presentation as overhead transparencies, paper copies, or 35-mm slides.

FIGURE C-22: Images created using paint, photo editing, and drawing software

▲ Paint software works well with realistic art and photos

▲ Photo editing software includes special features for touching up photographs

▲ Drawing software tends to create two-dimensional "cartoon-like" images

FIGURE C-23: Images created using 3-D graphics tools

▼ 3-D graphics software provides tools for creating a wireframe that represents a three-dimensional object

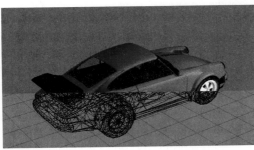

▲ Some 3-D software specializes in drawing figures

FIGURE C-24: A computer-based presentation

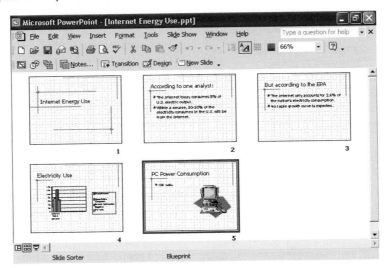

Defining business and science software

The terms business software and science software provide a broad umbrella for several types of software that are designed to help businesses and organizations accomplish routine or specialized tasks. These types of software provide a structured environment dedicated to a particular number-crunching task, such as money management, mathematical modeling, or statistical analysis.

INFO WEB
NUMERIC SOFTWARE

DETAILS

- **Accounting and finance software** helps you keep a record of monetary transactions and investments. In this software category, **personal finance software** is geared toward individual finances. **Tax preparation software** is a specialized type of personal finance software designed to help you gather your annual income and expense data, identify deductions, and calculate your tax payment.

- Some accounting and finance software is geared toward business. If you're an entrepreneur, **small business accounting software** can be a real asset. These easy-to-use programs don't require more than a basic understanding of accounting and finance principles. This type of software helps you invoice customers and keep track of what they owe. It stores additional customer data, such as contact information and purchasing history. Inventory functions keep track of the products that you carry. Payroll capabilities automatically calculate wages and deduct federal, state, and local taxes.

- **Vertical market software** is designed to automate specialized tasks in a specific market or business. Examples include patient management and billing software specially designed for hospitals, job estimating software for construction businesses, and student record management software for schools. Today, almost every business has access to some type of specialized vertical market software designed to automate, streamline, or computerize key business activities.

- **Horizontal market software** is generic software that can be used by just about any kind of business. **Payroll software** is a good example of horizontal market software. Almost every business has employees and must maintain payroll records. No matter what type of business uses it, payroll software must collect similar data and make similar calculations in order to produce payroll checks and W2 forms. Accounting software and project management software are additional examples of horizontal market software. **Accounting software** helps a business keep track of the money flowing in and out of various accounts. **Project management software** is an important tool for planning large projects, scheduling project tasks, and tracking project costs.

- **Groupware**, another umbrella term in the world of business software, is designed to help several people collaborate on a single project using network or Internet connections. It usually provides the capability to maintain schedules for all of the group members, automatically select meeting times for the group, facilitate communication by e-mail or other channels, distribute documents according to a prearranged schedule or sequence, and allow multiple people to contribute to a single document.

- One type of science-related software is **statistical software**, which helps you analyze large sets of data to discover relationships and patterns. It is a helpful tool for summarizing survey results, test scores, experiment results, or population data. Most statistical software includes graphing capability so that you can display and explore your data visually.

- **Mathematical modeling software**, such as MathCAD and Mathematica, provides tools for solving a wide range of math, science, and engineering problems. See Figure C-25. Students, teachers, mathematicians, and engineers, in particular, appreciate how this software helps them recognize patterns that can be difficult to identify in columns of numbers.

Why spreadsheet software is not always the best software for businesses

Spreadsheet software provides a tool to work with numeric models by using values, labels, and formulas. The advantage of spreadsheet software is its flexibility. You can create customized calculations according to your exact specifications. The disadvantage of spreadsheet software is that, aside from a few pre-designed templates, you are responsible for entering formulas and selecting functions for calculations. If you don't know the formulas, or don't understand the functions, you would do much better to purchase a business software package with those functions to meet your specific needs.

FIGURE C-25: Mathematical modeling software

$$\text{Solve}\left[\frac{P_x - q_x}{P_x - r_x} == \frac{P_y - q_y}{P_y - r_y} == \frac{P_z - q_z}{P_z - r_z}, \{q_x, q_y\}\right] /. \{P_x \to 0, P_y \to 0, P_z \to 1, q_z \to -1\}$$

▲ Mathematical modeling software helps you visualize the product of complex formulas; the points from a sphere are graphed onto a plane to demonstrate the principles behind the Astronomical Clock of Prague

FIGURE C-26

▲ **Microsoft Office Professional Edition 2003**
Word
Excel
Outlook
PowerPoint
Access

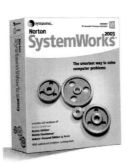

▲ **Norton SystemWorks**
Norton AntiVirus
Norton Utilities
Norton Password Manager
Norton CleanSweep
Norton GoBack Personal
    Edition

▲ **Adobe Creative Suite**
Adobe Illustrator CS
Adobe Photoshop CS
Adobe InDesign CS
Adobe GoLive CS
Adobe Acrobat
    Professional

What is a software suite?

A software suite is a collection of application software sold as a single package. See Figure C-26. Office suites, such as Microsoft Office, Star Office, Open Office, and WordPerfect Office, typically include applications to boost basic productivity: word processing, spreadsheet, and e-mail software. Graphics suites, such as Adobe Creative Suite, Macromedia Studio MX 2004, and CorelDRAW Graphics Suite, typically include paint, draw, and Web graphics tools. Software suites are available in many application categories, such as productivity, antivirus, and graphics.

Purchasing a software suite is usually much less expensive than purchasing the applications separately. Another advantage is usability. Because all the applications in a suite are produced by the same software publisher, they tend to use similar user interfaces and provide an easy way to transport data from one application to another. The disadvantage of a software suite is that it might include applications you don't need. If that is the case, you should calculate the price of the applications you do need and compare that to the cost of the suite.

Defining entertainment and education software

The computer can provide entertainment in many formats, including listening to music, watching videos, and playing games. Computer games are the most popular type of entertainment software. Software classified as educational can also be entertaining. When these software categories often overlap, the product is called edutainment.

 DETAILS

- It is easy to make your own digital voice and music recordings and store them on your computer's hard disk. Windows and Mac OS operating system utilities typically supply the necessary **audio editing software**, including Sound Recorder on PCs (see Figure C-27), and iTunes on iMacs. Audio editing software typically includes playback as well as recording capabilities. A specialized version of this software called karaoke software integrates music files and on-screen lyrics.

- **MP3** is a music compression file format that stores digitized music in such a way that the sound quality is excellent, but the file size remains relatively small—small enough to be easily downloaded from the Web. To listen to MP3 music on your computer, you need an **MP3 player**. Versions of MP3 player software are available for many handheld computers and for personal computers running Windows, Mac OS, and Linux.

- **Ear training software** targets musicians and music students who want to learn to play by ear, develop tuning skills, recognize notes and keys, and develop other musical skills. **Notation software** is the musician's equivalent of a word processor. It helps musicians compose, edit, and print the notes for their compositions. For non-musicians, **computer-aided music software** is designed to generate unique musical compositions simply by selecting the musical style, instruments, key, and tempo. **MIDI sequencing software** and software synthesizers are an important part of the studio musician's toolbox. They're great for sound effects and for controlling keyboards and other digital instruments.

- **Video editing software** provides a set of tools for transferring video footage from a camcorder to a computer, clipping out unwanted footage, assembling video segments in any sequence, adding special visual effects, and adding a sound track. Despite an impressive array of features, video editing software is relatively easy to use, as explained in Figure C-28.

- Computer games are generally classified into subcategories, such as multiplayer, role-playing, action, adventure, puzzles, simulations, and strategy/war games. Multiplayer games provide an environment in which two or more players can participate in the same game. Players can use Internet technology to band together in sophisticated visual environments. Massively multiplayer games operate on multiple Internet servers, each one with the capacity to handle thousands of players at peak times.

- Since it was established in 1994, the Entertainment Software Rating Board (ESRB) has rated more than 7,000 video and computer games. ESRB ratings have two parts: rating symbols that suggest what age group the game is best for, and content descriptors that tell you about content elements that may be of interest or concern. Rating symbols, shown in Figure C-29, can usually be found on the game box.

- **Educational software** helps you learn and practice new skills. For the youngest students, educational software teaches basic arithmetic and reading skills. Instruction is presented in game format, and the levels of play are adapted to the player's age and ability. For older students and adults, software is available for educational endeavors such as learning languages, training yourself to use new software, learning how to play the piano or guitar, preparing for standardized tests, improving keyboarding skills, and even learning managerial skills for a diverse workplace.

- **Reference software** provides you with a collection of information and a way to access that information. The reference software category spans a wide range of applications from encyclopedias to medical references, from map software to trip planners, and from cookbooks to telephone books. An encyclopedia on CD-ROM or the Web has several advantages over its printed counterpart. For example, in addition to containing text, graphics, and audio, it might also contain video clips and interactive timelines. Finding information is easier, since you can search using keywords or click hyperlinks to access related articles.

FIGURE C-27: Audio editing software

Menus provide additional digital editing features, such as speed control, volume adjustments, clipping, and mixing

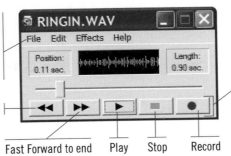

Rewind to beginning

Fast Forward to end | Play | Stop | Record

Audio editing software, such as Sound Recorder, provides controls much like a tape recorder

---

FIGURE C-28: Video editing software

▶ Video editing software, such as Adobe Premiere, helps you import a series of video clips from a camera or VCR, arrange the clips in the order of your choice, add transitions between clips, and add an audio track

The video and sound clips that you import for the project are displayed in a list so that you can easily select them in sequence

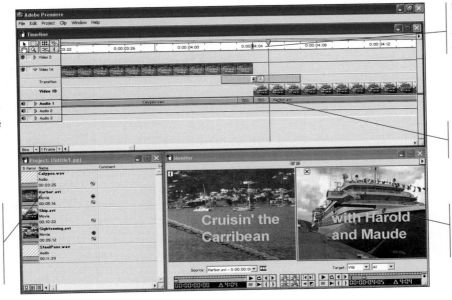

Use the timeline to indicate the sequence for your video clips and transitions

Arrange the audio tracks to synchronize with each video clip

Preview your video to see how the clips, transitions, and soundtrack all work together

---

FIGURE C-29: ESRB ratings and symbols

EARLY CHILDHOOD
Suitable for ages 3 and older. Contains no material that parents would find inappropriate.

TEEN
Suitable for 13 and older. May contain violent content, mild or strong language, and/or suggestive themes.

ADULTS ONLY
Content suitable only for adults. May include graphic depictions of sex and/or violence.

EVERYONE
Suitable for ages 6 and older. May contain minimal violence, some comic mischief, or crude language.

MATURE
Suitable for 17 and older. May contain mature sexual themes or more intense violence or language.

RATING PENDING
Product has been submitted, but a rating has not yet been assigned.

UNIT C

Understanding licenses and copyrights

Once you purchase a software package, you might assume that you can install it and use it in any way that you like. In fact, your "purchase" entitles you to use the software only in certain prescribed ways. In most countries, computer software, like a book or movie, is protected by a copyright. In addition to copyright protection, computer software is often protected by the terms of a software license. Copyright laws provide fairly severe restrictions on copying, distributing, and reselling software. However, a license agreement may offer some rights to consumers as well.

DETAILS

- A **software license**, or "license agreement," is a legal contract that defines the ways in which you may use a computer program. For personal computer software, you will find the license on the outside of the package, on a separate card inside the package, on the CD packaging, or in one of the program files.

- Typically, computer owners purchase the right to use software that is distributed under a **single-user license** that limits use of the software to only one person at a time. Schools, organizations, and businesses sometimes purchase a site license, multiple-user license, or concurrent-use license, which allows more than one person to use the software. A **site license** is generally priced at a flat rate and allows software to be used on all computers at a specific location. A **multiple-user license** is priced per user and allows the allocated number of people to use the software at any time. A **concurrent-use license** is priced per copy and allows a specific number of copies to be used at the same time.

- Most legal contracts require signatures before the terms of the contract take effect. This requirement becomes unwieldy with software; imagine having to sign a license agreement and return it before you can use a new software package. To circumvent the signature requirement, software publishers typically use two techniques to validate a software license: shrink-wrap licenses and installation agreements. When you purchase computer software, the distribution disks, CDs, or DVDs are usually sealed in an envelope, plastic box, or shrink wrapping. A **shrink-wrap license** goes into effect as soon as you open the packaging. Figure C-30 explains more about the mechanics of a shrink-wrap license.

- An **installation agreement** is displayed on the screen when you first install the software. After reading the software license on the screen, you can indicate that you accept the terms of the

license by clicking a designated button usually labeled "OK," "I agree," or "I accept."

- Software licenses are often lengthy and written in legalese, but your legal right to use the software continues only as long as you abide by the terms of the software license. Therefore, you should understand the software license for any software you use. When you read a software license agreement, look for answers to the following questions: Am I buying the software or licensing it? When does the license go into effect? Under what circumstances can I make copies? Can I rent the software? Can I sell the software? What if the software includes a distribution CD and a set of distribution disks? Does the software publisher provide a warranty? Can I loan the software to a friend?

- A **copyright** is a form of legal protection that grants the author of an original work an exclusive right to copy, distribute, sell, and modify that work, except under special circumstances described by copyright laws. Exceptions include the purchaser's right to copy software from a distribution disk or Web site to a computer's hard disk in order to install it; to make an extra, or backup, copy of the software in case the original copy becomes erased or damaged; and to copy and distribute sections of a software program for use in critical reviews and teaching.

- Most software displays a **copyright notice**, such as "© 2004 eCourseWare," on one of its screens. However, because this notice is not required by law, programs without a copyright notice are still protected by copyright law. People who circumvent copyright law and illegally copy, distribute, or modify software are sometimes called software pirates, and their illegal copies are referred to as pirated software.

FIGURE C-30: A shrink-wrap license

▶ When software has a shrink-wrap license, you agree to the terms of the software license by opening the package; if you do not agree with the terms, you should return the software in its unopened package

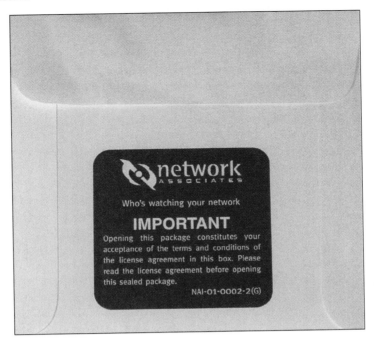

Reviewing software copyright protections

Commercial software is typically sold in computer stores or at Web sites. Although you buy this software, you actually purchase only the right to use it under the terms of the software license. A license for commercial software typically adheres closely to the limitations provided by copyright law, although it might give you permission to install the software on a computer at work and on a computer at home, provided that you use only one of them at a time.

Shareware is copyrighted software marketed under a try before you buy policy. It typically includes a license that permits you to use the software for a trial period. To use it beyond the trial period, you must send in a registration fee. A shareware license usually allows you to make copies of the software and distribute them to others. If they choose to use the software, they must send in a registration fee as well. These shared copies provide a low-cost marketing and distribution channel.

Registration fee payment relies on the honor system, so unfortunately many shareware authors collect only a fraction of the money they deserve for their programming efforts. Thousands of shareware programs are available, encompassing just about as many applications as commercial software.

Freeware is copyrighted software that is available without a fee. Because the software is protected by copyright, you cannot do anything with it that is not expressly allowed by copyright law or by the author. Typically, the license for freeware permits you to use the software, copy it, and give it away, but does not permit you to alter it or sell it. Many utility programs, device drivers, and some games are available as freeware.

Open source software makes the uncompiled program instructions available to programmers who want to modify and improve the software. Open source software may be sold or distributed free of charge, but it must, in every case, include the uncompiled source code. Linux is an example of open source software, as is FreeBSD—a version of UNIX designed for personal computers.

Public domain software is not protected by copyright because the copyright has expired or the author has placed the program in the public domain, making it available without restriction. Public domain software may be freely copied, distributed, and even resold. The primary restriction on public domain software is that you are not allowed to apply for a copyright on it.

No matter how you obtain a new software package, you must install it on your computer before you can use it.

Printed on the software package, or on the software publisher's Web site, are the **system requirements**, which specify the operating system and minimum hardware capacities for a software product to work correctly. When you **install** software, the new software files are placed in the appropriate folders on your computer's hard disk, and then your computer performs any software or hardware configurations necessary to make sure the program is ready to run.

Windows software typically contains a **setup program** that guides you through the installation process. Figure C-31 shows you what to expect when you use a setup program.

FIGURE C-31: Installing from distribution media

1.

▲ Insert the distribution disk, CD, or DVD. The setup program should start automatically. If it does not, look for a file called *Setup.exe* and then run it.

2.

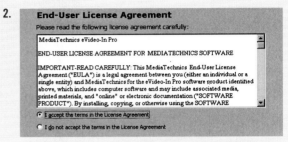

▲ Read the license agreement, if one is presented on the screen. By agreeing to the terms of the license, you can proceed with the installation.

3.

```
● Full Installation
○ Custom Installation
```

▲ Select the installation option that best meets your needs. If you select a full installation, the setup program copies all files and data from the distribution medium to the hard disk of your computer system. A full installation provides you with access to all features of the software.

If you select a custom installation, the setup program displays a list of software features for your selection. After you select the features you want, the setup program copies only the selected program files, support programs, and data files to your hard disk. A custom installation can save space on your hard disk drive.

4.

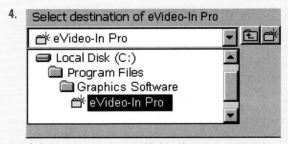

▲ Follow the prompts provided by the setup program to specify a folder to hold the new software program. You can use the default folder specified by the setup program or a folder of your own choosing. You can also create a new folder during the setup process.

5.

▲ If the software includes multiple distribution CDs, insert each one in the specified drive when the setup program prompts you.

6.

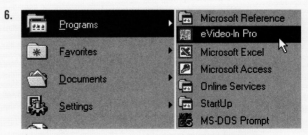

▲ When the setup is complete, start the program you just installed to make sure it works.

Downloadable software can be provided in several different formats. Some automatically install themselves, whereas others require manual procedures. A downloadable file typically is set up as a self-installing executable file, self-executing zip file, or non-executing zip file. Figure C-32 shows you what to expect when you download a program to install.

From time to time, you might also want to uninstall some of the software that exists on your computer. Operating systems, such as Windows and Mac OS, provide access to an **uninstall routine** that deletes the software's files from various directories on your computer's hard disk. The uninstall routine also removes references to the program from the desktop and from operating system files, such as the file system and, in the case of Windows, from the Windows Registry.

FIGURE C-32: Installing downloaded software

1.

▲ At the distribution Web site, locate any information pertaining to installing the software. Read it. You might also want to print it.

2.

▲ Click the download link.

3.

▲ If you are downloading from a trusted site and have antivirus software running, click the Open button in the File Download dialog box.

4.
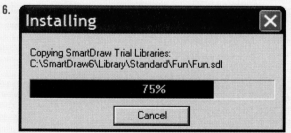

▲ Wait for the download to finish.

5.

▲ Specify a folder to hold the new software program. You can use the default folder specified by the setup program or a folder of your own choosing. You can also create a new folder during the setup process.

6.

Installing

Copying SmartDraw Trial Libraries:
C:\SmartDraw6\Library\Standard\Fun\Fun.sdl

75%

Cancel

▲ Wait for the setup program to uncompress the downloaded file and install the software in the selected directory. During this process, respond to license agreement and other prompts. When the installation is complete, test the software to make sure it works.

Tech Talk

Computers in Context Journalism

The news business is all about gathering and disseminating information as quickly as possible (see Figure C-33). In the ancient world, news spread by word of mouth, relayed by bards and merchants who traveled from town to town—in essence, they were the first reporters to "broadcast" the news. Throughout history, technology has played a major role in how news reporting has evolved into the modern 24-hour "live" news networks. Johann Gutenberg's printing press (ca. 1450), the first technological breakthrough in the news business, made it feasible to publish news as printed notices tacked to walls in the town square. As paper became more economical, resourceful entrepreneurs sold broadsheets to people eager for news, and the concept of a newspaper was born. The first regularly published newspapers appeared in Germany and Holland in 1609, and the first English newspaper, the *Weekly News*, was published in 1622.

But the news spread slowly. In the early 1800s, it took four weeks for newspapers in New York to receive reports from London. With the advent of the telegraph in 1844, however, reporters from distant regions could "wire" stories to their newspapers for publication the next day. The first radio reporters in the 1920s offered live broadcasts of sports events, church services, and variety shows. Before the 1950s, black-and-white newsreels shown in movie theaters provided the only visual imagery of news events; and it was television that gave viewers news images on a nightly basis.

Technology has benefited print journalism in many ways. For decades, typesetters transferred reporters' handwritten stories into neatly set columns of type. Today, reporters use computers and word processing software to type their stories and run a preliminary check of spelling and grammar. Stories are submitted via a computer network to editors, who use the same software to edit stories so they fit space constraints. The typesetting process has been replaced by desktop publishing software and computer to plate (CTP) technology. Digital pages produced with desktop publishing software are sent to a raster image processor (RIP), which converts the pages into dots that form words and images. A platesetter uses lasers to etch the dots onto a physical plate, which is then mounted on the printing press to produce printed pages. CTP is much faster and more flexible than typesetting, so publishers can make last-minute changes to accommodate late-breaking stories.

Personal computers have added a new dimension to the news-gathering process. Reporters who were once limited to personal interviews, observation, and fact gathering at libraries, can now make extensive use of Internet resources and e-mail. Web sites and online databases provide background information on all sorts of topics. Other resources include newsgroups and chat rooms, where reporters can monitor public opinion on current events and identify potential news sources.

FIGURE C-33

Most major networks maintain interactive Web sites that offer online polls and bulletin boards designed to collect viewers' opinions. Although online poll respondents are not a representative sample of the population, and the statistics are not scientifically valid, they can help news organizations gauge viewer opinions and determine whether news coverage is comprehensive and effective.

E-mail has changed the way reporters communicate with colleagues and sources. It's often the only practical method for contacting people in remote locations or distant time zones, and it's useful with reluctant sources, who feel more comfortable providing information under the cloak of anonymous Hotmail or Yahoo! accounts. "Vetting" e-mail sources—verifying credentials such as name, location, and occupation—can be difficult, however, so reporters tend not to rely on these sources without substantial corroboration.

For broadcast journalism, digital communications play a major role in today's "live on the scene" television reporting. Most news organizations maintain remote production vans, sometimes called "satellite news gathering (SNG) trucks," that travel to the site of breaking news. These complete mobile production facilities include camera control units, audio and video recording equipment, and satellite or microwave transmitters. They need only to raise their antennas to begin to broadcast.

On-the-scene reporting does not always require a truck full of equipment. Audiovisual editing units and video cameras have gone digital, making them easier to use and sized to fit in a suitcase. A new breed of "backpack journalists" carries mini-DV cameras, notebook computers, and satellite phones. Jane Ellen Stevens, a pioneer backpack journalist specializing in science and technology, has reported since 1997 from remote locations, such as a space camp in Russia. Backpack journalists can connect their minicams to notebook computers with a firewire cable, transfer their video footage to the hard disk, and then edit the footage using consumer-level video editing software. The resulting video files, compressed for transmission over a satellite phone, are sent to newsroom technicians, who decompress and then broadcast them—all in a matter of seconds. One drawback of backpack journalists' use of minicams and compression is that the video quality usually isn't as crisp as images filmed with studio cameras. News organizations with high standards were hesitant to use this lower quality video, but have found that viewers would rather see a low-quality image now than a high-quality image later. To many viewers, a few rough edges just make the footage seem more compelling, more "you are there."

Computers, the Internet, and communications technology make it possible to instantly broadcast live reports across the globe, but live reporting is not without controversy. A reporter who arrives at the scene of a disaster with microphone in hand has little time for reflection, vetting, and cross-checking, so grievous errors, libelous images, or distasteful video footage sometimes find their way into news reports.

Jeff Gralnick, former executive producer for ABC News, remarks, "In the old days, we had time to think before we spoke. We had time to write, time to research and time to say, 'Hey, wait a minute.' Now we don't even have the time to say, 'Hey, wait a nanosecond.' Just because we can say it or do it, should we?" Technology has given journalists a powerful arsenal of tools for gathering and reporting the news, but has also increased their accountability for accurate, socially responsible reporting.

Context

Is Piracy a Problem?

Software is easy to steal. You don't have to walk out of a Best Buy store with a Quicken Deluxe box under your shirt. You can simply borrow your friend's distribution CDs and install a copy of the program on your computer's hard disk. It seems so simple that it couldn't be illegal. But it is. Software piracy takes many forms. End-user piracy includes friends loaning distribution disks to each other and installing software on more computers than the license allows.

Counterfeiting is the large-scale illegal duplication of software distribution media and sometimes even its packaging. According to Microsoft, many software counterfeiting groups are linked to organized crime and money-laundering schemes that fund a diverse collection of illegal activities. Counterfeit software is sold in retail stores and online auctions—often the packaging looks so authentic that buyers have no idea they have purchased illegal goods.

Internet piracy uses the Web as a way to illegally distribute unauthorized software. Some pirated software has even been modified to eliminate serial numbers, registration requirements, expiration dates, or other forms of copy protection. The Business Software Alliance (BSA) estimates that more than 800,000 Web sites illegally sell or distribute software. In many countries, including the United States, software pirates are subject to civil lawsuits for monetary damages and criminal prosecution, which can result in jail time and stiff fines. Nonetheless, software piracy continues to have enormous impact. According to the Software and Information Industry Association (SIIA), a leading anti-piracy watchdog, revenue losses from business software piracy typically exceed $2 billion per year. This figure reveals only part of the piracy problem—it does not include losses from rampant game and educational software piracy, which are estimated to exceed $12 billion a year.

A small, but vocal, minority of software users, such as members of GNU (which stands for "Gnu's Not UNIX"), believes that data and software should be freely distributed. Richard Stallman writes in the GNU Manifesto, "I consider that the golden rule requires that if I like a program I must share it with other people who like it. Software sellers want to divide users and conquer them, making each user agree not to share with others. I refuse to break solidarity with other users in this way. I cannot in good conscience sign a nondisclosure agreement or a software license agreement."

As a justification of high piracy rates, some observers point out that people in many countries simply might not be able to afford software priced for the U.S. market. This argument could apply to China, where the average annual income is equivalent to about $3,500, and in North Korea, where the average income is only $900. A Korean who legitimately purchases Microsoft Office for $250 would be spending more than one-quarter of his or her annual income.

Most countries with a high incidence of software piracy, however, have strong economies and respectable per capita incomes. To further discredit the theory that piracy stems from poverty, India—which has a fairly large computer-user community, but a per capita income of only $1,600—is not among the top 10 countries with high rates of software piracy.

Is software piracy really damaging? Who cares if you use Microsoft Office without paying for it? Software piracy is damaging because it has a negative effect on the economy. Software production makes a major contribution to the United States economy, employing more than 2 million people and accounting for billions of dollars in corporate revenue. Software piracy in the United States is responsible for tens of thousands of lost jobs, millions in lost wages, and lost tax revenues. Decreases in software revenues can have a direct effect on consumers, too. When software publishers must cut corners, they tend to reduce customer service and technical support. As a result, you, the consumer, get put on hold when you call for technical support, find fewer free technical support sites, and encounter customer support personnel who are only moderately knowledgeable about their products. The bottom line—software piracy negatively affects customer service.

As an alternative to cutting support costs, some software publishers might build the cost of software piracy into the price of the software. The unfortunate result is that those who legitimately license and purchase software pay an inflated price.

If economic factors do not account for the pervasiveness of software piracy, what does? Some analysts suggest that people need more education about software copyrights and the economic implications of piracy. Other analysts believe that copyright enforcement must be increased by implementing more vigorous efforts to identify and prosecute pirates.

▼ INTERACTIVE QUESTIONS

○ Yes   ○ No   ○ Not sure   **1.** Do you believe that software piracy is a serious issue?

○ Yes   ○ No   ○ Not sure   **2.** Do you know of any instances of software piracy?

○ Yes   ○ No   ○ Not sure   **3.** Do you think that most software pirates understand that they are doing something illegal?

○ Yes   ○ No   ○ Not sure   **4.** Should software publishers adjust software publishing for local markets?

▼ EXPAND THE IDEAS

1. Do you believe that software piracy is a serious issue? Write a two-page paper supporting your position. Include the opposing side's arguments in your report. Be sure to include your resources.

2. Do you think there are ways that software publishers can control piracy in the United States? In other countries? Do you know of any recent attempts at doing so? Work in a small group to brainstorm ideas and research recent trends or events. Compile your ideas and findings into a short presentation to give to the class. Include handouts for the audience and cite any sources you used.

3. Do you think that most software pirates understand that they are doing something illegal? Design a marketing campaign that could be used to educate the public about the issue. Create a poster that could be used in the campaign.

4. Should software publishers try to adjust software pricing for local markets? How would you propose such a pricing structure? How would these policies be enforced? Can you think of any other industry that adjusts prices for local markets? Write a two-page paper discussing your proposals and explaining your findings. Be sure to cite your sources.

End of Unit Exercises

▼ KEY TERMS

3-D graphics software
Absolute reference
Accounting and finance software
Accounting software
Application software
Audio editing software
Automatic recalculation
Bootstrap program
CAD software
Cell
Cell reference
Clip art
Commercial software
Compiler
Computer-aided software design
Computer language
Computer program
Computer programmer
Concurrent-use license
Copyright
Copyright notice
Data file
Database
Database software
Desktop operating system
Desktop publishing software
Drawing software
DOS
Ear training software
Educational software

Executable file
Field
Footer
Format
Formula
Frames
Freeware
Function
Graphical user interface (GUI)
Graphics
Graphics software
Groupware
Header
High-level language
Horizontal market software
Install
Installation agreement
Interpreter
Kernel
Label
Linux
Mac OS
Machine language
Mathematical modeling software
Microsoft Windows
Midi sequencing software
MP3
MP3 player
Multiple-user license
Multitasking operating system

Multiuser operating system
Natural language query
Network operating system
Notation software
Object code
Open source software
Operating system
Page layout
Paint software
Palm OS
Payroll software
Personal finance software
Photo editing software
Presentation software
Programming language
Project management software
Public domain software
Query
Query by example
Query language
Record
Reference software
Relative reference
Resource
Server operating system
Setup program
Shareware
Shrink-wrap license
Single-user license
Single-user operating system

Site license
Slide
Small business accounting
    software
Software
Software license
Software suite
Source code
Spreadsheet
Spreadsheet software
SQL
Statistical software
Support program
System requirements
System software
Table
Tax preparation software
Uninstall routine
UNIX
User-executable file
Utilities
Value
Vertical market software
Video editing software
Web authoring software
Windows Mobil OS
Windows XP tablet edition
Word processing software
Worksheet

▼ UNIT REVIEW

1. Use your own words to define each of the bold terms that appear throughout the unit. List 10 of the terms that are least familiar to you and write a sentence for each of them.

2. Make sure that you can list and describe the three types of files that are typically supplied on a software distribution disk.

3. Explain the difference between a compiler and an interpreter.

4. List three types of system software and at least five categories of application software.

5. Describe how an operating system manages resources.

6. Sketch a simple worksheet like one you might find in a spreadsheet software program and label the following: columns, rows, cell, active cell, values, labels, formulas, and Formula bar.

7. List three types of "number crunching" software that you can use instead of spreadsheet software and tell how you might use each one.

8. Describe when you would use each type of graphics software described in this unit.

9. Create a table with these column headings: single-user, multiuser, network, multitasking, and desktop operating

system. List Linux, UNIX, Mac OS, and each version of Windows down the side of the table. Use a check mark to indicate which characteristics fit each operating system.

10. In your own words, explain what each of the ESRB ratings mean and how they would help you purchase software.

▼ FILL IN THE BEST ANSWER

1. Software can be divided into two major categories: application software and _____ software.

2. Software usually contains support programs and data files, in addition to a main _____ file that you run to start the software.

3. Instructions that are written in a(n) _____ -level language must be translated into _____ language before a computer can use them.

4. A(n) _____ translates all of the instructions in a program as a single batch, and the resulting machine language instructions are placed in a new file.

5. To run more than one program at a time, the operating system must allocate specific areas of _____ for each program.

6. A(n) _____ user interface provides a way for a user to interact with the software using a mouse and graphical objects on the screen.

7. A(n) _____ operating system is designed to deal with input, output, and processing requests from many users.

8. A(n) _____ operating system provides communications and routing services that allow computers to share data, programs, and peripheral devices.

9. Palm OS and Windows Mobil OS are two of the most popular operating systems for _____ computers.

10. Linux is an example of open _____ software.

11. Various kinds of document _____ software provide tools for creating and formatting printed and Web-based documents.

12. _____ software helps you work with wireframes, CAD drawings, photos, and slide presentations.

13. In a spreadsheet the rows are identified with _____ and the columns are identified with _____.

14. _____ market software is designed to automate specialized tasks in a specific market or business.

15. _____ art is a collection of drawings and photos designed to be inserted into documents.

16. _____ is a music compression file that stores digitized music in such a way that quality is excellent but the file size is relatively small.

17. _____ laws provide software authors with the exclusive right to copy, distribute, sell, and modify their work, except under special circumstances.

18. _____ is copyrighted software their is marketed with a "try before you buy" policy.

19. A(n) _____ license is generally priced at a flat rate and allows software to be used on all computers at a specific location.

20. Public _____ software is not copyrighted, making it available for use without restriction, except that you cannot apply for a copyright on it.

▼ PRACTICE TESTS

When you use the Interactive CD, you can take Practice Tests that consist of 10 multiple-choice, true/false, and fill-in-the blank questions. The questions are selected at random from a large test bank, so each time you take a test, you'll receive a different set of questions. Your tests are scored immediately, and you can print study guides to determine which questions you answered incorrectly. If you are using a Tracking Disk, insert it in the floppy disk drive to save your test scores.

▼ INDEPENDENT CHALLENGE 1

How you acquire software varies based on the software and your needs. If you have a home computer and own or have purchased software, complete the following independent challenge by writing a short paper discussing the issues raised below.

1. What software is installed on your computer? How did you acquire the software? What type of software does each package fall into based on the categories outlined in this unit?

2. Explain the differences between commercial software, shareware, open source software, freeware, and public domain software. Do you have any of these? If so, which ones? Why did you select one type over the other?

3. If possible, describe one experience installing software, describe the process of installing software from a distribution CD, and contrast it with the process of installing downloaded software.

4. Have you used software that has an ESRB rating? Based on your experience with the software, did you find that the rating was adequate and fair? Why or why not?

▼ INDEPENDENT CHALLENGE 2

When you use a software package, it is important to understand the legal restrictions on its use. For this independent challenge, make a photocopy of the license agreement for any software package. Read the license agreement, then answer these questions:

1. Is this a shrink-wrap license? Why or why not?

2. After you pay your computer dealer for the program covered by this license, who owns the program?

3. Can you legally have one copy of the program on your computer at work and another copy of the program on your computer at home if you use the software only in one place at a time?

4. Can you legally sell the software? Why or why not?

5. Under what conditions can you legally transfer possession of the program to someone else?

6. If you were the owner of a software store, could you legally rent the program to customers if you were sure they did not keep a copy after the rental period was over?

7. Can you legally install this software on one computer, but give more than one user access to it?

8. If you use this program for an important business decision and later find out that a mistake in the program caused you to lose $500,000, what legal recourse is provided by the license agreement?

▼ INDEPENDENT CHALLENGE 3

 There are so many software packages on the market today that it is often overwhelming to make a wise purchasing decision. The breadth of software available in each category is quite large, and no two packages claim all the same features. Do you base your decision to buy a new application package on word of mouth? Reviewer comments in professional magazines? Trying it out? To complete this independent challenge, you will research a type of software package that you intend to purchase.

1. Determine the type of package you want to select (graphics, DTP, word processing, Web development, e-mail, scheduling, or data management) and which operating system you plan to use.

2. Locate vendor ads either on the Internet or in local papers or trade magazines that sell software.

3. Read comparison reviews of the products. Create a chart detailing the features and prepare a competitive analysis of the three top candidates for your purchase.

4. Write a short summary of your findings, indicating which package you would buy and why.

▼ INDEPENDENT CHALLENGE 4

Copyrights and software piracy are very relevant issues for software users, developers, and educators. There is constant debate among all stakeholders as to the best models for software distribution, and how developers, publishers, or programmers should be compensated. To begin this project, log on to the Internet and use your favorite search engine or consult the Copyright and Piracy InfoWeb and link to the recommended Web pages to get an in-depth overview of the issue. Armed with this background, select one of the following viewpoints and statements and argue for or against it:

Viewpoints:

a. Free software advocates: As an enabling technology, software should be freely distributed, along with its modifiable source code.

b. Librarians: Copyright laws, especially the Digital Millennium Copyright Act, minimize the needs of the public and go too far in their efforts to protect the rights of software authors.

c. Software Publishers Association: Strong copyright laws and enforcement are essential for companies to publish and support high-quality software.

Directions:

1. Write a two- to five-page paper about this issue based on information you gather from the Internet.

2. Be sure to cite your sources and list them as part of the paper.

3. Follow your professor's instructions for formatting and submitting your paper.

▼ INDEPENDENT CHALLENGE 5

 The Computers in Context section of this unit focused on computer and communications technology used by reporters and journalists. Technology has had a major effect on "backpack journalists" who use small-scale digital devices to gather and report the news.

Log on to the Internet and use your favorite search engine to collect information on the advantages and disadvantages of backpack journalism. In your research, you should explore technical issues, such as the cost of equipment, video quality, and transmission capabilities. Also explore ethical issues pertaining to on-the-spot news reporting.

1. Create an outline of the major points you researched.

2. Summarize your research in a two- to four-page paper. Make sure you cite sources for your material.

3. Follow your professor's instructions for formatting and submitting your paper.

▼ LAB: USING THE WINDOWS INTERFACE

1. Start the interactive part of the lab. Insert your Tracking Disk if you want to save your QuickCheck results. Perform each of the lab steps as directed and answer all of the lab QuickCheck questions. When you exit the lab, your answers are automatically graded and your results are displayed.

2. Draw a sketch or print a screenshot of the Windows desktop on any computer that you use. Use ToolTips to identify all of the icons on the desktop and the taskbar.

3. Use the Start button and Accessories menu to start an application program called Paint. (If Paint is not installed on your computer, you can use any application software, such as a word processing program.) Draw a sketch or print a screenshot of the Paint (or other application) window and label the following components: Window title, title bar, Maximize/Restore button, Minimize button, Close button, menu bar, toolbar, and scroll bar.

4. Look at each of the menu options provided by the Paint software (or other application). Make a list of those that seem to be standard Windows menu options.

5. Draw a sketch of Paint's Print dialog box (or another application's Print dialog box). Label the following parts: buttons, spin bar, pull-down list, option button, and check boxes.

▼ LAB: INSTALLING AND UNINSTALLING SOFTWARE

1. Start the interactive part of the lab. Insert your Tracking Disk if you want to save your QuickCheck results. Perform each of the lab steps as directed and answer all of the lab QuickCheck questions. When you exit the lab, your answers are automatically graded and your results are displayed.

2. Browse the Web and locate a software application that you might like to download. Use information supplied by the Web site to answer the following questions:

   a. What is the name of the program and the URL of the download site?

   b. What is the size of the download file?

   c. According to the instructions, does the download file appear to require manual installation, is it a self-executing zip file, or is it a self-installing executable file?

3. On the computer that you typically use, look through the list of programs (click Start, then select Programs to see a list). List the names of any programs that include their own uninstall routine.

4. On the computer that you typically use, open the Control Panel and then open the Add/Remove Programs dialog box. List the first 10 programs that are currently installed on the computer.

▼ STUDENT EDITION LABS

Reinforce the concepts you have learned in this unit through the **Using Windows, Word Processing, Spreadsheets, Databases, Presentation Software, Installing and Uninstalling Software,** and **Advanced Spreadsheets** Student Edition Labs, available online at the Illustrated Computer Concepts Web site.

▼ SAM LABS

If you have a SAM user profile, you have access to additional content, features, and functionality. Log in to your SAM account and go to your assignments page to see what your instructor has assigned for this unit.

▼ VISUAL WORKSHOP

Figure C-34 shows images from handheld computer and tablet PC screens. The image on the left is the Palm OS, the image on the right is the Windows Mobile OS; and the image below is the Windows operating system designed specifically for tablet PCs.

FIGURE C-34

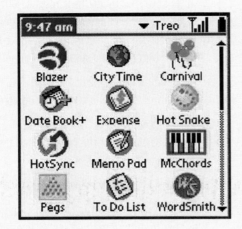

Log on to the Internet. Find Web sites that discuss each of the three operating systems shown above.

1. In your research find five facts about each of the operating systems. Write a brief statement explaining the similarities and differences among these operating systems.

2. Which devices are supported by each of these operating systems?

3. Which utilities are built into these operating systems? Are the utilities similar to utilities you find in personal computer desktop operating systems? Explain the differences.

4. List three applications that are supported by these operating systems. Are these available for personal computer desktop computers also? If so, list one major difference, if any, in the functionality of the software.

UNIT D

Digital Electronics and File Management

OBJECTIVES

Introduce digital data representation
Introduce integrated circuits
Explore processor performance factors
Understand computer memory: RAM
Explore computer memory
Introduce computer file basics
Understand file locations
Explore file management
Understand logical file storage
Use files
Understand physical file storage
Tech Talk: How a Processor Executes Instructions
Computers in Context: Astronomy
Issue: New Chip Technologies

In this unit, you will learn how data representation and digital electronics work together to make computers tick. You will learn about two of the most important components in a computer—the processor and memory. You will learn how they work and how they affect computer performance. You will learn about the different types of memory and how memory works to store and process data. You will get a general introduction to computer files and learn some very practical information about filenames. You will learn techniques for organizing computer files so that they are easy to access and update. You will also learn how an operating system stores, deletes, and tracks files. The Tech Talk section explains the details of how a processor executes instructions. You'll have the opportunity to look at computers in the context of astronomy. The Issue discusses new chip technologies and their impact on the future of computing.

Introducing digital data representation

Data representation refers to the form in which information is conceived, manipulated, and recorded. Because a computer is an electronic digital device, it uses electrical signals to represent data. A **digital device** works with discrete data or digits, such as 1 and 0, "on" and "off," or "yes" and "no." Data exists in the computer as a series of electronic signals represented as 1s and 0s, each of which is referred to as a **bit**. Most computer coding schemes use eight bits to represent each number, letter, or symbol. A series of eight bits is referred to as a **byte**. This lesson looks more closely at the coding schemes used in digital representation.

FYI

If you need to brush up on binary numbers, refer to the Working with Binary Numbers lab in Unit B.

DETAILS

● Just as Morse code uses dashes and dots to represent the letters of the alphabet, computers use sequences of bits to represent numbers, letters, punctuation marks, music, pictures, and videos. **Digital electronics** makes it possible for a computer to manipulate simple "on" and "off" signals to perform complex tasks. The **binary number system** allows computers to represent virtually any number simply by using 0s and 1s, which translate into electrical "on" and "off" signals.

● Digital computers use many different coding schemes to represent data. The coding scheme used by a computer depends on whether the data is numeric data or character data.

● **Numeric data** consists of numbers representing quantities that might be used in arithmetic operations. For example, your annual income is numeric data, as is your age. Computers represent numeric data using the binary number system, also called "base 2." The binary number system has only two digits: 0 and 1. These digits can be converted to electrical "ons" or "offs" inside a computer. The number 2 cannot be used in the binary number system; so instead of writing *2* you would write *10*, which you would pronounce as *one zero*. See Figure D-1.

● **Character data** is composed of letters, symbols, and numerals that will not be used in arithmetic operations. Examples of character data include your name, address, and hair color. Character data is also represented by a series of 1s and 0s.

● Several types of codes are used to represent character data, including ASCII, EBCDIC, and Unicode. **ASCII (American Standard Code for Information Interchange)** requires only seven bits for each character. For example, the ASCII code for an uppercase

"A" is 1000001. ASCII provides codes for 128 characters, including uppercase letters, lowercase letters, punctuation symbols, and numerals. A superset of ASCII, called **Extended ASCII**, uses eight bits to represent each character. See Figure D-2. The eighth bit provides codes for 128 additional characters, which are usually boxes, circles, and other graphical symbols. **EBCDIC (Extended Binary-Coded Decimal Interchange Code)** is an alternative 8-bit code, usually used by older IBM mainframe computers. **Unicode** uses 16 bits and provides codes for 65,000 characters, a real bonus for representing the alphabets of multiple languages. Most personal computers use Extended ASCII code, although Unicode is becoming increasingly popular.

● Because computers represent numeric data with binary equivalents, ASCII codes that represent numbers might seem unnecessary. Computers, however, sometimes distinguish between numeric data and numerals. For example, you don't use your social security number in calculations, so a computer considers it character data composed of numerals, not numbers.

● To work with pictures and sounds, a computer must **digitize** the information that makes up the picture (such as the colors) and the information that makes up the sound (such as the notes) into 1s and 0s. Computers convert colors and notes into numbers, which can be represented by bits and stored in files as a long series of 1s and 0s.

● Your computer needs to know whether to interpret those 1s and 0s as ASCII code, binary numbers, or the code for a picture or sound. Most computer files contain a **file header** with information on the code that was used to represent the file data. A file header is stored along with the file and can be read by the computer, but never appears on the screen.

FIGURE D-1: Comparing decimal and binary numbers

▶ The decimal system uses ten symbols to represent numbers: 0, 1, 2, 3, 4, 5, 6, 7, 8, and 9; the binary number system uses only two symbols: 0 and 1

DECIMAL (BASE 10)	BINARY (BASE 2)
0	0
1	1
2	10
3	11
4	100
5	101
6	110
7	111
8	1000
9	1001
10	1010
11	1011
1000	1111101000

FIGURE D-2: A sample of Extended ASCII code

▶ The Extended ASCII code uses a series of eight 1s and 0s to represent 256 characters, including lowercase letters, upper-case letters, symbols, and numerals. The first 63 ASCII characters are not shown in this table because they represent special control sequences that cannot be printed.

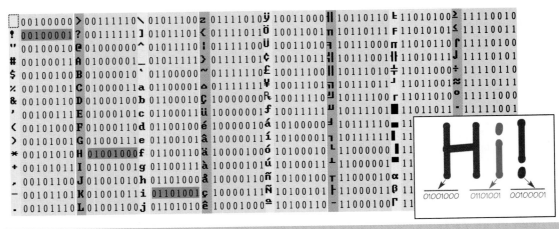

Quantifying bits and bytes

A bit is one binary digit and a byte is eight bits. The word "bit" can be abbreviated as a lowercase "b" and byte can be abbreviated as an uppercase "B."

Bits and bytes are used in different ways. Transmission speeds are usually expressed in bits, whereas storage space is usually expressed in bytes. The speed 56 Kbps means 56 kilobits per second; the capacity 8 GB means 8 gigabytes. "Kilo" is usually a prefix that means 1,000. For example, $50 K means $50,000. However, when it refers to bits or bytes, a "kilo" is 1,024 because computer engineers measure everything in base 2, and 2^{10} in base 2 is 1,024, not 1,000. So a **kilobit** (abbreviated Kb or Kbit) is 1,024 bits and a **kilobyte** (abbreviated KB or Kbyte) is 1,024 bytes. The prefix "mega" refers to a million, or in the context of bits and bytes, precisely 1,048,576 (the equivalent of 2^{20}). Mb or Mbit is the abbreviation for **megabit**. MB or Mbyte is the abbreviation for **megabyte**.

The prefix "giga" refers to a billion, or precisely 1,073,741,824. A **gigabit** (Gb or Gbit) is approximately one billion bits. A **gigabyte** (GB or GByte) is one billion bytes. Gigabytes are typically used to refer to RAM and hard disk capacity. Tera- (trillion), peta- (thousand trillion), and exa- (quintillion) are prefixes

for large amounts of data. Figure D-3 summarizes the commonly used terms to quantify computer data.

FIGURE D-3: Bits and bytes

Bit	One binary digit
Byte	8 bits
Kilobit	1,024 or 2^{10} bits
Kilobyte	1,024 or 2^{10} bytes
Megabit	1,048,576 or 2^{20} bits
Megabyte	1,048,576 or 2^{20} bytes
Gigabit	2^{30} bits
Gigabyte	2^{30} bytes
Terabyte	2^{40} bytes
Petabyte	2^{50} bytes
Exabyte	2^{60} bytes

Introducing integrated circuits

Computers are electronic devices that use electrical signals and circuits to represent, process, and move data. Bits take the form of electrical pulses that can travel over circuits. An **integrated circuit (IC)** is a super-thin slice of semi-conducting material packed with microscopic circuit elements such as wires, transistors, capacitors, logic gates, and resistors.

INTEGRATED CIRCUITS   MICROPROCESSOR UPDATE

DETAILS

- If it weren't for digital electronics, computers would be huge, and the inside of a computer's system unit would contain a jumble of wires and other electronic components. Today's computers contain relatively few parts. A computer's system unit contains circuit boards, storage devices, and a power supply that converts current from an AC wall outlet into the DC current used by computer circuitry. See Figure D-4.

- Integrated circuits can be used for processors, memory, and support circuitry. The terms computer chip, microchip, and chip originated as jargon for integrated circuit. Chips are classified by the number of miniaturized components they contain—from small-scale integration (SSI) of less than 100 components per chip to ultra large-scale integration (ULSI) of more than 1 million components per chip.

- The processor, memory modules, and support circuitry chips are packaged in a protective carrier or "chip package." Chip carriers vary in shape and size including small rectangular **DIPs (dual in-line packages)** with caterpillar-like legs protruding from a black, rectangular body; long, slim **DIMMs (dual in-line memory modules)**; pin-cushion-like **PGAs (pin-grid arrays)**; and cassette-like **SEC (single-edge contact) cartridges**, such as those pictured in Figure D-5. The pins on each chip package provide the electronic connection between the integrated circuit and other computer components.

- **Semiconducting materials** (or "semiconductors"), such as silicon and germanium, are used to make chips. The conductive properties of selective parts of the semiconducting material can be enhanced to create miniature electronic pathways and components, such as transistors.

- The computer's main circuit board, called a **motherboard** or main board, houses all essential chips and provides the connecting circuitry between them. See Figure D-6. Some chips are permanently soldered in place. Other chips are plugged into special sockets and connectors, which allow chips to be removed for repairs or upgrades. When multiple chips are required for a single function, such as generating stereo-quality sound, the chips might be gathered together on a separate small circuit board, such as a sound card, which can be plugged into a special slot-like connector on the motherboard.

- A **processor** (sometimes referred to as a microprocessor) is an integrated circuit designed to process instructions. It is the most important component of a computer, and usually the most expensive single component. Looking inside a computer, you can usually identify the processor because it is the largest chip on the motherboard. Depending on the brand and model, a processor might be housed in a cartridge-like SEC cartridge or in a square PGA. Inside the chip carrier, a processor is a very complex integrated circuit, containing as many as 300 million miniaturized electronic components.

Comparing today's processors

A typical computer ad contains a long list of specifications describing a computer's components and capabilities. Most computer specifications begin with the processor brand, type, and speed. Intel is the world's largest chipmaker and supplies a sizeable percentage of the processors that power PCs. In 1971, Intel introduced the world's first processor, the 4004. The company has continued to produce a steady stream of new processor models based on the 8088 processor.

AMD (Advanced Micro Devices) is Intel's chief rival in the PC chip market. It produces processors that work just like Intel's chips, but at a lower price. AMD's Athlon and Opteron processors are direct competitors to Intel's Pentium and Itanium lines and have a slight performance advantage according to some benchmarks.

Motorola is the main chip supplier for Apple computers. Transmeta Corporation specializes in chips for mobile computing devices, such as tablet computers.

The processors that are marketed with today's computers will handle most business, educational, and entertainment applications. While it is technically possible to upgrade your computer's processor, the cost and technical factors discourage processor upgrades.

FIGURE D-4: Inside a typical desktop computer

Power supply and fan

Processor with built-in fan

Expansion cards

CD-ROM drive

Floppy disk drive

Hard disk drive

Cables that transfer data from storage devices to motherboard

Main circuit board (motherboard)

FIGURE D-5: Integrated circuits

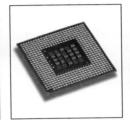

▲ A DIP has two rows of pins that connect the IC circuitry to a circuit board

▲ A DIMM is a small circuit board containing several chips, typically used for memory

▲ A PGA is a square chip package with pins arranged in concentric squares, typically used for processors

▲ An SEC cartridge was pioneered by Intel to house Pentium III processors

FIGURE D-6: The motherboard

▶ A computer motherboard provides sockets for chips, slots for small circuit boards, and the circuitry that connects all these components

Connectors for storage devices

DIMM module containing memory chips

SEC-style processor

Connector for power supply

Battery that powers the computer's real-time clock

Expansion slots hold additional expansion cards, such as a modem or sound card

Expansion card

DIP holding a ROM chip

Circuitry that transports data from one component to another

Exploring processor performance factors

All processors have two main parts: the arithmetic logic unit (ALU) and the control unit. To process data, each of these units performs specific tasks. The performance of a processor is affected by several factors, including clock speed, word size, cache size, instruction set, and processing techniques. This lesson looks at the two main parts of a processor and the factors that affect processor performance.

LAB
BENCHMARKING

DETAILS

- The **arithmetic logic unit (ALU)** is the circuitry that performs arithmetic operations, such as addition and subtraction. It also performs logical operations, such as comparing two numbers using the logical operators such as less than (<), greater than (>), or equal to (=). Logical operations also allow for comparing characters and sorting and grouping information. The ALU uses **registers** to hold data that is being processed. Figure D-7 illustrates how the ALU works.

- The processor's **control unit** fetches each instruction, as illustrated in Figure D-8. A processor executes instructions that are provided by a computer program. The list of instructions that a processor can perform is called its **instruction set**. These instructions are hard-wired into the processor's circuitry and include basic arithmetic and logical operations, fetching data, and clearing registers. A computer can perform very complex tasks, but it does so by performing a combination of simple tasks from its instruction set.

- How efficiently the ALU and the control unit work are determined by different performance factors. Processor speed is one of the most important indicators in determining the power of a computer system. The **processor clock** is a timing device that sets the pace (the clock speed) for executing instructions. The clock speed of a processor is specified in **megahertz (MHz)**—millions of cycles per second or **gigahertz (GHz)**—billions of cycles per second. A cycle is the smallest unit of time in a processor's universe. Every action that a processor performs is measured by these cycles. The clock speed is not equal to the number of instructions that a processor can execute in one second. In many computers, some instructions occur within one cycle, but other instructions might require multiple cycles. Some processors can even execute several instructions in a single clock cycle. A specification such as 2.8 GHz means that the processor's clock operates at a speed of 2.8 billion cycles per second.

- **Word size**, another performance factor, refers to the number of bits that a processor can manipulate at one time. Word size

is based on the size of the registers in the ALU and the capacity of circuits that lead to those registers. A processor with a 32-bit word size, for example, has 32-bit registers, processes eight bits at a time, and is referred to as a 32-bit processor. Processors with a larger word size can process more data during each processor cycle. Today's personal computers typically contain 32-bit or 64-bit processors.

- **Cache**, sometimes called RAM cache or cache memory, is special high-speed memory that a processor can access more rapidly than memory elsewhere on the motherboard. Cache capacity is usually measured in kilobytes.

- Another performance factor is the type of instruction set a processor uses. As chip designers developed various instruction sets for processors, they tended to add increasingly more complex instructions, each of which required several clock cycles for execution. A processor with such an instruction set uses **CISC (complex instruction set computer)** technology. A processor with a limited set of simple instructions uses **RISC (reduced instruction set computer)** technology. Most processors in today's Macs use RISC technology; most PCs use CISC technology. A processor's ability to handle graphics can be enhanced by adding specialized graphics and multimedia instructions to a processor's instruction set. 3DNow!, MMX, and SSE-2 are instruction set enhancements.

- The processing technique also affects performance. With **serial processing**, the processor must complete all of the steps in the instruction cycle before it begins to execute the next instruction. However, using a technology called **pipelining**, a processor can begin executing an instruction before it completes the previous instruction. Many of today's processors also perform **parallel processing**, in which multiple instructions are executed at the same time. Hyper-Threading refers to a technology that enables processors to execute multiple instructions in parallel.

FIGURE D-7: How the ALU works

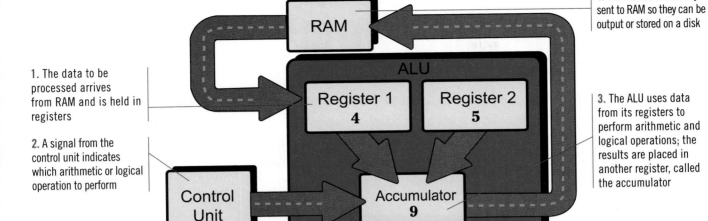

1. The data to be processed arrives from RAM and is held in registers

2. A signal from the control unit indicates which arithmetic or logical operation to perform

4. The results are usually sent to RAM so they can be output or stored on a disk

3. The ALU uses data from its registers to perform arithmetic and logical operations; the results are placed in another register, called the accumulator

FIGURE D-8: How the control unit works

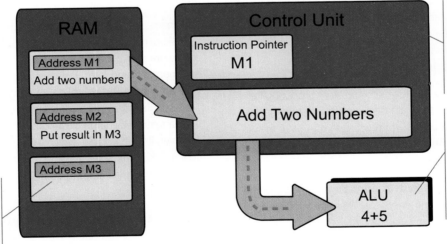

The control unit retrieves an instruction from RAM and puts it in the instruction register; the control unit interprets the instruction in its instruction register

Depending on the instruction, the control unit will get data from RAM, tell the ALU to perform an operation, or change the memory address of the instruction pointer

The RAM address of the instruction is kept in the instruction pointer; when the instruction has been executed, the address in the instruction pointer changes to indicate the RAM address of the next instruction to be executed

Benchmarking

All things being equal, a computer with a 2.8 GHz processor is faster than a computer with a 1.5 GHz processor and a computer with a processor that has a larger word size can process more data during each processor cycle than a computer with a processor that has a smaller word size. Furthermore, all things being equal, a computer with more Level 1 cache (L1), which is built into the processor chip, is faster than a computer with the same amount of Level 2 cache (L2), which is located on a separate chip and takes a little more time to get data to the processor.

But all things aren't equal. So how do you tell the overall performance of a computer and its processor? Various testing laboratories run a series of tests called **benchmarks** to gauge the overall speed of a processor. These results can be used to compare the results to other processors. The results of benchmark tests are usually available on the Web and are published in computer magazine articles.

Understanding computer memory: RAM

Memory is the electronic circuitry linked directly to the processor that holds data and instructions when they are not being transported from one place to another. Computers use four categories of memory: random access memory (RAM), virtual memory, read-only memory (ROM), and CMOS memory. Each type of memory is characterized by the type of data it contains and the technology it uses to hold the data.

DETAILS

- **RAM (random access memory)** is a temporary holding area for data, application program instructions, and the operating system. In a personal computer, RAM is usually several chips or small circuit boards that plug into the motherboard within the computer's system unit. Next to the processor, RAM is one of the most expensive computer components. The amount of RAM in a computer can, therefore, affect the overall price of a computer system. Along with processor speed, RAM capacity is the other most important factor in determining and comparing the power of a computer system.

- RAM is the "waiting room" for the computer's processor. Refer to Figure D-9. It holds raw data that is waiting to be processed and the program instructions for processing that data. In addition, RAM holds the results of processing until they can be stored more permanently on disk or tape.

- RAM also holds operating system instructions that control the basic functions of a computer system. These instructions are loaded into RAM every time you start your computer, and they remain there until you turn off your computer.

- People who are new to computers sometimes confuse RAM and disk storage, perhaps because both of these components hold data. To distinguish between RAM and disk storage, remember that RAM holds data in circuitry, whereas disk storage places data on storage media such as floppy disks, hard disks, or CDs. RAM is temporary storage; disk storage is more permanent. In addition, RAM usually has less storage capacity than disk storage.

- In RAM, microscopic electronic parts called capacitors hold the bits that represent data. You can visualize the capacitors as microscopic lights that can be turned on or off. Refer to Figure D-10. A charged capacitor is "turned on" and represents a "1" bit. A discharged capacitor is "turned off" and represents a "0" bit. You

can visualize the capacitors as being arranged in banks of eight. Each bank holds eight bits, or one byte, of data.

- Each RAM location has an address and holds one byte of data. A RAM address on each bank helps the computer locate data as needed for processing.

- In some respects, RAM is similar to a chalkboard. You can use a chalkboard to write mathematical formulas, erase them, and then write an outline for a report. In a similar way, RAM can hold numbers and formulas when you balance your checkbook, then hold the text of your English essay when you use word processing software. The contents of RAM can be changed just by changing the charge of the capacitors. Unlike a chalkboard, however, RAM is volatile, which means that it requires electrical power to hold data. If the computer is turned off, or if the power goes out, all data stored in RAM instantly and permanently disappears.

- The capacity of RAM is usually expressed in megabytes (MB). Today's personal computers typically feature between 128 and 256 MB of RAM. The amount of RAM needed by your computer depends on the software that you use. RAM requirements are routinely specified on the outside of a software package. If it turns out that you need more RAM, you can purchase and install additional memory up to the limit set by the computer manufacturer.

- RAM components vary in speed. RAM speed is often expressed in **nanoseconds,** or billionths of a second. Lower numbers mean faster transmission, processing, and storage of data. For example, 8 ns RAM is faster than 10 ns RAM. RAM speed can also be expressed in MHz (millions of cycles per second). Just the opposite of nanoseconds, higher MHz ratings mean faster speeds. For example, 400 MHz RAM is faster than 133 MHz RAM.

FIGURE D-9: Contents of RAM

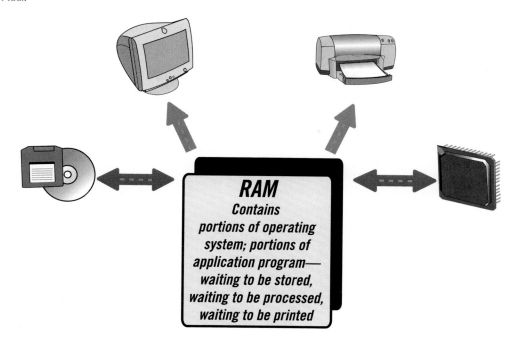

RAM
Contains
portions of operating
system; portions of
application program—
waiting to be stored,
waiting to be processed,
waiting to be printed

FIGURE D-10: How RAM works

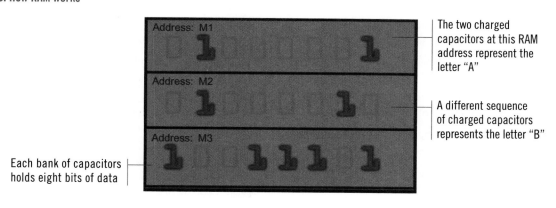

Address: M1

The two charged capacitors at this RAM address represent the letter "A"

Address: M2

A different sequence of charged capacitors represents the letter "B"

Address: M3

Each bank of capacitors holds eight bits of data

What is SDRAM?

Most of today's personal computers use SDRAM or RDRAM. **SDRAM (synchronous dynamic RAM)** is fast and relatively inexpensive. **RDRAM (rambus dynamic RAM)** was first developed for the popular Nintendo 64® game system and adapted for use in personal computers in 1999. Although more expensive than SDRAM, RDRAM is usually found in high-performance workstations with processors that run at speeds faster than 1 GHz. RAM is usually configured as a series of DIPs soldered onto a small circuit board, as shown in Figure D-11. SDRAM is the most popular type of RAM in today's computers. It is typically available on a small circuit board called a DIMM (dual inline memory module).

FIGURE D-11: RAM

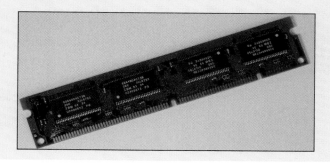

Exploring computer memory

In addition to RAM, a computer uses three other types of memory: virtual memory, ROM, and CMOS. This lesson looks at these types of computer memory and how all computer memory types work together.

DETAILS

● It might seem logical that the more you do with your computer, the more memory it needs. However, if you want to work with several programs and large graphics at the same time, personal computer operating systems are quite adept at allocating RAM space to multiple programs. If a program exceeds the allocated space, the operating system uses an area of the hard disk called **virtual memory** to store parts of a program or data file until they are needed. By selectively exchanging the data in RAM with the data in virtual memory, your computer effectively gains almost unlimited memory capacity.

One disadvantage of virtual memory is reduced performance. Too much dependence on virtual memory can have a negative affect on your computer's performance because getting data from a mechanical device, such as a hard disk, is much slower than getting data from an electronic device, such as RAM. Loading up your computer with as much RAM as possible will help your computer speed through all of its tasks.

● **ROM (read-only memory)** is a type of memory circuitry that holds the computer's startup routine. ROM is housed in a single integrated circuit, usually a fairly large, caterpillar-like DIP package that is plugged into the motherboard.

While RAM is temporary and volatile, ROM is permanent and non-volatile. ROM circuitry holds "hard-wired" instructions that remain in place even when the computer power is turned off. This is a familiar concept to anyone who has used a hand calculator, which includes various "hard-wired" routines for calculating square roots, cosines, and other functions. The instructions in ROM are permanent, and the only way to change them is to replace the ROM chip.

● When you turn on your computer, the processor receives electrical power and is ready to begin executing instructions. But, because the power had been off, RAM is empty and contains no instructions for the processor to execute. Now ROM plays its part. ROM contains a small set of instructions called the **ROM BIOS (basic input/output system)**. These instructions tell the computer how to access the hard disk, find the operating system, and load it into RAM. Once the operating system is loaded, the computer can understand your input, display output, run software, and access your data. While ROM BIOS

instructions are accomplished mainly without user intervention or knowledge, the computer will not function without the ROM chip and the BIOS instructions.

● In order to operate correctly, a computer must have some basic information about storage, memory, and display configurations. For example, your computer needs to know how much memory is available so that it can allocate space for all of the programs that you want to run. RAM goes blank when the computer power is turned off, so configuration information cannot be stored there. ROM would not be a good place for this information either because it holds data on a permanent basis. If, for example, your computer stored memory specification information in ROM, you could never add more memory; or if you were able to add it, you couldn't change the memory specification information in ROM. To store some basic system information, your computer needs a type of memory that's more permanent than RAM but less permanent than ROM.

● **CMOS memory (complementary metal oxide semiconductor)**, pronounced "SEE moss," is a type of memory that requires very little power to hold data. CMOS memory is stored on a chip that can be powered by a small, rechargeable battery integrated into the motherboard. The battery trickles power to the CMOS chip so that it can retain vital data about your computer system configuration even when your computer is turned off. To access the CMOS setup program, press and hold down the F1 key as your computer boots. But be careful! If you make a mistake with these settings, your computer might not be able to start.

When you change the configuration of your computer system by adding RAM, for example, the data in CMOS must be updated. Some operating systems recognize such changes and automatically perform the update; or you can manually change CMOS settings by running the CMOS setup program. See Figure D-12.

● Even though virtual memory, ROM, and CMOS have important roles in the operation of a computer, it is really RAM capacity that makes a difference you can notice. The more data and programs that can fit into RAM, the less time your computer will spend moving data to and from virtual memory. With lots of RAM, you'll find that documents scroll faster, and many graphics operations take less time than with a computer that has less RAM capacity.

FIGURE D-12: CMOS setup program

▶ CMOS holds computer configuration settings, such as the date and time, hard disk capacity, number of floppy disk drives, and RAM capacity

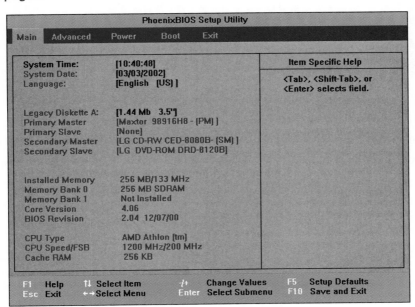

Understanding memory specified in computer ads

Most ads specify RAM capacity, speed, and type. When you see the specification "512 MB 400 MHz SDRAM (max. 2 GB)" in a computer ad similar to the one in Figure D-13, you'll know that the computer's RAM capacity is 512 megabytes (plenty to run most of today's software), that it operates at 400 megahertz (fairly fast), and that it uses SDRAM (a little slower and less expensive than RDRAM). You'll also have important information about the maximum amount of RAM that can be installed in the computer—2 GB, which is more than enough for the typical computer owner who does a bit of word processing, surfs the Web, and plays computer games.

FIGURE D-13: A computer ad typically specifies the amount and type of RAM

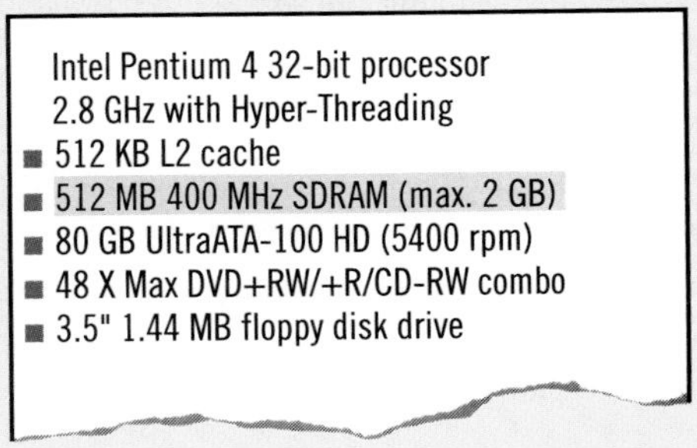

Intel Pentium 4 32-bit processor
2.8 GHz with Hyper-Threading
- 512 KB L2 cache
- 512 MB 400 MHz SDRAM (max. 2 GB)
- 80 GB UltraATA-100 HD (5400 rpm)
- 48 X Max DVD+RW/+R/CD-RW combo
- 3.5" 1.44 MB floppy disk drive

UNIT D

Introducing computer file basics

The term "file" was used for filing cabinets and collections of papers long before it became part of the personal computer lexicon. Today, a **computer file** or simply "file" is defined as a named collection of data that exists on a storage medium, such as a hard disk, floppy disk, CD, DVD, or tape. A file can contain a group of records, a document, a photo, music, a video, an e-mail message, or a computer program. This lesson looks at several common characteristics of computer files—type, filename, and format.

Info Web
FILE FORMATS

DETAILS

- There are several categories of files, such as data files, executable files, configuration files, and drivers. A computer file is classified according to the data it contains, the software that was used to create it, and the way you should use it. See Table D-1.

- Every file has a filename. The filename has two parts—the filename itself and the filename extension.

- A **filename** is a unique set of characters and numbers that identifies a file and should describe its contents. When you save a file, you must provide it with a valid filename that adheres to specific rules, referred to as **file-naming conventions**. Each operating system has a unique set of file-naming conventions. See Figure D-14.

  If an operating system attaches special significance to a symbol, you might not be able to use it in a filename. For example, Windows uses the colon (:) and the backslash (\) to separate the device letter from a filename or folder, as in C:\Music. A filename such as Report:\2004 is not valid because the operating system would become confused about how to interpret the colon and backslash.

  Some operating systems also contain a list of **reserved words** that are used as commands or special identifiers. You cannot use these words alone as a filename. You can, however, use these words as part of a longer filename. For example, under Windows XP, the filename Nul would not be valid, but you could name a file something like Nul Committee Notes.doc.

- A **filename extension** (or file extension) is separated from the main filename by a period, as in Paint.exe. A filename extension further describes the file contents. Generally, the software application you are using automatically assigns the filename extension when you save a file. If you don't see a filename extension

when you use the Save or Save As dialog box to save a file, the option to show filename extensions has been deactivated. When using Windows, you can choose to hide (but not erase) or display the filename extensions through the Folder Options setting in the Control Panel.

Knowledge of filename extensions comes in handy when you receive a file on a disk or over the Internet but you don't know much about its contents. If you are familiar with filename extensions, you will know the file format and, therefore, which application to use when you want to open the file.

- A filename extension is usually related to the **file format**, which is defined as the arrangement of data in a file and the coding scheme that is used to represent the data. Files that contain graphics are usually stored using a different file format than files containing text. Hundreds of file formats exist, and you'll encounter many of them as you use a variety of software. As you work with a variety of files, you will begin to recognize that some filename extensions, such as .txt (text file) or .jpg (graphics file), indicate a file type and are not specific to application software.

You will also recognize that other filename extensions, such as .doc (Word), .xls (Excel), and .zip (WinZip), can help you identify which application was used to create the file. These filename extensions indicate the **native file format**, which is the file format used to store files created with that software program. For example, Microsoft Word stores files in doc format, whereas Adobe Illustrator stores graphics files in ai format. When using a software application such as Microsoft Word to open a file, the program displays any files that have the filename extension for its native file format, as shown in Figure D-15.

FIGURE D-14: File-naming conventions

	DOS AND WINDOWS 3.1	WINDOWS 95/98/Me/XP/ NT/2000	MAC OS (CLASSIC)	UNIX/LINUX
Maximum length of filename	8-character filename plus an extension of 3 characters or less	Filename and extension cannot exceed 255 characters	31 characters (no extensions)	14–256 characters (depending on UNIX/Linux version) including an extension of any length
Spaces allowed	No	Yes	Yes	No
Numbers allowed	Yes	Yes	Yes	Yes
Characters not allowed	* / [ ] ; " = \ : ,	?	* \ : < >	" / ?	:	* ! @ # $ % ^ & ( ) { } [ ] " \ ? ; < >
Filenames not allowed	Aux, Com1, Com2, Com3, Com4, Con, Lpt1, Lpt2, Lpt3, Prn, Nul	Aux, Com1, Com2, Com3, Com4, Con, Lpt1, Lpt2, Lpt3, Prn, Nul	Any filename is allowed	Depends on the version of UNIX or Linux
Case sensitive	No	No	No	Yes (use lowercase)

FIGURE D-15: Filename extensions

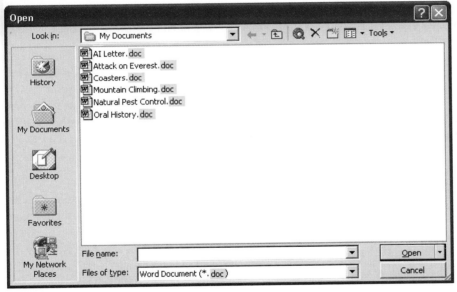

◀ If you don't see any filename extensions, in dialog boxes or in Explorer, the Windows setting that can hide (but not erase) filename extensions is set to hide file extensions. To view filename extensions, open Windows Explorer, click Tools on the menu bar, click Folder Options, then click the Hide file extensions check box to clear the mark.

TABLE D-1: Types of files

TYPE OF FILE	DESCRIPTION	EXTENSION
Configuration file	Information about programs that the computer uses to allocate the resources necessary to run them	.cfg .sys .mif .bin .ini
Help	The information that is displayed by online Help	.hlp
Temporary file	Contains data while a file is open, but that is discarded when you close the file	.tmp
Program files	The main executable files for a computer program	.exe .com
Support files	Program instructions that are executed in conjunction with the main .exe file for a program	.ocx .vbx .vbs .dll
Data files	Documents, images, spreadsheets, databases, music, sound, video, Web page, any file created with a program	.doc .bmp .jpg .gif .html .xls .mdb .mpg

Understanding file locations

Programs and data files have unique names and locations to ensure that the computer can find them. To designate a file's location, you must specify where the file is stored on the storage media. This lesson looks more closely at file locations—how to assign them and the information about each file that is available at the file's location.

DETAILS

- The Windows operating system labels storage devices with letters, such as A: and C:. See Figure D-16. The floppy disk drive is usually assigned device letter A and is referred to as "drive A." A device letter is usually followed by a colon, so drive A could be designated as A: or as 3½" Floppy (A:). The main hard disk drive is usually referred to as "drive C." Additional storage devices can be assigned letters from D through Z. Although most PCs use the standard of drive A for the floppy disk drive and drive C for the hard disk drive, the device letters for CD, Zip, and DVD drives are not standardized. For example, the CD-writer on your computer might be assigned device letter E, whereas the CD-writer on another computer might be assigned device letter R.

- An operating system maintains a list of files called a **directory** for each storage disk, tape, CD, or DVD. The main directory of a disk is referred to as the **root directory**. On a PC, the root directory is typically identified by the device letter followed by a backslash. For example, the root directory of the hard disk drive would be C:\. You should try to avoid storing your data files in the root directory of your hard disk, and instead store them in a subdirectory.

- A root directory is often subdivided into smaller **subdirectories**. When you use Windows, Mac OS, or a Linux graphical file manager, these subdirectories are depicted as **folders** because they work like the folders in a filing cabinet to store an assortment of related items. Each folder has a name, so you can easily create a folder called Documents to hold reports, letters, and so on. You can create another folder called Music to hold your MP3 files. Folders can be created within other folders. You might, for example, create a folder within your Music folder to hold your jazz collection and another to hold your reggae collection.

- A folder name is separated from a drive letter and other folder names by a special symbol. In Microsoft Windows, this symbol is the backslash (\). For example, the folder for your reggae music (within the Music folder on drive C) would be written as C:\Music\Reggae. Imagine how hard it would be to find a specific piece of paper in a filing cabinet that was stuffed with a random assortment of reports, letters, and newspaper clippings. By storing a file in a folder, you assign it a place in an organized hierarchy of folders and files.

- A computer file's location is defined by a **file specification** (sometimes called a **path**), which begins with the drive letter and is followed by the folder(s), filename, and filename extension. Suppose that you have stored an MP3 file called Marley One Love in the Reggae folder on your hard disk drive. Its file specification would be as shown in Figure D-17.

- A file contains data, stored as a group of bits. The more bits, the larger the file. **File size** is usually measured in bytes, kilobytes, or megabytes. Knowing the size of a file can be important especially when you are sending a file as an e-mail attachment. Your computer's operating system keeps track of file sizes.

- Your computer keeps track of the date on which a file was created or last modified. The **file date** is useful if you have created several versions of a file and want to make sure that you know which version is the most recent. It can also come in handy if you have downloaded several updates of player software, such as an MP3 player, and you want to make sure that you install the latest version.

- The operating system keeps track of file locations, filenames, filename extensions, file size, and file dates. See Figure D-18. This information is always available to you through a file management utility, which will be discussed in the next lesson.

FIGURE D-16: Labeling storage devices

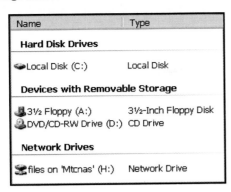

Name	Type
Hard Disk Drives	
Local Disk (C:)	Local Disk
Devices with Removable Storage	
3½ Floppy (A:)	3½-Inch Floppy Disk
DVD/CD-RW Drive (D:)	CD Drive
Network Drives	
files on 'Mtcnas' (H:)	Network Drive

FIGURE D-17: A file specification

C:\Music\Reggae\Marley One Love.mp3

Drive letter · Primary folder · Secondary folder · Filename · Filename extension

FIGURE D-18: File sizes and dates

Folders hold additional folders or files

Icon indicates application used to create file

Filename

Filename extension

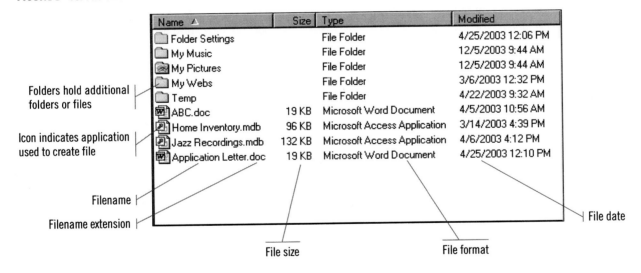

Name ▲	Size	Type	Modified
Folder Settings		File Folder	4/25/2003 12:06 PM
My Music		File Folder	12/5/2003 9:44 AM
My Pictures		File Folder	12/5/2003 9:44 AM
My Webs		File Folder	3/6/2003 12:32 PM
Temp		File Folder	4/22/2003 9:32 AM
ABC.doc	19 KB	Microsoft Word Document	4/5/2003 10:56 AM
Home Inventory.mdb	96 KB	Microsoft Access Application	3/14/2003 4:39 PM
Jazz Recordings.mdb	132 KB	Microsoft Access Application	4/6/2003 4:12 PM
Application Letter.doc	19 KB	Microsoft Word Document	4/25/2003 12:10 PM

File size · File format · File date

Deleting files

You may have noticed when using Windows that when you delete a file it is moved to the Recycle Bin. The Windows Recycle Bin and similar utilities in other operating systems are designed to protect you from accidentally deleting hard disk files that you actually need. The operating system moves the file to the Recycle Bin folder. The "deleted" file still takes up space on the disk, but does not appear in the usual directory listing. The file does, however, appear in the directory listing for the Recycle Bin folder, and you can undelete any files in this listing. It is important to remember that only files you delete from your hard disk drive are sent to the Recycle Bin; files you delete from a floppy disk drive are not sent to the Recycle Bin.

To delete data from a disk in such a way that no one can ever read it, you can use special file shredder software that overwrites "empty" sectors with random 1s and 0s. You might find this software handy if you plan to donate your computer to an organization, and you want to make sure that your personal data no longer remains on the hard disk.

Exploring file management

File management encompasses any procedure that helps you organize your computer-based files so that you can find and use them more efficiently. Depending on your computer's operating system, you may be able to organize and manipulate your files from within an application program, or by using a special file management utility provided by the operating system.

DETAILS

- Applications, such as word processing software or graphics software, typically provide file management capabilities for files created within the application. For example, most applications provide a way to open files and save them in a specific folder on a designated storage device. An application might also provide additional file management capabilities, such as deleting and renaming files.

- Most application software provides access to file management tasks through the Save and Open dialog boxes. These dialog boxes provided by Windows applications allow you to do more than just save a file. You can use them to perform other file management tasks such as rename a file, delete a file, or create a folder, as shown in Figure D-20. At times, however, you might want to work with groups of files, or perform other file operations that are inconvenient to perform within the Save or Open dialog boxes. Most operating systems

provide **file management utilities** that give you the "big picture" of the files you have stored on your disks and help you work with them. For example, Windows provides a file management utility called **Windows Explorer** that can be accessed from the My Computer icon or from the Windows Explorer command on the Start menu. On computers with Mac OS, the file management utility is called **Finder**. These utilities, shown in Figure D-21, help you view a list of files, find files, move files from one place to another, make copies of files, delete files, and rename files.

- File management utilities are designed to help you organize and manipulate the files that are stored on your computer. Most file management operations begin with locating a particular file or folder. A file management utility should make it easy to find what you're looking for by drilling down through your computer's hierarchy of folders and files.

The Save vs. Save As dialog box

Knowing how to save a file is a crucial file management skill. The Save As command is generally an option on the File menu. In addition to the Save As option, the menu also contains a Save option. The difference between the two options is subtle, but useful. The Save As option allows you to select a name and storage device for a file, whereas the Save option simply saves the latest version of a file under its current name and at its current location. When you try to use the Save option for a file that doesn't yet have a name, your application will display the Save As dialog box, even though you selected the Save option. The flow chart in Figure D-19 will help you decide whether to use the Save or the Save As command.

FIGURE D-19: Save or Save As

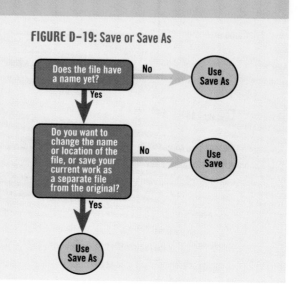

FIGURE D-20: The Save As dialog box

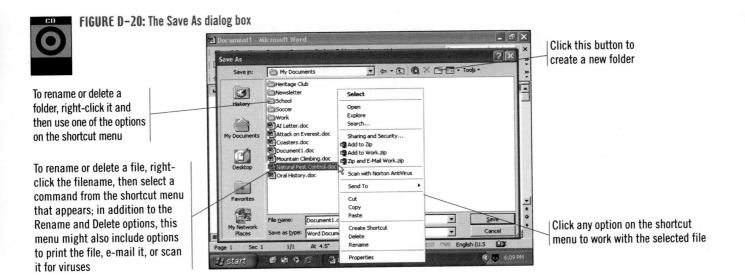

To rename or delete a folder, right-click it and then use one of the options on the shortcut menu

To rename or delete a file, right-click the filename, then select a command from the shortcut menu that appears; in addition to the Rename and Delete options, this menu might also include options to print the file, e-mail it, or scan it for viruses

Click this button to create a new folder

Click any option on the shortcut menu to work with the selected file

FIGURE D-21: Operating system file managers

► The Windows file manager utility, Windows Explorer, can be tailored to show files as icons or as a list

▼ Mac OS provides a file management utility called the Finder

Understanding logical file storage

File management utilities often use some sort of metaphor to help you visualize and mentally organize the files on your disks and other storage devices. These metaphors are sometimes referred to as **logical storage models** because they help you form a mental (logical) picture of the way in which your files are stored. Windows Explorer is based on logical file storage. This lesson looks at logical file storage metaphors and how Windows Explorer implements the models.

DETAILS

● After hearing so much about files and folders, you might have guessed that the filing cabinet is a popular metaphor for computer storage. In this metaphor, each storage device of a computer corresponds to one of the drawers in a filing cabinet. The drawers hold folders and the folders hold files, as illustrated in Figure D-22.

● You might also find it helpful to think of the logical storage model as an outline. In the hierarchy of an outline, the highest or top level is the general level (root directory). As you move down to lower levels in the outline you have greater detail (primary subfolders and then secondary subfolders and so on). When you expand a higher level (a folder), you can see all the subordinate (subfolder) levels for that folder.

● The tree metaphor as shown in Figure D-23 is also helpful. In this metaphor, a tree represents a storage device. The trunk of the tree corresponds to the root directory. The branches of the tree represent folders. These branches can split into small branches representing folders within folders. The leaves at the end of a branch represent the files in a particular folder. For practicality, storage metaphors are translated into screen displays. Figure D-24 shows how Microsoft programmers combined the filing cabinet metaphor with the tree structure metaphor within the Windows Explorer file management utility.

The Windows Explorer window is divided into two "window panes." The pane on the left side of the window lists each of the storage devices connected to your computer, plus several important system objects, such as My Computer, Network Neighborhood, and the Desktop. Each storage device is synonymous with a file drawer in the file cabinet metaphor.

An icon for a storage device or other system object can be "expanded" by clicking its corresponding plus-sign icon. Once an icon is opened, its contents appear in the pane on the right side of the Windows Explorer window. Opening an icon displays the next level of the storage hierarchy, usually a collection of folders. Each folder is synonymous with the folders in the file cabinet metaphor.

Any of these folders can contain files or subfolders. Files are synonymous with papers in the file cabinet metaphor. Subfolders can be further expanded by clicking their plus-sign icons. You continue expanding folders in this manner until you reach the file you need. The minus-sign icon can be used to collapse a device or folder to hide the levels of the hierarchy.

● To work with either a single or a group of files or folders, you must first select them. Windows Explorer displays all of the items that you select by highlighting them. Once a folder or file or a group of folders or files is highlighted, you can use the same copy, move, or delete procedure that you would use for a single item.

● In addition to locating files and folders, Windows Explorer provides a set of file management tools that will help you manipulate files and folders in the following ways:

- Rename. You might want to change the name of a file or folder to better describe its contents. When renaming a file, you should be careful to keep the same filename extension so that you can open it with the correct application software.

- Copy. You can copy a file or folder. For example, you can copy a file from your hard disk to a floppy disk if you want to send it to a friend or colleague. You might also want to make a copy of a document so that you can revise the copy and leave the original intact. When you copy a file, the file remains in the original location and a duplicate file is added to a different location.

- Move. You can move a file from one folder to another, or from one storage device to another. When you move a file, it is erased from its original location, so make sure that you remember the new location of the file. You can also move folders from one storage device to another, or from one folder to another.

- Delete. You can delete a file when you no longer need it. You can also delete a folder. Be careful when you delete a folder because most file management utilities also delete all the files (and subfolders) that a folder contains.

FIGURE D-22: A filing cabinet as a metaphor

The file cabinet represents all of the storage devices connected to a computer

Each drawer represents one storage device

A drawer can contain folders that hold documents and other folders

FIGURE D-23: A tree as a metaphor

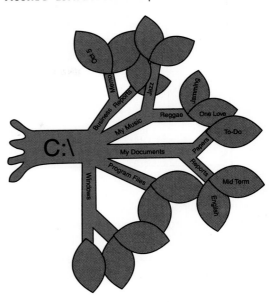

▲ You can visualize the directory of a disk as a tree on its side; the trunk corresponds to the root directory, the branches to folders, and the leaves to files

FIGURE D-24: Windows Explorer

▶ Windows Explorer borrows the folders from the filing cabinet metaphor and the branches on a tree from the tree metaphor and places them in a hierarchical structure, which makes it easy to drill down through the levels of the directory hierarchy to locate a folder or file

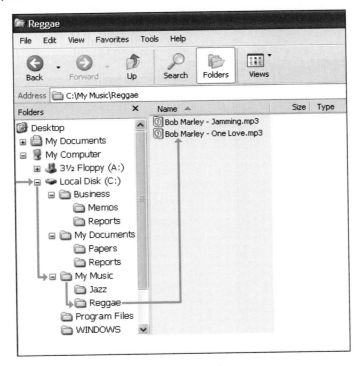

Using files

Creating, opening, saving, renaming, and starting are all actions that you perform on and with files as you work with software. A file management utility provides tools and procedures to help you keep track of your program and data files, but these tools are most useful when you have a logical plan for organizing your files and when you follow some basic file management guidelines.

DETAILS

● Before you can save or use files, you have to format the media to create the equivalent of electronic storage bins. Today, most floppy, Zip, and hard disks are preformatted at the factory; however, computer operating systems provide formatting utilities you can use to reformat some storage devices—typically floppy and hard disks. Formatting utilities are also supplied by the companies that manufacture hard disk drives, writable CD drives, and writable DVD drives. When you use a formatting utility, it erases any files that are on the disk, and then prepares the tracks and sectors necessary to hold data in new files. Refer to Figure D-25 which illustrates how to use Windows to format a floppy disk.

● Applications, such as word processing software or graphics software, typically provide a way to run a program file, open data files, and save data files on a designated storage device. A software application can typically open files that exist in its "native" file format, plus several additional file formats. For example, Microsoft Word opens files in its native document (.doc) format, plus files in formats such as HTML (.htm or .html), Text (.txt), and Rich Text Format (.rtf). Within the Windows environment, you can discover which formats a particular software program can open by looking at the Files of type list in the Open dialog box, as shown in Figure D-26.

● You use many files during a typical Windows application session.

- Start the program. Typically, you would open your word processing software. When you start the word processor, the necessary files are copied from the hard disk and placed in RAM. You then begin to type the document. As you type, the document is held in RAM. At some point, you'll want to save the document.

- Save a file. The Save As dialog box, shown in Figure D-27, allows you to specify a name for the file and its location on one of your computer's storage devices. To save a file in all Windows applications, click File on the menu bar, and then click Save As to open the Save As dialog box. You click the Look in list arrow to display a list of storage devices. Double-clicking any device displays its folders. You select a storage device and folder to indicate where you want the file to be stored, then type a name for the file in the File name text box. You can change the default file type by clicking the Files of type list arrow, then click the Save button.

- Retrieve a file. You click File on the menu bar, then click Open to open the Open Dialog box. You locate a file on the storage device by clicking the Look in list arrow, select the file, then click Open.

- Rename the file. Use the Save As command to save the current file using a new filename. The original file will be intact on the media and the open file will now have a new filename.

● The following tips pertain to managing files on your own computer.

- Use descriptive names. Give your files and folders descriptive names, and avoid using cryptic abbreviations.

- Maintain filename extensions. When renaming a file, keep the original file extension so that you can easily open it with the correct application software.

- Group similar files. Separate files into folders based on subject matter. For example, store your creative writing assignments in one folder and your MP3 music files in another folder.

- Organize your folders from the top down. When devising a hierarchy of folders, consider how you want to access files and back them up. For example, it is easy to specify one folder and its subfolders for a backup. If your important data is scattered in a variety of folders, however, making backups is more time consuming.

FIGURE D-25: Formatting a floppy disk

◀ Windows includes a floppy disk formatting utility, which can be accessed from the A: (Floppy disk) icon in the My Computer window or Windows Explorer

FIGURE D-26: Files of type list for an application

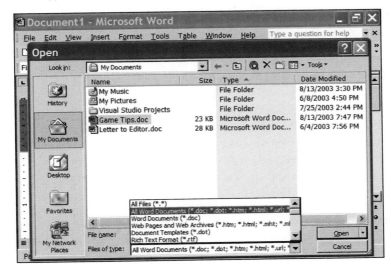

▶ An application's *Files of type* list usually displays the file formats a program can open. You can also look for an Import option on the File menu.

FIGURE D-27: Saving a file

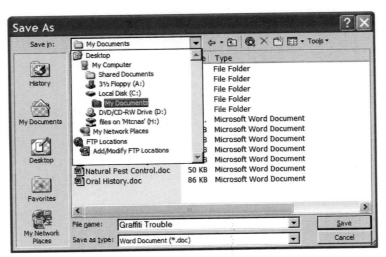

◀ The Save As dialog box is used to name a file and specify its storage location

Understanding physical file storage

So far, you've seen how an operating system like Windows can help you visualize computer storage as files and folders. The structure of files and folders that you see in Windows Explorer is called a "logical" model because it helps you create a mental picture. You have also seen how files are created, saved, and retrieved. What actually happens to a file when you save it is called physical file storage.

DETAILS

● When the storage medium is formatted it is divided into **tracks**, and each track is divided into wedge-shaped **sectors**. See Figure D-28. Tracks and sectors are numbered to provide addresses for each data storage bin. The numbering scheme depends on the storage device and the operating system. On CDs and DVDs, one or more tracks spiral out from the center of the disk; on floppy, Zip, and hard disks, tracks are arranged as concentric circles.

● The operating system uses a **file system** to keep track of the names and locations of files that reside on a storage medium, such as a hard disk. Different operating systems use different file systems. Most versions of Mac OS use the Macintosh Hierarchical File System (HFS). Ext2fs (extended 2 file system) is the native file system for Linux. Windows NT, Windows 2000, and Windows XP use a file system called New Technology File System (NTFS). Windows versions 95, 98, and ME use a file system called FAT32.

● To speed up the process of storing and retrieving data, a disk drive usually works with a group of sectors called a **cluster** or a "block." The number of sectors that form a cluster varies depending on the capacity of the disk and how the operating system works with files. A file system's primary task is to maintain a list of clusters and keep track of which ones are empty and which ones hold data. This information is stored in a special file.

● If your computer uses the FAT32 file system, for example, this special file is called the **File Allocation Table (FAT)**. If your computer uses NTFS, it is called the **Master File Table (MFT)**.

● Each of your disks contains its own index file so that information about its contents is always available when the disk is in use. Unfortunately, storing this crucial file on disk also presents a risk because if the index file is damaged by a hard disk head crash or scratch, you'll generally lose access to all the data stored on the disk. Index files become damaged all too frequently, so it is important to back up your data.

When you save a file, your PC's operating system looks at the index file to see which clusters are empty. It selects one of these clusters, records the file data there, and then revises the index file to include the filename and its location. A file that does not fit into a single cluster spills over into the next contiguous cluster unless that cluster already contains data. When contiguous clusters are not available, the operating system stores parts of a file in noncontiguous (nonadjacent) clusters. Figure D-29 helps you visualize how an index file, such as the MFT, keeps track of filenames and locations.

● When you want to retrieve a file, the OS looks through the index for the filename and its location. It moves the disk drive's read-write head to the first cluster that contains the file data. Using additional data from the index file, the operating system can move the read-write heads to each of the clusters containing the remaining parts of the file.

● When you click a file's icon and then select the Delete option, the operating system simply changes the status of the file's clusters to "empty" and removes the filename from the index file. The filename no longer appears in a directory listing, but the file's data remains in the clusters until a new file is stored there. You might think that this data is as good as erased, but it is possible to purchase utilities that recover a lot of this "deleted" data—law enforcement agents, for example, use these utilities to gather evidence from "deleted" files on the computer disks of suspected criminals.

● As a computer writes files on a disk, parts of files tend to become scattered all over the disk. These **fragmented files** are stored in noncontiguous clusters. Drive performance generally declines as the read-write heads move back and forth to locate the clusters that contain the parts of a file. To regain peak performance, you can use a **defragmentation utility** to rearrange the files on a disk so that they are stored in contiguous clusters. See Figure D-30.

FIGURE D-28: Tracks and sectors on a disk

▶ Formatting prepares the surface of a disk to hold data

Disks are divided into tracks and wedge-shaped sectors—each side of a floppy disk typically has 80 tracks divided into 18 sectors; each sector holds 512 bytes of data

On a typical CD, a single spiral track is divided into 336,000 sectors; each sector holds 2,048 bytes of data

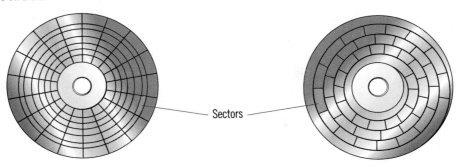

Sectors

FIGURE D-29: How the MFT works

▶ Each colored cluster on the disk contains part of a file. Bio.txt is stored in contiguous clusters. Jordan.wks is stored in noncontiguous clusters

A computer locates and displays the Jordan.wks file by looking for its name in the Master File Table

Master File Table

File	Cluster	Comment
MFT	1	Reserved for MFT files
DISK USE	2	Part of MFT that contains list of empty sectors
Bio.txt	3, 4	Bio.txt file stored in clusters 3 and 4
Jordan.wks	7, 8, 10	Jordan.wks file stored noncontiguously in clusters 7, 8, and 10
Pick.wps	9	Pick.wps file stored in cluster 9

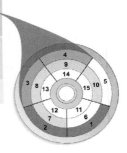

FIGURE D-30: Defragmenting a disk

▶ Defragmenting a disk helps your computer operate more efficiently; consider using a defragmentation utility a couple of times per year to keep your computer running in top form

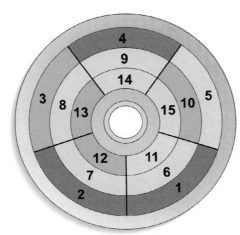

Fragmented disk

▲ On this fragmented disk, the purple, yellow, and blue files are stored in non-contiguous clusters

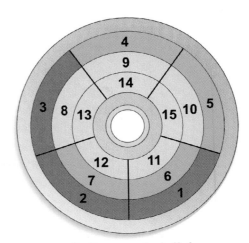

Defragmented disk

▲ When the disk is defragmented, the sectors of data for each file are moved to contiguous clusters

Remarkable advances in processor technology have produced exponential increases in computer speed and power. In 1965, Gordon Moore, co-founder of chip-production giant Intel Corporation, predicted that the number of transistors on a chip would double every 18 to 24 months. Much to the surprise of engineers and Moore himself, "Moore's law" accurately predicted 30 years of chip development. In 1958, the first integrated circuit contained two transistors. The Pentium III Xeon processor, introduced in 1999, had 9.5 million transistors. The Pentium 4 processor, introduced only a year later, featured 42 million transistors.

What's really fascinating, though, is how these chips perform complex tasks simply by manipulating bits. How can pushing around 1s and 0s result in professional-quality documents, exciting action games, animated graphics, cool music, street maps, and e-commerce Web sites? To satisfy your curiosity about what happens deep in the heart of a processor, you'll need to venture into the realm of instruction sets, fetch cycles, accumulators, and pointers.

A computer accomplishes a complex task by performing a series of very simple steps, referred to as instructions. An instruction tells the computer to perform a specific arithmetic, logical, or control operation. To be executed by a computer, an instruction must be in the form of electrical signals, those now-familiar 1s and 0s that represent "ons" and "offs." In this form, instructions are referred to as machine code. They are, of course, very difficult for people to read, so typically when discussing them, we use more understandable mnemonics, such as JMP, MI, and REG1.

An instruction has two parts: the op code and the operands. An op code, which is short for "operation code," is a command word for an operation such as add, compare, or jump. The operands for an instruction specify the data, or the address of the data, for the operation.

In the instruction JMP M1, the op code is JMP and the operand is M1. The op code JMP means jump or go to a different instruction. The operand M1 stands for the RAM address of the instruction to which the computer is supposed to go. The instruction JMP M1 has only one operand, but some instructions have more than one operand. For example, the instruction ADD REG1 REG2 has two operands: REG1 and REG2.

The list of instructions that a processor is able to execute is known as its instruction set. This instruction set is built into the processor when it is manufactured. Every task that a computer performs is determined by the list of instructions in its instruction set.

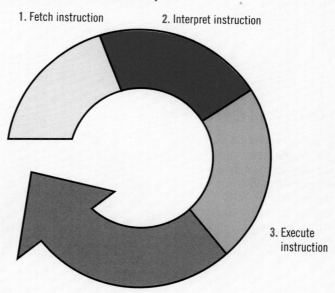

FIGURE D-31: The instruction cycle

1. Fetch instruction
2. Interpret instruction
3. Execute instruction
4. Increment instruction pointer

The term **instruction cycle** refers to the process in which a computer executes a single instruction. Some parts of the instruction cycle are performed by the processor's control unit; other parts of the cycle are performed by the ALU. The steps in this cycle are summarized in Figure D-31.

Like most modern scientists, astronomers use Web-based resources and computer-equipped tools to assist in their research. Even before leaving home to view the night sky, astronomers can use their desktop computers to access a special weather-forecasting Web site, which predicts ideal viewing conditions for the late evening. They can check the Web to find out whether any especially interesting objects, such as the international space station, might be viewable from their latitude and longitude that night. Many amateur and professional astronomers use sky map software to plan what they'll look at on a particular night. Based on the date, and coordinates for longitude and latitude, the software displays an image of the night sky and indicates key objects. For example, an astronomer could request the software to "show me the night sky looking south from Marquette, MI at 2 a.m. on May 15, 2005." The software responds with an image of the night sky, highlights constellations, and provides background information and photos for any selected celestial object.

Many astronomers' telescopes have a computerized positioning system, consisting of a handheld controller and a small computer mounted on the side of the telescope. The computer contains a database of thousands of celestial objects—stars, nebulae, planets, and galaxies. When astronomers set up a computerized telescope, they first align the computer by manually pointing the telescope at one or two stars that are easy to see with the naked eye, such as Polaris, the North Star, or Sirius, the Dog Star. After the computer "knows" the location of these stars, an astronomer can use the handheld controller to choose a celestial object from the database. The computerized positioning system finds the coordinates for the object and moves the telescope to point in the correct direction. Most computerized positioning systems also track the object—that is, as the object moves through the sky during the evening, the computer automatically moves the telescope so that the object is always centered in the eyepiece.

Amateur astronomers often carry specialized digital cameras that use CCD technology. A CCD (charge coupled device) is a light-sensitive integrated circuit that performs particularly well in low light, making it well suited for photographing dim objects, such as faraway galaxies and nebulae. Astrophotographers take pictures of celestial objects by mounting a CCD camera on a telescope. The CCD camera can take several pictures over a given time period or be adjusted to use a long exposure time—in some cases, over an hour—for extremely dim objects.

Taking a picture is only the first step in producing a spectacular celestial photograph. After photographing an object (see Figure D-32), astrophotographers upload the image to a desktop or notebook computer. Using graphics software, they can enhance the image by removing artifacts caused by external light sources, such as street lights, by emphasizing or reducing parts of the image, or by combining several images of the same object to create a clearer and brighter image. Many of the celestial images in magazines, on the Internet, and on television have been created by amateurs working in local parks, wilderness areas, or their own backyards.

Astrophotography isn't used only to take pretty pictures, however. With CCD imaging, both professional and amateur astronomers can document and analyze areas of the night sky and identify new celestial objects. "Comet hunters"—a slang term describing astronomers who specialize in finding and identifying new celestial objects—take several pictures of the same area of the sky over the span of many nights. The images are then combined and compared manually or with specialized software. Moving objects, such as comets or asteroids, show up as blurred or dotted lines when the time-lapse images are combined. Using this technique, both amateurs and professionals have discovered new asteroids, comets, exploding super-novae, and other objects.

When starlight passes through the atmosphere, it descends through many layers of different temperatures and densities. These atmospheric changes, called turbulence, distort the light and give stars their distinctive twinkling effect. Twinkling stars might be pretty to look at, but they're not good subjects for observation or research. Large earth-based telescopes, such as the one at the Gemini Observatory in Hawaii, use a computer-controlled technology called "adaptive optics" to manipulate a flexible mirror to negate atmospheric disturbance. Adaptive optics work by measuring the atmospheric distortion and bending a flexible mirror to eliminate these distortions. Light is gathered and sent to a wavefront sensor, which measures the level of atmospheric distortion in a light wave. Wavefront sensors in an adaptive optics system sample light waves entering the telescope many times a second. Data from these samples is routed to a computer attached to a flexible mirror called a "deformable mirror," which is usually a thin disk of quartz coated with a reflective layer of silver. Piston-like actuators attached to the back of the mirror push and pull its surface into the exact arc necessary to view a celestial object without atmospheric distortion.

FIGURE D-32

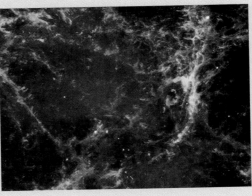

The need for more and more storage and faster and faster processors has teams of scientists in all the major labs around the world working on ways to create new chips. Ever since Robert Noyce and Jack Kilby constructed the first integrated circuits with components connected by aluminum lines on a silicon-oxide surface layer on a plane of silicon in 1959, scientists have been working to create ways of storing and processing data on smaller devices with greater reliability and speed. In 1965, Gordon Moore, head of research and development for Fairchild Semiconductor and co-founder of Intel, predicted that transistor density on integrated circuits would double every 12 months for the next ten years. This prediction, known as Moore's Law, was revised in 1975 to state that the density would double every 18 months. To everyone's amazement, including Moore himself, Moore's Law holds true even today, as scientists have continued to create faster and denser chips using silicon. If Moore's Law is to continue to hold true, then chip features must shrink or the technologies must greatly improve to keep increasing functionality and performance.

The limitations of silicon have been known for years, and the challenge has been to find new materials to take chip development to the next level. Current manufacturing processes use lithography to imprint circuits on semiconductor materials. While lithography has improved dramatically over the last two decades, it is widely believed that lithography is quickly approaching its physical limits. So where do chip developers go next?

The primary performance-enhancing strategy for over 30 years has been based on the scaling theory, which shrinks the dimensions and energy required by a processor's components. The result has been greater transistor density, faster transistors, and higher performance. Some scientists are researching nanotechnology, which is the "field of science whose goal is to control individual atoms and molecules to create computer chips and other devices that are thousands of times smaller than current technologies permit" (Webopedia), as a means of creating smaller, more powerful chips. What are the benefits of smaller and more powerful chips? One benefit is energy consumption. Smaller chips should consume less energy and should produce less heat, which should in turn make chips more environmentally friendly. But what is the best way to make these smaller chips? For more than a decade, Intel has been driving the pace of Moore's Law. Recent developments at Intel include a 90-nanometer processor.

To create this processor, Intel developed a new type of technology in the production of its processors that stretches atoms across the transistor to increase speed and efficiency. According to Intel, the technology uses "strained silicon," in which atoms in the 90-nanometer chips are spaced farther apart than normal. According to scientists at Intel, a strained silicon chip can function with less energy, which means devices consume less power and work faster. The technique of using strained silicon has been proven on larger transistors, but until the announcement of the 90-nanometer processor, it has remained a question as to whether or not it could work in significantly smaller scales. Intel officials have said that the company will be able to use nearly one-fourth of its existing manufacturing equipment with the new technology.

Are there alternatives to silicon-based chips? Yes, in fact, some of the most promising research involves carbon nanotubes, first discovered by Japanese scientist Sumio Iijima in 1991. A carbon nanotube is a single cylinder-shaped molecule about 10,000 times thinner than a human hair. The electrical properties of carbon nanotubes are similar to the semiconductors used in today's processors. Because carbon nanotubes are so small, they could be used for processors and memory. IBM researchers were able to construct a prototype carbon-nanotube transistor in 2001.

IBM has been working on molecular computing for years as it tries to find an alternative to silicon-based semiconductors. IBM scientists have built the tiniest computer circuit yet using individual molecules, a move they say advances their push toward smaller, faster electronics. IBM researchers at its Almaden Research Center in San Jose, California, have built and operated a computer circuit in which individual molecules of carbon monoxide move like toppling dominoes across a flat copper surface. This computer circuit involves nanotechnology and quantum computing.

Quantum computing is the application of quantum mechanics to computer systems. It has been described as a "bizarre, subatomic world in which two electrons can be two places at the same time." This description is fairly accurate. The subatomic bits used in quantum computing are called qubits. The good news for chip development is that qubits have the potential of representing not just a 1 or a 0, but of representing both a 1 and a 0 at the same time. This definitely means faster and more powerful computing. As research in these areas continues, the goal for chip developers is to translate the work in research labs into chips based on nanotechnology and quantum computing that can be manufactured and then used in products like cell phones and personal computers.

As scientists look at alternative methods for developing chips, some researchers are thinking beyond the physical restrictions of a chip and thinking instead about the computing process. These scientists are finding tremendous potential in a cheap, non-toxic, renewable material found in all living creatures—DNA. DNA (deoxyribonucleic acid) molecules are the material of which our genes are made. In fact, DNA is very similar to a computer hard drive in how it stores permanent information about your genes. DNA computing is the science of using DNA to code mathematical systems. In 1994, Leonard Adleman, a computer scientist at the University of Southern California, introduced the idea of using DNA to solve complex mathematical problems. Adleman is often called the inventor of DNA computers. Unlike conventional computers, DNA computers perform calculations parallel to other calculations. Parallel computing allows DNA to solve complex mathematical problems very quickly; DNA molecules have already been harnessed to perform complex mathematical problems. Whereas conventional computers might take hundreds of years, DNA computers can solve problems in hours. DNA might one day be integrated into a computer chip that will push computers even faster.

What is the future of computer chips? Will Moore's Law continue to hold with advances in computer chip technology? Current research suggests that Moore's Law might not be applicable to new mediums being considered for chips. But current research does suggest new chips will be faster, more energy efficient, and more environmentally friendly.

▼ INTERACTIVE QUESTIONS

○ Yes ○ No ○ Not sure   1. Do you think Moore's law will continue to be upheld?

○ Yes ○ No ○ Not sure   2. Should chipmakers be required to develop environmentally friendly chips?

○ Yes ○ No ○ Not sure   3. Will DNA computers become commercially viable?

▼ EXPAND THE IDEAS

1. We may be reaching the limit of Moore's Law as it applies to silicon-based chips. Research Moore's Law. Discover what scientists believe is the upper limit to Moore's Law and when they think we might reach that limit. Write a concluding paragraph indicating what will happen to computing if we reach the limit of Moore's Law and no alternative means for computing has been developed.

2. Advances in processor technology are announced frequently. Log on to the Internet and locate two news stories on recent advances. You can research developments at Intel by going to www.intel.com. What are the new barriers that are being broken? Is Moore's Law still being upheld? Write a short paragraph discussing your findings.

3. The new chips are becoming faster, more energy efficient, and able to solve problems more quickly. Will computers surpass human intelligence? How is human intelligence going to change? Will human and machine intelligence become intertwined? Research the work and writings of Raymond Kurzweil. Begin by looking at http://www.kurzweilai.net. Summarize your findings and write a short paragraph explaining your theory on how far computing "intelligence" can go.

End of Unit Exercises

▼ KEY TERMS

ALU	Directory	Gigahertz (GHz)	Processor clock
ASCII	EBCDIC	Instruction cycle	RAM
Benchmark	Extended ASCII	Instruction set	RDRAM
Binary number system	File Allocation Table (FAT)	Integrated circuit (IC)	Register
Bit	File date	Kilobit	Reserved word
Byte	File format	Kilobyte	RISC
Cache	File header	Logical storage model	ROM
Character data	File management	Master File Table	ROM BIOS
CISC	File management utility	Megabit	Root directory
Cluster	File-naming conventions	Megabyte	SDRAM
CMOS memory	File size	Megahertz (MHz)	SEC cartridge
Computer file	File specification	Motherboard	Sector
Control unit	File system	Nanosecond	Semiconducting material
Data representation	Filename	Native file format	Serial processing
Defragmentation utility	Filename extension	Numeric data	Subdirectory
Digital device	Finder	Parallel processing	Track
Digital electronics	Folder	Path	Unicode
Digitize	Fragmented file	PGA	Virtual memory
DIMM	Gigabit (Gb)	Pipelining	Windows Explorer
DIP	Gigabyte (GB)	Processor	Word size

▼ UNIT REVIEW

1. Review the bold terms in this unit. Then pick 10 terms that are most unfamiliar to you. Be sure that you can use your own words to define the terms you have selected.

2. Describe how the binary number system and binary coded decimals can use only 1s and 0s to represent numbers.

3. Describe the difference between numeric data, character data, and numerals. Then, list and briefly describe the four codes that computers typically use for character data.

4. Make sure that you understand the meaning of the following measurement terms; indicate what aspects of a computer system they are used to measure: KB, Kb, MB, Mb, GB, Kbps, MHz, GHz, ns.

5. List four types of memory and briefly describe how each one works.

6. Describe how the ALU and the control unit interact to process data.

7. Describe the difference between the Save and the Save As options provided by an application.

8. Explain the kinds of file management tasks that might best be accomplished using a file management utility such as Windows Explorer.

9. In your own words, describe the difference between a logical storage model and a physical storage model.

10. Make sure that you can describe what happens in the MFT when a file is stored or deleted.

▼ FILL IN THE BEST ANSWER

1. The _____ number system represents numeric data as a series of 0s and 1s.

2. ASCII is used primarily to represent _____ data.

3. Most personal computers use the _____ code to represent character data.

4. Digital _____ makes it possible for a computer to manipulate simple "on" and "off" signals to perform complex tasks.

5. An integrated _____ contains microscopic circuit elements, such as wires, transistors, and capacitors that are packed onto a very small square of semiconducting material.

6. The _____ in the processor performs arithmetic and logical operations.

7. The _____ in the CPU directs and coordinates the operation of the entire computer system.

8. The timing in a computer system is established by the _____.

9. In RAM, microscopic electronic parts called _____ hold the electrical signals that represent data.

10. The instructions for the operations your computer performs when it is first turned on are permanently stored in _____.

11. System configuration information about the hard disk, date, and RAM capacity is stored in battery-powered _____ memory.

12. An operating system's file-naming _____ provide a set of rules for naming files.

13. A file _____ refers to the arrangement of data in a file and the coding scheme that is used to represent the data.

14. The main directory of a disk is sometimes referred to as the _____ directory.

15. A file's location is defined by a file _____, which includes the drive letter, folder(s), filename, and extension.

16. Windows XP maintains a(n) _____ File Table, which contains the name and location of every file on a disk.

17. The _____ option on an application's File menu allows you to name a file and specify its storage location.

18. A(n) _____ storage model helps you form a mental picture of how your files are arranged on a disk.

19. On a floppy disk or hard disk, data is stored in concentric circles called _____, which are divided into wedge-shaped _____.

20. Windows Explorer is an example of a file _____ utility.

▼ PRACTICE TESTS

When you use the Interactive CD, you can take Practice Tests that consist of 10 multiple-choice, true/false, and fill-in-the blank questions. The questions are selected at random from a large test bank, so each time you take a test, you'll receive a different set of questions. Your tests are scored immediately, and you can print study guides to determine which questions you answered incorrectly. If you are using a Tracking Disk, insert it in the floppy disk drive to save your test scores.

▼ INDEPENDENT CHALLENGE 1

The three leading manufacturers of processors are Intel, AMD, and Transmeta. These companies manufacture processors for personal computers as well as other devices.

1. Based on what you read in this unit, list and describe the factors that affect processor performance. Create a table using the performance factors as column heads.

2. Use your favorite search engine on the Internet to research any two companies that produce processors.

3. List their Web sites and any other pertinent contact information for the companies that you chose.

4. List three of the models that each company produces as row labels in the table you created in Step 1. Complete the table to show how these models rate, that is, their specifications for each performance factor.

5. Write a brief statement describing any new research or new products that each company is developing.

▼ INDEPENDENT CHALLENGE 2

How quickly could you code a sentence using the Extended ASCII code? What is the history of coding and coding schemes? You can find a wealth of information about coding schemes that have been developed throughout the history of computing as well as coding used to transmit information.

1. Log onto the Internet, then use your favorite search engine to research the history of Morse code. Write a brief paragraph outlining your findings.

2. Use the International Morse Code alphabet to write your full name.

3. Research the history of the ASCII code. Write a one-page summary of your findings.

4. Use the extended ASCII code to write your full name.

5. Research the history of the EBCDIC code. Write a one-page summary of your findings.

6. Use the extended EBCDIC code to write your full name.

▼ INDEPENDENT CHALLENGE 3

How will you organize the information that you store on your hard drive? Your hard disk will be your electronic filing cabinet for all your work and papers. You can create many different filing systems. The way you set up your folders will guide your work and help you keep your ideas and projects organized so you can work efficiently with your computer. Take some time to think about the work that you do, the types of documents or files you will be creating, and then decide how you will create files and folders.

1. Read each of the following plans for organizing files and folders on a hard disk and comment on the advantages and disadvantages of each plan.

    a. Create a folder for each file you create.

    b. Store all the files in the root directory.

    c. Store all files in the My Documents folder.

    d. Create a folder for each application you plan to use and store only documents you generate with that application in each folder.

    e. Create folders for broad topics such as memos, letters, budget, art, personal, and then store all related documents and files within those folders.

    f. Create folders based on specific topics such as tax, applications, household, school, then store all related documents and files within those folders.

    g. Create a new folder for each month and store all files or documents created in that month in that appropriate folder.

2. Write up a summary of how you plan to organize your hard disk and explain why you chose the method you did.

▼ INDEPENDENT CHALLENGE 4

You can use Windows Explorer or any file management program on your computer to explore and find specific files and folders on your hard disk.

1. Start Windows Explorer then expand the My Computer icon. List the devices under My Computer.

2. Open the My Documents folder on the Local Disk C: (if not available, find the folder that has your documents). List how many folders are in the My Documents folder on your hard disk.

3. Open one of the folders in the My Documents folder, then display the Details View. Are filename extensions showing? If so, list them and identify which programs would open those files.

4. How many different types of files can you find on your hard disk? List up to 10.

5. Make a list of five filenames that are valid under the file-naming conventions for your operating system. Create a list of five filenames that are not valid and explain the problem with each one.

6. Create five filenames that meet the file-naming conventions for Windows and for MAC OS. Then create five filenames that do not meet the file-naming conventions for Windows or for MAC OS, and explain why these filenames do not meet the file-naming conventions.

7. Pick any five files on the computer that you typically use, and write out the full path for each one. If you can, identify the programs that were used to create each of the files you found.

▼ LAB: BENCHMARKING

1. Start the interactive part of the lab. Insert your Tracking Disk if you want to save your QuickCheck results. Perform each of the lab steps as directed and answer all of the lab QuickCheck questions. When you exit the lab, your answers are automatically graded and your results are displayed.

2. Use the System Info button that's available in Microsoft Word to analyze the computer that you typically use. Provide the results of the analysis along with a brief description of the computer that you tested and its location (at home, at work, in a computer lab, etc.).

3. From the Processor Benchmarks table above, which processor appears to be faster at graphics processing? Which processor appears to be better at overall processing tasks?

4. Explain why you might perform a benchmark test on your own computer but get different results from those that you read about in a computer magazine that tested the same computer with the same benchmark test.

5. Use a search engine on the Web to find benchmark ratings for Intel's Pentium 4 processors. What do these ratings show about the relative performance for 1.36 GHz, 1.5 GHz, and 1.7 GHz Pentium 4s?

▼ LAB: WORKING WITH WINDOWS EXPLORER

1. Start the interactive part of the lab. Insert your Tracking Disk if you want to save your QuickCheck results. Perform each of the lab steps as directed and answer all of the lab QuickCheck questions. When you exit the lab, your answers are automatically graded and your results are displayed.

2. Use Windows Explorer to look at the directory of the hard disk or floppy disk that currently contains most of your files. Draw a diagram showing the hierarchy of folders. Write a paragraph explaining how you could improve this hierarchy and draw a diagram to illustrate your plan.

3. Use a new floppy disk or format an old disk that doesn't contain important data. Create three folders on the disk: Music, Web Graphics, and Articles. Within the Music folder, create four additional folders: Jazz, Reggae, Rock, and Classical. Within the Classical folder, create two more folders: Classical MIDI and Classical MP3.

4. Use your browser software to connect to the Internet, then go to a Web site, such as www.zdnet.com or www.cnet.com. Look for a small graphic (remember, you only have 1.44 MB of space on your floppy disk!) and download it to your Web Graphics folder. Next, use a search engine like www.google.com or www.yahoo.com to search for "classical MIDI music." Download one of the compositions to the Music\Classical\Classical MIDI folder. Open Windows Explorer and expand all of the directories for drive A. Open the Music\Classical\Classical MIDI folder and make sure that your music download appears. Capture a screenshot. Follow your instructor's directions to submit this screenshot as a printout or e-mail attachment.

▼ STUDENT EDITION LABS

Reinforce the concepts you have learned in this unit through the **Understanding the Motherboard, Managing Files and Folders,** and **Binary Numbers** Student Edition Labs, available online at the Illustrated Computer Concepts Web site.

▼ SAM LABS

If you have a SAM user profile, you have access to additional content, features, and functionality. Log in to your SAM account and go to your assignments page to see what your instructor has assigned for this unit.

▼ VISUAL WORKSHOP

Your computer probably came with a specific amount of RAM. What if you wanted to upgrade to more RAM? How would you go about finding RAM to purchase? How much RAM is enough? Is there too much RAM? Figure D-33 shows the Web page for Kingston Technology, a leading distributor and manufacturer of computer memory. You can use the Internet for researching and buying RAM. You will research RAM and determine the best buy for your system.

FIGURE D-33

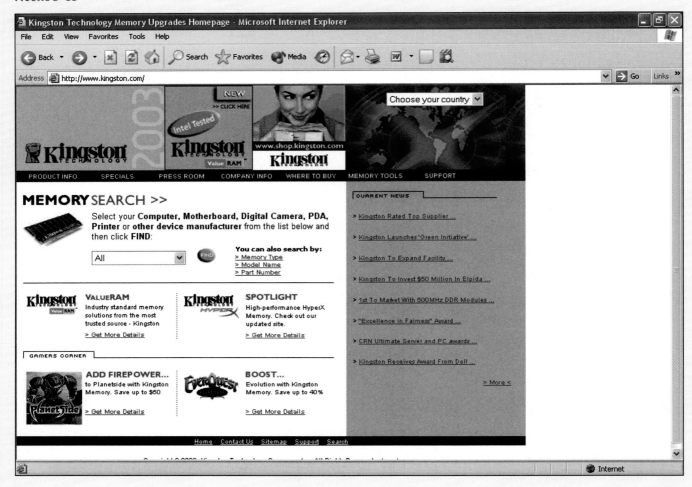

1. Use a search engine to search on RAM. What kinds of Web sites did you find? Did you need to be more specific in your search to find the RAM for your computer?

2. Complete a search on DRAM. Was this more successful in finding Web sites that would sell you chips to update the memory capacity on your computer?

3. Go to www.kingston.com, the page shown in Figure D-33. See if you can find the best memory for upgrading your system.

4. Write a brief summary of your findings.

5. Click the links for different types of memory. Read the pages and write a brief summary of what you read for two of the links.

Networks and the Internet

OBJECTIVES

Although network technology continues to evolve, it is based on a set of fairly stable concepts. This unit discusses network building blocks and evolving network technologies. The unit discusses not only the technology of simple local area networks (LANs) but also the technology behind a complex network—the Internet. You will learn about the devices, connections, and protocols that make it possible to communicate over networks. The unit compares and contrasts various options for accessing the Internet and concludes with a Tech Talk on installing and using a LAN. You have the opportunity to look at computers in the context of education. The Issue discusses Wi-Fi technology and how it enables Internet access.

Introducing networks

A **communications network** is the combination of hardware, software, and connecting links that transport data. In 1948, Claude Shannon, an engineer at the prestigious Bell Labs, published an article that described a communications system model. In this model, data from a source is "encoded," or changed from one form to another, and sent over a communications channel to its destination, where it is decoded. According to Shannon, effective communication depends on the efficiency of the coding process and the channel's resistance to interference, called noise. Figure E-1 illustrates Shannon's communications system model.

DETAILS

● In the early years of the personal computer's popularity, networks were scarce. Most personal computers functioned as standalone units, and computing was essentially a solitary activity in which one person interacted with a limited set of software tools, such as a word processor, spreadsheet, or database. Some computer engineers, however, had the foresight to anticipate that personal computers could be networked to provide advantages not available with standalone computers. One of the most significant network ideas was conceived by Bob Metcalfe in 1976. His plan for transporting data between computers, shown in Figure E-2, has become a key element in just about every computer network, including the Internet.

● Today, the pervasiveness of networks has dramatically changed the face of computing by offering **shared resources**—hardware, software, and data made available for authorized network users to access.

● Networks offer the following advantages:

Sharing networked hardware can:

- Reduce costs. Networked peripheral devices can be accessed by any authorized network users. For example, a single expensive color printer, scanner, or plotter can be purchased and attached to a network, instead of the expensive alternative of purchasing that same device for each computer.

- Provide access to a wide range of services. A network can allow multiple users to access Internet services through a single Internet connection.

Sharing networked software can:

- Reduce costs. Software site licenses for network use are typically less expensive than purchasing single-user versions of a product for each network user. Purchasing and installing a single software copy for an entire network might be technically possible, but it is typically not allowed under the terms of a single-user license agreement.

- Facilitate sharing data. Networks can provide authorized users with access to data stored on network servers or workstations.

- Enable people to work together. Using groupware and other specialized network application software, several people can work together on a single document, communicate via e-mail and instant messaging, and participate in on-line conferences and Webcasts—all over the network.

● Two disadvantages of networks are:

- Vulnerability to unauthorized access. Whereas a standalone computer is vulnerable to on-premises theft or access, network computers are vulnerable to unauthorized access from many sources and locations. Through unauthorized use of a network workstation, intruders can access data stored on the network server or other workstations. Networks connected to the Internet are vulnerable to intrusions from remote computers in distant states, provinces, or countries. Wireless networks can be tapped from a specially equipped "snooping" computer, usually located in a car that's being driven by a hacker.

- Susceptibility to malicious code. Whereas the most prevalent threat to standalone computers is disk-borne viruses, networks are susceptible to an ever-increasing number of worms, Trojan horses, and other threats.

● Most computer owners are enthusiastic about the benefits provided by networks and believe that those benefits outweigh the risks of intrusions and viruses—especially if their computers can be protected. You'll learn more about network security threats and countermeasures in Unit F.

● In the past, a great diversity of network technologies existed as engineers pioneered new ideas to make data transport faster, more efficient, and more secure. Today, networks are becoming more standardized, but some diversity remains necessary to accommodate networking environments that range from simple household networks to complex global banking networks.

FIGURE E-1: Claude Shannon's communications system model

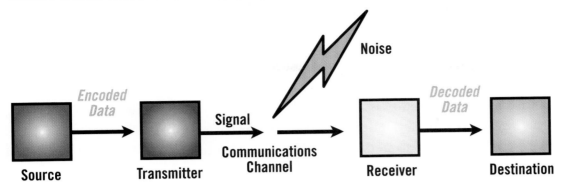

▲ A communications system sends information from a source to a destination; the path between the source and destination might appear to be straight as in the diagram, but the data may pass through several devices, which convert it to electrical, sound, light, or radio signals; beam it up to satellites; route it along the least congested links; or clean up parts of the signal that have been distorted by noise

FIGURE E-2: Bob Metcalfe's diagram of "Ethernet"

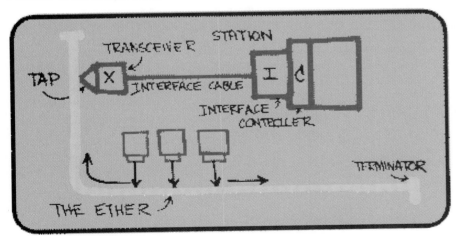

◄ In 1976, Bob Metcalfe drew this diagram of a network technology, which he called "Ethernet."

Classifying networks

Networks exist in many variations. Networks can be categorized by distinguishing characteristics, such as their geographical structure, organizational structure, topology, protocols, and so forth. In casual conversation, a network is often referred to by only one of the characteristics, even though that reference does not provide a complete description of the network and all the technologies it uses. Network classifications are described in Table E-1 and discussed in the next few lessons.

DETAILS

○ Geographical structure: From a geographic perspective, networks can be classified as PANs, LANs, MANs, and WANs.

- A **PAN (personal area network)** is a term sometimes used to refer to the interconnection of personal digital devices within a range of about 30 feet (10 meters) and without the use of wires or cables. For example, a PAN could be used to wirelessly transmit data from a notebook computer to a PDA or portable printer.

- A **LAN (local area network)** is a data communications network that typically connects personal computers within a very limited geographical area—usually a single building. LANs use a variety of wired and wireless technologies, standards, and protocols. School computer labs and home networks are examples of LANs.

- A **MAN (metropolitan area network)** is a public high-speed network capable of voice and data transmission within a range of about 50 miles (80km). Examples of MANs that provide data transport services include local ISPs, cable television companies, and local telephone companies.

- A **WAN (wide area network)** covers a large geographical area and typically consists of several smaller networks, which might use different computer platforms and network technologies. The **Internet** is the world's largest WAN. Networks for nationwide banks and multilocation "superstores" can be classified as WANs.

○ Organizational structure: Networks have an organizational structure that provides a conceptual model of the way data is stored and transported. The two most prevalent network organizational structures are client/server and peer-to-peer.

- **Client/server network** contains one or more computers configured with server software and other computers configured with client software that access the servers. The server provides a centralized repository for data and a transfer point through which data traffic flows. Web sites, retail point-of-sale networks, school registration systems, online databases, and Internet-based multiplayer games typically use a client/server organizational structure.

- **Peer-to-peer network (P2P)** treats every computer as an "equal" so that workstations can store network data, which can be transported directly to other workstations without passing through a central server. P2P technology forms the basis for file-sharing networks, such as Microsoft Networking provided with Windows. Figure E-3 contrasts the client/server structure with the peer-to-peer structure.

○ Localized networks typically include a small number of computers, which can be connected using basic equipment. As the area of network coverage expands, the number of workstations grows, specialized devices are sometimes required to boost signals, and the diversity of devices requires sophisticated management tools and strategies.

Licensing software for use on a network

Even though an application might run on a LAN, it is still subject to copyright law and the terms of the license agreement. A **single-user license** agreement typically allows one copy of the software to be in use at a time. A **multiple-user license** allows more than one person to use a particular software package. Multiple-user licenses are generally priced per user, but the price for each user is typically less than the price of a single-user license. A **concurrent-user license** allows a certain number of copies of the software to be used at the same time. This type of license is popular for application software that might be accessed throughout the day by 100 or more different people, but when no more than, for instance, 20 copies would be in use at any one time. A **site license** generally allows software to be used on any and all computers at a specific location, such as within a corporate office or on a university campus.

TABLE E-1: Network classifications

CATEGORY	DESCRIPTION	EXAMPLES
Geographical structure	The area in which network devices are located	PAN, LAN, MAN, WAN
Organizational structure	The hierarchy of devices connected to a network	Client/server, peer-to-peer
Physical topology	The physical layout and relationship between network devices	Star, bus, ring, mesh, tree
Network links	The technologies for cables and signals that carry data	Twisted-pair cable, coaxial cable, fiber-optic cable, RF signals, microwaves, infrared light, power line, phone line
Bandwidth	The capacity of a network for carrying data	Broadband, narrowband
Communications protocols	The transportation standards that provide an orderly way to package data and make sure data is not corrupted in transit	TCP/IP, SPX/IPX (Novell networks), NetBEUI/NetBIOS (Microsoft Networking), AppleTalk

FIGURE E-3: Comparing client/server and peer-to-peer networks

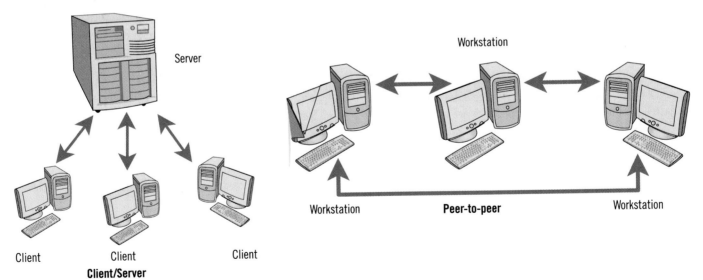

Server

Client   Client   Client

Client/Server

Workstation

Workstation   **Peer-to-peer**   Workstation

▲ In a client/server network, a server is the most important resource

▲ In a peer-to-peer network, every computer is treated as an equal resource

Understanding network topology

The physical arrangement of devices, wires, and cables on a network is called its **physical topology**. Figure E-4 illustrates the five common network topologies: star, ring, bus, mesh, and tree—each named for its inherent shape.

DETAILS

- A network arranged as a **star topology** features a central connection point for all workstations and peripherals. Many home networks are arranged in a star topology. The advantage of this topology is that any link can fail without affecting the rest of the network. Its primary disadvantage is that it requires quite a bit of cable to link all the devices—a disadvantage that disappears with wireless networks. Although the failure of a link does not affect the rest of the network, you can see from Figure E-4 that a device with a failed link would be cut off from the network; it would be unable to communicate with other devices on the network or to use the network resources.

- A **ring topology** connects all devices in a circle, with each device having exactly two neighbors. Data is transmitted from one device to another around the ring. This topology minimizes cabling, but failure of any one device can take down the entire network. Ring topologies, once championed by IBM, are infrequently used in today's networks.

- A **bus topology** uses a common backbone to connect all network devices. The backbone functions as a shared communication link, which carries network data. The backbone stops at each end of the network with a special device called a "terminator." Bus networks work best with a limited number of devices. Bus networks with more than a few dozen computers are likely to perform poorly, and if the backbone cable fails, the entire network becomes unusable.

- A **mesh topology** connects each network device to many other network devices. Data traveling on a mesh network can take any of several possible paths from its source to its destination. These redundant data pathways make a mesh network very robust. Even if several links fail, data can follow alternative functioning links to reach its destination—an advantage over networks arranged in a star topology.

- A **tree topology** is essentially a blend of star and bus networks. Multiple star networks are connected to form a bus configuration by a backbone. Tree topologies offer excellent flexibility for expansion—for example, a single link to the backbone can add an entire group of star-configured devices. Most of today's school and business networks are based on tree topologies.

- Each connection point on a network is referred to as a **node**. The pathways shown between nodes can be linked by physical cables or wireless signals. A network node typically contains one of the following:

  - **Server**: A computer responsible for storing data and programs.
  - **Workstation**: A personal computer connected to a network.
  - **Networked peripheral**: A device, such as a printer or scanner, directly connected to a network rather than to a workstation.
  - **Network device**: An electronic device that broadcasts network data, boosts signals, or routes data to its destination.

How to interconnect various networks

Two similar networks can be connected by a device called a **bridge**, which simply transfers data without regard to its format. Networks that use different topologies and technologies can be interconnected by using gateways. **Gateway** is a generic term for any device or software used to join two dissimilar networks by converting data sent from one network into a format compatible to the receiving network. A gateway can be implemented completely in software, completely in hardware, or as a combination of the two. The most commonly used gateway is a **router**, an electronic device that joins two or more networks. A router acts as one network's point of presence to another network. It shuttles data from one network to another network. It also accepts incoming data transmissions and distributes them to the devices attached to the local area network. A router typically connects a LAN to a WAN and filters transmissions between them. The router forwards messages destined for other networks (orange), but keeps local messages (green) within the network as shown in Figure E-5.

FIGURE E-4: Network topologies

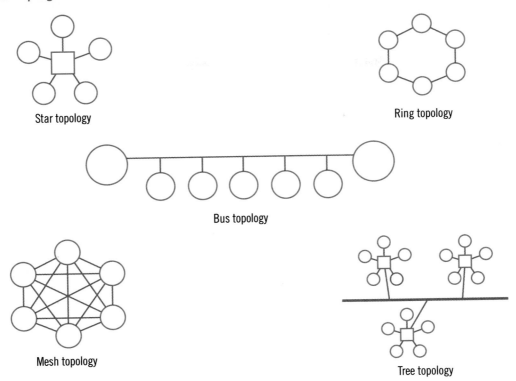

Star topology

Ring topology

Bus topology

Mesh topology

Tree topology

FIGURE E-5: What a router does

▶ A router typically connects a LAN to a WAN and filters transmissions between them

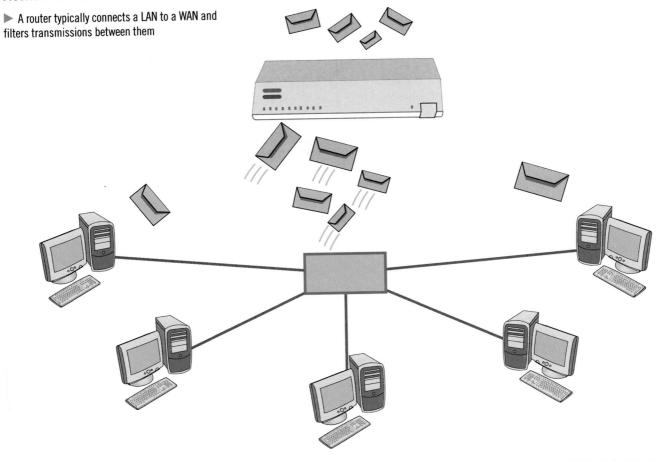

Exploring network hardware

Even though networks come in many sizes and configurations, they all require some basic network hardware components. Figure E-6 provides an overview of network hardware.

DETAILS

- Computers perform different functions on a network. For example, a computer might be a network server, a host computer, a workstation, or a client. A **server** refers to a computer connected to a network that "serves" or distributes resources to network users. A server contains the software to manage and process files for other network nodes. E-mail servers, communications servers, file servers, and Web servers are some of the most common servers on today's networks. A **host computer**, or "host," usually refers to any computer that provides services to network users. The terms "host" and "server" are often used interchangeably, but "host" is more commonly used in the context of the Internet. "Server" is used both in the context of the Internet and LANs.

  A **workstation** usually refers to a personal computer connected to a network. The term **client** usually refers to software on a computer that allows a user to access the services of a server. The terms client and workstation are sometimes used interchangeably, but client is more commonly used in the context of a personal computer that is connected to the Internet.

- A **network interface card (NIC)** is a small circuit board that converts the digital signals from a computer into signals that can travel over a network. Figure E-7 shows a NIC for a desktop computer that plugs into an expansion slot on the motherboard. An **Ethernet card** is a type of network interface card (NIC), or "network adapter," designed to support Ethernet protocols. You will learn about Ethernet protocols in a later lesson. Many desktop, notebook, and tablet computers include a preinstalled Ethernet card. Figure E-8 shows examples of Ethernet NICs. NICs send data to and from network devices such as workstations or printers over the network usually using cables.

  Instead of cables, a wireless network sends and receives data using a **transceiver** (a combination transmitter and receiver) that is equipped with an antenna. On a strictly wireless network, every network workstation, peripheral device, and hub must be equipped with a transceiver, which sends and receives data. See Figure E-9.

- A variety of devices connect computers over a network, either individually or in combination. These devices include modems, hubs, routers, gateways, and repeaters. A **modem** is a network device connected to a computer that converts the digital signals from a computer into signals that can travel over a network, such as the telephone system or the Internet.

  A **hub** is a network device that connects several nodes of a local area network. All of the devices that attach to a hub are part of the same local area network. Multiple hubs can be linked to expand a local area network. Today, most hubs also serve as routers and are available in many configurations offering various numbers of ports. A hub should have enough ports to accommodate the number of devices you plan to connect to the network. A five-port or an eight-port hub is typical for home networks. A 12-port hub, such as the one in Figure E-10, might be used in a small business. To connect more than one local area network or to connect a local area network to the Internet, an additional device, such as a router or a gateway, is necessary.

  A **router** is a network device that is connected to at least two networks. Routers make decisions about the best route for data based on the data's destination and the state of the available network links. A **gateway** is a network device that serves as an entrance to another network. A **repeater** is a network device that amplifies and regenerates signals so that they can retain the necessary strength to reach their destinations.

- Every node on a network, whether it is a computer or a network device, has an address. Every packet of data that travels over a network also has an address, which helps to route a packet to its destination, much like the address on a letter. A **physical address** is built into the circuitry of most network devices at the time they are manufactured. A device's physical address, however, is not always in a format that can be used by a particular network. If that is the case, a network device is assigned a **logical address**. Network software keeps track of which physical address corresponds to each logical address.

FIGURE E-6: Network hardware

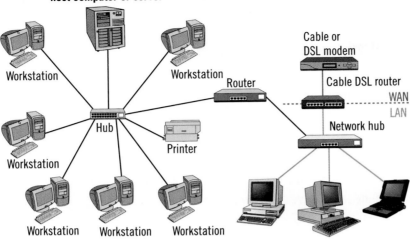

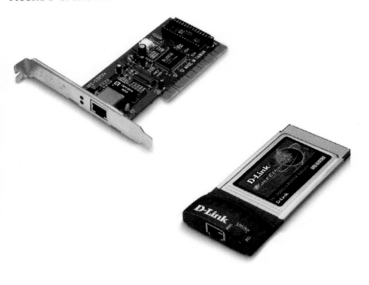

FIGURE E-7: Network interface card

▲ A desktop network interface card is an expansion card that can be used to connect a computer to a network using a cable

FIGURE E-8: Ethernet cards

FIGURE E-9: Wireless devices

Wireless network card
for workstation

Wireless hub

FIGURE E-10: Ethernet hub

Exploring communications channels

A **communications channel**, or "link," is a physical path or a frequency for a signal transmission. Data in a **wired network** travels from one device to another over cables. Data in a **wireless network** travels through the air, eliminating the need for cables. Computer networks use a variety of links to carry data between nodes; the most common being wired communications channels: twisted-pair cable, coaxial cable, and fiber-optic cable. Wireless communications channels include radio waves, microwaves, satellites, infrared light, and laser beams.

Info Web

FIBER OPTICS

DETAILS

Many networks use **twisted-pair cables** for data communications. See Figure E-11. Twisted-pair cables are similar to the telephone wiring in a house and can be shielded or unshielded. **STP (shielded twisted pair)** encases its twisted pairs with a foil shield, which reduces signal noise that might interfere with data transmission. **UTP (unshielded twisted pair)** contains no shielding and is less expensive than shielded cable but it is more susceptible to noise. UTP is commonly used for small networks.

Coaxial cable, shown in Figure E-12, is often called coax cable or co-ax. It is the cable of choice for cable television because its high capacity allows it to carry signals for more than 100 television channels and cable modem signals simultaneously.

Fiber-optic cable, shown in Figure E-13, is a bundle of extremely thin tubes of glass. Each tube, called an optical fiber, is much thinner than a human hair. Fiber-optic cables do not conduct or transmit electrical signals; instead, miniature lasers convert data into pulses of light that flash through the cables. Fiber-optic cables are an essential part of the Internet backbone.

In addition to wired communication channels, computer data can also travel via wireless communications channels. **RF signals (radio frequency signals)**, commonly called radio waves, are sent and received by a transceiver, which is equipped with an antenna. RF signals provide data transport for small home networks, campus networks, and business networks.

Microwaves provide another option for transporting data over wireless communications channels. Microwaves can be aimed in a single direction, have more carrying capacity than radio waves, and work best when a clear path exists between the transmitter and receiver. Microwaves cannot penetrate metal objects. Microwave installations typically provide data transport for large corporate networks and form part of the Internet backbone.

Radio and microwave transmissions cannot bend around the surface of the earth, so earth-orbiting **communications satellites** play an important role in long-distance communications. A signal can be relayed from a ground station to a communications satellite. A **transponder** on the satellite receives, amplifies, and retransmits the signal to a ground station on earth. Satellite transmissions are a key technology for the Internet backbone and provide a way for individuals to connect personal computers to the Internet.

Other wireless communications channels include infrared light, laser light, and airborne data transmission. **Infrared light** can carry data signals but only for short distances and with a clear line of sight. At the present time, its most practical use is for transmission of data between a notebook computer and a printer or between a PDA and a desktop computer, and in remote controls to change television channels. **Laser light** can stay focused over a larger distance but requires a clear line of sight; no trees, snow, fog, or rain. Airborne data transmission is currently in the experimental stage.

Defining broadband and narrowband

Bandwidth is the transmission capacity of a communications channel. The bandwidth of a digital channel is usually measured in bits per second (bps). A high-bandwidth communications channel can carry more data than a low-bandwidth channel. High-bandwidth communications systems, such as cable TV or DSL lines, are sometimes referred to as **broadband**; systems with less capacity, such as the telephone system, are referred to as **narrowband**. A dial-up connection, which allows speeds up to 56 Kbps, is an example of narrowband. A typical LAN, such as a college computer lab, might provide 100 Mbps bandwidth and is an example of broadband.

FIGURE E-11: Twisted-pair cable

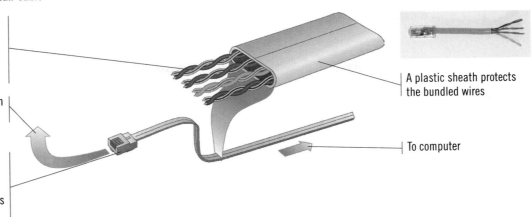

Each of the four pairs of copper wires is independently insulated and then twisted around each other

To communications system

Twisted-pair cables typically terminate with plastic RJ-11 plugs for telephones or RJ-45 plugs for computer networks

A plastic sheath protects the bundled wires

To computer

FIGURE E-12: Coaxial cable

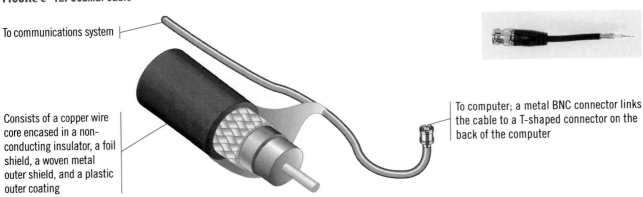

To communications system

Consists of a copper wire core encased in a non-conducting insulator, a foil shield, a woven metal outer shield, and a plastic outer coating

To computer; a metal BNC connector links the cable to a T-shaped connector on the back of the computer

FIGURE E-13: Fiber-optic cable

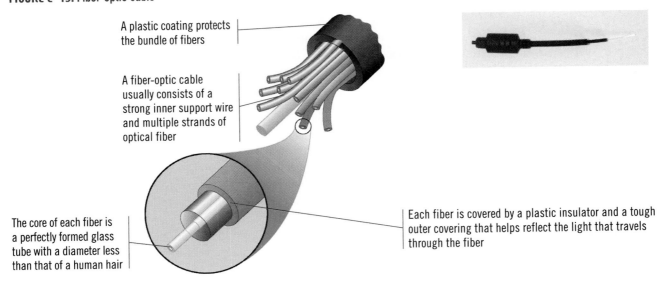

A plastic coating protects the bundle of fibers

A fiber-optic cable usually consists of a strong inner support wire and multiple strands of optical fiber

The core of each fiber is a perfectly formed glass tube with a diameter less than that of a human hair

Each fiber is covered by a plastic insulator and a tough outer covering that helps reflect the light that travels through the fiber

Transporting data

The way data is transported over a network depends on the network topology, the packet switching technology, and protocols. Topology is the configuration of a network. **Protocols** are rules that ensure the orderly and accurate transmission and reception of data. Protocols start and end transmission, recognize errors, send data at the appropriate speed, and identify the correct senders and recipients. Figure E-14 describes some common communications protocols. Packet switching technology determines how data is broken up so that it can be transported over a network.

DETAILS

- Protocols perform several important network functions, including: dividing messages into packets, affixing addresses to packets, initiating transmission, regulating the flow of data, checking for transmission errors, and acknowledging receipt of transmitted data.

- When you send a file or an e-mail message over a network, the file is actually broken up into small pieces called packets. A **packet** is a "parcel" of data that is sent across a computer network. See Figure E-15.

- The technology of dividing a message into several packets that can be routed independently to their destination to avoid out-of-service or congested links is called **packet switching**. Packet switching uses available bandwidth efficiently because packets from many different messages can share a single communications channel, or "circuit." Packets are shipped over the circuit on a "first come, first served" basis. If some packets from a message are not available, the system does not need to wait for them. Instead, the system moves on to send packets from other messages, resulting in a steady stream of data.

- Some communications networks, such as the telephone system, use a technology called **circuit switching**, which essentially establishes a dedicated, private link between one telephone and another for the duration of a call. Packet switching technology is a more efficient alternative to circuit switching. See Figure E-16. Today, packet switching is the technology used for virtually every computer network.

- The best-known protocol is TCP/IP—popular because it is the protocol that regulates Internet data transport. **TCP/IP** is a suite of protocols that includes TCP, IP, and others. **TCP (Transmission Control Protocol)** breaks a message or file into packets. **IP (Internet Protocol)** is responsible for addressing packets so that they can be routed to their destinations. TCP/IP is also used on LANs and WANs. A local area network that uses TCP/IP is called an **intranet**. Intranets are popular with businesses that want to store information as Web pages but not provide them for public access. An intranet that provides private, external access is called an **extranet**.

- There are several characteristics of communications protocols that decide the direction of the flow of data: **Simplex**, in which a signal travels in only one direction (for example, a TV set or a clock radio); **Half duplex**, in which it is possible to send and receive data, but not at the same time (for example, a walkie-talkie); and **Full duplex**, in which it is possible to send and receive at the same time over the same channel (for example, a telephone conversation).

- Protocols help two network devices negotiate and establish communications through a process called **handshaking**. The transmitting device sends a signal and waits for a signal from the receiving device. The two devices then negotiate a transmission speed that both can handle.

- Protocols also decide on how to coordinate the transmission. Using a **synchronous protocol**, the sender's signals and the receiver's signals are synchronized by a signal called a clock. The transmitting computer sends data at a fixed clock rate, and the receiving computer expects the incoming data at the same fixed rate. The rules for **asynchronous protocol** require the transmitting computer to send a start bit that indicates the beginning of a packet. Data is then transmitted as a series of bytes; the number of bytes that can be sent in each series is specified by the protocol. A stop bit marks the end of the data. Most data communications systems implement asynchronous protocol.

- Computers use error-checking protocols to ensure accurate delivery of data. Internet protocols use a simple **checksum**—a number that represents the total number of bits being sent. That number is affixed to each packet. As data arrives, a second checksum is calculated and compared to the original. If the checksums are not the same, the receiving device assumes that data has been corrupted and requests retransmission. Some LANs use an alternative error-checking calculation called a **cyclic redundancy check**.

FIGURE E-14: Communications protocols

Protocol	Main use
TCP/IP	Internet
NetBIOS/ NetBEUI	Microsoft networks
AppleTalk	Macintosh networks
IPX/SPX	Novell networks

FIGURE E-15: Messages are divided into packets

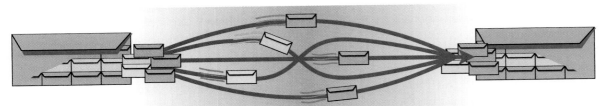

▲ Each packet contains the address of its sender, the destination address, a sequence number, and some data; dividing messages into equal-size packets makes them easier to handle than an assortment of different-sized files

▲ When a packet reaches an intersection in the network's communications channels, a router examines the packet's address; the router checks the address in a routing table and then sends the packet along the appropriate link toward its destination

▲ As packets arrive at their destination, they are reassembled into a replica of the original file

FIGURE E-16: Packet switching compared to circuit switching

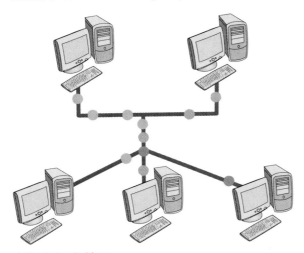

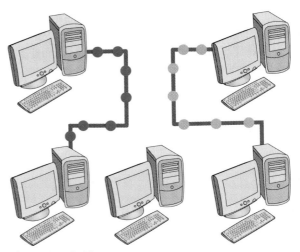

▲ **Packet switching**
Divides a message into several packets that can be routed independently to their destinations

▲ **Circuit switching**
Provides callers with a direct pipeline over which streams of voice data can flow; circuit switching is inefficient, for example, when someone is "on hold," no communication is taking place—because the circuit is reserved and cannot be used for other communications

Exploring LAN standards

LAN technologies are standardized by the Institute of Electrical and Electronics Engineers (IEEE) *Project 802 – Local Network Standards*. IEEE standards are available for most types of commercial networks. An IEEE designation number, such as IEEE 802.3, is sometimes used to refer to a network standard. IEEE designation numbers help identify compatible network technologies. Historically, several LAN standards have experienced popularity, including ARCnet, Token Ring, FDDI, and Ethernet.

Info Web
ETHERNET

DETAILS

● Introduced in 1977, **ARCnet (Attached Resource Computer network)** is one of the oldest, simplest, and least expensive LAN technologies. A special advantage of ARCnet permits twisted-pair, coax, and fiber-optic cables to be mixed on the same network to connect up to 255 workstations. Although no longer popular for LANs, ARCnet technology is now deployed for applications such as industrial control, building automation, transportation, robotics, and casino gaming.

● A **Token Ring network**, defined by the IEEE 802.5 standard, passes data around a ring topology using a signal called a "token" to control the flow of data. See Figure E-17. The original Token Ring standard carried data at 4 Mbps. In 1989, the speed was increased to 16 Mbps. By 1999, new network technologies offered faster and less expensive solutions than Token Ring. Token Ring technology, while still used with networks that are operational today, is not the technology of choice when new networks are established.

● **FDDI (Fiber Distributed Data Interconnect)** offers 100 Mbps speeds over fiber-optic cables. As defined by the IEEE 802.8 standards, an FDDI network supports up to 500 devices, cabled as a dual ring—the second ring provides redundancy in case the first ring fails. Like Token Ring networks, FDDI uses a token to control data transmission, as shown in Figure E-18.

● In 1980, **Ethernet** became commercially available. As defined by IEEE 802.3, Ethernet simultaneously broadcasts data packets to all network devices. A packet is accepted only by the device to which it is addressed. An integral part of Ethernet technology relies on **CSMA/CD protocol (Carrier Sense Multiple Access with Collision Detection)**. CSMA/CD takes care of situations in which two network devices attempt to transmit packets at the same time. See Figure E-19. A "collision" occurs as two signals travel over the network. CSMA/CD protocol detects the collision, deletes the colliding signals, and resets the network.

The original Ethernet standard carried data over a coaxial cable bus topology at 10 Mbps. Today, the term "Ethernet" refers to a family of LAN technologies that offer various data transmission rates over fiber-optic and twisted-pair cables arranged in a bus or star topology. Ethernet variations are 10BaseT Ethernet, Fast Ethernet, Gigabit Ethernet, and 10 Gig Ethernet IE. Fast Ethernet is currently the most popular for small to medium LANs, such as you might find in homes and small businesses.

Large Ethernet networks typically connect many workstations. Despite challenges from other technologies, Ethernet has emerged as the leading LAN technology. Ethernet's success is attributable to several factors: Ethernet networks are easy to understand, implement, manage, and maintain. As a nonproprietary technology, Ethernet equipment is available from a variety of vendors, and market competition keeps prices low. Current Ethernet standards allow extensive flexibility in network topology to meet the needs of small and large installations.

What equipment is required for a home Ethernet?

A basic Ethernet network requires an Ethernet card in each workstation and any peripheral device to be attached directly to the network. An Ethernet card is a type of network interface card (NIC) designed to support Ethernet protocols. A home Ethernet network also requires some type of link between network nodes—typically CAT 5 twisted-pair cable. These cables link workstations and peripherals to a central connection point called an Ethernet hub. Today, most Ethernet hubs also serve as routers. Ethernet hubs are available in many configurations offering various numbers of ports.

FIGURE E-17: How Token Ring networks work

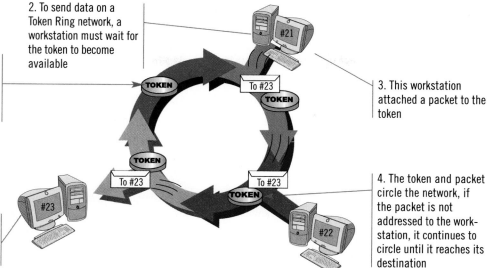

1. A signal called a token speeds over the network; the token is available when not escorting a packet

2. To send data on a Token Ring network, a workstation must wait for the token to become available

3. This workstation attached a packet to the token

4. The token and packet circle the network, if the packet is not addressed to the workstation, it continues to circle until it reaches its destination

5. This workstation sees its address on the packet and detaches the packet from the token

FIGURE E-18: How FDDI networks work

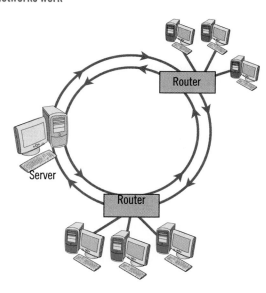

◀ FDDI networks connect routers and servers using a double ring topology; workstations connect to a router rather than to the ring

FIGURE E-19: How Ethernet's CSMA/CD works to avoid collisions

▶ On an Ethernet network, data travels on a first come first served basis; if two workstations attempt to send data at the same time, a collision occurs and that data must be resent

Data is sent from this workstation

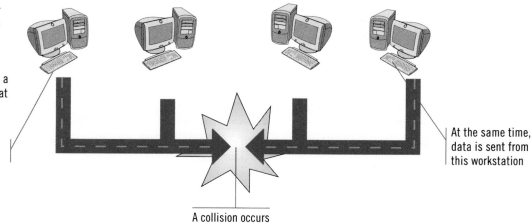

At the same time, data is sent from this workstation

A collision occurs

Exploring wireless

Wi-Fi (Wireless Fidelity) refers to a set of wireless networking technologies defined by IEEE 802.11 standards that are compatible with Ethernet. Wi-Fi is popular because of the absence of wires and cables running through walls and between floors. Wireless networks are desirable for notebook and tablet computers that don't otherwise need to be tethered to electrical outlets.

DETAILS

- When compared to wired networks, Wi-Fi has three disadvantages: speed (slow transmission rates), distance (susceptibility to interference), and lack of security.

  - Speed: A **Wi-Fi network** transmits data as radio waves over predefined frequencies, much like cordless telephones. Wi-Fi networks operate at 2.4 or 5 GHz. Wi-Fi standards are listed in Table E-2. The fastest Wi-Fi standards operate at a maximum speed of 54 Kbps, but actual throughput is about half the maximum speed.

  - Distance: In a typical office environment, Wi-Fi's range varies from 25 to 150 feet, although considerably more range is possible with additional equipment. Thick cement walls, steel beams, and other environmental obstacles can, however, drastically reduce this range to the point that signals cannot be reliably transmitted. Wi-Fi signals can also be disrupted by interference from electronic devices operating at the same frequency, such as 2.4 GHz cordless telephones.

  - Security: Wi-Fi signals that travel through the air are easy to intercept by any suitably equipped receiving device within the network's range of service. A practice called **war driving** or **LAN-jacking** occurs when hackers cruise around with a Wi-Fi-equipped notebook computer set up to search for Wi-Fi signals coming from home and corporate Wi-Fi networks. War drivers can access and use unsecured Wi-Fi networks to hack into files and gain unauthorized access to larger, wired networks.

- Encrypting transmitted data using **WEP (Wired Equivalent Privacy)** is an essential step in making data useless to intruders. The WEP algorithm has been broken, however, so although it is adequate for a typical home network, corporations must establish additional security measures.

- As with a wired Ethernet network, every workstation and network peripheral requires a network interface card. Figure E-20 illustrates various Wi-Fi equipment. A **Wi-Fi card** includes a transceiver and an antenna. A **wireless access point** provides a central point for data transmitted over a wireless network by broadcasting signals to any devices with compatible Wi-Fi cards. This is the same function as a hub or router in a wired Ethernet network. Many wireless access points also include a port for connecting to a wired Ethernet network or cable modem, allowing the network to extend beyond the set of workstations and peripherals on the wireless network.

- **Bluetooth** is a short-range wireless network technology that's designed to make its own connections between electronic devices, without wires, cables or any direct action from a user. Unlike Wi-Fi, Bluetooth is not typically used to connect a collection of workstations. Instead, Bluetooth connectivity replaces the short cables that would otherwise tether a mouse, keyboard, or printer to a computer. Bluetooth can also be used to link devices in a PAN, connect home entertainment system components, and to synchronize PDAs with desktop base stations.

  Bluetooth is built into some peripheral devices and can be added to personal computers using a variety of add-on cards. Bluetooth-enabled devices automatically find each other and strike up a conversation without any user input at all. Bluetooth operates at the same 2.4 GHz frequency as Wi-Fi but offers peak transmission rates of only 1 Mbps over a range of about 30 feet.

- Despite security concerns and other potential drawbacks, Wi-Fi is becoming increasingly popular in corporate, school, and home networks. Table E-3 summarizes network technologies, including Wi-Fi.

TABLE E-2: Wi-Fi standards

IEEE DESIGNATION	FREQUENCY	SPEED	RANGE	PROS/CONS
IEEE 802.11b	2.4 GHz	11 Mbps	100–150 feet	Original standard
IEEE 802.11a	5 GHz	54 Mbps	25–75 feet	Not compatible with 802.11b
IEEE 802.11g	2.4 GHz	54 Mbps	100–150 feet	Faster than, but compatible with, 802.11b

FIGURE E-20: Wi-Fi cards

▲ Wi-Fi cards for notebook or tablet computers plug into a PCMCIA slot

▲ Wi-Fi capability can be added to a desktop computer as a Wi-Fi card that fits into a system unit slot with the antenna protruding out of the back or as a small box that connects to a USB port

▲ A wireless adapter converts a standard Ethernet port into a wireless port

▲ A Wi-Fi access point provides a central point for data transmitted over a wireless network

TABLE E-3: Comparison of network technologies

NETWORK TYPE	ADVANTAGES	DISADVANTAGES	SPEED	
Ethernet	Inexpensive; reliable; standard technology; fast	Unsightly cables; might require running cables through walls	10 Mbps, 100 Mbps, 1 Gbps, 10 Gbps	
Wi-Fi	No cables required	Each device requires a transceiver, which adds costs; signals can be intercepted; susceptible to interference	11 Mbps 54 Mbps	(802.11b) (802.11a and 802.11g)
Bluetooth	Inexpensive; reliable; built into many popular devices	Slow; limited range; little security	700 Kbps	
HomePLC	No cables required; uses any standard electrical outlet	Susceptible to electrical interference; very slow	2 Mbps	
HomePNA	No cables required; uses existing telephone wiring	Requires telephone jacks near computers; slow transmission speed	10 Mbps	

What's HomePNA? What's HomePLC?

A **HomePNA** network utilizes existing telephone wiring to connect network devices. The HomePNA network standard uses a special NIC and cable to connect each computer to a standard telephone wall jack. The NICs contain circuitry that eliminates the need for hubs. When your computer is connected to a HomePNA network, you can typically use the phone to make a call and send information over the network at the same time because the network frequency is different from the voice frequency. You cannot, however, make a voice call while a dial-up Internet connection is active.

A **HomePLC** network, or "power line network," uses a special NIC to connect a computer to a standard electrical outlet. Data, transmitted as low-frequency radio waves, travels along the electrical wiring until it reaches another network device. Unfortunately, power line fluctuations caused by fluorescent lights, baby monitors, dimmer switches, amateur band radios, air-conditioning units, or other major appliances can disrupt the signal and cause momentary loss of network connections.

Understanding Internet connections

Even people who haven't used the Internet know about it from watching the news, reading magazines, and watching movies. With more than 200 million nodes and 500 million users, the Internet is huge. Although exact figures cannot be determined, it is estimated that Internet traffic exceeds 100 terabytes each week—about 100 trillion bytes. That's approximately ten times the amount of data stored in the entire printed collection of the U.S. Library of Congress. The Internet lets you browse Web sites, shop at the Net mall, send e-mail, and chat online. How does this one network provide so much information to so many people?

DETAILS

● The Internet is not "owned" or operated by any single corporation or government. It is a data communications network that grew over time as networks connected to other networks. The Internet backbone provides the main high-speed routes for data traffic consisting of high-speed fiber-optic links connecting high-capacity routers that direct network traffic. Backbone links and routers are maintained by **Network Service Providers (NSPs)**, such as AT&T, MCI, Qwest, Sprint, and UUNET. NSP equipment and links are tied together by network access points (NAPs), so that, for example, data that begins its journey on an AT&T link can cross over to a Sprint link, if necessary, to reach its destination.

● To access the Internet, you do not typically connect your computer directly to the Internet backbone. Instead, you connect to an ISP that in turn connects to the backbone. An **ISP (Internet Service Provider)** operates network devices that handle the physical aspects of transmitting and receiving data from your computer. Your computer connects to the Internet in one of two ways (see Figure E-21). It can link directly to an ISP connection, such as voiceband modem, cable modem, direct satellite service, or DSL. Or, if your computer is part of a LAN, an Internet connection can be provided by a LAN link.

● An ISP operates network devices that handle the physical aspects of transmitting and receiving data from your computer. For example, an ISP that offers telephone modem connections must maintain a bank of modems that answer when your computer dials the ISP's access number. Many ISPs operate e-mail servers to handle incoming and outgoing mail for their subscribers and Web servers for subscriber Web sites. ISPs can also maintain servers for chat groups, instant messaging, music file sharing,

FTP, and other file transfer services. Customers arrange for service for which they pay an installation charge and a monthly fee. Figure E-22 illustrates the equipment at a typical ISP.

● The Internet and many other networks use the TCP/IP suite of protocols, which is responsible for addressing packets so that they can be routed to their destination. TCP/IP provides a standard that is free, public, and fairly easy to implement. TCP/IP defines data transport on the Internet. In addition to TCP/IP, several other protocols are used on the Internet. Table E-4 briefly describes some of them.

● Internet pathways can be checked to be sure that they are open to Internet traffic. A software utility called **Ping (Packet Internet Groper)** sends a signal to a specific Internet address and waits for a reply. If a reply arrives, Ping reports that the computer is online and displays the elapsed time, or latency delay, for the round-trip message. Ping is useful for finding out if a site is up and running. Ping is also useful for determining whether the connection is adequate for online computer games or videoconferencing.

Data traveling over the Internet can be traced. A software utility called **Traceroute** records a packet's path, including intermediate routers, from your computer to its destination.

Using Ping or Traceroute, you can discover how long data is in transit from point A to point B. On average, data within the continental U.S. arrives at its destination 110-120 ms (milliseconds) after it is sent. Overseas transmissions usually require a little more time.

FIGURE E-21: Connecting your computer to the Internet

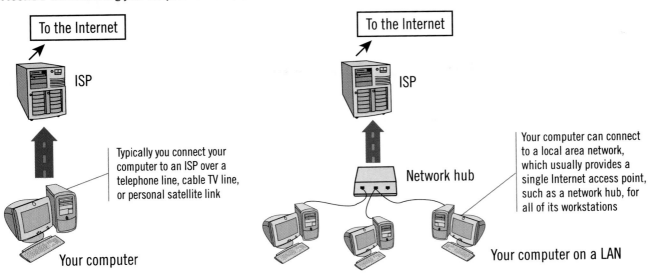

To the Internet

ISP

Typically you connect your computer to an ISP over a telephone line, cable TV line, or personal satellite link

Your computer

To the Internet

ISP

Network hub

Your computer can connect to a local area network, which usually provides a single Internet access point, such as a network hub, for all of its workstations

Your computer on a LAN

FIGURE E-22: ISP equipment

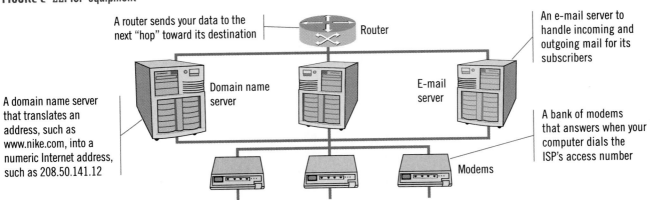

A router sends your data to the next "hop" toward its destination

Router

An e-mail server to handle incoming and outgoing mail for its subscribers

A domain name server that translates an address, such as www.nike.com, into a numeric Internet address, such as 208.50.141.12

Domain name server

E-mail server

A bank of modems that answers when your computer dials the ISP's access number

Modems

TABLE E-4: Protocols used on the Internet

PROTOCOL	NAME	FUNCTION
HTTP	Hypertext Transfer Protocol	Exchanges information over the Web
FTP	File Transfer Protocol	Transfers files between local and remote host computers
POP	Post Office Protocol	Transfers mail from an e-mail server to a client Inbox
SMTP	Simple Mail Transfer Protocol	Transfers e-mail messages from client computers to an e-mail server
IMAP	Internet Mail Access Protocol	An alternative to POP
TELNET	Telecommunications Network	Allows users who are logged on to one host to access another host
SSL	Secure Sockets Layer	Provides secure data transfer over the Internet

UNIT E
Introducing IP addresses and domain names

Computers on the Internet are identified using IP addresses. The "IP" part of TCP/IP defines the format for the IP addresses.

DETAILS

- Every ISP controls a unique pool of IP addresses, which can be assigned to subscribers as needed.

- An **IP address** is a series of numbers, such as 204.127.129.001. When written, an IP address is separated into four sections by periods for the convenience of readers. The number in a section cannot exceed 255. In binary representation, each section of an IP address requires 8 bits, so the entire address requires 32 bits. The four sections are used to create classes of IP addresses where each part is assigned based on the size, type of network, and other Internet functions.

- A permanently assigned IP address is called a **static IP address**. As a rule of thumb, computers that need a permanent IP address are servers or "hosts" on the Internet, for example, ISPs, Web sites, Web hosting services, or e-mail servers. Computers with static IP addresses usually are connected to the Internet all the time. For example, the computer that hosts the Course Technology Web site has a permanent address so that Internet users can always find it.

- A temporarily assigned IP address is called a **dynamic IP address**. Dynamic IP addresses are typically assigned by ISPs for most dial-up connections, and some DSL, ISDN, or cable modem connections. When you use a dial-up connection, for example, your ISP assigns a temporary IP address to your computer for use as long as your computer remains connected to the Internet. When you end a session, that IP address goes back into a pool of addresses that can be distributed to other subscribers when they log in. Your computer will rarely be assigned the same IP address it had during a previous dial-up session.

   Dynamic IP addresses are generally assigned to computers for client activities such as surfing the Web, sending and receiving e-mail, listening to Internet radio, or participating in chat groups.

- The IP address situation for ISP subscribers varies. Depending on the ISP, your computer might be assigned a static IP address, it might be assigned a dynamic address each time you connect, or it might be assigned a semi-permanent address that lasts for several months. If you want your computer to function as an

Internet server, ask your ISP about its method of IP address allocation and its policies on allowing server activities.

- Because your ISP assigns IP addresses, you usually do not need to know the IP address assigned to your computer. However, if you need to identify how your computer is connected to the Internet or troubleshoot your connection, you can see your computer's IP address by reviewing the Internet configuration settings.

- IP addresses work well for communication between computers, but people often have difficulty remembering a series of numbers. As a result, many host computers have an easy-to-remember name that translates directly to the computer's IP address. See Figure E-23. This name is the "fully qualified domain name" (FQDN), but most people just refer to it as a **domain name**.

- A domain name is a key component of URLs and e-mail addresses. It is the Web server name in a URL and the e-mail server name in an e-mail address. For example, in the URL www.course.com, the domain name is course.com. In the e-mail addresses jsmith@rutgers.edu and emilyb@course.com the domain names are rutgers.edu and course.com, respectively.

- A domain name ends with an extension that indicates its **top-level domain**. For example, in the domain name course.com, "com" indicates that the host computer is maintained by a commercial business, in this case, Course Technology. Top-level domains and their uses are listed in Table E-5. Other domains are also in use. For example, country codes also serve as top-level domains. Canada's top-level domain is ca; the United Kingdom's is uk; Australia's is au. Another domain with growing popularity is .tv. Originally assigned to the small Polynesian island of Tuvalu, the .tv domain has been obtained by a professional management team and is available for a fee to media-related Web sites.

- Every domain name corresponds to a unique IP address that has been entered into a database called the **domain name system**. Computers that host this database are referred to as **domain name servers**. A domain name must be converted into an IP address before any packets can be routed to it.

FIGURE E-23: How domain names convert to IP addresses

▶ When you type a domain name into your browser, a domain name request is routed through your ISP to your designated domain name server, which then searches through its database to find a corresponding IP address; the IP address can then be attached to packets, such as requests for Web pages

Domain name server

www.travelocity.com

ISP

www.travelocity.com

151.193.165.126

TABLE E-5: Top-level domains

DOMAIN	DESCRIPTION	DOMAIN	DESCRIPTION
biz	Unrestricted use; usually for commercial businesses	int	Restricted to organizations established by international treaties
com	Unrestricted use; usually for commercial businesses	mil	Restricted to U.S. military agencies
edu	Restricted to North American educational institutions	net	Unrestricted use; traditionally for Internet administrative organizations
gov	Restricted to U.S. government agencies	org	Unrestricted use; traditionally for professional and nonprofit organizations
info	Unrestricted use		

How your computer connects with a domain name server

An organization called **ICANN (Internet Corporation for Assigned Names and Numbers)** is recognized by the U.S. and other governments as the global organization that coordinates the technical management of the Internet's domain name system, the allocation of IP addresses, and the assignment of protocol parameters.

The domain name system is based on a distributed database. This database is not stored as a whole in any single location; it exists in parts all over the Internet. Your Internet connection is set up to access one of the many domain name servers that reside on the Internet. When you enter a domain name or URL, it is sent to your designated domain server, which can either send back the IP address that corresponds to the domain name, or if your domain name server does not have a record of the domain name, it can contact another domain name server and request the IP address. The servers in the domain name system supply IP addresses in a matter of milliseconds. Organizations or individuals can select a domain name and register it by using an online registration service, as shown in Figure E-24.

The first step in registering a domain name is to find out whether the name is currently in use or reserved for future use. If a domain name is not

available, consider using a different top-level domain, such as biz instead of com. After you've found an available domain name you like, you can continue the registration process by filling out a simple online form.

FIGURE E-24: Registering on the Web

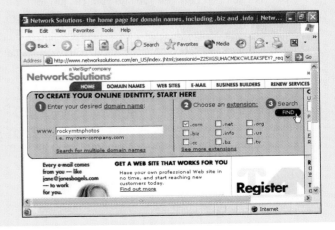

Connecting to the Internet using dial-up

The most difficult aspect of the Internet is getting connected. Although many high-speed Internet access options, such as cable modems, DSL, personal satellite dishes, and ISDN are available, most people's first experience connecting to the Internet begins with a dial-up connection. A dial-up connection uses **POTS (plain old telephone service)** to transport data between your computer and your ISP. This lesson explores dial-up connections.

Info Web · MODEM · Info Web · VOICE OVER IP

DETAILS

● The telephone communications system uses a tiered network to transport calls locally, cross-country, and internationally. At each level of the network, a switch creates a connection so that a call eventually has a continuous circuit to its destination. The first tier of this network uses a star topology to physically connect each telephone in a city to a switch in a "switching station," "local switch," or "central office." The second tier of the telephone network links several local switching stations. Connections then fan out to switches that are maintained by many different local and long-distance telephone companies.

● The telephone network uses a technology called circuit switching, which essentially establishes a continuous private link between two telephones for the duration of a call. This type of switching provides callers with a direct pipeline over which streams of voice data can flow. Because a circuit-switching network devotes an entire circuit to each call when someone is "on hold," no communication is taking place; yet the circuit is reserved and cannot be used for other communications.

● When you use a dial-up connection, your computer's modem places a regular telephone call to your ISP. Your call is routed through the telephone company's local switch and out to the ISP. When the ISP's computer answers your call, a dedicated circuit is established between you and your ISP, just as if you had made a voice call and someone at the ISP had picked up the phone. The circuit remains connected for the duration of your call and provides a communications link that carries data between your computer and the ISP. As your data arrives at the ISP, a router sends it out over the Internet. See Figure E-25.

● The signals that represent data exist in your computer as digital signals. The telephone system, however, expects to work with human voices, so the data that it carries must be in the format

of analog audio tones. A **voice band modem**, usually referred to as a modem, converts the digital signals from your computer into signals that can travel over telephone lines.

● Although telephone companies "went digital" long ago, their digital switches kick into action only after your call arrives at the local switching station. The technology between your telephone and your local switch is designed to carry analog voice signals. To transport data over this loop, the digital signals from your computer must be converted into analog signals that can travel over the telephone lines to your local switch. When these signals arrive at the local switch, they are converted into digital signals.

● The term modem is derived from the words "modulate" and "demodulate." In communications terminology, **modulation** means changing the characteristics of a signal, as when a modem changes a digital signal into an analog audio signal. **Demodulation** means changing a signal back to its original state, as when a modem changes an audio signal back to a digital signal. See Figure E-26.

● When your computer is connected to your ISP using a standard dial-up connection, data is transmitted over the same frequencies that are normally used for voice conversations. If you have only one telephone line, you cannot pick up your telephone receiver, dial your friend, and carry on a voice conversation while you are connected to your ISP. You can, however, use the Internet to carry voice signals from your computer's microphone through the dial-up connection to the sound card of another computer. This technology, called **voice over IP (VoIP)**, allows you to play games over the Internet and chat about your moves, all while you are online.

FIGURE E-25: Dialing in to the Internet

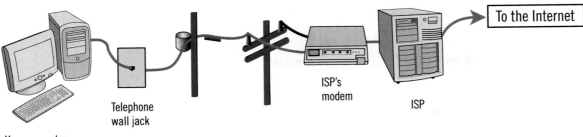

Your computer
and modem

Telephone
wall jack

ISP's
modem

ISP

To the Internet

▲ When you use an ISP to access the Internet, your data
travels through the local telephone switch to your ISP,
which sends it onto the Internet

FIGURE E-26: How a modem works

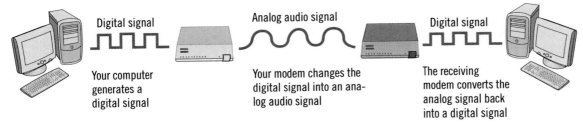

Digital signal

Analog audio signal

Digital signal

Your computer
generates a
digital signal

Your modem changes the
digital signal into an analog audio signal

The receiving
modem converts the
analog signal back
into a digital signal

▲ When you send data, your modem modulates the signal
that carries your data. A modem at the other end of the
transmission demodulates the signal

How fast is a modem?

When modems were a new technology, their speed was measured as **baud rate**, the number of times per second that a signal in a communications channel varies, or makes a transition between states. An example of such a transition is the change from a signal representing a 1 bit to a signal representing a 0 bit. A 300-baud modem's signal changes state 300 times each second; however, each baud doesn't necessarily carry one bit. So, a 300-baud modem might be able to transmit more than 300 bits per second. To help consumers make sense of modem speeds, they are now measured in bits per second. This is actually a measure of capacity, but everyone calls it "speed."

Actual data transfer speeds are affected by factors such as the quality of your local loop connection to the telephone switch. Even with a "perfect" connection, a 56 Kbps modem tops out at about 44 Kbps. Many Internet connection methods provide faster downstream (data received) transmission rates than upstream (data sent) rates. Dial-up connections are no exception: 44 Kbps is a typical downstream speed for a 56 Kbps modem; upstream, the

data rate drops to about 33 Kbps, or less. Slightly faster speeds might be possible with V.92 and V.44 modems (see Figure E-27), as they gain widespread support from dial-up ISPs.

FIGURE E-27: A modem

UNIT E

Connecting to the Internet using broadband

Although the standard equipment provided by telephone companies limits the amount of data that you can transmit and receive over a voice band modem, the copper wire that runs from your wall jacks to the switching station actually has a fair amount of capacity. This lesson discusses other Internet connection options, such as DSL, ISDN, T1, and T3, all of which offer high-speed digital communications links for voice and data.

DETAILS

- **DSL (Digital Subscriber Line)** is a high-speed, digital, always-on Internet access technology that uses standard phone lines to transport data. It is one of the fastest Internet connections affordable to the individual consumer.

- Several variations of DSL technology exist, including ADSL (asymmetric DSL with downstream speed faster than upstream speed), SDSL (symmetric DSL with the same upstream and downstream speed), HDSL (high-rate DSL), and DSL lite. This entire group of DSL technologies is sometimes called xDSL, but xDSL is not a variation of DSL.

  DSL is digital, so data doesn't need to be changed into analog form and then back to digital, resulting in fast data transmission over standard copper telephone cable. If permitted by your DSL provider, you can use your DSL line instead of your POTS line for voice calls. Figure E-28 illustrates how voice and data signals travel over DSL to a special device at the local telephone switching station, where they are divided and routed either to an ISP or to the regular telephone network.

  In many areas, DSL is a joint venture between the telephone company and the DSL provider. The telephone company is responsible for the physical cabling and voice transmission. The DSL provider is responsible for data traffic.

  The speed of a DSL connection varies according to the characteristics of your telephone line, the equipment at your local switch, and your DSL provider. Most **DSL modems** are rated for 1.5 Mbps downstream, compared to standard 56 Kbps for a dial-up connection. When shopping for a DSL connection, you should inquire about actual speed and find out if the upstream rate differs from the downstream rate.

  Currently, most DSL installations require trained service technicians. You can obtain service from a special DSL provider. A typical DSL installation begins when your local telephone company designates a telephone line for the DSL connection.

This line might utilize unused twisted-pair cables in your current telephone line, if they are available, or it might require a new line from the nearest telephone pole to the telephone box outside your house. This line is connected to a special type of DSL switch. A technician from the DSL provider has to run cables, install a DSL wall jack if necessary, and then connect a DSL modem to your computer's Ethernet card. See Figure E-29.

- **ISDN (Integrated Services Digital Network)** connections move data at speeds of 64 Kbps or 128 Kbps—not as fast as DSL or cable modems, but faster than a dial-up connection. ISDN is an all-digital service with the potential to carry voice and data. A device called an **ISDN terminal adapter** connects a computer to a telephone wall jack and translates the computer's digital signals into a different kind of digital signal that can travel over the ISDN connection. ISDN service is typically regarded as a high-speed Internet connection option for businesses that maintain small local area networks. The service is usually obtained from a local telephone company or a dedicated ISDN service provider.

- **T1** is a high-speed (1.544 Mbps) digital network developed by AT&T in the early 1960s to support long-haul voice transmission in North America. Similar service is available in Europe under CEPT (Conference of European Postal and Telecommunications) standards. A T1 line consists of 24 individual channels. Each channel has a capacity of 64 Kbps, and can be configured to carry voice or data. T1 lines provide a dedicated link between two points, so they are popular for businesses and ISPs that want a high-speed connection to the Internet, regardless of cost. A **T3** connection consists of 672 channels and supports data rates of about 43 Mbps. Sometimes referred to as DS3 (Digital Service-3) lines, T3 lines provide many of the links on the Internet backbone. Both T1 and T3 services are considered dedicated leased lines, which means that they are essentially rented from the telephone company and are not typically shared by other customers. T1 and T3 services are usually too expensive for individuals.

FIGURE E-28: How DSL carries voice and data

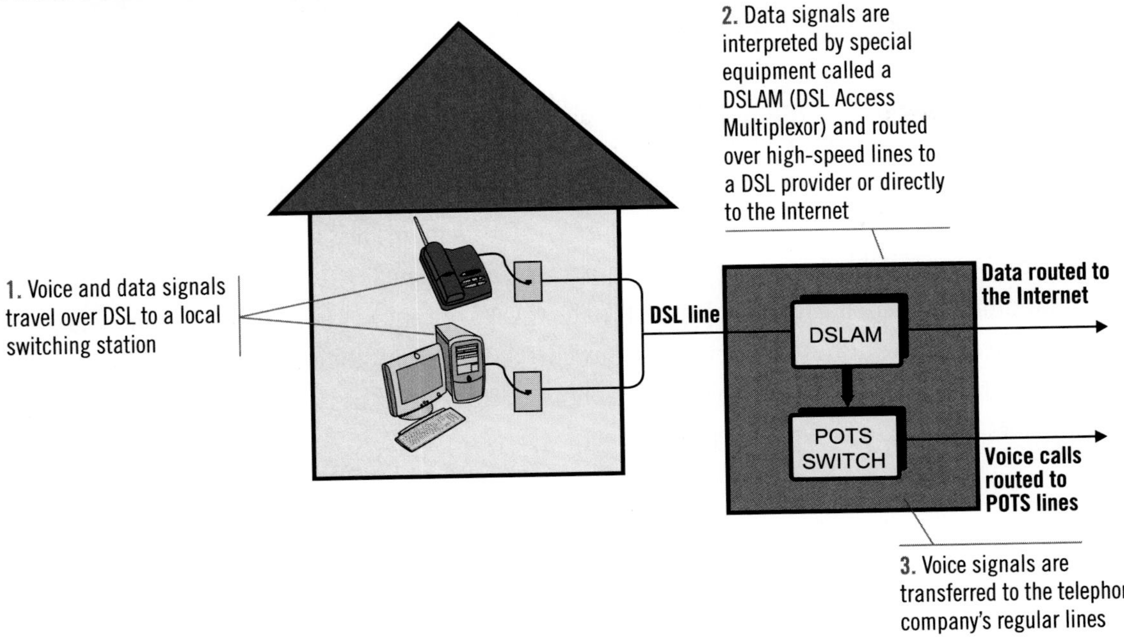

2. Data signals are interpreted by special equipment called a DSLAM (DSL Access Multiplexor) and routed over high-speed lines to a DSL provider or directly to the Internet

1. Voice and data signals travel over DSL to a local switching station

DSL line

Data routed to the Internet

DSLAM

POTS SWITCH

Voice calls routed to POTS lines

3. Voice signals are transferred to the telephone company's regular lines

FIGURE E-29: Connecting your computer to DSL

Ethernet port

In a typical DSL installation, a twisted-pair cable connects your computer's Ethernet card to a DSL modem, which is plugged into a wall jack

DSL modem

Security and always-on connections

Unlike a dial-up connection, which is only connected for the duration of your "call" or connection, an **always-on connection** is always connected, and it is "on" whenever your computer is powered up. With an always-on connection, you might have the same IP address for days, or even months, depending on your ISP. A hacker who discovers that your computer is always on can easily find your computer again, and its high-speed access makes it a very desirable target. When your computer is turned off, it is not vulnerable to attack. Therefore, it is a good idea to shut down your computer when you are not using it. Putting your computer into sleep mode or activating a screen saver is not sufficient protection. Your computer must be shut down and turned off. Additional steps you can take to protect yourself from security breaches through your cable connection to the Internet are discussed in Unit F.

Connecting to the Internet using cable

The cable television system was originally designed for remote areas where TV broadcast signals could not be received in an acceptable manner with an antenna. These systems were called "community antenna television," or CATV. The CATV concept was to install one or more large, expensive satellite dishes in a community, catch TV signals with these dishes, and then send the signals over a system of cables to individual homes. This system has been adapted and now provides Internet service to many homes.

Info Web

CABLE MODEM

DETAILS

- The satellite dish "farm" where television broadcasts are received and retransmitted is referred to as the head-end. From the head-end, a cabling system branches out and eventually reaches consumers' homes. The topology of a CATV system has the physical topology of a computer network.

- When your cable TV company becomes your Internet service provider, your computer becomes part of a neighborhood local area network, as shown in Figure E-30. A router and high-speed connection from the head-end to the Internet provide the potential for Internet connectivity over every cable in the system.

- To offer both television and Internet access, the cable's bandwidth is divided among three activities. As shown in Figure E-31, a CATV cable must provide bandwidth for television signals, incoming data signals, and outgoing data signals. Even dividing the bandwidth among these activities, the lowest-capacity coaxial cable used by the CATV system has a far greater carrying capacity than a POTS line.

- What do you need to configure your computer to access the Internet over a CATV system? When you configure your computer to access the Internet with a cable modem, you are essentially connecting to an Ethernet-style LAN that connects a neighborhood of cable subscribers. The two requirements for this type of connection are circuitry to handle Ethernet protocols and a cable modem, which converts your computer's signal into one that can travel over the CATV network. Some cable modems include Ethernet circuitry, so they can be connected to your computer using a USB cable. Otherwise, your computer must be equipped with an Ethernet card. Figure E-32 shows how to connect a cable modem to a desktop computer's Ethernet card.

- If you have only one CATV cable, you will need to use a splitter to connect both your cable modem and your television to that one CATV cable. If you have multiple CATV cables, you can connect your cable modem directly to any one of them. See Figure E-32.

- When your CATV connection is up and running, your computer becomes part of a neighborhood network because the cable from your computer and the cables from your neighbors' computers essentially connect at a centralized point.

- A communications channel like your CATV cable carries packets at a constant speed. The CATV cable also has a certain amount of bandwidth. As more and more neighbors use the service, data transport might seem to get slower.

- As for the security issue, in the early days of cable modem service, some cable modem users were unpleasantly surprised when they happened to open Windows Network Neighborhood, only to be greeted with a list of their neighbors' computers. When you have an Ethernet card in your PC, Windows automatically takes inventory of the LAN during boot up. It looks for any computers on the network that have file and printer sharing activated, and then lists them in the My Network Places window. Today, most cable companies use DOCSIS-compliant **cable modems** that block "crossover" traffic between subscribers. **DOCSIS (Data Over Cable Service Interface Specification)** is a security technology that filters packets to certain ports, including the port Windows uses for networking. DOCSIS secures your computer from your neighbors, but it does not close up all the security holes that are opened when you use an always-on connection.

FIGURE E-30: The topology of CATV

▶ Cables from the CATV head-end extend out as a series of "trunks;" the trunks are then connected to "feeders" that serve neighborhoods; the connection from a feeder to a subscriber's home is referred to as a "drop"

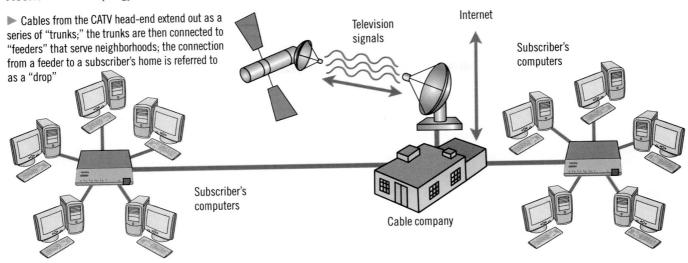

Television signals

Internet

Subscriber's computers

Subscriber's computers

Cable company

FIGURE E-31: CATV cable

▶ CATV cable has enough bandwidth to support TV channels and data flowing downstream, as well as data flowing upstream

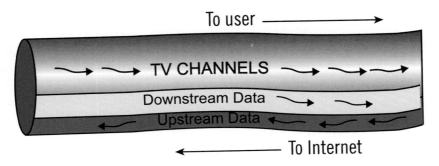

To user →

TV CHANNELS

Downstream Data

Upstream Data

← To Internet

FIGURE E-32: Connecting your computer to a CATV cable

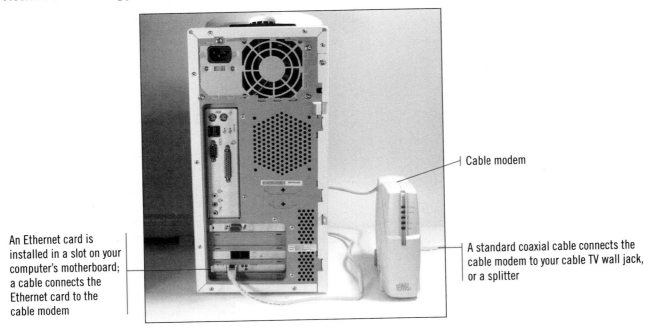

Cable modem

An Ethernet card is installed in a slot on your computer's motherboard; a cable connects the Ethernet card to the cable modem

A standard coaxial cable connects the cable modem to your cable TV wall jack, or a splitter

Connecting to the Internet without wires

You don't need wires to connect to the Internet. You can connect a computer to the Internet using several wireless options, including personal satellites and cellular telephones. Most people are familiar with services that provide access to "pay TV" over a personal satellite dish. Many of the companies that provide satellite TV also provide satellite Internet access.

DETAILS

- Satellite connections include direct satellite service and two-way satellite service. Both of these services are relatively expensive; but in some areas, particularly remote rural areas, they might be the only high-speed option available.

- **Direct satellite service (DSS)** uses a low-earth satellite to send television (such as DirectTV) or computer data (such as DirectTV DSL) directly to a satellite dish owned by an individual. Some direct satellite services provide only downstream data transport. If so, then upstream data transport, such as Web page requests, must be sent using a dial-up or DSL modem. See Figure E-33.

- Two-way satellite service sends both upstream and downstream data through the satellite. Two-way satellite service typically offers 500 Kbps downstream, but only 40–60 Kbps upstream. Satellite data transport is subject to delays of one second or more, which occur as your data is routed between your computer and a satellite that orbits 22,200 miles above the earth. Delays may not pose much of a problem for general Web surfing and downloading MP3 files, but they can become a showstopper for interactive gaming that requires quick reactions.

  As with cable modem service, satellite data transport speeds may decline when other users subscribe to the service because the bandwidth provided by the satellite is shared among all users.

- When you are not using a computer with access to your home Internet connection, you can use a mobile Internet connection to surf the Web and check your e-mail. Devices such as cell phones, PDAs, notebook computers, and tablet computers can be easily configured for mobile Internet access. Currently, the two most popular options for mobile Internet access are public Wi-Fi networks and WWAN networks.

- A **public Wi-Fi network** is a wireless LAN that provides open Internet access to the public. Public Wi-Fi networks are popping up in public places such as airports, hotels, and restaurants. The range of network coverage is called a **hotspot**. Any Wi-Fi

equipped device that enters a hotspot can gain access to the network's services. Some Wi-Fi public networks offer free service; others require a subscription or one-time use fee. A company that maintains a public Wi-Fi network is sometimes referred to as a WISP (wireless ISP).

- A **WWAN (wireless wide area network)** uses cellular phone networks to offer data communications and Internet access for cell phones, PDAs, and portable computers. There are two ways to use a WWAN for Internet access: you can use a cellular-ready modem to dial your usual ISP, or you can subscribe to a WAP plan offered by your cellular phone provider.

- **WAP (Wireless Access Protocol)** is a communications protocol that provides Internet access from handheld devices, such as cell phones and PDAs. WAP-enabled devices contain a microbrowser that simplifies Web and e-mail access on a small, low-resolution screen (see Figure E-34). You can obtain WAP-enabled devices and services from many mobile telecommunications providers, such as T-Mobile, Verizon, and CellularOne.

- **Cellular-ready modems** are packaged as PC cards that slip easily into the PCMCIA port of a notebook or tablet computer. You must have regular cellular phone service to use a cellular-ready modem. To activate the modem, call your cellular service provider, supply the **Electronic Serial Number (ESN)** printed on the back of your cellular modem, and then use the software provided with the modem to configure your computer. Currently, access speed over the cellular phone network is slow—about 14.4 Kbps, and that's less than half the speed of a dial-up connection. Some cellular providers offer high-speed data communications services priced separately from cellular service. As an example, AT&T's Global System for Mobile Communication/General Packet Radio Service (GSM/GPRS) high-speed wireless data network provides access speeds ranging from 56 to 114 Kbps.

FIGURE E-33: Connecting to the Internet via satellite

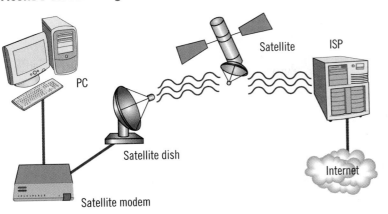

PC

Satellite

ISP

Satellite dish

Internet

Satellite modem

FIGURE E-34: WAP-enabled device

◀ The advantage of WAP-enabled devices is their portability. The disadvantage is their small, low-res screens. Although various schemes for scrolling over a full-sized Web page have been tried, most WAP users stick to Web sites specially designed for small screen devices

TABLE E-6: Internet access options

	DIAL-UP	ISDN	DSL	CABLE	SATELLITE	PUBLIC WI-FI	WWAN
Downstream speed (max)/(avg)	56 Kbps/ 44 Kbps	128 Kbps/ 128 Kbps	384 Kbps– 1.5 Mbps/ 384 Kbps	1.5 Mbps/ 800 Kbps	500 Kbps/ 400 Kbps	11 or 56 Mbps/ 4.5 or 27 Mbps	14.4, 56, or 114 Kbps/ 14.4 Kbps
Upstream speed (max)	33 Kbps	128 Kbps	128 Kbps– 1.5 Mbps	56–256 Kbps	40–60 Kbps	11 or 56 Mbps	14.4, 56, or 114 Kbps
Latency	100–200 ms	10–30 ms	10–20 ms	10–20 ms	1–3 seconds	3-4 ms	200–500 ms
Image file (2 MB) download time	6 minutes	2 minutes	43 seconds	20 seconds	40 seconds	4 seconds	29 minutes
Short video (72 MB) download time	4 hours	78 minutes	26 minutes	12 minutes	25 minutes	2.5 minutes	17 hours
Requirements	Telephone line, ISP, voiceband modem	Computer must be located within 3 miles of local telephone switch	Computer must be located within 3 miles of local telephone switch	CATV service that provides Internet access	Clear view of southern sky	Wi-Fi equipped computer or PDA, access to Wi-Fi hotspot	Cellular service, cable to connect modem to cell phone

What's the best Internet connection?

The best Internet connection depends on your budget and what's available in your area. Most people begin with a dial-up connection and eventually look around for a connection that offers higher access speeds. Cable modem service is usually the first choice, when available. If cable modem service is not available, or proves slower or less dependable than expected, the next choice would be DSL or satellite service, if available. If several Internet connection services are available to you, Table E-6 can help you evaluate their requirements, costs, advantages, and disadvantages.

Setting up a small LAN is easy. Equipment for HomePLC and HomePNA LANs are typically sold in kit form, with detailed instructions on setup procedures. To set up an Ethernet or Wi-Fi LAN, most consumers purchase parts from a computer, electronics, or office store, and follow the setup instructions provided with the hub or router. The Tech Talk provides an overview of Ethernet and Wi-Fi setup. Refer to Figure E-35.

Installing a LAN

FIGURE E-35

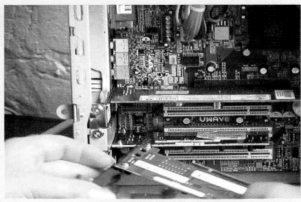

1. To begin, make sure every computer and peripheral you'll connect to the network contains a NIC. If a card is not built in, you must install one.

Devices you intend to connect using cables require Ethernet cards. Devices slated for wireless connections require Wi-Fi cards.

2. Place the hub or router in a central location and plug it in.

If you are planning to link your LAN to the Internet, connect the hub or router to your Internet connection.

3. For an Ethernet, run cables from the hub or router to the NIC in each device.

Turn on network devices one at a time. Windows should automatically detect the NICs and establish a connection to the network.

Using a LAN

How do I access network resources? If you use Windows, it automatically detects the network any time you turn on a workstation. Depending on your network setup, you might be asked to log in by entering a user ID and password. Once access is established, you can use any shared resources for which you have been given authorization.

How do I specify which resources can be shared by other workstations? Workstation owners can specify whether files and locally attached printers can be accessed from other workstations on the network. Windows allows you to designate a special folder for files you want to share with others. You can allow others to view and edit these files, or you can limit access only to viewing. You can also allow other network users to access your computer's entire hard disk or locally connected printer. For example, you can use My Computer to access shared resources listed under the My Network Places icon, or you can use **drive mapping** to assign a drive letter to a storage device located on a different workstation. See Figure E-36.

FIGURE E-36

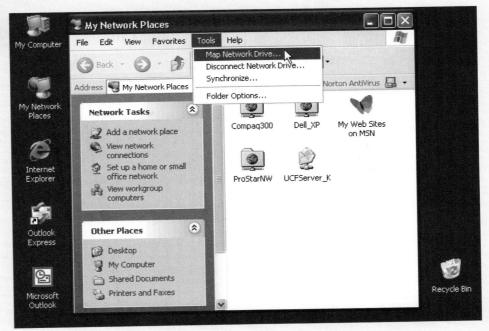

▲ In this drive mapping example, a server's drive C will be mapped as drive F by a workstation. After the mapping is complete, the server's hard disk will appear in the workstation's directory as drive F so it can be used just as though it were a drive connected directly to the workstation.

Computers in Context Education

The first educational application of computers emerged in the 1960s (see Figure E-37), when huge main-frames with clunky interfaces introduced students to computer-aided instruction (CAI). CAI uses basic drill and practice: The computer presents a problem, the student responds, and the computer evaluates the response. Studies in the 1970s indicated that CAI systems, such as PLATO (Programmed Logic for Automated Teaching Operations), improved student test scores, but students found the mainframe's monochrome display and the CAI's regimented drill format boring. More recent versions of CAI use colorful graphics and arcade formats to grab learners' attention.

Educators looking for ways to harness the computer's interactive and programmable nature arrived at the idea of computer-based training (CBT). CBT is formatted as a series of tutorials, beginning with a pretest to see whether students have the prerequisite skills and ending with a CAI-style drill and practice test to determine whether students can move on to the next tutorial segment.

Another educational approach, called computer-aided learning (CAL), uses the computer more as a source of information than an assessment mechanism. Students using CAL make decisions about their level of expertise, what material is relevant, and how to pace their own learning. Exploratory CAL environments included Seymour Papert's Logo programming language; students investigated geometry concepts by using Logo to program a graphical turtle on-screen.

In addition to CAI, CBT, and CAL, simulations were developed as an educational tool. In a simulation, the computer mimics a real-world situation through a narrative description or with graphics. Students are given options and respond with a decision or an action. The computer evaluates each response and determines its consequences. Oregon Trail, a simulation popular with elementary school students, describes events that beset a group of pioneers traveling in a wagon train. Students respond to each event, while learning bits of history, money-handling skills, conservation, and decision making. Even though this was one of the earliest simulations, it has kept up with advances in technology and is still popular today.

Most educators believe that computers can help create an individualized and interactive learning environment, which can make learning more effective and efficient. Although 99% of American public schools have computers and 93% of students use them in some way, these statistics can be deceiving. The reality falls far short of the ideal situation—every student having access to a computer throughout the school day. The challenge is to figure out how to realize computers' potential in an educational setting. Solutions have been tried with varying degrees of success. Some schools have installed learning labs where students go for scheduled "lab time." In elementary schools, often a few computers are placed in special work areas of classrooms and used for small group projects or individual drill and practice. Some schools have relegated most computers to the library, where they are connected to the Internet and used for research. In some classrooms, a single computer can be used as an effective presentation device. A few schools without the budget for enough desktop computers have opted for inexpensive PDAs. "Students need to use technology just as you and I do, not just one hour a day," says one teacher in support of PDAs. Students use standard PDA software for educational tasks: tracking nutritional intake for health class, collecting data from experiments in biology class, graphing functions in math class, translating phrases for French class, and maintaining to-do lists. The biggest drawback to more widespread educational use of PDAs, however, is a lack of software specifically designed for education.

As another option, some schools—primarily colleges— have confronted the problem of computer access by requiring all incoming first-year students to purchase notebook

FIGURE E-37

computers. Many colleges, for example, provide Internet connections in dorm rooms and library study carrels or offer campus-wide Wi-Fi service. Students can tote their notebook computers to class and take notes or outside for a study group. See Figure E-38. They can contact instructors via e-mail, use the Internet as a research resource, and run educational software.

Another educational use of computers can be seen in distance education (DE) or distance learning (DL) courses. Historically, distance education meant correspondence study or courses delivered by radio or television, but the meaning has been broadened to encompass any educational situation in which students and instructors aren't in the same place. Therefore, most DE courses today require students to have access to a computer and an Internet connection. DE courses are offered to K-12 students, college students, military personnel, business people, and the general public. Most students who choose DE courses do so because they want to learn at their own pace, at a convenient time, and in a location close to home. For example, single parents who must deal with the realities of day care, working professionals who cannot relocate to a college town, and physically disabled students who find DE handy. DE has the potential of increasing the pool of students for a course by making it financially feasible; for example, an advanced Kanji course could be offered at a Midwestern university with only 10 on-campus Japanese majors if enough DE students can boost enrollment.

The Internet hosts a wide variety of DE courses, both credit-earning and non-credit courses. Several course management systems (CMSs), such as Blackboard and WebCT, help teachers prepare and manage DE courses. These systems are popular with degree-granting institutions that offer credit-earning DE courses in their course catalogs (subject to the usual course fees and requirements). Course management software typically runs from a server maintained by a school system, college, or university. Using Web browsers, teachers access the CMS to post an online syllabus, develop Web pages with course content, create a database of questions for online assessment, manage e-mail, set up online discussion groups, and maintain a gradebook. Students using Internet-connected computers and standard Web browsers can access course materials, submit assignments, interact with other students, and take tests.

Computers and the Internet have opened opportunities for life-long learning. Prospective students can use a search engine to easily find non-credit courses and tutorials for a wide range of topics, including pottery, dog grooming, radio astronomy, desktop publishing, and drumming. Some tutorials are free, and others charge a small fee. Several Web sites, such as Barnes & Noble University and OnlineLearning.com, offer a good choice of fee-based or free courses. In a society that promotes learning as a life-long endeavor, the Internet has certainly made it possible for students of all ages to pursue knowledge and skills simply by using a computer and an Internet connection.

FIGURE E-38

Issue   Free Wi-Fi? Why or Why Not?

How would you like high-speed Internet access that requires no cables, no modem, and best of all—no subscription fees? Free community wireless access in cities as diverse as San Francisco, Miami, New York, Prague, and Amsterdam is made possible by free WLANs (wireless LANs). Dubbed "renegade WLANs" by some members of the press, these free networks are operated by public-spirited individuals who like to tinker with technology and want to provide a useful community service. Free WLAN operators typically subscribe to a DSL or cable provider for high-speed Internet access. They pay their monthly fees, but instead of curtailing access to their own personal use, they distribute their connections to friends, neighbors, and just about anyone who passes by with the right computer equipment.

Free WLANs are based on Wi-Fi technology, which uses the 802.11b networking standard to create wireless Ethernet-compatible LANs. The technology itself is not inherently renegade, in fact, it is used for many mainstream applications. Wi-Fi networks are popular in corporations and universities where users are mobile and the flow of information typically requires broadband capacity.

The 802.11b standard uses an unlicensed telecommunications spectrum, so it is perfectly legal to set up an antenna to transmit and receive Wi-Fi signals without obtaining a broadcast license or paying any fees to the Federal Communications Commission. Not only is it legal, setting up a Wi-Fi antenna is simple and inexpensive. A basic Wi-Fi antenna can be created with a few wires and an empty container. See Figure E-39. Using a Wi-Fi network is even cheaper and easier than setting one up. Many notebook computers have built-in Wi-Fi transceivers and software. If a transceiver is not built into your computer, you can add one for less than $100. With a Wi-Fi-ready computer, you can literally walk down the street, and your computer will look for and connect to any available Wi-Fi network.

Some free WLAN advocates envision a nationwide web of interconnected Wi-Fi networks that will form "a seamless broadband network built by the people, for the people." In this vision of a world connected by free WLANs, libraries can offer Internet access to people in low income neighborhoods. Local schools could get wired without exorbitant cabling expenses. Parents, kids, and grandparents, as well as corporate executives, could exchange e-mail and instant messages from locations that include the kitchen table, the corner coffee shop, and the Little League field.

But some broadband providers, such as AT&T and Time Warner Cable, fear that every user of a free wireless network is one less paying customer. According to one industry analyst, "The telecom industries are addicted to the one-wire, one-customer philosophy." Sharing an Internet connection that is intended for single-user access does not coexist with this philosophy. Most subscriber agreements contain wording that limits use of a broadband connection to one user and perhaps immediate family members. Although wording varies from one provider to another, most agreements expressly prohibit subscribers from using their connections for commercial purposes. Some free WLAN operators don't believe that sharing is commercial use. "I'm sharing it with people," says one free WLAN provider, "I'm not selling it. I'm not making a profit off it."

FIGURE E-39

Whether or not free WLANs are legal, their benefits are tempered by several potentially negative repercussions. For example, tightening up subscriber agreements to eliminate the sharing loophole could affect many broadband subscribers who currently operate private wired or wireless networks that link several computers to a single Internet connection. Broadband providers could force private network operators to purchase more expensive multi-user licenses—an option that might be too expensive for many home networks.

Most free WLANs are operated as a hobby. Some operators are very conscientious, but others have a laid-back attitude toward quality of service: If users are not paying for the service, they can't really complain when the network doesn't work. Consequently, free WLAN access can be unreliable. If broadband providers threaten to pull out of areas where free WLANs are popular, community members might have to choose between unreliable free WLAN service offered by hobbyists and more reliable, but more costly, services supplied by for-profit providers.

The wisdom of unregulated network availability is called into question by the proliferation of free WLANs. A publicly accessible LAN that requires no passwords or accounts can be used anonymously for a variety of illegal and dangerous activities. Like drug dealers who use public telephones to avoid taps and traces, terrorists and other criminals can simply walk into a free WLAN zone, tap into the Internet, and walk away without leaving a trace.

Widespread distribution of free WLANs can reduce the bandwidth available to paying customers. If your neighbor sets up a free WLAN that becomes popular with customers in a nearby coffee house, your previously sedate network neighborhood might suddenly become an overcrowded metropolis with major Internet access traffic jams.

Despite possible repercussions, the free WLAN movement appears to be growing and becoming more controversial. Some industry analysts expect a battle similar to the one that ensued when Napster's peer-to-peer music-sharing network was attacked by the music industry. The free WLAN controversy could pit a group of telecommunications giants against a rag-tag alliance of free WLAN advocates. The outcome has the potential to affect broadband subscribers everywhere.

▼ WHAT DO YOU THINK?

○ Yes ○ No ○ Not sure   1. Have you ever accessed a free WLAN?

○ Yes ○ No ○ Not sure   2. Do you believe that pirate WLANs can survive alongside for-profit broadband ISPs?

○ Yes ○ No ○ Not sure   3. Are broadband providers justified in limiting the terms of their service agreements to "one subscription, one customer"?

▼ EXPAND THE IDEAS

1. Research Wi-Fi technology. Write a brief description of what it is and how it works. Then consider: Is it ethical to set up a free Wi-Fi? Is it ethical to use one? Research two articles that present both viewpoints, for and against the unregulated use of free WLANs. Compare the viewpoints and then summarize the findings. Draw your own conclusion at the end of a short paper.

2. Do you believe that pirate WLANS can provide service alongside for-profit broadband ISPs? Why might one group prefer to use one service over the other? Might a for-profit broadband ISP consider offering Wi-Fi service? How could that be beneficial for the consumer? Write a short description of your ideas.

3. Are broadband ISPs justified in limiting the terms of their service agreements to "one subscription, one customer"? Relate broadband ISP services to other services such as telephone, cable TV, software licenses, radio, and print media. How are the services similar? How are they different? Does the difference justify the "one subscription, one customer" service agreements? Should exceptions be made for the following: same family users, same dwelling users, or home network users? Explain your position in a media presentation.

End of Unit Exercises

▼ KEY TERMS

Always-on connection
ARCnet (Attached Resource Computer network)
Asynchronous protocol
Bandwidth
Baud rate
Bluetooth
Broadband
Bus topology
Cable modem
Cellular-ready modem
Checksum
Circuit switching
Client
Client/server network
Coaxial cable
Communications channel
Communications network
Communications satellite
Concurrent-user license
CSMA/CD
Cyclic redundancy check
Demodulation
Direct satellite service
DOCSIS (Data Over Cable Service Interface Specification)
Domain name
Domain name server
Domain name system
Drive mapping
DSL

DSL modem
Dynamic IP address
Electronic Serial Number (ESN)
Ethernet
Ethernet card
Extranet
FDDI
Fiber-optic cable
Full duplex
Gateway
Half duplex
Handshaking
HomePLC
HomePNA
Host computer
Hotspot
Hub
ICANN
Infrared light
Internet Service Provider (ISP)
Intranet
IP address
ISDN
ISDN terminal adapter
LAN (Local Area Network)
LAN-jacking
Laser light
Logical address
MAN (metropolitan area network)
Mesh topology

Microwaves
Modem
Modulation
Multiple-user license
Narrowband
Network device
Network interface card (NIC)
Network Service Provider (NSP)
Networked peripheral
Node
Packet
Packet switching
PAN (personal area network)
Peer-to-peer network
Physical address
Physical topology
Ping
POTS
Protocols
Public Wi-Fi network
Repeater
RF signals
Ring topology
Router
Server
Shared resource
Simplex
Single-user license
Site license
Star topology

Static IP address
STP (shielded twisted pair)
Synchronous protocol
T1
T3
TCP/IP
Token Ring network
Top-level domain
Traceroute
Transceiver
Transponder
Tree topology
Twisted-pair cable
UTP (unshielded twisted pair)
Voice band modem
Voice over IP
WAN (Wide Area Network)
WAP (Wireless Access Protocol)
War driving
WEP (Wired Equivalent Privacy)
Wi-Fi (Wireless Fidelity)
Wi-Fi card
Wi-Fi network
Wired network
Wireless access point
Wireless network
Workstation
WWAN (wireless wide area network)

▼ UNIT REVIEW

1. Use your own words to define bold terms that appear throughout the unit. List the 10 terms that are least familiar to you and write a sentence for each of them.

2. List the four classifications for networks based on geographical structure and explain each. Then list the two classifications based on organization structure and explain each.

3. Create a table listing communications channels. Include advantages, disadvantages, relative speed/capacity, and quality of connection for each channel.

4. Explain three advantages and three disadvantages of wireless technology. List three wireless technologies discussed in this unit and write a brief explanation of each.

5. Make a list of the networks discussed in this unit, and then briefly describe each.

6. Make a list of four of the network hardware devices discussed in this unit. Explain how each device works within the network.

7. Draw diagrams of star, ring, and bus network topologies. Make sure that you can trace the route of data over a Token Ring network and an Ethernet network.

8. Explain the differences between permanent IP addresses, dynamic IP addresses, private IP addresses, and domain names.

9. Make a list of Internet access methods. Briefly describe each and include transmission rates.

10. Draw a diagram of the Internet that includes the following devices connected in a technically correct configuration so that data can flow from the personal computer to the Web server: a personal computer, voice band modem, ISP modem, e-mail server, ISP router, domain name server, two backbone routers, backbone repeater, and Web server.

▼ FILL IN THE BEST ANSWER

1. A communications _____ is the combination of hardware, software, and connecting links that transport data.

2. From a geographic perspective, networks can be classified as _____, _____, _____, and _____.

3. A local area network that uses TCP/IP is called a(n)_____ and are popular with businesses that want to store information as Web pages but not provide them for public access.

4. An intranet that provides private, external access is called a(n) _____.

5. The _____, or capacity, of a digital channel is usually measured in bps.

6. The _____ topology of a network refers to the layout of cables, devices, and connections; the _____ topology refers to the path of data over the network.

7. A technology called _____ switching divides messages into small parcels and handles them on a first come, first served basis.

8. _____ is one of the most widely used network technologies, and it uses a protocol called CSMA/CD to deal with collisions.

9. _____is a short-range wireless network technology that's designed to make its own connections between electronic devices, without wires, cables or any direct action from a user.

10. Protocols help two network devices negotiate and establish communications through a process called _____.

11. When you use a dial-up connection, your ISP gives you a temporary address, called a(n) _____ IP address, for use as long as you remain connected.

12. The database that keeps track of the names that correspond to IP addresses is called the _____ name system.

13. In communications terminology, _____ means changing the characteristics of a signal, whereas _____ means changing a signal back to its original state.

14. Although the speed of a modem was once measured by _____ rate, today's modem transmission speeds are measured in bps.

15. A software utility called _____ sends a signal to a specific Internet address and waits for a reply.

16. DSL, ISDN, _____, and T3 connections provide digital service over the telephone system's "local loop."

17. DSS service uses a low-earth _____ to send television, voice, or computer data directly to a dish owned by an individual.

18. A(n) _____ network uses radio frequencies not cables to send data from one node to another.

19. _____is a communications protocol that provides Internet access from handheld devices, such as cell phones and PDAs.

20. _____ technology is a standard for low-cost personal area network connections among mobile users that uses a globally available frequency range.

▼ PRACTICE TESTS

When you use the Interactive CD, you can take Practice Tests that consist of 10 multiple-choice, true/false, and fill-in-the-blank questions. The questions are selected at random from a large test bank, so each time you take a test, you'll receive a different set of questions. Your tests are scored immediately, and you can print study guides to determine which questions you answered incorrectly. If you are using a Tracking Disk, insert it in the floppy disk drive to save your test scores.

▼ INDEPENDENT CHALLENGE 1

You can connect to the Internet in a variety of ways, including dial-up connections, cable modem connections, DSL service, ISDN service, and direct satellite service. The Internet connection service you choose may be based more on availability than on what is the best and fastest technologically.

1. Write a brief statement explaining your Internet needs. Be sure to include whether you are planning to use the Internet for research, shopping, business, how often you need to log on, and if you need mobile access or high-speed access.

2. Research Internet connection options available in your area.

3. Create a table that lists the vendors for each available option and compares the options in terms of their setup cost, monthly fees, maximum speed upstream, and maximum speed downstream. Provide a summary of which Internet access options would be your first and second choices and why.

▼ INDEPENDENT CHALLENGE 2

You've decided to network a few computers in your home. This is the first time you have been put to this task, so you have to research and develop a plan for the project.

1. Describe the number, type, and location of the computers that will form your network.

2. Decide what type of network technology you want to use: Ethernet, HomePNA, wireless, or HomePLC.

3. Create a diagram showing the location of each computer, the wiring path (for Ethernet), the location of electrical outlets (for HomePLC), the location of telephone outlets (for HomePNA), or potential signal interference (for wireless).

4. Create a shopping list of the network components that you will need to purchase; research prices for each item on your list.

5. Indicate any software that you would have to purchase for the network.

▼ INDEPENDENT CHALLENGE 3

 The domain name system contains a vast array of names for businesses, organizations and institutions. When you see a URL in an advertisement or a book, you often know immediately what the company or organization is and what the site will be about when you get to the page.

1. Use your favorite search engine to research top-level domains; or you might start by visiting the ICANN Web site.

2. Find out the latest information about the new top-level domains (TLD).

3. Think about a URL that you might want to register, for example, yourname.com or something else that is important to you personally. Also think about a business venture that you might want to begin. What URL would you want for that business?

4. Find out if these URLS are available. Track your research. If the first choice was not available, list how you went about finding a URL that you could use. For example, if your name is Jennifer Dumont, would you want jenniferdumont.com? If that isn't available, would you go for jdumont.com? or Jenniferdumont.biz?

5. Submit a paper detailing your quest and the results you achieved.

▼ INDEPENDENT CHALLENGE 4

 Wireless services are available and expanding. You can get mobile news, e-mail, text messaging, and mobile access to the Internet. Wireless communication is already having an impact on the way people work. More and more people are working at least part-time from a remote location such as a satellite office or a home office. As this becomes the emerging business model, employees are finding that being connected is a necessity, not just a nicety.

1. Write a brief statement explaining your position and opinions on each of the following:

   a. how you think wireless e-mail is changing the way business is conducted;

   b. how it is changing the relationship between employer and employee; and

   c. how it is affecting personal relationships.

2. Wireless e-mail raises societal questions such as privacy issues, employer expectations vs. employee responsibilities, and impact on family life. Choose one societal issue impacted by wireless e-mail. Research the issue and write a paper presenting your findings.

3. Write a short summary of your findings. In your conclusion, compare your research findings with the opinions you expressed when you answered Step 1.

4. Be sure to include references and resources for your research.

▼ INDEPENDENT CHALLENGE 5

The Computers in Context section focuses on the many ways computers and Internet technology are used in education. You or someone you know may be currently enrolled in a DL or DE course; or in the past, you or someone you know may have taken a course through the Internet.

1. For this project, identify a topic you'd like to learn more about, such as a hobby or your academic major.

2. Use your word processor to create an outline using these headings: Topic Description, Available Tutorials, and Evaluation.

3. Under the heading "Topic Description," write a brief description of your topic and what you would like to learn about it.

4. Log onto the Internet and use a search engine, such as Google, to locate online tutorials about your topic. Take one of the free tutorials. Under the heading "Evaluation," describe the format for the tutorial, its ease of use, and what you learned.

LAB: TRACKING PACKETS

1. Start the interactive part of the lab. Insert your Tracking Disk if you want to save your QuickCheck results. Perform each of the lab steps as directed and answer all of the lab QuickCheck questions. When you exit the lab, your answers are automatically graded and your results are displayed.

2. Use the Ping utility that is supplied by Windows to ping www.abcnews.com. Record the IP address for the ABC News site, plus the minimum, maximum, and average times. For each time, indicate whether it would be considered poor, average, or good.

3. Use the Tracert utility that's supplied by Windows to trace a packet between your computer and the Web. Print the Traceroute report. Circle any pings on the report that indicate high latency.

4. Locate a Web-based Ping utility and use it to ping www.gobledegok.com. Include the URL for the Web site where you found the Ping utility. Explain the results of the ping.

5. Connect to the Internet Traffic Report Web site, make a note of the date and time, and then answer the following questions:

   a. What is the traffic index for Asia?

   b. How does the index for Asia compare with the traffic index for North America?

   c. During the previous 24 hours in Europe, what was the period with the worst response time?

LAB: SECURING YOUR CONNECTION

1. Start the interactive part of the lab. Insert your Tracking Disk if you want to save your QuickCheck results. Perform each of the lab steps as directed, and answer all of the lab QuickCheck questions. When you exit the lab, your answers are automatically graded and your results are displayed.

2. Use the Netstat utility to scan any computer that you typically use. Write out the Netstat report or print it. To print the report, copy it to Paint or Word, and then print. Explain what the Netstat report tells you about the security of that computer.

3. Connect to the grc.com site and access the Shields Up! tests. Test the shields and probe the ports for the same computer that you used for Assignment 2. Explain the similarities and differences between the Shields Up! report and the Netstat report for this computer. Which report indicates more security risks? Why?

4. In the lab, you learned which dialog boxes to use for disabling Windows file and print sharing, plus a technique for unbinding TCP from file and print sharing. Without actually changing the settings, use the dialog boxes to determine whether file and print sharing is active or disabled on your computer. Also, discover if file and print sharing is bound to TCP on your computer. Report your findings and indicate if these settings are appropriate in terms of network access and security.

▼ STUDENT EDITION LABS

Reinforce the concepts you have learned in this unit through the **Protecting Your Privacy Online**, **Connecting to the Internet**, **Getting the Most Out of the Internet**, **Networking Basics**, and **Wireless Networking** Student Edition Labs, available online at the Illustrated Computer Concepts Web site.

▼ SAM LABS

If you have a SAM user profile, you have access to additional content, features, and functionality. Log in to your SAM account and go to your assignments page to see what your instructor has assigned for this unit.

▼ VISUAL WORKSHOP

The Bluetooth wireless technology, see Figure E-40, is a standard for low-cost, personal area network connection among mobile computers, mobile phones and other devices. Using a globally available frequency range, Bluetooth eliminates the need for cables and provides secure, radio-based transmission of data and voice.

FIGURE E-40: Bluetooth technology

1. Log onto the Internet and go to the Bluetooth SIG (special interest group) Web site. Find the answers to the following questions: Who developed the Bluetooth wireless technology? When was it developed? What were the goals or reasons for developing the technology?

2. Bluetooth technology is being included in many new applications. List two applications that are discussed on the Web site.

3. Find the Web site of one of the companies using Bluetooth technology in their products. Describe one of the applications. Be sure to cite your sources.

UNIT F

Data Security

Understanding how to create, organize, and interpret your data is very important. However, if your data is not secure, it could be lost. This unit discusses factors that may work against you to destroy your data and ways to secure your computer and computer data. The unit begins with an introduction on what can go wrong and how to avoid data loss; later lessons discuss computer viruses and the potential attacks that affect files and disrupt computer operations. You will learn how to restrict unauthorized user access and how to use antivirus software to protect or recover your computer data. You will also learn one of the most important aspects of computing—how to back up your data. The Tech Talk discusses ways to secure a local area network. You will have the opportunity to read about computers in the context of law enforcement. The Issue looks at how our society views and prosecutes computer crime.

Knowing what can go wrong

In the context of computer systems, **risk management** is the process of identifying potential threats to computer equipment and data, implementing plans to avoid as many threats as possible, and developing steps to recover from unavoidable disasters. Although it might not be cost-effective or even possible to protect a computer system from all threats, a good risk management plan provides a level of protection that is technologically and economically feasible. Part of risk management is knowing what can go wrong. Computer systems are threatened by viruses, natural disasters (see Figure F-1), power outages, malicious hackers, software failures, hardware breakdowns, human error, security breaches, acts of war, and viruses.

DETAILS

- Hardware failure. The effect of a hardware failure depends on which component fails. Most hardware failures are simply an inconvenience. For example, if your monitor fails, you can obtain a replacement monitor, plug it in, and get back to work. A hard disk drive failure, however, can be a disaster because you might lose all stored data. Although an experienced computer technician might be able to recover some of the files on the damaged hard disk drive, it is more often the case that all programs and data files stored on the hard disk are permanently lost. Much of the computer hardware that fails does so within the first hours or days of operation. If this period passes without problems, hardware can be expected to work fairly reliably until it nears the end of its useful life. The risk of a breakdown increases as a hardware component ages. Many devices are rated with a **mean time between failures (MTBF)** statistic. For example, a MTBF rating of 125,000 hours means that, on average, a device could function for 125,000 hours before failing. MTBF ratings are averages, which means a device with a 125,000 MTBF rating might actually operate for only 10 hours before it fails.

- Human error. Human error or **operator error** refers to a mistake made by a computer operator or programmer. Common errors within a computing system include entering inaccurate data and failing to follow required procedures. Despite the sometimes sensational press coverage of computer criminals and viruses, the most common cause of lost and/or inaccurate data is a mistake made by a computer user; mistakes such as entering the wrong data or deleting a file that is still needed. One of the most well-known disasters due to human error was the loss of the Mars Climate Orbiter in 1999 (see Figure F-2).

- Power problems. Because computers are powered by electricity, they are susceptible to power failures, spikes, and surges. A **power failure** is a complete loss of power to the computer system, usually caused by something over which you have no control. Even a brief interruption in power can force your computer to reboot and lose all of the data in RAM. Although a

power failure results in lost data from RAM, it is unlikely to cause data loss from disks.

Two other common power-related problems are spikes and surges. Both of these can damage sensitive computer components. A **power spike** is an increase in power that lasts only a short time—less than one millionth of a second. A **power surge** lasts a little longer—a few millionths of a second. Spikes and surges can be caused by malfunctions in the local generating plant or the power distribution network, and they are potentially more damaging than a power failure. Both can destroy the circuitry that operates your hard disk drive or damage your computer's motherboard.

- Software failures. Software failure can be caused by bugs or flawed software design. A tiny memory leak might be undetectable in a small computing system, but it can be disastrous on a system consisting of hundreds or thousands of computers. Other bugs may cause security leaks. For example, hackers continue to discover bugs in Microsoft software that allow unauthorized access to servers. Security breaches might be the result of physical intrusions or deliberate sabotage and often result in stolen data.

- Acts of war once affected only computer systems located on battle fronts. With a recent increase in terrorist incidents, however, civilian areas have become targets. Acts of war, such as bombing, can cause physical damage to computer systems. **Cyberterrorism** can also cause damage, using viruses and worms to destroy data and otherwise disrupt computer-based operations, which now include critical national infrastructures such as power grids and telecommunications systems.

- **Computer viruses** can cause damage to just about any computer system. You might have experienced the nuisance of rooting out a virus from your computer. That inconvenience pales when compared to the potential effect of a virus on a large computing system. Viruses are explored in detail later in this unit.

FIGURE F-1: A disaster can destroy computers

◀ After a severe thunderstorm, a worker pokes a hole in a ceiling tile to let out water in the computer information systems department; employees covered most of the computers before too much damage was done

FIGURE F-2: Results of operator error

Intended orbit = 150 km altitude
Actual orbit = 60 km altitude

Image not drawn to scale

◀ In the Fall of 1999, a failure to recognize and correct an error in a transfer of information between the Mars Climate Orbiter spacecraft team in Colorado and the mission navigation team in California led to the loss of the Mars Climate Orbiter. Investigators determined the cause of the crash was a miscalculation by NASA scientists, who failed to convert rocket thrust calculations from English measurements to metric measurements. One team used English units (e.g., inches, feet and pounds) while the other used metric units for a key spacecraft operation. This information was critical to the maneuvers required to place the spacecraft in the proper Mars orbit. Since then, NASA has successfully landed spacecrafts on Mars, such as the Spirit and Opportunity Orbiters in January 2004, with spectacular results.

What if disaster strikes?

Despite the best risk prevention measures, disasters that destroy data can and do occur. One of the most destructive disasters in history was the attack on the World Trade Center and subsequent collapse on September 11, 2001. The personal loss and magnitude of loss for the world was incalculable and could never have been planned for. Although the human toll was staggering, very few companies affected by the disaster experienced critical data loss. Most companies were able to reconstitute their computer systems because the World Trade Center bombing eight years earlier prompted many companies in the towers to design disaster recovery plans. A **disaster recovery plan** is a step-by-step plan that describes the methods used to secure data against disaster, and explains how an organization will recover lost data if and when a disaster occurs. Kemper Insurance, located on the 35th and 36th floors of the north tower of the World Trade Center, designed a disaster recovery plan after the 1993 bombing. Kemper's disaster recovery plan not only detailed what to do in case of disaster, it also required a mock disaster recovery exercise at least once a year. In these yearly exercises, IT employees went through the process of reconstructing the company's computer system from scratch at an off-site location. They configured new hardware, installed the required software, and restored data from backup tapes. In response to the 9/11 catastrophe, Kemper Insurance IT employees followed the disaster recovery plan and recreated the computer system at another Kemper Insurance site. Kemper Insurance was up and running by 4:00 a.m. on September 12th—less than 24 hours after one of the largest and most devastating disasters in history.

Protecting systems

No computer system can be completely risk-free, but several proactive procedures can protect computer systems from threats. Preventative countermeasures shield the system from attack or reduce its impact if one occurs. These preventative countermeasures can be grouped into three categories: deterrent measures, detection activities, and corrective procedures.

DETAILS

● Deterrents. Deterrents are preventative countermeasures that reduce the likelihood of deliberate attack, hardware failure, or data loss. Deterrents include devices for protecting systems and restricting access to software and systems.

- Provide power protection. There are several devices that can help protect computer systems from power problems. See Figure F-3. A **UPS (uninterruptible power supply)** represents the best protection against power problems. A UPS is a device containing a battery that provides a continuous supply of power and other circuitry to prevent spikes and surges from reaching your computer. A UPS gives you enough time to save your files and exit your programs in the event of a power outage. A UPS is essential equipment for Internet and LAN servers. As a low-cost alternative, you can plug your computer into a **surge strip** (also called a **surge protector** or **surge suppressor**) to protect it from power spikes and surges. A surge strip does not contain a battery to keep the computer running and protect the data in RAM if the power fails. When you shop for a surge strip, do not mistakenly purchase a power strip. While the UPS and surge strip can help protect your computer systems, there are some situations (for example, an electrical storm) when it is best to simply unplug your computer equipment.

- Restrict Access. Physical deterrents for restricting access include providing only limited access to critical servers. If potential criminals cannot get to a computer or a terminal, stealing or damaging data becomes more difficult. Keep in mind, however, that restricting physical access will not prevent a determined criminal from stealing data. In today's web of interlaced computer technologies, it has become critical to restrict not only physical access but also user access to authorized users. Restricting the access of users—especially those who are logging in from sites thousands of miles away—is a critical step in data security. Passwords are a first line of defense against unauthorized access. Security features such as **authentication** and **password protection** identify authorized users. See Figure F-4.

- Establish user rights. One way to limit the amount of damage from a break-in is to assign **user rights**, which are rules that limit the directories and files that each user can access. They can restrict your ability to erase, create, write, read,

and find files. When you receive a user ID and password for a password-protected system, the system administrator gives you rights that allow you to access and perform specified tasks only on particular directories and files on the host computer or file server. Assigning user rights helps prevent both accidental and deliberate damage to data. If users are granted limited rights, a hacker who steals someone's password has only the same access as the person from whom the password was stolen. Monitoring software that tracks users, file updates, and changes to critical systems also acts as a deterrent. Firewalls, software that prevents unauthorized access to a system, are also a preventative countermeasure.

- Stop mistakes before they happen. To protect against operator error some companies establish **usage procedures**, which, if followed, can reduce operator error. Many organizations have reduced the incidence of operator error by using a **direct source input device**, such as a bar code reader, to collect data directly from a document or object. Computer software designers can also help prevent operator error by designing products that anticipate mistakes users are likely to make and that provide features to help users avoid those mistakes.

● Detection activities. Detection activities recognize attacks and trigger preventative countermeasures or corrective procedures. Theft or vandalism can be detected by periodic hardware inventories. Antivirus software detects viruses entering a system, and can be configured to automatically clean the system or quarantine infected files. Viruses will be discussed in detail in this unit.

● Corrective procedures. Corrective procedures reduce the effect of an attack. Data backups, disaster recovery plans, and the availability of redundant hardware devices all are examples of corrective procedures. Another corrective procedure is to carry proper insurance. Some insurance companies provide extra coverage for the data on your computer. With this type of coverage, you would receive a sum of money to compensate you for the time it takes to reload your data on a replacement computer. A good insurance policy provides funds to replace computer equipment, but the only insurance for your data is an up-to-date backup tape or disk. Backups and redundancy will be discussed in detail in this unit.

FIGURE F-3: A UPS, surge strip, and power strip

UPS

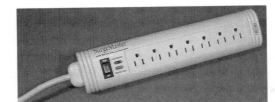

Surge strip

Power strip

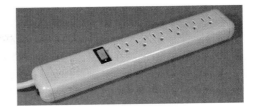

▲ To connect to a UPS, plug it into a wall outlet, then plug your computer and monitor cables into the outlets on the UPS; a light on the case lets you know that the UPS is charged and ready

▲ A surge strip contains the electronics to prevent power spikes and surges from damaging your computer

▲ Although a power strip contains multiple outlets for power plugs, it does not contain the electronics necessary to filter out power spikes and surges

FIGURE F-4: Equipment used to restrict physical access

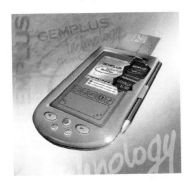

▲ Identity card reader

▲ Fingerprint scanner

▲ Retinal scanner

Ways to restrict physical access

Three methods of personal identification are used to restrict access: something a person carries, something a person knows, or some unique physical characteristic. Each of these methods has the potential to positively identify a person, and each has a unique set of advantages and disadvantages. *Something a person carries:* An identity badge or pass card featuring a photo, or perhaps a magnetic strip or bar code with unique coded information, remains a popular form of personal identification. Because an identity badge can be lost, stolen, or duplicated, however, it works best when used on site where a security guard verifies that the face on the badge is the face of the person wearing the badge. Without visual verification, the use of identity badges from a remote site is not secure, unless combined with a password or PIN (personal identification number) that is coded on the badge. *Something a person knows:* User IDs and passwords fall into this category of personal identification. When you work on a multiuser system or network, you

generally must have a user ID and password. Data security on a computer system that is guarded by user IDs and passwords depends on password secrecy. If users give out their passwords, choose obvious passwords, or write them down in obvious places, hackers can break in. The method of trying every word in an electronic dictionary to steal a password decreases in effectiveness if a password is based on two words, a word and number, or a nonsense word that does not appear in a dictionary.

Some unique physical characteristic: This third method of personal identification, called **biometrics**, bases identification on some physical trait, such as a fingerprint or the pattern of blood vessels in the retina of the eye. Unlike passwords, biometric data can't be forgotten, lost, or borrowed. Such technologies include hand-geometry scanners, voice recognition, face recognition, fingerprint scanners, and retinal scanners.

UNIT F Introducing computer viruses

Computer viruses invade all types of computers, including mainframes, servers, personal computers, and even handheld computers. Spreading a virus is a crime. Although the term virus technically refers to a type of program that behaves in a specific way, it has become a generic term that refers to a variety of destructive programs. To defend your computer against viruses, you should understand what they are, how they work, and how to use antivirus software.

DETAILS

● **Malicious code** refers to any program or set of program instructions that is designed to surreptitiously enter a computer and disrupt its normal operations. Malicious code, including viruses, worms, and Trojan horses, is created and unleashed by individuals referred to as "hackers" or "crackers." The term hacker originally referred to a highly skilled computer programmer. Today, however, the terms **hacker** and **cracker** usually refer to anyone who uses a computer to gain unauthorized access to data, steal information, or crash a computer system.

● A **computer virus** is a set of program instructions that attaches itself to a file, reproduces itself, and spreads to other files. It can corrupt files, destroy data, display an irritating message, or otherwise disrupt computer operations. A virus might deliver a **payload**, which could be as harmless as displaying an annoying message or as devastating as corrupting the data on your computer's hard disk. A **trigger event**, such as a specific date, can unleash some viruses. For example, the Michelangelo virus is designed to damage hard disk files on March 6, the birthday of artist Michelangelo.

● Viruses have the ability to lurk in a computer for days or months, quietly replicating themselves. While this is taking place, you might not even know that your computer has a virus, which makes it is easy to spread infected files to other people's computers inadvertently.

● A virus can be classified as a **file virus**, **boot sector virus**, or **macro virus**. For details, see Table F-1.

● A **Trojan horse** is a computer program that seems to perform one function while actually doing something else. See Figure F-5. Trojan horses are notorious for stealing passwords. Even handheld computers are susceptible. For example, a Trojan horse called PictureNote usually arrives as an e-mail attachment named Picture.exe, which leads you to believe you've received some type of graphics software. If you open this file, however, it searches for America Online (AOL) user information and tries to steal your login and e-mail passwords. Some Trojan horses delete files and cause other trouble. Although a Trojan horse is not defined as a program that replicates itself, some Trojan horses do contain a virus or a worm, which can

replicate and spread. Virus experts call this a blended threat because it combines more than one type of malicious program. In addition to Trojan horse/virus combinations, worm/virus combinations are also becoming prevalent.

● With the proliferation of network traffic and e-mail, worms have become a major concern. Unlike a virus, which is designed to spread from file to file, a **worm** is designed to spread from computer to computer. Most worms take advantage of communications networks (especially the Internet) to travel within e-mail and TCP/IP packets. See Figure F-6. Worms also deliver payloads that vary from harmless messages to malicious file deletions.

● Klez, for example, is a mass-mailing worm that sends itself to every address in the address book of an infected computer. To make the virus difficult to track, the "From" line of the infected message contains the e-mail address of a randomly selected person from the address book rather than the address of the computer that actually sent the mail. The infected e-mail message typically claims to contain an attachment that can be used to protect your computer against Klez, but it actually contains the worm, which can infect your computer when the message—not the attachment—is opened or previewed. Another notorious worm known as "Love Bug" arrives as an e-mail attachment called LOVE-LETTER-FOR-YOU.TXT.vbs. When you open the attachment, the worm overwrites most of the music, graphics, document, spreadsheet, and Web files on your disk. After trashing your files, the worm automatically mails itself to everyone in your e-mail address book, looking for other victims.

   The attachment LOVE-LETTER-FOR-YOU.TXT.vbs appears to have two filename extensions: TXT and vbs. That's a clue that should arouse your suspicions. The second filename extension, .vbs, is the real filename extension and it means that the file contains an executable program—potentially some type of malicious code.

● Some worms are designed to generate a lot of activity on a network by flooding it with useless traffic—enough to overwhelm the network's processing capability and essentially bring all communications to a halt. These **denial of service attacks** cut network users off from e-mail and Web browsing.

FIGURE F-5: A Trojan horse

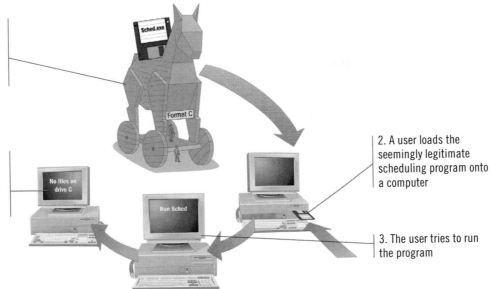

1. A Trojan horse pretends to be a legitimate scheduling program but is really a harmful formatting program

4. The command to run the program activates the format program and destroys the contents of the hard disk drive

2. A user loads the seemingly legitimate scheduling program onto a computer

3. The user tries to run the program

FIGURE F-6: A worm attack

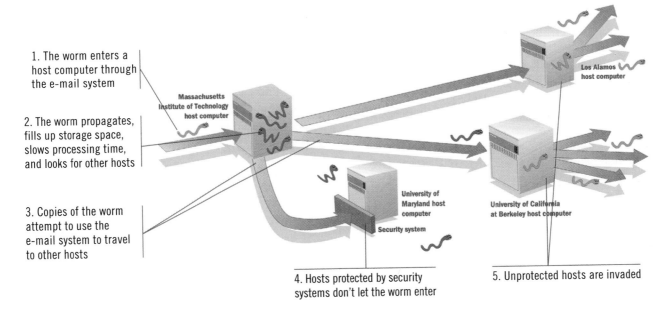

1. The worm enters a host computer through the e-mail system

2. The worm propagates, fills up storage space, slows processing time, and looks for other hosts

3. Copies of the worm attempt to use the e-mail system to travel to other hosts

4. Hosts protected by security systems don't let the worm enter

5. Unprotected hosts are invaded

TABLE F-1: Virus classifications

VIRUS TYPE	DESCRIPTION	EXAMPLE
File virus	Infects application programs, such as games	Chernobyl can infect any .exe file; its payload can overwrite sections of your hard disk
Boot sector virus	Infects the system files your computer uses every time you turn it on; causes widespread damage	The Stoned virus infects the boot sector; the payload corrupts some data on your computer's hard disk
Macro virus	Infects a set of instructions called a **macro**; when anyone views a document containing an infected macro, the macro virus duplicates itself into the general macro pool, where it is picked up by other documents	The two most common macro viruses are the Melissa virus, which attaches itself to Microsoft Word documents; and Codemas, which attaches itself to Microsoft Excel spreadsheets

Understanding how viruses spread

Viruses spread because people distribute infected files by exchanging disks and CDs, sending e-mail attachments, and downloading software from the Web. A virus infects the files with .exe, .com, or .vbs filename extensions by attaching itself to them. When you open an infected file, the attached virus instructions also open. These instructions then remain in RAM, waiting to infect the next program that your computer runs or the next file that it opens.

DETAILS

- Shared files are a common source of viruses. Figure F-7 illustrates how a single disk can easily infect many computers. Floppy disks, homemade CDs, and Web sites that contain games are the most common sources of viruses.

- E-mail attachments are another common source of viruses. A seemingly innocent attachment can harbor a file virus or a boot sector virus. Typically, infected attachments look like executable files, usually with .exe filename extensions, although in some cases they can have .sys, .drv, .com, .bin, .vbs, .scr, or .ovl extensions. These files cannot infect your computer unless you open them, which executes the virus code that they contain. You increase your chances of identifying "bad" e-mail attachments if you make sure that Windows is set to display all filename extensions. Never open a suspicious attachment without first checking it with antivirus software. If you don't want the attachment, simply delete the e-mail message to which it was attached.

- In addition to problems with e-mail attachments, e-mail messages themselves can carry viruses to unsuspecting recipients. This is particularly true if you receive your e-mail in HTML format, which allows you to use different fonts and different font formatting features (such as colors and sizes) for your messages. E-mail in HTML format can harbor viruses and worms hidden in program-like scripts that are embedded in the HTML tags. These viruses are difficult to detect even for antivirus software. To avoid the threat to data security, many people stick with plain text, non-HTML e-mail format for sending and receiving e-mail messages.

- Macro viruses can exist in documents created with Microsoft Word and spreadsheets created with Microsoft Excel. Infected files display the usual .doc or .xls filename extensions—there are no outward clues to the virus lurking within the file. Today, most software that executes macros includes security features that help protect your computer from macro viruses. See Figure F-8.

- Web sites that contain games and music are also a common source of viruses. When you download files from these sites, the downloaded files often contain scripts that can harbor viruses. You should scan all files with up-to-date antivirus software before downloading files.

- With the widespread use of the Internet, worms have become more prevalent than viruses. Looking toward the future, experts predict increasing numbers of blended threats that combine worm-like distribution with virus payloads. Table F-2 describes recent worms.

- When the write-protect window on a floppy disk is open, the disk is protected and all you can do is view or open the files on a disk. To save a new or modified file you must close the write-protect window; rendering the disk unprotected. A virus cannot jump onto your disk when it is write-protected, however, with the write protection removed, your disk is open to a virus attack.

What are the symptoms of a virus?

The symptoms depend on the virus. The following symptoms might indicate that your computer has contracted a virus, though some of these symptoms can have other causes: Your computer displays vulgar, embarrassing, or annoying messages; your computer develops unusual visual or sound effects; you have difficulty saving files, or files mysteriously disappear; your computer suddenly seems to work very slowly; your computer reboots unexpectedly; your executable files unaccountably increase in size; or your computer starts sending out lots of e-mail messages on its own.

It is important to remember, however, that some viruses, worms, and Trojan horses have no recognizable symptoms. Your computer can contract a worm, for example, that never displays an irritating message or attempts to delete your files, but which replicates itself through your e-mail until it eventually arrives at a server where it can do some real damage to a network communications system. You should use antivirus software to detect and remove viruses, worms, or Trojan horses in your computer.

FIGURE F-7: How a disk-borne virus spreads

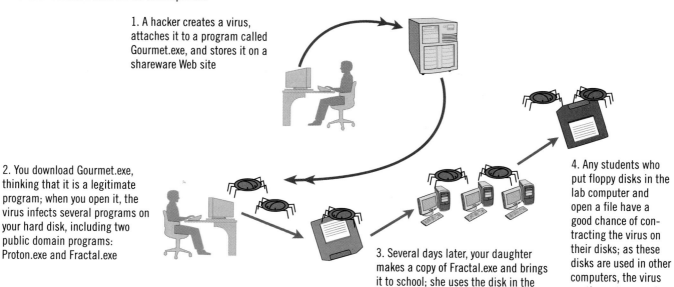

1. A hacker creates a virus, attaches it to a program called Gourmet.exe, and stores it on a shareware Web site

2. You download Gourmet.exe, thinking that it is a legitimate program; when you open it, the virus infects several programs on your hard disk, including two public domain programs: Proton.exe and Fractal.exe

3. Several days later, your daughter makes a copy of Fractal.exe and brings it to school; she uses the disk in the school lab, and the virus begins spreading to files on the computer she used

4. Any students who put floppy disks in the lab computer and open a file have a good chance of contracting the virus on their disks; as these disks are used in other computers, the virus continues to spread

FIGURE F-8: A Windows security warning

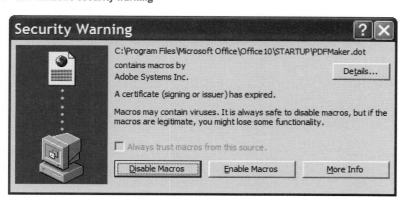

◄ Macro security features usually allow you to disable macros or warn you if a document contains a macro; macro security warnings do not necessarily mean that a document contains a macro infected with a virus; scanning the macro with anti-virus software, however, can detect the presence of a virus

TABLE F-2: How some malicious codes spread

NAME	TYPE	WHAT YOU SHOULD KNOW ABOUT THESE WORMS
Bugbear	worm	Arrives as an e-mail attachment with a double extension. Activates when its host e-mail message is opened or simply previewed. Sends itself to addresses in the inbox or address book. Can infect Registry files and programs. Records keystrokes and sends them to the worm's author. Attempts to disable antivirus software.
Code Red	worm	Defaces Web pages and floods NT/2000/XP servers with traffic so that they can't service legitimate requests. Defaces Web sites with the message "Hacked By Chinese." Originally targeted the Whitehouse.gov Web site.
Klez	worm	Arrives as an e-mail attachment with .bat, .exe, .pif, or .scr extension. Activates when opening or previewing its host message. Mass-mails itself to addresses in local address book. Carries the Elkern virus that tries to disable antivirus software.
Slammer	worm	Targets servers running Microsoft SQL Server software. At the height of its attack, Slammer clogged more than 225,000 company networks, disabled bank networks and ATMs, and slowed Internet access.
Sobig	worm	Arrives as an e-mail attachment that looks like it was sent from *support@microsoft.com*. Sends itself to addresses in local e-mail address book. Connects to a Web site and downloads a Trojan horse that allows a hacker to take control of the computer.

Using antivirus software

Antivirus software is a set of utility programs that looks for and eradicates a wide spectrum of problems, such as viruses, Trojan horses, and worms. Versions of antivirus software are available for handheld computers, personal computers, and servers. Figure F-9 shows a popular antivirus program. Considering the sheer number of existing viruses and the number of new viruses that debut every week, antivirus software is a must as part of your data security plan.

DETAILS

- Antivirus software uses several techniques to find viruses. The earliest antivirus software simply examined the programs on a computer and recorded their length. A change in the length of a program from one computing session to the next indicated the possible presence of a virus. This method of virus detection requires that you start with a virus-free copy of the program.

- In response to early antivirus software, hackers became more cunning. They created viruses that insert themselves into unused portions of a program file without changing its length. Of course, the people who designed antivirus software fought back. They designed software that examines the bytes in an uninfected application program and calculates a checksum. A **checksum** is a number that is calculated by combining the binary values of all bytes in a file. Each time you run an application program, the antivirus software calculates the checksum and compares it with the previous checksum. If any byte in the application program has changed, the checksum will be different, and the antivirus software assumes that a virus is present. The checksum approach also requires that you start with a copy of the program that is not infected with a virus. If the original copy is infected, the virus is included in the original checksum, and the antivirus software never detects it.

- Antivirus software also identifies viruses by searching your files for a **virus signature**, a unique series of bytes that can be used to identify a known virus, much as a fingerprint is used to identify an individual. Most of today's antivirus software scans for virus signatures. The signature search technique is fairly quick, but it identifies only those viruses with a known signature.

- Viruses try to escape detection in many ways. **Multi-partite viruses** are able to infect multiple types of targets. For example, a multi-partite virus might combine the characteristics of a file virus (which hides in .exe files) and a boot sector virus (which hides in the boot sector). If your antivirus software looks for that particular virus only in .exe files, the virus could escape detection by hiding in the boot sector as well. **Polymorphic viruses** mutate to escape detection by changing their signatures.

- **Stealth viruses** remove their signatures from a disk-based file and temporarily conceal themselves in memory. Antivirus software can find stealth viruses only by scanning memory. Some viruses called **retro viruses** are designed to attack antivirus software by deleting the files that contain virus descriptions or by corrupting the main executable virus program.

- The information that your antivirus software uses to identify and eradicate viruses, Trojan horses, and worms is stored in one or more files usually referred to as **virus definitions**. New viruses and variations of old viruses are unleashed just about every day. To keep up with these newly identified viruses, antivirus software publishers provide virus definition updates, which are usually available as Web downloads. You should check your antivirus publisher's Web site for the latest updates of antivirus software every few weeks or when you hear of a new virus making headlines (see Figure F-10).

   Most antivirus software allows you to specify what to check and when to check it (refer again to Figure F-10). You can, for example, start the program when you receive a suspicious e-mail attachment. Or, you can set it to look through all of the files on your computer once a week. The best practice, however, is to keep your antivirus software running full-time in the background so that it scans all files the moment they are accessed and checks every e-mail message as it arrives.

- Keeping a virus out of your computer and files is preferable to trying to eradicate a virus that has taken up residence. Once a virus infiltrates your computer, it can be difficult to remove, even with antivirus software. Certain viruses are particularly tenacious; just the process of booting up your computer can trigger their replication sequence or send them into hiding. As a result, antivirus software is not 100% reliable. On occasions, it might not identify a virus, or it might think that your computer has a virus when one does not actually exist. Despite these mistakes, the protection you get using antivirus software is worth the required investment of time and money.

FIGURE F-9: A Web site for an antivirus program

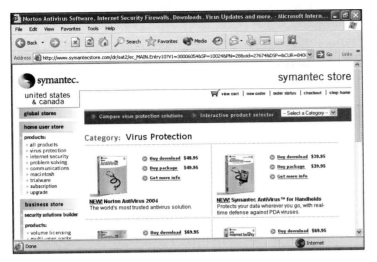

◀ You can buy the CD or download the program from the Internet; two popular antivirus programs for personal computers include McAfee VirusScan and Norton AntiVirus (shown here).

FIGURE F-10: Update the virus definitions and set the specifications

▶ It is important to get regular updates for your antivirus software; some antivirus vendors feature an electronic update service that you can set to automatically download and install updated virus definitions

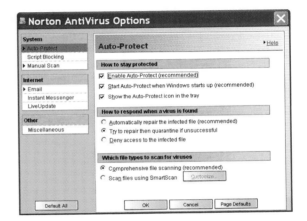

Virus hoaxes

Some viruses are very real, but you're likely to get e-mail about "viruses" that don't really exist. A **virus hoax** usually arrives as an e-mail message containing dire warnings about a supposedly new virus that is on the loose. The message typically suggests some strategy for avoiding the virus, and recommends that you forward the e-mail warning to all of your friends and colleagues. In most cases, however, the alleged virus does not exist, and the e-mail message is a prank designed to send people into a panic.

Bogus virus e-mail messages usually contain a long list of people in the To: and Cc: boxes; they have been forwarded many times. Most hoaxes include a recommended procedure for removing the virus, such as reformatting your computer's hard disk drive—a process that could cause more damage than the virus itself! Fake viruses are often characterized as being capable of bizarre acts. For example, check out the message about a phony virus in Figure F-11. If you follow the instructions in this e-mail, you will delete a legitimate program that debugs java programs.

When you receive an e-mail message about a virus, don't panic. Virtually all of them are hoaxes. If you are uncertain, check one of the many antivirus Web sites and look up the alleged virus by name to see if it is a

hoax or if it is a real threat. If the virus is a real threat, the antivirus Web site will provide the information that you need to check your computer and download an update to your antivirus software.

FIGURE F-11: A virus hoax

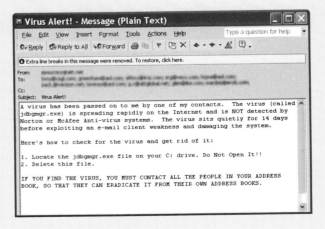

Introducing data backup

Have you ever mistakenly copied an old version of a document over a new version? Has your computer's hard disk drive gone on the fritz? Did a virus wipe out your files? Has lightning "fried" your computer system? These kinds of data disasters are not rare; they happen to everyone. Since you can't always prevent disasters from happening, you need a backup plan that helps you recover data that's been wiped out by operator error, viruses, or hardware failures. Computer experts universally recommend that you make backups of your data.

DETAILS

- A **backup** is a copy of one or more files that has been made in case the original files become damaged. A backup is usually stored on a different storage medium from the original files. For example, you can back up files from your hard disk to a different hard disk, a writable CD or DVD, tape, floppy disk, or Web site. The exact steps that you follow to make a backup depend on your backup equipment, your backup software, and your personal backup plan. Figure F-12 gives you a general idea of the steps that are involved in a typical backup session.

- You **restore** data from a backup to the original storage medium or its replacement. As with the procedures for backing up data, the process that you use to restore data to your hard disk varies, depending on your backup equipment, backup software, and exactly what you need to restore. After a hard disk crash, for example, you'll probably need to restore all of your backup data to a new hard disk. On the other hand, if you inadvertently delete a file, or mistakenly copy one file over another, you might need to restore only a single file from the backup. Most backup software allows you to select which files you want to restore.

- A good backup plan allows you to restore your computing environment to its pre-disaster state with a minimum of fuss. Unfortunately, no single backup plan fits everyone's computing style or budget. You must tailor your own backup plan to your particular computing needs. The checklist in Figure F-13 outlines the factors you should consider as you formulate your own backup plan.

- A **full backup** (also called a **full system backup**) contains a copy of every program, data, and system file on a computer. The advantage of a full backup is that you can easily restore your computer to its pre-disaster state simply by copying the backup files to a new hard disk. A full backup takes a lot of time, however, and automating the process requires a large-capacity tape backup device.

An alternative is to back up your most important data files. By doing so, you make sure that your computer-based documents and projects are protected from data disasters. You can back up these files on floppy disks, Zip disks, removable hard disks, CDs, or DVDs. The disadvantage of this backup strategy is that because you backed up only data files, you must manually reinstall all of your software, in addition to restoring your data files.

- Some applications, such as financial software, create files and update them without your direct intervention. If you have the option during setup, make sure that these files end up in a folder you always backup, such as My Documents.

- In addition to data files that you create, consider making backups of the following files:

  - Internet connection information. Your ISP's phone number and TCP/IP address, your user ID, and your password are often stored in an encrypted file somewhere in the Windows\System folder. Your ISP can usually help you find this file.

  - E-mail folders. If you're using POP e-mail software, your e-mail folder contains all of the e-mail messages that you've sent and received, but not deleted. Check the Help menu on your e-mail program to discover the location of these files.

  - E-mail address book. Your e-mail address book might be stored separately from your e-mail messages. Find the file by using the Help menu for your e-mail program.

  - Favorite URLs. If you're attached to the URLs that you've collected in your Favorites or Bookmarks list, you might want to back up the file that contains this list.

  - Downloads. If you paid to download any files, you might want to back them up so that you don't have to pay for them again. These files include software, which usually arrives in the form of a compressed .exe or .zip file that expands into several separate files as you install it. For backup purposes, the compressed file should be all that you need.

FIGURE F-12: Steps in a typical backup session

1. Insert the disk, CD, or tape on which you'll store the backup.

2. Start the software you're using for the backup.

3. Select the folders and files you want to back up.

4. Give the "go ahead" to start copying data.

5. Feed in additional disks, CDs, or tapes if prompted to do so.

6. Clearly label each disk, CD, or tape.

7. Test your backup.

FIGURE F-13: Backup tips

☑ Decide how much of your data you want, need, and can afford to back up.

☑ Create a realistic schedule for making backups.

☑ Make sure you have a way to avoid backing up files that contain viruses.

☑ Find out what kind of boot disks you might need to get your computer up and running after a hard disk failure or boot sector virus attack.

☑ Make sure you have a procedure for testing your restore procedure so that you can successfully retrieve the data that you've backed up.

☑ Find a safe place to store your backups.

☑ Decide what kind of storage device you'll use to make backups.

☑ Select software to handle backup needs.

Backing up the Windows Registry

The Windows Registry is an important file that is used by the Windows operating system to store configuration information about all of the devices and software installed on a computer system. If the Registry becomes damaged, your computer might not be able to boot, launch programs, or communicate with peripheral devices. It is a good idea to have an extra copy of the Registry in case the original file is damaged.

Backing up the Registry can present a problem because the Registry file is always open while your computer is on. Some backup software will not copy open files, and if this is the type of backup software that you are using, the Registry will never make its way onto a backup. Windows users whose backup plans encompass all of the files on the hard disk must make sure that their backup software provides an option for including the Windows Registry. Even if a full-system backup is not planned, many experts recommend that you at least copy the Registry file to a separate folder on the hard disk or to a floppy disk. If you do so, it is necessary to update this copy whenever you install new software or hardware.

Examining backup procedures

One of the most distressing computing experiences is to lose all of your data. This problem might be the result of a hardware failure or a virus. Whatever its cause, most users experience only a moment of surprise and disbelief before the depressing realization sinks in that they might have to recreate their data and reinstall their programs. A backup can pull you through such trying times, making the data loss a minor inconvenience rather than a major disaster.

DETAILS

- It is really frustrating when you restore data from a backup only to discover that the restored files contain the same virus that wiped out your data. If your antivirus software is not set to constantly scan for viruses on your computer system, you should run an up-to-date virus check as the first step in your backup routine.

- A **full backup** (Figure F-14) makes a copy of every file that exists in the folders on your computer. Because a full backup includes a copy of every file on a disk, it can take a long time to make one for a hard disk. Some users consider it worth the extra time, however, because this type of backup is easy to restore. You simply have the computer copy the files from your backup to the hard disk. It might, however, not be necessary to make a full backup on every backup date, especially if most of your files don't change from one backup session to another.

- A **differential backup** (Figure F-15) makes a backup of only those files that were added or changed since your last full backup session. After making a full backup, you will want to make differential backups at regular intervals. You maintain two sets of backups: a full backup that you make infrequently (once a week); and a differential backup that you make more frequently (once a day). It takes less time to make a differential backup than to make a full backup, but it is a little more complex to restore data from a differential backup. If you need to restore all of your files after a hard disk crash, first restore the files from your full backup, then restore the files from your latest differential backup.

- An **incremental backup** (Figure F-16) makes a backup of the files that were added or changed since the last backup, which might have been a full backup or an incremental backup. First you make a full backup, then when you make your first incremental backup, it will contain the files that have changed since the full backup. When you make your second incremental backup, it will contain only the files that changed since the first incremental backup. Incremental backups take the least time to make, and

they provide a little better protection from viruses than other backup methods because your backup contains a series of copies of your files. They are, however, the most complex type of backup to restore. If you need to restore all of your files after a hard disk crash, first restore the files from the full backup, then restore the files from each incremental backup, starting with the oldest and working your way to the most recent.

- Any data backup plan represents a compromise between the level of protection and the amount of time and resources you can devote to backup. Realistically you should perform backups at regular intervals (including copies of the Registry). The interval between backups will depend on the value of your data. If you're working on an important project, you might want to back up the project files several times a day. Under normal use, however, most people schedule a once-a-week backup.

- Make rotating sets of backups. One backup is good, but in case your backup gets corrupted, you should maintain a rotating set of backups. For example, if you are backing up to tape, you can use one tape for your first backup, then use a different tape for your next backup. Use even another tape for your third backup. For your fourth backup, you can overwrite the data on your first backup; for your fifth backup, you can overwrite the data on the second tape, and so on. Make sure that you write the date of the backup on the tape label so that you know which backup is the most recent.

- Test your backups. As soon as you make a backup, test your backup to be sure you can restore your data.

- Store your backups in a safe place. Don't keep them at your computer desk because a fire or flood that damages your computer could also wipe out your backups. In addition, a thief who steals your computer might also scoop up nearby equipment and media. Storing your backups at a different location is the best idea, but at least store them in a room apart from your computer.

FIGURE F-14: A full backup

▶ A full backup is simply a copy of all files on your hard disk

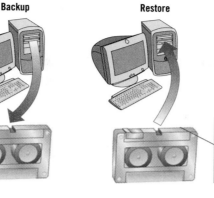

Backup

Restore

1. Back up all files from the hard disk drive to a backup tape

2. If the hard drive fails, you can restore all of the files from the backup to the hard disk drive

FIGURE F-15: A differential backup

▶ A differential backup copies any files that have changed since your last backup

1. Make a full backup on Monday evening

2. On Tuesday evening, use a different tape to back up only the files that have changed since the full backup

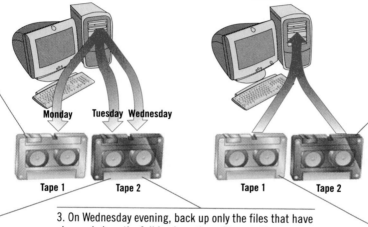

Backup

Monday   **Tuesday**   **Wednesday**

Tape 1   **Tape 2**

Restore

Tape 1   **Tape 2**

5. Next, load the data from the differential backup tape; this step restores the files you changed on Tuesday and Wednesday

4. Now, suppose the hard disk fails; to restore your data, first load the full backup onto the hard disk; this step restores the files as they existed on Monday evening

3. On Wednesday evening, back up only the files that have changed since the full backup; these files are the ones you changed or created on Tuesday and Wednesday; put these files on the same tape you used for Tuesday's backup

FIGURE F-16: An incremental backup

▶ Of the three backup techniques, an incremental backup takes the least time, but is the most complex to restore

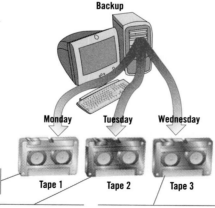

Backup

Monday   **Tuesday**   **Wednesday**

Tape 1   **Tape 2**   **Tape 3**

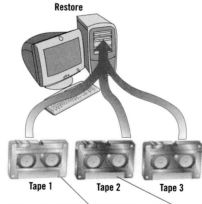

Restore

Tape 1   **Tape 2**   **Tape 3**

1. Make a full backup on Monday evening

2. On Tuesday evening, back up only the files that have been changed or created on Tuesday

3. On Wednesday evening, back up only the files that have been changed or created on Wednesday

4. Now, suppose the hard disk fails; to begin the restoration process, first load the data from the full backup

5. Next, load the data from Tuesday's incremental backup; this step restores the work you did on Tuesday

6. Finally, load the data from Wednesday's incremental backup; this step restores the work you did on Wednesday

UNIT F # Using backup devices

The hardware and media you use to backup your data is very important in determining the reliability and success of the procedure. The backup device that you select depends on the value of your data, your current computer configuration, equipment, and budget. There are several backup options available, some of which are discussed in this lesson and detailed in Table F-3.

DETAILS

● While floppy disks are inexpensive and just about every computer has a floppy disk drive, they are not an effective medium for a backup procedure. The 1.44 MB capacity of a floppy disk is suitable for storing several documents, but it does not provide enough capacity for digital photos or most MP3 music files.

● Several 750 MB Zip disks might be enough for backing up all your data files and could be feasible for a full system backup if you have not installed lots of application software.

● A second hard disk drive is a good backup option—especially if it has equivalent capacity to your main hard disk. This capacity allows the backup process to proceed unattended because you won't have to swap disks or CDs. Speed-wise, a hard disk is faster than many tape drives. Unfortunately, like your computer's main hard disk, a backup hard disk is susceptible to head crashes, making it one of the least reliable storage options. Internal hard disk drives are inexpensive, but they are not desirable backup devices because they are susceptible to electrical damage and any other catastrophe that besets your computer. External hard disk drives are preferred for backups because they can be disconnected from your computer and stored in a safe place. An internal hard disk drive with removable disks is also an acceptable option because the disks can be removed for safe storage.

● Today, most computers are equipped with a writable CD or DVD drive with adequate storage capacity for a typical computer owner's data files. An easy way to back up your important data is by copying selected files to a writable CD or DVD. The device driver for your CD or DVD writer includes a formatting routine, which prepares a disk to hold data. After a CD or DVD is formatted, you can use Windows Explorer or My Computer to select the files you want to copy as a backup.

Writable CDs and DVDs provide good storage capacity and blank disks are fairly inexpensive. You can typically use them to back up all of your data files. It might also be feasible to back up your entire system on a series of CDs or DVDs. You would, however, have to monitor the backup process and switch disks occasionally. The major disadvantage of writable CDs and DVDs is that the writing process is slower than writing data to tape or a removable hard disk.

● Tape drives are typically used in business computing situations, when a full-system backup is desirable. Some computer owners with a large amount of important data also install tape drives for their home systems. Tape drives are fairly inexpensive and fast enough to back up an entire hard disk in less than two hours. A tape drive with the capacity to hold the entire contents of a computer's hard disk can be left unattended as the backup proceeds.

Tape is a storage medium similar in reliability to floppy disks and Zip disks but not as durable as writable CDs and DVDs. Even though tape is simply too slow to be practical as your computer's main storage device, it is effective as a backup device. When you make a backup, you're simply copying lots of data onto the tape. You don't need to locate specific data or jump back and forth between different files. For a backup device, access time is less important than the time it takes to copy data from your hard disk to tape. The most popular types of tape drives for personal computers use tape cartridges, but there are several tape specifications and cartridge sizes.

● Remote storage is also an option for your backup. If your computer is connected to a local area network, you might be able to use the network server as a backup device. Before backing up your data to a network server, you want to check with the network administrator to make sure that you are allowed to store a large amount of data on the server. If you want to limit access to your data, ask the network administrator to let you store your data in a password-protected area. Also make sure that the server is backed up on a regular basis and that you have access to the backups in case you need to restore data to your local computer.

● Another possibility for remote storage is the Internet. Several Web sites offer fee-based backup storage space. When needed, you can simply download backup files from the Web site to your hard disk. These sites are an excellent idea for backups of your data files. When used in conjunction with a recovery CD, you can usually get your computer into functional condition after a data disaster. For most personal computer owners, however, a Web site might not be feasible for storing a backup image of an entire hard disk. First, it would be necessary to recover enough of your system files to get your computer connected to the Internet before the restoration files could be downloaded. In addition, the transfer time for several gigabytes of files could be days.

TABLE F-3: Backup media

	DEVICE COST*	MEDIA COST*	CAPACITY	COMMENTS
Floppy disk	$40-99	25¢	1.44 MB	Low capacity means that you have to wait around to feed in disks
Zip disk	$200 (average)	$15	750 MB	Holds much more than a floppy but a backup still requires multiple disks
External hard disk	$200 (average)	N/A	80 GB (average)	Fast and convenient, but might hold only one backup
Removable hard disk	$149 (average)	$100.00	2 GB (average)	Fast, limited capacity, but disks can be removed and locked in a secure location
CD-R	$200	50¢	680 MB	Limited capacity, can't be reused, long shelf life
CD-RW	$100-200	$1.25	680 MB	Limited capacity, reusable, very slow
Writable DVD	$400 (average)	$8.00	4.7 GB	Good capacity, not yet standardized
Tape	$300 (average)	$50.00	40 GB (average)	Great capacity, reasonable media cost, convenient—you can let backups run overnight
USB Flash drive	$20-$500	N/A	32 MB-2 GB	Convenient and durable, but high-capacity models are expensive
Web site	N/A	$5.95 per month	N/A	Transfer rate depends on your Internet connection; security and privacy of your data might be a concern

* Approximate cost at time this book was published

Creating a boot disk

If your computer's hard disk is out of commission, you might wonder how it can access the operating system files that are needed to carry out the boot process. If your hard disk failed, or a virus wiped out the boot sector files on your hard disk, you will not be able to use your normal procedures to boot your computer. A **boot disk** is a floppy disk or CD that contains the operating system files needed to boot your computer without accessing the hard disk.

A barebones boot disk simply loads the operating system kernel. You can make a boot disk using My Computer or Windows Explorer. The boot disk you create, however, boots DOS, not Windows.

A more sophisticated boot disk—sometimes referred to as a **recovery CD**—loads hardware drivers and user settings as well as the operating system.

Recovery CDs are sometimes included with new computer systems. Some computer manufacturer Web sites offer a download that creates a recovery CD. The operating system might also supply a method for creating recovery CDs. For example, the Windows XP Backup utility creates a set of **Automated System Recovery** disks.

The contents and capabilities of recovery CDs vary. Some are designed to restore your computer to its "like new" state and will wipe out all your data. Others attempt to restore user settings, programs, and data. Before you depend on a recovery CD, make sure you know what it contains and how to use it in case of a system failure.

Exploring backup software

Choosing the software you use to create your backups depends on your backup plan. If you are simply copying one or more data files to a floppy or Zip disk, you can use the Copy command that is provided by your operating system or a file management utility, such as Windows Explorer. However, many types of backup software are available if you want to go beyond a simple file backup.

DETAILS

● Many personal computer operating systems provide a **Copy Disk utility** that makes an exact copy of one floppy disk onto another disk of the same size and capacity. See Figure F-17. This utility is useful for students working in school computer labs, who often save and transport their files on floppy disks. This utility does not typically make copies of hard disks or CDs—only floppy disks—so its use for backups is limited to those occasions when you need a backup of a floppy disk.

● To make a tape backup, you typically use **backup software**—a set of utility programs designed to back up and restore files. Backup software usually provides options that make it easy to schedule periodic backups, define a set of files that you want to regularly back up, and automate the restoration process. Backup software differs from most copy routines because it typically compresses all the files for a backup and places them in one large file. Under the direction of backup software, this file can spread across multiple tapes if necessary. The file is indexed so that individual files can be located, uncompressed, and restored.

● Backup software is supplied with most tape drives. Some versions of Windows include Microsoft Backup software, which you can usually find by clicking the Start button, and then selecting

Accessories and System Tools. You can also purchase and download backup software from companies that specialize in data protection software.

● Backup software provides tools for scheduling backup dates and selecting the files you want to back up. The scheduling feature allows you to automate the backup process and reduces the chance that you'll forget to make regular backups. Backup software can also save time and storage space by offering options for full, differential, or incremental backups.

● Whatever backup software you use, remember that it needs to be accessible when it comes time to restore your data. If the only copy of your backup software exists on your backup disks, you will be in a "Catch-22" situation. You won't be able to access your backup software until you restore the files from your backup, but you won't be able to restore your files until your backup software is running! Make sure that you keep the original distribution CD for your backup software or that you have a separate backup that contains any backup software that you downloaded from the Web. Also be sure to make the required recovery disks so that you can restore Windows and get your backup program running.

Does a data center help to minimize risks?

The hardware and software for most enterprise and many high-performance computing systems are housed in a data center. A **data center** is a specialized facility designed to house and protect computer systems and data. A data center typically includes special security features, such as fireproof construction, earthquake proof foundations, sprinkler systems, power generators, secure doors and windows, and anti-static floor coverings. A typical data center may be located in the basement of a building, or even underground—providing some level of protection against natural disasters, such as storms and fires, and are not susceptible to extreme changes in surface temperature. In general, data centers are not

located in earthquake, flood, or tornado prone areas. Data centers typically include equipment to keep computers functioning during power outages. A data center must also protect and maintain its own power grid. For example, fuel tanks must be protected against explosions or fire, and batteries must be kept at room temperature for proper functioning. Most data centers limit physical access via fingerprint identification systems, badges, or security guards. Steel doors divide the centers into secure areas. Motion detectors and automated alarm systems prevent unauthorized movement through the building.

FIGURE F-17: The Copy Disk utility

1. Place the disk that you want to copy in the floppy disk drive; make sure that you also have a blank disk handy

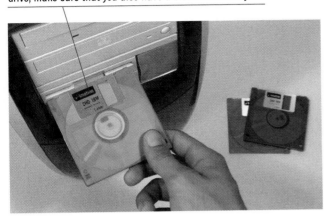

2. Double-click the My Computer icon

3. Right-click the 3½ Floppy (A:) icon

4. Click the Copy Disk option

5. Click the Start button; the contents of the disk are copied into RAM; when prompted, insert a blank disk in drive A so that the data can be copied from RAM to the blank disk

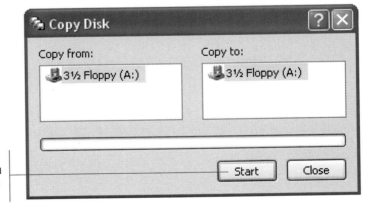

Local area networks are susceptible to internal security breaches, such as when a person at one workstation gains unauthorized access to the files on another workstation. If a LAN is equipped with an always-on Internet connection, it also becomes vulnerable to external attacks. Security is an issue you must address if you are on a LAN or if you are using an ISP or a cable modem to connect to the Internet.

Any home network that is connected to an always-on Internet connection is vulnerable to intrusions. You should make sure that password protection is enabled on every workstation.

Whether you are connecting a standalone computer or a LAN, Internet connections pose two kinds of risks: malicious code and intrusions. To deal with malicious code, such as viruses and worms, it is important to run antivirus software on standalone computers and all network workstations. Network administrators should make sure to keep up-to-date on security patches that apply to any network software providing network services or utilities, such as operating systems and browsers. A standalone computer with an always-on DSL, ISDN, or cable modem connection is particularly susceptible to intrusions. Without any visible sign or warning, hackers can infiltrate your computer to obtain personal information or use your computer to disguise themselves when they attack other machines.

For added protection, you might also want to purchase and install **personal firewall software**, which is designed to analyze and control incoming and outgoing packets. This software helps to keep your computer secure in several ways. It makes sure that incoming information was actually requested and is not an unauthorized intrusion. It blocks activity from suspicious IP addresses and, best of all, it reports intrusion attempts so that you can discover if any hackers are trying to break into your computer. Most firewall software allows you to set up various filters to control the type of packets that your workstation accepts. Most packages allow you simply to select a level of security, such as high, medium, or low.

Windows XP includes firewall protection you can activate and configure using the Control Panel's Network Connections option. When you turn off file and printer sharing (see Figure F-18), your files and printer cannot be accessed by other network users. When this box is not checked, file and printer sharing is deactivated. Tiny Personal Firewall and BlackICE are popular personal firewall products for computers with earlier versions of Windows or non-Windows operating systems.

You can also use **network address translation (NAT)** as a line of defense. Your ISP typically assigns an IP address to your high-speed connection; that is the address that's visible to the rest of the Internet. Within your LAN, however, the workstations should use private Internet addresses. When the IP addressing scheme was devised, three ranges of addresses were reserved for internal or "private" use: 10.0.0.010.255.255.255, 172.16.0.0172.31.255.255, and 192.168.0.0192.168.255.255. These private IP addresses cannot be routed over the Internet. If you've assigned private IP addresses to your workstations, they are essentially hidden from hackers, who only see the IP address for your router.

You might wonder how you can transmit and receive data from a workstation with a non-routable address. Your router maintains a network address translation table that keeps track of the private IP addresses assigned to each workstation. For outgoing packets, the router substitutes its own address for the address of the workstation. When a response to a packet arrives, the router forwards it to the appropriate workstation. In that way, only the router's address is publicly visible. The router should, of course, be protected by antivirus software and firewall software.

If you are connected to the Internet using a cable modem, and if you have an Ethernet card in your PC, Windows automatically takes inventory of the local area network during boot-up. It looks for any computers on the network that have file and print sharing activated, and then lists them in the Network Places window. Today, many cable companies use DOCSIS-compliant cable modems to block this "crossover" access among computers owned by their cable modem subscribers. **DOCSIS (Data Over Cable Service Interface Specification)** is a security technology that filters packets to certain ports, including the port that Windows uses for networking. DOCSIS secures your computer from your neighbors, but it does not close up all of the security holes that are opened when you use an always-on connection, such as a cable modem or DSL.

Unlike a dial-up connection that's only connected for the duration of your call, an always-on connection is always connected, and it is "on" whenever your computer is powered up. With an always-on connection, you might have the same IP address for days, or even months, depending on your ISP. A hacker who discovers that your computer has a security weakness can easily find it again, and its high-speed access makes it a very desirable target.

When your computer is turned off, it is not vulnerable to attack. It is a good idea to shut down your computer when you are not using it. Putting your computer into sleep mode or activating a screen saver is not sufficient protection. Your computer must be shut down and turned off.

FIGURE F-18: Turning off file and printer sharing

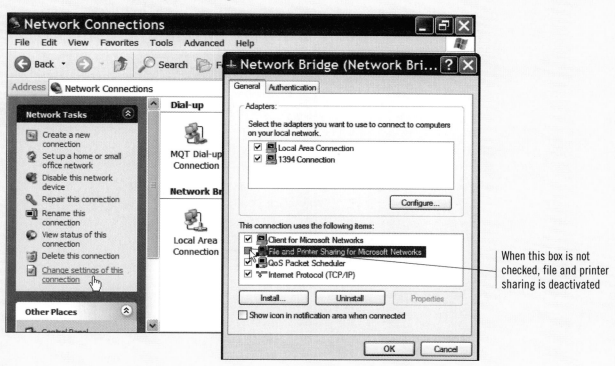

When this box is not checked, file and printer sharing is deactivated

Mounted in the dashboard of marked and unmarked police cars, a mobile data computer resembles a notebook computer with its flat-panel screen and compact keyboard. See Figure F-19. Unlike a consumer-grade notebook, however, the computers in police cruisers use hardened technology designed to withstand extreme conditions, such as high and low temperatures in parked vehicles. The dashboard-mounted computer communicates with an office-based server using a wireless link, such as short-range radio, CDPD (cellular digital packet data) technology, or Wi-Fi. With this wireless link, police officers can access data from local, state, and national databases.

One national database, the National Crime Information Center (NCIC), is maintained by the FBI and can be accessed by authorized personnel in local, state, and federal law enforcement agencies. The system can process more than 2.4 million queries per day related to stolen vehicles, wanted criminals, missing persons, violent gang members, stolen guns, and members of terrorist organizations. For example, the officers who pull over a speeding car might receive information from the NCIC that the car was stolen. If they do, they arrest the car's occupant and take him to the police station for booking. At the police station, digital cameras flash and the suspect's mug shot is automatically entered into an automated warrants and booking system. The system stores the suspect's complete biographical and arrest information, such as name, aliases, addresses, social security number, charges, and arrest date. The system also checks for outstanding warrants against the suspect, such as warrants for other thefts. Booking agents assign the new inmate to a cell, log his personal items, and print a photo ID or wrist band. Automated warrants and booking systems have been proved to increase police productivity. New York City's system handles more than 300,000 bookings per year, with gains in productivity that have put nearly 300 officers back into action investigating crimes and patrolling neighborhoods.

As part of the booking process, the suspect is fingerprinted. A standard fingerprint card, sometimes called a "ten-print card," contains inked prints of the fingers on each hand, plus name, date of birth, and other arrest information. Now, however, instead of using ink, a biometric scanning device can electronically capture fingerprints. See Figure F-20. Text information is entered via keyboard and stored with digital fingerprint images. The fingerprint information can be transmitted in digital format from local law enforcement agencies to the FBI's Automated Fingerprint Identification System (AFIS). This biometric identification methodology uses digital imaging technology to analyze fingerprint data. Using sophisticated algorithms, AFIS can classify arriving prints for storage or search the collection of 600 million fingerprint cards for matching prints.

FIGURE F-19

Computer crimes can be separated into two categories. The first includes crimes that use computers, such as transmitting trade secrets to competitors, reproducing copyrighted material, and distributing child pornography. The second includes crimes targeted at computers, such as denial-of-service attacks on servers, Web site vandalism, data theft, and destructive viruses. Conventional crimes, such as car theft, are often solved by using standard investigative techniques with information from computer databases. To solve cybercrimes, however, often the special skills of computer forensic investigators are required. Computer forensics is the scientific examination and analysis of data located on computer storage media, conducted to offer evidence of computer crimes in court.

Computer forensics can be applied to both categories of computer crimes. Whether a computer is suspected as the origin of a cyber attack or is suspected of holding evidence, the first step in the forensic process is to use disk imaging software to make an exact replica of the information stored on the hard disk. The disk image is then collected on a write-once medium that cannot be altered with "planted" evidence, and the forensic scientist begins analyzing the disk image data with simple search software that looks through files for keywords related to the crime. In the case of the "Gap-Toothed Bandit" who was convicted for robbing nine banks, analysis of the disk image revealed word processing files containing notes he handed to tellers demanding money. Criminals typically attempt to delete files with incriminating evidence, but a good forensic scientist can retrieve data from deleted files with undelete software or data recovery software. Temporary Internet or cache files can also yield evidence, pointing law enforcement officers to Web sites the suspect visited that might be fronts for illegal activity.

When a computer is a target of a cyber attack, forensic investigators use three techniques to track the source. The first option is to make an immediate image of the server's hard disk and look through its log files for evidence of activity coming from unauthorized IP addresses. A second technique is to monitor the intruder by watching login attempts, changes to log files, and file access requests. Sophisticated intruders might be able to detect such monitoring, however, and cover their tracks. A third technique is to create a "honeypot"—an irresistible computer system or Web site containing fake information to lure any criminal activity. It allows investigators to monitor hackers until identification is possible.

Despite the many techniques and tools available to forensic investigators, they have three main constraints. First, they must adhere to privacy regulations and obtain warrants to set up wiretaps or gather information from ISPs about their customers. Second, they must scrupulously document their procedures so that the evidence they produce cannot be discredited in court as "planted" or fabricated. Third, forensic investigators must examine a wide range of alternatives pertaining to the crime, such as the chance that an IP or e-mail address used to commit a cybercrime doesn't belong to an innocent bystander being spoofed by the real hacker. Privacy, documentation, and evidentiary constraints cost forensic investigators time, and failure to adhere to strict standards can sometimes allow criminals to avoid conviction and penalties. But even within these constraints, careful forensic investigation is an important aspect of catching and convicting high-tech criminals.

FIGURE F-20

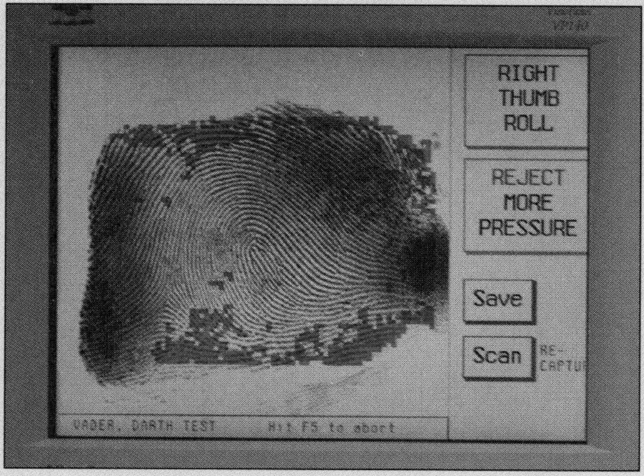

Issue   Is It a Crime?

It doesn't take any special digital expertise to mastermind every computer crime. Setting fire to a computer doesn't require the same finesse as writing a stealthy virus, but both can have the same disastrous effect on data. "Old-fashioned" crimes, like arson, that take a high-tech twist because they involve a computer, can be prosecuted using traditional laws. Traditional laws do not, however, cover the range of possibilities for computer crimes. Suppose a person unlawfully enters a computer facility and steals backup tapes. That person might be prosecuted for breaking and entering. But would breaking and entering laws apply to a person who uses an off-site terminal to "enter" a computer system without authorization? And what if a person copies a data file without authorization? Has that file really been "stolen" if the original remains on the computer?

Computer crimes are costly to organizations and individuals. Crimes include virus distribution, data diddling—unauthorized alterations to data stored on a computer system, identity theft—unauthorized copying of personal information, redirecting small, unnoticeable amounts of money from large amounts, denial of service attacks, information theft, and vandalism. Many computer criminals are caught and prosecuted. One of the first computer crime cases involved a worm unleashed on the ARPANET in 1990 that quickly spread through government and university computer systems. The worm's author, Robert Morris, was convicted and sentenced to three years' probation, 400 hours of community service, and a $10,000 fine. This relatively lenient sentence was imposed because Morris claimed he had not intended to cripple the entire network. In a recent court case, the author of the Anna Kournikova worm was caught by Dutch police and sentenced to 150 hours of community service after he admitted creating the worm to call attention to the fact that too few people were taking precautions to avoid computer viruses. At the end of the 2003, a Web page developer from Norco, California admitted to federal authorities that he was responsible for defacing the Web site maintained by Arabic-language news station Al Jazeera.

Many countries have computer crime laws that specifically define computer data and software as personal property. These laws also define as crimes the unauthorized access, use, modification, or disabling of a computer system or data. But laws don't necessarily stop criminals. In a 1995 case, a computer hacker named Kevin Mitnick was accused of breaking into dozens of corporate, university, government, and personal computers. Before being arrested, Mitnick reportedly stole thousands of data files and more than 20,000 credit card numbers. U.S. attorney Kent Walker commented, "He was clearly the most wanted computer hacker in the world." Mitnick's unauthorized access and use of computer data are explicitly defined as criminal acts by computer crime laws in most countries.

Mitnick denied many, but not all, of the accusations against him. Although vilified in the media, Mitnick had the support of many hackers and other people who believed that the prosecution grossly exaggerated the extent of his crimes. Nonetheless, Mitnick was sentenced to 46 months in prison, and ordered to pay restitution in the amount of $4,125 during his three-year period of supervised release. The prosecution was horrified by such a paltry sum, an amount that was much less than its request for $1.5 million in restitution.

Forbes reporter Adam L. Penenberg took issue with the 46-month sentence imposed by Judge Marianne Pfaelzer, and wrote, "This in a country where the average prison term for manslaughter is three years. Mitnick's crimes were curiously innocuous. He broke into corporate computers, but no evidence indicates that he destroyed data. Or sold anything he copied. Yes, he pilfered software but in doing so left it behind. This world of bits is a strange one, in which you can take something and still leave it for its rightful owner. The theft laws designed for payroll sacks and motor vehicles just don't apply to a hacker."

Unfortunately for Mitnick, the jail term and $4,125 fine were, perhaps, the most lenient part of his sentence. Mitnick, who had served most of his jail term while awaiting trial, was scheduled for a supervised release soon after sentencing. The additional conditions of Mitnick's supervised release included a ban on access to computer hardware, software, and any form of wireless communication. He was prohibited from possessing any kind of passwords, cellular phone codes, or data encryption devices. And just to make sure that he didn't get into any trouble with technologies that are not specifically mentioned in the terms of his supervised release, Mitnick was prohibited from using any new or future technology that performs as a computer or provides access to one. Perhaps worst of all, he could not work for a company with computers or computer access on its premises.

The Mitnick case and the opposing views that swirled around it illustrate our culture's attitude toward hackers. On the one hand, they are viewed as evil cyberterrorists who are set on destroying the glue that binds together the Information Age. From this perspective, hackers are criminals who must be hunted down, forced to make restitution for damages, and prevented from creating further havoc. From another perspective, hackers are viewed more as moderately bothersome entities whose pranks are tolerated by the computer community, along with software bugs and hardware glitches.

Which perspective is right? Are hackers dangerous cyberterrorists or harmless pranksters? Before you make up your mind about computer hacking and cracking, you might want to further investigate the Mitnick case and similar cases by following the Computer Crime InfoWeb links.

▼ INTERACTIVE QUESTIONS

○ Yes   ○ No   ○ Not sure

1. Should it be a crime to steal a copy of computer data while leaving the original data in place and unaltered?

○ Yes   ○ No   ○ Not sure

○ Yes   ○ No   ○ Not sure

2. Was Mitnick's sentence fair?

3. Should hackers be sent to jail if they cannot pay restitution to companies and individuals who lost money as the result of a prank?

○ Yes   ○ No   ○ Not sure

4. Do you think that a hacker would make a good consultant on computer security?

▼ EXPAND THE IDEAS

1. Should it be a crime to steal a copy of computer data while leaving the original data in place and unaltered? Why or why not? Write a short paper detailing your opinion and supporting your position.

2. Who's in cybercrime news these days? Are there any new techniques being used to catch cybercriminals? Research the current news items and past stories. Who is Mafiaboy and what has happened to him? Where is Kevin Mitnick today? Compile your findings in a short report. Include your resources as part of the report.

3. Should hackers be sent to jail if they cannot pay restitution to companies and individuals who lost money as the result of a prank? Do you think that a hacker would make a good consultant on computer security? Why or why not? Based on what you read, do you think Mitnick's sentence was fair? Write a short paper detailing your opinion and supporting your positions.

End of Unit Exercises

▼ KEY TERMS

Antivirus software
Authentication
Automated System Recovery
Backup
Backup software
Biometrics
Boot disk
Boot sector virus
Checksum
Computer virus
Copy Disk utility
Cracker
Cyberterrorism
Data center
Denial of service attack

Differential backup
Direct source input device
Disaster Recovery Plan
DOCSIS
File virus
Full system backup
Hacker
Incremental backup
Macro
Macro virus
Malicious code
MTBF
Multi-partite virus
Network address translation
   (NAT)

Operator error
Password protection
Payload
Personal firewall software
Polymorphic virus
Power failure
Power spike
Power surge
Recovery CD
Restore
Retro virus
Risk management
Stealth virus
Surge protector

Surge strip
Trigger event
Trojan horse
UPS (uninterruptible power
   supply)
Usage procedures
User rights
Virus
Virus definition
Virus hoax
Virus signature
Windows Startup Disk
Worm

▼ UNIT REVIEW

1. Use your own words to define bold terms that appear through-out the unit. List 10 of the terms that are least familiar to you and write a sentence for each of them.

2. Create a chart to review the factors that cause data loss or misuse. List the factors you learned about in this unit in the first column. Then place an X in the appropriate column to indicate whether that factor leads to data loss, inaccurate data, stolen data, or intentionally damaged data. Some factors might have more than one X.

3. Summarize what you have learned about viruses, Trojan horses, and software worms.

4. Make a checklist of steps to follow if you suspect that your computer is infected with a virus.

5. You receive three e-mail messages as follows:

   a. an e-mail attachment called Read this.txt.vbs. Because it appears to have two filename extensions, should you assume that this file harbors a virus?

   b. an e-mail message from a friend that says, "My antivirus software says that an attachment I received from you contains the QAZ virus." Would you assume that this message from your friend is a hoax?

   c. a message from an address you can't recognize with several lines of forwarded text that states that "If you receive an e-mail entitled "Badtimes," delete it IMMEDIATELY. Do not open it. Apparently this one is pretty nasty. It will not only erase everything on your hard drive, but it will also delete anything on disks within 20 feet of your computer." Do you believe it? Would you assume that this message is a hoax?

6. List the filename extensions of files that might typically harbor a virus.

7. Explain how antivirus software works and how it is able to catch new viruses that are created after the software is installed on your computer.

8. Explain the differences among the backup devices discussed in this unit.

9. Describe the various types of boot disks that might help you recover from a hard disk crash.

10. Devise a backup plan for the computer you use regularly. Explain how you would implement your plan.

▼ FILL IN THE BEST ANSWER

1. A(n) _____ is a device containing a battery that provides a continuous supply of power and other circuitry to prevent spikes and surges from reaching your computer.

2. Although a(n) _____ contains multiple outlets for power plugs, it does not contain the electronics necessary to filter out power spikes and surges.

3. The _____ is calculated by observing test equipment in a laboratory, then dividing the number of failures by the total number of hours of observation.

4. As part of a risk management program, preventative countermeasures can be grouped into three categories: deterrent measures, detection activities, and _____ procedures.

5. A method of personal identification called _____ bases identification on some physical trait, such as a fingerprint or the pattern of blood vessels in the retina of the eye.

6. User _____ are rules that limit the directories and files that each user can access.

7. A computer _____ is a program that attaches itself to a file and reproduces itself so as to spread from one file to another.

8. A boot _____ virus infects the system files that your computer uses every time you turn it on.

9. A Trojan _____ is a computer program that seems to perform one function while actually doing something else.

10. Viruses often attach themselves to a program file with a(n) _____ extension so that when you run the program, you also run the virus code.

11. Unlike a virus, which is designed to spread from file to file, a(n) _____ is designed to spread from computer to computer.

12. A virus can enter a computer as an e-mail attachment or as a script in an e-mail message formatted as _____.

13. Antivirus software calculates a(n) _____ to make sure that the bytes in an executable file have not changed from one computing session to another.

14. The process of identifying potential threats to computer systems, implementing plans to avoid threats, and developing steps to recover from disasters is referred to as _____ management.

15. A virus that doesn't really exist is referred to as a virus _____.

16. Some full-system backups miss the Windows _____ because that file is always open while the computer is on.

17. The three types of backup plans are full, _____, and differential.

18. A(n) _____ CD contains the operating system files needed to start your computer without accessing the hard disk.

19. A(n) _____ center is a facility specifically designed to house and protect computer systems and data.

20. Many personal computer operating systems provide a(n) _____ utility that makes an exact copy of a floppy disk.

▼ PRACTICE TESTS

When you use the Interactive CD, you can take Practice Tests that consist of 10 multiple-choice, true/false, and fill-in-the-blank questions. The questions are selected at random from a large test bank, so each time you take a test, you'll receive a different set of questions. Your tests are scored immediately, and you can print study guides to determine which questions you answered incorrectly. If you are using a Tracking Disk, insert it in the floppy disk drive to save your test scores.

▼ INDEPENDENT CHALLENGE 1

Losing data can be devastating to a business and certainly upsetting to an individual. We have all experienced that moment of panic when we go to retrieve a file only to receive some error message when we try to open it or find that it isn't where we thought we saved it. Describe a situation in which you or someone you know lost data stored on a computer.

Write a brief essay that answers the following questions:

1. Was the data lost, stolen, or just inaccessible? What caused the data loss?

2. What steps could have been taken to prevent the loss?

3. What steps could you or this other person have taken to recover the lost data?

▼ INDEPENDENT CHALLENGE 2

Do you have a plan for data recovery in place for your computer data? Are you working at a company that practices data backup and recovery on a regular basis? Is there antivirus software in place on the computer you use regularly? Assess the risk to the programs and data files stored on the hard disk drive of your computer.

Write a brief essay that answers the following questions:

1. What threats are likely to cause your data to be lost, stolen, or damaged?

2. How many data files do you have?

3. If you add up the size of all your files, how many megabytes of data do you have?

4. How many of these files are critical and would need to be replaced if you lost all of your data?

5. What would you need to do to reconstruct the critical files if the hard disk drive failed and you did not have any backups?

6. What measures could you use to protect your data from the threats you identified in Question 1? What is the cost of each of these measures?

7. Taking into account the threats to your data, the importance of your data, and the cost of possible protective measures, what do you think is the best plan for the security of your own data?

▼ INDEPENDENT CHALLENGE 3

If you suspect your computer has become infected with a virus, it is prudent to activate virus detection software to scan your files immediately. With the continued spread of viruses, virus detection software has become an essential utility in today's computing environment. Many virus detection software packages are available in computer stores, on computer bulletin boards, and on the Internet.

1. Find information about three virus detection software packages. Write a brief report on each one, and compare and contrast the features and benefits of each.

2. Microsoft Word documents can harbor macro viruses. Using library or Internet resources, find symptoms for a Word macro virus. Write a one-page report describing the Word macro virus.

3. Use the latest version of your virus protection software to check your disks to see whether you have the Word macro virus and to check the list of signatures in your virus software to see whether the virus is listed there.

▼ INDEPENDENT CHALLENGE 4

 An Internet worm created concern about the security of data on military and research computer systems, and it raised ethical questions about the rights and responsibilities of computer users. Select one of the following statements and write a two-page paper that argues for or against it. Use the Internet or library resources to learn more about each viewpoint. Be sure to include the resources you used in a bibliography. Whatever viewpoint you decide to present, make sure that you back it up with facts and references to authoritative articles and Web pages.

1. People have the right to hone their computing skills by breaking into computers. As a computer scientist once said, "The right to hack is held higher than the right of someone to tell you not to. It's an inalienable right."

2. If problems exist, it is acceptable to use any means to point them out. The computer science student who created the Internet worm was perfectly justified in claiming that he should not be prosecuted because he was just trying to point out that security holes exist in large computer networks.

3. Computer crimes are no different from other crimes, and computer criminals should be held responsible for the damage they cause by paying for the time and cost of replacing or restoring data.

▼ INDEPENDENT CHALLENGE 5

Obtain a copy of your school or work place's student/employee code or computer use policy. If your school or work place does not have a student/employee code or a computer use policy, use your favorite search engine to find one on the Internet. Use the document you select to write a brief paper that answers the following questions:

1. To whom does the policy apply: students, faculty, staff, community members, others?

2. What types of activities does the policy specifically prohibit?

3. Does the policy state the penalties for computer crimes? If so, what are they?

▼ INDEPENDENT CHALLENGE 6

Suppose that you work as a reporter for a local television station. Your boss wants the station to run a 90-second story about virus hoaxes and gives you the responsibility for writing the script. The basic objectives of the story are: (1) to remind people not to panic when they receive e-mail about viruses and (2) to provide a set of concrete steps that a person could take to discover whether a virus threat is real or a hoax.

1. Write the script for the story and create a storyboard that outlines the first few scenes.

2. Use your favorite search engine to research recent hoaxes (e.g., visit www.urbanlegends.com). Write a summary of two hoaxes to include in the script.

▼ INDEPENDENT CHALLENGE 7

Is it a good idea to use the Web to backup your data? Is this something that individuals as well as businesses should consider? At what point would a small business choose this option? What are the benefits and risks?

1. Log onto the Internet and then investigate a Web site that provides storage for data backups.

2. Find out the cost of using the site and investigate the site's terms and conditions for use. Try to discover if data stored at the site would be secure and private. Also try to determine whether the backup and restore procedures seem feasible. Try to determine whether a plan exists for notifying customers if the site is about to go out of business. You might also look for a review of the backup provider at sites such as www.zdnet.com or www.cnet.com.

3. After completing your research, submit a two-page paper that explains whether or not you would use the site for storing your backups.

▼ LAB: BACKING UP YOUR COMPUTER

1. Start the interactive part of the lab. Insert your Tracking Disk if you want to save your QuickCheck results. Perform each of the lab steps as directed and answer all of the lab QuickCheck questions. When you exit the lab, your answers are automatically graded and your results are displayed.

2. Describe where most of your data files are stored and estimate how many megabytes of data (not programs) you have in all of these files. Next, take a close look at these files and estimate how much data (in megabytes) you cannot afford to lose. Finally, explain what you think would be the best hardware device for backing up this amount of data.

3. Draw a sketch or capture a screenshot of the Microsoft Backup window's toolbar. Use ToolTips or the window's status bar to find the name of each toolbar button. Use this information to label the buttons on your sketch or screenshot.

4. Assume that you will use Microsoft Backup to make a backup of your data files. Describe the backup procedure you would use to specify the folders that you must include. It is not necessary to list individual files unless they are not within one of the folders that you would back up. Make sure that you indicate whether or not you would use password protection, the type of compression that you would select, and how you would handle the Windows Registry.

▼ STUDENT EDITION LABS

Reinforce the concepts you have learned in this unit through the **Keeping Your Computer Virus Free** and **Backing Up Your Computer** Student Edition Labs, available online at the Illustrated Computer Concepts Web site.

▼ SAM LABS

If you have a SAM user profile, you have access to additional content, features, and functionality. Log in to your SAM account and go to your assignments page to see what your instructor has assigned for this unit.

▼ VISUAL WORKSHOP

As network technologies continue to emerge, security will always be a factor, and businesses and consumers will find themselves asking, "How vulnerable is our business data?" Virtual private networks (VPNs) are an advancement in network systems that are used to provide secure private network access over an otherwise insecure public access network, typically the Internet. VPNs are generally less expensive than establishing and maintaining a private network over private lines. VPNs allow businesses to provide secure communications and connections over the Internet. Figure F-21 shows a Web page from a company that provides VPN services.

FIGURE F-21

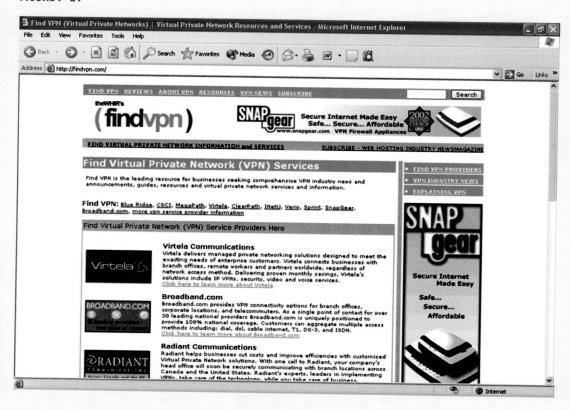

Log onto the Internet and use a favorite search engine to find businesses that offer VPN service.

1. Review three Web sites.

2. Use the information on the Web site and other resources to define VPN and briefly describe how it works.

3. Create a table that compares the VPN services offered by the three companies you researched.

4. Summarize by stating why you would or would not use a VPN as a backup resource.

UNIT G
The Web and E-commerce

Unit G focuses on the Web and the variety of key technologies that make the Web what it is today. The unit begins with an introduction to the technologies that bring the Web to your computer screen. The unit continues by exploring the tools that make it possible to create and enhance Web pages while providing a consistent look across all pages in a Web site. You will also explore e-commerce topics and learn about buying and selling merchandise and services over the Web. The unit wraps up with a Tech Talk on encryption. You will read about computers in the context of politics. The Issue explores how to evaluate the information you receive through the Internet and determine its validity.

Exploring Web technology

Although many people use the terms interchangeably, there is a difference between the Web and the Internet. The Internet is basically a collection of computers and cables that forms a communications network. The Internet carries a variety of data, including e-mail, videoconferences, and instant messages. The Internet also carries text, graphical, and audio data that form Web pages. The Web is a collection of documents that can be accessed over the Internet and can be related by using links. This lesson discusses technologies (HTTP, HTML, Web servers, URLs, and browsers) behind the Web.

DETAILS

● Two of the most important elements of the Web are **Hypertext Transfer Protocol (HTTP)** and **Hypertext Markup Language (HTML)**. HTTP is the communications protocol used to transport data over the Web. HTML is the set of specifications used to create Web pages. Notice that both of these Web elements contain hypertext in their names. **Hypertext** is a key concept for understanding the Web.

The idea of hypertext originated much earlier than the Web, or even the Internet. In 1945, an engineer named Vannevar Bush wrote the article "As We May Think," which described a microfilm-based machine called the Memex that linked associated information or ideas through "trails." The idea resurfaced in the mid-1960s, when Harvard graduate Ted Nelson coined the term hypertext to describe a computer system that could store literary documents, link them according to logical relationships, and allow readers to comment and annotate what they read. Nelson sketched the diagram shown in Figure G-1 to explain his idea. This early sketch of project Xanadu, a distant relative of the Web, used the terms links and web.

In 1990, a British scientist named Tim Berners-Lee developed specifications for HTML, HTTP, and URLs. He hoped that these technologies would help researchers share information by creating access to a sort of web of electronic documents. In the words of Berners-Lee, "The Web is an abstract (imaginary) space of information. On the Net, you find computers; on the Web, you find documents, sounds, videos, and information. On the Net, the connections are cables between computers; on the Web, connections are hypertext links."

● A **Web server** stores one or more Web pages that form a Web site. Each page is stored as a file called an **HTML document**—a text or ASCII document with embedded HTML tags. Some tags specify how the document is to be displayed when viewed in a browser. Other tags contain **hypertext links** (or simply links) to related documents, graphics, and sound files that are also stored on Web servers. You can click a hypertext link—an underlined word, phrase, or graphic—to access related documents. In addition to storing these files, a Web server runs software that handles requests for specific Web pages.

As an alternative to HTML documents, Web servers can also store Web page data in other types of files, such as databases. This data can be assembled into HTML format "on the fly" in response to Web page requests.

● Every Web page is a document stored on a Web server and identified by a unique address called a **URL (Uniform Resource Locator)**.

● You use Web client software called a **browser** to view Web pages. When you type a URL into the browser's address box, you are requesting the HTML document for the Web page that you want to view. Your browser creates a request for the specified file using a command provided by the HTTP communications protocol. The request is sent to a Web server, which has been listening for HTTP requests. When your request arrives, the Web server examines it, locates the HTML document that you requested, and sends it back to your computer. If additional elements are needed to view the Web page correctly—a graphic, for example—your browser must issue a new request to the server for that element. The cycle continues until the Web page appears in your browser window. Figure G-2 illustrates the entire process.

FIGURE G-1: Ted Nelson's early sketch of project Xanadu

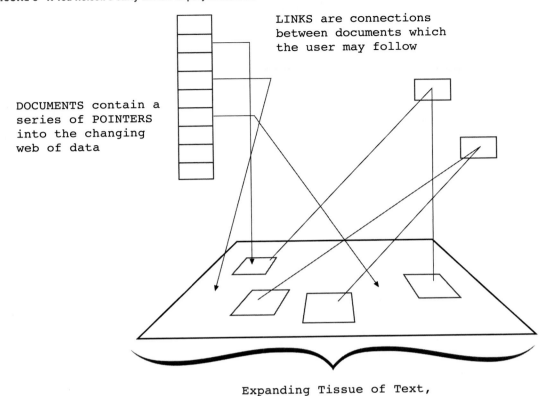

LINKS are connections
between documents which
the user may follow

DOCUMENTS contain a
series of POINTERS
into the changing
web of data

Expanding Tissue of Text,
Data, and Graphics

FIGURE G-2: How browsers and Web servers exchange HTTP messages

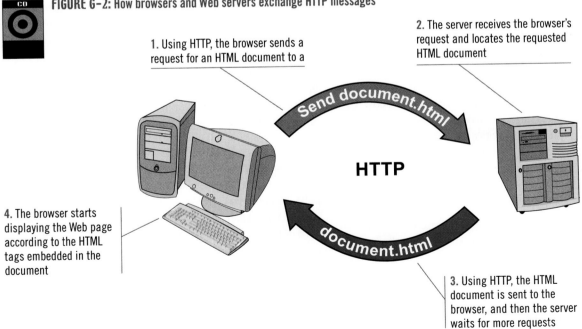

1. Using HTTP, the browser sends a request for an HTML document to a

2. The server receives the browser's request and locates the requested HTML document

Send document.html

HTTP

document.html

4. The browser starts displaying the Web page according to the HTML tags embedded in the document

3. Using HTTP, the HTML document is sent to the browser, and then the server waits for more requests

Exploring HTML

HTML (Hypertext Markup Language) is a set of specifications for creating HTML documents that a browser can display as a Web page. HTML is called a **markup language** because authors mark up their documents by inserting special instructions called **HTML tags** that specify how the document should appear when displayed on a computer screen or printed. The original HTML specifications that were developed by Tim Berners-Lee in 1990 have been revised several times by an organization called the **World Wide Web Consortium (W3C)**. This lesson discusses how the current HTML specifications work to display the lines of text on your computer screen in the right color and size and to position graphics in your browser.

DETAILS

- HTML has had several versions. **XHTML** is the follow-up version to HTML 4. Rather than calling it HTML 5, the W3C preferred to name it XHTML 1.0 to reflect its extensibility. XHTML, which includes all HTML 4 tags, can be extended by adding customized tags. Today's Web operates according to XHTML standards, even though people commonly refer to the technology simply as HTML.

- The term **Web page** refers to both the HTML document and the corresponding Web page that is displayed by your browser. The term "source" is used to refer to the document that has the HTML tags. Most browsers include a menu option that allows you to view the source HTML document with its HTML tags. For example, when using the Internet Explorer browser, you can click View on the menu bar, then click Source. See Figure G-3.

- In an HTML document, HTML tags, such as <b> and <hr />, are enclosed in angle brackets. These tags are treated as instructions to the browser. When your browser displays a Web page on your computer screen, it does not show the tags or angle brackets. Instead, it attempts to follow the tags' instructions. Most HTML tags work in pairs. An opening tag begins an instruction, which stays in effect until a closing tag appears. Closing tags always contain a slash. For example, the following sentence contains opening and closing bold tags:

  <b>Caterpillars</b> love sugar.

  When displayed by a browser, the word "Caterpillars" will be bold, but the other words in the sentence will not.

  The <hr /> tag produces a horizontal line on a Web page. The <hr /> tag is called a **self-closing tag**, which is a single tag that includes a closing "/" symbol. A space between the "hr" and "/" is included for maximum compatibility with various browsers.

- HTML is not a case-sensitive language, but XHTML style requires tags to be lowercase so that they work on case-sensitive servers. Notice, too, that in self-closing tags such as <hr />, the slash comes at the end of the tag, whereas in a closing tag such as </b>, the slash comes at the beginning.

- HTML documents contain no graphics. So, in addition to specifying how text should be formatted, HTML tags can be used to specify how to incorporate graphics on a page. The <img src> tag is used to specify the name and location of a graphic file that is to be displayed as part of a Web page. Figure G-4 illustrates how browsers use HTML tags to display content.

- HTML tags also produce the links that connect you to other Web documents. The <a href> tag specifies the information necessary to display the links that allow you to jump to related Web pages. The <a href> HTML tag contains the URL for the linked page. Text between the <a href> and </a> tags appears as an underlined link when the Web page is displayed in a browser. Refer again to Figure G-3, "Volunteers" in <a href = "http://www.expn.com/volunteers.htm">volunteers</a>) appears as underlined text.

- HTML includes hundreds of tags. For convenience, tags are classified into four groups. **Operational tags** specify the basic setup for a Web page, provide ways for users to interact with a page, and offer ways for Web pages to incorporate information derived from databases. **Formatting tags** change the appearance of text and work much like the formatting options in a word processor to create bold and italic text, adjust the size of text, change the color of text and backgrounds, arrange text in table format, or align text on a page. **Link tags** specify where and how to display links to other Web pages and e-mail addresses. **Media tags** specify how to display media elements, such as graphics, sound clips, or videos.

FIGURE G-3: Viewing the source HTML document

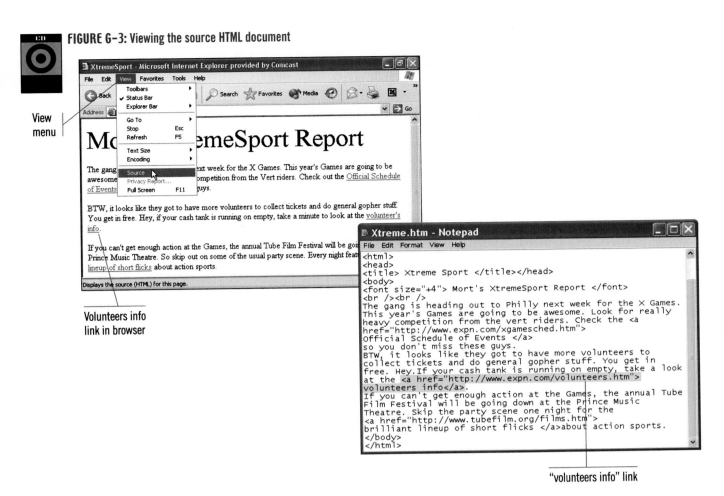

View menu

Volunteers info link in browser

"volunteers info" link

FIGURE G-4: How browsers interpret HTML tags

This <hr /> tag produces one horizontal rule

The <img src> tag produces a graphic

JPG image file

HTML document

Web page in browser with horizontal rules and image

UNIT G

Using Web browsers

A **Web browser**, usually referred to simply as a browser, is a software program that runs on your computer and helps you access Web pages. Technically, a browser is the client half of the client/server software that facilitates communication between a personal computer and Web server. The software on the Web server is the server side of the system. The browser is installed on your computer, and the Web server software is installed on a host computer on the Internet. This lesson gives an overview of the various browsers that are available, and explains how helper applications, plug-ins, and players work with your browser to display Web pages.

DETAILS

● Your browser plays two roles in accessing and displaying Web pages. First, a browser uses HTTP to send messages to a Web server—usually a request for a specific HTML document. Second, when it receives an HTML document from a Web server, your browser interprets the HTML tags in order to display the requested Web page.

Popular browsers include Internet Explorer (IE), Netscape Navigator, and Opera. See Figure G-5. Internet Explorer and Netscape Navigator share similar features—perhaps because they evolved from the earliest graphical browser, Mosaic. Opera is an alternative that offers unique features such as a multidocument display, which IE and Navigator do not offer. Table G-1 provides a brief history of popular Web browsers.

● All browsers are designed to interpret HTML documents. Modern browsers also handle additional file formats, such as GIF and JPEG graphic formats. However, if you click a link that leads to a file that your browser cannot handle, you will see a message that directs you to download the software necessary to read the file format. For example, you might be directed to the Adobe Web site to download the Acrobat Reader software, which handles PDF (Portable Document Format) files and lets you view documents created from a variety of desktop publishing applications uniformly on any system. To display an animation, you might need Shockwave software that handles SWF files. For movies, you might need QuickTime software to handle MOV files.

● The software your browser uses to read non-native file formats can be a helper application, plug-in, or player. A **helper application** is a program that understands how to work with a specific file format. When a helper application is installed, it updates your computer system so that your browser knows which file formats it can accept. Whenever your browser encounters a non-HTML file format, it automatically runs the corresponding helper application, which in turn opens the file. A helper application opens a new window for displaying the file.

● A **plug-in** is similar to a helper application, but it displays files within the browser window. A plug-in that was pioneered by Netscape developers is activated from an <embed> tag inserted in an HTML document. For example, <embed src = "sample.swf"> instructs a browser to activate the plug-in that works with the SWF file format, which in turn opens the sample.swf file. Recent versions of Internet Explorer, however, do not respond to the <embed> tag and, therefore, are not able to use Netscape-style plug-ins. Instead, IE uses ActiveX components, which are activated by the <object> tag.

Helper applications and plug-ins are very similar from the user's perspective. The current trend is to use the term "player" to refer to any helper application or plug-in that helps a browser display a particular file format.

● It is a good idea to upgrade when a new version of your browser is available. You can get up-to-date browser functionality and often increased security simply by spending a few minutes downloading and installing an update. Because Web pages may depend on new HTML features that are supported only by the latest browser versions, you might encounter errors as your browser tries to display a page, but cannot interpret some of the HTML without the latest upgrade. In other cases, your browser might display the Web page without errors, but you will not see all of the intended effects.

Another important reason to upgrade is increased security. As hackers discover and take advantage of security holes, browser publishers try to patch them. Upgrades typically contain patches for known security holes, though new features in the upgrade may open new security holes.

FIGURE G-5: Popular browsers—Internet Explorer, Netscape Navigator, and Opera—all displaying Google's main page

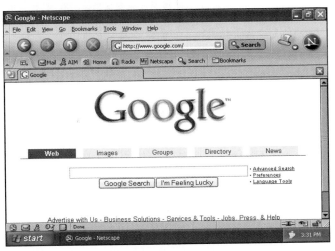

TABLE G-1: A brief history of browsers

BROWSER	IMPORTANT DATES	DESCRIPTION
Mosaic Available for Macintosh, PC, and UNIX	Introduced November 1993, NCSA discontinued Mosaic support in 1997	The earliest graphical browsers, developed at the University of Illinois National Center for Supercomputing Applications (NCSA), also licensed and sold as Spyglass
Netscape Navigator Available for Mac and PC platforms, Linux and several versions of UNIX	Version 1.0 published in December 1994; in 1998 became available as open source software through an organization called Mozilla; version 6.0 appeared in 2001	Developed by a group of programmers who worked on Mosaic; quickly became the most popular browser, numerous revisions added pioneering features such as frames, plug-ins, and JavaScript support
Internet Explorer (IE) Available for Mac and PC platforms, Linux and several versions of UNIX	Version 1.0 was published by Microsoft in August 1995; version 4.0 appeared in 1997; version 6.0 appeared in 2001	Original IE 1.0 browser code was licensed from Spyglass; not until 1997 did it match and then surpass Navigator's popularity
Opera Available for Windows, Linux, UNIX, and Mac OS	Published in December 1996	Opera began as a Telenor (Norwegian phone company) project to develop a small and fast browser for computers with meager memory and processing resources; Opera was written from scratch, and as a result, it has some unique features, such as page zoom and a multidocument display

Understanding HTTP and Web servers

HTTP is a communications protocol that works in conjunction with the TCP/IP communications protocol to get Web resources to your desktop. A **Web resource** is any data file that has a URL, such as an HTML document, a graphic, or a sound file. This lesson explains how HTTP works with Web servers to send and receive Web resources.

DETAILS

- HTTP includes commands called methods that help browsers communicate with Web servers. GET is the most frequently used HTTP method and is typically used to retrieve the text and graphics files necessary for displaying a Web page. HTTP transports a request for a Web resource to a Web server, then transports the Web server's response back to a browser.

- An HTTP communications transaction takes place over a pair of sockets. A **socket** is an abstract concept that represents one end of a connection. In an HTTP communications transaction, your browser opens a socket, connects to a similar open socket at the Web server, and issues a command like "send me an HTML document." The server receives the command, executes it, and sends a response back through the socket. The sockets are then closed until the browser is ready to issue another command. Figure G-6 illustrates how the messages flow between your browser and a Web server in order to retrieve an HTML document.

- HTTP is classified as a **stateless protocol**, which generally allows one request and one response per session. As a result, your browser can request an HTML document during a session, but as soon as the document is sent, the session is closed, and the Web server will forget that your browser ever made a request. To make additional requests, your browser must make another HTTP request. This is why assembling a complex Web page with several graphics, buttons, and sounds requires your browser to make many HTTP requests to the Web server.

- A Web server's response to a browser's request includes an **HTTP status code** that indicates whether or not the browser's request can be fulfilled. You may have encountered the "404 Not Found" message that a browser displays when a Web server sends a 404 status code to indicate that the requested resource does not exist. HTTP status codes are summarized in Table G-2.

- A Web server is configured to include HTTP software, which is always running when the server is up and ready to fulfill requests. One of the server's ports is dedicated to listening for HTTP requests. When a request arrives, the server software analyzes the request and takes whatever action is necessary to fulfill it. The computer that runs Web server software might have other software running on it as well. For example, a computer might operate as a Web server, as an e-mail server, and as an FTP (File Transfer Protocol) server all at the same time! To handle these diverse duties efficiently, a computer devotes one port to HTTP requests (usually Port 80), another to handling SMTP e-mail (usually Port 25), and a third to FTP requests (usually Port 21).

- The way that a computer allocates one port to each service helps explain how it is possible for a Web service to be down when the Web server is still up and running. A Web server runs separate software for each service it offers. As long as the right software is running, the service is available.

- A single port on a Web server can connect to many sockets carrying requests from browsers. The number of socket connections a port can handle depends on the server's memory and operating system, but at minimum, hundreds of requests can be handled at the same time. Some large-volume sites, such as yahoo.com and amazon.com, have more traffic than any single Web server can handle. These sites tend to use a group of multiple servers, also known as a **server farm**, to handle the thousands of requests that come in each second. See Figure G-7.

  Excessive demand can occur when special circumstances attract people to a Web site or when a worm launches a denial-of-service attack. When traffic exceeds capacity, a Web server can take a long time to fulfill Web page requests—some requests might even produce a "page not found" error.

- Most Web server software can be configured so that the server responds to requests addressed to more than one IP address or domain name. In such a case, one computer running one Web server program can act like multiple Web sites. This type of shared hosting is typically supplied to small Web sites that don't have enough traffic to justify the cost of a dedicated server.

FIGURE G-6: How HTTP messages flow between a browser and a Web server

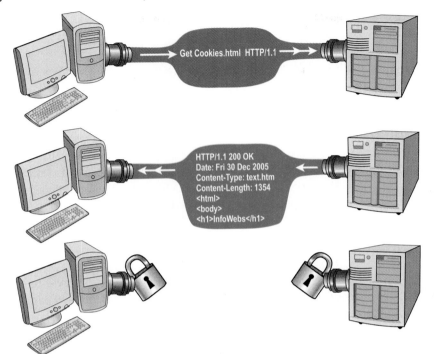

1. The URL in the browser's Address bar contains the domain name of the Web server that your browser contacts

Address | www.infoweblinks.com/Cookies.html

Get Cookies.html HTTP/1.1 →

2. Your browser opens a socket and connects to a similar open socket at the Web server; next, your browser generates and sends an HTTP message through the socket

HTTP/1.1 200 OK
Date: Fri 30 Dec 2005
Content-Type: text.htm
Content-Length: 1354
<html>
<body>
<h1>InfoWebs</h1>

3. The server sends back the requested HTML document through the open sockets so you can view the page in your browser

4. After sending the response, the server closes its socket and the browser closes its socket

FIGURE G-7: A server farm

◄ Large-volume Web sites often use a server farm to handle thousands of Web page requests

TABLE G-2: HTTP status codes

CODE	MESSAGE	DESCRIPTION
200	OK	The request succeeded, and the resulting resource, such as a file or script output, was sent.
301	Moved Permanently	The resource was moved.
302	Moved Temporarily	The resource is temporarily unavailable.
303	See Other	The resource moved to another URL and should be automatically retrieved by the client.
404	Not Found	The requested resource doesn't exist.
500	Server Error	An unexpected server error, such as encountering a scripting error, occurred.

UNIT G
Introducing Web page authoring

Info Web

WEB AUTHORING TOOLS

With today's Web page authoring tools, it is easy to create your own Web pages. You have several choices when it comes to Web page authoring tools. In this lesson, you'll explore these different tools and get an overview of the basic components of a Web page.

DETAILS

● At the most basic level, you can use a text editor such as NotePad to create Web pages. A **text editor** is similar to word processing software. Unlike word processing software, however, a text editor creates a plain text ASCII document with no hidden formatting codes. See Figure G-8. The only codes included in a document created with a text editor are the HTML tags you type along with the text that you want your browser to display.

When you save the document you create with a text editor, you must specify an appropriate filename extension, such as .html or html so that browsers will recognize it as an HTML document. If you want to create Web pages using a text editor, you will need a good HTML reference book.

● A second way to create Web pages is to use the HTML conversion option included with many software applications. Microsoft Word, for example, allows you to create a standard .doc file and then use the File menu's Save As Web Page option to convert the document into HTML format. Most recent versions of spreadsheet, presentation, or desktop publishing software include HTML capabilities. To discover whether an application has an HTML option, click File on the menu bar, then click Save As or click Export. Converting a document into HTML format sometimes produces an unexpected result because some of the features and formatting in your original document might not translate well into HTML.

● A third option for creating Web pages is to use the online Web page authoring tools provided by some ISPs and other companies that host Web pages. Working with these tools is typically quite simple. You type, select, drag, and drop elements onto a Web page. These simple tools are great for beginners, but they sometimes omit features that are included with more sophisticated authoring tools.

● A fourth way to create Web pages is to use a special category of software called **Web authoring software**, which provides tools specifically designed to enter and format Web page text, graphics, and links. See Figure G-9. Most Web authoring software includes features that help you manage an entire Web site, as opposed to simply creating Web pages. Web site management

tools include the capability to link the pages within a site automatically and easily change those links. They are also capable of checking all of the external links at a site to make sure that they still link to valid Web pages. Popular Web authoring software packages include Microsoft FrontPage and Macromedia Dreamweaver.

● Whether you create Web pages using a very basic text editor or a very sophisticated Web authoring program, all Web pages have common characteristics. Figure G-10 illustrates the basic components of a typical Web page.

● The HTML document for a Web page is divided into two sections: the head and the body. If you create an HTML document using a text editor, you must manually enter the tags that begin and end these two sections. If you use Web authoring software, these tags are automatically entered for you. The **head section** begins with the <head> HTML tag and contains information that defines some global properties for the document, but it is not displayed by your browser. Information in the head section of an HTML document can include the following: the title of your page as it will appear in the title bar of your browser window, global formatting information, information about your page that can be used by search engines, and scripts that add interactivity to your page.

The **body section** of an HTML document begins with the <body> HTML tag. It contains the text that you want the browser to display, the HTML tags that format the text, plus a variety of links, including links to graphics. Most Web pages use headers to break up the text into organized sections. A **Web page header** or header is simply a subtitle that appears in a font that is a different size or color than the normal text on the page. HTML supports six pre-defined levels of headers, with H1 using the largest font and H6 using the smallest font.

Other common characteristics of Web pages include navigation tools such as scroll bars and navigation bars, hyperlinks such as hypertext or graphics, Web page components such as search features, visual elements such as graphics, and multimedia elements such as video, audio, and animation.

FIGURE G-8: Notepad as a Web page authoring tool

When using a text editor, a Web page author types the text for the page, and also types the HTML codes that will produce various formats and effects

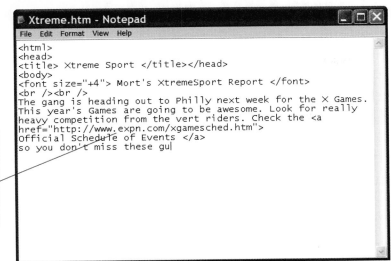

FIGURE G-9: Web authoring software

When creating a Web page, you can type the text without worrying about HTML tags; to format words, phrases, or paragraphs, simply use the formatting buttons on the toolbars

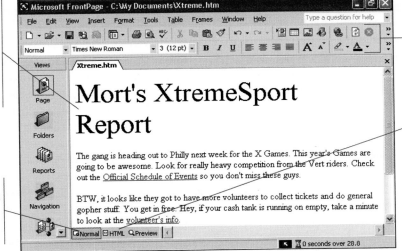

If you've done any word processing with Microsoft Word, most of the controls on the tool-bars should look familiar

In HTML view, you can see all of the HTML tags that were inserted into your text

In Normal view, the FrontPage window displays your Web page similar to how it will appear in a browser window

FIGURE G-10: Elements in a typical Web page

Web page title

Theme elements

Header

Graphical link

Navigation links

Graphic

Text link

Enhancing Web pages

Web pages consist of visual elements that enhance the way the information is conveyed. Whether you are creating a Web page or a Web site, it is important that these visual elements have a consistent look and feel. This lesson discusses styles, style sheets, themes, and sound and graphics, which enhance Web pages and create visual consistency.

DETAILS

- A **style** is a combination of attributes—colors, sizes, and fonts—that specify the way text is displayed. When working with Web page authoring software, you can simply highlight the text that you want to format and select the formatting attributes from a list. When you create Web pages with a text editor, you can format text by inserting the appropriate HTML tags. Table G-3 provides a list of basic HTML formatting tags.

- A **style sheet**, also called a **cascading style sheet (CSS)**, acts as a template to control the layout and design of Web pages. Style sheets work in conjunction with HTML tags to make it easy to change the format of elements in a Web page globally and consistently. They allow Web page authors to separate the format specifications for an element from the element itself. A style sheet allows you simply to define the style for an element, such as a price list, once at the beginning of the HTML document, then apply it by using a single HTML tag (if you are using a text editor), or by selecting the format from a list (if you are using Web page authoring software). You can also set up an **external style sheet** that contains formatting specifications for a group of Web pages. All Web pages in a Web site can use the external style sheet by means of a link placed in their head sections.

  Style sheets make it easy to apply styles and change them consistently. For example, if you define the style for prices in a price list as centered, italic, and red, then every time this style is applied to the prices in a price list they will be centered, italic, and red. If later you decide to change the style associated with prices to different specifications, such as right-aligned, bold, and blue, you change the specification for the prices style once in the style sheet, not each time the prices style is used. Changing the style in the style sheet causes the change to cascade through the entire Web page or Web site so that all occurrences associated with the prices style are changed. The main disadvantage of style sheets is that some features are not uniformly supported by all browsers.

- In addition to styles, themes are often used to enhance Web pages. A **theme** is a collection of coordinated graphics, colors, and fonts applied to individual pages or all pages in a Web site. Themes are generally available as part of Web authoring software.

- You can enhance Web pages by including sound files. The Web page can show a popup window containing sound controls, or the music can play completely in the background. The <a href> tag creates a foreground link that visitors can click to hear the sound. You can use the <embed> tag to attach a sound file that starts to play "background sound" as soon as a browser displays the Web page.

- Another way to enhance Web pages is through the use of graphics. The HTML document that your browser receives does not contain any graphics but does contain an HTML tag that references a graphic. If you use a text editor to create a Web page, you must enter the complete tag manually. For example, <img src = "truck.gif"> includes the filename for the truck.gif graphic. When using Web page authoring software, you typically use a menu option to select the graphic from a list of files that are stored on your computer. Figure G-11 illustrates how you insert a graphic when creating a Web page using FrontPage. Most of the graphics used for Web pages are stored in **GIF (Graphics Interchange Format)**, **JPEG (Joint Photographics Experts Group)**, or **PNG (Portable Network Graphics)** format. Keeping graphics files small helps Web pages download and appear quickly in the browser window.

- An **animated GIF** is a graphic file that consists of a sequence of frames or related images. When an animated GIF is displayed, your browser cycles through the frames, resulting in a simple, repeating animation. Animated GIFs, see Figure G-12, are one of the easiest ways to add simple animation to a Web page. **Flash animation** is a proprietary technology developed by Macromedia. You have to download the Flash client software which is free and required for viewing flash animation. Flash provides more flexibility than animated GIFs and can be used for more complex animations.

- Video is also used to enhance Web pages. Popular video formats, such as **QuickTime**, **MPEG**, and **AVI**, are used for Web-based and disk-based video playback. Variations of these formats are specially designed to handle the communications details for Web playback. To play video, your computer needs corresponding player software, usually specified at the Web site.

TABLE G-3: HTML formatting tags

TAG	USE
<font size="xxx">	Specify a font size by inserting a number between the quotation marks
<font color="color">	Specify a color name or number between the quotation marks
<b> </b>	Bold text
<i> </i>	Italicize text
<u> </u>	Underline text
<align="direction">	Specify paragraph alignment by inserting right, center, or left between the quotation marks
<bgcolor="color">	Specify a background color for the entire page

 FIGURE G-11: Inserting a graphic in a Web page

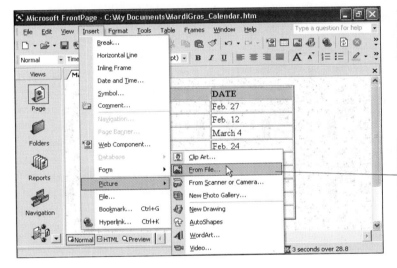

◄ Web authoring software makes it easy to specify the graphics you want to include on a Web page

Use the From File menu option to view a list of graphics stored on your hard disk, and select the one you want to use

 FIGURE G-12: Simple animation on a Web page

► When an animated GIF is displayed, your browser cycles through the frames, resulting in a simple repeating animation; in this example, the spacecraft spins

Exploring navigation elements

For a Web page or Web site to be effective, visitors must be able to move intuitively to the information they want. Web pages should include clear and consistent navigation elements. This lesson looks at navigation elements, such as hypertext links, graphics links, hot spots, and navigation bars, used to make navigating a Web page or Web site easy.

DETAILS

● **Links** (also called **hyperlinks**) open a location in the same Web page, a different Web page, or a different Web site. Links, whether they are text or graphics, provide the fundamental tools for navigating Web pages. An **internal link** (also called a local link or page link) links to other pages within the same Web site. An **external link** (also called a remote link) links to pages outside of the Web site. You can create links to any Web site in the world, but it is a good idea to check the site's policies on external links. An **interpage link** (also called an "anchor link") is a type of link usually used to jump to a different location within the current Web page. These links are handy for a long page divided into sections. For example, user group FAQs are often structured as a long page of questions and answers. The page begins with a list of questions, each of which is linked to its answer, which appears farther down the page. A **mailto link** automatically opens a pre-addressed e-mail form that can be filled in and sent. These links are typically used to provide a method for contacting the Webmaster, the Web site's author, or a customer service representative.

● Typically, a link appears on a Web page as underlined, blue text, but a link can also be a graphic such as a picture or a button. The arrow-shaped pointer changes, usually to a pointing hand, when it moves over any text or graphics link in the browser window.

● The HTML that specifies a link typically has two parts: a destination and a label. See Figure G-13. The <a href> link tag also allows a Web page author to specify whether the linked page will appear in the current browser window or in a new browser window. You've probably encountered Web page links that create a new window. When used effectively, new windows help you easily return to previous pages. However, too many new windows can clutter your screen.

● Instead of a text label, you can use an image as a clickable link. These graphical links can connect to other Web pages or graphics. You might have encountered graphical links called **thumbnails** that expand in size when clicked. Graphical links can even look like buttons, complete with labels and icons. Figure G-14 shows the HTML tag you might use to create a clickable image in a Web page.

● While browsing the Web, you've probably encountered graphics that are divided into several clickable areas. These images might be maps that allow you to click a geographic region to view a list of local attractions, businesses, or dealers. You also might encounter technical diagrams that link to information about the part that you click. You might even come across a Web site with a photo on the main page that is divided into areas representing different parts of the Web site.

A clickable map, photo, or diagram is referred to as an **image map**, and each of the links within the image map is sometimes referred to as a **hot spot**. To create an image map with a text editor, a Web page author uses a set of HTML tags that specify the coordinates and destination page for each clickable hot spot. A Web page authoring tool typically makes it easy to drag over an area of an image, then use menus and dialog boxes to specify the destination page for each hot spot. See Figure G-15.

● A Web page link only works as long as a file with the corresponding URL exists on the server. A non-functioning link is called a **broken link**. If a Webmaster moves, deletes, or changes the name of the requested file, the link will not function properly. If a broken link points to a non-existent HTML document, your browser typically produces a 404 Page Not Found error. When a broken link points to a non-existent graphic or other non-HTML format file, your browser typically displays a broken link icon (for example ☒ or ☒).

● It is the responsibility of Web page authors to check the links on their Web pages periodically to make sure they work. To test links, an author can click through them manually or use the link-checking feature of Web authoring software. Bad links must be removed or edited to reflect the correct URL for a destination page.

FIGURE G-13: A link to display another Web page

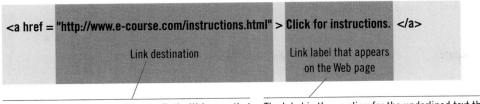

`<a href = "http://www.e-course.com/instructions.html" > Click for instructions. </a>`

Link destination — Link label that appears on the Web page

The destination specifies a URL, usually the Web page that will appear as a result of clicking the link

The label is the wording for the underlined text that appears on the Web page as the clickable link

FIGURE G-14: A link to display a graphic

▼ This link is an image of a sports car from the file sports car.jpg; when clicked, this graphical link displays the information contained in the file named features.html

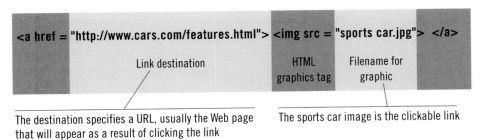

`<a href = "http://www.cars.com/features.html"> <img src = "sports car.jpg"> </a>`

Link destination — HTML graphics tag — Filename for graphic

The destination specifies a URL, usually the Web page that will appear as a result of clicking the link

The sports car image is the clickable link

FIGURE G-15: Web page with hot spots

▶ Using Web page authoring software, hot spots can be defined by dragging over areas of the graphic; in this example, hot spots define areas of the solar system; clicking one of these hot spots produces information about that planet

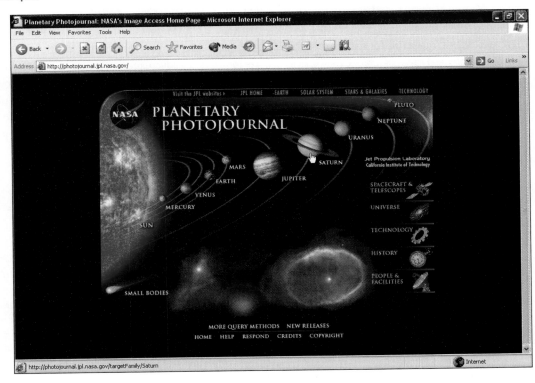

Organizing Web pages

Tables and frames are tools you can use to help organize areas of text or graphics on a page. This lesson explains how to use tables and frames to layout the content on a Web page. Once you have finished your pages, you must test and publish them. See Table G-4.

Info Web

WEB PAGE DESIGN TIPS

DETAILS

● A **Web page table** (usually referred to simply as a "table") is a grid of cells that can be used as a layout tool for specifying the placement of text and graphics on a Web page. Tables are an important part of Web page design because HTML does not include a formatting feature for multiple columns. Without tables, authors have less control over the position of text and graphics displayed in the browser window. The effectiveness of tables is illustrated in Figure G-16, where one Web page uses tables and the other page does not.

● Web tables provide Web page designers with flexibility. For example, the table cells can contain text or graphics; columns and rows in a table can be different sizes. Individual cells can be sized according to the material they contain and their contents can be formatted individually. Many Web page designers put the entire contents of a Web page into one table.

● Tables are very easy to use, whether you create them with Web authoring software or with word processing software that converts documents into HTML format. You simply define the number of columns and rows for a table, then specify the size for each row and each column. You can merge two or more cells to create a larger cell, or you can split a cell to make smaller cells.

Creating tables with a text editor is more of a challenge. You use HTML tags to specify the beginning of the table, each row, and each cell in the row. What makes this task difficult is that you cannot see the table as you construct it. To view the table, you must preview your Web page using your browser.

● An **HTML form** (or "form") is a series of fill-in blanks created using the HTML <form> and <input> tags. Forms are used to collect user input for e-commerce orders, site registrations, opinion polls, and so on. See Figure G-17. The information you enter into an HTML form is held in the memory of your computer, where your browser creates temporary storage bins that correspond to the input field names designated by the form's HTML tags. When you click a Submit button, your browser gathers the data from memory and sends it to a specially designated program on an HTTP server, where it can be processed and stored.

● In addition to Web tables and forms, some designers use frames to create Web pages. An **HTML frame** (or simply "frame") scrolls independently of other parts of the Web page. The main advantage of frames is the ability to display multiple documents at once. A typical use of frames, shown in Figure G-18, is to display a stationary banner at the top of a page and a set of links on the left side of the screen that do not move as you scroll through the main text on the Web page.

TABLE G-4: Steps for testing and publishing Web pages

STEPS	DESCRIPTION
Test each page locally	You must test your Web page locally to verify that every element is displayed correctly by any browsers that might be used by visitors to your Web page. You can accomplish this task without connecting to the Web. Simply open a browser, then enter the local filename for the HTML document that you created for your Web page. Because your hard disk drive is much faster than a dial-up connection, the text and graphics for your Web page will appear faster during your local test than when viewed over the Internet.
Transfer pages to a Web server	Whether you're publishing a single page, a series of pages, or an entire Web site, you must put your pages on a Web server. Although Web server software is available for your home computer, you probably will not want to leave your computer continually linked to the Internet. Instead, you should look for a Web hosting site that will host your pages, usually for a monthly fee.
Review all content and test all links	After you publish your pages on a Web server, make sure that all content appears as expected. Be sure to test the links between your pages, as well as the links to pages on other sites.
Update your site to keep it current	Periodically, you should review the information on your Web pages and verify that the links still connect to existing Web pages. You can easily change your pages and then test them offline before reposting them.

FIGURE G-16: Using tables

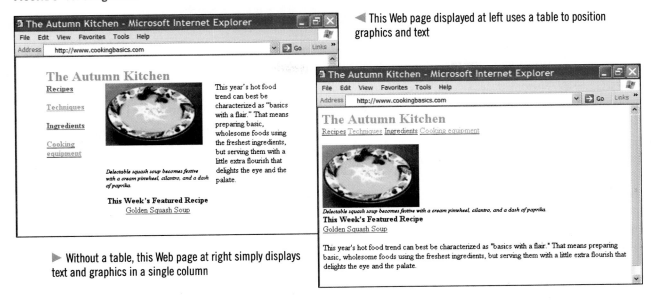

◀ This Web page displayed at left uses a table to position graphics and text

▶ Without a table, this Web page at right simply displays text and graphics in a single column

FIGURE G-17: An HTML form

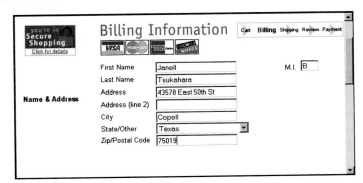

◀ HTML forms are typically used to collect payment and shipping information at the "checkout counter" of e-commerce Web sites

FIGURE G-18: Using frames

▶ A frame can be stationary, or it can scroll independently of the text and graphics in other frames

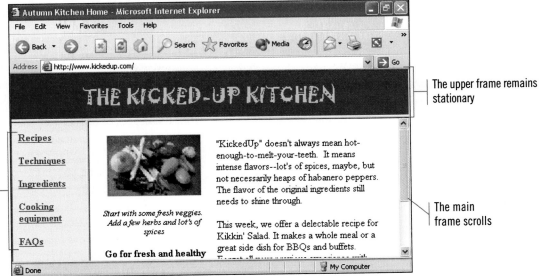

The upper frame remains stationary

The left frame remains stationary

The main frame scrolls

UNIT G

Introducing cookies

While browsing the Web, you might encounter a message like "Do you want to accept a cookie?" This message is not a joke or a malicious virus preparing to attack your computer. This message is a polite way of asking if you'll permit a Web site to collect and store some information about you. Not all sites ask your permission before creating cookies; in fact, most sites proceed on the assumption that you'll have no objection to the use of cookies. This lesson explains what cookies are and how they work on the Web.

DETAILS

● A **cookie** is data generated by a Web server and stored in a text file on your computer. Cookies allow a Web site to store information on a client computer for later retrieval. Cookies are used to remind a Web server who you are each time your browser makes a request. Cookies can also be used to store information necessary to keep track of your preferences and activities while visiting a Web site.

● Web sites use cookies to track your path through a site—to help the site remember the pages you viewed or the items you purchased. Cookies provide information that allows the Web site to display ad banners targeted to products you purchased previously at that Web site. Cookies retain the personal information that you typed into a Web page form.

● When your browser connects to a Web site that uses cookies, it receives an HTTP Set-cookie message from the Web server. This cookie message contains some information that your browser stores on your computer's hard disk. The cookie information can include a customer number, a shopping cart number, a part number, or any other data. In addition, the cookie usually contains the date the cookie expires and the domain name of the Web server that created the cookie. Any server that creates a cookie can request it the next time you connect to one of its Web pages.

● Cookies provide a way to store information as you link from one page to another page on a Web site. Because the data is stored on your computer rather than on the Web server, it doesn't require server space, it requires very little server processing time, and the Web server is not responsible for the security of the cookie data.

● Cookies don't use your name for identification purposes. Instead, a Web server provides your browser with a randomly generated number, which is saved in the cookie and used to identify you and keep track of your activity on the site. Your name is not associated with your cookies unless you entered it into a form, which is then transferred to the cookie.

● Cookies are a relatively safe technology and have several important privacy features. A cookie is data, not a computer program or script; so while a cookie is sent to your computer and stored

there, it cannot be executed to activate a virus or worm. In addition, only the site that created the cookie can access it. Finally, a cookie can contain only as much information as you disclose while using the Web site that sets the cookie. For example, a cookie cannot rummage through your hard disk to find the password for your e-mail account, the number for your checking account, or the PIN number for your credit card. However, if you enter your credit card number in the process of making an online purchase, it is possible for the cookie to store that number. Most reputable Web sites do not store such sensitive information; you can read a Web site's privacy policy for more information on this important privacy and security topic.

● Most browsers allow you to set your security level to block cookies. See Figure G-19. On many Web sites, cookies are the only mechanism available for tracking your activity or remembering your purchases. If you set the security level to block cookies, then you will not be able to access all the activities when you visit these Web sites.

A more sophisticated approach to cookie security is provided by **P3P (Platform for Privacy Preferences Project)**, which defined a standard set of security tags that become part of the HTTP header for every cookie. This header, called a **Compact Privacy Policy**, describes how cookie data is used by a Web site. Based on your security preferences, your browser can use this header data to decide whether or not to accept the cookie. Compact Privacy Policy headers are supported by recent versions of browsers.

● Cookies can be deleted from your hard drive automatically or you can delete them manually. To delete cookies automatically, you let the cookie expire. When a cookie reaches the end of its pre-defined lifetime, your browser simply erases it. A cookie is programmed to time out by the site's Web developer. To delete cookies manually, you must know where the cookies are stored on your hard drive. Netscape Navigator stores the cookie files in the Netscape folder in one large file called Cookies.txt on the PC or in Magiccookie on the Macintosh. IE stores each cookie in a separate file, usually in the Windows/Cookies folder. See Figure G-20.

FIGURE G-19: Blocking cookies

▶ Most browsers allow you to block cookies, but doing so might make it impossible to shop at some Web sites

Drag to allow or block cookies on your computer

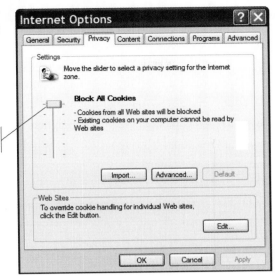

FIGURE G-20: Cookies stored on a hard disk

IE typically stores cookies as small individual files on your computer's hard disk in a folder called Cookies

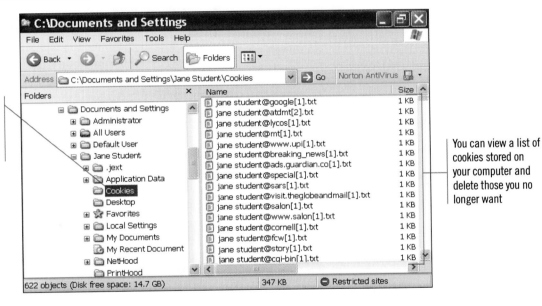

You can view a list of cookies stored on your computer and delete those you no longer want

Why would you want to use cookies?

When Web users first hear about cookies, they often wonder: Why use cookies at all? To answer that question, pretend that you use your browser to visit a popular online music store. You search for your favorite groups, listen to some sample tracks, and select a few CDs that you want to purchase. After browsing through 20 or 30 pages, you eventually go to the checkout counter, where you see a list of the CDs that you selected. You fill out a form that requests your name, shipping address, and payment information.

Because HTTP is a stateless protocol, each time that you connect to a different page, the server regards it as a new visit. So, while it seems to you that you're connected to the music site for the length of your visit, from the perspective of the Web site's server, it seems like 20 or more people have

made 20 or more successive visits. In order to keep track of you and your purchases, the Web site's server uses cookies to distinguish your requests from those of other people visiting the site. The cookies track your activity so that the Web server can compile a list of your purchases.

If you set your security level to turn off cookies, you probably won't be able to make online purchases, you'll have to enter your user IDs and passwords manually, and you won't be able to take advantage of targeted marketing (for example, when a music Web site keeps track of your favorite bands and shows you their new CDs). In the end, an individual must weigh privacy issues against convenience when deciding whether to use cookies or not use cookies.

Introducing DHTML and XML

The very first Web pages were static. In the early days of the Web, a Web page was downloaded and displayed in a browser window to be viewed; it did not change and was not interactive. To address these deficiencies, technologies such as Web page extensions, scripts, and programming tools were developed. Students who plan careers as Web page designers need to learn how to use these tools. However, to browse the Web, a basic awareness of these tools is also valuable.

DETAILS

- With basic HTML, the only way to change a Web page was to download an update to the entire page. Suppose, for example, that the Web designer wanted a star to appear next to any item selected from a list displayed on a Web page. With only Basic HTML as the toolkit, the designer made the list item a hot spot, and linked it to a copy of the same page in which a star appeared next to the selected item. Basic HTML does not provide much flexibility in two key areas. First, it does not allow Web pages to change in appearance after they are downloaded and displayed, and second, it does not provide a convenient way for users to interact with Web pages.

- **DHTML (Dynamic HTML)** is typically used to describe the combination of HTML tags, cascading style sheets, and scripts that enables Web page authors to animate the pages they create. DHTML allows the appearance of a Web page to change after it's loaded into the browser, without any additional communication with the Web server for an update. DHTML is sometimes described as "animating HTML." For example, after a Web page appears in the browser window, a section of text can change color or a graphic can move from one location to another, in response to some user action, such as a mouse movement or mouse click. See Figure G-21. DHTML is not a replacement for HTML. In fact, DHTML is not a scripting language at all. It is simply a term used to describe a method for using HTML in combination with a few other technologies to make Web pages more dynamic.

  All of today's popular personal computer browsers support DHTML. However, each browser supports DHTML somewhat differently. As a result, the tags and scripts that a Web page author uses for dynamic effects to be displayed by the Netscape browser differ from the tags required to achieve the same effects with Internet Explorer. If you ever noticed a message such as "This site is best when viewed with Netscape," you might have encountered a Web page that includes DHTML effects that work only when the page appears in the Netscape browser window. When you encounter these Web pages, you might be able to obtain information from the site regardless of the browser you use, but you might not be able to see all the dynamic affects if you are not using the recommended browser.

- **XML (eXtensible Markup Language)** is a method for putting structured data, such as spreadsheet data or database records, into a text file. As with HTML, XML uses tags and attributes to mark up the contents of a file. Whereas HTML tags, such as <b>, focus on the format or appearance of a document, XML tags essentially define fields of data. For example, XML tags, such as <part number>, <price>, and <weight>, explicitly identify a particular kind of information. As the name suggests, XML is **extensible**, which means that individual users and groups of users can create their own tags and even their own markup languages. Table G-5 lists some markup languages created with XML.

  Suppose an automobile manufacturing group wants a standard way to store and exchange information about car features and prices. The group can specify new tags, such as <dealer_price> and <suggested_retail_price>, which can be inserted into XML documents along with corresponding data. Of course, these new tags must be defined somewhere, so the XML specifications provide for **DTD files (Document Type Definition files)**, which contain the tags used in an XML file. DTD files can exist in the same location as the XML file or on a server elsewhere on the Web. This flexibility makes it possible for an entire industry to define and use the same tags by referencing a DTD file on a known server. The tool for reading XML documents is referred to as an **XML parser** and is included in all of today's popular browsers.

- **XSL (eXtensible Stylesheet Language)** is a technology that's similar to XML, but can be used to create customized tags that control the display of data in an XML document. The files containing the definition for the new XSL tags can be stored in the same location as the XML file, or they can be referenced from a server anywhere on the Internet. XSL and XML work well together to produce customized, flexible, and platform-independent Web pages.

FIGURE G-21: DHTML

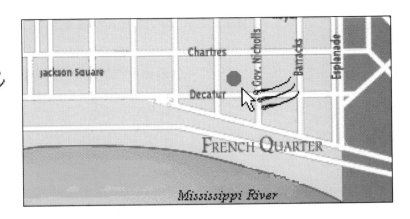

▲ DHTML effects usually activate as a result of a "mouseover." In this example, moving the mouse over the map zooms the map to a larger size

TABLE G-5: XML applications

INDUSTRY	DESCRIPTION
Real Estate Transaction Standard (RETS)	Designed to allow realtors and county clerks to access real estate transaction information.
Green Building XML	Helps architects, engineers, and builders obtain and calculate energy efficiency data for construction projects.
Robotic Markup Language (RoboML)	Allows researchers, designers, and manufacturers to communicate and archive data used by human-robot interface agents.
OpenGIS Geography Markup Language	Designed for geographers and mapmakers to record and exchange topographic details and coordinate reference points.
SportsML	Helps recruiters, sportswriters, and coaches, record and exchange sports scores, schedules, standings, and statistics for a wide variety of competitions.
DocBook	Enables authors and technical writers to create and store the contents of books and papers about computer hardware and software.
Chemical Markup Language	Helps researchers record, exchange, and display chemical information, particularly at the molecular level.

Introducing e-commerce

The Internet was first opened to commercial use in 1991. Since that date, thousands of businesses have taken up residence at Web sites, making online shopping a popular Web activity. The economics of the Web go beyond retail catalogs; even small businesses, individual artists, and isolated craftsmen can post Web pages that display their wares.

DETAILS

● **E-commerce** is used to describe financial transactions conducted over a computer network. E-commerce activities include online shopping, electronic auctions, and online stock trading.

● E-commerce includes many kinds of physical products, digital products, and services. Physical products include clothing, books, toys, and even cars. Most of these products can be shipped to buyers or can be picked up by buyers at a designated spot, generally a storefront. Digital products are news, music, video, databases, software, and all types of knowledge-based items. The unique feature of these products is that they can be transformed into bits and delivered over the Web. Consumers can get them immediately upon completing their orders, so there are no shipping costs.

E-commerce merchants also sell services, such as arranging trips, medical consultation, and remote education. E-commerce services can be delivered electronically; for example, an e-ticket, which is confirmation that an airline reservation is being held in your name. You print the e-ticket and use it instead of a ticket issued by an airline.

● E-commerce enhances traditional business models by offering efficiency and opportunities for automation and computerization. As with a traditional "brick and mortar" business, profit in an e-commerce business is the difference between income and expenses. E-commerce increases profit margins by cutting costs.

● E-commerce merchants also gain income by hosting advertising space for banner and popup ads. A **banner ad** is an advertisement, typically embedded at the top of a Web page. A **popup ad** is an advertisement that appears in a separate window when you enter a Web site or connect to Web pages. When you click a banner or popup ad, your browser connects directly to the advertiser's Web site, where you can find product information and make a purchase. Banner and popup ads earn revenue for hosting merchants based on **click-through rate**—the number of times that site visitors click the ad to connect to the advertiser's site. The hosting merchant is paid a small fee for each click through. Click-through rates have declined in recent years because most

consumers simply ignore the ads or install ad-blocking software to prevent ads from appearing on their screens.

● E-commerce seems simple from the perspective of a shopper who simply connects to an online store, browses the electronic catalog, selects merchandise, and then pays for it. Figure G-22 illustrates a typical shopping session.

● Behind the scenes, e-commerce is based on a Web site and technologies that track shoppers' selections, collect payment data, guard customers' privacy, and protect credit card numbers. An e-commerce site's domain name, such as www.amazon.com, acts as the entry to the online store. A Web page at this location welcomes customers and provides links to various parts of the site. The goods and services for sale appear in a customer's browser window. An e-commerce site usually includes some mechanism for customers to select merchandise and then pay for it. Most e-commerce businesses use as much automation as possible; their order-processing systems automatically update inventories, and then print packing slips and mailing labels.

● An **online shopping cart** is a cyberspace version of the cart that you wheel around a store and fill up with merchandise. Most shopping carts work by using cookies to store information about your activities on a Web site. An e-commerce site might use cookies as a storage bin for all of the items that you load into your shopping cart, as shown in Figure G-23.

● Some e-commerce sites use cookies simply to identify each shopper uniquely. These sites use your unique number to store your item selections in a server-side database. When you connect to a merchant's site, the server sends your browser a cookie that contains your unique shopping cart number. When you select an item to purchase, your browser reads your shopping cart ID number from the cookie, and then sends this number to the merchant's Web server. The Web server sends this number and your merchandise selection to the database, where it is stored in a record that corresponds to your shopping cart number. When you check out, your browser sends your shopping cart number to the server, which retrieves all your selections from the database.

FIGURE G-22: A typical shopping session on the Web

A shopping cart keeps track of the merchandise you want to purchase; as you browse, you can drop items into your electronic shopping cart; at the checkout counter, you enter the information necessary to pay for the items you selected

You can find items by browsing through the catalog, or by searching for specific items

FIGURE G-23: Storing shopping cart items in a cookie

1. When you click the Add to Cart button, the merchant's server sends a message to your browser to add that item number to the cookie, which is stored on your computer

ITEM #B7655

2. When you check out, the server asks your browser for all of the cookie data that pertains to your shopping cart items

3. Your browser sends those cookies along with a request for an order summary

Your order:
1 Blender   29.95
1 Wok   38.49

4. The Web server uses the cookies to produce a Web page listing the items you want to purchase

Identifying e-commerce categories

E-commerce activities fall into different categories depending on the seller and buyer. Most of the e-commerce activities that the typical Web surfer enjoys are classified as **B2C (business-to-consumer)** e-commerce. In the B2C model, businesses supply goods and services to individual consumers. In another popular e-commerce model, consumers sell to each other. This **C2C (consumer-to-consumer)** model includes wildly popular online auctions and rummage sales. **B2B (business-to-business)** e-commerce involves one enterprise buying goods or services from another enterprise. **B2G (business-to-government)** e-commerce aims to help businesses sell to governments.

Securing e-commerce transactions

After you wheel your cyber shopping cart over to the checkout line, you must verify the items you plan to purchase and you must pay for the merchandise online before your transaction can be completed. This lesson explores secure transactions and some of the ways you pay for merchandise and services you purchase on the Web.

DETAILS

● Customers often worry about the security of their online transactions. They want to be sure their credit card and other personal information is secure. Several encryption technologies are used to secure online transactions. **Encryption** is the science of coding data. You will learn more about encryption in the Tech Talk in this unit.

A **packet sniffer** (also called a "protocol analyzer") is a computer program that monitors data as it travels over networks. A packet sniffer can observe and open any packet traveling on the network. Packet sniffers have legitimate uses in system maintenance, but hackers can also use them to pilfer data as it travels from customers' computers to e-commerce sites. To protect your data, you should engage in electronic transactions only over a secure connection. A **secure connection** encrypts the data transmitted between your computer and a Web site. Even if a hacker can capture the packets containing your payment data, this data must be decrypted before it can be used for illicit purposes. Technologies that create secure connections include SSL and S-HTTP.

SSL (Secure Sockets Layer) protocol encrypts the data that travels between a client computer and an HTTP server. This encryption protocol creates what's called an SSL connection using a specially designated port, typically Port 443 rather than Port 80, which is used for unsecured HTTP communication. You will notice https: instead of http: in the URL of Web pages that provide an SSL connection.

S-HTTP (secure HTTP) is an extension of HTTP that encrypts the text of an HTTP message before it is sent. Although SSL and S-HTTP both use encryption techniques to transmit data securely, they are technically different. Whereas SSL creates a secure connection between a client and a server over which any amount of data can be sent securely, S-HTTP is designed simply to encrypt and transmit an individual message.

From the consumer's perspective, however, either one of these security measures can do an excellent job of protecting the data you send over the Internet.

● Securing your credit card number as it travels over the Internet solves only half of the security problem. Both parties in an e-commerce transaction must make sure that they are dealing with authorized and reputable entities. Consumers want to make sure that a merchant is legitimate. Merchants want to make sure that the credit card charges are authorized by the card's rightful owner. Your browser helps you identify when you are using a secure connection. See Figure G-24.

SET (Secure Electronic Transaction) is a security method that relies on cryptography and digital certificates to ensure that transactions are legitimate and secure. A **digital certificate** is a specially coded electronic attachment to a file that verifies the identity of its source. SET uses digital certificates and secure connections to transfer consumers' credit card numbers directly to a credit card processing service for verification.

● An **electronic wallet** (also called a digital wallet) is software that stores and handles the information a customer submits when finalizing an e-commerce purchase. It typically holds your name, shipping address, and the number, expiration date, and billing address for one or more credit cards. It might also hold a digital certificate that verifies your identity. You can create an electronic wallet by subscribing at the wallet provider's site. See Figure G-25.

Most wallets implement SET (Secure Electronic Transaction)—a security method that relies on cryptography and digital certificates to ensure that transactions are legitimate as well as secure. Even if a hacker gains access to your wallet file, the data it contains will be difficult to decode. Your wallet is protected by a password, which acts as a PIN to prevent unauthorized use.

FIGURE G-24: Identifying secure connections

When a secure connection is about to be activated, your browser usually displays a dialog box

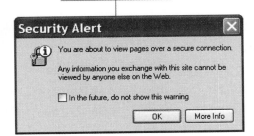

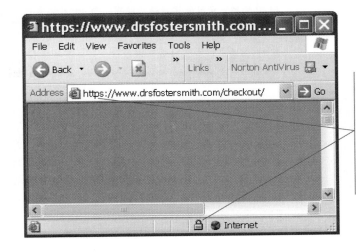

While a secure connection is active, the URL begins with *https://* and the taskbar typically displays a closed padlock icon

▲ Secure connections are indicated by a dialog box, URL, and taskbar icon

FIGURE G-25: An electronic wallet

▶ When you proceed to an online checkout, software on the merchant's server sends an HTTP message to your PC that looks for and activates compatible wallet software; by clicking a Submit button, your payment data is transferred from your electric wallet to the server

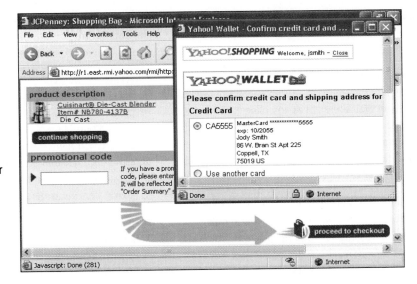

Understanding transaction privacy and security

Web sites can secretly collect data about your browsing and purchasing habits. Merchants who market goods and services are eager to get the attention of prospective customers, but they sometimes use spyware that has the potential to compromise your privacy. In the context of the Web and e-commerce, **spyware** is any technology that secretly gathers information and relays it to advertisers or other interested parties. Web-based marketers use several spyware techniques, including ad-serving cookies and clear GIFs.

When you connect to a Web site, you expect it to store an innocuous cookie on your computer's hard disk. Some Web sites, however, feature banner ads supplied by third-party marketing firms. If you click the ad, this third party can create an **ad-serving cookie** and use it to track your activities at any site containing banner ads from that third party. The marketing firms that distribute

ad-serving cookies maintain that this data is simply used to select and display ads that might interest you, but privacy advocates are worried that shopper profiles can be compiled, sold, and used for unauthorized purposes.

A **clear GIF** or **"Web bug"** is typically a 1x1 pixel graphic on a Web page. Clear GIFs can be used to set cookies to third party Web sites. Unlike ad-serving cookies, you don't have to click a banner ad to receive a GIF-activated cookie. Simply viewing the page that contains a clear GIF sets the cookie. Cookies created with clear GIFs have the same uses and potential for misuse as ad-serving cookies.

Several software products are designed to block ad-serving cookies, clear GIFs, and other spyware—some even block banner and popup ads altogether. These products are becoming quite popular, despite their tendency to slow your browser's response time slightly.

Avoiding fraud when shopping online

Fraud is a serious concern. Credit card numbers can be stolen and used without authorization. You may find yourself a victim of fraud even if you shop using traditional stores or through phone order services. Computers store credit card and shopping information for all businesses. This lesson explores several ways you might be defrauded and how to protect yourself when shopping.

DETAILS

- Security-conscious e-commerce merchants protect their databases by limiting access and encrypting data. Unfortunately, not all businesses follow these practices. Even when databases seem secure, hackers might find security holes and retrieve sensitive data. In fact, an increasing number of businesses report that their customer databases have been accessed without authorization. In some cases, thousands of credit card numbers are stolen.

- Secure connections differ from secure Web sites. A secure connection encrypts the data transmitted between your computer and a Web site. A secure Web site, such as an online banking site, uses password security to prevent unauthorized access to pages on the site. As a consumer, you cannot prevent database break-ins, but you can take steps to ensure that the credit card number stored in a merchant's database is of little use to a hacker.

- An online break-in into the database of a merchant or credit card processing service is a fairly high-tech crime, but your credit card number can be compromised by low-tech methods as well. If a merchant collects your credit card number instead of routing it directly to a credit card processing service, a dishonest employee who works for the merchant might be able to obtain your card number while processing your order. Individual consumers can't do much to prevent this type of theft, but the likelihood of it occurring is low—you take a similar risk every time you pay for a meal by allowing a waiter to take your credit card back to a cashier station or give your credit card number over the phone.

- A fake storefront appears to be an online store, but is in fact a fraudulent Web site, designed exclusively for the purpose of collecting credit card numbers from unwary shoppers. These sites might have all the trappings of a real e-commerce site—they might even offer a secure connection for transmitting your credit card number. When your data is received, however, it is stored in a database that belongs to a hacker, who can use the data for illegitimate transactions. Figure G-26 explains how you can avoid fake storefronts.

- Several credit card companies offer one-time-use credit card numbers, which allow consumers to make purchases while keeping their actual card numbers hidden. A one-time-use credit card number works for a single online purchase. Your credit card company tracks the purchases you incur with one-time-use numbers and adds the charges to your monthly credit card statement. One-time-use numbers cannot be used twice, so even if a hacker steals the number, it will not be accepted for any online or offline purchases.

- A **person-to-person payment** (sometimes called an on-line payment) offers an alternative to credit cards. It can be used to pay for auction items and wire money over the Internet. A service called PayPal pioneered person-to-person payments and has since been copied by several other service providers. The process begins when you open an account at a person-to-person payment service. As with a checking account, you deposit some money in your account by using your credit card. You receive a user ID and password that allows you to access your account to make purchases and deposit additional funds. Money can be sent to anyone who has an e-mail account, as shown in Figure G-27.

FIGURE G-26: How you can avoid fake storefronts

▶ The URLs for fake storefronts often differ from the real thing by a single character. For example, hackers might create a fake storefront using the URL *www.ediebauer.com*—similar to the legitimate store at *www.eddiebauer.com*. To protect yourself from fake storefronts, make sure to type the URL correctly. Better yet, type the store name—Eddie Bauer, for example—in a search engine such as Google, and use the link provided to reach the site's home page.

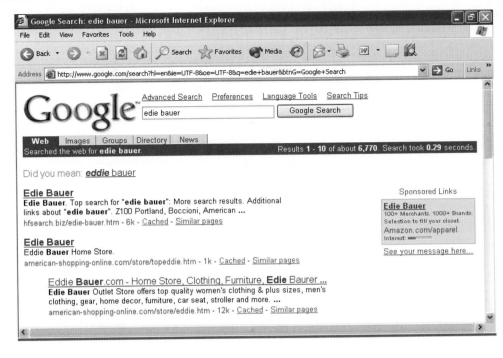

FIGURE G-27: Using a person-to-person payment service

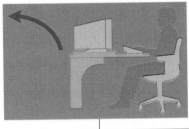

1. To use a person-to-person payment service, simply log into your account, enter the recipient's e-mail address, and indicate the payment amount

2. The recipient immediately receives an e-mail notification of your payment

3. The recipient connects to the payment site to pick up the money by transferring the funds to a checking account, requesting a check, or sending the funds to someone else

Tech Talk Encryption

Encryption is one of the most important technologies for maintaining your privacy and the security of important information, such as your credit card number. Encryption makes a message illegible to unauthorized users, and is designed to keep messages secret. Its purpose, therefore, is quite different from simple coding schemes, such as ASCII and EBCDIC, which are designed to transform data into formats that are publicly known and shared.

An original message that has not yet been encrypted is referred to as **plaintext** or cleartext. An encrypted message is referred to as **ciphertext**. The process of converting plaintext into ciphertext is called **encryption**. Reconverting ciphertext to plaintext is called **decryption**. In an e-commerce transaction, for example, your credit card number exists as plaintext, which is encrypted into ciphertext for its journey over a secure connection to the merchant. When the ciphertext arrives at its destination, it is decrypted back into the original plaintext credit card number.

Messages are encrypted using a cryptographic algorithm and key. A **cryptographic algorithm** is a specific procedure for encrypting or decrypting a message. A **cryptographic key** (usually just called a key) is a word, number, or phrase that must be known in order to encrypt or decrypt a message. An encryption method called simple substitution uses a transformation table like the one in Figure G-28 to encrypt or decrypt messages.

The simple substitution key is an example of **weak encryption**, because it is easy to decrypt even without the algorithm and key. Unauthorized decryption is sometimes referred to as breaking or cracking a code. **Strong encryption** is loosely defined as very difficult to break. Of course, with continuous advances in technology, strong encryption is a moving target. For example, several encryption methods that were considered impossible to break 10 years ago have recently been cracked using networks of personal computers. The encryption methods that are used for most e-commerce transactions are considered strong but not unbreakable.

Encryption methods can be broken by the use of expensive, specialized, code-breaking computers. The cost of these machines is substantial, but not beyond the reach of government agencies, major corporations, and organized crime. Encryption methods can also be broken by standard computer hardware—supercomputers, mainframes, workstations, and even personal computers. These computers typically break codes using a **brute force method**, which consists of trying all possible combinations.

Suppose that a criminal steals an ATM card. The card cannot be used, however, without the correct PIN. A four-digit PIN could be one of 10,000 possible combinations. If you're mathematically inclined, you'll realize that each digit of the PIN could be one of 10 possibilities: 0, 1, 2, 3, 4, 5, 6, 7, 8, or 9, so 10^4 or 10x10x10x10 possible PINs exist. To discover a PIN number by brute force, a criminal must try, at most, 10,000 possibilities. Although it would take a person quite a long time to figure out and try all 10,000 possibilities, a computer could polish them off as quickly as the ATM would accept them.

FIGURE G-28: Simple substitution

Ciphertext letters:

D E F **G** H I J K L M N O P Q R S T U V W X Y Z A B C

Equivalent plaintext letters:

A B **C** D E F G H I J K L M N O P Q R S T U V W X Y Z

The simple substitution encryption method is an example of **symmetric key encryption**, which is also called secret key or conventional encryption. With symmetric key encryption, the same key used to encrypt a message is also used to decrypt a message. Symmetric key encryption is often used to encrypt stationary data, such as corporate financial records. It is not, however, a very desirable encryption method for data that's on the move. The person who encrypts the data must get the key to the person who decrypts the data, without the key falling into the wrong hands. On a computer network, key distribution is a major security problem because of the potential for interception.

To eliminate the key-distribution problem, Whitfield Diffie and Martin Helman introduced a concept called **public key encryption (PKE)** in 1975. It uses asymmetric key encryption, in which one key is used to encrypt a message, but another key is used to decrypt the message. Figure G-29 illustrates how public key encryption works. Public key encryption is a crucial technology for the Web and e-commerce. When you use an SSL (secure socket layer) connection to transmit your credit card number, the server sends a public key to your browser, which uses this public key to encrypt the credit card number. Once encrypted, no one can use this public key to decrypt the message. The encrypted message is sent to the Web server, where the private key is used to decrypt it.

RSA (named for its inventors—Ron Rivest, Adi Shamir, and Leonard Adleman) is the most commonly used public key encryption algorithm. In addition to being the technology used for SSL connections, RSA is used to encrypt the data in most digital certificates. **DES (Data Encryption Standard)** is an encryption method based on an algorithm developed by IBM and the U.S. National Security Agency. It uses 56-bit symmetric key encryption. Although it was once the cornerstone of government encryption, DES is being replaced by AES, which offers stronger encryption. **AES (Advanced Encryption Standard)** is an encryption standard that uses three key sizes of 128, 192, or 256 bits. It is based on the Rijndael (pronounced "rain doll") encryption algorithm.

FIGURE G-29: Public key encryption

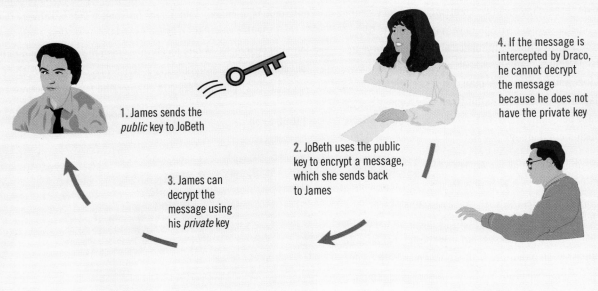

1. James sends the *public* key to JoBeth

2. JoBeth uses the public key to encrypt a message, which she sends back to James

3. James can decrypt the message using his *private* key

4. If the message is intercepted by Draco, he cannot decrypt the message because he does not have the private key

Computers in Context Politics

The word "politicians" conjures up images of candidates vying for votes during an election campaign, paid political advertising, and personal appearances replete with glad-handing, back slapping, and baby kissing. However, the Web has added a new dimension to today's political campaigns. Information technology, such as Web sites and e-mail, has become a valuable supplement to traditional campaign tools. According to Bruce Bimber, Director of the Center for Information Technology and Society at the University of California, Santa Barbara, "Rather than creating political attention as television can do, the Web serves to engage and sustain those already attentive."

Internet anthropologists credit Republican presidential candidate Bob Dole with a technology first for announcing the URL of his campaign Web site during a 1994 televised debate. As the next election cycle looms, few campaigns would be complete without a Web site containing position statements and an easy way for supporters to donate money. A few candidates have experimented with mass e-mail solicitations, based on demographic databases similar to those telemarketers use. Because many voters view unsolicited e-mail as "spam," however, political strategists believe it's more likely to backfire than gain new supporters.

After they're elected to office, politicians at local, state, and national levels continue to use computer technology. Many state governments supply notebook computers to legislators, and some maintain information technology departments that offer computer training to lawmakers and their staffs. Lawmakers use notebook computers to do research, view bills, create amendments, communicate with colleagues, and correspond with constituents. One politician describes the growing influence of e-mail: "Five years ago, it was 10 percent e-mail and 90 percent paper. Now, it's 10 percent paper and 90 percent e-mail. I still see literally dozens of people a day in my office, and nothing will ever replace personal contact on really personal issues, but, frankly, technology allows me to be a much more thorough legislator."

Political action groups, such as the ACLU and League of Women Voters, maintain sophisticated Web sites to advance their political agendas and urge supporters to write to their local, state, or national representatives. In the past, many people didn't know their representatives' names or addresses, but now they can enter a ZIP code at a political action group's Web site to find complete contact information for their representatives. They can download template letters that express concern about an issue and then customize, print, and mail or fax these letters. Constituents can gather political information from a variety of online sources. They can read the full content of pending and passed legislation posted on government Web sites. They can also read voter guides, maintained by allegedly impartial organizations, for information about elections, candidates, campaign funding, and other public issues. Some Web sites offer public forums and electronic "town hall" meetings where people can express their opinions and engage in debate.

Even with online access to information, interest in politics continues to decline in the United States. Voter turnout, for example, ranks among the lowest of the world's established democracies. Many political analysts expected that "cyberpolitics" might reverse that trend by improving access to political information and engaging citizens in interactive online political activities. Some observers hoped that information technology might increase levels of political knowledge and reduce the gap between the most and least engaged citizens. Studies leading up to the 2000 presidential election showed increasing use of the Internet to find political information. However, even citizens who specifically sought political information on the Internet were no more likely to vote than those who did not. More studies are needed to assess the current level of political interest and its relationship to new technologies.

Computer technology has also had a remarkable effect on the voting process. The 2000 presidential election "hanging chad" fiasco highlighted problems with old optical ballot readers. Legislators swung into action and passed the Help America Vote act in 2001, which provided $4 billion for new voting machines (see Figure G-30)—computer kiosks called DREs (direct recording electronics) that use touch-screen technology similar to an ATM. A DRE displays candidate names, numbers, and photos on-screen. Voters activate the machine with a one-time-use key card, similar to pass cards used for hotel door locks. Voters touch the screen to select a candidate; for voters with visual handicaps or those who cannot read, there is a voice-guided option. Voters can change and review selections until

FIGURE G-30

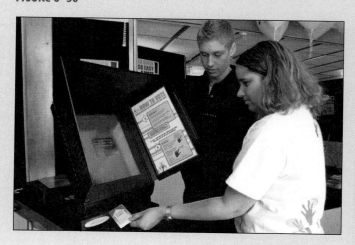

they are ready to activate the Cast Vote option. Votes are stored on the machine's hard disk and at least one removable device, such as a cartridge or SmartCard. When the poll closes, the removable storage device is extracted and transported to a central computer, which records, tallies, and combines the votes with those from other machines. To prevent hackers and viruses, the machines are not networked. Integrated backup battery power ensures continual service in case of a power outage.

Touch-screen voting machines are not without detractors, however. One complaint is that voting machine software is shrouded in secrecy, which prevents election officials from verifying the method for recording votes. Detractors fear that programmers at voting machine companies could surreptitiously insert code that shifts some votes from one party to another. According to voting machine company spokespeople, however, a simple pre-election test run can verify a machine's accuracy. Voting machine companies also state that maintaining secrecy about the software is a security measure to prevent outsiders from making unauthorized modifications that might invalidate votes.

The controversy over touch-screen voting machines is minor compared to the uproar caused by online voting. Arizona Democrats held the first binding election in which votes could be cast from conventional voting machines or via the Internet. More than 35,000 voters cast online votes in that primary election. The Voting Integrity Project criticized the Internet vote, however, because minorities and the poor did not have equal access to voting. While the sociological debate about Internet voting continues, so does the technological debate. A secret and valid ballot is the cornerstone of democracy. Many experts doubt that current Internet technology can provide secrecy or validity in voting if skilled hackers could capture and change electronic votes, launch a denial-of-service attack to overload vote collecting servers, or devise viruses that disable e-voting software. Although the Internet might not be ready for primetime voting, it has changed the face of politics by increasing grass roots access to the political process.

context

Is The Truth Out There?

In a classic episode of the X-Files, Agent Scully warns Mulder about his search into the unexplored realm of extraterrestrial and paranormal phenomena: "The truth is out there, but so are lies." And so it is on the Internet, where truth mingles with lies, rumors, myths, and urban legends. The Internet is uncensored and unregulated. Anyone with a Web page or an e-mail account can rapidly and widely distribute information, which is often redistributed and forwarded like a chain letter on steroids.

You might have received an e-mail from a Nigerian businessman claiming "to know of you in my search for a reliable person to handle a very confidential transaction which involves the transfer of a huge sum of money to a foreign account." Yes, this businessman is willing to transfer millions of dollars (U.S.) into your bank account so that it can be smuggled out of the country for the bereaved widow of a martyred freedom fighter or the son of a deposed dictator. For your trouble, you will receive a substantial handling fee. All you have to do is supply your bank account number! Called an "advance fee fraud," this many layered scam begins with a request for your bank account number and then progresses to pleas for advance handling fees. Although it seems improbable that anyone would believe such an outlandish proposal, the U.S. Secret Service reports, "Advance fee fraud grosses hundreds of millions of dollars annually and the losses are continuing to escalate. In all likelihood, there are victims who do not report their losses to authorities due to either fear or embarrassment." According to the U.S. State Department, some victims have been lured abroad to complete the transaction, kidnapped, and held for ransom. A bookkeeper for an Illinois law firm reportedly embezzled $2.1 million and sent it to Nigerian scam artists as handling fees for the transfer of many more millions to the woman's personal bank account. E-mail and the Internet make it possible for scam artists to reach millions of victims.

FIGURE G-31

The Internet has also been blamed for circulating reports that the U.S. Navy shot down TWA Flight 800. Pierre Salinger, an ex-TV reporter and a former advisor to President John F. Kennedy, made front-page headlines in November 1996 when he displayed documents that described how the Navy was testing missiles off Long Island and accidentally hit Flight 800. Although Salinger would not reveal the source of the documents, it turned out that they had been circulated on the Internet months earlier. The Chicago Tribune described Salinger's error as "merely the latest outbreak of the disturbing new information-age phenomenon of bogus news," and went on to say that "America is awash in a growing and often disruptive avalanche of false information that takes on a life of its own in the electronic ether of the Internet, talk radio, and voice mail until it becomes impervious to denial and debunking."

In a more recent debacle, a seemingly legitimate news wire flashed over the Internet: "A city still mourning the death of punk rock innovator Joey Ramone has endured another tragedy as Velvet Underground leader Lou Reed was found dead in his apartment last night, apparently from an overdose of the painkiller Demerol." Lou Reed was not dead, but the fake wire story fooled several radio stations, which reported it as hard news.

But is it fair to say that the Internet has a monopoly on false information? Probably not. Even well-established newspapers, magazines, and television news shows report stories that are later found to be misleading or untrue. In an article published online in Salon, Scott Rosenberg asks, "Who's more responsible for the spread of misinformation, the Internet or the news media? Well, ask yourself how you first heard of Salinger's memo: was it from the Net or from a TV broadcast? The sad truth is that the old media are far more efficient disseminators of bogus news than the new."

Before the Internet became a ubiquitous part of modern life, certain rules of thumb helped distinguish truth from lies and fact from fiction. In *The Truth About URLs*, Robin Raskin writes, "When printed junk mail floods our overcrowded mailboxes we have some antennae for the bogus causes and the fly-by night foundations. We've come to expect *The New York Times* to be a credible source of information (see Figure G-31); we're not as sure about *The National Enquirer*. It takes years to establish these sorts of cultural cues for knowing whether we're getting good information or a bum steer." Perhaps the Internet has not been around long enough for us to establish the cultural cues we need to distinguish fact from fiction in Web pages, e-mails, online chats, and discussion groups. You can, however, get some help from the Web itself. Several sites keep track of the myths and so-called urban legends that circulate on the Internet. Before you spread rumors about the demise of Lou Reed, or call a press conference to report a government cover-up, you might want to check one of these sites for the real scoop.

Who should be responsible for the accuracy of information? Holding writers accountable for their "facts" does not seem to work, and governments, already overburdened with other problems, have scant resources available to sift through mountains of information and set the record straight. It seems, then, that the burden of verifying facts is ultimately left to the reader. Many people, however, do not have the time, motivation, expertise, or resources to verify facts before they pass them through the information mill. We live in an information age. Ironically, much of the information that we hear and read just isn't true. False and misleading information is not unique to our time, but now it propagates more rapidly, fed by new technologies and nurtured by spin doctors. As one commentator suggested, "The danger is that we are reaching a moment when nothing can be said to be objectively true, when consensus about reality disappears. The Information Age could leave us with no information at all, only assertions."

▼ INTERACTIVE QUESTIONS

○ Yes   ○ No   ○ Not sure   1. Would you agree that it sometimes seems difficult to determine whether information is true or false?

○ Yes   ○ No   ○ Not sure   2. Do older people tend to be more susceptible than younger people to false information that's disseminated over the Internet?

○ Yes   ○ No   ○ Not sure   3. Have you ever received an e-mail that contained false information or visited a Web site that provided inaccurate information?

○ Yes   ○ No   ○ Not sure   4. Do you have your own set of rules to help you evaluate the truth of information that's disseminated over the Internet?

▼ EXPAND THE IDEAS

1. Do older people with less Internet experience tend to be more naïve about Internet information than younger people who have been raised on the Internet? Find several examples of articles, documentaries, or news stories on verifying facts and data on the Internet. Write a summary of each article or media piece. Analyze your findings. Was the media voice consistent? Why or why not?

2. Can you think of another way in which information spreads so quickly? How does society monitor and check the facts for other media, like newspapers and television? Find several examples of articles, documentaries, or news stories on integrity in journalism. Form a discussion group and share your articles. Compile a group presentation on your articles, summarizing them for the class. How are the situations in the articles similar and how are they different? What steps were taken to verify the facts? Were these steps appropriate? Sufficient? What else would you have done to monitor the facts?

3. Do you have your own set of rules to help you evaluate information on the Internet? Write a two-page paper detailing how you evaluate information. Do you follow an existing model? Be sure to include your resources.

Issue

End of Unit Exercises

▼ KEY TERMS

Ad-serving cookie
AES (Advanced Encryption Standard)
Animated GIF
AVI
B2B
B2C
B2G
Banner ad
Body section
Broken link
Browser
Brute force method
C2C
Cascading style sheet
Ciphertext
Clear GIF
Click-through rate
Compact Privacy Policy
Cookie
Cryptographic algorithm
Cryptographic key
Decryption
DES (Data Encryption Standard)
DHTML (Dynamic HTML)
Digital certificate
DTD files (Document Type

Definition files)
E-commerce
Electronic wallet
Encryption
Extensible
External link
External style sheet
Flash animation
Formatting tag
GIF
Head section
Helper application
Hot spot
HTML
HTML document
HTML form
HTML frame
HTML tag
HTTP
HTTP status code
Hyperlink
Hypertext
Hypertext link
Image map
Internal link
Interpage link
JPEG

Link
Link tag
Mailto link
Markup language
Media tag
MPEG
Online shopping cart
Operational tag
P3P
Packet sniffer
Person-to-person payment
Plaintext
Plug-in
PNG
Popup ad
Public key encryption
QuickTime
RSA
Secure connection
Self-closing tag
Server farm
SET
S-HTTP
Socket
Spyware
SSL
Stateless protocol

Strong encryption
Style
Style sheet
Symmetric key encryption
Text editor
Theme
Thumbnail
URL
Weak encryption
Web authoring software
Web browser
Web bug
Web page
Web page header
Web page table
Web resource
Web server
World Wide Web Consortium (W3C)
XHTML
XML (eXtensible Markup Language)
XML parser
XSL (eXtensible Stylesheet Language)

▼ UNIT REVIEW

1. Use your own words to define bold terms that appear throughout the unit. List 10 of the terms that are least familiar to you and write a sentence for each of them.

2. Draw a multi-panel cartoon that shows how a Web server and browser interact. Include the following terms: Web server, browser, HTTP, HTML, Port 80, socket, HTML document, graphic file, and URL.

3. Create a timeline of the history of HTML and browsers based on the information provided in this unit. Your timeline should begin in 1990 and continue through 2004.

4. In a short paragraph, explain the relationship between an HTML document and a Web page.

5. List and describe in your own words the classifications of HTML tags as presented in this unit.

6. List the port numbers that are traditionally used for HTTP traffic, SMTP e-mail, and FTP.

7. List the major security and privacy features of cookies.

8. Describe the advantages and disadvantages of each type of Web page development tool that was discussed in this unit.

9. Locate a Web page, print it out, and then identify the following parts of the Web page: title, header, graphic, link, button, menu, and frame.

10. Describe some of the ways that Web page designers use links. Describe external links, mailto links, and internal links.

▼ FILL IN THE BEST ANSWER

1. The _____ is a collection of documents that can be related by links.

2. HTML is called a markup language because authors insert special instructions called HTML _____ that specify how a document should appear when printed or displayed on a computer screen.

3. A(n) _____ is the client half of the client/server software that facilitates communication between a personal computer and Web server.

4. _____ is a protocol that works in conjunction with TCP/IP to get Web resources to your desktop.

5. A Web server usually listens for HTTP requests on _____ 80.

6. If you use a text _____ to create an HTML document, you must manually enter HTML tags.

7. _____ is a method for putting structured data, such as spreadsheet data or database records, into a text file.

8. A(n) _____ style sheet allows you to create an HTML document that contains style specifications for multiple Web pages.

9. A(n) _____ is a collection of coordinated graphics, colors, and fonts applied to individual pages or all pages in a Web site.

10. The <img src> _____ tag is used to reference an image that will appear on a Web page.

11. A(n) _____ is an advertisement, typically embedded at the top of a Web page; a(n) _____ is an advertisement that appears in a separate window when you enter a Web site or connect to Web pages.

12. A(n) _____ link is used to send an e-mail message to an address specified by the Web page author.

13. A diagram that contains clickable hot spots is referred to as an image _____.

14. Many Web page authors and designers use _____ as a layout tool for positioning the elements of a Web page.

15. On a Web page, a(n) _____ scrolls independently of other parts of the page.

16. _____ is typically used to describe financial transactions conducted over a computer network.

17. Most shopping carts work because they use _____ to store information about your activities on a Web site.

18. A(n) _____ wallet stores and handles the information that a customer typically submits when finalizing an e-commerce purchase.

19. _____ e-commerce involves one enterprise buying goods or services from another enterprise, whereas _____ e-commerce aims to help businesses sell to governments.

20. In the context of the Web and e-commerce, _____ is technology that secretly gathers information and relays it to advertisers or other interested parties.

▼ PRACTICE TESTS

When you use the Interactive CD, you can take Practice Tests that consist of 10 multiple-choice, true/false, and fill-in-the-blank questions. The questions are selected at random from a large test bank, so each time you take a test, you'll receive a different set of questions. Your tests are scored immediately, and you can print study guides to determine which questions you answered incorrectly. If you are using a Tracking Disk, insert it in the floppy disk drive to save your test scores.

▼ INDEPENDENT CHALLENGE 1

Many people have their own home pages. A home page is a statement of who you are and what your interests may be. You can design your own home page. Depending on the tools you have available, you might be able to create a real page and publish it on the Web. If these tools are not available, you will still be able to complete the initial design work.

1. Write a brief description of the purpose of your home page and your expected audience. For example, you might plan to use your home page to showcase your résumé to prospective employers.

2. List the elements you plan to include on your home page. Briefly describe any graphics or media elements you want to include.

3. Create a document that contains the information you want to include on your home page.

4. Make a sketch of your home page showing the colors you plan to use and the navigation elements you plan to include. Annotate this sketch to describe how these elements follow effective Web page design guidelines.

▼ INDEPENDENT CHALLENGE 2

Surfing the Web will take you to many interesting sites. As you visit each one, you will notice differences among Web pages. To some extent, good design is a matter of taste; when it comes to Web page design, there are usually many possible solutions that will provide a pleasing look and efficient navigational tools. On the other hand, some designs just don't seem to work because they make the text difficult to read or navigate.

1. Select a Web page or several pages that have many of the elements described in this unit, including hot spots, image maps, links, images, or other media.

2. Find the page by browsing on the Web; save and print the page or pages.

3. Using colored markers or pens, identify each of the elements and write a brief explanation of how each element enhances or detracts from the message of the page.

4. What tools do you think the Web page designer used to organize the information on the page? Was it done effectively? Identify the sections of content on the printouts.

5. Do you think styles were used in developing the page? Do you see common fonts and colors in the text portions? Identify these elements on the printout.

6. Next, find one Web page that you think could use improvement. Use colored pencils or markers to sketch your plan for improving the page. Annotate your sketch by pointing out the features you would change and explain why you think your makeover will be more effective than the original Web page.

▼ INDEPENDENT CHALLENGE 3

Shopping on the Web has benefits for consumers as well as merchants. You will take a quick shopping tour of the Web and compare a few sites to see how they differ. You do not have to make any purchases to complete this independent challenge.

1. Find three retailers on the Internet. If possible find e-commerce retailers that also have "brick and mortar" stores, for example, Bed, Bath, and Beyond.

2. Besides the name of the Web site, what clues on the Web page help you identify the products or services being offered?

3. For each of the retailers, search for two items and place them in a shopping cart. Do not complete the purchase and do not enter any credit card or personal information.

4. Create a chart with three columns, one for each retailer. Complete the chart by answering the questions that follow:

   a. What procedures did you go through to find the merchandise?

   b. Was there a shopping cart or comparable way of gathering your purchases?

   c. What methods of payment did they offer you?

   d. Were there any warning dialog boxes that opened in your browser during the shopping trip?

   e. Did the retailer make use of cookies? Could you find them on your computer after you exited the retailer?

   f. Select one store that has a brick and mortar counterpart. Would you prefer to shop online or at its brick and mortar counterpart? Write a brief summary supporting your response.

▼ INDEPENDENT CHALLENGE 4

The World Wide Web Consortium is required to maintain standards for working on the Web. New versions of browsers are constantly appearing with new features. Companies develop plug-in and add-in programs that have to be compatible with browsers, and then the media have to be available on the Web sites to make downloading the additional software worthwhile for consumers. Keeping up with all this change can make any Web surfer dizzy. How can you keep up?

1. Go to the World Wide Web Consortium site at www.w3c.org and find two recent news items that relate to updates in programming Web pages and write a brief summary of your findings. Be sure to include the sources.

2. Go to the Microsoft Web site at www.microsoft.com and find one recent news item about the latest release of the Internet Explorer Web browser. Write a brief summary of your findings. Be sure to include the sources.

3. Go to the Netscape Web site at www.netscape.com, click the Download link, and find one recent news item about the latest release of the Netscape Web browser. Write a brief summary of your findings. Be sure to include the sources.

4. Go to the Opera Web site at www.opera.com and find one recent news item about the latest release of the Opera Web browser. Write a brief summary of your findings. Be sure to include the sources.

5. Write a summary of the features that are advertised for each of the three browsers. Which features are similar and which are different.

▼ INDEPENDENT CHALLENGE 5

The Computers in Context section of this unit focused on computers in politics, discussing their use by politicians and citizens. For this independent challenge, select a current political event, personality, or issue that interests you. Your topic should incorporate the influence of technology on the event. Create a question about your topic that you will answer based on research you will conduct on the Web.

1. Log onto the Internet, and then use the Web to research your topic and find an answer to your question. Use your favorite search engine to find relevant sites on the Web.

2. As you browse the Web, maintain a log describing the Web sites you visit. For each site, include its URL, the name of the organization that maintains the Web site, a brief description of the site's content, and your assessment of the information's reliability and validity on the site.

3. Write a short essay describing your findings. Your essay should include an answer to the question you originally posed. Include a summary paragraph on how the Internet and computers influenced the topic, and how the Internet facilitated your research.

▼ LAB: WORKING WITH COOKIES

1. Start the interactive part of the lab. Insert your Tracking Disk if you want to save your QuickCheck results. Perform each of the lab steps as directed and answer all of the lab QuickCheck questions. When you exit the lab, your answers are automatically graded and your results are displayed.

2. Use Windows Explorer to look at the cookies stored on your computer. Indicate how many cookies are currently stored. Examine the contents of one cookie and indicate whether or not you think it poses a threat to your privacy.

3. Indicate the name and the version of the browser that you typically use. To find this information, open your browser and select the About option from the Help menu. Next, look at the cookie settings provided by your browser. Describe how you would adjust these settings to produce a level of privacy protection that is right for your needs.

4. Adjust your browser settings so that you are prompted whenever a Web server attempts to send a cookie to your computer. Go to several of your favorite Web sites and watch for third-party cookies. When you receive a message from a third-party Web site, record the name of the third-party site and the contents of the cookie that it is attempting to send. Finally, indicate whether or not you would typically accept such a cookie.

▼ STUDENT EDITION LABS

Reinforce the concepts you have learned in this unit through the **Creating Web Pages**, **E-Commerce**, and **Web Design Principles** Student Edition Labs, available online at the Illustrated Computer Concepts Web site.

▼ SAM LABS

If you have a SAM user profile, you have access to additional content, features, and functionality. Log in to your SAM account and go to your assignments page to see what your instructor has assigned for this unit.

▼ VISUAL WORKSHOP

The presence of visual media enhances any experience. If you are at a news site or a retailer, seeing a video or interacting online helps you understand what the concepts are or just makes it more fun. The Web site shown in Figure G-32 has many media elements and links to radio, music, and video. You can go to the site shown in the figure or to another one.

FIGURE G-32

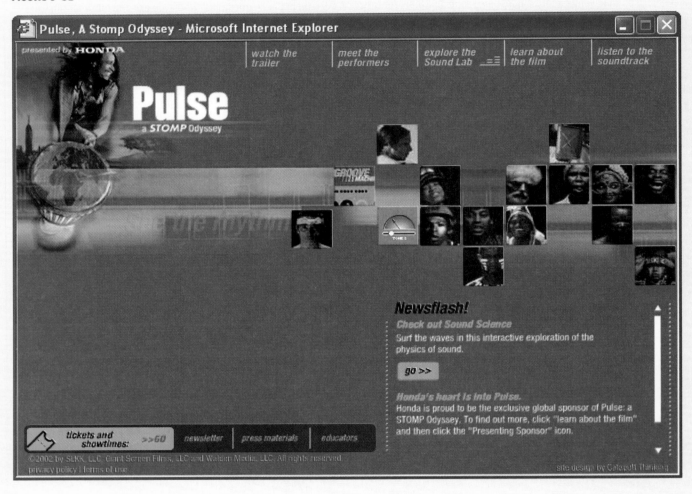

1. What type of media is available at the site you chose? Try to download or listen to at least one music file. Try to view one video file.

2. What players, if any, did you have to use to view or play the media files?

3. What types of images were on the site (what was the file format)? To find out, right-click the image and click Save or Save Picture as. The file format should appear in the Save Picture dialog box.

4. Find two different ways to listen to Internet radio through your computer. What were they and how did they differ?

UNIT H Digital Media

OBJECTIVES

Introduce bitmap graphics

Modify bitmap graphics

Introduce color depth

Introduce vector graphics

Create vector graphics

Explore 3-D graphics

Introduce desktop video

Explore video equipment

Edit and process desktop video

Introduce digital sound

Explore synthesized sound

Tech Talk: Data Compression

Computers in Context: Film

Issue: Who's Got the Rights?

This unit explores digital media, taking a close look at bitmap graphics—the most popular graphics for photographs and Web use. You will learn about vector graphics, which are often used for clip art and provide the underlying technology for 3-D graphics and 3-D animations. You will explore desktop video technology. You will learn about digital sound, including the different music formats, speech synthesis, and techniques for combining voice recognition with word processing. The Tech Talk explores the topic of compression—you'll find out how it works, and you'll learn how to use a popular compression utility. You will also have an opportunity to look at computers in the context of the film industry. The Issue discusses the implications of sharing, through the Internet, all types of digital media, including graphics, animations, music, and videos.

Introducing bitmap graphics

Bitmap graphics are images that are composed of a grid of colored dots. Bitmap graphics are often used to create realistic images, such as photographs. There are many sources for bitmaps: photos from a digital camera, images converted by a scanner, photos that you send or receive as e-mail attachments, as well as most Web page graphics.

DETAILS

- A bitmap graphic, also called a raster graphic, or simply a bitmap, is composed of a grid of dots. The color of each dot is stored as a binary number. Think of a grid superimposed on a picture. The grid divides the picture into cells, called pixels. Each pixel is assigned a color, which is stored as a binary number.

- You can create a bitmap graphic from scratch using the tools provided by graphics software—specifically **paint software**. Paint software provides tools for freehand sketching, filling in shapes, adding realistic shading, and creating effects that look like oil paints, charcoal, or watercolors.

- When you already have a printed image, such as a photograph, you can use a **scanner** to convert the printed image into a bitmap graphic. A scanner divides an image into a fine grid of cells and assigns a digital value for the color of each cell. These values are transferred to your computer's RAM. The values can then be saved and stored as a bitmap graphic file on the hard disk. Scanners, such as the one pictured in Figure H-1, are relatively inexpensive and easy to use.

- While a scanner digitizes printed images, a **digital camera** creates digitized images of real objects—that is, converts the images of real objects into bitmap graphics files. Instead of taking a photo with a conventional camera, developing the film, then digitizing it with a scanner, you use a digital camera, such as the one in Figure H-2, to take a photo in digital format.

- **Storing images:** Some digital cameras store images on floppy disks, CDs, mini-CDs, or miniature hard disk drives. Other digital cameras store images on removable solid-state storage media, sometimes called memory cards. Solid state storage is a popular technology for digital cameras. Like RAM, it can be erased and reused. Unlike RAM, solid state storage holds data without consuming power, so it doesn't lose data when the camera is turned off. Figure H-3 illustrates several digital camera storage options, including memory cards and a miniature hard disk drive.

- **Retrieving images:** Digital cameras allow you to preview images while they are still in the camera and delete those that you don't want. The photos that you want to keep can be transferred directly to some printers, but typically, you'll transfer the photo data to your computer's hard disk. This transfer can be achieved in several ways, depending on your camera.

Media transfer. If your camera stores data on floppy disks or CDs, you can simply remove the media from your camera and insert it into the appropriate drive of your computer.

Direct cable transfer. If your computer and your camera have FireWire ports (also called IEEE-1394 ports), you can connect a cable between these two ports to transfer the photo data. You can use a cable if your computer and camera have USB ports or serial ports. A USB-2 port provides good transfer speed. A USB-1 port is slower, while a serial port is the slowest.

Infrared port. Some cameras can "beam" the data from your camera to your computer's infrared port. This method eliminates the need for a cable, but is much slower than using a FireWire, USB, or serial port.

Card reader. A **card reader** is a small device connected to your computer's USB or serial port and designed to read data contained in a solid state memory card. A card reader acts in the same way as an external disk drive by treating your memory cards like floppy disks. To transfer the photo data from a memory card, you remove it from the camera and insert it into the card reader, as shown in Figure H-4.

Floppy disk adapter. A **floppy disk adapter** is a floppy disk-shaped device that contains a slot for a memory card. You simply insert the memory card into the floppy disk adapter, and then insert the adapter into your computer's floppy disk drive.

- Regardless of the technology that you use, transferring photo data from your camera to your computer requires software, which may be supplied along with your camera, with your card reader, or by a standalone graphics software package, such as Adobe Photoshop. This software allows you to select a file format, specify a filename, and determine the location for each image file. After you store your digital photos on your computer's hard disk, you can modify them, send them as e-mail attachments, print them, post them on Web pages, or archive them onto a CD.

FIGURE H-1: A scanner

To scan an image:
1. Turn on the scanner and start your scanner software
2. Place the image face down on the scanner glass
3. Use the scanner software to initiate the scan
4. The scanned image is stored in RAM
5. Save the image on your computer's hard disk

FIGURE H-2: A digital camera

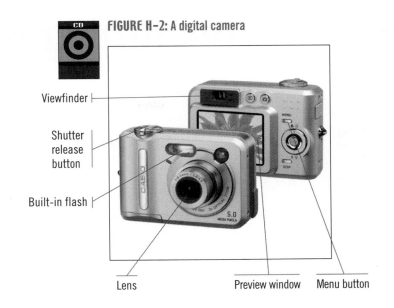

Viewfinder

Shutter release button

Built-in flash

Lens   Preview window   Menu button

FIGURE H-3: Storage options for a digital camera

▼ Storage options for digital cameras vary in capacity from 8 MB to 1 GB; the number of photos that can be stored depends on their resolution; high-resolution photos require more storage space than low-resolution photos; as few as two high-resolution photos might fit on a 32 MB card, whereas the same card might hold hundreds of low-res images

CompactFlash Card

Memory Stick

SmartMedia Card

xD-Picture Card

Microdrive

FIGURE H-4: A card reader

▼ A card reader transfers photo data from a memory card to your computer's hard disk

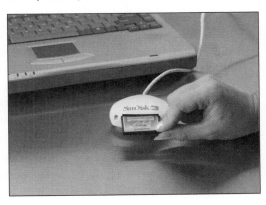

Modifying bitmap graphics

Because bitmap graphics are coded as a series of bits that represent pixels, you can use graphics software to modify or edit this type of graphic by changing individual pixels. You can retouch or repair old photographs to eliminate creases, spots, and discoloration. In order to modify bitmap graphics images, you need an understanding of image resolution, density, and file formats.

LAB
WORKING WITH
BITMAP GRAPHICS

DETAILS

- Whether you acquire images from a digital camera or from a scanner, bitmap graphics tend to require a lot of storage space. Each pixel in a bitmap graphic is stored as one or more bits. The more pixels in a bitmap graphic, the more bits needed to store the file. So while a large bitmap graphic file might provide the necessary data for a high-quality printout, these files take up space on your hard disk, can require lengthy e-mail transmission times, and make Web pages seem sluggish.

- Unlike a photograph, a bitmap graphic has no fixed physical size. The size at which a bitmap graphic is displayed or printed depends on the resolution, as well as the density, of the image grid.

- **Resolution**, the dimensions of the grid that forms a bitmap graphic, is usually expressed as the number of horizontal and vertical pixels that it contains. For example, a small graphic for a Web page might have a resolution of 150×100 pixels: 150 pixels across and 100 pixels high. High-resolution graphics contain more data and look better at any size than low-resolution graphics. With more data, it is possible to display and print high-quality images that are smoother and cleaner. Bitmap graphics are **resolution dependent**, which means that the quality of the image depends on its resolution.

  Camera manufacturers sometimes express the resolution of digital cameras in **megapixels** (millions of pixels), the total number of pixels in a graphic. A resolution of $1,600 \times 1,200$ would be expressed as 1.9 megapixels (1,600 multiplied by 1,200); a bitmap graphic image that has 3.1 megapixels contains more pixels and is a higher quality. If you reduce the resolution from $2,160 \times 1,440$ (3.1 megapixels) to $1,080 \times 720$ (.8 megapixels), the image grid becomes a quarter of its original size. The file size is reduced by a similar amount. Data is lost when you reduce the pixels, thereby reducing image quality.

- The concept of stretching and shrinking a bitmap graphic without changing resolution is important for understanding what happens when bitmap graphics are displayed on a monitor and printed on paper. The denser the grid, the smaller the image will appear. See Figure H-5. The **density** of an image grid can be expressed as dots per inch (dpi) for a printer or scanner, or as pixels per inch (ppi) on a monitor. When viewing an image that is larger than the screen, you must scroll to see all parts of the image, or set the

zoom level of your graphics software to less than 100 percent. Changing the zoom level only stretches or shrinks the size of the image grid; it has no effect on the size at which a graphic is printed, or the size of the file in which the graphic is stored.

- Most graphics software allows you to specify the size at which an image is printed without changing the resolution of the bitmap graphic. You'll get the highest print quality if the resolution of the graphic meets or exceeds the printer's dpi. An ink jet printer with a resolution of $1,440 \times 720$ dpi produces a very dense image grid. If each pixel of a $1,600 \times 1,200$ graphic was printed as a single dot on this printer, the resulting image would be very high quality, but just a bit wider than 1 inch. You can specify a larger size for the printout, in which case the printer must create additional data to fill the print grid. This process can produce a fuzzy and blocky image if the printed image gets very large.

  If you attempt to enlarge a bitmap by increasing its resolution, your computer must somehow add pixels because no additional picture data exists. Most graphics software uses a process called **pixel interpolation** to create new pixels by averaging the colors of nearby pixels. See Figure H-6.

- Sometimes the resolution and corresponding file size of a graphic might not be right for your needs. For example, a photo taken with a 5 megapixel camera is unsuitable for a Web page or as an e-mail attachment. Not only would it take a long time to download, but it would be larger than most screens. If you reduce the resolution, the computer eliminates pixels from the image, reducing the size of the image grid. The file size is reduced by a similar amount, and image quality is reduced.

- Another way to reduce the size of a bitmap graphic is to crop it. **Cropping** refers to the process of removing part of an image, just like cutting out a section of a photograph. Cropping decreases file size by reducing the number of pixels in a graphic. The visual presentation changes to reflect the cropped changes.

- Bitmap graphics can be saved in a variety of graphics file formats. Most graphics software provides a choice of popular formats, such as BMP, TIFF, JPEG, GIF, and PNG. The file format you use depends on a variety of factors. See Table H-1.

FIGURE H-5: Two views of an image with a 24 × 24 resolution

▶ Imagine that each bitmap image and its grid comes on a surface that you can stretch or shrink, as you shrink the surface, the grid becomes smaller and more dense

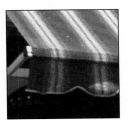

24 × 24 resolution

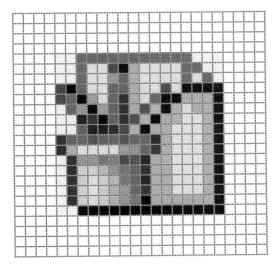

▶ As you stretch the surface, the grid maintains the same number of horizontal and vertical cells, but each cell becomes larger and the grid becomes less dense

24 × 24 resolution

FIGURE H-6: Increasing resolution can reduce image quality

▶ The smaller figure has a resolution of 130 × 130; the larger figure was changed to a resolution of 260 × 260; for some graphics, pixel interpolation results in an image that appears very similar to the original; other images, particularly those that contain strong curved or diagonal lines, develop an undesirable pixelated, or bitmappy, appearance

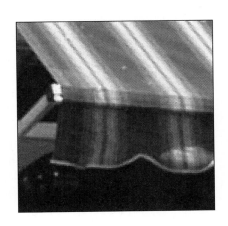

TABLE H-1: Popular file formats for graphics

FORMAT	DESCRIPTION
BMP	Native bitmap graphic file format of the Microsoft Windows environment; creates BMP graphics files; supports True Color; used for graphical elements, such as buttons and other controls used in computer programs, as well as, for a wide variety of graphics applications
TIFF	A highly flexible and platform-independent graphics file format that is supported by most photoediting software packages; supports True Color; used for high resolution scanned images and digital photos
JPEG	Joint Photographic Experts Group; a graphics format with built-in compression that stores True Color bitmap data efficiently in a small file; used for photographic or scanned images that might be used in a variety of applications, such as Web pages, where flexibility in file size is important
GIF	Graphics Interchange Format; specifically designed to create images that can be displayed on multiple platforms, GIF graphics are limited to 256 colors; used for Web graphics; the compression algorithm built into GIF format is patented by UniSys
PNG	Graphics format designed to improve upon the GIF format; a PNG graphic can display up to 48-bit True Color (trillions of colors); unlike GIF, PNG is a pubic domain format without any restrictions on its use; used as an alternative to GIF for Web graphics

Introducing color depth

Color depth refers to the number of colors available for use in an image. As the color depth increases, image quality improves and file size increases. You can adjust color depth in order to decrease the size of the file required for a graphic. This lesson looks at color depth and how it affects your bitmap graphics.

DETAILS

● When monitors were simple monochrome (one-color) devices, each screen pixel was either on or off. A **monochrome bitmap** would be displayed by manipulating the pattern of on and off pixels displayed on the screen. To store the data for a monochrome bitmap, an on pixel is represented by a 1 bit. An off pixel is represented by a 0 bit. Each row of the bitmap grid is stored as a series of 0s and 1s, as shown in Figure H-7. Monochrome bitmaps require very little storage space. Each pixel is set to display either a black dot or a white dot, and so requires only one bit for storage. Therefore, the number of bits required to represent a full-screen picture is the same as the number of pixels on the screen.

● Color monitors require a more complex storage scheme. Each screen pixel displays a color based on the intensity of red, green, and blue signals that it receives. A pixel appears white if the red, green, and blue signals are set to maximum intensity. If red, green, and blue signals are equal but at a lower intensity, the pixel displays a shade of gray. If the red signal is set to maximum intensity, but the blue and green signals are off, the pixel appears in brilliant red. A pixel appears purple if it receives red and blue signals, and so on.

Each red, green, and blue signal is assigned a value ranging from zero to 255, from absence of color to the highest intensity level for that color. These values produce a maximum of 16.7 million colors. A graphic that uses this full range of colors is referred to as a **True Color bitmap** or a **24-bit bitmap**. The data for each pixel requires three bytes of storage space: eight bits for red, eight bits for green, and eight bits for blue, for a total of 24 bits per pixel. True Color bitmaps produce photographic-quality images, but they also produce very large files.

A **32-bit bitmap** displays 16.7 million colors just like a 24-bit bitmap. The extra eight bits are used to define special effects, such as the amount of transparency, for a pixel. 32-bit bitmap graphics files are even larger than 24-bit bitmap graphics files.

● To reduce the size of a bitmap file, you can reduce its color depth by using graphics software to work with color palettes. A **color palette** (also called a color lookup table or color map) holds the selection of colors and allows you to select a group of colors to use for a bitmap graphic. If a palette contains only

256 colors, you can store the data for each pixel in eight bits instead of 24 bits, which reduces the file to one third the size required for a True Color bitmap. A color palette is stored as a table within the header of a graphic file. Figure H-8 explains how this table works.

● Most graphics software offers a selection of ready-made palettes that you can select using the color palette or color picker tool. Ready-made palettes usually include a grayscale palette, a system palette, and a Web palette. A **grayscale palette** displays an image using shades of gray, which looks similar to a black-and-white photograph. Most grayscale palettes consist of 256 colors. Figure H-9 illustrates a grayscale bitmap graphic and a grayscale palette.

A **system palette** is the selection of colors used by the operating system for the graphics that represent desktop icons and controls. Windows, for example, uses a system palette that contains 20 permanent colors and 236 colors that can be changed, depending on the application. A **Web palette** contains a standard set of colors used by Internet Web browsers. Because most browsers support this palette, it is typically regarded as a safe choice when preparing graphics for Internet distribution. Figure H-10 shows the collection of colors used by system and Web palettes. Additional palettes may be provided by your graphics software.

● A particular 256-color palette sometimes does not contain the right selection of colors for an image. For example, the Windows system palette does not provide a wide enough selection of orange tones for a Halloween or sunset photo. To make up for the lack of colors, your graphics software can dither the image. **Dithering** uses patterns composed of two or more colors to produce the illusion of additional colors and shading, relying on the human eye to blend colors and shapes. Most graphics software provides options that let you control the dithering.

● As a rule of thumb, bitmap graphics that you want to print should remain in True Color format. Any graphics that will be sent as e-mail attachments, posted on a Web site, or viewed only on screen should be reduced to a 256-color palette.

FIGURE H-7: Monochrome bitmap graphic

1. The image can originate as a black-and-white silhouette, as a black-and-white photograph, or even as a color photo

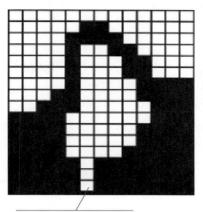

2. The computer divides the picture into a matrix

```
1 1 1 1 1 1 1 1 1 1 1 1
1 1 1 1 0 0 1 1 1 1 1 1
1 1 1 0 0 0 0 1 1 1 1 1
1 1 1 0 1 1 0 0 1 1 1 1
1 1 1 1 0 1 1 0 0 1 1 1
1 1 1 1 0 1 1 0 0 1 1 1
1 1 1 1 0 1 1 1 0 0 0 0
1 1 1 0 0 1 1 1 0 0 0 0
1 1 0 0 0 1 1 1 1 0 0 0
0 0 0 0 1 1 1 1 1 0 0 0
0 0 0 0 1 1 1 1 1 0 0 0
0 0 0 0 1 1 1 1 1 0 0 0
0 0 0 0 1 1 1 1 0 0 0 0
0 0 0 0 0 1 0 0 0 0 0 0
0 0 0 0 0 1 0 0 0 0 0 0
0 0 0 0 0 1 0 0 0 0 0 0
```

3. If a cell is white, it is coded as a 1; if the cell is black, it is coded as a 0

FIGURE H-8: The color palette

▶ A color palette is a subset of all possible colors; each color in the palette is numbered and its number points to the full 24-bit RGB value that is stored in the graphic file header

0	2	2
1	1	3
2	4	4
3	3	253

Pixels in the upper-left corner of an image

Color Palette	
Index #	RGB Value
0	000 000 000
1	060 000 255
2	020 167 167
3	120 060 060
4	180 060 060
5	255 000 000
.	
.	
253	255 060 060
254	255 000 255
255	255 255 255

FIGURE H-9: Grayscale bitmap graphic and grayscale palette

FIGURE H-10: Other palettes

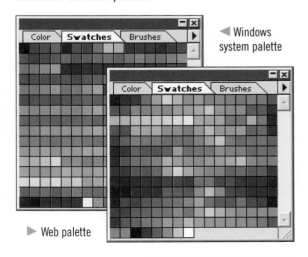

◀ Windows system palette

▶ Web palette

UNIT H

Introducing vector graphics

A **vector graphic** consists of a set of instructions for creating a picture. Unlike a bitmap graphic file, which superimposes a grid of pixels over an image and stores the color value for each pixel, a vector graphic file contains the instructions that the computer needs to create the shape, size, position, and color for each object in an image. This lesson explains the basics of two-dimensional vector graphics and how they differ from bitmap graphics.

DETAILS

- The parts of a vector graphic are created as separate objects, as seen in the Stonehenge image in Figure H-11.

- It is difficult to identify a vector graphic just by looking at an on-screen image. One clue that an image might be a vector graphic is a flat, cartoon-like quality. Think of clip art images, which are typically stored as vector graphics. For a more definitive identification, however, you should check the filename extension. Vector graphics files have filename extensions such as .wmf, .dxt, .mgx, .eps, .pict, and .cgm.

- Vector graphics are suitable for most line art, logos, simple illustrations, and diagrams that might be displayed and printed at various sizes. When compared to bitmaps, vector graphics have several advantages and disadvantages. You should take the following distinctions into account when deciding which type of graphic to use for a specific project.

  - Vector graphics resize better than bitmap graphics. When you change the physical size of a vector graphic, the

objects change proportionally and maintain their smooth edges. See Figure H-12.

  - Vector graphics usually require less storage space than bitmap graphics. Each instruction requires storage space, so the more lines, shapes, and fill patterns in the graphic, the more storage space it requires.

  - It is easier to edit an object in a vector graphic than in a bitmap graphic. In some ways, a vector graphic is like a collage of objects. Each object can be layered over other objects but moved and edited independently. You can individually stretch, shrink, distort, color, move, or delete any object in a vector graphic. See Figure H-13.

  - Vector graphics tend not to produce images that are as realistic as bitmap images. Most vector images tend to be more cartoon-like than the realistic appearance of a photograph. The cartoon-like characteristic of vector images results from the use of objects filled with blocks of color. Because your options for shading and texturing vector graphics are limited, vector graphics tend to have a flat appearance.

Vector graphics on the Web

Web browsers were originally designed to support a limited number of exclusively bitmap graphics formats. Built-in browser support for vector graphics has been slow, but plug-ins and players are currently available for several of the most popular Web-based vector graphics formats.

A graphics format called **SVG**, or **Scalable Vector Graphics**, is designed specifically for the Web. Graphics in SVG format are automatically resized when displayed on different screens or when printed. SVG supports gradients, drop shadows, multiple levels of transparency, and other effects, along with transportability to other platforms like handheld computers and cellular phones. SVG graphics objects can include regular and irregular shapes, images, and text, and they can be animated. You can add SVG files to HTML and XML documents using the <embed> tag.

Macromedia's Flash software, which requires a browser plug-in to be viewed, creates a popular vector graphics format designed for Web use that is stored in swf files with .swf extensions. **Flash graphics** can be static or

animated, and typically require less storage space than SVG graphics. Flash animations have advantages over animated GIFs. GIF files are fairly large because they are bitmap images; most Flash animations are smaller because they fit in compact files. As a result, they can be transferred from a Web server to a browser more rapidly than animated GIFs.

Vector graphics files require little storage space and can be transmitted swiftly from a Web server to your browser. On Web pages, vector graphics appear with the same consistent quality on all computer screens, making it possible for browsers to adjust the size of an image instantaneously to fit correctly on a screen, regardless of its size or resolution. Any text contained in a vector image is stored as actual text, not just a series of colored dots. This text can be indexed by search engines so that it can be included in keyword searches, and the image can turn up in the list of search results.

FIGURE H-11: A vector graphic

▶ A vector graphic is formed from lines and shapes, which can be colored or shaded; this image was created with a series of roughly rectangular objects for the stones and a circular object for the sun

FIGURE H-12: Resizing vector graphic image vs. resizing bitmap graphic image

▼ Unlike bitmaps, vector graphics can be resized without becoming pixelated; for example, a circle in a vector graphic appears as a smooth curve at any size

▼ Images in a bitmap graphic might appear to have jagged edges after the graphic is enlarged

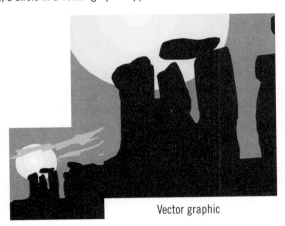

Vector graphic

Bitmap graphic

FIGURE H-13: Vector graphics are layered

▶ Vector graphic objects are layered, so it is easy to move and delete objects without disrupting the rest of the image

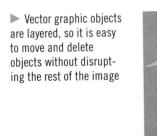

Vector graphic

Deleting a shape from a bitmap image leaves a hole because the image is only one layer of pixels

Bitmap graphic

Creating vector graphics

To create vector graphics images, you cannot use scanners or digital cameras. Instead, you must have special tools and software that work together to generate the instructions for the image. This lesson discusses the hardware and software you need to create and edit vector graphics and how to create vector graphics from bitmap graphics.

DETAILS

● Usually, vector graphics are created from scratch using vector graphics software, referred to as **drawing software**. Drawing software is sometimes packaged separately from the paint software used to produce bitmap graphics. In other cases, it is included with bitmap software as a graphics software suite. Vector graphics software provides an array of drawing tools that you can use to create objects, position them, and fill them with colors or patterns. For example, you can use the filled circle tool to draw a circle that is filled with a solid color. You can create an irregular shape by connecting points to outline the shape. Figure H-14 illustrates how to use drawing tools to create a vector graphic.

● Vector graphics software helps you edit individual objects easily within a graphic by changing their sizes, shapes, positions, or colors. For example, the data for creating the circle is recorded as an instruction, such as CIRCLE 40 Y 200 150, which means: create a circle with a 40-pixel radius, color it yellow, and place the center of the circle 200 pixels from the left of the screen and 150 pixels from the top of the screen. If you move the circle to the right, the instruction that the computer stores for the circle changes to something like CIRCLE 40 Y 500 150, which means the circle is now 500 pixels from the left instead of 200 pixels.

● When filling in a shape with color, your vector graphics software might provide tools for creating a gradient. A **gradient** is a smooth blending of shades from one color to another or from light to dark. Gradients can be used to create shading and three-dimensional effects. See Figure H-15.

● Some vector graphics software provides tools that apply bitmapped textures to vector graphics objects, giving them a more realistic appearance. For example, you can create a vector drawing of a house and then apply a brick-like texture that's derived from a bitmap photograph of real bricks. These graphics that contain both bitmap and vector data are called **metafiles**.

● Sometimes a special input device, called a digitizing tablet, is used to create vector graphics. A **digitizing tablet** provides a flat surface for a paper-based drawing, and a pen or puck is used to click the endpoints of each line on the drawing. The endpoints are converted into vectors and stored. Architects and engineers sometimes use a digitizing tablet, like the one in Figure H-16, to turn a paper-based line drawing into a vector graphic.

● To change a bitmap graphic into a vector graphic, you must use special tracing software. **Tracing software** locates the edges of objects in a bitmap graphic image and converts the resulting shapes into vector graphic objects. This software works best on simple images and line drawings, but does not typically provide acceptable results when used on photos.

Using rasterization to create bitmap graphics from vector graphics

You can create a bitmap graphic from a vector graphic through a process called rasterization. **Rasterization** works by superimposing a grid over a vector graphic and determining the color for each pixel. This process is typically carried out by graphics software, which allows you to specify the output size for the final bitmap image.

It is important to output your rasterized images at the size you will ultimately need. If you rasterize a vector image at a small size and then try to enlarge the resulting bitmap image, you will likely get a poor-quality pixelated image. It is also important to know that once a vector graphic is converted to a bitmap, the resulting graphic no longer has the qualities of a vector graphic; you cannot edit the resulting bitmap graphic as you would the original vector graphic. For example, if you convert the Stonehenge vector graphic into a bitmap, you cannot grab the entire sun object and move it or change its color.

FIGURE H-14: Drawing vector graphic images

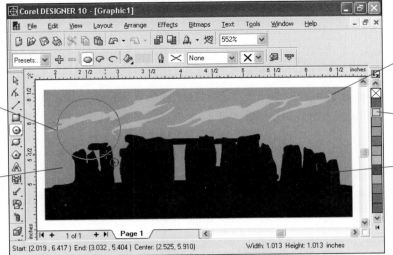

To draw a circle, select the circle tool; drag the pointer to indicate the location and size of the circle

The background is a filled rectangle

The clouds are created as a series of short line segments and filled with color

A color palette allows you to select the circle color

The stones are created as a series of short line segments and filled with black

FIGURE H-15: Gradients can create shading and three-dimensional effects

The sun is a circle filled with a gradient

▲ The use of a gradient makes this shape appear to be a tube

FIGURE H-16: A digitizing tablet

▶ A digitizing tablet allows you to create vector graphics

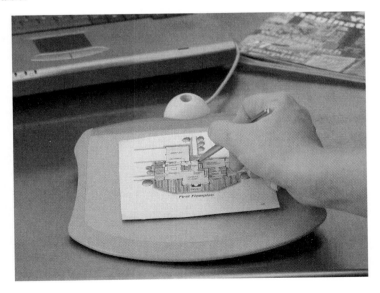

UNIT H

Exploring 3-D graphics

Now that you have covered the basics for two-dimensional graphics, this lesson expands what you learned to introduce static 3-D graphics and animated 3-D graphics. If you've played any computer games recently or watched a hit movie like Shrek or Monsters, Inc., you've seen the product of computer-generated, 3-D, animated graphics. This lesson discusses 3-D graphics in more detail.

DETAILS

● Like vector graphics, 3-D graphics are stored as a set of instructions. For a 3-D graphic, however, the instructions contain the locations and lengths of lines that form a wireframe for a three-dimensional object. The **wireframe** provides a framework for the 3-D graphic. A 3-D wireframe can be covered with surface texture and color to create a graphic of a 3-D object. The process of covering a wireframe with surface color and texture is called **rendering**. The rendering process outputs a bitmap image. See Figure H-17.

● For added realism, the rendering process can take into account the way that light shines on surfaces and creates shadows. The technique for adding light and shadows to a 3-D image is called **ray tracing**. Ray tracing adds realism to 3-D graphics by adding highlights and shadows that are produced by a light source. Before an image is rendered, the artist selects a location for one or more light sources. The computer applies a complex mathematical algorithm to determine how the light source affects the color of each pixel in the final rendered image. This process can take hours for a complex image, even using today's most powerful personal computers. Figure H-18 shows the image from the previous figure rendered with an additional light source using ray tracing.

● To create 3-D graphics, you need 3-D graphics software, such as AutoCad or Caligari trueSpace. 3-D graphics software provides the tools that you need to draw a wireframe and view it from any angle. See Figure H-19. It provides rendering and ray tracing tools, along with an assortment of surface textures and colors that you can apply to individual objects. 3-D graphics software runs on most personal computers, though some architects and engineers prefer to use high-end workstations. A fast processor, lots of RAM, and a fast graphics card with its own video RAM all speed up the rendering process.

● 3-D graphics can be animated to produce special effects for movies or create interactive animated characters and environments for 3-D computer games. Animated special effects are created by rendering a sequence of bitmaps in which one or more objects are moved, or otherwise changed, between each rendering. In traditional hand-drawn animation, a chief artist draws the key frames, and then a team of assistants creates each of the in-between images. There are 24 images for each second of animation. For 3-D computer animation, the computer creates the in-between

images by moving the object and rendering each necessary image. All of the images are then combined into a single file, creating essentially a digital movie.

Graphic design companies like Pixar Animation Studios and DreamWorks use 3-D animation techniques to produce animated feature films, as well as special effects. The first full-length animated 3-D movie was "Toy Story," released in 1995 by Walt Disney Studios and Pixar. Digitally animated films, such as "Finding Nemo," "Ice Age," and "The Incredibles," illustrate the growing sophistication of 3-D animation. An important characteristic of special effects and animated films is that the rendering can be accomplished during the production phase of the movie and incorporated into the final footage.

● In contrast, 3-D computer game animation happens in real time. Each frame that makes the image seem to move must be rendered while you are playing the game—a process that requires an incredible amount of computer power. Consider a game displayed on a computer monitor at $1,024 \times 768$ resolution so the screen contains 786,432 pixels. If the game is presented in 32-bit color, each frame of the animation requires 25,165,824 bits (multiply 786,432 by 32). Computer game designers believe that onscreen animation looks smoothest at 60 frames per second, which means that your computer must handle 1,509,949,440—that's more than 1 billion—bits of information every second just to put the 3-D image onto the screen. In addition, the computer must process even more data to keep track of the movements of each player.

● To handle all of this data, your computer's main processor gets help from a graphics processor located on your computer's graphics card. These graphics processors vary in their capabilities. For the fastest graphics capability, look for graphics cards billed as 3-D accelerators.

● You can create 3-D animations on a desktop computer using commercially available software, but many of the best software packages are expensive and have a steep learning curve. These commercial products used by professionals result in higher quality and require powerful computer hardware. If you want to experiment with 3-D animations before making an expensive software investment, you might try one of the shareware programs.

FIGURE H-17: Creating a 3-D graphic

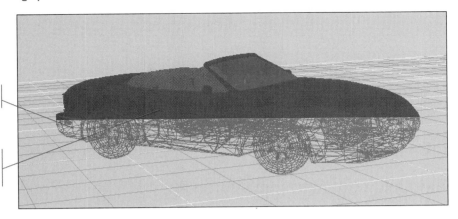

3-D graphics are based on a wireframe...

...which can be rendered into a bitmap image that looks three-dimensional

FIGURE H-18: Ray tracing

Light source

Shadow

Highlight

FIGURE H-19: 3-D graphics software

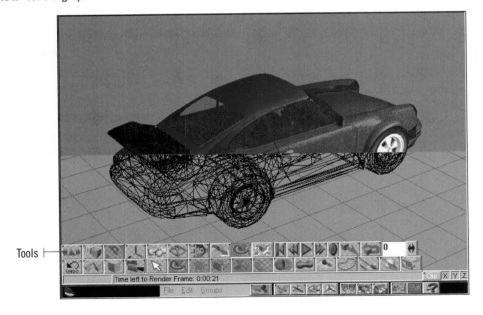

Tools

Time left to Render Frame: 0:00:21

File Edit Groups

Introducing desktop video

UNIT H

Desktop videos are constructed and played using a personal computer. These videos can be stored on a hard disk or distributed on CDs, DVDs, videotapes, or the Web. Typically, the footage for a desktop video is captured by a video camera or converted into digital format from videotape. You can use a consumer-quality camera and your personal computer to create videos that are suitable for a variety of personal and professional uses.

DETAILS

- A **video** is composed of a series of frames. See Figure H-20. Each frame is essentially a still picture that can be stored as a bitmap graphic. **Frame rate** refers to the number of frames shown per second; the higher the frame rate the better the video image. Feature films are typically projected at a rate of 24 frames per second (fps). Most desktop videos have a frame rate of only 15 fps.

- The basic process of creating desktop videos consists of the following steps: shoot the video footage; transfer the footage to your computer's hard disk; edit the video and soundtrack; output the video in its final format by selecting frame rate, window size, file format, and compression levels. See Figure H-21.

- Once the video footage is captured and transferred to your computer's memory, you must save the video footage to the hard drive. Several file formats are popular for desktop videos including **AVI**, **QuickTime**, **MPEG**, **RealMedia**, and **ASF**. Table H-2 provides some basic information about each one.

- Although video playback requires no special hardware, it does require a software player that's designed to work with the file format in which the video is stored. Players for most video file formats are available on the Web at no cost. The most popular players are Microsoft Media Player and QuickTime. Figure H-22 illustrates how to use Media Player. Apple's QuickTime player is popular for both the PC and Mac platforms. It is available for download at the Apple Web site.

- Most of today's personal computers are well-equipped for viewing videos; however, playback quality can vary depending on your computer's microprocessor, RAM capacity, and the capabilities of its graphics card. When viewing Web-based videos, the speed of your Internet connection also affects video quality. Your computer displays video frames as fast as they are received and processed. On a slow computer or using a dial-up Internet connection, videos might appear in a very small window on the screen, images might appear choppy and pixelated, and the sound might get out of sync with the action.

TABLE H-2: Popular desktop video file formats

FORMAT	EXTENSION	PLATFORM	PLAYERS	DESCRIPTION
AVI (Audio Video Interleave)	.avi	PC	Microsoft Media Player	Sometimes called "Video for Windows," AVI is the most common format for desktop video on the PC platform
QuickTime Movie	.mov	PC, Mac, UNIX, Linux	QuickTime, Microsoft Media Player	Originally developed for the Mac platform, QuickTime movies are one of the most popular formats for Web videos
MPEG (Moving Picture Experts Group)	.mpg or .mpeg	PC, Mac, UNIX, Linux	Microsoft Media Player	MPEG is one of the most sophisticated digital video formats; used both for desktop videos and DVD movies
RealMedia	.rm	PC, Mac, UNIX, Linux	RealPlayer, Microsoft Media Player	RealMedia, produced by RealNetworks, is a popular format for streaming Web videos
ASF	.asf	PC	Microsoft Media Player	ASF is Microsoft's video format for streaming video over the Web

FIGURE H-20: A video is a series of frames

FIGURE H-21: Steps to create a desktop video

1. Shoot the video footage

2. Transfer the footage to your computer's hard disk

3. Edit the video and soundtrack

4. Output the video in its final format

FIGURE H-22: Playing a desktop video

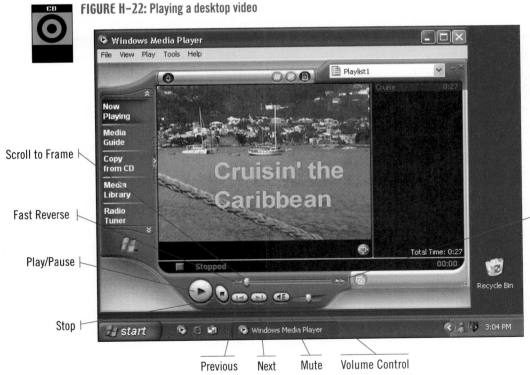

◄ Windows Media Player is shipped with Windows and is designed to be used on the PC platform; updates for this player can be obtained from the Microsoft Web site

Exploring video equipment

To create a desktop video, you need a video camera. To edit and modify video footage, you transfer the video footage from your video camera to your computer. This lesson explores cameras you can use to capture the video and the equipment that you need for transferring the video footage from your camera to your computer. This lesson also discusses computer devices, such as cards and cables that you will need to transfer the video to a computer for editing.

DETAILS

● You can use either a digital or an analog video camera to shoot the footage for desktop video. A **digital video camera** stores footage as a series of bits. The video data is stored on a tape in much the same way that digital data is stored on a backup tape. Digital video tape formats include miniDV, DVCPro, and DVCam. MiniDV is used by most consumer digital video cameras.

You can also use an **analog video camera** to shoot the footage for your desktop video. As with digital video cameras, the footage is stored on tape; but instead of storing bits, an analog video camera stores the video signal as a continuous track of magnetic patterns. The three most popular analog video formats are Hi8, S-VHS, and VHS. VHS produces lower quality video than Hi8 or S-VHS.

● In addition to video cameras, you might also be familiar with the small inexpensive videoconferencing cameras (often called a "Web camera" or "Web cam") that attach directly to a computer. See Figure H-23. These cameras capture video data in digital format and are designed mainly for talking head applications, such as online video chats and videoconferences.

● Digital cameras generally produce higher quality video than analog or videoconferencing cameras. Images produced using digital video cameras tend to be sharper and more colorful. Generally speaking, the higher the quality of the original video, the better the final video will look.

● In order to digitally edit, process, and store a desktop video, you must transfer the video footage from your camera to your computer. A digital video camera captures video data in digital format, which can then be transferred directly to a computer for editing. See Figure H-24. You can transfer video footage from a digital camera to a hard disk by a cable connecting the video camera and computer. Most digital cameras provide a **FireWire port** or **USB port** for this purpose. Your computer needs a corresponding port to accept the cable from the camera. Figure H-25 shows computers with built-in FireWire and USB ports.

Once the footage is transferred and stored on a random-access device, such as your computer's hard disk, you can easily cut out unwanted footage, divide the remaining footage into separate clips, and rearrange clips.

● Analog video footage must be converted into digital format before it is stored on your computer's hard disk. This analog-to-digital conversion process is referred to as capturing a video. A **video capture device** converts the camera's analog signal into digital data. If your computer's graphics card does not include video capture capabilities, you can purchase a separate video capture device that connects to your computer's USB port or a video capture card that plugs into one of your computer's PCI slots. A video capture card is shown in Figure H-26.

● Whether you're transferring footage from an analog camera or a digital camera, you must use **video capture software**, which allows you to start and stop the transfer and select the display size, frame rate, filename, and file format for your video footage. Your video will be easier to edit if you divide it into several files, each containing a one-to-two-minute segment of footage.

Creating good desktop videos

When desktop videos are processed and stored, some of the image data is eliminated to reduce the video file to a manageable size. Simpler videos tend to maintain better quality as they are edited, processed, and stored. Camera movements, fast actions, patterned clothing, and moving backgrounds all contribute to the complexity of a video. The following techniques will help you produce video footage that maintains good quality as it is edited and processed:

• Use a tripod to maintain a steady image

• Move the camera slowly if it is necessary to pan from side to side

• Zoom in and out slowly

• Direct your subjects to move slowly, when possible

• Position your shot to eliminate as much background detail and movement as possible

• Ask the subjects of your video to wear solid-colored clothing, if possible

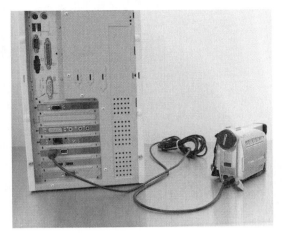

▲ A cable connects a digital video camera and computer;
when the transfer is complete, the cable can be disconnected

FIGURE H-25: FireWire and USB ports

▼ FireWire ports (left) and USB ports
(right) can be located on the front or the
back of the computer's system unit

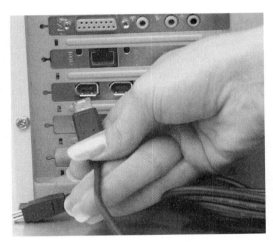

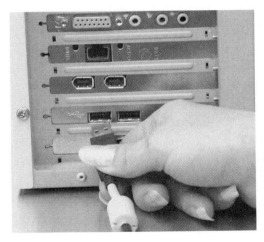

FIGURE H-26: A video capture card

◄ After it has been installed in your computer, a video capture card transforms
analog video footage into digital format

Editing and processing desktop video

Before video cameras went digital, editing a video consisted of recording segments from one videotape onto another. This process, called **linear editing**, required at least two VCRs. Today's **non-linear editing** simply requires a computer hard disk and video editing software, and has the advantage of using a random-access device to edit and arrange footage. The disadvantage is that video footage requires a lot of available storage space.

DETAILS

● Once your video footage is transferred to your computer and stored on the hard disk, you can edit it using **video editing software**. Your completed video consists of video tracks containing video segments and transitions, plus audio tracks containing voices and music. You arrange the video tracks and the audio tracks on a timeline. Most video editing software allows you to overlay a video track with several audio tracks. See Figure H-27.

● After you modify your video tracks and audio tracks, your video editing software combines the data from all of the selected tracks into a single file. This file is stored on your computer's hard disk as a desktop video using a video file format, such as AVI or QuickTime.

● The video footage that you capture and transfer to your computer contains more data than can fit on a CD, DVD, or hard disk. For a desktop video to fit on a personal computer storage device, it is necessary to reduce the number of bits used to represent the video data. To shrink videos to a more manageable size, you can decrease the size of the video window, reduce the number of frames displayed per second, and select a compression technique.

  • Decrease the size of the video window. When creating desktop video, you can specify the size of the window in which your video appears. A smaller window contains fewer pixels than a full-screen window and requires fewer bits to represent the data, but some details become difficult to see.

  • Reduce the **frame rate**. The smooth motion that you expect from commercial films is achieved in a desktop video by displaying 24 fps. Reducing the frame rate to 15 fps—a typical rate for desktop video—cuts the file size almost in half. However, reducing the frame rate tends to increase the blurriness of a video, especially for fast-action sequences.

  • Compress the video data. Several compression techniques were created specifically to reduce the size of video files. A **codec (compressor/decompressor)** is the software that compresses a file when a desktop video is created and decompresses the file when the video is played. Popular codecs include MPEG, Indeo, Cinepak, DivX, and Video 1. Each of these codecs uses a unique compression algorithm and allows you to specify the level of compression that you desire. The three videos associated with Figure H-28 illustrate the differences in image quality and file size that result from using different compression techniques.

● Most video editing software allows you to set the file format, frame rate, color depth, and compression levels as you are saving the video in its final form.

Web-based video

A video for a Web page is stored on a Web server in a file. Usually a link for the video file appears on the Web page. When you click the link, the Web server transmits a copy of the video file to your computer. If you have the correct video player installed on your computer, the video appears on your computer screen. Sometimes your computer has to wait until it receives the entire video file before starting to play it. An alternative method, called **streaming video**, sends a small segment of the video to your computer and begins to play it while your computer continues to receive it. Streaming video is possible with QuickTime, ASF, and RealMedia video formats.

You can add two styles of video to your Web pages. The first style, called **external video**, uses an HTML tag to display a link to a video file. When the link is clicked, the video file is downloaded, the video player is opened, and the video is displayed in a separate window. A second style of Web video uses the <embed> tag to create an **internal video**, or in-place video. Instead of opening a separate window for the video player, an internal video plays within the Web page. See Figure H-29.

Although it is possible to play streaming videos over a dial-up connection, it is truly an unsatisfying experience. High-speed Internet connections provide much more bandwidth for streaming video. Videos that are designed to be played over high-speed connections can have a larger video window and less compression, resulting in better quality. Until everyone has a high-speed connection, however, many Web sites provide one video file that's optimized for dial-up connections and a better-quality video file optimized for DSL, cable, and ISDN connections.

FIGURE H-27: Video editing software

Use the video tracks on the timeline to indicate the sequence for your video clips and transitions

Use the audio tracks to add sound clips

The video and sound clips that you import for the project appear in a list

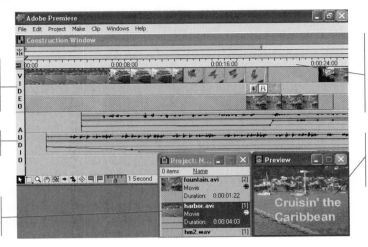

A timeline stretches across the top of the video editing window and provides the structure for each second of your video

Preview your video to see how the video segments, transitions, and soundtrack all work together

FIGURE H-28: Comparing compression and frame rates

▶ To achieve the best compression for a particular video, experiment with different codecs, compression levels, and frame rates; the codec used to compress a video also must be used to decompress the video when it is played; videos should use one of the codecs included in popular video players, such as QuickTime or Windows Media Player; missing codecs account for a high proportion of desktop video glitches

Compression ratio: 35:1
Frame rate: 3
File size: 35 KB

Compression ratio: 14:1
Frame rate: 10
File size: 76 KB

Compression ratio: 3:1
Frame rate: 15
File size: 353 KB

FIGURE H-29: An external Web video vs. an internal, or in place, video

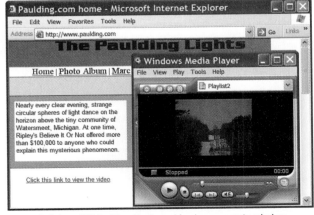

▲ External Web video displays video in a separate window

▲ Internal Web video plays "in place"

Introducing digital sound

Computers can record, store, and play sounds, such as narrations, sound effects, and music. Swapping music files over the Internet is currently a popular use of digital sound, but digital sound also plays a key role in many other interesting applications. This lesson introduces digital sound concepts and technologies.

DETAILS

● **Waveform audio** is a digital representation of sound. Music, voice, and sound effects can all be recorded as waveforms. To record sound digitally, samples of the sound are collected at periodic intervals and stored as numeric data. Figure H-30 shows how a computer digitally samples a sound wave.

● **Sampling rate** refers to the number of times per second that a sound is collected or measured during the recording process and is expressed in hertz (Hz). One thousand samples per second is 1,000 Hz or 1 KHz (kilohertz). Higher sampling rates increase the quality of the sound recording but require more storage space than lower sampling rates. The audio clips associated with Figure H-31 illustrate how sampling rate affects sound quality.

● Your computer's **sound card** contains a variety of input and output jacks plus audio-processing circuitry. It contains the circuitry responsible for transforming the bits stored in an audio file into music, sound effects, and narrations. See Figure H-32. You will usually find a desktop computer's sound card plugged into a PCI expansion slot inside the system unit. Sound card circuitry is sometimes built into the motherboard of notebook computers.

A sound card is typically equipped to accept input from a microphone and provide output to speakers or headphones. For processing waveform files, a sound card contains a special type of circuitry called a **digital signal processor**, which transforms digital bits into analog waves when you play back a waveform audio file, transforms analog waves into digital bits when you make a sound recording, and handles compression and decompression, if necessary.

● Waveform audio can be stored in a variety of file formats. Table H-3 presents some of the advantages and disadvantages of the most popular waveform audio file formats. Wave format files are supported by most Web browsers, so it is a popular audio file format. RealAudio, AIF, and MP3 can also be delivered over the Web. Web-based waveform audio is often delivered in streaming format over the Internet so it plays as it is downloaded. Streaming audio avoids lengthy delays while the entire audio file is downloaded and provides the technology for real-time Internet radio broadcasts and voice chat sessions.

● To play an audio file, you must use an audio player, such as Microsoft Media Player. These players tend to support several audio file formats. In the Windows environment you can use Microsoft Media Player to play Wave, AIF, and MP3 formats, but you cannot use it to record sound. For recording, you must use Microsoft's Sound Recorder software.

TABLE H-3: Popular waveform audio file formats

AUDIO FORMAT EXTENSION	ADVANTAGES	DISADVANTAGES
Wave (.wav)	Good sound quality; supported in browsers without a plug-in	Audio data is stored in raw, uncompressed format, so files are very large
Audio Interchange Format (.aif)	Good sound quality; supported in browsers without a plug-in	Audio data is stored in raw, uncompressed format, so files are very large
MP3 (also called MPEG-1 Layer 3) (.mp3)	Good sound quality even though the file is compressed; can be streamed over the Web	Requires a stand-alone player or browser plug-in
RealAudio (.ra)	High degree of compression produces small files; data can be streamed over the Web	Sound quality is not up to the standards of other formats; requires a player or plug-in

FIGURE H-30: Sampling a sound wave

▼ The height of each sample can be saved as an 8-bit number for radio-quality recordings or as a 16-bit number for high-fidelity recordings; professional audio CDs are recorded at a sampling rate of 44.1 KHz, which means a sample of the sound is taken 44,100 times per second; sixteen bits are used for each sample; stereo effects require two of these 16-bit samples; therefore, each sample requires 32 bits of storage space

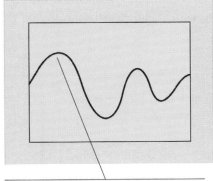

An analog sound wave is a smooth curve of continuous values

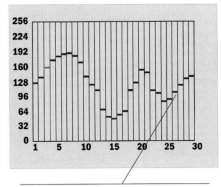

To digitize a sound wave, it is sliced into vertical segments, called samples; for purposes of illustration, this one-second sound wave was sliced into 30 samples

Sample	Sample Height (Decimal)	Sample Height (Binary)
1	130	10000010
2	140	10001100
3	160	10100000
4	175	10101111
5	185	10111001

The height of each sample is converted into a binary number and stored; the height of sample 3 is 160 (decimal), so it is stored as its binary equivalent—10100000

FIGURE H-31: Comparing audio clips

FIGURE H-32: How sound cards convert signals

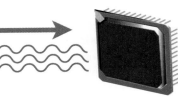
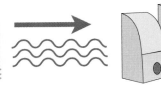

The sound card receives data from the processor

The sound card's digital signal processor decompresses data and converts it to analog signals

The sound card sends analog signals to speakers

Exploring synthesized sound

SPEECH SYNTHESIS AND RECOGNITION

Waveform audio is a digital version of an analog sound signal. In contrast, **synthesized sound** is artificially created. This lesson explores synthesized sounds, which include MIDI music and synthesized speech.

DETAILS

- **MIDI (Musical Instrument Digital Interface)** specifies a standard way to store music data for synthesizers, electronic MIDI instruments, and computers. MIDI is a music notation system that allows computers to communicate with music synthesizers. Unlike waveform sound files, which contain digitized recordings of real sound passages, MIDI files contain instructions for creating the pitch, volume, and duration of notes that sound like various musical instruments. MIDI files are much more compact than waveform audio files.

- The computer encodes the music as a **MIDI sequence** and stores it as a file with a .mid, .cmf, or .rol filename extension. A MIDI sequence contains instructions specifying the pitch of a note, the point at which a note begins, the instrument that plays the note, the volume of the note, and the duration of the note.

- Most computer sound cards are equipped to capture music data from a MIDI instrument as well as generate music from MIDI files. A MIDI-capable sound card contains a **wavetable** (sometimes called a patch set), which is a set of pre-recorded musical instrument sounds. The sound card accesses these sounds and plays them as instructed by the MIDI file.

- MIDI files are much more compact than waveform audio files. Depending on the exact piece of music, three minutes of MIDI music might require only 10 kilobytes of storage space, whereas the same piece of music stored in a high-quality, uncompressed waveform file might require 15 megabytes of storage space.

- MIDI is not suitable for vocals, and it does not have the full resonance of waveform audio sound. Most musicians can easily identify MIDI recordings because they simply lack the tonal qualities of symphony-quality sound, as illustrated in the audio clips associated with Figure H-33.

- MIDI is a good choice for adding background music to multimedia projects and Web pages. Using a procedure similar to that for waveform audio files, you can add a link to a MIDI file by inserting a tag within an HTML document. Most browsers include built-in support for MIDI music.

- You can use MIDI software to compose your own tunes, or you can get permission to use MIDI files that you find on the Web. For composing your own MIDI music, you can input the notes from a MIDI instrument, such as an electronic keyboard, directly to your computer. The input is typically handled by MIDI composition software, similar to that shown in Figure H-34, which you can also use to edit the notes and combine the parts for several instruments.

- **Speech synthesis** is the process by which machines, such as computers, produce sound that resembles spoken words. **Speech recognition** (or voice recognition) refers to the ability of a machine to understand spoken words.

- Speech synthesis is a key technology in wireless communication, such as accessing your e-mail via cell phone—a speech synthesizer reads your e-mail messages to you. A speech synthesizer can also read a computer screen aloud, which unlocks access to computers and the Internet for individuals with disabilities. Most speech synthesizers string together basic sound units called **phonemes**. A basic speech synthesizer consists of **text-to-speech software**, which generates sounds that are played through your computer's standard sound card; other speech synthesizers are special-purpose hardware devices.

- A speech recognition system typically collects words spoken into a microphone that's attached to the sound card. The sound card's digital signal processor transforms the analog sound of your voice into digital data, which is then processed by speech recognition software. **Speech recognition software** analyzes the sounds of your voice and breaks them down into phonemes. Next, the software analyzes the content of your speech and compares the groups of phonemes to the words in a digital dictionary that lists phoneme combinations along with their corresponding English (or French, Spanish, and so on) words. When a match is found, the software displays the correctly spelled word on the screen.

- Speech recognition can be used to activate Windows controls instead of using a mouse. Most speech recognition software also works with your browser, allowing you to "voice surf" the Web. Windows XP includes speech recognition software that you can activate by using the Speech icon in the Control Panel. The first step in using XP's speech recognition feature is training the computer to recognize your speaking style—your accent, pronunciation, and idiomatic expressions—using the Voice Training Wizard. See Figure H-35. When training is complete, you can use the speech recognition feature to verbally issue commands in Windows and dictate text in applications, such as Microsoft Word and Excel, which support the speech recognition feature.

 FIGURE H-33: MIDI music

 FIGURE H-34: MIDI composition software

▼ You can also place notes
on the staff using your mouse

FIGURE H-35: The Windows Voice Training Wizard

▼ The Windows Voice Training Wizard displays short text passages; as you read each passage, the computer listens to the way your pronounce each word and stores it in your speech profile

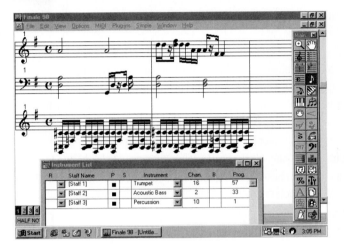

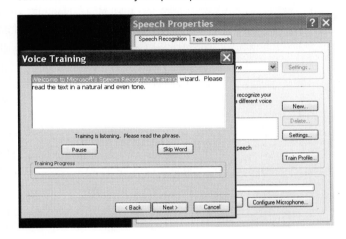

What is MP3?

MP3 is a compressed waveform audio format that stores digitized music, vocals, and narrations in such a way that the sound quality is very good, but the file size remains relatively small—small enough to download from the Web. A CD track that requires 32 MB of storage space shrinks to approximately 3 MB in MP3 format. Famous performing artists and aspiring rock stars use MP3 files to post sample sound tracks from their albums on Web sites.

MP3 files are available from several Web sites, but you can also create your own MP3 files from audio CDs. Software called a CD ripper grabs tracks from an audio CD and stores them in Wave format. After ripping a CD into Wave format, you can use an **MP3 encoder** to convert the Wave file into MP3 format. MP3 files can be stored on your computer's hard disk, transferred to a CD, or relocated to a portable MP3 player. A portable MP3 player (see Figure H-36) is a hardware device that plays MP3 files stored in flash memory, on CDs, or on a mini hard disk drive. Although MP3 is currently the most popular audio file format, newer standards provide better sound quality and compression. Apple is promoting AAC (Advanced Audio

Compression) format on its iTunes Web site. Microsoft is promoting its WMA (Windows Media Audio) format.

FIGURE H-36

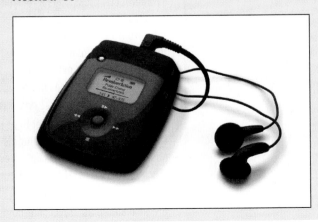

Digital media files can be quite large. They need lots of storage space, require lengthy transmission times, and easily become fragmented, which reduces the efficiency of your computer's hard disk drive. Reducing the size of a file would minimize these problems. **Data compression** is the general term used to describe the process of recoding data so that it requires fewer bytes of storage space; bytes are removed, which reduces the file size. Because data compression is reversible, bytes previously removed from a file can be restored. The process of reversing data compression is sometimes referred to as uncompressing, decompressing, extracting, or expanding a file.

The amount of shrinkage produced by data compression is referred to as the **compression ratio**. A compression ratio of 20:1, for example, means that a compressed file is 20 times smaller than the original file. Data compression is based on a **compression algorithm**—the steps that are required to shrink the data in a file and reconstitute the file to its original state. A compression algorithm is incorporated into a codec, which is used by a computer to compress and decompress file data. Some compression algorithms are designed to shrink text files; other algorithms are for graphics, sound, or video data. Some compression algorithms are generalized and work for any type of data.

Compression that reduces the file size without any data loss, **lossless compression**, provides the means to compress a file and then reconstitute all of the data into its original state. In contrast, **lossy compression** throws away some of the original data during the compression process. Lossy compression can be applied to graphics, videos, and sounds because, in theory, the human eye or ear won't miss the lost information. Most lossy compression techniques provide adjustable compression levels so that you can decide how much data you can afford to lose.

Although most of today's codecs contain sophisticated compression algorithms that are beyond the scope of this book, we can look at some examples of simple compression algorithms to get a general idea of how they work.

Dictionary-based compression replaces common sequences of characters with a single codeword, or symbol, that points either to a dictionary of the original characters or to the original occurrence of the word.

Statistical compression, such as the well-known Huffman algorithm, takes advantage of the frequency of characters to reduce file size. Characters that appear frequently are recoded as short bit patterns, while those that appear infrequently are assigned longer bit patterns.

Spatial compression takes advantage of redundant data within a file by looking for patterns of bytes and replacing them with a message that describes the pattern. **Run-length encoding (RLE)** is an example of a lossless, spatial compression technique that replaces a series of similarly colored pixels with a code that indicates the number of pixels and their colors. JPEG is a lossy version of run-length encoding that can be applied to images, such as photographs, that don't have large areas of solid color. A True Color photograph might not have any adjoining pixels of the same color. Applying run-length encoding to such a photo would not result in any compression whatsoever. JPEG "pre-processes" an image by tweaking the colors in adjoining pixels so that they are the same color whenever possible. Once this pre-processing is complete, run-length encoding techniques can be applied with more success.

Temporal compression is a technique that can be applied to video footage or sound clips to eliminate redundant or unnecessary data between video frames or audio samples. In the case of video, for example, if you are working with a video of a talking head, the background image is likely to contain lots of redundant information that doesn't change from one frame to the next. As the temporal compression algorithm begins to analyze the frames, the first frame becomes a **key frame** that contains all of the data. As the compression algorithm analyzes subsequent frames in the video, it stores only the data that is different from the data in the key frame.

Some file formats, such as PCX, GIF, and MP3, always compress data. Other file formats allow you to select not only whether or not you want to compress the file, but also the level of compression. The software that you use to save and open these files contains the codecs necessary to compress and decompress them. Codecs for JPEG, MPEG, AVI, ASF, and QuickTime files typically allow you to select compression levels before saving a graphic or video file. Some TIFF files are compressed, but others are not—it depends on the software used to store the file.

Most files that contain documents and databases are not stored in compressed format. BMP and Wave files are also stored as "raw," non-compressed bits. If you want to compress these files before sending them as e-mail attachments, for example, you can do so manually. BMP and DOC file sizes might shrink by as much as 70 percent. Other non-compressed file formats, such as Wave, may compress by about 20 percent. File formats such as GIF, MP3, MPEG, and JPEG hardly shrink at all when you zip them because they are already stored in a compressed format.

To manually compress a file, such as a Word document or a Windows bitmap image, you can work with a **file compression utility**, to shrink one or more files into a single new file. You cannot use this compressed file until it has been decompressed. WinZip, a file compression utility, produces compressed files with .zip extensions. Compressing a file is called **zipping**; decompressing a file is called **unzipping**. Figure H-37 shows files that were zipped using WinZip software.

Windows XP includes a built-in compression feature that allows you to create compressed folders. Any files that you drag into a compressed folder are automatically compressed. Compressed folders provide fairly transparent compression. You don't have to do anything special to open a file from a compressed folder. Simply double-click the filename as usual and Windows automatically decompresses the file before displaying its contents. When you create a compressed folder, Windows automatically adds a .zip extension to the folder name. In this way, the folder is treated like a zipped file by other compression utilities, such as PKZIP and WinZip. For example, if you want to e-mail several bitmap graphics, you can create a zipped folder to store the graphic files. First, you save them in BMP format. Next, create a compressed folder called Photos (see Figure H-38). Drag the bitmap graphics into the Photos folder. Attach the Photos folder to your e-mail message. The attachment will be named Photos.zip. The recipient of your e-mail can open the attachment using Windows or a file compression utility, such as PKZIP or WinZIP.

FIGURE H-37: The WinZip window

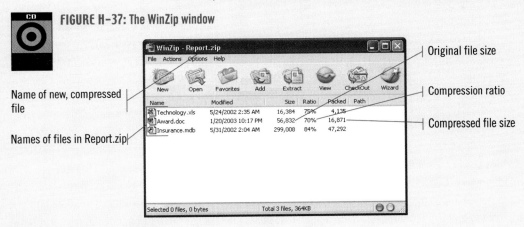

Name of new, compressed file

Names of files in Report.zip

Original file size

Compression ratio

Compressed file size

FIGURE H-38: Compressed folders

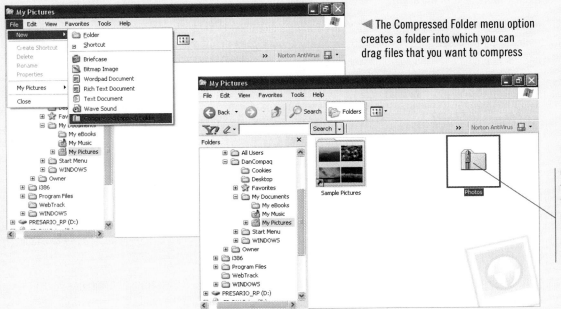

◀ The Compressed Folder menu option creates a folder into which you can drag files that you want to compress

Compressed folder icons feature a zipper; the folder name has a .zip extension, which is only visible if you have file extensions turned on in Windows

In 1895, eager Parisians crowded into a busy café to watch the first public presentation of an exciting new invention—the Cinematograph. The 10-minute film, mostly scenes of everyday life, was a smashing success and ushered in the motion picture era.

Early films were short, grainy, grayscale, and silent, but technology quickly improved. In the New York debut of *The Jazz Singer* (1927), Al Jolson spoke the first words in a feature film, "Wait a minute, wait a minute. You ain't heard nothin' yet!" The audience rose to its feet, applauding wildly. In 1935, RKO studios released *Becky Sharp*, the first feature-length movie filmed from beginning to end in Technicolor—a real milestone for the film industry. Even before "talkies" and Technicolor, filmmakers sought ways to escape the bounds of reality through special effects. As early as 1925, directors such as Willis O'Brien used stop-motion photography to animate dinosaurs, giant gorillas, and sword-wielding skeletons. Special-effects technologies—miniatures, blue screens, puppets, claymation, and composite shots—were used with varying degrees of skill over the next 50 years.

FIGURE H-39

Films such as Stanley Kubrick's masterpiece, *2001: A Space Odyssey* (1968), and George Lucas's original *Star Wars* (1977) stretched these technologies to their limits, but audiences demanded even more spectacular, yet "realistic," effects. In 1982, Disney released *TRON*, a movie about a computer programmer who becomes trapped in the depths of a computer where programs are humanlike creatures at the whim of an evil Master Control Program. The movie included the first primitive attempts at computer-generated footage—30 minutes of computer-generated imagery (CGI) created by two Cray XMP supercomputers. CGI uses rendering techniques to create a 3-D scene from a 2-D image, a camera angle, and a light source. Sophisticated algorithms determine how textures, colors, and shadows appear in the rendered scene. Camera angles can be changed at will, and fantastic effects can be created by bending or stretching the image, manipulating light, creating textures, and adding movement to the scene.

Rendered scenes can be set in motion with computer animation techniques. Manual animation requires a painstaking process called "in-betweening," in which an artist draws a series of incrementally different images to produce the illusion of movement. Today, computers can easily generate in-between images and free up human animators for even more challenging work.

A captivating animation special effect called morphing was first seen on the big screen in James Cameron's *Abyss* (1989) and later used in *Terminator II* (1991) and other movies. Like in-betweening, morphing starts out with animators defining the morph's start and end points—for example, in *Terminator II*, the liquid metal face of the T-1000 robot and actor Robert Patrick's face. The start and end points are rendered into digital images, and then the computer generates all the in-between images. Human animators tweak the images by inserting small discrepancies for a touch of less-than-perfect realism in the final image.

Although the process might sound simple, morphing complex objects realistically and believably takes a tremendous amount of time and computer power. The five-minutes morphing sequence in *Terminator II* took special-effects company Industrial Light and Magic one year to create.

Memorable computer-generated scenes from 2002 blockbusters include the breathtaking aerial scenes in *Spiderman*, a furry blue monster careening downhill in *Monsters, Inc.*, and the endless army of Uruk-hai marching down the valley toward Helm's Deep in *The Two Towers*. Spiderman's acrobatic swing through Manhattan was generated with three professional rendering products: Maya, Houdini, and RenderMan. The Uruk-hai were created with MASSIVE, a custom program that gave each computer-generated warrior a unique sequence of actions. To individually animate each of Sully's 2,320,413 blue hairs, animators developed software called Fizt, a dynamic simulator.

Rendering, morphing, and other special-effects processing require sophisticated computer systems. Pixar Inc., the company that provided the technology behind *Toy Story*, *Finding Nemo*, *Monsters Inc.*, and many other feature-length animated films, uses a cluster of computers dubbed the "RenderFarm." Consisting of more than 100 Sun SPARCstation computers, the network can process 16 billion instructions per second. A movie such as *Toy Story* took more than 800,000 computer hours to produce using the RenderFarm. That might seem like a long time, but if Pixar animators had attempted to use a single-processor computer, it would have taken 43 years to finish the job!

Other CGI variations are being used for increasingly sophisticated effects. Special-effects guru John Gaeta developed bullet time and image-based rendering for *The Matrix* (1999) and *The Matrix: Reloaded* (2003). Bullet time produces reality-defying action sequences that slow time to a tantalizing crawl and then crank it back up to normal speed as the camera pivots rapidly around the scene. The effect requires a computer to meticulously trigger a circular array of more than 100 still cameras in sequence. Image-based rendering generates a digital image based on photos of objects, scenes, or people. The 2-D photos can be digitally manipulated to create 3-D objects, eliminating the need for conventional CGI's computationally intensive 3-D wireframes and raytracing. Neo battles hundreds of Agent Smiths in a world created by image-based rendering.

Sophisticated animation and rendering techniques now come close to producing realistic human figures. Animations were once clearly two-dimensional and far from lifelike, but CGI renderings are becoming more difficult to distinguish from real actors. What might happen in the

FIGURE H-40

future is the subject of *Simone* (2002), starring Al Pacino as a washed-up director who is given a hard disk containing code for a computer-generated movie star. Pacino uses her as the leading lady in a string of hits, all the while keeping her identity secret. According to reviewer Leigh Johnson, it becomes clear that Simone, a computer generated image, is more authentic than the people watching her. It is one of the film's main themes, expressed by Pacino's character: "Our ability to manufacture fraud now exceeds our ability to detect it." The implications of computer-generated actors are just emerging. Not only do they blur the line between reality and fiction, but they also raise puzzling questions for actors and their agents, directors, and programmers. Is it possible to create CGI doubles for long-dead actors, such as Marilyn Monroe and James Dean? If so, who controls their use and profits from their work? Can aging actors sign contracts for use of their "young" CGI counterparts? Would it be legal and ethical for programmers to create and market virtual characters based on real actors or a compilation of the best traits of popular stars? As is often the case, new technologies present issues along with their benefits—issues you might want to consider the next time you watch a movie.

Who's Got the Rights?

In early 1999, an 18-year-old student named Shawn Fanning developed a Web-based technology for sharing MP3 music files. This technology, dubbed "Napster" after Shawn's nickname, quickly became one of the hottest applications on the Internet. In less than a year, its user base exceeded 25 million. Almost immediately, Napster ran afoul of the Recording Industry Association of America (RIAA), a watchdog organization that represents record companies, such as Columbia Records, Motown Records, and Epic Nashville. The RIAA compiled a list of 12,000 copyrighted songs that Napster technology made available as free downloads. In December of 1999, the RIAA filed suit, accusing Napster of contributing to copyright infringement, which considerably reduced the revenues of record companies and artists. The ensuing court battle stirred up a caldron of issues that relate to the use and abuse of digital media, including music, photos, and videos.

To get a handle on the controversy, it is necessary to understand how Napster works. Napster was created as a peer-to-peer network technology that could run over the Internet. Anyone with an Internet connection could become part of the Napster network simply by registering at the Napster Web site, downloading the Napster client software called MusicShare, and installing it.

Registered users make their MP3 files available over the Napster Network by placing the files in a user library folder on their own computers' hard disks. Whenever a registered Napster user logs in at the Napster Web site, the names of his or her MP3 files are uploaded to the Napster server and incorporated into a master database. These MP3 filenames only remain in the database and accessible while the registered Napster user is logged in.

Any Napster member can search the master database to find the name of a specific music file. Once found, the file is transferred directly between the hard disks of the users. No MP3 files are stored on Napster servers, nor do these files travel through Napster servers as they are transferred from one user to another. No copyrighted material is ever in Napster's possession. So how can Napster be held responsible for copyright violation? The argument went something like the following:

RIAA: Napster is providing technology that is infringing on copyrights held by record companies and recording artists.

Napster: No copyrighted material was ever stored on our servers.

RIAA: But you knew that your registered users were using your technology to illegally exchange copyrighted music files.

Napster: What's illegal about it? The Audio Home Recording Act of 1992 allows people to make recordings and lend them out to people, provided it is not done for commercial purposes. Our members were not getting paid for allowing others to copy their MP3 files, so our network has nothing to do with commercial use.

RIAA: Even though money is not changing hands, Napster-style copying is commercial use for two reasons: First, Napster users are distributing files, not to their friends, but to Napster users they have never met. Second, by getting files for free, Napster users don't buy the music through legitimate channels, and that has tangible commercial repercussions.

Napster: But Napster can't be held responsible for users who break the law. Remember that the courts refused to hold video tape recorder manufacturers and retailers responsible when their machines were used to make tapes of copyrighted television shows. Also, remember that the Digital Millennium Copyright Act protects Internet Service Providers from being liable for illegal actions on the part of their subscribers.

RIAA: Ah, but ISPs are only protected if they have no knowledge of their subscribers' illegal actions. We asked the court to subpoena your e-mail records, and there is clear evidence that you knew what your members were doing! Just look at the names of the files in your database "Yellow Submarine by the Beatles," and "Celebrity - N Sync."

Napster: Even if we knew, how could we stop them? Suppose that instead of calling a file "Yellow Submarine by the Beatles," one of our users named it "Light-Colored Underwater Craft by a Famous British Rock Group?" We would have no way to screen that file out of our database.

RIAA: If you can't find a way to police your network, we'll ask for damages to the tune of $5 million.

In 2001, U.S. courts suspended Napster activity, and in 2002, the file-sharing site officially closed. Despite this setback, similar sites have appeared. Some operate legally by making sure that the files, especially MP3 files, are in the public domain, or posted with permission from the artist and record company. With the apparent success of Apple's iTunes music for purchase site, Napster reopened in 2003 as Napster 2.0, a legal site for digital music and offering a catalog of more than 500,000 songs for downloading. Napster offers a way to purchase single songs as well as a premium subscription service.

Other music-sharing networks, such as Morpheus, Kazaa, and Grokster, provide access to copyrighted material, but use peer-to-peer file-sharing technologies, such as Gnutella, which are subtly different from the technology used by Napster. Unlike Napster, Gnutella networks require no central database. In true peer-to-peer fashion, client software installed on one user's computer searches for other similar clients. For example, as soon as a Gnutella client comes online, it sends a signal to another Gnutella client. That client then tells eight other clients that it has established contact with the new client. Each of those eight then tells seven others, who tell six others, and so on. In this way, each client tells many other clients it is online, and what content it has available. P2P utilities that employ this decentralized approach provide another unique set of legal challenges. Because there is no central server maintaining an index of users, there is no easy way to police the use of the network and its software.

In a 2003 court decision against Metro-Goldwyn-Mayer Studios, the court sided with Grokster, which claimed it merely supplied peer-to-peer client software and had no control over how customers used it. Many content developers in music, video, and similar creative industries are beginning to realize that fundamental changes are on the horizon.

▼ INTERACTIVE QUESTIONS

○ Yes ○ No ○ Not sure
1. Do you think that most people realize that copyright law gives musicians and record companies the exclusive right to distribute their music?

○ Yes ○ No ○ Not sure
2. Do you believe that music-sharing networks should not allow their members to swap copyrighted music without the permission of the copyright holder?

○ Yes ○ No ○ Not sure
3. Can you envision any way to monitor Gnutella networks to make sure that they don't contribute to illegal activities?

▼ EXPAND THE IDEAS

1. Do you believe that it is not against the law to take music off the Web and create CDs or to copy purchased music for personal use? Why or why not? Write a short paper supporting your position.

2. Research three current music-sharing networks. Are their policies stated on their Web sites? What restrictions, if any, do they impose on music taken from their sites? Find a site that charges for downloading music. Create a table to compile your findings. Write a brief summary comparing and contrasting the trends that you found.

3. Can you envision any way to monitor Gnutella networks to make sure that they don't contribute to illegal activities? What monitoring strategies are currently in place or in development? Write a short paper discussing your findings. Be sure to include your sources.

Issue

End of Unit Exercises

▼ KEY TERMS

24-bit bitmap
32-bit bitmap
Analog video camera
ASF
Audio Interchange Format
AVI
Bitmap graphic
Bitmap image
BMP
Card reader
Codec
Color depth
Color palette
Compression algorithm
Compression ratio
Cropping
Data compression
Density
Desktop video
Dictionary-based compression
Digital camera
Digital signal processor
Digital video camera
Digitizing tablet

Dithering
Drawing software
External video
File compression utility
FireWire port
Flash graphic
Floppy disk adapter
Frame rate
GIF
Gradient
Grayscale palette
Internal video
JPEG
Key frame
Linear editing
Lossless compression
Lossy compression
Megapixels
Memory card reader
Metafile
MIDI
MIDI sequence
Monochrome bitmap
MP3

MP3 encoder
MPEG
Non-linear editing
Paint software
Phoneme
Pixel interpolation
PNG
QuickTime
Rasterization
Ray tracing
RealAudio
RealMedia
Rendering
Resolution
Resolution dependent
Run-length encoding
Sampling rate
Scanner
Sound card
Spatial compression
Speech recognition
Speech recognition software
Speech synthesis

Statistical compression
Streaming video
SVG
Synthesized sound
System palette
Temporal compression
Text-to-speech software
TIFF
Tracing software
True Color bitmap
Unzipping
USB port
Vector graphic
Video
Video capture device
Video capture software
Video editing software
Wav
Waveform audio
Wavetable
Web palette
Wireframe
Zipping

▼ UNIT REVIEW

1. Use your own words to define bold terms that appear throughout the unit. List 10 of the terms that are least familiar to you and write a sentence for each of them.

2. Make a list of the file extensions that were mentioned in this unit and group them according to digital media type: bitmap graphic, vector graphic, digital video, waveform audio, and MIDI. Circle any formats that are used on the Web.

3. Make a list of the software mentioned in this unit, indicating the type of task that it helps you accomplish.

4. Describe the devices that transfer photos from a digital camera to a computer. Explain the different procedures required to transfer analog or digital video from camera to computer.

5. Describe how resolution and color depth contribute to the size of a graphic file.

6. Explain how a computer monitor displays color, and how a color palette can be used to reduce file size.

7. Explain how the concept of layering relates to your ability to modify a vector graphic.

8. Make a list of the advantages and disadvantages of bitmaps and vector graphics.

9. Explain how streaming audio and video work and contrast them to non-streaming technology.

10. Explain sampling rate. Be sure to discuss how it affects sound quality and file size.

▼ FILL IN THE BEST ANSWER

1. While a(n) _____ digitizes printed images, a digital _____ digitizes images of real objects.

2. JPEG, _____, and PNG are bitmap graphics formats and are supported by most browsers.

3. The dimensions of the grid that forms a bitmap graphic are referred to as its _____.

4. Bitmap graphics are resolution _____, which means that the quality of an image relies on its resolution.

5. Color _____ refers to the number of colors available for use in a bitmap graphic.

6. A color _____ holds the selection of colors and allows you to select a group of colors to use for a bitmap graphic.

7. A(n) _____ graphic contains the instructions that a computer needs to create the shape, size, position, and color for each graphic.

8. _____ graphics tend to have a cartoon-like rather than a realistic appearance.

9. Graphics that contain both bitmap and vector data are called _____.

10. The process of applying color and texture to a 3-D graphic wireframe is called _____.

11. Ray _____ is the process of adjusting the colors in a rendered image to coincide with the highlights and shadows that would be produced by a light source.

12. _____ editing moves footage from one videotape to another, whereas _____ editing uses a random-access device, such as a hard disk, to hold both the original footage and finished video.

13. The _____ of a video file can be reduced using three techniques: reducing the frame rate, decreasing the size of the video window, and compressing the video data.

14. AVI, QuickTime, MPEG, and RealMedia are examples of _____ video formats.

15. When you transfer footage from an analog or digital camera to your computer, you must use either a(n) _____ port or a(n) _____ port.

16. You use video _____ software to start and stop the transfer and select the display size, frame rate, filename, and file format for your video footage.

17. A(n) _____, such as MPEG or Indeo video, is the software that compresses a video.

18. The number of times per second that a sound wave is measured is referred to as the _____ rate.

19. The popular waveform audio format that is based on MPEG is called _____.

20. Speech _____ is the process by which machines, such as computers, produce sound that resembles spoken words.

▼ PRACTICE TESTS

When you use the Interactive CD, you can take Practice Tests that consist of 10 multiple-choice, true/false, and fill-in-the-blank questions. The questions are selected at random from a large test bank, so each time you take a test, you'll receive a different set of questions. Your tests are scored immediately, and you can print study guides to determine which questions you answered incorrectly. If you are using a Tracking Disk, insert it in the floppy disk drive to save your test scores.

▼ INDEPENDENT CHALLENGE 1

Do you own a digital camera? Do you know someone who does? If you look at the advertisements that come with the local papers, you will see that most electronic retailers are selling digital cameras. How can you know which is best for you?

1. Research the latest offerings in digital cameras. Find three leading manufacturers of digital cameras.

2. List and compare the features and prices for the cameras that are being sold in your area.

3. What is the range of prices? How is price related to megapixels?

4. Select three models, one in each price range (inexpensive, moderate, and expensive) that you might consider purchasing.

5. List any accessories that you would have to purchase with the camera.

6. Create a table comparing features and prices. Determine what is the best value. Write a summary of your findings and which camera you might purchase.

▼ INDEPENDENT CHALLENGE 2

Do you own a digital video camera? Do you know someone who does? If you look at the advertisements that come with the local papers, you will see that most electronic retailers are selling digital video cameras as well as the Hi8 and VHS format video cameras.

1. Research the latest offerings in digital video cameras. Find three leading manufacturers of digital video cameras.

2. List and compare the features and prices for the cameras that are being sold in your area.

3. What is the range of prices? How is price related to features?

4. Select three digital models, one in each price range (inexpensive, moderate, and expensive) that you might consider purchasing. Also select one Hi8 or VHS video camera.

5. List any accessories that you would have to purchase with the camera.

6. Create a table comparing features and prices. Determine which is the best value. Write a summary of your findings and which camera you might purchase.

▼ INDEPENDENT CHALLENGE 3

 The Web has a wide variety of music, video, and sound files available for download. You can sample new artists and, if you like what you hear, you can purchase the CD.

1. Log onto the Internet and search for music by your favorite artist.

2. Download and listen to the audio file. Was it the entire song? What was the format of the file? Write a brief summary of how you found the music, the source of the file, what software you used to download and then listen to the music.

3. Locate, download, and view a video file from the Internet.

4. What was the content of the video? Was it an inline or external video? Did the video play all at once or did it stream? What was the format of the file? Write a brief summary of how you found the video, and what software you used to download and then view the video.

▼ INDEPENDENT CHALLENGE 4

The GIF format is very popular for Web graphics. Its use is controversial because the GIF format uses the LZW compression technology, which is owned by UniSys. Currently, UniSys allows individuals to use GIF graphics on Web sites freely, as long as these graphics were created by software approved and licensed by UniSys.

Although the GIF format is popular, some Web developers express concern about further restrictions or fees that UniSys might require in the future.

1. Research the GIF controversy. Write a short paper that includes information answering the following questions.

    a. Who invented LZW compression and when was the information first published?

    b. When was the LZW compression technique incorporated into the GIF format?

    c. Why did GIF become so popular?

    d. What are the alternative non-proprietary graphics formats that can replace GIF?

    e. What information about GIF usage restrictions has been provided by UniSys?

    f. What is the current status of the GIF controversy?

2. Make sure you incorporate specific bibliographic information to indicate the sources of your answers in your report.

▼ INDEPENDENT CHALLENGE 5

The hardware used for digital media is evolving at a very rapid pace. Technology once the toolbox of professionals is now readily available for the consumer market. You can research and purchase printers, cameras, and a variety of input devices in local electronics shops.

1. Form a group with two–four of your classmates.

2. Use the local paper or Internet advertisements to research and then select a graphics-related digital device, such as a photo printer, scanner, digital camera, Web camera, digital video camera, video capture card, digitizing tablet, or accelerated 3-D graphics card. If one of the members of your group owns the device, ask them to bring it in.

3. Create materials for a tradeshow booth featuring your "product." Create a poster and marketing materials. You might include a product photo, list of specifications, and a short instruction manual. Be sure to research and include technical specifications as well as a list of applications.

4. If possible, create a two–three minute video commercial for the product. If you cannot film the commercial, create a storyboard of the commercial.

5. If time permits, your instructor might ask your group to provide the rest of the class with your sales presentation or a demonstration for your device.

▼ INDEPENDENT CHALLENGE 6

The Computers in Context section of this chapter focused on digital special effects technology used in recent films, such as *Spiderman II* and *The Matrix: Revolutions*. For this independent challenge, conduct your own exploration of the special effects that have appeared in your favorite movies.

1. Select two of your favorite films that incorporated computerized special effects.

2. Log onto the Internet, look for information about the specific movies using Web sites, such as the Internet movie database (www.imdb.com). Many movies also have dedicated Web sites, which you can find using a search engine.

3. Browse through the material presented in the Web sites.

4. Use your favorite search engine to research special effects software used in filmmaking.

5. Write a two–four page movie review that focuses on how its special effects contribute to the movie's overall quality. Try to incorporate information about how the special effects were developed—the company that provided the effects and the type of equipment used. You can also consider comparing the special effects in your chosen movies with the effects in other movies. You might also incorporate some frames from the film as illustrations in your paper. Before doing so, however, make sure that you understand its copyright restrictions.

6. Follow your professor's instructions for formatting and submitting your movie review.

▼ LAB: WORKING WITH BITMAP GRAPHICS

1. Start the interactive part of the lab. Insert your Tracking Disk if you want to save your QuickCheck results. Perform each of the lab steps as directed and answer all of the lab QuickCheck questions. When you exit the lab, your answers are automatically graded and your results are displayed.

2. Use the Start button to access the Programs menu for the computer that you typically use. Make a list of the available bitmap graphics software.

3. Capture a photographic image from a digital camera, scanner, or Web page. Save it as "MyGraphic." Open the image using any available graphics software. Use this software to discover the properties of the graphic. Indicate the source of the graphic, then describe its file format, file size, resolution, and color depth.

4. Prepare this graphic file to send to a friend as an e-mail attachment that is less than 200 KB. Describe the steps that were required.

5. Suppose that you want to post this image on a Web page. Make the necessary adjustments to file size and bit depth. Describe the resulting graphic in terms of its resolution, bit depth, palette, and dithering.

▼ LAB: VIDEO EDITING

1. Start the interactive part of the lab. Insert your Tracking Disk if you want to save your QuickCheck results. Perform each of the lab steps as directed and answer all of the lab QuickCheck questions. When you exit the lab, your answers are automatically graded and your results are displayed.

2. Use the Control Panel's Add/Remove Programs icon to view and make a list of the video players that are available on your computer.

3. Locate a video clip on the Web and indicate the URL of the Web page on which it can be found. Describe the video's properties, including file size and format.

4. Play the video that you located for Lab Assignment #3. Describe the visual and sound qualities of the video and discuss how they relate to your Internet connection speed. Also describe the length and content of the video, the use of transitions or special effects (if any), and the use of sound tracks. If you could edit this video yourself, what changes would you make to make it more effective?

▼ STUDENT EDITION LABS

Reinforce the concepts you have learned in this unit through the **Working with Graphics**, **Working with Audio**, and **Working with Video** Student Edition Labs, available online at the Illustrated Computer Concepts Web site.

▼ SAM LABS

If you have a SAM user profile, you have access to additional content, features, and functionality. Log in to your SAM account and go to your assignments page to see what your instructor has assigned for this unit.

▼ VISUAL WORKSHOP

Digital photography and digital cameras have changed the way we view images. Without having to incur the cost of film or the cost and time for developing to see your images, you can enjoy the freedom of taking as many pictures as your digital camera memory card will permit. You can send and share pictures instantly with friends and family in your home or across the world. Online photo sites such as Ofoto and Snapfish make it possible to instantly upload the images and then send e-mail notification to anyone you want. Viewing the photos online is free, and then you or whoever views your online photo album can order the prints. The International Imaging Industry Association (I3A)—a nonprofit trade group supported by Eastman Kodak, Hewlett-Packard, Fujifilm, and others—announced plans for the Common Picture eXchange environment (CPXe). The CPXe is a ground-breaking initiative by the digital photography industry to advance growth in the consumer digital photo services category. See Figure H-41.

Digital image manipulation is readily available at the consumer level with affordable software packages that put professional tools right on the desktop. Adobe Photoshop and ULead PhotoImpact are two of many commercial packages that are available. This software includes professional digital editing tools for your photos. Most digital cameras come with some kind of proprietary software to not only download and save files but also to erase lines and reduce redeye through airbrush and other tools.

FIGURE H-41

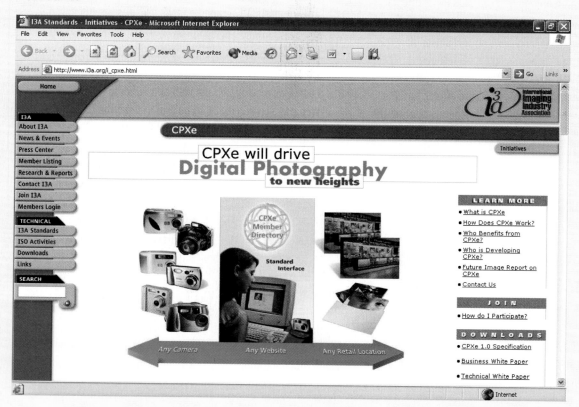

1. Log onto the Internet and search for information on CPXe. You can go to the Web site www.I3A.org. List three advantages of CPXe for photo companies, for consumers, for retailers, and for camera and software manufacturers.

2. Use your favorite search engine to find three online photo sites. Two suggested sites are Ofoto.com and Snapfish.com. Create a comparison chart for the three sites. List and compare features such as services offered, pricing, and various options.

3. Review digital image manipulation software packages that are available today. Make a comparison chart for at least three software packages. Write a summary paragraph indicating how the packages are alike, how they are different, and why a consumer might purchase one over the other.

Buyer's Guide Worksheets

Whether you are a first-time buyer or you are upgrading your computer system, when the time comes to make your computer buying decision, you might find yourself overwhelmed by the vast amount of information available. There are thousands of computer advertisements on the Web, on television, in magazines, and in newspapers that list detailed technical product specifications. To get the best deal on a computer that meets your needs, you need to understand what these technical specifications mean and how they will affect your computing power. You need to establish the budget for your computer system. This Buyer's Guide will help you to organize your purchasing decisions.

▼ ORGANIZE YOUR FINDINGS: A BUYER'S GUIDE SUMMARY

You can refer to the table below to organize your research on purchasing a computer system.

CONSIDERATIONS	NOTES
Basic computer system	
Desktop or notebook?	
Platform: Macintosh or IBM-compatible PC?	
Case type: tower, desktop?	
Display device: type, size, and resolution	
Computer architecture	
Which processor?	
How much RAM?	
What type of video card?	
Special considerations for notebook computers	
Display size and resolution	
External monitor	
PCMCIA slot	
Weight	
Power source/battery type	
Pointer type	
Carrying case	
Peripheral devices and storage	
Hard disk capacity	
CD-ROM/DVD	
Sound card/speakers	
Floppy disk drive	
Zip disk drive	
Pointing device	
Printer	
Fax modem/modem	
Expansion cards	
Scanner	
Digital camera	
Web cam	
Backup system	
Surge protector/UPS	
Networking considerations	
Wired or Wireless?	
Interface card	
Hub	
Router	
System and application software	
Operating system	
Software for basic applications	
Virus protection	
Internet service	
Wireless? DSL? Cable? Dial-up?	
Internet Service Provider	
Web browser	
E-mail client	

▼ COMPARING COMPUTERS: A BUYER'S SPECIFICATION WORKSHEET

Before you make a decision, shop around to collect information on pricing, features, and support. You can find comparative pricing at Web-based price-quote sites. When you use a price-quote site, be aware that some of these sites search only those merchants that have paid to participate. Although you might be tempted to buy the computer with the lowest price and best features, don't forget to consider the warranty and the quality of the support you are likely to get from the vendor.

Use the worksheet that follows to organize the information you gather about pricing, features, and support. Complete the worksheet for each computer system you are considering, then compare the information.

Manufacturer: _____

Model: _____

Price: _____

Processor model: _____

Processor speed: _____

RAM capacity: _____

Hard disk drive capacity: _____

Hard disk drive type and speed: _____

Speaker description: _____

Graphics card slot type (desktop only): _____

Graphics card video RAM capacity: _____

Display type (LCD/CRT/Plasma): _____

Display screen size and dot pitch: _____

Type of pointing device: _____

Number/type of expansion ports: _____

Number/type of expansion slots: _____

CD/DVD access drive speed: _____

CD/DVD writer: _____

Zip drive included: _____

Modem speed: _____

Sound card model: _____

Overall weight (notebook only): _____

Battery type/time (notebook only): _____

Operating system version: _____

Bundled software: _____

▼ QUESTIONS TO BE SURE TO ASK ABOUT SERVICE AND SUPPORT

• What is the warranty period? _____ years

• Can I get my computer fixed in an acceptable time period?

• Does the warranty cover parts and labor?

• Are the costs and procedures for fixing the computer acceptable?

• Does the vendor have a good reputation for service?

• Are technical support hours adequate?

• Are other users satisfied with this brand and model of computer?

• Is there a toll-free number for technical support?

• Can I contact technical support without waiting on hold for a long time?

• Is the vendor likely to stay in business?

• Are the computer parts and components standard?

• Are technical support people knowledgeable?

Refer to the online Buyer's Guide at www.course.com/illustrated/concepts5e for up-to-date information about current pricing and offerings as you gather information before purchasing your computer system.

 TRENDS

Trends in Technology

OBJECTIVES

Exploring evolving trends in ...

Computer I/O components

Processors and memory

Storage

Networking and wireless connectivity

Security and privacy

The Internet and e-mail

Software

Leisure technology

Tech Talk: Internet Access Security

Computers in Context: Fashion Industry

Issue: Should the Internet be regulated?

Technologies once the domain of science fiction writers and filmmakers are now integral to people's daily lives. Today, you can pick up a device small enough to fit comfortably in your pocket, press a few keys, and then communicate by speaking or exchanging images instantly with anyone anywhere in the world. Now, you can have access to vast amounts of knowledge through the Web. Learning about and understanding the technology that makes this all possible is fascinating and overwhelming—fascinating because of the way technology impacts our daily lives, overwhelming because the science behind the technologies continually changes and evolves at rapid rates. For the average consumer it is not important to fully understand or keep up with every aspect of technology. However, it is important to have a general idea of market trends. This unit highlights a sampling of emerging trends in computer technology. Because technology changes so rapidly some of these trends may be well on their way to becoming mainstream, while others may have almost entirely disappeared. Regardless of their current state, though, these trends play an important role in the ongoing technology revolution.

Exploring evolving trends in ... Computer I/O components

The trend in PC development (desktop, notebook, and handheld computers) is to produce systems that are more powerful, smaller, faster, cheaper, and lighter than their previous counterparts. This lesson explores recent developments and trends in computers and in the external input and output components that are part of a computer system.

DETAILS

- **Supercomputers:** Supercomputers are often based on computer clusters, which are capable of **high–performance computing (HPC)**. Processing speeds of HPC systems are measured in **FLOPS (floating point operations per second)** or **MIPS (millions of instructions per second)**. The TOP500 compiles a list of the world's 500 most powerful supercomputers. National Energy Research Scientific Computing Center (NERSC), which uses supercomputers, is a world leader in accelerating scientific discovery through computation.

- **Handheld computers:** Newer PDAs (personal digital assistants) and "smart" cell phones (known as **smartphones**) are converging into a single handheld technology that provides keypad input, color screen, digital camera, PDA software, voice communications, text messaging, Web browsing, and e-mail.

- **Display technologies:** Imagine being able to fold a monitor into your pocket and then simply roll it out when you need it. **Organic light emitting diode (OLED)** is a technology used to create display devices that are thinner, have higher resolutions, and are more power efficient than the dominant technologies used in monitor displays today: Cathode Ray Tube (CRT) displays or Liquid Crystal Displays (LCD). Universal Display is a leader in flexible flat panel display, like the one shown in Figure T-1. Roll-up computer screens and TVs for the mainstream consumer market are still a few years away.

  A new technology called **Field Emission Display (FED)** is being developed for use in flat panel displays (FPDs). FED technology makes possible the thin panel of today's LCDs, offers a wide field of view, provides a high image quality, and requires less power than today's CRT displays. Some believe FPD monitors using FED technology are more environmentally friendly both when in use (because they emit less radiation and are more energy efficient) and when they are discarded (because they are not made with mercury, lead, and glass like CRT monitors).

- **Input devices:** Keyboard technology has continued to evolve. Researchers are working on **membrane keyboards**, which cost less than keyboards with mechanical switches and, because they can be sealed, work in a variety of conditions. Some keyboards are flexible and can be rolled up for portability. Advances have been made in wireless keyboards that work with IR (infrared) devices to transmit input to the computer and that can be used up to 50 feet from a computer or printer. There are new keyboard designs that offer alternatives to the typical layout, such as keyboards designed to be used by just one hand.

  Recent developments in pointing devices include mice that use **force feedback technology**, optical technology, or wireless connections. Force feedback means you can feel motion coming back to you though the pointing device, which is useful in medical applications and training situations. Research into interface technology includes devices that transport motion into commands without the use of keys. University of Delaware researchers have developed a device called iGesture, which uses a touch pad as the input device.

- **Assistive technology:** Recent advances in input and output device technology have enhanced technology products available for individuals with special needs, especially in the areas of auditory, vision, cognitive, mobility, and ergonomic. The purpose of **assistive technology** is to make the technology so pervasive in our daily lives accessible to all regardless of ability. Modified keyboards, voice activated input devices, and mouse emulator programs make it possible for persons with cognitive, learning, fine motor, mobility or upper-extremity disabilities to use a computer and have the functionality of a mouse (clicking, right-clicking, dragging, and so on). A keyboard-style mouse gives "points of compass" control over the mouse pointer. Specially designed word processors and other application programs designed for use by individuals with oral or written communication disabilities include features such as word prediction, multiple access modes, spell checking, and built-in scanning options. Display technologies using assistive technology enhance images or provide Braille on screen for people with vision disabilities. Web sites, such as those sponsored by NIDRR, provide access to an extensive database of products and services for persons with disabilities. See Figure T-2.

FIGURE T-1: FOLED technology

▶ Rollout or flexible display panels use a more efficient production method, which effectively prints a special type of OLED on a surface. Hopes for the technology are high because such displays do not require a back light. This makes rollout displays energy efficient and thin—so thin they can be folded.

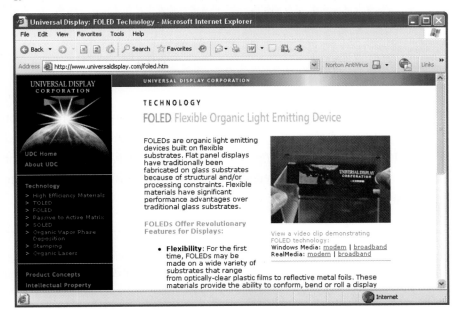

FIGURE T-2: Web site providing information about assistive technology

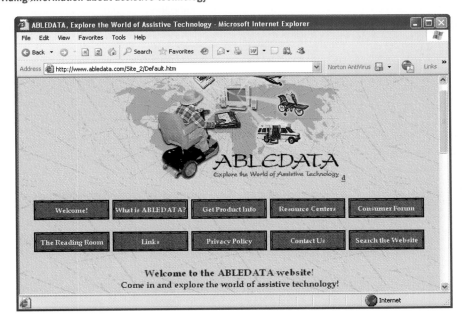

Government initiatives on assistive technology

The National Institute on Disability and Rehabilitation Research (NIDRR) is a national leader in sponsoring research in assistive technology. NIDRR is one of three components of the Office of Special Education and Rehabilitative Services (OSERS) at the U.S. Department of Education. The mission of NIDRR is to generate, disseminate, and promote new knowledge to improve the technology-related options available to disabled persons. The ultimate goal is to allow these individuals to perform their regular activities in the community and to bolster society's ability to provide full opportunities and appropriate supports for its disabled citizens. New technology initiatives sponsored by the NIDRR are designed to advance trends in assistive technology.

Another initiative includes The Department of the Interior's (DOI) Accessible Technology Program, which was established in June 2000 to support employees with disabilities by determining the appropriate assistive technology and ergonomic solutions for the individual. These accommodations enable employees with a disability to equal access to information technology that is essential in today's workplace.

Exploring evolving trends in ... Processors and memory

Processors for mobile computing, desktop computing, and consumer electronics are driving technology trends in computing. Chipmakers continue to enhance processor speed and capabilities while reducing size and energy consumption. The terms "memory" and "storage" used to be clearly distinct, but the line for differentiating these concepts as they relate to computers is blurring. This lesson explores processors and memory.

DETAILS

● **Processors:** Generally, a company manufactures several lines of processors; each one in a series builds on and improves the features and the functionality of the processor that came before it. When it comes to chip manufacturing, smaller is better. A nanometer (nm) is a billionth of a meter, or a millionth of a millimeter. Advances in chip manufacturing technology have made it possible for the leading chipmakers to move from 130-nanometer processors to 90-nanometer processors. This was not easy. The major chipmakers had to overcome technology hurdles in order to pack more transistors in a smaller space and to create chips that operate faster, use less energy, and are more efficient. The leading manufacturers of processors are Intel, Advanced Micro Devices (AMD), and Transmeta.

● **Intel:** Intel is leading the way with research for a 65-nanometer processor. Intel has recently changed the way they identify their processors. The new trend, the Processor Number Nomenclature system, uses a combination of the processor brand, processor name, and processor number. See Figure T-3.

● **Advanced Micro Devices (AMD):** AMD processors include the **Athlon**, **Geode**, and **Duron** family of processors. These processor families are designed for desktop, mobile, server, and workstation computers. AMD also has a line of flash memory processors, **Spansion**, for mobile applications. In addition to processors for the PC, AMD offers solutions for wireless connectivity. New technology advances in the **Alchemy** processor for Wireless LAN include low power consumption, compact design, and increased battery life. AMD's **Opteron** is a family of enterprise-class processors for servers and workstations.

● **Transmeta:** Transmeta's flagship product is the **Crusoe** processor. With Crusoe, Transmeta pioneered **Code Morphing** software. Transmeta has gone to the next level with its Advanced Code Morphing software for its next generation processors. The **Efficeon** processor is Transmeta's newest line of processors, which is designed to deliver more performance than the Crusoe processor in this era of energy-efficient computing. The Efficeon processor has increased performance and responsiveness, features three new high-performance I/O interfaces, uses a faster engine with wider execution paths, has a fully re-engineered instruction set, and boasts higher frequency capabilities. In response to the escalating threat of computer virus attacks, Transmeta introduced a new feature in its Efficeon processors, called AntiVirusNX, that can detect common viruses and render them harmless for Transmeta Efficeon processor-based computers.

● **Memory:** Flash memory, memory sticks, and smart media are referred to as memory, but these components don't lose their contents when the power goes off, making them more like storage. Digital cameras and portable devices (such as PDAs, portable computers, and cell phones) make use of these memory technologies.

Flash memory, memory sticks, and smart media are based on solid state technology. Trends in solid state storage are not that different than trends in processor technology: solid state storage is becoming smaller, faster, and more energy efficient. Traditional flash memory chips were able to store only a single bit of data in each of two cells. AMD researchers have developed **MirrorBit**, a technology that enables storage of two bits in each cell. Its newest flash memory technology is the development of a 4-bit flash memory chip for storing data in wireless devices, such as mobile phones, PDAs, and handheld gaming devices. SanDisk Corporation continues to advance its line of flash memory cards to fulfill the storage needs of multimedia mobile phone users. The needs of mobile phone users are driving advancements in solid state storage technology. Mobile phones are evolving so that they include still and video cameras, Web browsers, as well as MP3 audio players. Nokia Corporation has a full line of mobile phones that typify these features. See Figure T-4.

FIGURE T-3: How to interpret Intel processor names

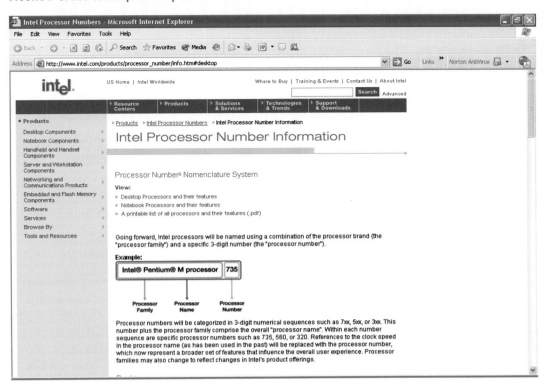

FIGURE T-4: Nokia mobile phones

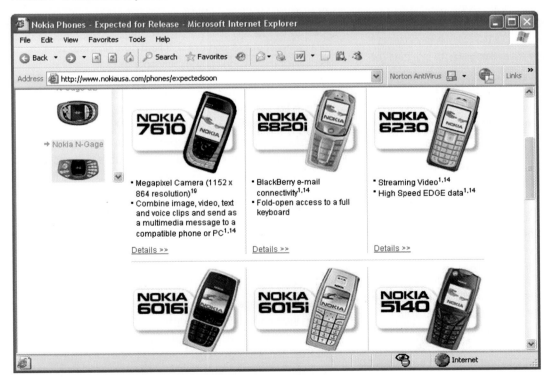

◄ Cellular phones can be portable gaming devices, MP3 players, still or video cameras, and computers

Exploring evolving trends in ... Storage

There was a time when a one gigabyte hard disk drive (hard drive) was unimaginable. Today, basic desktop systems come equipped with hard drives with a minimum of 40 GB; capacities greater than 400 GB are available. This lesson explores the recent trends in storage devices and technologies.

DETAILS

● **Hard drives:** Hard drive trends include hard drives that have gotten smaller in physical size and greater in capacity. As a result, massive amounts of data can now be stored on desktop computers. For example, Hitachi Global Storage Technologies has a 400 GB hard drive—that is the storage capacity for about 200 movies.

At the other end of the spectrum are MP3 players. Many MP3 players are usually built around a 1.8-inch hard drive with storage between 10GB-60GB. The class of players built with microdrives, such as the Apple iPod mini (see Figure T-5), include a built-in 4 GB hard disk drive.

● **MEMS-based storage:** MEMS (MicroElectroMechanical Systems) technology combines storage and processing on one chip. **MEMS-based storage** is expected to have access times much faster than conventional disks. Being able to integrate the processor and the storage device will improve power consumption and cost. MEMS-based storage is not currently available commercially; however, MEMS-based storage is laying the foundation for advances in systems and storage devices.

● **Removable storage:** Removable storage devices allow you to store your data in a safe place. Another benefit is the ability to work on a computer, remove the storage device, then plug it into another computer in another location and continue to work. Removable storage devices plug into USB ports and many are platform independent. One drawback is that removable storage devices tend to have slower transfer rates and lower capacities than high-capacity hard drives installed in a computer.

CDs and DVDs provide another option for removable storage. CD and DVD technology continues to improve, but progress is hindered by the lack of one standard for DVD technology. Improvements include increased storage capacity (DVDs can now hold up to 9.4 GB) and writing to both sides of a DVD. CD and DVD drives are now included as standard hardware in desktop systems.

DVD burners have taken the next step. Manufacturers have introduced **double-layer DVD** burners. Although it is still early

and the technology has drawbacks, double-layer DVD burners allow home users to create CDs and DVDs up to 8.5 GB.

● **USB Flash Drives: USB flash drives** are compact, light-weight, and easy-to-use devices for transferring data files. Because these devices plug into a USB port, they are device independent, which makes them more versatile than other types of solid state storage. Compatible with most PCs, USB flash drives can be used to share information between computers or to bring documents between work and home, often eliminating the need to transport laptops back and forth. The drive is powered through the USB port, and it uses no batteries or power cord. USB flash drives are easier to use than rewritable CDs and DVDs, and they have capacities ranging from 16 MB up to 2 GB, which is many times the storage space of a compact disk. A portable USB flash drive slips into your pocket, or it can hang conveniently on a keychain.

● **Network drives:** The trend today when more than one computer is being used is to network computers— in the workplace and at home. **Network drives** are drives that are directly connected to a network and are accessible from all computers on the network. One advantage to a network drive is shared space. There are some security risks in having access to shared folders and drives on a network. A new storage technology known as self-securing storage is becoming available in a business environment. **Self-securing storage** devices keep all versions of all data for a specified period of time and continually monitor requests. This allows system administrators to review requests and determine if data has been compromised.

● **Tape:** Tape storage is still used for backup and storage. While CDs are an inexpensive way to quickly back-up data for a personal system, CDs may not hold all the data that a business user needs to back up. Tape technology has advanced to the point where storing terabytes of data is possible. IBM was the first to record 1 terabyte (TB) of data to a linear digital tape. One terabyte is equal to 16 days of continuously running DVD movies.

FIGURE T-5: Hard drive capacities for some Apple iPods

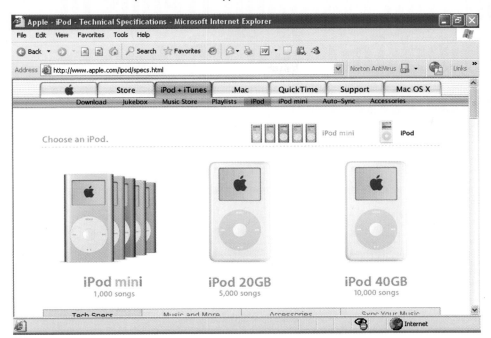

◄ An iPod includes a screen, batteries, and at 3.5 cubic inches weighs only 3.6 ounces, which is smaller than most cell phones.

FIGURE T-6: The "How Much Information?" project

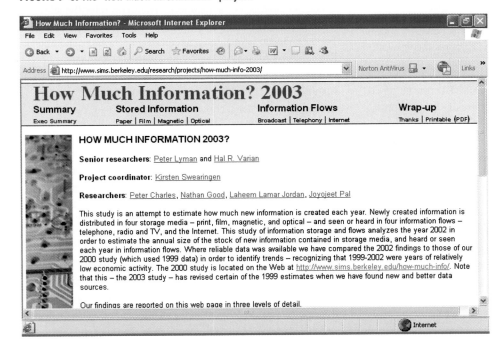

How much storage?

As the capacities of storage media increases, one of the questions is what information should people store? Are people storing every bit of electronic data that crosses their path or are they storing only information that is vital for archival reasons? Before we can answer these questions, we need to know what and how much information is being stored. The "How much information?" project is a study that is being conducted by faculty and students at the School of Information Management and Systems at the University of California at Berkeley with financial support from Microsoft Research, Intel, Hewlett-Packard, and EMC (a corporation whose product line is information management and storage service and solutions). This annual study is an attempt to estimate how much new information is created and stored and distributed each year. See Figure T-6.

Exploring evolving trends in ... Networking and wireless connectivity

Networks drive connectivity. Whether by cable, satellite, radio, or telephone, networks define our interconnected world. Remote and wireless connectivity has freed the user from the physical limits of cables.

DETAILS

● **Virtual Local Area Network (VLAN):** A VLAN is a group of personal computers, servers, and other network resources that are on physically different segments of a network but that communicate as though they are on the same segment. A VLAN is a logical grouping rather than a physical grouping. It is a network created by software that combines stations and network devices. Advantages include: changes do not have to be hard wired, users and resources that are likely to work together can be grouped in common VLANs to optimize the network, and VLANs free up bandwidth to boost traffic through the network and allow more control in securing the network.

● **Radio frequency identification (RFID): RFID** technology is based on "smart tags" applied to a component such as a product or document, or even a person. RFID tags consist of chips and an antenna that can transmit data, such as identification and tracking information, to a wireless receiver. See Figure T-7. Despite its advantages, privacy advocates have concerns about the use of RFID technology and its potential for tracking of individuals.

● **Clustering: Cluster computing** allows computers to work together to maximize performance. A **cluster** is a group of devices that share a server or group of servers. The computers in a cluster can share processing tasks or they can provide backup in case any of the connected servers fail. Clustering technology is essential to e-business, and it is used to balance traffic on high-traffic Web sites.

● **Free Space Optics (FSO):** An up-and-coming technology being used to bridge the connection between businesses and the Internet's fiber optic backbone is **Free Space Optics (FSO)** technology. FSO uses lasers to provide optical bandwidth

connections with line of sight technology and can be used with various protocols including ATM, IP, and Ethernet networks. It's capable of sending up to 2.5 Gbps of data, voice, and video communications simultaneously.

● **Cellular technology:** Cellular technology is evolving rapidly and generates acronyms, such as G1, AMPS, CDMA, GSM, and GPRS. "G" stands for "generation." The trend is for the latest generation, such as G3 cell phones, to offer always-on broadband connections with faster speeds than previous generations. See Table T-1 for features associated with each generation. A cellular service provider's network typically uses only one technology and so cellular telephones using that service must be compatible with the technology offered.

● **Expanding Wireless connectivity:** To help bridge the digital gap often found in rural areas, FCC partnerships, such as the partnership between the FCC's wireless Telecommunications Bureau and the USDA's Rural Utilities Service, have been formed. The objective of this partnership is to encourage greater access and deployment of wireless services to enhance economic development throughout rural America.

Another area for wireless connectivity growth is **m-Commerce (mobile commerce)**, which gives consumers the ability to communicate and conduct business transactions through mobile devices, such as cell phones and PDAs.

One area of concern associated with wireless connectivity involves security and privacy issues. Consumers will need to be assured their wireless transmissions are secure. Another concern involves health issues that might arise because of increased and prolonged exposure to potentially dangerous radio waves.

FIGURE T-7: Buying gas using an RFID keychain tag

◄ As long as RFID tags are within the range of a wireless reading device, the device can read hundreds of RFID tags a second simultaneously and automatically. RFID technology has been used in e-payment systems, such as highway toll collection systems, for some years now. ExxonMobile Speedpass users can now buy gasoline by simply pointing the RFID keyrings at readers that are by the pumps. The Speedpass device can also be used for convenience store purchases.

TABLE T-1: Cellular Network Technologies

GENERATION/SERVICE	FEATURES	GENERATION/SERVICE	FEATURES
G1/AMPS (advanced mobile phone service)	Analog voice service No data service	G2.5/GPRS (general packet radio service)	Adds always-on data transfers
G2/CDMA (code division multiple access)	Digital voice service 9.6 Kbps-14.4 Kbps speed	G3/W-CDMA (wide-band code division multiple access)	Superior digital voice service
TDMA (time division multiple access	Enhanced calling features, such as caller ID	UTMS (universal mobile telecommunications system)	Always-on data service
PDC (personal digital cellular)	NO always-on data connection	CDMA-2000 (code-division multiple access)	Broadband multimedia data services
GSM (global system for mobile communications)	Messages are stored if the phone is off/out of range		

The role of the FCC in wireless connectivity

The FCC regulates many aspects of wireless connectivity in the United States. The Wireless Telecommunications Bureau (WTB), a division of the FCC, handles nearly all FCC domestic wireless telecommunications programs, policies, and outreach initiatives. Wireless communications services include Amateur, Cellular, Paging, Broadband PCS, Public Safety, and more.

One benefit of wireless connectivity is the deployment of **E911 (Enhanced911)** technology in all mobile phones. See Figure T-8. E911 technology seeks to provide 911 dispatchers with better information from wireless calls, such as the caller's location.

FIGURE T-8: Enhanced 911

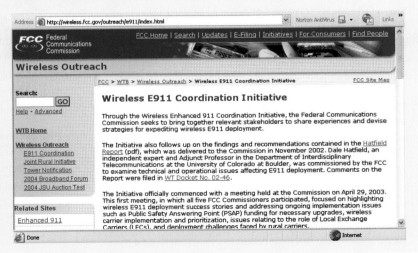

Exploring evolving trends in ... Security and privacy

Security and privacy related to computers have been the focus of many articles, new products, and grave concerns. This lesson focuses on trends in computer security and related privacy issues.

DETAILS

Hardware and data security: If your computer is lost or stolen, you can make it difficult to access your data by setting up your system to require a password. Until the password is entered, your data is off limits. A thief might be able to boot up the Windows desktop but will not be able to look at the data in your folders easily without the password. Because many new computers are shipped with a standard administrator password that everyone knows, it is critical that you create a secure password for your computer as soon as you get it. If your computer includes a preset guest account, you should disable this "guest" account or assign it a secure password.

Identity theft: A major concern today is identify theft, which is when someone steals a person's identity and uses that identity as his or her own. How does a thief get the personal information in the first place? If the proper precautions are not taken, then every time you provide personal information (such as your date of birth, account numbers, or mother's maiden name) when you fill out a form, submit an insurance claim, shop online, or complete a survey, you are putting your identity at risk. With increased use of computers for commerce, banking, health, and recreation, identity theft is on the rise and it is more than just an annoyance. People whose identity has been stolen have lost time, money, and in some cases have been accused of illegal activities. Privacy advocates have been fighting educational institutions, health insurers, and other companies demanding that they stop using a person's Social Security number as the ID number.

Phishing: Another trend on the rise is **phishing**—an illegal activity that involves unlawful people who send out e-mails that imitate legitimate companies to entice people to share personal and account information. As shown in Figure T-9, an e-mail is sent from the potential thief to an unsuspecting individual. The e-mail appears to come from a legitimate source such as Support@YourCreditCardCompany.com (it could be Visa, MasterCard, American Express, or Discover). The e-mail message directs the recipient to click a link to update billing information at a Web site "Billing Center." If you do this, you run a high risk of exposing yourself to identify theft, fraud, and misuse of your funds and credit. Remember that legitimate companies do not ask for personal or account information to be submitted via e-mail.

Credit card companies are trying to educate the consumer about phishing. For example, Discover Card provides the following list of signs to help you know if an e-mail is fraudulent: A false sense of urgency, such as threatens to "close/suspend your account," or to charge a fee for not keeping your account up-to-date; suspicious-looking links & popups, such as links containing all or part of a real company's name asking you to submit personal information; misspellings or poorly written message. If any of these signs are present, you should be suspicious about the legitimacy of the e-mail.

Viruses and worms: Several units in this book have included discussions related to the origin, nature, and reasons for avoiding and detecting viruses and worms on your computer. Unfortunately, the trend is for more and more viruses to attack computer systems worldwide. Symantec, a leader in antivirus software, reported that there were more than $4\frac{1}{2}$ times as many viruses and worms targeting Windows systems in the first half of 2004 than in the same period in 2003.

Spyware: When you access Web sites, some ActiveX components and spyware have the potential to search your computer for passwords and credit card numbers, install viruses, block your access to legitimate Web sites, or surreptitiously use your computer as a staging area for illicit activities. Spyware often piggybacks on popup ads and activates if you click the ad window or the Close button. How can you block spyware? The first line of defense is to never click popup ads. To close an ad, right-click its button on the taskbar at the bottom of your screen, and then select the Close option from the menu that appears. Some browsers can be configured to block spyware and popup ads. Your antivirus software might offer similar options. You can also install software specially designed to block spyware and popup ads.

Highjacked PCs: Another trend is to highjack PCs and use them for illegal or personal use. A **zombie PC** or **zombie PC network** is one that has been hijacked by hackers for illegal or personal use. US-CERT, see Figure T-10, a nonprofit security coordination center reports large increases in zombie networks and hackers using these networks for illegal and personal activities on the Internet.

FIGURE T-9: An example of phishing

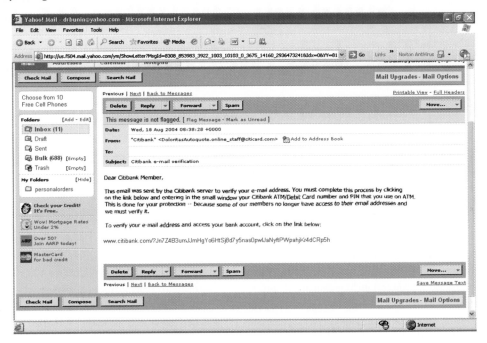

FIGURE T-10: US-CERT Web site

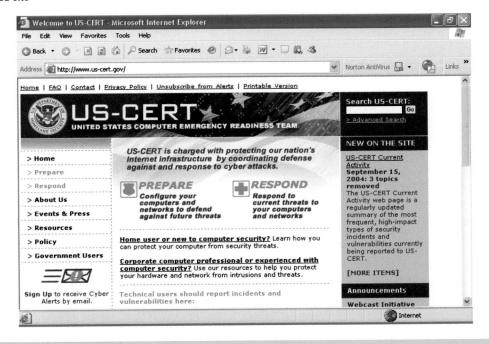

Protecting Your Computer:

Firewall software provides a protective barrier between a computer and the Internet. If your computer is connected directly to the Internet, it should have active firewall software. If your computer connects to a local area network for Internet access, the network should have a device called a router to block infiltration attempts. When a firewall is active, it watches for potentially disruptive incoming data called "probes." When a probe is discovered, your firewall displays a warning and asks what to do. If the source looks legitimate, you can let it through, if not, you should block it. The trend is for operating systems and antivirus software to include a firewall as part of the installation. For example, Windows XP includes a built-in Firewall called Windows Internet Connection Firewall (ICF) or Windows Firewall. Third-party, shareware, and freeware firewall programs are also available. So, if your computer uses an earlier version of Windows, you can download and install one of these programs.

Exploring evolving trends in ... The Internet and e-mail

Internet-related technologies are developing quickly. For example, browsers, which are the window to the Web, have become more sophisticated, user-friendly, and ubiquitous as they are now being built into PDAs, cars, cell phones, and watches. They include a variety of new security and usability controls. This lesson explores recent trends related to the Internet and e-mail.

DETAILS

● **Browsers:** Browser technology is not new, but advances in components integrated into browsers are new. As the Web continues to change, so too, must the browsers used to navigate the Web. New versions of browsers include enhanced and integrated search and explorer bars, security features, popup and spyware control, and instant messaging (IM) capabilities. AIM (AOL Instant Messaging), YahooMessenger, MSN Messenger (see Figure T-11), and ICQ (I Seek You) are instant messaging communities.

Windows XP was released in 2001, and the next version of Windows is expected in 2006. Microsoft is limiting security upgrades to Windows XP versions of IE, so unless a user pays to upgrade to Windows XP, he or she will not be able to install the security upgrades, putting his or her computer, as well as any computer he or she connects to, at risk for security–related problems.

For those who do not have Windows XP, users can use browsers, such as Safari and Firefox. Safari is a Web browser developed by Apple Computer, Inc. for its Mac OS X operating system (see Figure T-12). Firefox is the upgraded open source Windows platform browser from Mozilla. Thunderbird 0.8 is Mozilla's next generation e-mail client.

● **Internet2:** A consortium of researchers and universities are working together with high-tech corporations and some government agencies to build the next generation of the Internet—Internet2. Internet2 is not a separate physical network and will not replace the Internet. Internet2 researchers are performing experiments using new and existing resources, including **middleware**. Middleware is intelligent software that prioritizes packets on the Internet. It is the "glue" that binds together major applications and negotiates communications between them. Middleware is used to help applications work more effectively over advanced networks through standardization and interoperability.

● **Gmail:** Google, the popular search engine, developed an e-mail system called **Gmail** (see Figure T-13). Gmail was announced on April 1st and many industry analysts thought it was an April Fool's joke. This was followed with privacy advocates alleging that the

service violates privacy laws because of Gmail's proposed data-retention and data-sharing policies. The data collected would be used by third-party vendors for advertising that would specifically relate to keywords found in a user's e-mail. Google programmed Gmail in such a way that users will not be able to permanently delete e-mail messages sent to their accounts and e-mails will be scanned by third-party computers in order to provide targeted advertising links. Google offers Gmail subscribers 1GB of free storage.

● **Managing e-mail:** The storage, management, and organization requirements for personal and business e-mail has companies searching for solutions. Companies with hundreds to several thousands of e-mail users have to seek storage and software to help consolidate and manage years of e-mail messages on a single networked storage system.

● **File sharing:** Napster was the pioneer in providing music MP3 files through peer-to-peer networking. Eventually Napster encountered legal difficulties, and the courts determined Napster was infringing on intellectual property. Other Web sites continue to offer similar file-sharing services, but the trend is moving toward creating ways for P2P users to purchase MP3 files rather than to share them. Napster returned as a paid service, competing with Apple iTunes and various other legal download services.

● **SPAM:** One disadvantage to e-mail is spam—unwanted electronic junk mail that arrives in your online mailbox. Spam is generated by marketing firms that harvest e-mail addresses from mailing lists, membership applications, and Web sites. Globally, spam accounts for about 75% of all e-mail messages. The trend is for all new e-mail systems and browsers to be developed with built-in spam control. U.S. lawmakers enacted the CAN-SPAM Act in an attempt to control the flood of unwanted e-mail. The act allows spam, but requires messages to be labeled so they can be filtered by ISPs or users. However, legislation to minimize spam has not met expectations.

FIGURE T-11: MSN Messenger home page

FIGURE T-12: Safari: the default browser for the Mac

FIGURE T-13: Google's e-mail service

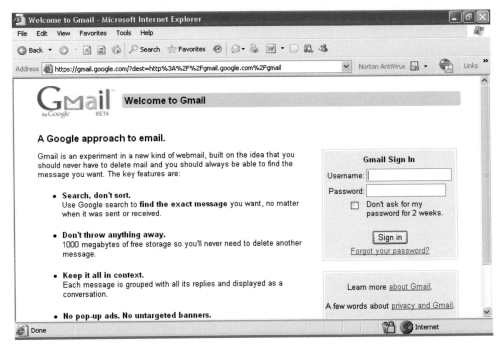

Using cell technology to send and receive e-mail, text, and pictures

Cellular or mobile phone technology has converged with browsers and e-mail clients. It is now quite simple and very common to use a cell phone to send and receive not only text messages, but also games, music files, e-mail, and images. All the major carriers (Sprint, Verizon, AT&T, Cingular, and CellularOne) have the capability of sending and receiving e-mail, text, and pictures through their networks.

The camera phone is one consumer commodity that is driving the need for this service. These phones are often given away free for the signing of a 1- or 2-year contract. With just one click, a digital image is captured; with just a few more clicks, it is sent via the network to one or a group on an e-mail list.

The implications for privacy surrounding cell technology in general and camera phones specifically are significant. For example, society would never allow a camera in a locker room or restroom, however, up until camera phones, no one questioned a person making a cell phone call in either of those spaces. In reaction to the misuse of camera cell phones in public places, some communities and organizations are banning their use in locker rooms, restrooms, and other places where privacy could be an issue.

Exploring evolving trends in ...
Software

Software is what keeps many machines, particularly computers, running. Many devices have some software component. In addition to the obvious software in your desktop, laptop, or even handheld computer, software adds functionalities to cars, home appliances, cameras, medical devices, retail and banking machines, and much more. As electronic communication becomes more prevalent, connectivity software, such as e-mail and instant messaging, are used by more people on a daily basis. This lesson looks toward the future of software—not only exciting new applications and new features being added to existing products, but also to the ways software is applied and delivered.

DETAILS

- **Updates and patches:** After you purchase and install software, you might have to update it. A software update can be distributed as a new version, patch, or service pack. A new version of software entirely replaces an old version, and it is installed in much the same way as the original software was installed. In contrast, a **software patch** is a section of program code that replaces part of the software currently installed to correct a security breach, to add functionality, or to enhance the existing program in some way. The term **service pack**, which applies to operating system updates, is a set of patches that correct problems and address security vulnerabilities. In 2004, Microsoft released a major upgrade to Windows XP, Service Pack 2. See Figure T-14. Patches and service packs are usually distributed via the Internet and auto-matically install themselves when you download them. The trend is for a Web-based program to scan your operating system or soft-ware and determine if it most up-to-date.

- **Software development trends:** The future of software development depends on many unsettled issues. One trend is the use of open source software development. Leading open source operating systems, such as Linux, have changed the development and marketing rules. Open source advocates have been fighting for years to force publishers, particularly Microsoft, to release their code. Apple's response to the open source movement was the release of the core of Mac OS X; called **Darwin**, it is a completely open source kernel. Most recently, Microsoft has agreed to give out the code for a few of its programs but it is still fighting to hold on to its propriety Windows and Office code.

- **Productivity software for the office:** Recent advances in database, word processing, presentation graphics, e-mail client, scheduling, and spreadsheet technologies include greater

integration with the Web and greater potential for collaboration. For corporate administrative functions, the trend has been to use improved B2B communications software as well as integrated software tools to improve production and hold down costs.

- **Graphics and imaging software:** Digital cameras and digital video cameras are changing the way many businesses capture and process their images and video. Real estate professionals, artists, law enforcement officials, medical professionals, and educators are using digital cameras for digital imaging and video editing.

- **DVD authoring software:** With the growing popularity of writable DVD drives, desktop video authors now want to trans-fer their productions to DVDs and watch them on standard DVD players connected to televisions or projectors. **DVD authoring software** offers tools for creating DVDs, which include menu selections such as Play Movie, Scene Selection, and Special Features. You can use the remote control for your DVD player to scroll through and select menu options.

- **Web-based Application Service Providers (ASPs):** Many businesses are turning to the Web as a delivery system for their software needs. Clients no longer have their software on com-pany servers; instead, ASPs charge customers via a contract for access to Web-hosted applications. Advantages to using ASPs include automatically having the most recent version of software and having fixes to known bugs already installed in the soft-ware. However, hosted applications have some disadvantages. They work only when you are connected to the Internet. If you lose the connection, you are no longer able to access the appli-cation. Performance depends on the speed of the connection; therefore, high-speed connections are required.

FIGURE T-14: Windows Update

▶ A user can click a link to have his or her computer scanned to identify any critical updates needed for installations of Office or Windows.

FIGURE T-15: Government initiatives in telemedicine

Trends in telemedicine

Advances in productivity software are making technology transparent and pervasive. Categories of productivity software will need to be expanded to include areas such as robotics and artificial intelligence. For example, doctors are using cutting-edge productivity software to perform robot-assisted surgery. The Web provides a wealth of information to doctors and providers of telemedicine. The Telemedicine Information Exchange (TIE) was created and is maintained by the Telemedicine Research Center. The TIE is funded with Federal funds from the National Library of Medicine National Institutes of Health. Government initiatives in several states are helping rural areas benefit from telemedicine technology. See Figure T-15. They are using communications productivity software to

practice telemedicine, which is the transmission of healthcare data—such as a consultative diagnosis.

Medical facilities are exploring wearable PCs so technicians and specialists can have access to their productivity software at all times. Some wearable PCs are projected to be voice-controlled so they can be used hands-free. Advances in telemedicine technology will also benefit the business sector and its needs. No matter what advances in productivity software are made, the basic premise—that productivity software increases user ability to perform tasks—will never change.

Exploring evolving trends in ... Leisure technology

Leisure is defined as what you do in your free time. It follows then that leisure technology is the technology that helps you accomplish what you want to do in your free time. Because of 24/7 connectivity, the lines between business technologies and leisure technologies are becoming blurred. Leisure technologies include advances in television, reading, gaming, and other leisure activities. As you explore these trends, think about how these systems change the way you live and play.

DETAILS

Television: Not only do people like to spend their leisure time watching TV, they like to watch it when it is convenient for them to do so. Until recently, video recorders provided the main technology to record TV programs and play movies. However, the trend is moving toward enhanced **Digital Video Recorders (DVRs)**, which allow viewers to record TV and video digitally. Personal TV services, such as TiVo (see Figure T-16), are computer-based systems that allow you to control how and when you watch television. TiVo powers a DVR and works with every TV system. It is a subscription-based service that automatically records programs that you specify. Because TiVo is computer-based, you can pause, rewind, and instantly replay live TV.

Many set-top box devices, those devices that sit on top of your television to access services that display through the television, have begun to use IBM's STBP (Set-Top Box Peripheral) chip technology. These are designed for use in a wide range of digital television products including **integrated digital television (IDTV)** sets, **personal video recorders (PVRs)**, and satellite, cable, and digital terrestrial receivers. IBM's new set-top box processors also support the emerging **multimedia home platform (MHP)**, considered to be an integral component to the future success and expansion of digital interactive television—an emerging leisure technology.

Reading: In addition to watching TV, reading is another favorite leisure pastime. Online magazines and eBooks are similar to their print versions but with electronic features linked directly to your computer. Software makes it easier to read the content on a computer display because of the improved text display. Adobe Acrobat eBook Reader and Microsoft Reader are provided free via the Internet and enable you to read eBooks on your computer. Zinio Reader for Windows is an example of a digital magazine reader. Zinio sells subscriptions to digital versions of popular magazines that are delivered via the Internet to your computer.

Games: Online gaming (see Figure T-17) and computer gaming are expanding multimillion dollar a year businesses. New technologies, such as VR and animation, have been driven, in part, by the gaming industry. Next generation gaming devices have dual screens, IP interfaces, and can operate as personal video players (PVP).

Music: The digital music revolution has changed the way the world enjoys, shares, and creates music. Most current music is recorded and played in digital format. CDs, DVDs, solid state storage and hard drives, are the media of choice. The delivery systems have changed, with many listeners downloading music from the Internet or creating music through their computers. Digital radio provides access to hundreds of clear music channels. Satellite radio allows you to get digital radio in your car, home, or wherever you take the satellite radio unit. Software for downloading files is available through the Internet, and swapping files using this download software both legally and illegally has sparked new industries, lawsuits, legislation and a host of new products and services. Convergence has brought voice and images to MP3 players so you can save your photos and hear your music on your iPod, or other MP3 player, if you chose.

FIGURE T-16: Tivo

FIGURE T-17: Online gaming

Screen shot reprinted by permission from Microsoft Corporation.

Art and Photography

Art: The digital art revolution is driven by the current technology for graphics software, printers, and display devices. Newer monitors designed specifically for graphics have increased resolution and wide aspect ratios for video production. Paint software tools permit enhancements to art that give artists free reign expressively.

Photography: Digital photography has made great strides in allowing people the freedom to take as many photographs as they want. Digital cameras with 8 Megapixels are well within the range of affordability. Without the cost of film or the price of developing, people are feeling free to experiment with photography as never before. Photo-editing software, such as Adobe Photoshop, provides tools for enhancing pictures. Adobe is pushing for the Digital Negative Specification (DNG) photo standard, which could make archiving and editing digital photos even easier. The goal is to create a public industry standard to make the archiving and editing process compatible across all types of cameras and photo software.

Internet Access Security

Whether you work with a standalone computer or a LAN, Internet connections pose two kinds of risks: malicious code and intrusions. To deal with malicious code, such as viruses and worms, it is important to run antivirus software on standalone computers and all network workstations. To prevent intrusions, you need to take additional precautions. This Tech Talk explains the most important steps you can take to secure Internet access on your Windows-based computer. These steps are summarized in Table T-2.

TABLE T-2: Standalone Computer Security Checklist

• Turn your computer off when not in use
• Make sure operating system security patches and service packs are up to date
• Disable file and printer sharing
• Check security settings in Internet Explorer
• Enable the Internet Connection Firewall
• Configure your computer for Automatic Updates

A standalone computer with an always-on DSL, ISDN, or cable modem connection is particularly susceptible to intrusions. Without any visible sign or warning, hackers can infiltrate your computer to obtain personal information or use your computer as a launching pad for attacks on other machines. If you have an always-on connection, you should take steps to secure your computer from intrusions. One of the easiest steps to enhance your computer's security is to turn it off when you are not using it. When your computer is off, it is not vulnerable to intrusions. Putting your computer into sleep mode or activating a screen saver is not sufficient protection. Your computer must be shut down and turned off.

You should also keep your computer up-to-date with the latest Windows security patches and service packs. Hackers look for holes or vulnerabilities in Windows and Internet Explorer and work out ways to exploit them to gain unauthorized access to computers. As Microsoft develops security patches, they are posted at www.windowsupdate.microsoft.com. Check the site frequently to download the most recent patches. You can also use the Windows Automatic Updates feature to check periodically for updates. To configure Automatic Updates, go to Control Panel, select System, and select a setting from the Automatic Updates tab. When updates are available, you will see the New Updates icon on the taskbar.

Your computer should be configured to run firewall software, which is designed to analyze and control incoming and outgoing packets. This software helps keep your computer secure in several ways. It makes sure that incoming information was actually requested and is not an unauthorized intrusion. It blocks activity from suspicious IP addresses and—best of all—it reports intrusion attempts so that you can discover whether any hackers are trying to break into your computer.

Windows XP includes firewall software called Internet Connection Firewall (ICF) or Windows Firewall. To activate and configure it, use the Control Panel's Network Connections option. See Figure T-18. For earlier Windows versions or non-Windows operating systems, ZoneAlarm, Tiny Personal Firewall, and BlackICE are popular personal firewall products.

You should also check Internet Explorer's security options. Most experts agree that the Medium setting allows maximum flexibility for browsing while providing a good level of protection from intrusions. To check this setting, open Internet Explorer and select Internet Options from the Tools menu.

FIGURE T-18: An example of firewall software

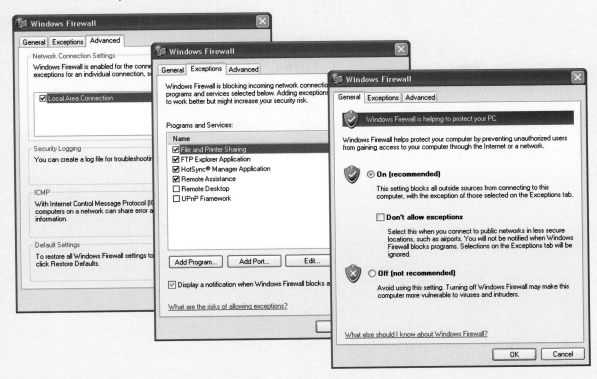

If your computer is used for access to a public Wi-Fi network, you should deactivate file and printer sharing. When you turn off file and printer sharing, your files and printer cannot be accessed by other network users.

What about LAN security? Many security measures for LANs are the same as for standalone computers. You should not, however, deactivate file and printer sharing, which would defeat the purpose of having a network. Instead, use firewall software designed for networks. LAN managers should establish user IDs and passwords for all users and close all "backdoors," such as default passwords.

LAN managers also should consider using Network Address Translation (NAT) to add another layer of security. A LAN requires a device with routing capabilities, and that device can become part of a network's security defenses. NAT uses private IP addresses to hide LAN workstations from Internet intruders. Your ISP typically assigns an IP address to your high-speed connection. This address is visible to the rest of the Internet. Within your LAN, however, workstations can use "hidden" private Internet addresses. When the IP addressing scheme was devised, three ranges of addresses were reserved for internal or "private" use: 10.0.0.0—10.255.255.255, 172.16.0.0—172.31.255.255, and 192.168.0.0—192.168.255.255. These Private IP addresses cannot be routed over the Internet. If you assign private IP addresses to your workstations, they are essentially hidden from hackers, who see only the IP address for your router. You might wonder how you can transmit and receive data from a workstation with a nonroutable address. Your router maintains a NAT table that keeps track of the private IP addresses assigned to each workstation. For outgoing packets, the router substitutes its own address for the address of the workstation. When a response to a packet arrives, the router forwards it to the appropriate workstation. In that way, only the router's address is publicly visible. The router should, of course, be protected by antivirus software and firewall software.

Telecommuters and sales representatives often have to access corporate networks by using a remote connection from home or a customer's office. It is possible to secure these remote connections by using virtual private network (VPN) access to a remote server that uses Point-to-Point Tunneling Protocol or Layer Two Tunneling Protocol. To initiate a VPN connection, dial your ISP as usual. After the connection is established, a second connection to the remote access server creates an encrypted channel for data transmission. Windows XP and several standalone products provide VPN software.

Fashion is big business. Worldwide, clothing sales generate more than $200 billion in revenue. Shoes, accessories, and jewelry bump this industry's revenue even higher. Competition is tough as designers, manufacturers, and retailers compete for customer dollars. In the fashion industry, trends are difficult to predict and change quickly. As the saying goes, "Today's style is tomorrow's markdown." Fashion industry players look for every competitive advantage. Technology plays a major role in this industry.

Fashion runway extravaganzas set off fashion trends that eventually work their way to retail stores. Fashion runway events ventured into Internet territory in 1999 when lingerie manufacturer Victoria's Secret produced a Webcast watched by over 1 million eager viewers. It was the combination of the technology and the fashion that drew the audience. Now, young designers without the cash to stage elaborate runway shows can turn to companies such as Nouveau Media, a video production company that creates "Fashion Video Shorts." These short digital runway videos can be produced on DVDs and displayed on TV monitors in retail stores or broadcast as commercials. In streaming media format, the videos can be accessed from a Web site.

Although runway fashions are typically conceived with a sketch and stitched by hand, designs are adapted for the ready-to-wear market by using computer-assisted design (CAD) tools, such as pattern-making software. CAD is also used to construct garments by digitally sewing together sections of fabric that form arms, fronts, backs, collars, and so forth. The set of templates used to cut fabric sections is called a pattern. Pattern-making is a tricky 3-D challenge because flat pieces of fabric eventually become garments shaped to conform to curved body contours. Pattern-making software helps designers visualize how flat pieces fit together and drape when sewn. Once a master pattern is complete, pattern-making software automatically generates a set of patterns for each garment size.

Computers play a major role in fabric design and manufacturing. Computer software, such as ArahWeave, lets fabric designers experiment with colors, yarns, and weaves while viewing detailed, realistic onscreen samples. Fabric designs can be stored in a variety of formats for weaving machines. Since a few of the older mechanical weaving machines are controlled by punched cards, digital fabric designs can be transferred to punched cards with a dedicated punch card machine. Most of today's weaving mills use computerized machinery that directly accepts digital input to control threads and patterns. Networks are used to tie weaving looms to CAD stations and to the Internet. Fabric designs can be stored in XML format, transmitted to a fabric manufacturer via the Internet, and used directly by computerized weaving machines.

FIGURE T-19

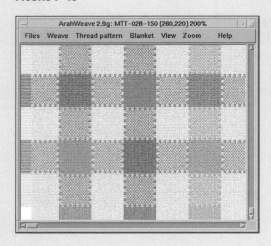

Clothing production, warehousing, and shipping are also highly automated. Benetton's high-tech facility at Castrette, Italy, can produce over 110 million garments per year. Its automated distribution center uses a workforce of only 24 people to handle 40,000 boxes of merchandise daily. Radio frequency identification (RFID) tags—sometimes called "smart labels"—can be attached to individual garments or to packing boxes as an important tool for controlling inventory.

RFID technology uses a tiny computer chip with a built-in antenna and the capacity to store between 64 and 128 bits of data about a garment—its SKU number, size, model, dye lot, manufacturing date, and so on. An RFID reader that can retrieve data from tags is used to track merchandise from the manufacturing plant through the distribution chain to the retailer. RFID tags are becoming popular for all types of merchandise. Businesses that use them can save time and money. For example, RFID tags can significantly reduce the time it takes to do a physical inventory by a factor of 10. Privacy advocates, however, are worried because these tags remain active even after you bring your merchandise home. Could a thief circle your house with an RFID scanner to find out what's inside? After customers protested a plan to attach RFID tags to every sweater, Benetton currently uses the tags only on shipping cartons.

Online shopping has become routine, but one drawback to catalog and online ordering is the cost associated with restocking returned merchandise. Can an online customer find out how a garment will fit and look before ordering it? In 1998, Lands' End introduced the "My Virtual Model" technology that allows shoppers to create a custom model of themselves by choosing from a variety of hair colors, face shapes, and body types. The model can "try on" clothes to show online customers how they would look when wearing the garments.

More recently, Land's End toured the country with a body-scanning device to collect actual measurements from thousands of customers. Body-scanning devices use cameras and lasers to capture approximately 300,000 data points that can be pieced together into a 3-D image.

Body scanners are also helping the fashion industry by collecting data. Sizing standards fell by the wayside as "vanity sizing" added an inch or two to a garment so that consumers can feel good about themselves by fitting into smaller sizes. In the U.S. clothing industry, a comprehensive study of body shapes and sizes can help standardize sizing and eliminate much of the trial and error involved in finding apparel that fits.

No discussion of fashion and computers would be complete without highlighting wearable technology. Clothing that contains digital devices has made its way out of the laboratory and onto store shelves. For example, Burton Snowboards, electronic fabric manufacturer SOFTswitch, and Apple teamed up to create the limited-edition Burton Amp, a jacket with integrated iPod controls designed for snowboarders to control music from the sleeve of their jackets without fumbling with zippers, gloves, and small control buttons.

Another "wearable," originally popular with secret service agents, is the SCOTTeVEST, a jacket with pockets for cell phone, PDA, MP3 player, and built-in wiring to connect these devices into a personal area network (PAN). Available as a jacket or vest and in men's and women's sizes, the jacket can now be purchased by civilians.

With a growing emphasis on the use of technology in fashion design and manufacturing, fashion degree programs at colleges and technical schools have added courses such as computer-aided fashion design, computer-based pattern drafting, pattern grading and computer-aided drafting, and wearable computers.

Originally thought to be the truest venue for unregulated free expression, it seems that the Internet may fall under restrictions and regulations once thought impossible. With the advent of new technologies and some recent laws (both national and international), it seems that online regulation of content and expression may not only be possible but probable.

Those who favor Internet restrictions and monitoring do so for a variety of reasons. In its communication "Illegal and harmful content on the Internet," the Commission of European Communities summarized the reasons governments feel pressure to regulate the Internet:

- national security (fear of terrorist activities, bomb-making instructions)

- protection of minors (from violence, pornography)

- protection of human dignity (from racial hatred or racial discrimination)

- economic security (protection against fraud)

- information security (protection from malicious hacking)

- protection of privacy (unauthorized distribution of personal data such as medical records)

- protection of reputation (libel)

- intellectual property (unauthorized distribution of copyrighted works)

Those groups and governments who favor regulating the Internet will soon have sophisticated tracking programs to do just that. Such programs will be capable not only of stopping the transfer of selected content on the Web, but also of locating those users who work outside the regulations. In addition to regulating content, there are a variety of issues related to business conducted over the Internet that some groups feel need to be regulated.

Software programs currently exist that provide for Internet regulation by individuals, parents, or organizations. Programs can filter out inappropriate subject matter to protect users from unwanted content. Some parents, schools, and libraries find these programs a first step in regulating the Internet. However, the bigger issue—should there be global regulation of the Internet—remains.

There are many questions that must be answered before regulating the Internet fairly can become a reality. First, what would be the purpose of regulating the Internet? Presumably, the purpose would be to address the concerns listed previously. Next, who would make up the regulations?

One challenge that faces those who believe the Internet should be regulated is the global aspect of the Internet. Each country and its government bring a different set of rules and a different cultural perspective to the Internet. These must all be understood and respected if regulation of the Internet is to succeed. Finally, who would monitor the Internet and enforce the regulations? Once again, the global nature of the Internet makes this a difficult question to answer.

Even if the "right" answers to the above questions can be found, there are those who do not believe the Internet should be regulated and who believe in the original premise of the Internet—free and open communication. Groups such as the Electronic Frontier Foundation (EFF) and the American National Standards Institute (ANSI) are working with policy-makers to ensure the Internet remains a venue for free and open communication. The EFF, for example, has as one of its goals "to educate the press, policymakers and the general public about civil liberties issues related to technology." [Source: http://www.eff.org/about]

Some movement has already been made to regulate the Internet. For example, with the Internet quickly becoming the global marketplace, the Federal Trade Commission (FTC) in the United States has been implementing various regulations regarding protection of consumer privacy information. Internationally, governments are proposing legislation to regulate business dealings on the Internet by providing basic rules to ensure that transactions and contracts completed online have the same protections and guidelines as those done face-to-face or on paper. In addition, new laws are being considered regarding ways to collect taxes on the sales of goods that fall outside the jurisdiction of a state's ability to collect taxes. There has also been talk of charging and taxing Internet use. The Federal Communications Commission (FCC), which has been in favor of lifting some of the existing telecommunications restrictions in order to bring high-speed Internet access into homes, also, has been debating what, if any, restrictions they should place on the content that is delivered.

All these ideas are contrary to the original premise of the Internet, which was developed to provide an open, unregulated, and free forum for the exchange of ideas. With the Internet such a vital component in areas such as commerce and education, however, are laws to regulate the Internet necessary?

▼ EXPAND THE IDEAS

1. Log onto the Internet, then use your favorite search engine and the key phrase "regulate the Internet." Create an outline of the key ideas related to regulating the Internet discovered in your research. Write a brief summary indicating your answer to the question: Should the Internet be regulated? Be sure to provide support through your research for your conclusion.

2. Is regulating the Internet a good idea? Consider such laws as the following that were passed by the U.S. Congress: The U.S. Communications Decency Act (1996) and the Child Online Privacy Protection Act (2000). Research these laws. Are they still in effect today or have they been overturned? If still in effect, summarize how they regulate the Internet, who is protected, and who monitors the regulations. If overturned, summarize on what grounds.

3. Will the new laws as described above hamper trade and e-commerce, or will they provide a secure and stable environment to promote and expand Internet trade and commerce? Research recent proposals and developments regarding e-commerce both in the U.S. and around the world. Write a short paper on your findings. In your conclusion, state how the proposals regulate the Internet. Do you think the proposals will work? Why or why not?

4. In the United States, the FCC regulates cable and broadcast television. If the Internet is provided via cable through television, does regulation fall within the FCC's jurisdiction? What are the issues and recent regulations? Write a short paper discussing your findings.

Issue

End of Unit Exercises

▼ KEY TERMS

Advanced Micro Devices (AMD)
Alchemy
Assistive technology
Athlon
Cluster
Cluster computing
Code Morphing
Crusoe
Darwin
Digital video recorder (DVR)
Double-layer DVD
Duron
DVD authoring software
E911 (Enhanced 911)

Efficeon
Field Emission Display (FED)
FLOPS (floating point operations per second)
Force feedback technology
Free Space Optics (FSO)
Geode
Gmail
High-performance computing (HPC)
Integrated digital television (IDTV)
Internet2
Intel

m-Commerce (mobile commerce)
Membrane keyboard
MEMS-based storage
Middleware
MIPS (Millions of instructions per second)
MirrorBit
Multimedia home platform (MHP)
Network drive
Opteron
Organic light emitting diode (OLED)

Personal video recorder (PVR)
Phishing
RFID
Self-securing storage
Service pack
Smart media storage
Smartphone
Software patch
Spansion
USB Flash Drive
VLAN
Wireless Application Protocol (WAP)
Zombie PC
Zombie PC network

▼ UNIT REVIEW

1. Review all of the bold terms in this unit to gain a better understanding of current terminology. In your own words define each term. Use online resources to explore the terms in more detail.

2. Look at the objectives list in the unit opener. Without referring to the lesson itself, write about one trend discussed for that lesson. Write additional questions you have about that trend and list resources where you might find information.

3. Create a three-column table for each lesson. List the trends mentioned in each lesson in column 1. In column 2, record the status of the trend—e.g., is it having an impact in that technology sector, is it no longer a player in that technology sector, has it had its day but is now replaced by a newer trend [name the trend that has supplanted the one named in column 1]. In column 3, write your reaction to the status of the trend—e.g., to be expected, disappointing, it never caught the imagination of the consumer, and so on.

4. By definition, some "trends" become integrated into society (like VHS for videotaping and CDs for data and music storage) and others disappear, never to be heard of again (like Beta, the competitor to VHS in the early days of videotaping, and 8-track tapes for music). In the lesson on networking and wireless connectivity, you read about trends related to wireless communication. Describe them. What are the possible conflicts between the technologies? Do you think newer technologies will be developed to facilitate the way we communicate wirelessly? Why or why not? To answer these questions, you may choose to use additional resources to expand your understanding of wireless connectivity technologies.

5. Ways to access the Internet, as well as browsers and Web services have evolved. Answer these questions: How do you access and use the Internet? What devices do you use to log on and access Web sites? What other features of the Internet (discussion groups, forums, e-mail, e-commerce) do you use? Make lists in answer to the questions. Then put an asterisk next to each item that uses a technology or trend discussed in these lessons.

6. Review the lesson on software. List the types of applications named in the lesson and some enhancements that have been made in those areas. Then consider other software you use in your daily life such as browsers, eBooks, photo-editing, graphics, music, games, word processors, graphics programs, and any technical packages. Discuss whether or not this software could be considered an example of a new trend, or discuss any trends you see in the software you are using. Write a concluding paragraph identifying trends you see in software.

7. The lesson on leisure technology discussed new trends in leisure activities such as music, art, and photography. Make a four-column table and list the technologies discussed, who or what devices and software are used with each type of technology. If you would like to enhance the information in your table, you might log onto the Internet and use your favorite search engine to search for links to trends in digital radio, photography standards, new gaming devices, and recent computer gaming trends. Review the site for any new standards and advances in any of these technologies. Add your findings to the table.

▼ FILL IN THE BEST ANSWER

1. Field emission display (FED) technology is being developed for use in _____ displays.

2. _____ is the flagship scientific computing facility for the Office of Science in the U.S. Department of Energy.

3. The _____ compiles a list of the world's 500 most powerful supercomputers.

4. Most removable storage devices plug into _____ ports and are platform independent.

5. _____-layer DVD burners allow home users to create CDs and DVDs up to 8.5 GB.

6. MEMS-based storage combines _____ and _____ on one chip.

7. One or more information systems that share data and typically provide information to very large groups of users is _____ computing.

8. _____ is the illegal activity in which an attempt is made to obtain a user's personal information by imitating the e-mails of legitimate companies.

9. A(n) _____ is a group of personal computers, servers, and other network resources that are connected logically but are on physically different segments of a network.

10. A software _____ is a section of program code that replaces part of the currently installed program, usually to enhance existing software.

11. _____ is a powerful and controversial technology that offers self identification for products and perhaps people through radio frequency.

12. A _____ is a group of devices that share a server or a group of servers that share processing tasks and can provide backup in case of failure of any of the connected servers.

13. The open source operating system offered by Apple Computer, Inc. is called _____.

14. U.S. lawmakers enacted the _____ Act in an attempt to control the flood of unwanted e-mail.

15. AIM, ICQ, and MSN are _____ messaging communities.

16. The intelligent software that prioritizes packets on the Internet and binds major applications together is called _____.

17. _____ software provides a protective barrier between a computer and the Internet.

18. The e-mail client offered through Google is called _____.

19. Unwanted electronic junk mail generated by marketing firms that arrives in your online mailbox is called _____.

20. A leading open source operating system is called _____.

▼ INDEPENDENT CHALLENGE 1

How have PC components changed over time? Did the first computer look similar to the current offering by computer companies? As with automobiles, the basic appearance of a desktop computer has not changed. You still have the keyboard, the system unit, and the monitor or display device. Accessories have improved and expanded. The general consumer first used the mouse in 1983 on the Apple Lisa computer. What have been some other developments and major changes to the computer?

1. Research the history of the desktop computer for major developments and historic moments in personal computers.

2. Include photos from the Web, if you can find them, of the TRS-80, early external modems, early mice, and dot-matrix printers. Be sure to credit your sources.

3. What technological development do you think is the most significant? Why? What new technologies do you think will be driving forces in the way PCs look, feel, and work?

4. Based on your research, what have been the trends in PC development? Do you expect future trends to continue along the same path? Explain.

▼ INDEPENDENT CHALLENGE 2

It is your job as an office manager in a new startup company to select the computers and office productivity software package that will be used by your employees. Your offices are in a new four-story office building in a commercial office park off a major highway. The building is wired with network cable and you are renting 1,000 square feet on one floor. Your advertising is mostly local, although you have a new Web site and are planning to expand your client base.

1. What computers will you purchase? Components? Will they be standalone or networked? If networked, explain any special considerations.

2. The three leading office suites are Corel WordPerfect, Microsoft Office, and Lotus SmartSuite. Which package is best for you? Create a chart of features for each, and list which ones are most important and why.

3. What e-mail client will you select and why? Research available software packages.

4. What current trends discussed in this unit, such as anti-spam software and anti-spyware technology, will you include in your plan? Discuss why you would include each. Is knowing whether or not the trend is fully-functional and supported an important consideration? Explain.

5. Write a report detailing your plan.

▼ INDEPENDENT CHALLENGE 3

Electronic game consoles are a large sector in the consumer market. You have to create a marketing campaign for a new console that your company MyCoolGAMZ is creating.

1. Research the current markets and trends in electronic gaming and prepare a statement that compares the top sellers.

2. List the top-selling games, and explain if they are marketed across platforms.

3. Draw a set of plans that lists the features that you would include in your gaming console. Name the device and list the price and ways consumers can buy and access games designed for your system.

4. Which strategies are in use to market the new console you are creating?

5. What trends or technologies discussed in this unit would you include as part of your gaming console? Explain why you would include them.

6. Create a poster that sells your new product. Emphasize the new trends or technologies that make your product the one that will take consumers into the future of gaming.

▼ INDEPENDENT CHALLENGE 4

 Medical science is often at the frontline of computer advances. People are benefiting greatly from new technologies that help in all fields of medicine. There are new techniques to assist those with disabilities, there are new tools to deliver insulin to diabetics, and there are systems in place in hospitals that help nurses track tests and medications that have been dispensed to patients. As mentioned in the unit, new technology and software are providing opportunities for robot-assisted surgery and telemedicine. The field is wide open and fascinating in its trend-setting efforts.

1. Log onto the Internet and use your favorite search engine to research new applications for computers in the medical field.

2. Reseach new hardware for persons with disabilities.

3. Create a list of five new computer-based products that have been introduced in the field of medicine.

4. Create a list of two devices that assist people with hearing, vision, and mobility special needs.

5. Print out any Web pages that show images of a device or application.

6. Write a summary report detailing your findings. Write a concluding paragraph summarizing any trends you see emerging or opportunities for cross-applications, that is, technologies developed for assistive technologies and the medical field that might have uses in another area.

▼ INDEPENDENT CHALLENGE 5

 The Internet was visualized and made a reality by pioneers. People such as Vannevar Bush, J.C.R. Licklider, Larry Roberts, and Tim Berners-Lee have all had instrumental roles in shaping the Internet. Who are the Internet pioneers? What contributions did they make?

1. Log onto the Internet. Use your favorite search engine and the key phrase "Internet Pioneers." Follow links to several pioneers and read briefly about them.

2. Select one pioneer to research in more depth. Prepare a short paper on your findings. Be sure to include information about the individual's contribution to the Internet.

3. Discuss whether the contribution was viewed as a trend, a passing fancy, or an innovation when it was originally conceived.

4. Discuss what pieces had to be in place to make the innovation a reality.

5. Conclude your report with a brief statement about what surprised you the most as you researched Internet pioneers.

UCITA (Uniform Computer Information Transactions Act) was drafted by the Chicago-based National Conference of Commissioners on Uniform State Laws (NCCUSL) and sent to all 50 states for their consideration as part of an effort to develop uniform commercial laws easing interstate commerce. This law is intended to govern all contracts involving computer software and information that you get electronically. It would apply to software, multimedia products, computer data and databases, online information, and any software product. This includes software from CDs, Web sites, and file transfers. The proposed law would cover software that is in most consumer electronics products today, including televisions, cars, and cell phones.

The rules set forth in UCITA have significant opposition from consumer groups and many corporate users. The opponents, who set up a group called Americans for Fair Electronic Commerce Transactions, claim that UCITA is too favorable to software vendors. See Figure T-21. For example, UCITA grants new rights to software and information publishers. Essentially, it says that, by default, the software developer or distributor is liable for flaws in the program, but allows a shrink-wrap license to override the default. UCITA backers argue that the measure has been misunderstood and erroneously maligned. In order for UCITA to become law, it must be ratified by each state through the state's legislature. Several states have adopted the law including Maryland and Virginia.

FIGURE T-21: UCITA opponents

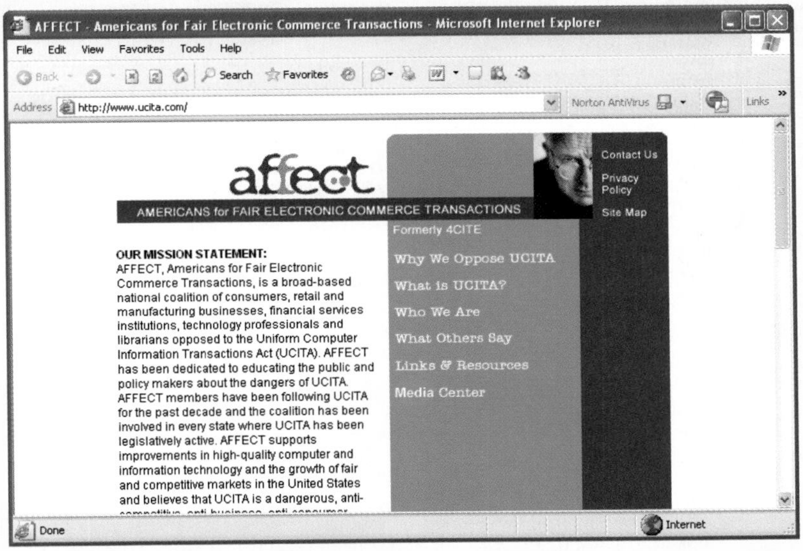

1. Research UCITA. What is it all about? What is the current status of UCITA? What is the status in your state? Based on your findings, do you support the act? If so, explain why. If not, explain why not.

2. If UCITA is not the answer, what is? Research other proposals that address software contracts and electronic information today. Identify one to study in more detail. Write a brief summary of your research. Include responses to these questions: What is the purpose of the proposal? Who supports it? Why? Who opposes it? Why? Summarize your opinion of the proposal based on your research.

3. There are many organizations that are interested in policy-making as it relates to technology today and tomorrow. Research several of these organizations. A good starting point is the Electronic Frontier Foundation (EFF), the IEEE (I triple E), the American Library Association (ALA), and the W3C. Review the mission statement and goals of each organization you research. Make a chart to help compare the organizations. Summarize your findings. Are these organizations working toward similar goals or are they at cross-purposes? Do these organizations support or oppose UCITA?

You finish school with a degree in computer science and want to go out into the world to get a job in the computer information systems area at a major company. Are your qualifications enough? You read through the classified want ads in the local paper only to find that many companies are requiring certifications that you did not take as part of your undergraduate training. You also look back and find that want ads from two years ago had certification requirements that don't seem to exist now. Certification and training classes are costly and time consuming. You know that various companies, such as Microsoft and Cisco (see Figure T-22), offer information about certification related to their software. How can you know which certificate you should pursue?

FIGURE T-22: A certification site

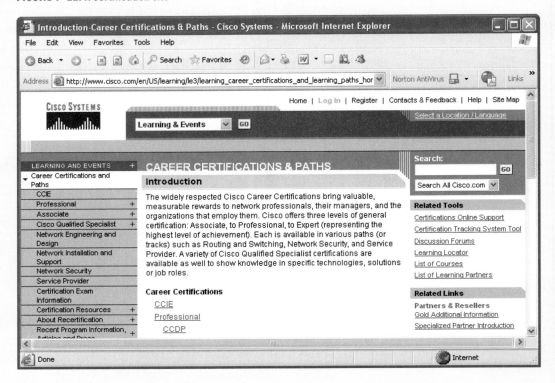

1. Log on to the Internet and research current certifications that are available for computer specialists. Look on the Microsoft, Oracle, Sun, Novell, and Cisco sites. What types of certifications are offered?

2. Typically, where are certification courses offered? How much do they cost? How long is the training for each certification? What types of jobs require the certification? Which companies require employees to be certified? Make a chart for three certifications and answer the questions just stated to complete the chart. Add a final column to your chart to include other information you found interesting or helpful but that is not covered by the questions.

3. Look in the local want ads or research online job sites such as monster.com, job-hunt.org, and flipdog.com. Do a keyword search on the certifications you found in Step 1. What did you find? Do these jobs require certification? Summarize your findings.

Bonus Issues and Up-To-Dates

Unit	Issue	Up-To-Date
A	E-mail-privacy—Who is reading your mail?	Buying computers
B	How do storage technologies impact piracy and privacy?	Advances in computer display technology
C	What's all the fuss about open source development?	E-voting: questions and concerns
D	Outsourcing and offshoring— what are the issues?	Global Positioning System (GPS) monitoring
E	Junk: spam, e-mail spoofing, phishing—how to deal with it?	The advertising assault on your computer
F	Spyware—a virus or a legal business practice?	Controlling security breaches in software
G	How does the Information Age impact business ethics?	Internet2
H	Digital rights management— how does it impact you?	DNG: an archival file format for digital images
Computers in Context: Banking		Online banking

Since computers affect almost all aspects of daily life, you should know about basic computer concepts and about recent advances in computer technology. It is nearly impossible, however, to keep up with advances in all areas. What you should know are general trends and significant developments. Sometimes an innovation that seems significant one year has minor impact on society or business and is gone within months, and sometimes a development that is barely noticed at first turns out to lead the way for technological advances for years to come. Advances in technology usually do not come without a price. Each new development has controversy, proponents, and opponents. The unit presents issues that have been generated by advances in technology and up-to-date projects to help you explore recent trends.

E-mail privacy—Who is reading your e-mail?

When you drop an envelope into the corner mailbox, you probably expect it to arrive at its destination unopened, with its contents kept safe from prying eyes. When you make a phone call, you might assume that your conversation will proceed unmonitored by wiretaps or other listening devices. Can you also expect an e-mail message to be read only by the person to whom it is addressed?

In the United States, the Electronic Communications Privacy Act of 2000 prohibits the use of intercepted e-mail as evidence unless a judge approved a search warrant. But, that doesn't mean the government isn't reading your mail. Heightened security concerns after the September 11, 2001 terrorist attacks resulted in the rapid passage of the Patriot Act, which became law on October 26, 2001. In an effort to assist law enforcement officials, the Patriot Act relaxes the rules for obtaining and implementing search warrants and lowers the Fourth Amendment standard for obtaining a court order to compel an ISP to produce e-mail logs and addresses.

To eavesdrop on e-mail from suspected terrorists and other criminals, the FBI developed a technology called Carnivore, which scans through messages entering and leaving an ISP's e-mail system to find e-mail associated with a person who is under investigation. Privacy advocates are concerned because Carnivore scans all messages that pass through an ISP, not just those messages sent from or received by a particular individual.

Although law enforcement agencies are required to obtain a court order before intercepting e-mail, no such restriction exists for employers who want to monitor employee e-mail. According to the American Management Association, 27% of U.S. businesses monitor employee e-mail. But this intentional eavesdropping is only one way in which the contents of your e-mail messages might become public. The recipient of your e-mail can forward it to one or more persons—people you never intended for it to reach. Your e-mail messages could pop up on a technician's screen in the course of system maintenance, updates, or repairs. Also, keep in mind that e-mail messages—including those you delete from your own computer—can be stored on backups of your ISP's e-mail server. You might wonder if such open access to your e-mail is legal. The answer in most cases is yes.

The United States Omnibus Crime Control and Safe Streets Act of 1968 and the Electronic Communications Privacy Act of 1986 prohibit public and private employers from engaging in surreptitious surveillance of employee activity through the use of electronic devices. However, two exceptions to these privacy statutes exist. The first exception permits an employer to monitor e-mail if one party to the communication consents to the monitoring. An employer must inform employees of this policy before undertaking any monitoring. The second exception permits employers to monitor employees' e-mail if a legitimate business need exists and the monitoring takes place within the business-owned e-mail system.

Employees generally have not been successful in defending their rights to e-mail privacy because courts have ruled that an employee's right to privacy does not outweigh a company's rights and interests. Courts seem to agree that because a company owns and maintains its e-mail system, it has the right to monitor the messages it carries.

Like employees of a business, students who use a school's e-mail system cannot be assured of e-mail privacy. When a CalTech student was accused of sexually harassing a female student by sending lewd e-mail to her and her boyfriend, investigators retrieved all the student's e-mail from the archives of the e-mail server. The student was expelled from the university even though he claimed that the e-mail had been "spoofed" to make it look as though he had sent it, when it had actually been sent by someone else.

Why would an employer want to know the contents of employee e-mail? Why would a school be concerned with the correspondence of its students? It is probably true that some organizations simply snoop on the off chance that important information might be discovered. Other organizations have more legitimate reasons for monitoring e-mail. An organization that owns an e-mail system can be held responsible for the consequences of actions related to the contents of e-mail messages on that system. For example, a school has a responsibility to protect students from harrassment. If it fails to do so, it can be sued along with the author of the offending e-mail message. Organizations also recognize a need to protect themselves from false rumors and industrial espionage. For example, a business wants to know if an employee is supplying its competitor with information on product research and development.

Many schools and businesses have established e-mail privacy policies, which explain the conditions under which you can and cannot expect your e-mail to remain private. These policies are sometimes displayed when the computer boots or a new user logs in. Court decisions, however, seem to support the notion that because an organization owns and operates an e-mail system, the e-mail messages on that system are also the property of the organization. The individual who authors an e-mail message does not own all rights related to it. The company, school, or organization that supplies your e-mail account can, therefore, legally monitor your messages. You should use your e-mail account with the expectation that some of your e-mail will be read from time to time. Think of your e-mail as a postcard, rather than a letter, and save your controversial comments for face-to-face conversations.

▼ EXPAND THE IDEAS

1. Do you think most people believe that their e-mail is private? Do you believe that your e-mail probably won't be read by anyone besides your intended recipient? Knowing that your e-mail is not private, will you be more careful in what you send via the e-mail system? Why or why not?

2. Should the laws be changed to make it illegal for employers to monitor e-mail without court approval? Why or why not?

3. Would you have different privacy expectations regarding an e-mail account at your place of work compared to an account you purchase from an e-mail service provider?

If you don't have a computer, it is only a matter of time before you will find that you need to have one. Whether for school, a job, or household chores, computers have become essential daily appliances. If you already have a computer, it is often the need to upgrade your software that drives the need to upgrade your existing computer or to buy a new one because new software and newer operating systems often require more hardware resources. It seems that as soon as you purchase a computer and as soon as you get your computer home and out of the box, a more powerful one supercedes the model you bought. It is indeed difficult to keep up with this fast-paced industry. At some point, however, you need to buy a computer, upgrade an existing one, or build your own. No matter which path you take, you need to know that the computer you end up with is capable of doing the work you need to do. Figure 1 shows the Web site for the Buyer's Guide available online for this book.

FIGURE 1: The online Buyer's Guide

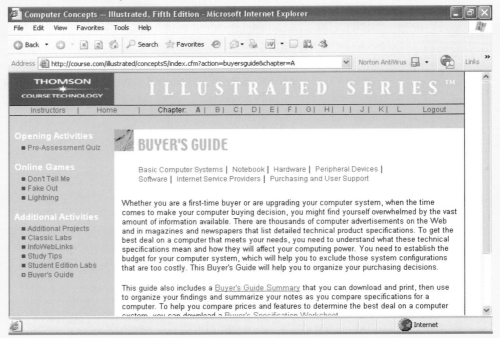

1. Log onto the Internet, and then go to http://www.course.com/downloads/illustrated/concepts5. Click the link for any unit, then click the Buyer's Guide link.

2. Click the link for Basic Computer Systems and read through the links on that page.

3. Click the Hardware link, then click and read through each of the links for architecture considerations. Click the Notebook link and read about notebook computers.

4. Use a search engine to locate at least one online retailer for computer systems. Consider the features you read about in Step 3, and then locate three different computer systems that fall into distinct pricing categories: inexpensive, moderate, and expensive. Create a chart that compares the price, features, and retailers for the three computers. Repeat by comparing three notebook computers.

5. Write a short summary answering the following questions:

   • Were you able to find computers for sale in a large price range?

   • What feature, if any in particular, created the largest price gap?

   • What features do newer models offer?

   • Write a paragraph summarizing decisions you need to make when selecting your computer system.

How do storage technologies impact piracy and privacy?

Bytes, kilobytes, megabytes, gigabytes, terabytes … New storage technologies are creating ways to store more data reliably and efficiently. But what does this mean to the consumer? On the personal computing front, new technologies allow users to save large amounts of data easily. Removable drives make it possible for you to work on a computer, remove the drive, take it across the country, and then place it in a bay or plug it into a USB port in a different computer and continue working as if you never left the original computer system. From a personal computing viewpoint, the increase in storage capabilities often means increases in efficiency—no more digging through lots of disks to find a file since files are all able to be stored in one place.

In addition to computer use, consumers are seeing the benefits of new storage technologies in consumer products. For example, the TiVo and Replay TV units come with hard drives that can store hours of recorded television. Hard-drive manufacturers are using hard disks as portable storage devices for set-top boxes, game consoles, and digital stereo receivers. Consumers can slide drives containing music, digital photos, or recorded TV programs into an empty bay, similar to the bay on PCs that holds CD drives. Great for the consumer, but some movie and record companies are objecting to these devices. They are concerned that the increase in storage capability will mean more people will be storing their own movies and music, which will result in a decrease in revenues. They are also concerned that consumers will fast forward through the commercials and advertisers will find other avenues for product exposure. These piracy fears are similar to the ones that the movie industry expressed when VCRs were first introduced.

The consumer is also affected by the way these advances in storage technologies are being used by businesses and the government. The U.S. government digitally stores and retrieves a variety of data about all its citizens, including tax forms and other legal documents. The trend toward digital passports is another way databases can be used to coordinate efforts to help identify potential threats on a global scale. By incorporating digital encoding into passports, border patrols can more readily identify and validate persons entering and exiting countries. European countries, such as Belgium and the United Kingdom, are moving forward with their programs to have passports contain encrypted personal information, such as fingerprint information and iris scans. Going a step further, the U.S. State Department has mandated as part of its Visa Waiver Program that passports contain biometric data. The Visa Waiver Program allows people from selected countries (currently 27) to travel to the United States for tourism or business for 90 days without a visa, but they must still have a passport.

In an August 2004 press release, a State Department Deputy Spokesman in Washington, D.C., stated, "The requirement for Visa Waiver travelers to have biometrics included in passports was mandated in the Enhanced Border Security and Visa Entry Reform Act of 2002. The passage of H.R. 4417 and the signing by the President extends for one year, to October 26, 2005, the deadline by which new passports issued must be biometrically enabled. This extension was necessary to avoid potential disruption of international travel and to provide the international community adequate time to develop viable programs for producing a more secure, biometrically enabled passport. The original legislation required that Visa Waiver Program country passports issued on or after October 26, 2004, be biometrically enabled for use in Visa Waiver travel. European travelers may also soon be required to carry passports containing biometric information. In June 2003 the European Union agreed to spend 140 million euros on the development of an interoperable biometric system." *source:* http://www.state.gov/r/pa/prs/ps/2004/35066.htm

Volumes of data about consumers are stored by insurance companies, manufacturers, telephone companies, and advertisers. Large databases are everywhere and they are getting larger. In order to manage these large databases, high-tech documents, also known as smart documents, have to be able to access the databases. These documents need to make the proper connections to the databases and then gather the appropriate information without gathering information that was not requested. The technology has to be highly secure in order to protect the privacy of all individuals, that is, secure when accessed, secure when data is retrieved, secure when in use and during data transmission. For example, if the smart document is looking specifically for information about J.Q. Public, then the only information it should be able to gather in the database should be information about J.Q. Public and no one else.

With all of this gathering being done electronically, you might wonder how can these database systems be secure and what happens when a system housing a database becomes obsolete? With so much personal data stored on so many computer systems, how can we be sure that once the system is no longer needed, the data is not just put out in the trash heap to be salvaged by anyone with even a remote curiosity as to what is on the hard drive? Millions of computers become obsolete each year. What happens to those computers? Are they 'stripped' of their data? Does a simple "File Delete" command remove all sensitive data from a doctor's computer? an insurance computer? a government computer? As you know, file recovery programs are readily available. What's to stop anyone from digging into that trash heap and recovering medical records? bank numbers? visa and passport information?

But the concern is not only about large database but also about data we carry with us. Smart cards are an example of a new storage technology that is being embraced by businesses and organizations. This technology is raising concerns among individuals. A smart card is similar to a credit card, but it contains a computer chip that stores information and can transfer data to and from a central database. For example, some universities are using smart cards as ID cards. These smart ID cards serve multiple purposes: students can use their smart cards as an ID card to retrieve their student records, as a library card to keep track of books borrowed and returned, as an e-wallet to keep track of purchases and a prepaid balance on the card, and as a health card to provide access to medical records. Some consumers are concerned about the amount of data and type of data being stored on smart cards. They claim privacy issues are at stake.

The amount of stored data is growing exponentially. The concern is not so much that data is being stored, but rather what is being done with that data. Advocates of new storage technologies point out that these advances mean a wealth of information is available and that with proper search techniques it is easily accessible. Those opposed to excessive storage raise piracy, privacy, and security concerns.

▼ EXPAND THE IDEAS

1. Research smart cards. How are they being used? How are they being received by the general public? Write a brief paper listing the benefits and drawbacks. Discuss ways that security and privacy concerns are being addressed.

2. Personal information (such as birth, banking, loans, health, and marriage) was stored in different locations and with differing levels of accuracy, so it was often difficult to gather lots of information about one individual. Today, the Internet provides access to a wide range of personal data. Use your favorite search engine to find out what type of personal information is available over the Internet. Make a list of your findings. Write a short paragraph stating your opinion of whether or not accessibility to such information should raise privacy or security concerns.

3. How do you feel about biometric data being a required component of passports and visas? Write a brief paper discussing the issue and supporting your position.

Up-To-Date Advances in computer display technology

Advances in computer display technology have taken displays in two very distinct directions: very large displays and very small displays. Small displays are making it possible for portable computers and cell phones to have full application functionality. A user can view photographs, work with documents, and view Web pages through the display on a cell phone. Small display technology allows for bright images, lower power consumption, and flat panels.

Large displays are being developed for cinema and graphics applications. Computer displays with high-resolution, wide-aspect ratios, and wide-viewing displays permit users to watch videos through the DVD players on their computers without any loss of image quality. Why? Because the wide-viewing displays allow more graphics and information to be displayed across the screen from left to right and the use of wide-aspect ratio imitates a cinema screen. For example, new high-end Dell portable computers feature a 15.4-inch LCD with an aspect ratio of 16:10, instead of the standard CRT and LCD ratio of 4:3. See Figure 2.

FIGURE 2: An LCD with a wide-aspect ratio

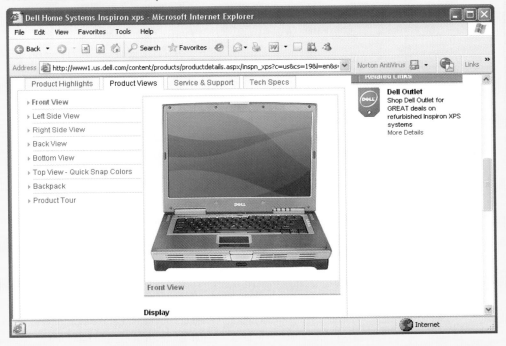

1. Log onto the Internet and use your favorite search engine to research display technology. Use the results of your research to answer the questions: What is the current trend for desktop computer displays? What is the current trend in portable computer displays? What is the current trend for cell phone displays? List a typical product in each of the three categories. Then, list basic specifications for each computer display.

2. Is it beneficial to use a display with a wide-aspect ratio (16:10) for viewing videos? Explain.

3. Research the latest developments in OLED (organic light-emitting diode) technology. What recent developments have been applied or implemented in consumer products?

4. Describe recent developments in displays for cell phones and portable computers. What is the latest trend?

What's all the fuss about open source development?

To understand the fuss, you need to understand what open source development is: the development and use of free software code. Open source development means that the source code for a software package or operating system is freely available. Developers who use the open source source code for other projects often suggest changes to the original source code to fix bugs or provide improvements. These "fixes" are then incorporated into the code so that all users have access to them. As the saying goes, "Many hands make light work," but in the case of open source development projects some would say, "Many programmers make for a stronger source code."

The non-profit corporation Open Source Initiative (OSI) is dedicated to promoting an understanding of open source as a software development model. The OSI Web site lists examples of open source software that is being used for commercial purposes and that can be found readily on the Internet. For example:

- Apache—the server software that runs over 50% of the world's Web servers

- Perl—the software behind most of the "live content" on the Web

- BIND (Berkeley Internet Domain Name)—the software that provides the DNS (domain name service) for the entire Internet

- sendmail™—a widely used e-mail transport software on the Internet

- DomainKeys—a software program used to control spam

So what's all the fuss about? The word "free" in the definition should give a clue to part of the controversy. Commercial companies spend a tremendous amount of money on research and development of software. Commercial companies are generally not open to the idea of the development and use of free software since their goal is to make money. But the Internet has opened the door for open source development and there are some companies that are embracing it—and still making money. Examples of open source development projects include Netscape Navigator, Linux, and Apache.

Netscape is a leading proponent of open source development. It pioneered the distribution of software online when it offered Netscape Navigator for no fee over the Internet. A few years later, Netscape became the first commercial company to make its source code for Netscape Communicator free for modifications. Netscape has been both praised and criticized for its role in the open source development strategy.

Linux, developed under the GNU General Public License, is a free Unix-based operating system that was originally developed by Linus Torvalds. The source code for Linux is distributed freely and is available to anyone who wants it. Linux is available in several formats called distributions. These are distributed for no charge by developers either by File Transfer Protocol (FTP) or for a nominal fee for shipping and handling by CD. The Linux tools and utilities that are available include Linux applications for administration, multimedia, graphics, system development, scientific applications, communications, and graphics. Even though the source code is free, the applications that are developed using Linux are not.

Linux has been making inroads into the personal digital assistant markets (PDAs). In addition, several large corporations that have traditionally used Windows NT servers to handle various computing tasks—such as Corel, Oracle, and SAP—are moving their tasks onto IBM mainframe computers running Linux. In fact, IBM has been boosting its support for Linux by launching new Unix servers that make bringing Linux into large corporate systems easy. Major software developers have created alliances with Linux and are developing their applications to run under the Linux system. As a result of the successes of these alliances, Linux has created an interesting dilemma for the Microsoft developers who have always resisted and been able to avoid the release of the source code for their operating systems. The operating system code is the intellectual property that is so highly coveted by Microsoft and is what the company bases its success on.

Versions of the Microsoft operating system have gone from MS-DOS in 1980 to Windows XP in 2001. Since the beginning of the PC revolution, Microsoft's operating systems have dominated the market. Microsoft, to date, has not made source code available to developers. Recently, Microsoft has come under increasing pressure to "open up." The company has been trying to overcome negative public images and, after settling the antitrust suit with the U.S. government, has determined that it is time to address this problem. One solution might be for Microsoft to provide access to its source code.

Apple Computer Company is also using open source projects to allow developers to enhance and customize Apple software for its computers. MAC OS X is based on the Darwin open source project. Darwin is the core of the MAC OS X. The Darwin project combined the efforts of Apple engineers and programmers in the open source community to create the source code for MAC OS X. Apple continues to make open source development a key component of its software development strategy and invites users to participate in the Darwin open source project.

Overwhelming world-wide public opinion is that open source operating systems, such as Linux, are viable and cost effective alternatives to proprietary operating systems, such as Windows. With Linux or other open source software, products can be customized and upgraded on the user's schedule, and upgrades don't necessarily erase customized code. Some recent open source software releases include the following: In 2000, Sun Microsystems released the source code to StarOffice to the open source community as part of the continuing open source project OpenOffice.org. Recently, Sun Microsystems released Solaris 10, which is its proprietary server operating system as an open source project. Then, it quietly released a version of its Java Desktop System software, which is based on Solaris. The Mozilla Foundation plans to release its FireFox v1 browser in late 2004. It is already available for preview as a download and at the time of this writing the program had been downloaded over 5 million times. This open source browser movement is expected to open the markets for new browsers other than Internet Explorer so that users can have more options for browsing the Internet.

The unexpected early success of Linux has led some experts to rethink the software development model—moving from a closed model to the open source model. Is it possible that more and more companies will share their source code in the hope of developing better software products? Will the consumer benefit from such a change in software development?

▼ EXPAND THE IDEAS

1. What is the GNU General Public License? The GNU General Public License differs from other software licenses in that it provides for the sharing, understanding, and modification of free software. Research the various software licenses that are available and create a comparison chart. In the chart explain, for each type of distribution license, who owns the software, and what provisions for distribution and change exist for each type of software license.

2. Is the open source approach to software distribution the way to go? What is Microsoft doing to meet the demands of the open source movement? You can find out more about open source principles by going to www.opensource.org and www.fsf.org. Research existing arguments for and against the GNU. Write a brief paper on how you think it will affect the software development market in the future.

3. Some software programs developed using the open source software model were listed in this Issue. Research other products developed using the open source software model. Create a list of these software programs. Do these programs have competitive programs that were developed using the closed development model? Which product is more widely used? Why do you think that is?

E-voting: questions and concerns

Throughout history and the world, finding ways to ensure that voting is accessible to all eligible citizens and that the ballots are counted accurately has been a challenge for each generation. From paper ballots to punch cards, countries find a way to administer elections. Advances in technology have had an impact on voting. Voting systems with touch-screen computerized voting machines have been developed. But, these new direct recording electronic (DRE) voting machines have proven to be vulnerable to some of the same problems other systems using computer technology experience, including crashes, power-outages, viruses, and hacking. Another concern is the lack of a voter verifiable paper trail (VVPT). A VVPT is a permanent paper record of a vote. The voter uses the VVPT to check for accuracy before the vote is cast. The VVPT must be deposited in a secure ballot box for use if a manual recount or audit is needed. There are organizations to monitor e-voting (see Figure 3).

FIGURE 3: Verifying the vote

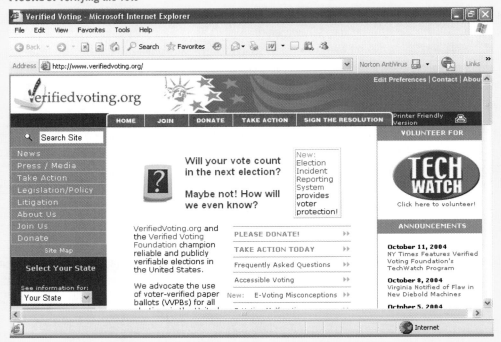

1. Write a list of the three major concerns you have about the use of these machines in general elections. Log onto the Internet and use your favorite search engine to research electronic voting machines. What steps are the manufacturers of these machines taking to ensure that every vote is counted? that votes are not lost? that hackers don't intervene and change votes? Did these sites address the concerns you recorded earlier? Based on your research, do you think Internet voting can be fair and secure?

2. Why are VVPTs necessary? Do current DRE systems use VVPTs? Do you believe that we must insist on a paper trail? If we do, why bother with electronic voting at all?

3. Do you agree that electronic voting is the way of the future and we must find ways to overcome the security, verification, and special influence issues? Write a brief essay explaining your position.

Outsourcing and Offshoring—what are the issues?

Have you ever called a customer service number and encountered a friendly voice with a foreign accent on the other end of the line? Has it ever occurred to you that this support technician might be sitting at a desk on the other side of the world—in India, Singapore, or the Philippines, for example?

Outsourcing is an established business practice that can reduce product costs, cut consumer prices, and help businesses remain competitive. The range of outsourced jobs includes manufacturing; electrical engineering; back-office functions like accounting, human resources, call centers, and data analysis; and IT-related work, such as software development, maintenance, support, and quality assurance.

Outsourcing seemed a good business practice and did not generate much controversy when jobs remained within national boundaries. As jobs were outsourced to other countries that could provide significantly cheaper labor, the term "offshoring" was born and analysts became increasingly concerned about its effect on unemployment at home. **Offshoring** is defined as relocating business processes, such as development and production, to lower-cost locations in other countries. U.S. computer companies have established manufacturing and development facilities in countries such as India, Malaysia, Thailand, and Mexico, where labor is inexpensive but reliable. Companies such as Microsoft and Oracle make extensive use of programmers based in India, who telecommute via the Internet. Some computer companies make use of offshoring to help keep product costs low. As some businesses have taken offshoring to a new level by creating illegal offshore ventures or tax safe-havens for their companies, the practice of offshoring has become increasingly controversial.

Computer and telecommunications technologies have made it possible for companies such as American Express, America Online, and Dell to move their call centers to India, the Philippines, and other countries. You might not, however, be able to determine a call center's location because according to an article in the *New York Times*, many offshore customer service representatives are not allowed to disclose their locations to customers.

Outsourcing and offshoring have come under increasing criticism. Some analysts believe these business practices are causing unemployment in many sectors of the U.S. economy—including the IT industry. Other experts disagree, and view outsourcing and offshoring as part of economic globalization.

Electronic Data Systems (EDS), founded in 1962 by Ross Perot, gets credit for turning IT outsourcing into a major business. In 1969, when Blue Shield of Pennsylvania could no longer handle the state's Medicare processing workload, EDS took over responsibility for managing the system and hiring employees. India, the first country to host offshore contact centers for U.S. businesses, is currently on the leading edge of IT offshoring. China, the Philippines, Mexico, Canada, and Russia are also considered strong contenders.

The major lure of offshoring is reduced cost of labor in developing nations. Whereas the salary for a U.S.-based programmer with three to four year's experience would be $45,000 to $55,000 a year, programmers in India charge a fraction of the cost—around $15,000 to $19,000 a year. News reports cite several high-tech U.S. workers who claim they were laid off after training their offshore replacements.

The downside of offshoring is rooted in language barriers and cultural differences. For example, in several Asian countries, it is customary to answer indirectly instead of giving an outright "yes" or "no" as would normally be the case in the U.S. An Asian technician who says "Very difficult" might actually mean "no."

Miscommunication can be costly. A major computer company was forced to discontinue its offshore business-customers call center because of mounting complaints about "bad service." New York financial services firm Lehman Brothers stopped offshoring its computer help desk to a company in India because of unsatisfactory feedback. On both the national and state levels, politicians are faced with a dilemma: Should they focus on protecting their constituents' jobs or helping the businesses keep costs down and grow their business? Voters are clearly voicing their anxiety over job security. Because it became a major election issue, the State of Indiana prematurely ended a $15.2 million offshoring contract to upgrade the state's unemployment claims computer system, even though the contract saved taxpayers $8.1 million.

Consumers, however, vote with their wallets, and few are willing to pay more for U.S.-produced goods and services. Businesses that maintain a high-cost onshore workforce could find themselves unable to compete in a global marketplace. If the business goes bankrupt, all its employees join the unemployment ranks.

It is difficult to precisely assess the pros and cons of offshoring. A survey conducted by CFO magazine reported that some companies had no cost savings whatsoever, or only nominal savings of less than 15%. Less than half of the companies in the study reported savings of more than 20%. In contrast to this data, Forrester Research, an independent technology research company, claims that its offshoring clients typically reap benefits ranging from 25% to 45%. How many domestic jobs have moved offshore? Estimates vary, the range is between 300,000 and 1 million—less than 2 tenths of one percent of all U.S. workers. Forrester Research projects a loss of 3.4 million jobs by 2015.

As the offshoring debate continues, IEEE-USA, an organizational unit of the world's largest technical professional society, recommends the following:

- The Federal Government must collect and publish reliable statistics on the kinds and numbers of manufacturing and service jobs that are being moved offshore.

- Government procurement rules should favor work done in the United States and should restrict the offshoring of work in any instance where there is not a clear long-term economic benefit to the nation or where the work supports technologies that are critical to our national economic or military security.

- New U.S. workforce assistance programs should be created to help displaced high-tech workers regain productive employment and ensure that employed workers can acquire the knowledge and skills they need to remain competitive.

- A coordinated national strategy must be developed to sustain U.S. technological leadership and promote jobs creation in response to the concerted strategies other countries are using to capture U.S. industries, jobs, and markets.

Not since the industrial revolution has technology provided tools for such a significant change as economic globalization. Our response as individuals and as a nation is likely to have a far-reaching effect on future lifestyles, so keeping tabs on this issue is important.

▼ EXPAND THE IDEAS

1. Have you ever contacted a support center that you suspected was located outside the United States? Why did you call the support center? Were your questions answered? Write a brief paragraph describing your experience. Do you believe the outcome would have been different if the support center was located in the United States? Explain.

2. Are you surprised that high-tech jobs, such as software engineering, requiring advanced skills can be handled by offshore firms? What are some challenges companies who do offshoring might encounter? What impact might these differences have on the end product? Create a list of several issues and challenges an offshoring company would face that a company that retains the jobs domestically would not. Explain how these might be overcome.

3. Are you for or against offshoring? Before answering the question, use the Internet to research two recent articles on offshoring. Write a summary of each article, then use information in the article to answer the question and support your position.

Many consumer applications today use GPS (Global Positioning System)—a tracking technology. Today, GPS is built into standalone devices, cars, cell phones, and other electronic equipment. For example, GPS can be found in many cars today and that technology can help you find your way home and provide exact location information if you call for help. There are several competing services such as OnStar and Magellan. Refer to Figure 4.

A U.S. mandate requires cell phones to use GPS technology so that emergency workers can locate people who use their cell phones to place 911 calls. The use for tracking technology continues to grow. But, the use of tracking technology is not without controversy. For example, there is a call by some employers to be able to use the GPS in cell phones to help track employees. You can place a chip on just about any thing, or perhaps anyone, and then use GPS technology to find it, him, or her.

FIGURE 4: Magellan

1. Log onto the Internet and use your favorite search engine to research the GPS system. What exactly is a GPS system? How does it work? What are the benefits? Who controls it? What are the implications? What are the limitations? Why was it created? Write a brief report of your findings.

2. What are the new applications for GPS technology? Log onto the Internet and use your favorite search engine to find out how governments and industries are mandating and using GPS technology. Write a brief summary of your findings.

3. What are the controversies surrounding GPS technology used to locate children? people? workers? How do you feel about your boss using a company cell phone to track your activities? Write a few paragraphs supporting your comments.

4. RFID (Radio Frequency Identification) can be used to track goods, but can it also be used to track people. Use your favorite search engine to research current uses of RFID and GPS. How do the two technologies differ? How are they similar? Summarize your findings.

Junk: spam, e-mail spoofing, and phishing—how to deal with it?

The Internet provides access to a virtually bottomless pool of information, but in its vast depths, truth mingles with lies, rumors, myths, and urban legends. The Internet is uncensored and unregulated. Anyone with a Web page or an e-mail account can distribute information rapidly and widely, which is then often redistributed and forwarded. Even with so many rumors, myths, and fake e-mails circulating on the Internet, is it fair to say that the Internet has a monopoly on false information? Probably not, since even well-established newspapers, magazines, and television news shows report stories that are later found to be misleading or untrue. But as an online consumer, as an Internet user, and as you become more dependent on the Internet, you have to learn how to sort out the fact from fiction. Not only do you have to question the veracity of the stories and information you read on the Web, you also have to learn to sort out valid sources from the fake ones as you use the Web sites and e-mail for commercial transactions.

While there has been a lot of news and discussion about viruses and spyware, three of the greatest challenges facing legitimate businesses and Internet users today are spam, e-mail spoofing, and phishing.

Spam is unwanted electronic junk mail. Typically, spam tries to sell medical products, low-cost loans, adult entertainment, and fake software upgrades. Today's proliferation of spam is generated by marketing firms that harvest e-mail addresses from mailing lists, membership applications, and Web sites. Globally, spam accounts for about 75% of all e-mail messages.

E-mail spoofing is the forging of another person's or company's e-mail address. E-mail spoofing can be a very convincing way to get users to trust and open a message. E-mail spoofing leads to **phishing**, which is the fraudulent solicitation for account information (such as credit card numbers and passwords) by impersonating the domain and e-mail content of a company to which users have entrusted the storage of these data. Well-known companies such as banks, utilities, and e-commerce services, commonly send transactional e-mail to consumers. As an online bank customer, for example, you will certainly open an e-mail and perhaps comply with its requests if you believe the e-mail was sent by your bank. But how can you know the e-mail really is from your bank and not from an illegal source phishing for your private information?

Without sender authentication, verification, and traceability, e-mail recipients and providers can never know for certain if a message is legitimate or forged. Do ISPs and e-mail providers have an obligation to their customers to ensure that all e-mail delivered through their systems is legitimate? What determines legitimacy? Are Internet service providers responsible for making educated guesses on behalf of their users regarding what to deliver, what to block, and what to quarantine? Or, is it the responsibility of the companies, such as banks, utilities, and e-commerce services, who use e-mail for transactional services? For companies that use e-mail for transactional services, protecting their users from fraudulant e-mails translates directly into user protection, user satisfaction, reduced customer care costs, and brand protection. All parties (ISPs, companies conducting transactional services, and consumers) need to work together to prevent spoofing and phishing attacks.

Since incidents of spam, e-mail spoofing, and phishing are on the rise, new technologies are being developed to combat these growing threats. **E-mail authentication software** technology (such as DomainKeys, which was developed as a joint venture between Yahoo and Gmail, and Caller ID for E-Mail, which is being developed by Microsoft) helps eliminate domain spoofing and increases the effectiveness of spam filters. For example, the goal of Caller ID for E-Mail is to verifying what domain a message came from—similar to the way caller ID for telephones shows the phone number of the person calling. Caller ID for E-Mail is intended to verify that an e-mail message came from the domain it claims to have come from.

The ultimate goal of DomainKeys is similar to Caller ID for E-Mail. DomainKeys gives e-mail providers a mechanism for verifying both the domain from which each e-mail message was sent and the integrity of the message (i.e., that it was not altered during transit). According to the developers of DomainKeys, "once the domain can be verified, it can be compared to the domain used by the sender in the From: field of the message to detect forgeries. If the e-mail message is a forgery, then it is spam or fraud and it can be dropped without impact to the recipient. If it is not a forgery, then the domain is known and matches the "From" field. A persistent reputation profile can be established for that domain and it can be tied into antispam policy systems, shared between service providers, and even exposed to the user." Source: *http://antispam.yahoo.com/domainkeys*. A domain associated with a persistent reputation profile is likely to be viewed as spam when it is encountered by DomainKeys in subsequent reviews. The effect of being 'blacklisted' or 'blocked' will keep that sender's spam out of the e-mail system.

For consumers, industry support for sender authentication technologies will mean that they can start trusting e-mail again. Yahoo and Gmail plan to make their DomainKeys software freely available to open-source developers, hoping that it will be adopted, installed, and implemented throughout the Internet.

Until these technologies really take off and until is is possible to avoid spam, you can reduce it as well as protect yourself from e-mail spoofing and phishing attacks by following a few simple guidelines, such as the ones that follow. When you receive a message that seems suspect, read it carefully and look for clues that might indicate it is a forgery. Call your bank before giving any personal information out in e-mail. Never reply to spam when you receive it. Don't click any links in the spam message; one click can send the spammer verification that the spam reached a valid account. Provide your e-mail address only to people from whom you want to receive e-mail. Be wary of providing your e-mail address at Web sites, entering it on application forms, or posting it in public places such as online discussion groups. If your e-mail client offers a **spam filter** to block unwanted messages, put it to use. If your e-mail client does not provide a spam filter, you can download and install one from a shareware site on the Web. A spam filter automatically routes advertisements and other junk mail to either the Deleted Items or Junk folder maintained by your e-mail client. Although spam filters can be effective for blocking spam and other unwanted e-mails, it sometimes blocks e-mail messages you want. After activating spam filters, periodically examine your Junk and Deleted Items folder to make sure the filters are not overly aggressive. If your e-mail provider offers a way to report spam, use it. The only way to really stop spam once your e-mail address has been spread through the lists is to change your e-mail address.

▼ EXPAND THE IDEAS

1. Who do you think is responsible for the authentication and verification of e-mail— the recipients? Senders? or ISPs? Do you believe that recipients should be in charge of the e-mail they receive by taking the responsibility of using spam filters and of not responding to spoofing or phishing? Or, should the legitimate companies bear the responsibility to protect the consumers? Write a paper explaining your position.

2. Have you ever received a spoofed e-mail? If so, how did you know it was not legitimate? Explain the tools you can use to protect yourself from spam, e-mail spoofing, and phishing.

3. Log onto the Internet and research the current state of technology to protect consumers from spam, e-mail spoofing, and phishing. Which companies are working together in these ventures? What new systems are in place? Are they successful in stopping the attacks? Summarize your findings in an essay.

It seems each time you sign onto the Internet you are bombarded with popup ads, popunder ads, and a barrage of unwanted advertisements. Spam is junk e-mail advertising products and services, often from very questionable sources, that fills up your inbox. Many ISPs are promoting services that block ads as part of their sign-on promotions. Popups are a result of deliberate programming code embedded inside a Web page. Typically, a Web scripting language such as JavaScript or VBScript is used. You can disable or limit the ability of scripting in your browser, but then you will also disable functionality that you might want. For example, scripting languages enable useful Web functions like buttons that change when you move the cursor over them. Popups have spawned many software programs that stop or reduce the occurence of popups (see Figure 5). It seems that just as each new technology promises to control the flood, advertisers find new ways to display their products and services on your machine—without your consent. Newer browsers, such as Firefox, promise to stop this advertising assault. Can it be done?

FIGURE 5: Ad-blocking software

1. Log onto the Internet and go to the following sites: www.msn.com, yahoo.com, google.com, and www.aol.com. Create a list of features that they are using as promotion for their newest service. What do they offer to stop popup and popunder ads? Are these services free? Or, do you have to pay for them? What are the differences? Is controlling unwanted popup ads a big factor in the services offered by any of these major Internet players?

2. In addition to the one shown here, what other products are commercially available that can be used to block these marketing activities? Why might some people not want to block the ads? Use your favorite search engine to research software products available for blocking popup and popunder ads. Review three products and make a comparison table. Summarize by saying why you would or would not use one of these products.

3. Spammers are using new ways to get through filters by eliminating the known keywords in the subject text box. They also use common names in the sender field to bypass the blocker lists at ISPs and e-mail clients. Use your favorite search engine to find Web sites devoted to Domainkeys technology. List the sites that you found and their strategies for using DomainKeys to control spam on the Internet.

Spyware—a virus or a legal business practice?

Spyware: just the name sounds ominous. Loosely defined, spyware is a software program that is installed on your computer without your knowledge. To be functional, spyware requires an Internet connection. Spyware is used for various purposes, such as advertising, collecting marketing data, or CPU sharing—also known as distributed processing. These activities can be accomplished without asking for permission each time—or ever. Bottom line: spyware is used to gather data about a person without the person knowing it, and then to send that information to advertisers or other interested parties, usually for commercial use.

One source of spyware is via a computer virus. Another source is via software that you download, which guarantees that the user of these programs has an Internet connection. For example, shareware and free-ware programs are often downloaded over the Internet and can include spyware. When you install the down-loaded program, the spyware program is also installed. Once installed, spyware works behind the scene, making it difficult for the end user to detect. In fact, spyware works even when you are not using the applica-tion that installed the spyware.

Adware is a type of program that displays ads, usually in banners, whenever a program is running. It is simi-lar to spyware in that it is included in a software package to help offset the cost of development and to help keep the cost down for consumers. Developers, for example, might agree to include an adware program as part of their program because an advertising company will pay them to do so. It is different from spyware, however, because the user can readily see that the program is running and, perhaps most importantly, it does not include a tracking component. This means that no data about the user is being collected when the adware program is running. Adware crosses the line and becomes spyware when a tracking component is added to the adware program that allows the program to track user data stealthily.

In addition to privacy and security concerns, spyware and adware can cost you time and money. Both can cause your computer to run significantly slower or make your system crash. If your CPU is being used by oth-ers for their purposes, you do not know what you are contributing your resources to—you are not asked. So, in addition to reduced performance and the risk of browser crashes or system crashes, you are blindly volun-teering your CPU. If you pay for time online, services running advertisements and hidden communications with servers cost you money.

Spyware and adware should not be confused with common e-business practices such as banner ads and cookies. Banner ads that appear on your computer as you work on the Internet are different from both spy-ware and adware because, unlike spyware and adware, banner ads are not installed on your computer. Banner ads, though annoying, can ultimately be removed by you despite the fact that some banner ad devel-opers have tried to find their way around "easy removal." For example, they have tried to hide the close but-ton or continue to play the sound in closed windows. Banner ads differ significantly from spyware because they do not track data about the person viewing them. Although banner ads may be annoying, they do not pose privacy or security threats.

Another e-business practice is the use of cookies, which are commonly used by Web site developers to store information on a user's computer. Cookies are often used to track the contents of an online shopping cart or to remember the geographic location of requested weather information. While it is true that cookies are stored on a user's computer, there are several major differences between cookies and spyware: users can set their preferences to know when cookies are being saved to their computers, users can delete cookies, and, perhaps most importantly, no tracking component is included with cookies.

When you install shareware, you are often asked to agree to license requirements. Sometimes you are asked to register and even pay a fee. Disclaimers are sometimes hard to find. If you are not sure whether or not a program includes spyware, you should pay particular attention to the licensing agreement and registration information requested at the time of the program's installation. Most people simply click the Agree button on these installation screens just to get through the installation; however, you may be granting unlimited access to your computer and your data by doing so. Take, for example, the shareware program Kazaa. When you accept the Kazaa fair use agreement, you grant the right to the folks at Kazaa to farm out CPU time on your computer to others. In addition, the spyware program installed when you install Kazaa can collect information from you and send it back to the advertisers who pay for the right to be installed with the Kazaa shareware.

Download sites, such as ZDNet Downloads and CNET, have begun posting notices on applications that use ad-sponsored spyware. In many cases, a non-ad-sponsored version of the application is also available, usually for a fee. Several of these sites have compiled lists of known installation offenders. You can find out which programs to watch for, how to opt out of some installation traps, and what your safest bets are for uninstalling unwanted software.

When you decide that you no longer want to use the free application on your PC, you can usually remove it via Windows Add/Remove Programs Wizard. Unfortunately, the spyware that was installed with the free application will remain on your computer, often buried within the Windows System Registry. Generally, you need a program such as Ad-Aware from www.lavasoftusa.com to remove the spyware. Ad-Aware is a free multi-spyware removal utility that scans your memory, registry, and hard drives for known spyware components and lets you remove them safely. Similar to virus protection programs such as Norton AntiVirus, it is updated frequently so you can always have the latest definitions.

Why should you worry about spyware? Why would you agree to use a program that installs spyware? According to companies that promote spyware, while it is true that data is collected, none of the data is sensitive and all of it is anonymous. The companies that incorporate spyware into their shareware say they are very clear about the fact that the spyware is part of the shareware program. Despite the public's awareness of the inclusion of spyware, it seems that some download programs remain quite popular even though they include spyware that secretly transmits user information via the Internet to advertisers in exchange for free use of the downloaded software.

▼ EXPAND THE IDEAS

1. Log onto the Internet and then use your favorite search engine to research spyware. Has there been any movement toward regulating spyware? Find two articles that discuss the current situation. Do you think spyware should be illegal? Write a short paper on your findings and support your position with your research.

2. What are the current trends in spyware removal? Use a search engine to find sites based on keywords such as spychecker, spybot, or lavasoft. Follow some of the links to see how spyware has spawned a whole new type of software for spyware removal. Find three types of software that claim to rid your computer of spyware. Create a comparison chart of your findings. Select the one that you think is most effective, and then support your claim in a short paragraph explaining why you think it is the best.

3. As discussed in this Issue, some very popular programs available for download include spyware. Make a list of popular downloads that include spyware. Research each of the download programs. Are there any commercially available programs that could be used for the same purposes? Why do people put up with the spyware? Write a short paper discussing your findings.

People trying to do harm using computers often take advantage of security breaches in commercial software. These breaches are flaws in the program that permit unauthorized access to the computer on which the software is installed. The software might allow malicious programmers to hide a virus within a file that is commonly used in the software program. Hackers might gain access to computers through back doors—a program function that provides administrative access to a program usually during program development—or other security breaches in software. Computer viruses, the most common form of destructive activity, often take advantage of security breaches in commercial software.

Microsoft devotes several pages on its Web site to security updates (see Figure 6) and privacy concerns. These security updates, which often include security patches, are not the same as virus protection; however, they do help protect against viruses and other malicious attacks by patching potential security holes. When using commercial software, it is critical that you stay informed about security breaches and ways to fix them.

FIGURE 6: Safeguarding against security breaches

1. Visit the Microsoft Web site at www.microsoft.com. Click the Security link under resources, then click through some of the links for home users. Find one article that you find relevant. Write a brief paper summarizing why users might or might not follow the advice given in the article.

2. What is a security patch? How does it help to protect against security breaches in commercial software? Are they all the same or is each unique to a particular software package? Write a brief paper describing how security patches can work to guard your safety and secure your computer.

3. Use your favorite search engine and the keywords "software security breach." Make a two-column chart. In column one, list software that has experienced security breaches; in column two, describe how the developer of the software recommends protecting against the security breach. Add a concluding paragraph indicating what type of software seems to be most vulnerable and why.

How does the Information Age impact business ethics?

What are ethics? According to the Cambridge Unabridged Dictionary, ethics are "a system of accepted beliefs which control behavior, especially such a system based on morals." Personal ethics help to guide one's personal behavior and business ethics help to guide one's business behavior.

Ethics often impact business decisions—such as the products a business sells or does not sell and the way it treats its employees. The debate about ethics is not new, but the issues employees are facing as a result of the Information Age are new. In today's fast paced business world, the technology may outpace current ethical guidelines, which leaves business leaders with ambiguous situations about which they must make ethical decisions. Sometimes, the technology may provide tempting avenues for unethical behavior.

What types of ethical questions does the Information Age pose? One that is prevalent centers on privacy issues related to databases. The Information Age has made it possible to create large, detailed databases that store incredible amounts of data about consumers. These databases might be generated by marketing firms which gather information submitted by consumers when they fill out registration information for a new product, by healthcare companies or insurance companies which keep detailed records of patients, by political groups which track membership through surveys, and so on.

Businesses are constantly struggling with the issue of selling their databases. Why would a business want to sell its database? Sometimes the company needs to make a quick profit or needs to show quick monetary gain, and selling its database is one way to do that. Other times, the database is sold as part of bankruptcy proceedings. Some e-commerce businesses have no assets besides their databases, so these are sold to help pay off debtors. Interested parties, often marketing firms, purchase the information in the database to target segments of the population. Most business leaders agree that losing consumer confidence by selling consumer information may result in short-term gain, but it is bad for long-term growth.

The impact of selling a business' databases must be considered not only from a financial viewpoint but also from an ethical viewpoint. Did the consumer whose data is stored in the database know that the information could be used for financial gain? Does the company have the right to use an individual's data for financial gain? Did the consumer willingly agree to have the information sold? Will sharing the information cause harm to individuals listed in the database—for example, does a health-related database contain sensitive data that could keep an individual from acquiring health insurance? These are ethical questions that a company must consider when deciding whether or not to sell its database.

The Information Age poses other ethical questions for businesses as well, especially for e-businesses. A business must always decide what type of merchandise it will sell. For example, the nationwide drugstore chain Walgreens sold alcoholic beverages for years, but when it reorganized a few years ago, the Walgreens leadership decided to discontinue the sale of alcoholic beverages in its stores (in most cases). This decision could have been made for financial reasons (removing alcoholic beverages from its footprint might leave more space for other merchandise) or for ethical reasons (removing alcoholic beverages, which are generally not considered healthy, might be more in keeping with the company's main merchandise health-related products).

Brick-and-mortar stores that sell products such as alcoholic beverages and cigarettes have systems in place for checking the age of consumers. But what about e-businesses that sell these same products? For example, studies have shown that underage smokers can bypass state and federal regulations prohibiting sales of tobacco products to minors by purchasing cigarettes through Web sites. How do e-businesses ensure that they are meeting the requirements of the law by not selling to minors? Is it enough to say that they will not sell to anyone who does not have a credit card (which assumes the holder is 18 years of age or older)? Is it enough to have the Web visitor click a disclaimer stating that he or she is over 18 years of age and therefore legally able to purchase the merchandise? Should the e-business be held responsible if indeed the merchandise is being sold and shipped to minors? Should the shipping companies be responsible for checking whether these products are being sold and delivered to minors? These are some of the ethical questions e-businesses face regarding the merchandise they sell. The technology of the Information Age makes it much easier for minors to obtain merchandise that they cannot readily obtain at brick-and-mortar stores.

Today, electronic transmission of data raises other ethical questions. Take, for example, the high-ranking financial official at Lockheed Martin who received a bid template with a competitor's information, including financial data, in the bid where blank lines should have been. Having this information gave Lockheed Martin a financial, as well as an unethical, advantage because Lockheed Martin would know exactly how to underbid its competitor. The problem could not be easily solved simply by deleting the file or erasing the information. To protect Lockheed Martin, its lawyers needed to be involved. The company releasing the bid template had to be notified that the template contained sensitive data. The Lockheed Martin IT staff needed to be consulted, and they had to adjust how they normally back up the files. The template needed to be backed up to a secure site and then removed from the mainstream correspondence so that no one else would have access to it. The original file needed to be returned to the sender. A company with less sophisticated knowledge of business ethics may not have known how to handle this situation.

Another point of discussion involving business ethics is the use of electronic monitoring to track employee activities or to log customer activities. Still other ethical issues related to the Information Age involve the use of business resources for personal activities such as sending personal e-mail via the company ISP, visiting online auctions via the company Internet connection, playing games online during business hours, checking stock prices for one's personal portfolio, and downloading inappropriate files to one's company computer.

The Information Age has spawned many new technologies and with it ethical questions regarding their use. What is being done to help business leaders sort through the ethical dilemmas they face? Many business schools recognize the need to offer courses in business ethics that relate specifically to e-business issues. Some companies, like Lockheed Martin, require employees to take an ethics course offered by the company once a year, thereby bringing all employees up to speed on ethical issues facing the company and how the company is responding to those issues. Still other companies, like Lands' End, test their IT administrators on ethical issues. As explained by Linda Severson, director of business systems at Lands' End, "We test to make sure they make data available only to those who should see it....You have to have tests that continually challenge your security and privacy processes. Ethics has to become more of a way of life, not a one-time policy posting."

▼ EXPAND THE IDEAS

1. Log onto the Internet and use your favorite search engine to research ethics in e-commerce. Read three articles. Do the articles agree on how to approach ethical questions, or do they contradict one another? Why might that be? Write a short summary of each article, and be sure to cite your sources.

2. Research course offerings at major universities or colleges on ethics and e-business. What are the types of courses offered? Do you believe that ethical issues in e-business are that much different from ethical issues in brick-and-mortar business? Write a short paper supporting your views and citing your findings.

3. Universities and businesses often have a code of ethics that must be followed. Research to find out whether or not your school or business has a code of ethics. If it does, read the code. If it does not, visit the Web sites of major corporations and look for links to their code of ethics, or use your favorite search engine using the keywords "code of ethics" to find a code of ethics. Read the code. Write a short paper summarizing the code of ethics. Indicate if the code applies to business in general or if it applies specifically to e-business activities.

More than 200 universities, industry leaders, and government agencies are developing Internet2 to create the next generation Internet. Just as the original Internet was a collaborative effort, so too is Internet2. Developers want a leading edge network that can provide connectivity for a wide variety of applications. Tele-immersion, virtual laboratories, digital libraries, and distributed instruction are just a few examples of Internet2 applications areas. Internet2 allows users to collaborate and access information in ways that the current Internet cannot handle. Internet2 developers have plans for advanced digital laboratories where people can interact with high-definition images in real time. Exciting showcases are being conducted using this technology. There are many initiatives (see Figure 7), including End to End performance initiatives, Arts and Humanities, Digital Video, and Distributed Storage, just to name a few.

FIGURE 7: Internet2

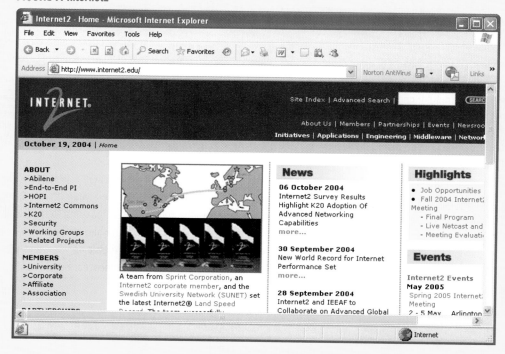

1. Log onto the Internet, then use your favorite search engine to find out more about Internet2. You might start at www.internet2.edu. Write a short paper on the goals of Internet2. Include information as to who is currently involved in the development of Internet2. Be sure to list at least 5 partners in the project. Describe one of the initiatives in detail.

2. The Internet was originally developed to enhance communication. But over time, the Internet has become "clogged" by commercial interests. Even though access speeds are improving, some still describe their Internet experiences as the World Wide Wait. Perhaps this is because the Internet is not regulated. What will Internet2 have to do to ensure that it does not get clogged with commercial interests and that the bandwidth for the applications being developed for Internet2 is available? Research to find out if Internet2 will be regulated. Write a short paper explaining the issues involved in regulating the Internet and Internet2. Provide a concluding paragraph stating your opinion regarding whether or not either should be regulated.

3. Browse the Internet2 Web site, then answer the question: Why is middleware important for Internet2?

Digital rights management—how does it impact you?

Suppose you purchase a music CD of your favorite recording group. Now you want to transfer the music to your computer, rip the best tracks, and transfer the files to your portable audio player. As you begin the process using legitimately purchased software, you discover that the CD is copy protected and your computer CD drive won't read it. You believe that since you purchased the CD that you should be able to listen to the music on any device you choose. Can companies stop you from doing so? The answer is "yes" and "no." Yes, copyright law gives you the right to make copies for your personal use and to transfer works into a format that works on your equipment. However, the growing pervasiveness of digital rights management may curtail your ability to exercise these rights.

Before the digital age, copies of images produced by photocopiers and copies of music produced by audio tape dubbing machines were of considerably poorer quality than the originals. But copying digital files is cheap and fast. On top of that, copies of digital materials, such as sound files or digital image files are indistinguishable from the originals, and that factor has encouraged an alarming increase in software, music, graphics, and movie piracy.

Piracy made world headlines in a dispute about sharing music on Napster. Many music lovers downloaded hundreds of songs without paying for any of them. The culture of file sharing has created a generation of music buyers who believe that content should be free.

Almost immediately, Napster ran afoul of the Recording Industry Association of America (RIAA), a watchdog organization that represents record companies, such as Columbia Records, Motown Records, and Epic Nashville. The RIAA compiled a list of 12,000 copyrighted songs that Napster technology made available as free downloads.

The RIAA filed suit, accusing Napster of contributing to copyright infringement, which considerably reduced the revenues of record companies and artists. The ensuing court battle stirred up a caldron of issues that relate to the use and abuse of digital media, including music, photos, and videos. After shutting down Napster's free download network, music piracy continued unabated. Many other Web sites offered free music file sharing for anyone with an Internet connection. Some flourish, and some have gone. The Napster experience hardened the resolve of digital stakeholders to stop illegal copying. The RIAA then initiated a series of lawsuits targeting individuals who allegedly maintained large collections of pirated music.

In addition to file sharing via Web sites, new technology broadcasts digital music directly to radio receivers via satellite radio. For example, XM radio broadcasts 101 channels of continuous digital programming from its two satellites (named Rock and Roll). XM revenue comes from listener subscriptions and some advertising. So, what are the implications of this new technology as it relates to file sharing? It means that listeners can quickly and easily make copies of their favorite songs as they are played, without ever buying the original. XM has radios for the car or home. Digital satellite broadcast has no static or distortion, so copies of music made from a digital broadcast are clear and CD-quality perfect.

Digital TV broadcasts are similiar to digital radio broadcasts in that they send clear, perfect images of films directly to TVs across the country. With the new hard drive TV systems, such as TiVo and ReplayTV, you can watch your favorite shows or films on your schedule. An even larger issue is that these systems have software that allows you to easily skip the commercials. This directly impacts the way media giants generate revenue. In addition, people receiving television directly to hard drive systems can store, copy, and then redistribute these image-perfect video files. It seems that file sharing has come of age for digital TV as well.

The battle against piracy took shape as a concept called digital rights management (DRM), which is vigorously supported by Microsoft and backed by a host of industry leaders. Today, digital rights management encompasses a variety of technologies implemented by copyright holders, such as record companies and software publishers, which restrict the usage of digital material. DRM systems address piracy by using a variety of technologies for manipulating data, media, devices, and transactions.

Cable television has a long history of signal scrambling and encryption to prevent piracy. Consumers seem to tolerate this form of DRM because once the signal arrives, it is descrambled and can be archived to TiVo or video tape just as any broadcast television program can be archived. Because of advances in DVR technology and DVD storage, it is now technically possible to save a feature length film from cable to a TiVo and then burn it onto a DVD. How will the industry respond to this?

The United States is currently in the process of transferring to a new system of Digital Television (DTV). Content owners such as Hollywood film producers are demanding that DRM technologies be built into the system in order to afford them a level of content protection. The FCC and Congress are in intense negotiations with broadcasters, rights owners, and device manufacturers to set up a system that works for consumers as well as for suppliers. Many consumers are not aware that they pay a surcharge for every blank audio tape or CD they purchase. Collected revenues from this surcharge go to music publishers to compensate recording artists for the fact that many people duplicate works without authorization.

Most of today's music download sites encrypt music files and embed codes that limit the number of times they can be copied and the devices on which they can be played. Apple's FairPlay DRM system is used on the iTunes Music Store, Microsoft's DRM-enabled Windows Media Player 9 is used on Walmart's Music Download site, and RealNetworks secure RealAudio (.rax) format protects files downloaded from the RealPlayer Music Store. These formats are not compatible with each other and require different players. Music from several different download sites cannot be compiled into a single playlist. Commercial movie DVDs use CSS (Content-Scrambling System) encryption to make DVDs playable only on authorized DVD players equipped with decryption key circuitry. Movies purchased in the United States and Canada cannot be played on devices manufactured for the European or Asian markets, so continent-jumping travelers have to take along their DVD players or abandon their DVD collections.

Despite DRM technologies and the inconveniences imposed on consumers, digital piracy remains rampant. Current DRM technologies do not seem able to distinguish between pirates and legitimate consumers. As a result, DRM technologies essentially pose restrictions on consumers that go beyond the intended limitations of copyright law. Circumventing DRM is possible and it would seem OK to do so for legitimate reasons, such as making a backup copy. However, the Digital Millennium Copyright Act, makes it illegal to circumvent any technological measure that controls access to a work. The current status of DRM seems to conflict with the original intent of copyright law, which is to allow consumers to manipulate and copy works for their own use. Can technology eventually offer a solution that prevents piracy, but allows individuals to exercise their rights to fair use of copyrighted materials?

▼ EXPAND THE IDEAS

1. Do sites like the iTunes Music Store provide consumers with enough flexibility for copying files and creating playlists? Do you subscribe to such a service? Do you think that this is the future of music distribution? Write a brief essay on the topic.

2. Why are digital rights management advocates concerned about DTV? Use the Internet to research the current state, vist the EFF.org and FCC.org and FCC.gov Web sites and write a brief report on your findings.

3. Explain why DRM technologies will evolve to meet the continuing technologies that enable piracy. Research new DRM technologies and write a brief report.

At the moment, digital camera manufacturers and, in fact, most digital camera models save the captured image—the raw data—in a format that is proprietary to that manufacturer or that camera. Digital camera users see the raw data as a negative. So, just as you could take a film negative to any developer and have it processed, digital camera users want to be able to take a digital negative and use it with any photo-related media or photo-editing software.

The bothersome question becomes—will future software be able to read the digital negatives stored using proprietary file formats? This is an ongoing question for all digital media, and is similar to the issue of trying to standardize DVD formats. Adobe is hoping that its new .DNG format will become the new industry standard, meaning that all digital cameras would save the raw image using the .DNG format (see Figure 8). If the digital negative (.DNG) format catches on, it will be a great breakthrough for photo-enthusiasts and photo-professionals. Why? Because digital camera users who want to archive their digital negatives could use the .DNG format to do just that, without the worry that the format won't be able to read in the future.

FIGURE 8: Digital Negative (DNG)

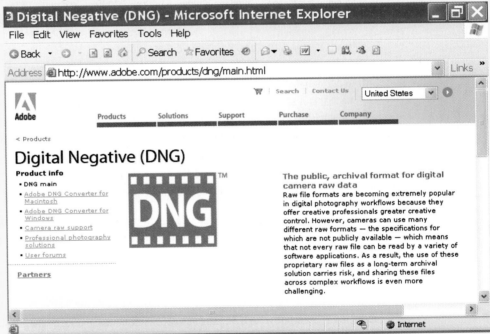

1. Log onto the Internet and search for information on standards for digital images. What is being done to create file formats that can be created by all cameras and edited in various software packages? Research DNG. What is being done to further the standard? Which companies are working on this standard? What would be the benefits?

2. Use your favorite search engine to find information about new technologies in digital cameras. What are the current specifications for digital photography? How are consumers embracing more elaborate digital cameras? Summarize the state of the consumer market for high end and middle of the market cameras. What features are new? Which features only exist in high-end cameras?

3. Review digital image manipulation software packages that are available today. Make a comparison chart for at least three software packages. Write a summary paragraph indicating how the packages are alike, how they are different, and why a consumer might purchase one over the other.

For most of history, banks used low-tech methods to track one of the world's most cherished commodities—wealth. Checking accounts were in widespread use as early as 1550, when wealthy Dutch traders began depositing money with cashiers for safekeeping. The use of printed checks became popular in England in the late 18th century—so popular that banks found it difficult to process a steadily increasing stream of checks, including those drawn on accounts from other banks.

An unverified story that has become part of bank lore describes the origin of a solution to the check processing problem. As the story goes, a London bank messenger stopped for coffee and got to talking with a messenger from another bank. Realizing that they were delivering checks drawn on each other's banks, the two messengers decided to exchange checks there in the coffee house. This event evolved into a system of check clearinghouses where representatives from various banks met periodically to exchange checks and reconcile totals in cash. By 1839, British clearinghouses were annually processing in excess of £954 million of checks—equivalent to $250 billion in today's money.

Bank clearinghouses were described in an essay, "The Economy of Machinery and Manufactures", written by Charles Babbage in 1832. He also included a reference to the "possibility of performing arithmetical calculations by machinery" along with a description of the Difference Engine, then under construction in his workshop.

This dream of automated check clearing did not, however, become reality until more than a century later when S. Clark Beise, senior vice president at Bank of America, contracted with Stanford Research Institute (SRI) to develop a computer system to automate check processing. SRI completed a prototype in 1955 that used mechanical sorting equipment to queue up each check and MICR (Magnetic Ink Character Recognition) technology to read check numbers. In 1959, the first ERMA (Electronic Recording Machine-Accounting) system went into service. With ERMA handling calculations, 9 employees could handle the job that once required 50 people. By 1966, 32 regional ERMA systems operated by Bank of America were processing more than 750 million checks per year. ERMA and similar check processing technologies quickly integrated with bank transaction processing systems to become the bedrock of today's banking technology.

Output from check sorting machines can be submitted to the Automated Clearing House (ACH) network, which offers a secure, batch-oriented data exchange system that can be accessed by financial institutions. On a daily basis, banks submit check data and receive a report of balances due to other banks. These balances can be reconciled by electronic funds transfer over the Federal Reserve's FedWire telecommunications network.

An upswing in check fraud during the 1960s made it increasingly difficult to cash checks at local merchants. As an alternative to trying to cash checks at banks and local merchants, automatic teller machines (ATMs) were first installed in the 1970s. A typical ATM connects to a bank's front-end processor—a computer that maintains account balances for in-network customers and monitors the bank's main computer system for security.

Some ATMs exchange data with the front-end processor by using dedicated dial-up telephone lines. Other ATMs use always-on leased lines. Legacy protocols such as SNA and 3270 bisync, are being replaced by the standard Internet Protocol (IP) that can be routed through more affordable connections, such as cable, ISDN, DSL, or Internet VPN.

ATMs are expensive—not only to purchase a machine and install it, but also to operate it. Banks have offset this cost by charging transaction fees and reducing the number of bank tellers. Although bank tellers continue to accept deposits, process withdrawals, and cash payroll checks, they are increasingly pressed into customer service roles—opening new accounts, issuing ATM cards, resolving disputed transactions, and assisting customers who have lost bank cards or checkbooks. Despite this shift in job description, the number of bank teller jobs is expected to fall at least 10% by 2010.

ATMs offer access to bank services from convenient locations where customers shop, eat, and hang out with friends. The Internet takes banking convenience one step further and provides round-the-clock account access from customers' homes, schools, or work PCs. Today, most banks and credit unions offer some type of online banking (also called home banking, Internet banking, or electronic banking).

Basic online banking services allow customers to access checking account and bankcard activity, transfer funds between checking and savings accounts, view electronic images of checks and deposit slips, download and print monthly statements, and reorder checks. Customers can also pay bills online by scheduling payment dates and amounts. Many credit card and utility companies offer e-billing services that automatically forward electronic bills to customers' online banking accounts. For monthly fixed-amount bills, such as car loans, online banking offers automatic payment options that deduct funds from specified checking or savings accounts.

For managing assets more effectively, online banking sites also offer sophisticated tools, including account aggregation, stock quotes, rate alerts, and portfolio management programs. Most online banking sites are also compatible with personal finance software, such as Managing Your Money, QuickBooks, Microsoft Money, and AOL BankNOW, so that transaction data can be shuttled between customer's local computers and their online banking services.

A cadre of customer support personnel staff online help desks for customers with questions about online banking. Webmasters, computer security specialists, and network technicians are also part of banking's new job corps.

Online banking services are typically housed on a secure Web server, and customers are not allowed direct access to the bank's transaction processing system. Customer privacy is maintained by the use of passwords and SSL connections that encrypt data as it is sent to and from customers' browsers.

Successful banks are built on good business decisions. Bank managers are increasingly working with business intelligence tools to look for trends in customer behavior, analyze competing financial institutions, and examine current business practices. Tools for these activities include data warehouses that collect and organize data, data mining software that organizes and analyzes data in a meaningful way, and statistical tools that formulate comparisons and trendlines.

Today, banking rests on multilayered technologies that incorporate check processing equipment, transaction processing systems, business intelligence software, ACH networks, FedWire, ATM networks, the Internet, and Web servers. Many banking practices originated from batch check processing, and only gradually have banks begun to move to more modern online transaction processing (OLTP) systems that store scanned images of checks and instantly update accounts when a purchase is made or a bill is paid.

Most major banks now offer free online banking as part of their basic service to customers. As a banking customer, you can now manage your bank accounts through the convenience of the Internet, while sitting at any computer. You no longer have to go to a drive up window, an ATM, or into a bank lobby to see the balances in an account, transfer funds, or pay bills. See Figure 9. Many online bank services also offer tax and finance tips in addition to investment options.

As competing banks offer more services to their customers, online banking has become a very large selling point. Almost all banks offer free bill paying. After you set up your accounts, you can transfer money from your bank account to pay your bills with a simple click. Reconciling your bank statements is easy.

Some people are concerned about the security of online banking. They worry about the security of their accounts and about privacy issues, especially related to identity. Advances in technology continue to address issues such as authenticating users (is it really *you* accessing your money?), paper trails (I paid that bill, but there is no returned check), and fraud (where did my money go?). But how long will it be before users fully embrace online banking? Or, have they already?

FIGURE 9: Online Banking

1. Does your local bank offer online banking? What are the fees, if any? What are the services offered? Are there minimum balances for participation? Go to a local bank and get information about its online banking offerings. Write a brief summary of your findings.

2. What concerns do you have with online banking? Do you feel that the technology has advanced to the point that you can trust the security of the system? How are banks addressing these concerns and assuring their customers of the privacy and security of the systems? Research the issues and write a brief summary of your findings, include a discussion of advances that are taking place to maintain the integrity of the system in your report.

3. Do you use online banking? Why or why not? Summarize your reasons.

Glossary

10BaseT network ▶ An Ethernet network that uses twisted-pair cables with a maximum length of 100 meters and supports data transmission rates of 10 Mbps.

100BaseT network ▶ An Ethernet network that uses 100BaseT cables and supports data transmission rates of 100 Mbps.

24-bit bitmap ▶ A True Color graphic that requires 24 bits for each pixel, used for photographic-quality images that can include any of 16.7 million colors.

32-bit bitmap ▶ A True Color graphic that requires 32 bits for each pixel, used for photographic-quality images that can include any of 16.7 million colors.

3-D graphic ▶ A type of digital graphics format that represents a three-dimensional image in a two- dimensional space.

3-D graphics software ▶ The software used to create three-dimensional wireframe objects and render them into images.

802.11b ▶ A popular wireless network standard that operates between 200 and 400 Kbps, with a range of up to 300 feet.

Absolute reference ▶ In a worksheet formula, cell references (usually preceded by a $ symbol) that cannot change as a result of a move or copy operation.

Access time ▶ The estimated time for a storage device to locate data on a disk, usually measured in milliseconds.

Accounting and finance software ▶ A category of software that helps you keep a record of monetary transactions and investments.

Accounting software ▶ See Accounting and Finance Software.

Active matrix screen ▶ A type of LCD technology that produces a clear, sharp image because each pixel is controlled by its own transistor.

ActiveX control ▶ A compiled computer program that can be referenced from within an HTML document, downloaded, installed on your computer, and executed within the browser window to add interactive features to Web pages.

Ad-serving cookie ▶ A cookie distributed by marketing firms that is used to track activities at any site containing banner ads from that third party. Used to target ads to users, but privacy advocates can be worried that shopper profiles can be compiled, sold, and used for unauthorized purposes.

AES (Advanced Encryption System) ▶ An encryption standard based on the Rijndael encryption algorithm that uses three key sizes of 128, 192, or 256 bits.

AGP (accelerated graphics port) ▶ A type of interface, or slot, that provides a high-speed pathway for advanced graphics.

AIF ▶ See Audio Interchange Format.

ALU (arithmetic logic unit) ▶ The part of the CPU that performs arithmetic and logical operations on the numbers stored in its registers.

Always-on connection ▶ A permanent connection, as opposed to a connection that is established and dropped as needed.

Analog device ▶ A device that operates on continuously varying data, such as a dimmer switch or a watch with a sweep second hand.

Analog video camera ▶ A device used to collect, store, and process video in an analog format on a magnetic tape.

Animated GIF ▶ A type of GIF image that displays a sequence of frames to create the appearance of continuous motion.

Antivirus software ▶ A computer program used to scan a computer's memory and disks to identify, isolate, and eliminate viruses.

Application software ▶ Computer programs that help you perform a specific task such as word processing. Also called application programs, applications, or programs.

Archive ▶ The process of moving infrequently used data from a primary storage device to a storage medium such as a CD-R.

ARCnet (Attached Resource Computer network) ▶ One of the oldest, simplest, and least expensive LAN technologies that permits twisted-pair, coax, and fiber-optic cables to be mixed on the same network to connect up to 255 workstations.

ASF (Advanced Streaming Format) ▶ Microsoft's video format for streaming video on the Web.

ASCII (American Standard Code for Information Interchange) ▶ A code that represents characters as a series of 1s and 0s. Most computers use ASCII code to represent text, making it possible to transfer data between computers.

Assistive technology ▶ Products available for individuals with special needs, especially in the areas of auditory, vision, cognitive, mobility, and ergonomic workspaces to make the technology accessible to all regardless of ability.

Asynchronous protocol ▶ A data transmission method in which the sender and receiver are not synchronized by a clock signal, and which uses start and stop bits to control the beginning and ending of transmissions.

ATM (asynchronous transfer mode) ▶ A network technology that transmits all packets in a message over the same channel.

Audio editing software ▶ A category of software that includes sound playback as well as recording capabilities. Windows and Mac OS operating system utilities typically supply audio editing software. Menus provide additional digital editing features, such as speed control, volume adjustments, clipping, and mixing of sounds.

Audio Interchange Format (.aif) ▶ A popular cross-platform audio format developed by Apple.

Authentication Security feature ▶ A way to restrict access to computer systems; used to positively identify a person as an authorized user by verifying the person through one of three methods: something a person carries, something a person knows, or some unique physical characteristic.

Automated System Recovery disk ▶ Created by the Windows XP Backup utility, or any operating system as a method for recovering system or data lost in a disk crash.

Automatic recalculation ▶ A feature found in spreadsheet software that automatically recalculates every formula after a user makes a change to any cell.

AVI (Audio Video Interleave) ▶ A video file format developed by Microsoft that is the most common format for desktop video on the PC.

B2B (business-to-business) ▶ An e-commerce exchange of products, services, or information between businesses.

B2C (business-to-consumer) ▶ An e-commerce transaction involving products, services, or information between businesses and consumers.

B2G (business-to-government) ▶ An e-commerce transaction involving products, services, or information between businesses and governments.

Backup ▶ A duplicate copy of a file, disk, or tape. Also refers to a Windows utility that allows you to create and restore backups.

Backup software ▶ The software used to copy program and data files to a storage media for backup purposes; most provide options that make it easy to schedule periodic backups, define a set of files that you want to regularly back up, and automate the restoration process.

Bandwidth ▶ The data transmission capacity of a communications channel.

Banner ad ▶ An advertisement typically embedded at the top of a Web page.

Baud rate ▸ The transmission speed of a modem measured as the number of times per second that a signal in a communications channel varies; a 300-baud modem's signal changes state 300 times each second; however, each baud doesn't necessarily carry one bit, so a 300-baud modem might be able to transmit more than 300 bits per second.

Beep code ▸ A series of audible beeps used to announce diagnostic test results during the boot process.

Benchmark ▸ A test used to measure computer hardware or software performance.

Binary digits ▸ Series of 1s and 0s representing data.

Binary number system ▸ A method for representing numbers using only two digits, 0 and 1; contrast this system to the decimal system, which uses ten digits: 0, 1, 2, 3, 4, 5, 6, 7, 8, and 9.

Biometrics ▸ A method of personal identification based on some unique physical trait, such as a fingerprint or the pattern of blood vessels in the retina of the eye.

Bit ▸ A bit is the smallest unit of information handled by a computer. A bit can hold one of two values, either a 0 or a 1. Eight bits comprise a byte, which can represent a letter or number.

Bit depth ▸ The number of bits that determines the range of possible colors that can be assigned to each pixel. For example, an 8-bit color depth can create 256 colors. Also called color depth.

Bitmap graphic ▸ An image, such as a digital photo, that is stored as a gridwork of colored dots.

Bitmap image ▸ See Bitmap graphic.

Blog ▸ Derived from the phrase "WeB LOG," refers to a personal journal focusing on a single topic or covering a variety of issues posted on the Web for access by the general public.

Bluetooth ▸ A wireless technology used in conjunction with standard Ethernet networks that allows data transfer rates between 200 and 400 Kbps, up to a maximum range of 35 feet.

BMP ▸ The native bitmap graphic file format of the Microsoft Windows OS.

Bookmark ▸ A link to a Web page; a list of saved URLS in a browser. Click the URL to return to the page. Also called Favorites.

Body section ▸ A part of a Web page that begins with the <BODY> HTML tag and contains the text, graphics, and links.

Boot disk ▸ A floppy disk or CD that contains the essential instructions needed for the boot process.

Boot process ▸ The sequence of events that occurs within a computer system between the time the user starts the computer and the time it is ready to process commands.

Boot sector virus ▸ A computer virus that infects the sectors on a disk containing the data a computer uses during the boot process.

Bootstrap program ▸ A program stored in ROM that loads and initializes the operating system on a computer.

Broadband ▸ A term used to refer to communications channels that have high bandwidth.

Broken link ▸ A non-functioning hyperlink on a Web page.

Browser ▸ A program that communicates with a Web server and displays Web pages.

Brute force method ▸ A method of breaking encryption code by trying all possible encryption keys, usually employing supercomputers.

Bus topology ▸ A network topology that uses a common backbone to connect all network devices. The backbone functions as a shared communication link, which carries network data, and stops at each end of the network with a "terminator."

Byte ▸ An 8-bit unit of information that represents a single character.

C2C (consumer-to-consumer) ▸ An e-commerce exchange of products, services, or information between consumers.

Cable ▸ Used to connect a peripheral device to a computer through a port.

Cable modem ▸ A communications device that can be used to connect a computer to the Internet via the cable TV infrastructure.

Cable modem service ▸ Internet access offered to a cable company's customers for an additional monthly charge. The connection usually requires two pieces of equipment: a network card and a cable modem.

Cache ▸ Special high-speed memory that gives the CPU rapid access to data that would otherwise be accessed from disk. Also called RAM cache or cache memory.

CAD software ▸ A special type of 3-D graphics software designed for architects and engineers who use computers to create blueprints and product specifications.

Card reader ▸ A small device connected to your computer's USB or serial port to read the data that's contained in a flash memory card; acts just like an external disk drive by treating your flash memory card like a floppy disk.

Cascading style sheet (CSS) ▸ A template that can be set to control the layout and design of Web pages.

CD ▸ See CD-ROM disc.

CD-DA (compact disc digital audio) ▸ The format for commercial music CDs. Music is typically recorded on audio CDs by the manufacturer.

CD drive ▸ See CD-ROM drive.

CD-R ▸ An acronym for compact disc-recordable. CD-R is a type of optical disc technology that allows the user to create CD-ROMs and audio CDs.

CD-ROM disc ▸ An optical storage media that can store up to 700 MB of data. There are a wide variety of CDs including CD-ROM, CD-R, and CD-RW.

CD-ROM drive ▸ A storage device that uses laser technology to read data from a CD-ROM.

CD-RW ▸ An acronym for compact disc-rewritable. CD-RW is a type of optical disc technology that allows the user to write data onto a CD, then change that data.

CD-writer ▸ A general term for recordable CD technologies such as CD-R and CD-RW.

Cell ▸ In spreadsheet terminology, the intersection of a column and a row. In cellular communications, a limited geographical area surrounding a cellular phone tower.

Cell reference ▸ The column letter and row number that designates the location of a worksheet cell. For example, the cell reference C5 refers to a cell in column C, row 5.

Cellular-ready modem ▸ A device that is packaged as a PC card that slips into the PCMCIA port of a notebook or tablet computer used to dial your ISP through a plan offered by your cellular phone provider.

Central processing unit ▸ See CPU.

Character data ▸ Letters, symbols, or numerals that will not be used in arithmetic operations (name, social security number, etc.).

Chat group ▸ A discussion in which a group of people communicates online simultaneously.

Checksum ▸ A value calculated by combining all the bytes in a file that is used by virus detection programs to determine whether any bytes have been altered.

Ciphertext ▸ An encrypted message.

Circuit switching ▸ The method used by the telephone network to temporarily connect one telephone with another for the duration of a call.

CISC (complex instruction set computer) ▸ A general-purpose processor chip designed to handle a wider array of instructions than a RISC chip.

Clear GIF ▸ A 1x1 pixel graphic on a Web page that can be used to set cookies to third party Web sites. Unlike ad-serving cookies, you don't have to click a banner ad to receive a GIF activated cookie. Also called Web bug.

Click-through rate ▸ The number of times that site visitors click an ad on a Web site to connect to the advertiser's site. The hosting merchant is paid a small fee for each click through.

Client ▸ A computer or software that requests information from another computer or server.

Client/server network ▸ A network where processing is split between workstations (clients) and the server.

Client-side script ▸ Scripting statement, embedded in an HTML document, that is executed by a client's browser.

Client/server network ▸ A network where processing is split between workstations (clients) and the server.

Clip art ▸ Graphics designed to be inserted into documents, Web pages, and worksheets, usually available in CD-ROM or Web-based collections.

Cluster ▸ A group of devices that share a server or group of servers.

Cluster ▸ A group of sectors on a storage medium that, when accessed as a group, speeds up data access.

Cluster computing ▸ System that allows computers to work together to maximize performance.

CMOS (complementary metal oxide semiconductor) memory ▸ A type of battery-powered integrated circuit that holds semi-permanent configuration data.

CMYK color ▸ A printing technology used by most ink jet printers that requires only cyan (blue), magenta (pink), yellow, and black inks to create a printout that appears to have thousands of colors.

Coaxial cable ▸ A type of cable with BNC connectors made of a center wire surrounded by a grounded shield of braided wire and used to connect nodes on a network. Also called coax cable.

Codec (COmpressor/DECom-pressor) ▸ Hardware or software routine that compresses and decompresses digital graphics, sound, and video files.

Code morphing ▸ Software used by Transmeta in processor development.

Color depth ▸ The number of bits that determines the range of possible colors that can be assigned to each pixel. For example, an 8-bit color depth can create 256 colors. Also called bit depth.

Color palette ▸ The selection of colors used in graphics software.

Commercial software ▸ Copyrighted computer applications sold to consumers for profit.

Communications channel ▸ Any pathway between the sender and receiver; channel may refer to a physical medium or a frequency.

Communications network ▸ A combination of hardware, software, and connecting links that transports data.

Communications protocol ▸ A set of rules for ensuring orderly and accurate transmission and reception of data.

Communications satellite ▸ Satellite used to send to and receive data from ground stations.

CompactFlash (CF) card ▸ A solid state storage device that is about the size of a matchbook and provides high storage capacities and access speeds; includes a built-in controller that reads and writes data within the solid state grid; are ideal for use on high-end digital cameras that require megabytes of storage for each photo.

Compact Privacy Policy ▸ The HTTP header defined in a standard set of security tags that becomes part of the header for every cookie, that describes how cookie data is used by a Web site.

Compiler ▸ Software that translates a program written in a high-level language into low-level instructions before the program is executed.

Compression algorithm ▸ The steps required to shrink data in a file and restore it to its original state.

Compression ratio ▸ A measurement of the amount of shrinkage when data is compressed.

Compression software ▸ A type of software, such as WinZip, that effectively reduces the size of files. See file compression utility.

Computer ▸ A device that accepts input, processes data, stores data, and produces output.

Computer-aided design software (CAD) ▸ A type of 3-D graphics software designed for architects and engineers who use computers to create blueprints and product specifications.

Computer file ▸ A single collection of data stored on a storage medium.

Computer language ▸ A set of tools that allows a programmer to write instructions that a computer can execute.

Computer network ▸ A collection of computers and related devices, connected in a way that allows them to share data, hardware, and software.

Computer program ▸ A set of detailed, step-by-step instructions that tells a computer how to solve a problem or carry out a task.

Computer programmer ▸ A person who codes or writes computer programs.

Computer projection device ▸ An output device that produces a large display of the information shown on the computer screen.

Computer system ▸ The hardware, peripheral devices, and software working together to input data, process data, store data, and produce output.

Computer virus ▸ A program designed to attach itself to a file, reproduce, and spread from one file to another, destroying data, displaying an irritating message, or otherwise disrupting computer operations.

Concurrent-user license ▸ Legal permission for an organization to use a certain number of copies of a software program at the same time.

Control unit ▸ The part of the ALU that directs and coordinates processing.

Controller ▸ A circuit board in a hard drive that positions the disk and read-write heads to locate data.

Cookie ▸ A message sent from a Web server to a browser and stored on a user's hard disk, usually containing information about the user.

Copy Disk utility ▸ A utility program that duplicates the contents of an entire floppy disk.

Copyright ▸ A form of legal protection that grants certain exclusive rights to the author of a program or the owner of the copyright.

Copyright notice ▸ A line such as "Copyright 2002 ACME Co." that identifies a copyright holder.

CPU (central processing unit) ▸ The main processing unit in a computer, consisting of circuitry that executes instructions to process data.

Cracker ▸ Refers to anyone who writes malicious code, including viruses, worms, and Trojan horses, to use a computer to gain unauthorized access to data, steal information, or crash a computer system.

Cropping ▸ The process of selecting and removing part of an image.

CRT (cathode ray tube) ▸ A display technology that uses a large vacuum tube similar to that used in television sets.

Cryptographic algorithm ▸ A specific procedure for encrypting and decrypting data.

Cryptographic key ▸ A specific word, number, or phrase that must be used to encrypt or decrypt data.

CSMA/CD (Carrier Sense Multiple Access with Collision Detection) ▸ A method of responding to an attempt by two devices to use a data channel simultaneously; used by Ethernet networks.

Cursor ▸ A symbol that marks the user's place on the screen and shows where typing will appear.

Cylinder ▸ A vertical stack of tracks that is the basic storage bin for a hard disk drive.

Cyberterrorism ▸ Threatening computer systems using viruses and worms to destroy data and otherwise disrupt computer-based operations, including critical national infrastructures such as power grids and telecommunications systems.

Cyclic redundancy check ▸ An error-checking protocol used by some LANs to ensure accurate delivery of data.

Darwin ▸ Open source kernel for the Mac OS X.

Data ▸ In the context of computing and data management, the symbols that a computer uses to represent facts and ideas.

Data bus ▸ An electronic pathway or circuit that connects the electronic components (such as the processor and RAM) on a computer's motherboard.

Data center ▸ A specialized facility designed to house and protect computer systems and data; typically includes special security features, such as fireproof construction, earthquake proof foundations, sprinkler systems, power generators, secure doors and windows, and anti-static floor coverings.

Data compression ▸ The process of condensing data so that it requires fewer bytes of storage space.

Data file ► A file containing words, numbers, or pictures that the user can view, edit, save, send, or print.

Data module ► A file linked to a program that provides data necessary for certain functions of the program.

Data representation ► The use of electrical signals, marks, or binary digits to represent character, numeric, visual, or audio data.

Data security ► Techniques that provide protection for data.

Data transfer rate ► The amount of data that a storage device can move from a storage medium to computer memory in one second.

Database ► A collection of information that may be stored in more than one file.

Database software ► The category of software designed for tasks associated with maintaining and accessing data stored in files in the form of a database. Sometimes called data management software.

Decryption ► The process of converting ciphertext into plaintext.

Defragmentation utility ► A software tool used to rearrange the files on a disk so that they are stored in contiguous clusters.

Demodulation ► The process of restoring a received signal to its original state. For example, when a modem changes an audio signal back to a digital pulse.

Denial of Service attack ► The result of hackers sending malicious software that is designed to overwhelm a network's processing capabilities, shutting it down.

Density ► A measure of an image, expressed as dots per inch (dpi) for a printer or scanner, or as pixels per inch (ppi) on a monitor. The denser the grid, the smaller the image will appear.

DES (Data Encryption Standard) ► An encryption method based on an algorithm developed by IBM and the U.S. National Security Agency that uses 56-bit symmetric key encryption.

Desktop computer ► Computer small enough to fit on a desk and built around a single processor chip.

Desktop operating system ► An operating system, such as Windows XP or Mac OS X, that is specifically designed for personal computers.

Desktop publishing software (DTP) ► A category of software used to create high-quality output suitable for commercial printing. DTP software provides precise control over layout.

Desktop video ► Video stored in digital format on a PC's hard disk or CD.

Device driver ► The software that provides the computer with the means to control a peripheral device.

DHTML (dynamic HTML) ► A variation of the HTML format that allows elements of Web pages to be changed while they are being viewed.

Dial-up connection ► A connection that uses a phone line to establish a temporary Internet connection.

Dictionary-based compression ► A data compression scheme that uses a codeword to represent common sequences of characters.

Differential backup ► A copy of all the files that changed since the last full backup of a disk.

Digital ► Any system that works with discrete data, such as 0s and 1s, in contrast to analog.

Digital camera ► An input device that records an image in digital format.

Digital certificate ► A security method that identifies the author of an ActiveX control.

Digital device ► A device that works with discrete (distinct or separate) numbers or digits.

Digital electronics ► Circuitry that's designed to work with digital signals.

Digital signal processor ► Circuitry that is used to process, record, and playback audio files.

Digital video camera ► A device used to collect, store, and process video in a digital format.

Digital video recorder (DVR) ► A device that allows viewers to digitally record TV and video. Features include pause, rewind, and instant replay of broadcast TV.

Digitize ► The conversion of non-digital information or media to a digital format through the use of a scanner, sampler, or other input device.

Digitizing tablet ► A device that provides a flat surface for a paper-based drawing, and a "pen" used to create hand-drawn vector drawings.

DIMM (dual in-line memory module) ► A small circuit board that holds RAM chips. A DIMM has a 64-bit path to the memory chips.

DIP (dual in-line package) ► A chip configuration characterized by a rectangular body with numerous plugs along its edge.

Directory ► A list of files contained on a computer storage device.

Direct satellite service (DSS) ► A service that uses a geosynchronous or low earth orbit satellite to send television, voice, or computer data directly to satellite dishes owned by individuals.

Direct source input device ► An input device, such as a bar code reader, that collects data directly from a document or object; used to reduce the incidence of operator error.

Disaster Recovery Plan ► A step-by step plan that describes the methods used to secure data against disaster, and explains how an organization will recover lost data if and when a disaster occurs.

Disk density ► The closeness of the particles on a disk surface. As density increases, the particles are packed more tightly together and are usually smaller.

Display device ► The main output device for a computer; one of two key components of a display system—a monitor or a screen uses one of three technologies: CRT, LCD, gas plasma, and OLED.

Distribution disks ► One or more floppy disks or CDs that contain programs and data, which can be installed to a hard disk.

Dithering ► A means of reducing the size of a graphics file by reducing the number of colors. Dithering uses patterns composed of two or more colors to produce the illusion of additional colors and shading.

DMA (direct memory access) ► A technology that allows a computer to transfer data directly from a drive into RAM, without intervention from the processor.

DOCSIS (Data Over Cable Services Interface Specification) ► A security technology used for filtering packets to certain ports.

Document production software ► Computer programs that assist the user in composing, editing, designing, and printing documents.

Domain name ► An identifying name by which host computers on the Internet are familiarly known; for example, coca-cola.com. Also referred to as fully qualified domain name.

Domain name server ► Computers that host the domain name system database.

Domain name system ► A large database of unique IP addresses that correspond with domain names.

DOS (disk operating system) ► The operating system software shipped with the first IBM PCs and used on millions of computers until the introduction of Microsoft Windows.

Dot matrix printer ► A printer that creates characters and graphics by striking an inked ribbon with small wires called "pins," generating a fine pattern of dots.

Dot pitch ► The diagonal distance between colored dots on a display screen. Measured in millimeters, dot pitch helps to determine the quality of an image displayed on a monitor.

Double-layer DVD ► DVDs that have storage on both sides of the DVD to bring storage capacity up to 8.5 GB.

Downloading ► The process of transferring a copy of a file from a remote computer to a local computer's disk drive.

Dpi (dots per inch) ► Printer resolution as measured by the number of dots it can print per linear inch.

Drawing software ► Programs that are used to create images with lines, shapes, and colors, such as logos or diagrams.

Drive bay ► An area within a computer system unit that can accommodate an additional storage device.

Drive mapping ► In network terminology, assigning a drive letter to a network server disk drive.

DSL (Digital Subscriber Line) ▶ A high-speed Internet connection that uses existing telephone lines, requiring close proximity to a switching station.

DSL modem ▶ A device that sends to and receives digital data from computers over telephone lines.

DSLAM (DSL Access Multiplexor) ▶ Special equipment used to interpret, separate, and route digital data in telephone lines for DSL providers.

DSS (Digital Satellite System) ▶ A type of Internet connection that uses a network of satellites to transmit data.

DTD (Document Type Definition) file ▶ A type of file that defines how markup tags are interpreted by a browser.

Duty cycle ▶ Determines how many pages a printer is able to print out; is usually measured in pages per month.

DVD authoring software ▶ Software tools for creating DVDs.

DVD (digital video disc or digital versatile disc) ▶ An optical storage medium similar in appearance and technology to a CD-ROM but with higher storage capacity.

DVD drive ▶ An optical storage device that reads data from CD-ROM and DVD disks.

DVD+R (digital versatile disc recordable) ▶ A DVD disc that stores data using recordable technology similar to a CD-R, but with DVD.

DVD+RW (digital versatile disc rewritable) ▶ A DVD disk that stores data using rewritable technology similar to CD-RW, but with DVD storage.

DVD-ROM ▶ A DVD disc that contains data that has been permanently stamped on the disc surface.

DVD-Video (digital versatile disc video) ▶ The format for commercial DVDs that contain feature-length films.

DVD-writer ▶ A device that can be used to create and copy CDs and DVDs.

Dye sublimation printer ▶ An expensive, color-precise printer that heats ribbons containing color to produce consistent, photograph-quality images.

Dynamic IP address ▶ A temporarily assigned IP address usually provided by an ISP.

E911 (Enhanced 911) ▶ Technology that provides 911 dispatchers with information, such as the caller's location, from wireless calls.

Ear training software ▶ The category of software that targets musicians and music students who want to learn to play by ear, develop tuning skills, recognize notes and keys, and develop other musical skills.

EBCDIC (Extended Binary-Coded Decimal Interchange Code) ▶ A method by which digital computers, usually mainframes, represent character data.

E-commerce (electronic commerce) ▶ A business connected over the Internet, including online shopping, linking businesses to businesses (sometimes called e-business or B2B), online stock trading, and electronic auctions.

Educational software ▶ A category of software that helps you learn and practice new skills.

Electronic Serial Number (ESN) ▶ A unique number that is printed on the back of a cellular modem or other electronic devices used to activate service through a provider.

Electronic wallet ▶ Software that stores and processes customer information needed for an e-commerce transaction.

EIDE (enhanced integrated drive electronics) ▶ A type of drive that features high storage capacity and fast data transfer.

E-mail (electronic mail) ▶ A single electronic message or the entire system of computers and software that handles electronic messages transmitted between computers over a communications network.

E-mail account ▶ A service that provides an e-mail address and mailbox.

E-mail address ▶ The unique address for each mailbox on the Internet, which typically consists of a user ID, an @ symbol, and the name of the computer that maintains the mailbox.

E-mail attachment ▶ A separate file that is transmitted along with an e-mail message.

E-mail authentication software ▶ A technology, such as DomainKeys and Caller ID for E-Mail, that helps eliminate domain spoofing and increases the effectiveness of spam filters by verifying the sender of an e-mail message.

E-mail client software ▶ A category of software that is installed on a client computer and has access to e-mail servers on a network. This software is used to compose, send, and read e-mail messages.

E-mail message ▶ A computer file containing a letter or memo that is transmitted electronically via a communications network.

E-mail server ▶ A computer that uses special software to store and send e-mail messages over the Internet.

E-mail spoofing ▶ The forging of another person's or company's e-mail address.

E-mail system ▶ The collection of computers and software that works together to provide e-mail services.

Encryption ▶ The process of scrambling or hiding information so that it cannot be understood without the key necessary to change it back into its original form.

Ethernet ▶ A type of network on which network nodes are connected by coaxial cable or twisted-pair wire; the most popular network architecture, it typically transmits data at 10 or 100 megabits per second.

Ethernet card ▶ A type of network interface card (NIC), or network adapter, designed to support Ethernet protocols sending data to and from network devices such as workstations or printers over the network usually using cables.

Exa- ▶ Prefix for a quintillion.

Executable file ▶ A file, usually with an .exe extension, containing instructions that tell a computer how to perform a specific task.

Expansion bus ▶ The segment of the data bus that transports data between RAM and peripheral devices.

Expansion card ▶ A circuit board that is plugged into a slot on a PC motherboard to add extra functions, devices, or ports.

Expansion port ▶ A socket into which the user plugs a cable from a peripheral device, allowing data to pass between the computer and the peripheral device.

Expansion slot ▶ A socket or slot on a PC motherboard designed to hold a circuit board called an expansion card.

Extended ASCII ▶ Similar to ASCII but with 8-bit character representation instead of 7-bit, allowing for an additional 128 characters.

Extensible ▶ A term used when describing XML tags that define fields of data by explicitly identifying a particular kind of information; means individual users and groups of users can create their own tags and even their own markup languages.

External link ▶ A hyperlink to a location outside the Web site.

External style sheet ▶ A template that contains formatting specifications for a group of Web pages.

External video ▶ A video on the Web that downloads and opens in a media player window when its link is clicked.

Extranet ▶ A network similar to a private internet that also allows outside users access.

Favorites ▶ A list of URLs for Web sites that you can create for your browser to store so that you can revisit those sites easily.

FDDI (Fiber Distributed Data Interconnect) ▶ A high-speed network that uses fiber-optic cables to link workstations.

Fiber-optic cable ▶ A bundle of thin tubes of glass used to transmit data as pulses of light.

Field ▶ The smallest meaningful unit of information contained in a data file.

Field Emission Display (FED) ▶ Technology used in developing flat panel displays.

File ▶ A named collection of data (such as a computer program, document, or graphic) that exists on a storage medium, such as a hard disk, floppy disk, or CD-ROM.

File allocation table (FAT) ▶ A special file that is used by the operating system to store the physical location of all the files on a storage medium, such as a hard disk or floppy disk.

File compression utility ▸ A type of data compression software that shrinks one or more files into a single file that occupies less storage space than the separate files.

File date ▸ Saved as part of the file information, the date on which a file was created or last modified; useful if you have created several versions of a file and want to make sure that you know which version is the most recent.

File format ▸ The method of organization used to encode and store data in a computer. Text formats include DOC and TXT. Graphics formats include BMP, TIFF, GIF, and PCX.

File header ▸ Saved as part of the file, information that can be read by the computer, but never appears on the screen on the about code that was used to represent the file data.

File management software ▸ A category of operating system software that helps the user organize and find files and folders on the hard drive or other storage media.

File management utility ▸ Software, such as Windows Explorer, that helps users locate, rename, move, copy, and delete files.

File-naming conventions ▸ A set of rules established by the operating system that must be followed to create a valid filename.

File size ▸ The physical size of a file on a storage medium, usually measured in kilobytes (KB).

File specification ▸ A combination of the drive letter, subdirectory, filename, and extension that identifies a file (for example, A:\word\ filename.doc). Also called a path.

File system ▸ A system that is used by an operating system to keep files organized.

File virus ▸ A classification of computer virus to describe those viruses that infect application program files.

Filename ▸ A set of letters or numbers that identifies a file.

Finder ▸ On computers with Mac OS, the file management utility that helps you view a list of files, find files, move files from one place to another, make copies of files, delete files, and rename files.

Filename extension ▸ A set of letters and/or numbers added to the end of a filename that helps to identify the file contents or file type.

File virus ▸ A computer virus that infects executable files, such as programs with .exe filename extensions.

FireWire port ▸ A port on a digital camera or computer used to transfer photo data. Also called IEEE-1394 port.

Flash animation ▸ A proprietary technology developed by Macromedia; it is one of the most popular animation formats and provides more flexibility than animated GIFs and can be used for more complex animations. You have to download the Flash client software which is free and required for viewing flash animation.

Flash graphics ▸ A popular vector graphics format developed by Macromedia that can be used for still images or animations.

Flash memory ▸ A type of memory module that can store data without power consumption. It can be reused, making it popular for digital camera memory.

Floppy disk ▸ A removable magnetic storage medium, typically 3.5" in size, with a capacity of 1.44 MB.

Floppy disk drive ▸ A storage device that writes data on, and reads data from, floppy disks.

Floppy disk adapter ▸ A device that contains a slot for a flash memory module that, when inserted into a floppy disk drive, enables users to transfer data to their PCs.

FLOPS (Floating poing operations per second) ▸ Meausre of processing speed.

Folder ▸ The subdirectory, or subdivision, of a directory that can contain files or other folders.

Font ▸ A typeface or style of lettering, such as Arial, Times New Roman, and Gothic.

Footer ▸ In a document, text that you specify to appear in the bottom margin of every page.

Force feedback technology ▸ Allows you to feel the motion coming back through the pointing device.

Format ▸ Refers to how all text, pictures, titles, and page numbers appear on the page.

Formatting tag ▸ HTML code that is used to change the appearance of text.

Formula ▸ In spreadsheet terminology, a combination of numbers and symbols that tells the computer how to use the contents of cells in calculations.

Fragmented file ▸ A file stored in scattered, noncontiguous clusters on a disk.

Frame ▸ An outline or boundary frequently defining a box. For document production software, a predefined area into which text or graphics may be placed.

Frame rate ▸ Refers to the number of frames displayed per second in a video or film.

Free Space Optics (FSO) ▸ A technology being used to bridge the connection between businesses and the Internet's fiber optic backbone that uses lasers to provide optical bandwidth connections with line of sight technology and can be used with various protocols.

Freeware ▸ Copyrighted software that is given away by the author or owner.

Frequency ▸ The number of times that a wave oscillates (moves back and forth between two points) per second. Short wave lengths have high frequencies.

Full duplex ▸ A system that allows messages to be sent and received simultaneously.

Full system backup ▸ A copy of all the files for a specified backup job. Also called full backup.

Fully justified ▸ The horizontal alignment of text in which the text terminates exactly at both margins of the document.

Function ▸ In worksheets, a built-in formula for making a calculation. In programming, a section of code that manipulates data but is not included in the main sequential execution path of a program.

Function key ▸ One of the keys numbered F1 through F12 located at the top of the computer keyboard that activates program specific commands.

Gateway ▸ An electronic link that connects one computer system to another.

GIF (Graphics Interchange Format) ▸ A bitmap graphics file format popularized by CompuServe for use on the Web.

Giga- ▸ Prefix for a billion.

Gigabit (Gb) ▸ Approximately one billion bits.

Gigabyte (GB) ▸ One billion bytes, typically used to refer to RAM and hard disk capacity.

Gigahertz (GHz) ▸ A measure of frequency equivalent to one billion cycles per second, usually used to measure speed.

GMail ▸ The e-mail system provided by Google.

Gradient ▸ A smooth blending of shades of different colors from light to dark.

Graphical user interface (GUI) ▸ A type of user interface that features onscreen objects, such as menus and icons, manipulated by a mouse. Abbreviation is pronounced "gooey".

Graphics ▸ Any pictures, photographs, or images that can be manipulated or viewed on a computer.

Graphics card ▸ A circuit board inserted into a computer to handle the display of text, graphics, animation, and videos. Also called a video card.

Graphics software ▸ Computer programs for creating, editing, and manipulating images.

Graphics tablet ▸ A device that accepts input from a pressure-sensitive stylus and converts strokes into images on the screen.

Grayscale palette ▸ Digital images that are displayed in shades of gray, black, and white.

Groupware ▸ Business software designed to help several people collaborate on a single project using network or Internet connections.

Hacker ▸ Refers to anyone who writes malicious code, including viruses, worms, and Trojan horses, to use a computer to gain unauthorized access to data, steal information, or crash a computer system.

Half duplex ▸ A communications technique that allows the user to alternately send and receive transmissions.

Handheld computer ▸ A small, pocket-sized computer designed to run on its own power supply and provide users with basic applications.

Handshaking ▸ A process where a protocol helps two network devices communicate.

Hard disk ▸ See hard disk drive.

Hard disk drive ▸ A computer storage device that contains a large-capacity hard disk sealed inside the drive case. A hard disk is not the same as a 3.5" floppy disk that has a rigid plastic case.

Hard disk platter ▸ The component of a hard disk drive on which data is stored. It is a flat, rigid disk made of aluminum or glass and coated with a magnetic oxide.

Hardware ▸ The electronic and mechanical devices in a computer system.

Head crash ▸ A collision between the read-write head and the surface of the hard disk platter, resulting in damage to some of the data on the disk.

Header ▸ Text that you specify to appear in the top margin of every page automatically.

Head section ▸ A part of a Web page that begins with the <HEAD> HTML tag and contains information about global properties of the document.

Helper application ▸ A program that understands how to work with a specific file format.

High-level language ▸ A computer language that allows a programmer to write instructions using human-like language.

High-performance computing (HPC) ▸ Systems whose performance is measured in FLOPS or MIPS.

History list ▸ A list that is created by your browser of the sites you visited so that you can display and track your sessions or revisit the site by clicking the URL in the list.

Home page ▸ In a Web site, the document that is the starting, or entry, page. On an individual computer, the Web page that a browser displays each time it is started.

HomePLC ▸ A network that uses a building's existing power line cables to connect nodes.

HomePNA ▸ A network that uses a building's existing phone lines to connect nodes.

Horizontal market software ▸ Any computer program that can be used by many different kinds of businesses (for example, an accounting program).

Host computer ▸ A computer system that stores and processes data accessed by multiple terminals from remote locations. In Internet terminology, any computer connected to the Internet.

Hot spot ▸ A clickable image, photo, or diagram within an image map on a Web page.

Hotspot ▸ The range of network coverage in a public Wi-Fi network that provides open Internet access to the public. Any Wi-Fi equipped device that enters a hotspot can gain access to the network's services.

HTML (Hypertext Markup Language) ▸ A standardized format used to specify the format for Web page documents.

HTML document ▸ A plain text or ASCII document with embedded HTML tags that dictate formatting and are interpreted by a browser.

HTML form ▸ An HTML document containing blank boxes prompting users to enter information that can be sent to a Web server. Commonly used for e-commerce transactions.

HTML frame ▸ Part of a Web page that scrolls independently of other parts of the Web page.

HTML tag ▸ An instruction, such as ..., inserted into an HTML document to provide formatting and display information to a Web browser.

HTTP (Hypertext Transfer Protocol) ▸ The communications protocol used to transmit Web pages. HTTP:// is an identifier that appears at the beginning of most Web page URLs (for example, http://www.course.com).

HTTP status code ▸ A code used by Web servers to report the status of a browser's request.

Hub ▸ A network device that connects several nodes of a local area network.

Hyperlink ▸ Provides the fundamental tool for navigating Web pages. Click a text or graphic hyperlink to jump to a location in the same Web page, open a different Web page, or go to a different Web site. Also called link.

Hypertext ▸ A way of organizing an information database by linking information through the use of text and multimedia.

Hypertext link ▸ An underlined word or phrase that, when clicked, takes you to its designated URL; also called link.

ICANN (Internet Corporation for Assigned Names and Numbers) ▸ A global organization that coordinates the management of the Internet's domain name system, IP addresses, and protocol parameters.

Image map ▸ An area on a Web page consisting of a single graphic image containing multiple hot spots.

IMAP (Internet Messaging Access Protocol) ▸ A protocol similar to POP that is used to retrieve e-mail messages from an e-mail server, but offers additional features, such as choosing which e-mails to download from the server.

Incremental backup ▸ A copy of the files that changed since the last backup.

Information ▸ The words, numbers, and graphics used as the basis for human actions and decisions.

Infrared light ▸ A wireless transmission technology that uses a frequency range just below the visible light spectrum to transport data signals for short distances with a clear line of sight. Its most practical uses seem to be transmission of data between a notebook computer and a printer, between a PDA and a desktop computer, and in remote controls to change television channels.

Infrared port ▸ Device that accepts infrared light containing photo data that was beamed by a camera to a computer. This method, though slow, eliminates the need for a cable.

Ink jet printer ▸ A non-impact printer that creates characters or graphics by spraying liquid ink onto paper or other media.

Input ▸ As a noun, "input" means the information that is conveyed to a computer. As a verb, "input" means to enter data into a computer.

Input device ▸ A device, such as a keyboard or mouse, that gathers input and transforms it into a series of electronic signals for the computer.

Insertion point ▸ Appears on the screen as a flashing vertical bar or flashing underline and indicates where the characters you type will appear on the screen. Change the location insertion point using the arrow keys or the mouse pointer. Also called cursor.

Install ▸ The process by which programs and data are copied to the hard disk of a computer system and otherwise prepared for access and use.

Installation agreement ▸ A version of the license agreement that appears on the computer screen when software is being installed and prompts the user to accept or decline.

Instant messsaging ▸ A private chat in which users can communicate with each other.

Instruction cycle ▸ The steps followed by a computer to process a single instruction; fetch, interpret, execute, then increment the instruction pointer.

Instruction set ▸ The collection of instructions that a CPU is designed to process.

Integrated circuit (IC) ▸ A thin slice of silicon crystal containing microscopic circuit elements, such as transistors, wires, capacitors, and resistors; also called chips and microchips.

Integrated digital television (IDTV) set ▸ Television with a built-in digital receiver.

Internal link ▸ A hyperlink to a location within the same Web site.

Internal video ▸ A video on the Web that plays within a frame inside the Web page when its link is clicked.

Internet ▸ The worldwide communication infrastructure that links computer networks using TCP/IP protocol.

Internet2 ▸ A consortium of researchers and universities working together with high-tech corporations and some government agencies to build the next generation of the Internet—Internet2.

Internet backbone ▸ The major communications links that form the core of the Internet.

Internet Service Provider ▸ See ISP.

Internet telephony ▸ A set of hardware and software that allows users to make phone-style calls over the Internet, usually without a long-distance charge.

Interpage link ▸ A hyperlink that links to a different location on the same Web page.

Interpreter ▸ A program that converts high-level instructions in a computer program into machine language instructions, one instruction at a time.

Intranet ▸ A LAN that uses TCP/IP communications protocols, typically for communications services within a business or organization.

IP (Transmission Control Protocol) ▸ One of the main protocols of TCP/IP that is responsible for addressing packets so they can be routed to their destination.

IP address ▸ A unique identifying number assigned to each computer connected to the Internet.

ISA (Industry Standard Architecture) ▸ A standard for moving data on the expansion bus. Can refer to a type of slot, a bus, or a peripheral device. An older technology, it is rapidly being replaced by PCI architecture.

ISDN (Integrated Services Digital Network) ▸ A telephone company service that transports data digitally over dial-up or dedicated lines.

ISDN terminal adapter ▸ A device that connects a computer to a telephone jack and translates the data into a signal that can travel over an ISDN connection.

ISP (Internet Service Provider) ▸ A company that provides Internet access to businesses, organizations, and individuals.

Joystick ▸ A pointing input device used as an alternative to a mouse.

JPEG (Joint Photographic Experts Group) ▸ A file format that uses lossy compression to store bitmap images. JPEG files have a .jpg extension.

Kernel ▸ The core module of an operating system that typically manages memory, processes, tasks, and disks.

Keyboard ▸ An arrangement of letter, number, and special function keys that acts as the primary input device to the computer.

Keyboard shortcut ▸ The use of the [Alt] or the [Ctrl] key in combination with another key on the keyboard to execute a command, such as copy, paste, or cut.

Key frame ▸ Frames at equal intervals in a digital video clip that contain all data for that frame. The rest of the frames in the video contain only the information that is different from the last key frame.

Keyword ▸ A word or term used as the basis for a database or Web-page search.

Kilobit (Kbit or Kb) ▸ 1,024 bits.

Kilobyte (KB) ▸ Approximately 1,000 bytes; exactly 1,024 bytes.

Label ▸ In a worksheet, any text that is used to describe data.

LAN (local area network) ▸ An interconnected group of computers and peripherals located within a relatively limited area, such as a building or campus.

Lands ▸ Non-pitted surface areas on a CD that represents digital data.

LAN-jacking ▸ A practice that occurs when hackers cruise around with a Wi-Fi-equipped notebook computer set up to search for Wi-Fi signals coming from home and corporate Wi-Fi networks so they can access and use unsecured Wi-Fi networks to hack into files and gain unauthorized access to larger, wired networks. Also called war driving.

Laser printer ▸ A printer that uses laser-based technology, similar to that used by photocopiers, to produce text and graphics.

Laser light ▸ A focused beam of light that, with a clear line of sight, can transmit data over long distances.

LCD (liquid crystal display) ▸ A type of flat panel computer screen, typically found on notebook computers.

LCD screen ▸ See LCD.

Linear editing ▸ A video editing technique that records segments of video from one tape to another.

Link ▸ Provides the fundamental tool for navigating Web pages. Click a text or graphic hyperlink to jump to a location in the same Web page, open a different Web page, or go to a different Web site. Also called hyperlink.

Link tag ▸ HTML code that is used to designate text as a hyperlink in a document.

Linux ▸ A server operating system that is a derivative of UNIX and available as freeware.

Logical address ▸ A network address that is assigned to a network device when the physical address is in an incorrect format.

Logical storage model ▸ Any visual aid or metaphor that helps a computer user visualize a file system.

Logical topology ▸ Network topology that corresponds with the way messages flow across the network, not necessarily identical to the network's physical topology.

Lossless compression ▸ A compression technique that provides the means to restore all of the data in the original file.

Lossy compression ▸ Any data compression technique in which some of the data is sacrificed to obtain more compression.

Mac (Macintosh computer) ▸ A personal computer platform designed and manufactured by Apple Computer.

Mac OS ▸ The operating system software designed for use on Apple Macintosh and iMac computers.

Machine code ▸ Program instructions written in binary code that the computer can execute directly.

Machine language ▸ A low-level language written in binary code that the computer can execute directly.

Macro ▸ A small set of instructions that automates a task. Typically, a macro is created by performing the task once and recording the steps. Whenever the macro is played back, the steps are repeated.

Macro virus ▸ A computer virus that infects the macros that are attached to documents and spreadsheets.

Magnetic storage ▸ The recording of data onto disks or tape by magnetizing particles of an oxide-based surface coating.

Mailing list server ▸ Any computer and software that maintains a list of people who are interested in a topic and that facilitates message exchanges among all members of the list.

Mailto link ▸ A link on a Web page that automatically opens a pre-addressed e-mail form.

Main executable file ▸ A program that is used to start and run software, usually with an .exe file extension.

Mainframe computer ▸ A large, fast, and expensive computer generally used by businesses or government agencies to provide centralized storage processing and management for large amounts of data.

Malicious code ▸ Any program or set of program instructions that is designed to surreptitiously enter a computer and disrupt its normal operations. Malicious code, including viruses, worms, and Trojan horses, is created and unleashed by individuals referred to as "hackers" or "crackers."

MAN (metropolitan area network) ▸ A public, high-speed network that can transmit voice and data within a range of 50 miles.

Markup language ▸ A language that provides text and graphics formatting through the use of tags. Examples include HTML, XML, and SGML.

Master File Table (MFT) ▸ Special files used by the operating system of NTFS computers to keep track of the names and locations of files that reside on a storage medium, such as a hard disk.

Mathematical modeling software ▸ A category of software such as MathCAD and Mathematica, that provides tools for solving a wide range of math, science, and engineering problems.

M-Commerce (Mobile commerce) ▸ Gives consumers the ability to communicate and conduct business transactions through mobile devices, such as cell phones, PDAs, and wireless networks.

Media tag ▸ HTML code that specifies how to display media elements in a document.

Megabit (Mb or Mbit) ▸ Approximately 1 million bits; exactly 1,048,576 bits.

Megabyte (MB) ▸ Approximately 1 million bytes; exactly 1,048,576 bytes.

Megahertz (MHz) ▸ A measure of frequency equivalent to 1 million cycles per second.

Megapixels ▸ A million pixels; used to express the resolution and quality of an image.

Membrane keyboard ▸ Sealed keyboards designed to work in a variety of environmental conditions.

Memory ▸ The computer circuitry that holds data waiting to be processed.

Memory card reader ▶ A device that connects to a PC via a USB or Serial cable that reads data from a flash memory module.

MEMS-based (MicroElectroMechanical Systems) storage ▶ Technology that combines storage and processing on one chip.

Mesh topology ▶ A network topology that connects each network device to many other network devices. Data traveling on a mesh network can take any of several possible paths from its source to its destination.

Metafile ▶ Graphics file that contains both vector and bitmap data.

Microcomputer ▶ A category of computer that is built around a single processor chip.

Microprocessor ▶ An integrated circuit that contains the circuitry for processing data. It is a single-chip version of the central processing unit (CPU) found in all computers. Often called processor.

Microsoft Windows ▶ An operating system developed by Microsoft Corporation that provides a graphical interface. Versions include Windows 3.1, Windows 95, Windows 98, Windows ME, Windows 2000, Windows XP, and Windows NT.

Microwave ▶ Electromagnetic wave with a frequency of at least 1 gigahertz.

Middleware ▶ Intelligent software that prioritizes packets on the Internet binding together major applications and negotiating communications.

MIDI (Musical Instrument Digital Interface) ▶ A standardized way in which sound and music are encoded and transmitted between devices that play music.

MIDI sequence ▶ Digitally encoded music stored on a computer. Usually a file with a .mid, .cmf, or .rol file extension.

MIDI sequencing software ▶ A category of software used for creating sound effects and for controlling keyboards and other digital instruments.

Millisecond (ms) ▶ A thousandth of a second.

MIME (Multipurpose Internet Mail Extension) ▶ A conversion process used for formatting non-ASCII messages so that they can be sent over the Internet.

MIPS (millions of instructions per second) ▶ A measure of processing speed for HPC computers.

MirrorBit ▶ Technology used by AMD researchers to advance solid state storage by storing two bits in each cell.

Modem ▶ A device that sends and receives data to and from computers over telephone lines.

Modem card ▶ A device that provides a way to transmit data over phone lines or cable television lines.

Modifier key ▶ The [Ctrl], [Alt], or [Shift] key, used in conjunction with another key to expand the repertoire of available commands.

Modulation ▶ The process of changing the characteristics of a signal. For example, when a modem changes a digital pulse into an analog signal.

Monitor ▶ A display device that forms an image by converting electrical signals from the computer into points of colored light on the screen.

Monochrome bitmap ▶ Displayed by manipulating the pattern of off and on pixels on the screen. Each pixel is set to display either a black dot or a white dot. Monochrome bitmaps require very little storage space.

Motherboard ▶ The main circuit board in a computer that houses chips and other electronic components.

Mouse ▶ An input device that allows the user to manipulate objects on the screen by moving the mouse on the surface of a desk.

MP3 ▶ A file format that provides highly compressed audio files with very little loss of sound quality.

MP3 player ▶ Software that plays MP3 music files.

MP3 encoder Software that compresses a WAV file into an MP3 file.

MPEG (Moving Pictures Expert Group) ▶ A highly compressed file format for digital videos. Files in this format have a .mpg extension.

MPEG-2 ▶ A special type of data coding for movie files that are much too large to fit on a disk unless they are compressed.

MTBF (mean time between failures) ▶ The reliability of computer components as calculated by observing test equipment in a laboratory, then dividing the number of failures by the total number of hours of observation. This statistic is an estimate based on laboratory tests of a few sample components.

Multifunction device ▶ A hardware device that works both as input and output devices to combine the functions of a printer, scanner, copier, fax, and answering machine.

MultiMedia card (MMC) ▶ Solid state storage that includes a built-in controller in a package about the size of a postage stamp that was initially used in mobile phones and pagers, but now also used in digital cameras and MP3 players.

Multimedia home platform (MHP) ▶ A standard of multimedia for IDTV that is hardware, vendor, and software independent.

Multi-partite virus ▶ A computer virus that is able to infect many types of targets by hiding itself in numerous locations on a computer.

Multiple-user license ▶ Legal permission for more than one person to use a particular software package.

Multitasking operating system ▶ An operating system that runs two or more programs at the same time.

Multiuser operating system ▶ An operating system that allows two or more users to run programs at the same time and use their own input/output devices.

Nanosecond ▶ A unit of time representing 1 billionth of a second.

Narrowband ▶ A term that refers to communications channels that have low bandwidth.

Native file format ▶ A file format that is unique to a program or group of programs and has a unique file extension.

Natural language query ▶ A query using language spoken by human beings, as opposed to an artificially constructed language such as machine language.

Navigation keypad ▶ On a keyboard, the keypad with the Home, End, and arrow keys, which you can use to efficiently move the screen-based insertion point or cursor.

Netiquette ▶ Internet etiquette or a set of guidelines for posting messages and e-mails in a civil, concise way.

Network address translation (NAT) ▶ An Internet standard that allows a LAN to use one type of IP address for LAN data and another type of address for data to and from the Internet.

Network card ▶ An expansion board mounted inside a computer to allow access to a local area network.

Network device ▶ An electronic device that broadcasts network data, boosts signals, or routes data to its destination.

Network drive ▶ Drives that directly connect to a network and are accessible from all computers that are on the network.

Network interface card (NIC) ▶ A small circuit board that sends data from and collects incoming data for a workstation over a network.

Network operating system ▶ Programs designed to control the flow of data, maintain security, and keep track of accounts on a network.

Network service provider (NSP) ▶ Company that maintains a series of nationwide Internet links.

Networked peripheral ▶ A device, such as a printer or scanner, directly connected to a network rather than to a workstation.

Newsgroup ▶ An online discussion group that centers around a specific topic.

Node ▶ Each device on a network, including workstations, servers, and printers; in a hierarchical database, a segment or record type.

Non-linear editing ▶ A digital video editing technique that requires a PC and video editing software.

Notation software ▶ A category of software used to help musicians compose, edit, and print musical scores.

Notebook computer ▶ Small, lightweight, portable computer that usually runs on batteries. Sometimes called laptop.

Numeric data ▶ Numbers that represent quantities and can be used in arithmetic operations.

Numeric keypad ▶ Calculator-style input devices for numbers located towards the right side of a keyboard.

Object code ▶ The low-level instructions that result from compiling source code.

Object-oriented database ▶ A database model that organizes data into classes of objects that can be manipulated by programmer-defined methods.

Offshoring ▶ Relocating business processes, such as development and production, to lower-cost locations in other countries.

OLED (organic light emitting diode) ▶ Technology used to create display devices that are thin, light, and conserve power.

Online ▶ Refers to being connected to the Internet.

Online shopping cart ▶ An e-commerce cookie that stores information about items selected and collected for purchase.

Op code (operation code) ▶ An assembly language command word that designates an operation, such as add (ADD), compare (CMP), or jump (JMP).

Open source software ▶ A category of software, such as Linux, that includes its uncompiled source code, which can be modified and distributed by programmers.

Operand ▶ The part of an instruction that specifies the data, or the address of the data, on which the operation is to be performed.

Operating system (OS) ▶ Software that controls the computer's use of its hardware resources, such as memory and disk storage space.

Operational tag ▶ HTML code used to specify the basic setup and database integration for Web pages.

Operator error ▶ The most common cause of lost and/or inaccurate data; mistakes made by a computer user such as entering the wrong data or deleting a needed file.

Optical storage ▶ A means of recording data as light and dark spots on a CD, DVD, or other optical media.

Organic light emitting diode (OLED) ▶ A technology used to create display devices that are thin, have high resolutions, and low power consumption.

Output ▶ The results produced by a computer (for example, reports, graphs, and music).

Output device ▶ A device, such as a monitor or printer, that displays, prints, or transmits the results of processing from the computer memory.

Outsourcing ▶ Hiring workers outside your company for specific job functions or projects so that another company provides services for your company that could be or usually have been provided in-house.

P3P (Platform for Privacy Preferences Project) ▶ A specification that allows Web browsers to detect a Web site's privacy policies automatically.

Packet ▶ A small unit of data transmitted over a network or the Internet.

Packet sniffer ▶ A computer program that monitors data as it travels over networks to observe and open any packet traveling on the network. Also called a protocol analyzer.

Packet switching ▶ A technology used by data communications networks, such as the Internet, in which a message is divided into smaller units called "packets" for transmission.

Page layout ▶ The physical positions of elements on a document page, such as headers, footers, page numbers, and graphics.

PAN (personal area network) ▶ A term used to refer to the interconnection of personal digital devices within a range of about 30 feet (10 meters) and without the use of wires or cables. For example, to wirelessly transmit data from a notebook computer to a PDA or portable printer.

Paint software ▶ The software required to create and manipulate bitmap graphics.

Palm OS ▶ One of the two dominant operating systems of handheld computers.

Parallel port ▶ Commonly used to connect most printers to a computer; however some printers are designed to connect to a USB port or a serial port.

Parallel processing ▶ A technique by which two or more processors in a computer perform processing tasks simultaneously.

Password ▶ A special set of symbols used to restrict access to a computer or network.

Password protection ▶ Security feature used to identify authorized users and are a way to restrict access to a computer system.

Path ▶ A file's location in a file structure. See File specification.

Payload ▶ The virus instructions that are delivered by the virus; might be as harmless as displaying an annoying message or as devastating as corrupting the data on your computer's hard disk.

Payroll software ▶ Horizontal market software used by business to maintain payroll records, collect data and make calculations in order to produce payroll checks and W2 forms.

PC ▶ A microcomputer that uses Windows software and contains an Intel-compatible processor.

PC card ▶ A credit card-sized circuit board used to connect a modem, memory, network card, or storage device to a notebook computer.

PCI (Peripheral Component Interconnect) ▶ A method for transporting data on the expansion bus. Can refer to type of data bus, expansion slot, or transport method used by a peripheral device.

PCMCIA (Personal Computer Memory Card International Association) slot ▶ An external expansion slot typically found on notebook computers.

PDA (Personal Digital Assistant) ▶ A computer that is smaller and more portable than a notebook computer. Also called a palm-top computer.

Peer-to-peer network (P2P) ▶ The arrangement in which one workstation/ server shares resources with another workstation/server; each computer on such a network must act as both a file server and workstation.

Peripheral device ▶ A component or equipment, such as a printer or scanner, that expands a computer's input, output, or storage capabilities.

Personal computer ▶ A microcomputer designed for use by an individual user for applications such as Internet browsing and word processing.

Personal finance software ▶ A category of software designed to help manage individual finances.

Personal firewall software ▶ A category of software designed to analyze and control incoming and outgoing packets.

Personal video recorder (PVR) ▶ Device that allows a user to record television based on personal viewing preferences.

Person-to-person payment ▶ An e-commerce method of payment that bypasses credit cards and instead uses an automatic electronic payment service.

PGA (pin-grid array) ▶ A common chip design used for processors.

PGP (Pretty Good Privacy) ▶ A popular program used to encrypt and decrypt e-mail messages.

Phishing ▶ The fraudulent solicitation for account information (such as credit card numbers and passwords) by impersonating the domain and e-mail content of a company to which users have entrusted the storage of these data.

Phoneme ▶ Unit of sound that is a basic component of words; can be produced by speech synthesizers.

Photo editing software ▶ A category of software that provides tools and wizards that simplify common photo editing tasks; includes features specially designed to fix poor-quality photos by modifying contrast and brightness, cropping out unwanted objects, and removing red eye.

Physical address ▶ An address built into the circuitry of a network device at the time of its manufacture.

Physical storage model ▶ The way data is stored on a storage media.

Physical topology ▶ The actual layout of network devices, wires, and cables.

Ping (Packet Internet Groper) ▶ A command on a TCP/IP network that sends a test packet to a specified IP address and waits for a reply.

Pipelining ▸ A technology that allows a processor to begin executing an instruction before completing the previous instruction.

Pits ▸ Dark spots that are burned onto the surface of a CD to represent digital data.

Pixel (picture element) ▸ The smallest unit in a graphic image. Computer display devices use a matrix of pixels to display text and graphics.

Pixel interpolation ▸ A process used by graphics software to average the color of adjacent pixels in an image.

Plaintext ▸ An original, un-encrypted message.

Plasma screen technology ▸ Display device technology that is used in gas plasma screens to create an onscreen image by illuminating miniature colored fluorescent lights arrayed in a panel-like screen. The name "plasma" comes from the type of gas that fills fluorescent lights and gives them their luminescence. Plasma screens are compact, lightweight, and more expensive than CRT monitors.

Platform ▸ A family or category of computers based on the same underlying software and hardware.

Plug and Play ▸ The ability of a computer to recognize and adjust the system configuration for a newly added device automatically.

Plug-in ▸ A software module that adds a specific feature to a system. For example, in the context of the Web, a plug-in adds a feature to the user's browser, such as the ability to play RealVideo files.

PNG (Portable Network Graphics) ▸ A type of graphics file format similar to, but newer than, GIF or JPEG.

Pointing stick ▸ Pointing device typically used with notebook computers as an alternative to a mouse that looks like the tip of an eraser and is embedded in the keyboard of a notebook computer. Push up, down, or sideways to move the onscreen pointer. Also called TrackPoint.

Polymorphic virus ▸ Virus that can escape detection by antivirus software by changing its signature.

POP (Post Office Protocol) ▸ A protocol that is used to retrieve e-mail messages from an e-mail server.

POP server ▸ A computer that receives and stores e-mail data until retrieved by the e-mail account holder.

Popup ad ▸ An advertisement that appears in a separate window when you enter a Web site or connect to Web pages.

PostScript ▸ A printer language developed by Adobe Systems that uses a special set of commands to control page layout, fonts, and graphics.

POTS ▸ An acronym for plain old telephone service.

Power failure ▸ A complete loss of power to the computer system, usually caused by something over which you have no control.

Power-on self-test (POST) ▸ A diagnostic process that runs during startup to check components of the computer, such as the graphics card, RAM, keyboard, and disk drives.

Power spike ▸ An increase in power that lasts only a short time—less than one millionth of a second. Spikes can be caused by malfunctions in the local generating plant or the power distribution network, and they are potentially more damaging to your computer system and data than a power failure.

Power strip ▸ A device that provides additional outlets for power but provides no protection against power spikes, surges, or failures.

Power surge ▸ A fluctuation in power that lasts a little longer than a power spike—a few millionths of a second. Surges can be caused by malfunctions in the local generating plant or the power distribution network, and they are potentially more damaging to your computer system and data than a power failure.

Presentation software ▸ A category of software that provides tools to combine text, graphics, graphs, animation, and sound into a series of electronic slides that can be output on a projector, or as overhead transparencies, paper copies, or 35-millimeter slides.

Printer ▸ A peripheral device used to create hard copy output.

Printer Control Language (PCL) ▸ A standard language used to send page formatting instructions from a computer to a laser or ink jet printer.

Private IP address ▸ IP address that cannot be routed over the Internet.

Processing ▸ The manipulation of data using a systematic series of actions.

Processor ▸ An integrated circuit that contains the circuitry for processing data. It is a single-chip version of the central processing unit (CPU) found in all computers.

Processor clock ▸ A device on the motherboard of a computer responsible for setting the pace of executing instructions.

Programming language ▸ Provides the tools that a programmer uses to create software. Also called computer language.

Project management software ▸ A category of software specifically designed as a tool for planning, scheduling, and tracking projects and their costs.

PROM (programmable read-only memory) ▸ Memory that can be created using a special machine through a process called burning.

Protocols ▸ Rules that ensure the orderly and accurate transmission and reception of data. Protocols start and end transmission, recognize errors, send data at the appropriate speed, and identify the correct senders and recipients.

Public domain ▸ A category of software that is available for use by the public without restriction, except that it cannot be copyrighted.

Public key encryption (PKE) ▸ An encryption method that uses a pair of keys—a public key (known to everyone) that encrypts the message, and a private key (known only to the recipient) that decrypts it.

Public Wi-Fi network ▸ A wireless LAN that provides open Internet access to the public.

Query ▸ A search specification that prompts the computer to look for particular records in a file.

Query by example (QBE) ▸ A type of database interface in which users fill in a field with an example of the type of information that they are seeking.

Query language ▸ A set of command words that can be used to direct the computer to create databases, locate information, sort records, and change the data in those records.

QuickTime ▸ A video and animation file format developed by Apple Computer that can also be run on PCs. QuickTime files have a .mov extension.

RAM (random access memory) ▸ A type of computer memory circuit that holds data, program instructions, and the operating system while the computer is on.

Random access ▸ The ability of a storage device (such as a disk drive) to go directly to a specific storage location without having to search sequentially from a beginning location.

Rasterization ▸ The process of superimposing a grid over a vector image and determining the color depth for each pixel.

Ray tracing ▸ A technique by which light and shadow are added to a 3-D image.

RDRAM (Rambus dynamic RAM) ▸ A fast (up to 600 MHz) type of memory used in newer personal computers.

Read-write head ▸ The mechanism in a disk drive that magnetizes particles on the storage disk surface to write data, or senses the bits that are present to read data.

RealAudio (.ra) ▸ An audio file format developed by Real Networks especially for streaming audio data over the Web.

RealMedia ▸ A video file format developed by Real Networks that is popular for streaming Web videos.

Record ▸ In the context of database management, a record is the set of fields of data that pertain to a single entity in a database.

Recordable technology ▸ Optical storage technology used to create CDs and DVDs.

Recovery CD ▸ A CD that contains all the operating system files and application software files necessary to restore a computer to its original state.

Reference software ▸ A category of software that provides you with a collection of information and a way to access that information; spans a wide range of applications.

Register ▶ A "scratch pad" area of the ALU and control unit where data or instructions are moved so that they can be processed.

Relational database ▶ A database structure incorporating the use of tables that can establish relationships with other similar tables.

Relative reference ▶ In a worksheet, cell references that can change if cells change position as a result of a move or copy operation.

Rendering ▶ In graphics software, the process of creating a 3-D solid image by covering a wireframe drawing and applying computer-generated highlights and shadows.

Repeater ▶ A network device that receives and retransmits amplified signals so that they can retain the necessary strength to reach their destinations.

Rescue disk ▶ A boot disk that contains operating system files plus antivirus software.

Reserved word ▶ Special words used as commands in some operating systems that may not be used in filenames.

Resolution ▶ The density of the grid used to display or print text and graphics; the greater the horizontal and vertical density, the higher the resolution.

Resolution dependent ▶ Graphics, such as bitmaps, for which the quality of the image is dependent on the number of pixels comprising the image.

Restore ▶ The act of moving data from a backup storage medium to a hard disk in the event original data has been lost.

Resource ▶ In the context of a computer system, refers to any component that is required to perform work such as the processor, RAM, storage space, and peripherals.

Retro virus ▶ Virus designed to corrupt antivirus software.

Revolutions per minute (rpm) ▶ A unit of measure that specifies how many times a platter spins each minute: used for the speed of a hard disk drive and to classify the access time for a hard disk.

Rewritable technology (RW) ▶ An optical storage technology that uses "phase change" technology to alter a crystal structure on the disc surface to create patterns of light and dark spots. RW makes it possible for stored data to be recorded and erased or modified multiple times much like on a hard disk. Examples of CDs and DVDs using rewritable optical technology are CD-RW (compact disc rewritable) discs and DVD+RW (digital versatile disc rewritable) discs.

RF signals (radio frequency signals) ▶ Data that is broadcast and received via radio waves with a transceiver.

RFID (Radio frequency identification) ▶ Technology based on "smart tags" that can be applied to a component such as a product or document, or even a person; consists of chips and an antenna that can transmit data, such as identification and tracking information, to a wireless receiver.

RIMM (Rambus in-line memory module) ▶ A memory module using RDRAM.

Ring topology ▶ A network topology that connects all devices in a circle, with each device having exactly two neighbors, so that data is transmitted from one device to another around the ring.

RISC (reduced instruction set computer) ▶ A processor chip designed for rapid and efficient processing of a small set of simple instructions.

Risk management ▶ The process of weighing threats to computer data against the amount of expendable data and the cost of protecting crucial data.

ROM (read-only memory) ▶ One or more integrated circuits that contain permanent instructions that the computer uses during the boot process.

ROM BIOS (basic input/output system) ▶ A small set of basic input/output system instructions stored in ROM that causes the computer system to load critical operating files when the user turns on the computer.

Root directory ▶ The main directory of a disk.

Router ▶ A device found at each intersection on the Internet backbone that examines the IP address of incoming data and forwards the data towards its destination. Also used by LANs.

RSA ▶ The most commonly used public key encryption algorithm used to encrypt the data in most digital certificates; the technology used for SSL connections. RSA is named for its inventors—Ron Rivest, Adi Shamir, and Leonard Adleman.

Run-length encoding ▶ A graphics file compression technique that looks for patterns of bytes and replaces them with messages that describe the patterns.

Safe Mode ▶ A menu option that appears when Windows is unable to complete the boot sequence. By entering Safe Mode, a user can gracefully shut down the computer then try to reboot it.

Sampling rate ▶ The number of times per second a sound is measured during the recording process; a higher sampling rate means higher-quality sound.

Scanner ▶ An input device that converts a printed page of text or images into a digital format.

Screen size ▶ On a display device, the measurement in inches from one corner of the screen diagonally across to the opposite corner.

Script ▶ Program that contains a list of commands that are automatically executed as needed.

Scripting error ▶ An error that occurs when a browser or server cannot execute a statement in a script.

SCSI (small computer system interface) ▶ An interface standard used for attaching peripheral devices, such as disk drives. Pronounced "scuzzy."

SDRAM (synchronous dynamic RAM) ▶ A type of RAM that synchronizes itself with the CPU, thus enabling it to run at much higher clock speeds than conventional RAM.

Search engine ▶ Program that uses keywords to find information on the Internet and return a list of relevant documents.

Search operator ▶ A word or symbol that has a specific function within a search, such as "AND" or "+".

SEC (single edge contact) cartridge ▶ A common, cassette-like chip design for processors.

Sector ▶ Subdivision of the tracks on a storage medium that provide a storage area for data.

Secure connection ▶ Technology that encrypts data transmitted between a computer and a Web site to protect the data during electronic transactions so that the data must be decrypted before it can be used. Technologies that create secure connections include SSL and S-HTTP.

SecureDigital (SD) card ▶ Solid state storage device popular for MP3 storage featuring fast data transfer rates and cryptographic security protection for copyrighted data and music.

Self-closing tag ▶ Any single HTML tag that includes a closing "/" symbol, such as the <hr/> tag which produces a horizontal line on a Web page. The slash comes at the end of the tag, whereas in a closing tag such as </b>, the slash comes at the beginning.

Self-securing storage ▶ Devices that keep all versions of date for a time period and continually monitor requests for access and storage for security purposes.

Semiconducting material ▶ Materials such as silicon and germanium that are used to make chips. The conductive properties create miniature electronic pathways and components, such as transistors. Also called semiconductors.

Sequential access ▶ A form of data storage, usually on computer tape, that requires a device to read or write data one record after another, starting at the beginning of the medium.

Serial processing ▶ Processing of data that completes one instruction before beginning another.

Server ▶ A computer or software on a network that supplies the network with data and storage.

Server farm ▶ A group of multiple Web servers used to handle large volumes of requests.

Server-side script ▶ Scripting statements that are executed by a Web server in response to client data.

Server operating system, ▶ Provides communications and routing services that allow computers to share data, programs, and peripheral devices by routing data and programs to each user's local computer, where the actual processing takes place. Also called network operating system.

Server ▶ A category of software used by servers to locate and distribute data requested by Internet users.

Service pack ▶ A software update, usually to an operating system.

SET (Secure Electronic Transaction) ▶ A system that ensures the security of financial transactions on the Web.

Setup program ▶ A program module supplied with a software package for the purpose of installing the software.

Shared resource ▶ On a network, hardware, software, and data made available for authorized network users to access.

Shareware ▶ Copyrighted software marketed under a license that allows users to use the software for a trial period and then send in a registration fee if they wish to continue to use it.

Shrink-wrap license ▶ A legal agreement printed on computer software packaging that goes into effect when the package is opened.

S-HTTP (Secure HTTP) ▶ A method of encrypting data transmitted between a computer and a Web server by encrypting individual packets of data as they are transmitted.

Simplex ▶ A communications technique that allows communication in only one direction.

Single-user license ▶ A legal agreement that typically allows only one copy of the software to be in use at a time.

Single-user operating system ▶ A type of operating system that is designed for one user at a time with one set of input and output devices.

Site license ▶ A legal agreement that generally allows software to be used on any and all computers at a specific location, such as within a corporate office or on a university campus.

Slides ▶ The 'canvas' for the delivery of ideas in presentation software that combines text, graphics, graphs, animations, and sound; a series of electronic slides display on a monitor for a one-on-one presentation or on a computer projection device for group presentations.

Small business accounting software ▶ A category of software that is geared towards small businesses to help invoice customers, keep track of what they owe, store customer data, such as contact information and purchasing history. Inventory functions keep track of the products. Payroll capabilities automatically calculate wages and deduct federal, state, and local taxes.

SmartMedia card ▶ The least durable of the solid state storage media, was originally called "solid state floppy disk card" because it looks like a miniature floppy disk, it does not include a built-in controller, so it requires a SmartMedia reader to manage the read/write process.

Smartphone ▶ PDA that offers convergent technology to provide keypad input, color screen, digital camera, PDA software, voice and text communications, Web browsing, and e-mail.

SMTP (Simple Mail Transfer Protocol) server ▶ A computer used to send e-mail across a network or the Internet.

Socket ▶ A communication path between two remote programs.

Software ▶ The instructions that prepare a computer to do a task, indicate how to interact with a user, and specify how to process data.

Software license ▶ A legal contract that defines how a user may use a computer program.

Software patch ▶ Section of software that replaces existing code to improve a feature or fix a problem.

Software suite ▶ A collection of application software sold as a single package.

Solid ink printer ▶ A printer that creates images on pages by melting sticks of crayon-like ink and then spraying the liquefied ink through the print head's tiny nozzles. The ink solidifies before the paper can absorb it, and a pair of rollers finishes fusing the ink onto the paper. A solid ink printer produces vibrant colors on most types of paper and is used for professional graphics applications.

Solid state storage ▶ A variety of compact storage cards, pens, and sticks that stores data in a non-volatile, erasable, low-power chip in a microscopic grid of cells.

SO-RIMM (small outline Rambus in-line memory) module ▶ A small memory module that contains RDRAM, used primarily in notebook computers.

Sound card ▶ A circuit board that gives the computer the ability to accept audio input from a microphone, play sound files stored on disks and CD-ROMs, and produce audio output through speakers or headphones.

Source code ▶ Computer instructions written in a high-level language.

SPAM ▶ Unwanted and unsolicited e-mail usually selling products, also called junk e-mail.

SPAM filter ▶ Software to block unwanted messages and automatically route advertisements and other junk e-mail to either the Deleted Items or Junk folder maintained by the e-mail client.

Spatial compression ▶ A data compression scheme that replaces patterns of bytes with code that describes the patterns.

Speakers ▶ Output devices that receive signals for the computer's sound card to play music, narration, or sound effects.

Speech recognition software ▶ The process by which computers recognize voice patterns and words and convert them to digital data.

Speech recognition ▶ A category of software that analyzes voice sounds and converts them into phonemes.

Speech synthesis ▶ The process by which computers produce sound that resembles spoken words.

Spreadsheet ▶ A numerical model or representation of a real situation, presented in the form of a table.

Spreadsheet ▶ A category of software for creating electronic worksheets that hold data in cells and perform calculations based on that data.

Spyware ▶ On the Web, any technology that secretly gathers information and relays it to advertisers or other interested parties.

SQL (Structured Query Language) ▶ A popular query language used by mainframes and microcomputers.

SSL (secure sockets layer) ▶ A security protocol that uses encryption to establish a secure connection between a computer and a Web server.

Star topology ▶ A network topology that features a central connection point for all workstations and peripherals.

Stateless protocol ▶ A protocol that allows one request and response per session, such as HTTP.

Static IP address ▶ A permanently assigned and unique IP address, used by hosts or servers.

Statistical compression ▶ A data compression scheme that uses an algorithm that recodes frequently used data as short bit patterns.

Statistical software ▶ A category of software that helps you analyze large sets of data to discover relationships and patterns, summarize survey results, test scores, experiment results, or population data. Most statistical software includes graphing capability.

Stealth virus ▶ Virus that can escape detection from antivirus software by removing its own signature and hiding in memory.

Storage ▶ The area in a computer where data is retained on a permanent basis.

Storage capacity ▶ The amount of data that can be stored on a storage media.

Storage device ▶ A mechanical apparatus that records data to and retrieves data from a storage medium.

Storage medium ▶ The physical material used to store computer data, such as a floppy disk, a hard disk, or a CD-ROM.

Storage technology ▶ Defines the data storage systems used by computers to store data and program files. Each data storage system has two main components: a storage medium and a storage device.

Store-and-forward technology ▶ A technology used by communications networks in which an e-mail message is temporarily held in storage on a server until it is requested by a client computer.

Stored program ▶ A set of instructions that resides on a storage device, such as a hard drive, and can be loaded into memory and executed.

STP (shielded twisted pair) ▶ A type of cable consisting of two wires that are twisted together and encased in a protective layer to reduce signal noise.

Streaming video ▶ An Internet video technology that sends a small segment of a video file to a user's computer and begins to play it while the next segment is sent.

Strong encryption ▶ Encryption that is difficult to decrypt without the encryption key.

Structured file ▶ A file that consists of a collection of records, each with the same set of fields.

Style ▶ A combination of attributes—colors, sizes, and fonts—that specify the way text is displayed.

Style sheet ▶ Acts as a template to control the layout and design of Web pages. Style sheets work in conjunction with HTML tags to make it easy to change the format of elements in a Web page globally and consistently. Also called cascading style sheet (CSS).

Subdirectory ▶ A directory found under the root directory.

Supercomputer ▶ The fastest and most expensive type of computer, capable of processing more than 1 trillion instructions per second.

SuperDisk ▶ A storage technology manufactured by Imation. Disks have a capacity of 120 MB and require special disk drives; a standard floppy disk drive will not read them. However, they are backward-compatible with standard floppy disk technology, which means you can use a SuperDisk drive to read and write to standard floppy disks.

Support module ▶ A file that can be called by the main executable program to provide auxiliary instructions or routines.

Support program ▶ A file that can be called by the main executable program to provide auxiliary instructions or routines.

Surge strip ▶ A low-cost device used to protect computer systems from power spikes and surges. Also called surge protector or surge suppressor.

SVG (Scalable Vector Graphics) ▶ A graphics format designed specifically for Web display that automatically resizes when displayed on different screens.

Symmetric key encryption ▶ An encryption key that is used for both encryption and decryption of messages.

Synchronous protocol ▶ Sender's signals and receiver's signals are synchronized by a signal called a clock; the transmitting computer sends data at a fixed clock rate, and the receiving computer expects the incoming data at the same fixed rate.

Synthesized sound ▶ Artificially created sound, usually found in MIDI music or synthesized speech.

System palette ▶ A selection of colors that are used by an operating system to display graphic elements.

System requirements ▶ Specifications for the operating system and hardware configuration necessary for a software product to work correctly. The criteria that must be met for a new computer system or software product to be a success.

System software ▶ Computer programs that help the computer carry out essential operating tasks.

System unit ▶ The case or box that contains the computer's power supply, storage devices, main circuit board, processor, and memory.

T1 ▶ A high-bandwidth telephone line that can also transmit text and images. T1 service is often used by organizations to connect to the Internet.

T3 ▶ A type of ISDN service that uses fiber-optic cable to provide dedicated service with a capacity of 45 megabits per second.

Table ▶ An arrangement of data in a grid of rows and columns. In a relational database, a collection of record types with their data.

Tablet computer ▶ A portable computing device featuring a touch-sensitive screen that can be used as a writing or drawing pad.

Tape ▶ A sequential magnetic storage technology that consists of a tape for the storage medium and a tape drive for the storage device.

Tape backup ▶ A copy of data from a computer's hard disk, stored on magnetic tape and used to restore lost data.

Tape cartridge ▶ A removable magnetic tape module similar to a cassette tape.

Tax preparation software ▶ A specialized type of personal finance software designed to help you gather your annual income and expense data, identify deductions, and calculate your tax payment.

TCP (Transmission Control Protocol) ▶ One of the main protocols of TCP/IP that is responsible for establishing a data connection between two hosts and breaking data into packets.

TCP/IP (Transmission Control Protocol/Internet Protocol) ▶ A standard set of communication rules used by every computer that connects to the Internet.

Telnet ▶ A common way to remotely control another computer or server on a network or the Internet.

Temporal compression ▶ A data compression scheme that, when applied to video or audio data, eliminates unnecessary data between video frames or audio samples.

Tera- ▶ Prefix for a trillion.

Text editor ▶ A program similar to a word processor that is used to create plain, unformatted ASCII text.

Text-to-speech ▶ A category of software that generates speech based on written text, that is played back through a computer's sound card.

TFT (thin film transistor) ▶ An active matrix screen that updates rapidly and is essential for crisp display of animations and video.

Theme ▶ A collection of coordinated graphics, colors, and fonts applied to individual pages or all pages in a Web site. Themes are generally available as part of Web authoring software.

Thermal transfer printer ▶ An expensive, color-precise printer that uses wax containing color to produce numerous dots of color on plain paper.

Thumbnail ▶ A graphical link that expands in size when clicked.

TIFF (Tag Image File Format) ▶ A file format (.tif extension) for bitmap images that automatically compresses the file data.

Toggle key ▶ A key that switches back and forth between two modes, such as Caps Lock on or Caps Lock off.

Token Ring network ▶ A type of network on which the nodes are sequentially connected in the form of a ring; the second most popular network architecture.

Top-level domain ▶ The major domain categories into which groups of computers on the Internet are divided: com, edu, gov, int, mil, net, and org.

Touchpad ▶ An alternative input device often found on notebook computers.

Traceroute ▶ A network utility that records a packet's path, number of hops, and the time it takes for the packet to make each hop.

Tracing ▶ A category of software that locates the edges of objects in a bitmap graphic and converts the resulting shape into a vector graphic.

TrackPoint ▶ An alternative input device often found on notebook computers.

Trackball ▶ Pointing input device used as an alternative to a mouse.

Tracks ▶ A series of concentric or spiral storage areas created on a storage medium during the formatting process.

Transceiver ▶ A combined transmitter/receiver used to send and receive data in the form of radio frequencies.

Transponder ▶ A device on a telecommunications satellite that receives a signal on one frequency, amplifies the signal, and then retransmits the signal on a different frequency.

Tree topology ▶ A network topology that is a blend of star and bus networks to offer excellent flexibility for expansion. Multiple star networks are connected to form a bus configuration by a backbone.

Trigger event ▶ An event that activates a task often associated with a computer virus.

Trojan horse ▶ A computer program that appears to perform one function while actually doing something else, such as inserting a virus into a computer system, or stealing a password.

True Color bitmap ▶ A color image with a color depth of 24 bits or 32 bits. Each pixel in a True Color image can be displayed using any of 16.7 million different colors.

Typing keypad ▶ The basic keys on a computer keyboard that include the keys or buttons with letters and numbers as well as several keys with characters and special words to control computer-specific tasks. You use the keys to input commands, respond to prompts, and type the text of documents.

Twisted-pair cable ▶ A type of cable used to connect nodes on a network; has RJ-45 connectors on both ends and two separate strands of wire twisted together.

UDMA (Ultra DMA) ▶ A faster version of DMA technology.

Ultra ATA ▶ A disk drive technology that is an enhanced version of EIDE. Also referred to as Ultra DMA or Ultra IDE.

Unicode ▶ A 16-bit character representation code that can represent more than 65,000 characters.

Uninstall routine ▶ A program that removes software files, references, and Windows Registry entries from a computer's hard disk.

UNIX ▶ A multi-user, multitasking server operating system developed by AT&T's Bell Laboratories in 1969.

Unzipped ▶ Refers to files that have been uncompressed.

Unzipping ▶ Restoring files that have been compressed to their original size.

Uplink port ▶ A connection port on a router to which additional hubs can be attached.

Uploading ▶ The process of sending a copy of a file from a local computer to a remote computer.

UPS (uninterruptible power supply) ▶ A device containing a battery that provides a continuous supply of power and other circuitry to prevent spikes and surges from reaching your computer. It represents the best protection against power problems because it is designed to provide enough power to keep your computer working through momentary power interruptions.

URL (Uniform Resource Locator) ▶ The address of a Web page.

Usage procedures ▶ A set of rules established so that, if followed, can reduce operator error.

USB (Universal Serial Bus) port ▶ A device-independent interface between a computer and peripheral device; used to transfer data to and from a computer.

USB flash drive ▶ A portable storage device featuring a built-in connector that plugs directly into a computer's USB port.

Usenet ▶ A worldwide Internet bulletin board system of newsgroups that share common topics.

User-executable file ▶ At least one of the files included in a software package designed to be launched, or started, by users. On PCs, these programs are stored in files that typically have .exe filename extensions. Also called executable file.

User ID ▶ A combination of letters and numbers that serves as a user's identification. Also referred to as user name.

User interface ▶ The software and hardware that enable people to interact with computers.

User rights ▶ Rules that limit the directories and files that each user can access; they can restrict the ability to erase, create, write, read, and find files.

Utility ▶ A subcategory of system software designed to augment the operating system by providing ways for a computer user to control the allocation and use of hardware resources. Also called utilities.

UTP (unshielded twisted pair) ▶ A type of cable consisting of two unshielded wires twisted together. It is less expensive but has more signal noise than a shielded twisted pair.

Value ▶ A number used in a calculation.

Vector graphic ▶ Image generated from descriptions that determine the position, length, and direction in which lines and shapes are drawn.

Vertical market software ▶ Computer programs designed to meet the needs of a specific market segment or industry, such as medical record-keeping software.

Video ▶ A recorded series of images that displays motion with sound.

Video capture device ▶ A device that is used to convert analog video signals into digital data stored on a hard drive.

Video capture ▶ A category of software used to control the capture process of digital and analog video data.

Video editing ▶ A category of software that provides tools for capturing and editing video from a camcorder.

Videogame console ▶ A computer specifically designed for playing games using a television screen and game controllers.

Viewable image size (vis) ▶ A measurement of the maximum image size that can be displayed on a monitor screen.

Viewing angle width ▶ Measurement of a monitor or display device that indicates how far to the side you can still clearly see the screen image.

Virtual Local Area Network (VLAN) ▶ A group of personal computers, servers, and other network resources that are on physically different segments of a network but that communicate as though they are on the same segment.

Virtual memory ▶ A computer's use of hard disk storage to simulate RAM.

Virus ▶ A set of program instructions that attaches itself to a file, reproduces itself, and spreads to other files. It can corrupt files, destroy data, display an irritating message, or otherwise disrupt computer operations. A virus generally infects files executed by your computer—files with extensions such as .exe, .com, or .vbs. Also called computer virus.

Virus definition ▶ A file that stores the information that your antivirus software uses to identify and eradicate viruses, Trojan horses, and worms.

Virus hoax ▶ A message, usually e-mail, that makes claims about a virus problem that doesn't actually exist.

Virus signature ▶ The unique computer code contained in a virus that helps with its identification. Antivirus software searches for known virus signatures.

Voice band modem ▶ The type of modem that would typically be used to connect a computer to a telephone line. See Modem.

Voice over IP (VoIP) ▶ A technology that allows computer users with Internet access to send and receive both data and voice simultaneously.

Volatile ▶ Data that can exist only with a constant power supply.

WAN (wide area network) ▶ An interconnected group of computers and peripherals that covers a large geographical area, such as multiple branches of a corporation.

WAP (Wireless Access Protocol) ▶ A communications protocol that provides Internet access from handheld devices, such as cell phones and PDAs. WAP-enabled devices contain a microbrowser that simplifies Web and e-mail access on a small, low-resolution screen.

War driving ▶ A practice that occurs when hackers cruise around with a Wi-Fi-equipped notebook computer set up to search for Wi-Fi signals coming from home and corporate Wi-Fi networks so they can access and use unsecured Wi-Fi networks to hack into files and gain unauthorized access to larger, wired networks. Also called LAN-jacking.

Wave (.wav) ▶ An audio file format created as Windows "native" sound format.

Waveform audio ▶ A digital representation of sound in which a sound wave is represented by a series of samples taken of the wave height.

Wavetable ▶ A set of pre-recorded musical instrument sounds in MIDI format.

Weak encryption ▶ Encryption that is relatively simple to decrypt without the encryption key.

Web (World Wide Web) ▸ An Internet service that links documents and information from computers distributed all over the world using the HTTP protocol.

Web authoring software ▸ Computer programs for designing and developing customized Web pages that can be published electronically on the Internet.

Web-based e-mail ▸ An e-mail account that stores, sends, and receives e-mail on a Web site rather than a user's computer.

Web browser ▸ A software program that runs on your computer and helps you access Web pages. Also called a browser.

Web bug ▸ A 1x1 pixel graphic on a Web page that can be used to set cookies to third party Web sites. Unlike ad-serving cookies, you don't have to click a banner ad to receive a GIF activated cookie. Also called clear GIF.

Web cam ▸ An input device used to capture live video and transmit it over the Internet.

Web page ▸ A document on the World Wide Web that consists of a specially coded HTML file with associated text, audio, video, and graphics files. A Web page often contains links to other Web pages.

Web page header ▸ A subtitle that appears at the beginning of a Web page, also called "header."

Web page table ▸ A grid of cells that is used as a layout tool for elements such as text and graphics placement on a Web page.

Web palette ▸ A standard selection of colors that all Internet browsers can display.

Web resource ▸ Any data file that has a URL, such as an HTML document, a graphic, or a sound file.

Web server ▸ A computer that uses special software to transmit Web pages over the Internet.

Web site ▸ Location on the World Wide Web that contains information relating to specific topics.

WEP (Wired Equivalent Privacy) ▸ A security method that encrypts transmitted data so that the data is useless to intruders who may intercept and try to steal it by LAN Jacking or other methods.

Wi-Fi (Wireless Fidelity) ▸ A set of wireless networking technologies defined by IEEE 802.11 standards. Wi-Fi networks operate at 2.4 or 5 GHz. In a typical office environment, Wi-Fi's range varies from 25 to 150 feet, although considerably more range is possible with additional equipment.

Wi-Fi card ▸ Required for transmission on a Wi-Fi network, required by every workstation and network peripheral; includes a transceiver (transmitter and receiver) and an antenna to transmit signals. Wi-Fi cards for notebook or tablet computers plug into a PCMCIA slot.

Wi-Fi network ▸ A wireless network that transmits data as radio waves over predefined frequencies, much like cordless telephones.

Windows Explorer ▸ A file management utility included with most Windows operating systems that helps users manage their files.

Windows Mobil OS ▸ A version of the Windows operating system designed for portable or mobile computers.

Windows Registry ▸ A crucial data file maintained by the Windows operating system that contains the settings needed by a computer to correctly use any hardware and software that has been installed on the system. Also called the Registry.

Windows Startup Disk ▸ A disk that is created by the user to load the operating system and the CD-ROM drivers, allowing for system restoration.

Windows XP tablet edition ▸ A version of the Windows operating system designed for tablet computers.

Wired network ▸ A type of network in which the data travels over cables or wires from one device to another.

Wireframe ▸ A representation of a 3-D object using separate lines, which resemble wire, to create a model.

Wireless access point ▸ Provides a central point for data transmitted over a wireless network by broadcasting signals to any devices with compatible Wi-Fi cards.

Wireless network ▸ A type of network that uses radio or infrared signals (instead of cables) to transmit data from one network device to another.

Word processing software ▸ Computer programs that assist the user in producing documents, such as reports, letters, papers, and manuscripts.

Word size ▸ The number of bits a CPU can manipulate at one time, which is dependent on the size of the registers in the CPU and the number of data lines in the bus.

Worksheet ▸ A computerized, or electronic, spreadsheet.

Workstation ▸ (1) A computer connected to a local area network. (2) A powerful desktop computer designed for specific tasks.

World Wide Web Consortium (W3C) ▸ An international consortium of companies involved with the Internet and developing open standards.

Worm ▸ A software program designed to enter a computer system, usually a network, through security "holes" and then replicate itself.

Write-protect window ▸ A small hole and sliding cover on a floppy disk that restricts writing to the disk.

WWAN (wireless wide area network) ▸ A network over a large geographic area that uses cellular phone networks to offer data communications and Internet access for cell phones, PDAs, and portable computers.

XHTML ▸ The follow-up version to HTML 4, set of specifications for creating HTML documents that a browser can display as a Web page. XHTML, which includes all HTML 4 tags, is extensible, therefore it can be extended by adding customized tags.

XML (eXtensible Markup Language) ▸ A document format similar to HTML that allows the Web page developer to define customized tags generally for the purpose of creating more interactivity.

XML parser ▸ A tool in most browsers used for reading XML documents.

XSL (eXtensible Stylesheet Language) ▸ A technology that is similar to XML, used to create customized tags for displaying data in an XML document.

Zip disk ▸ Floppy disk technology manufactured by Iomega available in 100 MB, 250 MB, and 750 MB versions.

Zipped ▸ Refers to files that have been compressed.

Zipping ▸ The process of compressing files.

Zombie PC ▸ A PC that has been hijacked by hackers for illegal or personal use.

Zombie PC network ▸ A network that has been hijacked by hackers for illegal or personal use.

Index

B

Back button of browsers, 20, 21
Back Thru the Future Micro Computer, Inc., 64
backbone, 14, 15
backpack journalists, 97
backslash (in filenames, 116, 118
backup(s), 188–195
    devices, 192–193
    procedures, 190–191
    software, 194–195
    Windows Registry, 189
backup software, 194–195
bandwidth, 146
banking, computer use, Enhanced 54–55
banner ads, 228, Enhanced 44, Enhanced 45
basic input/output system (BIOS), 114
baud rate, 159
B2B (business-to-business) e-commerce, 229
Bcc: feature, e-mail, 23
Becky Sharp (film), 270
beep code, 24
benchmarking, 111
Berners-Lee, Tim, 208
B2G (business-to-government) e-commerce, 229
Bimber, Bruce, 236
binary number system, 10, 106, 107
biomechanics, 26
biometrics, 181
BIOS (basic input/output system), 114
bit(s), 10, 106, 107
bit depth, 52
bitmap graphics, 246–249, 252, 253
    color depth, 250–251
    creating from vector graphics, 254
    modifying, 248–249
bitmap images, 252, 253
.biz extension, 157
Block feature, e-mail, 23
blocking cookies, 224, 225
blogs, 15
Bluetooth, 152, 153
BMP file format, 249
body scanners, fashion industry, Enhanced 21

body section of Web pages, 216
bogus news, 238
Bookmarks list, 20, 21
boot disk, creating, 193
boot process, 24–25
boot sector viruses, 182, 183
bootstrap programs, 76
bridges, 142
broadband connections, 160–161
broadband systems, 146
broken links, 220
browsers, 20–21, 208, 212–213, Enhanced 12, Enhanced 13
brute force method, 234
Bugbear worm, 185
bull backups, 190, 191
bull system backups, 190, 191
Burton Snowboards, Enhanced 21
bus topology, 142, 143
Bush, Vannevar, 208
business ethics, Enhanced 48–49
business software, 88, 89
business-to-business (B2B) e-commerce, 229
business-to-consumer (B2C) e-commerce, 229
business-to-government (B2G) e-commerce, 229
buyer's guide worksheets, 279–280
buying computers, Enhanced 32
bytes, 10, 106, 107

C

cable connections, 162–163, 165
cable connectors for peripheral devices, 58, 59
cable modem(s), 16, 17, 162
cable modem service, 16, 17
caches, 110
CAD (computer addiction disorder), 29
CAD (computer-aided design) software, 27, 86
    fashion industry, Enhanced 20
CAI (computer-aided instruction), 168
CAL (computer-aided learning), 168
Caller ID for E-Mail, Enhanced 42
CAM (computer-aided manufacturing) software, 27

camera(s)
    digital, 58, 59, 246, 247, 260, 261
    Web cams, 58, 59, 260, 261
camera phones, Enhanced 13
CAN-SPAM Act, Enhanced 12
carbon nanotubes, 130
card readers, 48, 246, 247
careers, Enhanced 28
Carnivore, Enhanced 30
Carrier Sense Multiple Access with Collision Detection (CSMA/CD), 150, 151
cascading style sheets (CSSs), Web pages, 218
cathode ray tube (CRT) monitors, 52, 53
CATV cable, 162, 163, 165
    topologies, 163
CBT (computer-based training), 168
Cc: feature, e-mail, 23
C2C (consumer-to-consumer) e-commerce, 229
CCD (charge coupled device), 129
CD(s) (compact discs), 37, 46–47, Enhanced 6
    capabilities, 47
    capacity, 41
    inserting, 47
CD drives, 46
CD-DA (compact disc digital audio), 46
CD-R (compact disc recordable) discs/drives, 46, 47
CD-ROM (compact disk read-only memory) discs/drives, 8, 9, 37, 46, 47
CD-RW (compact disc rewritable) discs/drives, 46, 47
    capacity, 41
CD-writers, 8
celestial photography, 129
cell(s), 82, 83
cell references, 82, 83
cellular technology, Enhanced 8, Enhanced 9
    e-mail, Enhanced 13
    pictures, Enhanced 13
    text, Enhanced 13
cellular-ready modems, 164
central processing units (CPUs), 4
certification, Enhanced 28
CF (CompactFlash) cards, 48, 49, 247

queries, 84

natural language, 84

query by example (QBE), 84

query language, 84

QuickTime, 218, 258

R

radio frequency identification (RFID) technology, Enhanced 8, Enhanced 9

fashion industry, Enhanced 20–21

radio frequency (RF) signals, 146

radio shows, Internet, 14

RAM (random access memory), 24, 36, 112–113

allocation by OS, 76, 77

rambus dynamic RAM (RDRAM), 113

random access, 40

random access memory (RAM), 24, 36, 112–113

allocation by OS, 76, 77

Raskin, Robin, 238

raster graphics. *See* bitmap graphics

raster image processor (RIP), 96

rasterization, 254

ray tracing, 256, 257

RDRAM (rambus dynamic RAM), 113

read-only memory (ROM), 114

read-only (ROM) technology, 46

read-write head, 38, 39

RealAudio files, 264

RealMedia file format, 258

record(s), databases, 84, 85

recordable technology, 46, 47

Recording Industry Association of America (RIAA), 272, Enhanced 51

recovery CD, 193

Recycle Bin, 119

recycling computers, 64–65

Reduced Instruction Set Computing (RISC), 110

reference software, 90

registers, 110

Registry, 60–61

backing up, 189

relative references, 82, 83

remote links, 220

remote storage, backing up on, 192

removable storage, Enhanced 6

renaming files, 124

rendering, 256

renegade WLANs, 170

repeaters, 144

Reply feature, e-mail, 23

reserved words, 116

resolution

bitmap graphics, 248, 249

monitors, 52, 53

resolution dependent graphics, 248

resources, 76

restoring data, 188

retinal scanners, 181

retrieving

files, 124

images, 246

retro viruses, 186

revolutions per minute (rpms), 44

rewritable technology, 46, 47

RF (radio frequency) signals, 146

RFID (radio frequency identification) technology, Enhanced 8, Enhanced 9

fashion industry, Enhanced 20–21

RIAA (Recording Industry Association of America), 272, Enhanced 51

ring topology, 142, 143

RIP (raster image processor), 96

RISC (Reduced Instruction Set Computing), 110

risk management, 178

Rivest, Ron, 235

RLE (run-length encoding), 268

ROM (read-only memory), 114

ROM BIOS (basic input/output system), 114

ROM (read-only) technology, 46

root directory, 118

routers, 14, 142, 143, 144

rpms (revolutions per minute), 44

RSA encryption algorithm, 235

.rtf files, 124

run-length encoding (RLE), 268

Rural Utilities Service, Enhanced 8

S

Safari, Enhanced 12, Enhanced 13

Safe Mode, 25

Salinger, Pierre, 238

sampling rate, 264

satellite connections, 16

satellite news gathering (SNG) trucks, 97

Satellite radio, Enhanced 51

Save As dialog box, 120, 121, 124, 125

Save dialog box, 120

saving files, 124, 125

Scalable Vector Graphics (SVG), 252

scaling theory, 130

scams, 238

scanners, 58, 59, 246, 247

science software, 88, 89

SCOTTeVEST, Enhanced 21

screen size, 52

SCSI C-50F connectors, 59

SCSI (small computer system interface) technology, 44

SD (SecureDigital) cards, 48, 49

SDRAM (synchronous dynamic RAM), 113

SDSL (Symmetric Digital Subscriber Line), 16, 160

search engines, 19

searching Web pages, 20

SEC (single-edge contact) cartridges, 108, 109

sectors, 126, 127

secure connections, 230

Secure Electronic Transaction (SET), 230

secure HTTP (S-HTTP), 230

Secure Sockets Layer (SSL), 155, 230

SecureDigital (SD) cards, 48, 49

security, 177–201

always-on connections, 161

breaches in commercial software, Enhanced 47

computer crime, 199–201

computer viruses. *See* computer viruses

data, Enhanced 10

data backup. *See* backup(s)

e-commerce, 230–231

evolving trends, Enhanced 10, Enhanced 11

firewall software, Enhanced 11, Enhanced 18, Enhanced 19

hardware, Enhanced 10

Internet access, Enhanced 18–19

LANs, 196–197

patches, Enhanced 18

storage media, 36, 37

   comparison, 40–41

storage technologies, 36–39

   comparing, 38–39

   devices, 36, 37

   media, 36, 37

   piracy and privacy, Enhanced 33–34

store-and-forward technology, 22

stored programs, 5

storing images, 246

STP (shielded twisted-pair) cable, 146

streaming video, 262

strong encryption, 234

Structured Query Language (SQL), 84

style(s), Web pages, 218

style feature, document production
   software, 80

style sheets, Web pages, 218

subdirectories, 118

Sun Microsystems, source code, Enhanced 37

supercomputers, 6, Enhanced 2

SuperDisks, 42, 43

   capacity, 41

support files, 117

support programs, 72

surge protectors, 180, 181

surge strips, 180, 181

surge suppressors, 180, 181

SVG (Scalable Vector Graphics), 252

switching stations, 158

Symmetric Digital Subscriber Line
   (SDSL), 160

symmetric key encryption, 235

synchronous dynamic RAM (SDRAM), 113

synchronous protocol, 148

synthesized sound, 266–267

system palette, 250

system requirements, 94

system software, 12, 13, 72, 73

system unit, 8, 9

   storage devices, 37

System.dat file, 60

T

T1 service, 160

T3 service, 160

table(s)

   databases, 84, 85

   documents, 80

tablet computers, 6, 7

tape(s), capacity, 41

tape cartridges, 37, 45

tape drives, 37

   backing up on, 192, 193

tape storage, 45, Enhanced 6

Target Acquisition Designation Sights, 62

tax preparation software, 88

TCP (Transmission Control Protocol), 148

TCP/IP (Transmission Control
   Protocol/Internet Protocol), 14, 148, 149

Technicolor, 270

Telecommunications Network (TELNET), 155

teleconferencing, 14

telemedicine, Enhanced 15

Telemedicine Information Exchange (TIE),
   Enhanced 15

telescopes, 129

television

   digital, Enhanced 51

   evolving trends, Enhanced 16,
      Enhanced 17

TELNET (Telecommunications Network), 155

temporal compression, 268

temporary files, 117

ten-print cards, 198

terminator, 142

Terminator II (film), 270

text, cellular technology, Enhanced 13

text editors, Web page authoring, 216, 217

text messaging, 28–29

text-to-speech software, 266

themes, Web pages, 218

thermal transfer printers, 54

32-bit bitmaps, 250

3-D graphics, 256–257

3-D graphics software, 86, 87, 256, 257

3M, 65

thumbnails, 220

Thunderbird 0.8, Enhanced 12

TIE (Telemedicine Information Exchange),
   Enhanced 15

TIFF file format, 249

TiVo, Enhanced 16, Enhanced 17

Token Ring networks, 150, 151

top-level domains, 156, 157

topologies, CATV cable, 163

Torvalds, Linus, 78

touch-screen voting machines, 237

toxic substances in computers, 64–65

Toy Story (film), 271

Traceroute, 154

tracing software, 254

track(s), 126, 127

trackballs, 50, 51

trackpads, 50, 51

TrackPoints, 50, 51

transceivers, 144

Transmeta Corporation, 108

   evolving trends in processors,
      Enhanced 4, Enhanced 5

Transmission Control Protocol (TCP), 148

Transmission Control Protocol/Internet
   Protocol (TCP/IP), 14, 148, 149

transponders, 146

tree metaphor for file storage, 122, 123

tree topology, 142, 143

trigger events, 182

Trojan horses, 182, 183

TRON (film), 270

True Color bitmaps, 250

The Truth About URLs (Raskin), 238

24-bit bitmaps, 250

twisted-pair cables, 146, 147

The Two Towers (film), 271

2001: A Space Odyssey (film), 270

typing keypads, 50

U

UCITA (Uniform Computer Information
   Transactions Act), Enhanced 27

UDMA (Ultra DMA) technology, 44

ULSI (ultra-large-scale integration), 108

Ultra ATA (AT attachment), 44

Ultra DMA (UDMA) technology, 44

ultra-large-scale integration (ULSI), 108

Unicode, 106

Uniform Computer Information
   Transactions Act (UCITA), Enhanced 27

uninstall routine, 95

uninterruptible power supplies (UPSs), 180, 181

Universal Resource Locators (URLs), 18, 19, 208

  backing up favorites, 188

  URL boxes, 20, 21

UNIX, 12, 78

  file-naming conventions, 117

unshielded twisted-pair (UTP) cable, 146

unzipping, 269

updates

  Automatic Updates, Enhanced 18

  security, Enhanced 47

  software, Enhanced 14, Enhanced 15

uploading, 14, 15

UPSs (uninterruptible power supplies), 180, 181

urban legends on Internet, 238–239

URL(s) (Universal Resource Locators), 18, 19, 208

  backing up favorites, 188

URL boxes, 20, 21

usage procedures, 180

USB connectors, 59

USB flash drives, 48, 49, Enhanced 6

USB ports, 56, 260, 261

US-CERT, Enhanced 10, Enhanced 11

Usenet, 14

user IDs, 16

user rights, 180

User.dat file, 60

user-executable files, 72, 73

utilities, 76, 77

UTP (unshielded twisted-pair) cable, 146

V

values in spreadsheets, 82

vector graphics, 252–255

  creating, 254–255

  on Web, 252

vertical market software, 88

VGA HDB-15 connectors, 59

video, 246–263, 258. See also desktop video

  bitmap graphics, 246–249

  color depth, 250–251

  desktop. See desktop video

  external, 262, 263

  internal, 262, 263

  streaming, 262

  3-D graphics, 256–257

  vector graphics, 252–255

video cameras, analog, 261

video capture devices, 260, 261

video capture software, 260

video editing software, 90, 91, 262, 263

videogame consoles, 6, 7

viewable image size (vis), 52

viewing angle width, 52

Virtual Local Area Networks (VLANs), Enhanced 8

virtual memory, 114

virtual private networks (VPNs), Enhanced 19

virus(es). See computer viruses

virus definitions, 186

virus hoaxes, 187

virus signatures, 186

vis (viewable image size), 52

Visa Waiver Program, Enhanced 33

VLANs (Virtual Local Area Networks), Enhanced 8

voice band modems, 16, 17, 158, 159

voice over IP (VoIP), 158

Voice Training Wizard, 266, 267

VoIP (voice over IP), 158

volatility of RAM, 36

voter verifiable paper trail (VVPT), Enhanced 38

voting, electronic, Enhanced 38

voting machines, 236–237

VPNs (virtual private networks), Enhanced 19

VVPT (voter verifiable paper trail), Enhanced 38

W

Walker, Kent, 200

WANs (wide area networks), 140, 141

WAP (Wireless Application Protocol), 164, 165

war driving, 152

.wav file extension, 264

Wave files, 264

waveform audio, 264

wavetable, 266

W3C (World Wide Web Consortium), 210

weak encryption, 234

wearable computer and communications equipment, 63, Enhanced 21

  medical uses, Enhanced 15

Web

  development, 208

  Internet versus, 208

  search engines, 19

  vector graphics on, 252

Web authoring software, 80, 216, 217

Web browsers, 20–21, 208, 212–213

Web bugs, 231

Web cams, 58, 59, 260, 261

Web page(s), 18, 19

  animation, 218, 219

  components, 216, 217

  copying, 20

  enhancing, 218–219

  graphics, 218, 219

  links, 18, 19

  navigation elements, 220–221

  organizing, 222–223

  printing, 20, 21

  publishing, 222

  videos, 262

Web page authoring, 216–217

Web page headers, 216, 217

Web page tables, 222, 223

Web palettes, 250

Web resources, 214

Web servers, 18, 208, 214–215

Web sites, 14, 15, 18

  backing up on, 192, 193

  favorites list, 20, 21

  home pages, 18

  viruses spread by, 184

Web-based e-mail, 22

Webcasts, fashion industry, Enhanced 20

WEP (Wired Equivalent Privacy), 152

wide area networks (WANs), 140, 141

Wi-Fi (Wireless Fidelity), free, 170–171

Wi-Fi cards, 152, 153

Wi-Fi networks, 152, 153

Windows Explorer, 120, 121, 122, 123

Windows Firewall, Enhanced 18